DECISIONS OF THE WORLD COURT RELEVANT TO THE UN CONVENTION ON THE LAW OF THE SEA

The International Court of Justice in public sitting during the delivery of the *Difference Relating to Immunity from Legal Process* Advisory Opinion on 29 April 1999.
On the right of President Stephen M. Schwebel: Judges Shigeru Oda, Gilbert Guillaume (subsequently the President in 2000-2003), Géza Herczegh, Carl-August Fleischhauer, Vladlen S. Vereshchetin, Gonzalo Parra-Aranguren and José F. Rezek.
On the left of President Schwebel: Vice-President Christopher G. Weeramantry, Judges Mohammed Bedjaoui, Raymond Ranjeva, Shi Jiuyong (subsequently the Vice-President in 2000-2003 and the President in 2003-2006), Abdul G. Koroma, Dame Rosalyn Higgins (subsequently the President in 2006-2009), Pieter H. Kooijmans and Registrar Eduardo Valencia-Ospina (succeeded in 2000 by Philippe Couvreur).
At the table below the Bench: Deputy Registrar Jean-Jacques Arnaldez.
Photography courtesy International Court of Justice.

Members of the International Court of Justice of 9 January 2010.
On the left side of President Hisashi Owada: Vice-President Peter Tomka and Judges Abdul G. Koroma and Thomas Buergenthal. On the right side of President Owada: Judges Shi Jiuyong [Vice-President in 2000-2003 and President in 2003-2006], Awn Shawkat Al-Khasawneh [Vice-President in 2006-2009] and Bruno Simma.
Standing from left to right: Judges Christopher Greenwood, Antonio A. Cancado Trindade, Mohamed Bennouna, Sir Kenneth Keith, Ronny Abraham, Bernardo Sepulveda Amor, Leonid Skotnikov and Abdulqawi Ahmed Yusuf.
Standing first on the right side: Registrar Philippe Couvreur.
Photography courtesy International Court of Justice.

DECISIONS OF THE WORLD COURT RELEVANT TO THE UN CONVENTION ON THE LAW OF THE SEA

A REFERENCE GUIDE
SECOND REVISED EDITION

by

BARBARA KWIATKOWSKA

MARTINUS
NIJHOFF
PUBLISHERS

LEIDEN • BOSTON
2010

This book is printed on acid-free paper.

Library of Congress Cataloging-in-Publication Data

Kwiatkowska, Barbara.
Decisions of the World Court relevant to the UN Convention on the Law of the Sea : a reference guide second revised edition / by Barbara Kwiatkowska.
p. cm.
ISBN 978-90-04-18429-9 (hardback : alk. paper)
1. Law of the sea—Cases. 2. International Court of Justice. I. Title.
KZA1123 2010
341.4'5—dc22

2010006388

ISBN 978 90 04 18429 9

PRINTED BY A-D DRUK BV - ZEIST, THE NETHERLANDS

To Stephen M. Schwebel,

Judge (1981-2000) and the President (1997-2000) of the International Court of Justice,

President of the Administrative Tribunal of the International Monetary Fund (1994-2009) and Member of the World Bank Administrative Tribunal (2007-),

President of the Annex VII *Southern Bluefin Tuna* Arbitral Tribunal (1999-2000) and Member of the *Eritrea/Yemen* Arbitral Tribunal (1996-1999)

Member of the UN *Eritrea/Ethiopia Boundary* Commission (2001-2008) and *North/South Sudan Abyei Boundary* Arbitral Tribunal (2008-2009)

President of the Annex VII *Barbados/Trinidad and Tobago* Arbitral Tribunal (2004-2006) and the ICSID *MHS v. Malaysia Sunken Treasure* Committee (2007-2009)

TABLE OF CONTENTS

PREFACE

"The content of customary international law, or the governing interpretation of a treaty, may be influenced or even determined by a judgment of the Court. The Court's decisions thus enjoy, as Lauterpacht has put it, an 'intrinsic' authority within the international community. [...] The 'intrinsic' authority of the Court's decisions and the coherence of its case-law are fundamental factors which enable it to contribute to the development of international law."

Stephen M. Schwebel, The Contribution of the International Court of Justice to the Development of International Law, in Wybo P. Heere ed., *International Law and The Hague's 750th Anniversary* 405, 407 (T.M.C. Asser Press 1999), quoting Sir Hersch Lauterpacht, *The Development of International Law by the International Court* 22 (Revised Edition, Cambridge 1982).

This *Reference Guide* is the product of many years of work carried out prior to publication of its first edition in 2002 and thereafter in reliance on two inter-related premises. One of them consists of significant contributions which have been made by the International Court of Justice (ICJ) to the development of the law of the sea – along with the law of the United Nations, the law of human rights, the law of treaties and the environmental law – as a part of general international law and as a part of the global system of peace and security.[1] The law of the sea related cases have continued to feature prominently in the voluminous annals of the World Court ever since the 1923 *S.S. Wimbledon (France, Britain, Italy, Japan v. Germany; Poland*

---

1 See especially the emphasis on such "unquestioned" contributions by the then ICJ President Stephen M. Schwebel, Fifty Years of the World Court: A Critical Appraisal, in *Are International Institutions Doing Their Job? 90th ASIL Annual Meeting, Washington D.C., 27-30 March 1996* 339, 345 (1997); S.M. Schwebel, The Impact of the International Court of Justice, in *Boutros Boutros-Ghali Amicorum Discipulorumque Liber* 663, 669-670 (Bruylant 1998); S.M. Schwebel, The Contribution of the International Court of Justice to the Development of International Law, in W.P. Heere ed., *International Law and The Hague's 750th Anniversary* 405-416 (T.M.C. Asser Press 1999); S.M. Schwebel, The Inter-Active Influence of the International Court of Justice and the International Law Commission, in *Liber Amicorum in Memoriam of Judge José Maria Ruda* 479, 480, 484-487, 492-495 (Kluwer International 2000); M.N. Shaw, *International Law* 527-540 (5th Edition 2003).

Cf. appraisal by Sir Gerald Fitzmaurice, GCMG QC, Judicial Innovation – Its Uses and Its Perils – As Exemplified in Some of the Work of the International Court of Justice During Lord McNair's Period of Office, in *Cambridge Essays in International Law in Honour of Lord McNair* 24, 39-47 (London/New York 1965); former ICJ President Sir Humphrey M. Waldock, The International Court and the Law of the Sea (Cornelis van Vollenhoven Memorial Lecture, T.M.C. Asser 1979); Eduardo Jimenez de Aréchaga, Customary Law and the Law of the Sea, in Jerzy Makarczyk ed., *Essays in Honour of Judge Manfred Lachs* 575-585 (Martinus Nijhoff 1984); Jean-Pierre Queneudec, The Role of the International Court of Justice and Other Tribunals in the Development of the Law of the Sea, in Alfred H.A. Soons ed., *Implementation of the Law of the Sea Convention Through International Institutions* 574-600 (University of Hawaii 1990); Barbara Kwiatkowska, *The Contribution of the International Court of Justice to the Development of the Law of the Sea – Stockholm Lecture* (2002) at: http://vandeplaspublishing.com, Environmental Law, and NILOS website at: www.uu.nl/nilos/onlinepapers; B. Kwiatkowska, The Law of the Sea Related Cases in the International Court of Justice During the Presidency of Judge Stephen M. Schwebel (1997-2000) and Beyond, 16 *International Journal of Marine and Coastal Law* (IJMCL) 1-40 (2001), as extended and revised, in G. Ziccardi Capaldo Editor-in-Chief, 2 *Global Community Yearbook of International Law and Jurisprudence* (YILJ) 2002, 27-75 (2003) at: www.oceanalaw.com/main_product_details.asp?ID=298 and NILOS website *supra*; ICJ President Gilbert Guillaume, *La Cour Internationale de Justice a l'aube du XXIeme siecle: Le Regard d'un Juge* 287-318 (Editions A. Pedone 2003); Raymond Ranjeva, Aux origines de l'Article 287.1.b de la Convention des Nations Unies sur le Droit de la Mer, in *La Mer et son Droit – Melanges offerts a Laurent Lucchini et Jean-Pierre Queneudec* 545-550 (Editions A. Pedone 2003); B. Kwiatkowska, Equitable Maritime Boundary Delimitation, as Exemplified in the Work of the International Court of Justice During the Presidency of Judge Gilbert Guillaume (2000-2003) and Beyond, 5 YILJ 51-171 (2005 Vol. I) at http://www.oceanalaw.com/main_product_

Intervening) and the 1948-1949 *Corfu Channel (UK/Albania)* Judgments, which inaugurated the contentious jurisprudence of the Permanent Court of International Justice (PCIJ) and its successor, the ICJ, respectively, by cases that arose out of incidents involving vessels and that have proven to have far-reaching implications for navigational rights and freedoms (in the context of the legal regimes of interoceanic canals, international straits, territorial sea, and the use of mines at sea).[2]

The other premise is that these – like all other – contributions of the Court substantiate what its former President Stephen M. Schwebel has perceived as fundamental factors of "the intrinsic" authority of the Court's decisions and the coherence of its jurisprudence which are characteristic of the unique role of the ICJ as the principal judicial organ of the United Nations and the world's most senior Court with the broadest material jurisdiction.[3] The Court's role in advancing the development

---

details.asp?ID=417 and Vols 1-6 (2001-2006) www.us.oup.com/us/catalog/general/subject/Law/?view=usa&ci=037921475X; S.M. Schwebel, Panel on *The International Judge*, together with Cesare Romano and Daniel Terris, U.S. Carnegie Council (CCEIA), 19 March 2008 at www.cceia.org/resources/video/data/000047 & www.cceia.org/resources/transcripts/0033.html.

2 PCIJ Series A, No.1, 11, 15; ICJ Reports 1947-1948, 15, and 1949, 1, 244. In the former case, the British steamship *Wimbledon*, proceeding from Salonica to the Polish Naval Base at Danzig (Gdansk), was refused passage through the Kiel Canal by Germany. In the latter case, during the incident, which occurred in the Strait of Corfu in 1946, two British destroyers struck mines, the explosion of which caused damage to the vessels and heavy loss of life.

3 Schwebel, The Contribution, *supra* note 1, at 407, relying on the concept of "intrinsic" authority of the Court's decisions as expounded by Sir Hersch Lauterpacht, *The Development of International Law by the International Court* 22 (Revised edn, Cambridge 1982); also quoted as the motto to this Preface and *infra* note 8. On Judge Schwebel's faithful continuation of attainments of Sir Hersch which remain unsurpassed by any international lawyer of this century, see Kwiatkowska, The Law of the Sea Related Cases, *supra* note 1, at 3; Peter H. Kooymans, Two Remarkable Men Have Left the International Court of Justice, 13 *Leiden Journal of International Law* (LJIL) 343, 345 (2000) at: http://www.cambridge.org/journals/ljl/ifc – All Issues; Judge Schwebel's review of Sir Hersch Lauterpacht, *Collected Papers*, Vol.5 (Cambridge 2004), in 99 *American Journal of International Law* (AJIL) 726-729 (2005); Remarks of Former ICJ President Stephen M. Schwebel on Sir Hersch Lauterpacht at www.law.cam.ac.uk/faculty-resources/summary/the-function-of-law-in-the-international-community-keynote--open-discussion/6188, in J. Crawford and M. Young eds., *The Function of Law in the International Community: An Anniversary Symposium* (Lauterpacht Centre for International Law, 11-12 July 2008)

of international law, including law of the sea,[4] finds expression in two paramount functions exercised by the ICJ along with its primary role as a factor and actor in the maintenance of international peace and security and today, peacemaking, including by means of "preventive diplomacy".[5] The two functions pertaining to the development of law include – as is consistently stressed in annual Statements of the Court's Presidents to the UN General Assembly and the ILC[6] and instruments implementing

at www.lcil.cam.ac.uk/25th_anniversary/book.php and Sir Hersch Lauterpacht at http://en.wikipedia.org/wiki/Hersch_Lauterpacht.

4 See remarks of President Schwebel, The Contribution, *supra* note 1, at 407, that: "Of course, Article 59 of the Statute of the Court provides that '[t]he decision of the Court has no binding force except between the parties and in respect of that particular case.' Nevertheless, it is undeniable that the decisions and opinions of the Court may have an influence extending beyond that particular case". Cf. also S.M. Schwebel, *Justice in International Law – Selected Writings of Judge Stephen M. Schwebel* 10-11 (Cambridge 1994 as republished in 2008) www.cambridge.org/catalogue/catalogue.asp?isbn=9780521462846; Sir Robert Jennings, The Role of the International Court of Justice, 68 *British Yearbook of International Law* (BYIL) 1, 39-44 (1997); review by Judge Schwebel of the book of John Collier and Vaughan Lowe, *The Settlement of Disputes in International Law* (Oxford 2000), 95 AJIL 464, 466 (2001); Guillaume, *La Cour Internationale de Justice*, *supra* note 1, at 38-41; review by Judge Schwebel of *Liber Amicorum Oscar Schachter: International Responsibility Today* (2005), 101 AJIL 237-241 (2007 No.1); *ASIL Video Forum on The International Court of Justice: The Road Ahead*, with participation of Former ICJ President Stephen M. Schwebel (Chairman), David A. Colson, Ruth Wedgwood and John R. Crook, Washington D.C., 3 October 2007 at http://fora.tv/2007/10/03/International_Court_of_Justice_Road_Ahead & http://intellibriefs.blogspot.com/2007/10/international-court-of-justice-road.html.

5 For an analysis of this Court's role in preventive diplomacy as elucidated in Statements of President Schwebel, *infra* note 6, see Malcolm N. Shaw, Peaceful Resolution of "Political Disputes": The Desirable Parameters of Jurisdiction of the International Court of Justice, in *Peaceful Resolution of Major International Disputes* 49, 55-56 (United Nations 1999); remarks on impacts of judicial and arbitral settlements as between the parties by Barbara Kwiatkowska, *Peaceful Settlement of Oceans and Other Environmental Disputes Under International Agreements* (2002) at: http://vandeplaspublishing.com, originally presented at the UNESCO Global Conference on Oceans and Coasts at Rio+10: Toward the 2002 Johannesburg World Summit, Paris, 3-7 December 2001 at: http://www.udel.edu/CMS/csmp/globaloceans/index.html, "Participants use only": password <OCR+10PA>; Shaw, *International Law* (2003), *supra* note 1, at 113.

6 For an excellent appraisal of all three fundamental functions of the ICJ, see Statements of Judge Stephen M. Schwebel, President of the International Court of Justice, to the 52nd General Assembly, UN Doc. A/52/PV.36, 1-5, 27 October 1997, *reprinted in ICJ*

the United Nations Millennium Declaration[7] – the ICJ's role as the most authoritative interpreter of the legal obligations of states in disputes between them and its role in both advisory and contentious proceedings as the

---

Yearbook 1997-1998 288-300 (No.52), 92 AJIL 612-517 (1998), to the 53rd General Assembly, UN Doc. A/53/PV.44, 1-5, 27 October 1998, *reprinted in ICJ Yearbook 1998-1999* 316-323 (No.53) and to the 54th General Assembly, UN Doc. A/54/PV.39, 1-5, 26 October 1999, *reprinted in ICJ Yearbook 1999-2000* 282-288 (No.54); Statements of Judge Gilbert Guillaume, President of the International Court of Justice, to the 55th General Assembly, 26 October 2000, *reprinted in ICJ Yearbook 2000-2001* 319-326 (No.55), to the 56th-57th General Assembly, UN Docs A/56/PV.32, 30 October 2001, A/57/PV.37, 29 October 2002, *reprinted in ICJ Yearbook 2001-2002* 308-313 (No.56) and *ICJ Yearbook 2002-2003* 327-335 (No.57); Statements of President Shi Jiuyong to the 58th-60th General Assembly, *ICJ Press Releases* No.2003/36, 31 October 2003, No.2004/32, 4 November 2004 and No.2005/21, 27 October 2005; *reprinted in ICJ Yearbook 2003-2004* 324-331 (No.58); Statement of Judge Rosalyn Higgins, President of the International Court of Justice, to the 61st General Assembly, *ICJ Press Release* No.2006/34 of 26 October 2006, *summarized in* www.un.org/apps/news/story.asp?NewsID=20391&Cr=international&Cr1=court and UN Doc.GA/10523 of 26 October 2006, also including the ensuing Statements of Finland, New Zealand, Egypt, Sudan, Madagascar, Nigeria, Tunisia, Mexico, India, South Africa, Peru, Poland, Cameroon, Pakistan and Syria at www.un.org/News/Press/docs/2006/ga10523.doc.htm; President Higgins' Statements to the 6th Committee of 27 October 2006 at www.un.org/News/Press/docs/2006/gal3305.doc.htm, to the UN Meeting of Legal Advisers of 23 October and the AALCC of 20 October 2006; Statements of ICJ President Rosalyn Higgins to the 62nd UNGA of 1 November 2007 at www.un.org/apps/news/story.asp?NewsID=24516&Cr=international&Cr1=justice, to the 62nd UNGA Legal Advisers of 29 October 2007 and to the 59th ILC of 10 July 2007 and the 60th ILC of 19 May and 22 July 2008; to the 63rd UNGA of 30 October 2008 at www.un.org/News/Press/docs//2008/ga10774.doc.htm and the 6th UN Legal Committee of 31 October 2008 at www.un.org/News/Press/docs//2008/gal3355.doc.htm; Statements of ICJ President Hishasi Owada to the 64th-66th General Assembly – Statement of ICJ President Owada to the 64th General Assembly of 29 October 2009, *summarized in ICJ Press Release* No.2009/31 of 2 November 2009, www.un.org/News/Press/docs//2009/ga10878.doc.htm, also including the ensuing Statements of Canada (on behalf of Australia and NZ), Denmark (on behalf of the Nordic States), Senegal, Philippines, South Africa, Peru, Egypt, Singapore, Chile, Kenya, Pakistan, Portugal, India, Sudan, Japan, Brazil, DRC, RoK, Costa Rica, Tunisia and Ghana; and President Owada's Statement to the 6th UN Legal Committee of 30 October 2009 at www.un.org/News/Press/docs//2009/gal3377.doc.htm & http://www.icj-cij.org.

[7] See General Assembly Resolution 55/2 on the United Nations Millennium Declaration of 8 September 2000, reaffirming commitment to "the purposes and principles of the Charter of the United Nations, which have proved timeless and universal" and to "resolution of disputes by peaceful means and in conformity with the principles of justice and

supreme interpreter of the United Nations Charter and of its associated instruments. In his illuminating reflections on these functions, Sir Robert Jennings observed that:

> Even where a court develops the law in the sense of adapting, modifying, filling gaps, interpreting, or even branching out in a new direction, the decision must be seen to emanate reasonably and logically from existing and previously ascertainable law. A court has no purely legislative competence. Naturally the court in probably most difficult cases – and for the most part it is only difficult cases that are brought before international tribunals – may have to make a choice between probably widely differing solutions. It may even choose a course which has elements of novelty. But whatever juridical design it decides to construct in its decision, it must do so, and be seen to do so, from the building materials available in already existing law. The design may be an imaginative artifact, but the bricks used in its construction must be recognizable and familiar.[8]

---

international law" (paras 3-4), and resolving "to strengthen the International Court of Justice, in order to ensure justice and the rule of law in international affairs" (para.30), and Resolutions 56/95 and 57/144 of 14 December 2001 and 16 December 2002; WWSD Johannesburg Declaration and Plan of Implementation of 4 September 2002 at www .iisd.ca/wssd/portal.html and UN Doc.A/CONF.199/20 (2002); General Assembly Resolution 57/26 on Prevention and Peaceful Settlement of Disputes of 19 November 2002 and UN Security Council Statement on The Role of the Security Council in the Pacific Settlement of Disputes, UN Doc. S/PRST/2003/5 of 13 May 2003; 2005 *UN World Summit Outcome*, reaffirming [para.3] dedication to the UN Millennium Declaration and [paras 5, 73, 134(f)] "the important role of the ICJ, the principal judicial organ of the United Nations" in pacific settlement of disputes at http://www.un.org/summit2005/; UN Security Council High-Level Meeting on Mediation and Settlement of Disputes – Presidential Statement, UN Doc. S/PRST/2008/36 of 23 September 2008 at www.un .org/News/Press/docs//2008/sc9452.doc.htm and UN Secretary-General's Statement at www.un.org/News/Press/docs//2008/sgsm11807.doc.htm, www.un.org/apps/news/story .asp?NewsID=28189&Cr=ki-moon&Cr1 & www.un.org/apps/sg/sgstats.asp?nid=3416. Cf. *infra* notes 27 and 45.

8 Jennings, *supra* note 4, at 43. See also Sir Gerard Fitzmaurice, *supra* note 1, at 24-47 and Sir Humphrey Waldock, *supra* note 1, at 16. For detailed surveys, see Giuliana Ziccardi Capaldo, *Repertory of Decisions of the International Court of Justice (1947-1992)*, Vols I-II (Martinus Nijhoff 1995); Hugh Thirlway, The Law and Procedure of the International Court of Justice 1960-1989, Part I, 60 BYIL 1-157 (1989); Part II, 61 BYIL 1-133 (1990); Part III, 62 BYIL 1-75 (1991); Part IV, 63 BYIL 1-96 (1992); Part V, 64 BYIL 1-54 (1993);

The critical role of consistency of the decisions of the ICJ and its predecessor PCIJ in the foregoing process was accurately appraised by Judge Stephen M. Schwebel as follows:

> The Court itself has characteristically followed its own reasoning, although it is not bound by precedent. It has good reasons for doing so: its decisions are a repository of legal analysis and experience to which it is natural to adhere. They embody what the Court has considered or determined to be the law. Respect for decisions given in the past makes for legal certainty and continuity, for a measure of predictability; it enhances stability. The coherence and consistency of its decisions has strengthened the Court's legitimacy, thereby promoting respect for its jurisprudence.[9]

Part VI, 65 BYIL 1-102 (1994); Part VII, 66 BYIL 1-96 (1995); Part VIII, 67 BYIL 1-73 (1996); Part IX, 69 BYIL 1-83 (1998); Part X, 70 BYIL 1-63 (1999); Part XI, 71 BYIL 71-180 (2000); Part XII, 72 BYIL 37-182 (2001); Part XIII, 74 BYIL 7-114 (2003); Supplement 2005, 76 BYIL 1-120 (2005); Supplement 2006: Part III, 77 BYIL 5-120 (2006); Supplement 2007: Parts IV, V and VI, 78 BYIL 1-115 (2007). This series continues a series of articles published by Sir Gerald Fitzmaurice in BYIL in 1950-1959, and then in tribute to Sir Hersch Lauterpacht in 1961-1963. Another prominently valuable series is that of annual Judicial Activity of the International Court of Justice, carried out for the first five years since 2000 by John R. Crook and thereafter by Stephen Mathias, both of U.S. State Department, including: for 2000 ICJ, 95 AJIL 685 (2001); for 2001 ICJ, 96 AJIL 397 (2002); for 2002 ICJ, 97 AJIL 352 (2003); for 2003 ICJ, 98 AJIL 309 (2004); for 2004 ICJ, 99 AJIL 450 (2005); for 2005, 100 AJIL 629 (2006); for 2006 ICJ, 101 AJIL 602 (2007); for 2007 ICJ, 102 AJIL 588 (2008); for 2008 ICJ, 103 AJIL 527 (2009).

9 Schwebel, The Contribution, *supra* note 1, at 407, excerpted from the motto to this Preface; and *supra* notes 3-4. Cf. Manley O. Hudson, *The Permanent Court of International Justice, 1920-1942: A Treatise* 612-615 (The Macmillan Company 1943); Sir Hersch Lauterpacht, *supra* note 3, at 387, remarking that "it is incumbent upon courts to examine all available evidence in a manner revealing the factual links of judicial reasoning resulting in the acceptance or rejection of practices as constituting binding custom"; Rosalyn Higgins, *Problems and Process: International Law and How We Use It* 202-204 (Oxford 1994); Mohamed Shahabuddeen, *Precedent in the World Court* (Hersch Lauterpacht Memorial Lectures, Cambridge 1996); Shabtai Rosenne, *The Law and Practice of the International Court, 1920-1996* 1609-1615 (Martinus Nijhoff 1997) and *1920-2005* 1555-1558 (Martinus Nijhoff 2006); *Cameroon v. Nigeria (Preliminary Objections)* Judgment, ICJ Reports 1998, 292, para.28, as reaffirmed by the eight *Legality of Use of Force (Preliminary Objections)* Judgments with Belgium, para.98, Britain and Germany, para.96, Canada, Italy and France, para.97, the Netherlands, para.97 and Portugal, para.100, *ICJ Press Releases* Nos

Consequently, when the ICJ departs from precedents, it is – notwithstanding their non-binding nature – very careful in explaining its reasons, as is exemplified by the legal reasoning found in the 2007 *Nicaragua v. Honduras Territorial and Maritime Dispute in the Caribbean Sea* with respect to the Court's use of a bisector line (that is to say the line formed by bisecting the angle created by the linear approximations of the coastlines),[10] instead of non-mandatory, though widely used in equitable maritime delimitation *infra legem*, equidistance boundary.[11]

Whereas, so construed, coherence and consistency of the jurisprudence of the Court has been mutually reinforcing with the distinguished line of arbitral awards dating back to the 1794 Jay Treaty,[12] the recent phenomenon

---

2004/39-46, 15 December 2004, 279 at www.icj-cij.org; 44 ILM 299 (2005); Schwebel, *International Judge*, *supra* note 1; Interviews with ICJ Presidents Schwebel (1997-2000) and Higgins (2006-2009) featured, in Dispute Settlement Video: Program 7, Seaton Hall University's Law School at http://law.shu.edu/faculty/fulltime_faculty/defeisel/intlawtv/intlaworder.htm.

10 *Nicaragua v. Honduras Territorial and Maritime Dispute in the Caribbean Sea*, ICJ Reports 2007, paras 262-298, as presented in ICJ President Higgins' Statements to the 60th ILC (2008), *supra* note 6, at 1-3, and to the 63rd UN General Assembly (2008), *id*., at 2, where President Higgins stressed that: "In view of the particular geographical circumstances of the area, it was impossible for the Court to follow the preferred practice of establishing an equidistance line" and that: "The bisector method provided the delimitation line with greater stability as it was less affected by the changing nature of the coastline. It also greatly reduced the risk of error".

11 For appraisal of the law of equitable maritime delimitation, combining the need for predictability and stability within the rule of law and the need for flexibility (entailing certain degree of judicial discretion) in the outcome, see 2006 *Barbados/Trinidad and Tobago (Jurisdiction and Merits)* Award, President Stephen M. Schwebel, paras 219-245 [45 ILM 800 (2006); XXVII UNRIAA 147 at www.un.org/law/riaa & http://untreaty.un.org/cod/riaa/cases/vol_XXVII/147-251.pdf; *PCA Awards Series*, Vol.V (2007) at www.pca-cpa.org] and *Romania v. Ukraine Maritime Delimitation in the Black Sea* Judgment, President Rosalyn Higgins, ICJ Reports 2009, paras 115-122: Delimitation Methodology at www.icj-cij.org. See also *A Reference Guide*: Settlement of Disputes – First Woman Judge and President Rosalyn Higgins in the PCIJ-ICJ History *infra*, noting that the 2009 *Romania v. Ukraine* Judgment was rendered unanimously in appreciation of Judge Higgins' outstanding Presidency and her being the first woman in the World Court's history.

12 On the unquestionably equal authority of ICJ Judgments and Awards of Inter-State Arbitral Tribunals, see Hersch Lauterpacht, *The Function of Law in the International Community* 380 (1933), as discussed by Sir Robert Jennings, *supra* note 4, at 5-9. For a definition of inter-state arbitration, see *Qatar v. Bahrain Maritime Delimitation and*

of the so-called "proliferation of international courts and tribunals" added a new dimension to the need of preserving such consistency. As the then President Schwebel (1997-2000) remarked and Presidents Rosalyn Higgins (2006-2009) and Hisashi Owada (2009-2012) reiterated: "The Court's standing appears undiminished by the availability of arbitration and the recent appearance on the scene of other international tribunals with specific mandates, such as the International Tribunal for the Law of the Sea (ITLOS) and the International Criminal Tribunal for the Former Yugoslavia (ICTY). [...] The Court with its distinguished record remains pre-eminent".[13] Similarly, in the view of Shabtai Rosenne: "While there

---

Territorial Questions (Merits) Judgment, para.113, ICJ Reports 2001, 76-77, *reprinted in* 40 ILM 847 (2001). See also Shabtai Rosenne, The International Court of Justice and International Arbitration, 6 LJIL 297-321 (1993); John G. Merrills, *International Dispute Settlement* 88-120 (Cambridge 1998); and J.G. Merrills, The Contribution of the Permanent Court of Arbitration to International Law and to the Settlement of Disputes by Peaceful Means, in *The Permanent Court of Arbitration: International Arbitration and Dispute Resolution, Summaries of Awards, Settlement Agreements and Reports* 3-27 (Kluwer 1999); A. Eyffinger, Role and Record of the 1907 Hague Peace Conference, 54 *Netherlands International Law Review* (NILR) 197, 218-223 (2007); J.G. Merrills, The Mosaic of International Dispute Settlement Procedures: Complementary or Contradictory?, *id.*, at 361-393; J.J. van Haersolte-van Hof, The Revitalization of the Permanent Court of Arbitration, *id.*, at 395-413.

13 Schwebel, The Impact, *supra* note 1, at 673. Cf., e.g., Elihu Lauterpacht, *Aspects of the Administration of International Justice* 9-22 (Hersch Lauterpacht Memorial Lectures, Cambridge 1991); Antonio Cassese, *International Law* 219-220 (Oxford 2001); Former ICJ President Stephen M. Schwebel, Reflections on International Adjudication (Yale 2004) at: www.law.yale.edu/documents/pdf/Reflections_on_International_Adjudication.pdf and His UN Audiovisual Library Lecture on The Merits (and Demerits) of International Adjudication and Arbitration of 28 October 2008 at http://untreaty.un.org/cod/avl/faculty/Schwebel.html; IWPR Interview with Newly Elected ICJ President Rosalyn Higgins of 10 February 2006 at: www.iwpr.net/?p=tri&s=f&o=259503&apc_state=henh and *ICJ Press Release* No.2006/5 of 6 February 2006 at: www.icj-cij.org; *ASIL Video Forum on The International Court of Justice* (2007), with participation of Former ICJ President Stephen M. Schwebel (Chairman), David A. Colson, Ruth Wedgwood and John R. Crook, *supra* note 4; Schwebel, *The International Judge* (2008), *supra* note 1; Statements of ICJ President Higgins to the 61st and 62nd UN General Assembly and of other ICJ Presidents, as well as the ensuing Statements of numerous states, *supra* note 6, invariably appreciating judicial supremacy of the ICJ as the uniquely principal judicial organ of the United Nations and the only international Court of a universal character with general jurisdiction; other works quoted *infra* notes 14-23. The confirmation by this *Reference Guide* of the leadership of the ICJ as the principal judicial organ of the

is no formal hierarchy of international courts and tribunals, the pre-eminence of the Permanent Court and the present International Court is today generally accepted. Any other international adjudicatory body which ignored relevant dicta and decisions of the International Court would jeopardize its credibility. The constant accretion of judicial precedents is creating what is now a substantial body of international case-law".[14] The awareness of this effect is also reflected in a survey of the law and practice of ITLOS by Judge Gudmundur Eiriksson, who stresses that while the general question of respect for the ICJ decisions is shared with other international tribunals, this question is of particularly outstanding relevance for the ITLOS, which is an autonomous treaty organ within the United Nations system and whose Statute and Rules are modelled on those of the ICJ.[15]

United Nations was particularly appreciated in this *Reference Guide*'s reviews by Jean-Pierre Queneudec, Giuliana Ziccardi Capaldo and David Freestone, *infra* note 47.

14 Rosenne, *The Law and Practice*, *supra* note 9, at 1609. Cf. holding that: "The current range of international legal obligations benefits from a process of accretion and cumulation", in the 2000 *Southern Bluefin Tuna (Jurisdiction and Admissibility)* Award, para.52, rendered by the Arbitral Tribunal presided over by Judge Schwebel. See 39 ILM 1359 (2000); 119 ILR 508; http://www.worldbank.org/icsid; *Oceans and the Law of the Sea – Report of the Secretary-General*, UN Doc. A/56/58, 80-81 (2001) at: http://www.un.org/Depts/los; and *infra* notes 35, 43 and 45. See also Shabtai Rosenne, An Introduction to International Litigation, in *Preparing for Boundary Litigation/Arbitration* 57, 60 (International Boundaries Research Unit 1999), noting that: "It is unlikely that these specialised bodies would produce conflicting decisions on matters of general international law. In that respect, the general supremacy of the ICJ is not really at risk"; Rosalyn Higgins, The ICJ, the ECJ and the Integrity of International Law, 52 *International and Comparative Law Quarterly* 1, 11, 18-19 (2003) and the 2006-2007 Statements of President Higgins to the 61st and 62nd UNGA quoted *infra* notes 16-17; The Revitalization of the PCA (2007), *supra* note 12.

15 Gudmundur Eiriksson, *The International Tribunal for the Law of the Sea* 146-147 (Martinus Nijhoff 2000). On Article 33 of the ITLOS Statute which mirrors Article 59 of the ICJ Statute (referred to *supra* note 4), see *id.*, at 271-272. Note that Agreements on Cooperation and Relationship Between the United Nations and the International Sea-Bed Authority of 14 March 1997 (in force: 26 November 1997, Article 5, UNGA Resolution 52/27; 1967 UNTS 256; 36 ILM 1492 (1997)) and the ITLOS of 18 December 1997 (in force: 8 September 1998, Article 4(1)(iii), UNGA Resolution 52/251) provide for furnishing, subject to requirements of confidentiality, of information requested by the ICJ. On the law and practice of the ITLOS, see also especially Shabtai Rosenne, Establishing the ITLOS, 89 AJIL 806-814 (1995); S. Rosenne, ITLOS: 1996-97 Survey, 13 IJMCL 487-514 (1998), 1998 Survey, 14 IJMCL 453-465 (1999), and 1999 Survey, 15

The current practice of ITLOS and Arbitral Tribunals has substantiated Judge Schwebel's anticipation – shared by ICJ Presidents Rosalyn Higgins (2006-2009) and Hisashi Owada (2009-2012) and other international lawyers – of interplay and interaction between the Court and other international tribunals, as well as their belief that, as then President Schwebel put it, "the fabric of international law and life is resilient enough[16] to sustain

IJMCL 443-474 (2000); V. Lowe, 2000 Survey, 16 IJMCL 549-570 (2001); V. Lowe and R. Churchill, 2001 Survey, 17 IJMCL 463-484 (2002); 2002 Survey, 18 IJMCL 470-495 (2003); 2003 Survey, 19 IJMCL 369-382 (2004); 2004 Survey, 21 IJMCL 1-14 (2006); R. Churchill, UNCLOS Dispute Settlement: 2006 Survey, 22 IJMCL 463-490 (2007); 2007 Survey, 23 IJMCL 601-642 (2008); 2008 Survey, 24 IJMCL 603-616 (2009). For a summary, see *ITLOS Press* No.58, 18 October 2001; Y. Tanaka, Some Reflections on the ITLOS Jurisprudence, 51 NILR 237-271 (2004); 10th ITLOS Anniversary, *ITLOS Press* No.105 of 29 September 2006 at http://www.itlos.org; 22 IJMCL (2007 No.3 – Special Issue); S. Karagiannis, La demande de prompte mainlevee de l'immobilisation d'un navire devant le TIDM, *Journal du Droit International* 809-851 (2009 No.3); 2008-2009 Statements of ITLOS President Jose L. Jesus, *infra* note 19. On the *Ireland v. UK Mox Plant (Provisional Measures)* Order, rendered pending the 2003 OSPAR and the then ongoing Annex VII *Mox Plant* Arbitrations (PCA), see *ITLOS Press* No.62, 3 December 2001 and PCA at: http://www.pca-cpa.org; B. Kwiatkowska, The *Ireland v. United Kingdom (Mox Plant)* Case: Applying the Doctrine of Treaty Parallelism, 18 IJMCL 1-57 (2003) at: http://www.brill.nl/product.asp?ID=18253 and Kwiatkowska, A Reply to the Article by David A. Colson and Dr. Peggy Hoyle, *infra* note 35. See also *European Commission v. Ireland Mox Plant* Case C-459/03 of the European Court of Justice (ECJ), OJEC C 7/24 (2004) at http://europa.eu.int/eur-lex/pri/en/oj/dat/2004/c_007/c_00720040110en00240024.pdf and Opinion of Advocate General Poiares Maduro of 12 Jan 2006 [*UNSG Oceans Report*, UN Doc. A/61/63, para.275 (2006)] and the ECJ *EC v. Ireland Mox Plant* Judgment of 30 May 2006 at http://curia.eu.int/jrisp/cgi-bin/form.pl?lang=EN&Submit=rechercher&numaff=C-459/03 & Cases since 1989 at http://curia.eu.int/en/content/juris/index.htm and PR No.45/06 at http://curia.eu.nt/en/actu/communiques/cp060045en.pdf & www.asil.org/ilib060706.htm; Annex VII *Ireland v. UK Mox Plant (Suspension of Reports by the Parties)* Order of 22 January 2007 and *Mox Plant (Termination of Proceedings)* Order No.6 of 6 June 2008 at PCA, *supra*. See also ECJ *International Association of Independent Tank Owners (Intertanko) v. Secretary of State for Transport* Judgment, Case C-308/06 of 3 June 2008 at http://eur-lex.europa.eu and *Intertanko* Case Report, 103 AJIL 555-561 (2009).

16 For an example of testing such resilience, see the 1995 *Loizidou v. Turkey* Judgment of the Strasbourg Court of Human Rights [90 AJIL 98 (1996)], whose insistence on separateness was found to be "disquieting" by Sir Robert Jennings, The Judiciary, International and National, and the Development of International Law, 45 *International and Comparative Law Quarterly* 1, 5-6 (1996). See also criticism raised in the 55th UNGA Statement of

such occasional differences as may arise".[17] While welcoming the creation of specialized international tribunals as making "international law more effective", President Stephen M. Schwebel reiterated in his Statement on the occasion of the closing of the Second and the opening of the Third Millennium that:

> A greater range of international legal fora is likely to mean that more disputes are submitted to international judicial settlement. The more international adjudication there is, the more there is likely to be: the "judicial habit" may stimulate healthy imitation.[18]

President Guillaume, *supra* note 6, of the application in the ICTY *Prosecutor v. Tadic* Judgment, paras 88-145 [38 ILM 1518 (1999); 94 AJIL 571 (2000)], of an "overall control" standard being less strict than an "effective control" standard which was applied by the *Nicaragua v. USA (Merits)* Judgment, ICJ Reports 1986, 45-65 and was rejected by Dissenting Opinion of Judge Stephen M. Schwebel, paras 154 *et seq*. Cf. *Report of the International Law Commission (ILC) 53rd Session*, UN Doc. A/56/10, 105-107 (2001) and authoritative explanation of differences between the *Tadic* and *Nicaragua v. USA* standards, in ICJ President Higgins' Speech to the 59th ILC (2007), *supra* note 6, as further quoted *infra* note 21.

17 Statement of President Schwebel to the 53rd UNGA, *supra* note 6, also welcoming the first instance of judicial activity of ITLOS as "a notable event in the life of international courts"; Schwebel, The Contribution, *supra* note 1, at 406; B.H. Oxman, Comments on the "Horizontal" Growth of International Courts, in *The Legalization of International Relations, Proceedings of the 96th Annual ASIL, Washington D.C., 13-16 March 2002* 373, 375-376 (2002); 2006 Statement of President Higgins to the 61st UNGA, *supra* note 6, at 6, stressing that growth in the number of new courts and tribunals has generated certain concerns about the potential for a lack of consistency in the enunciation of legal norms and the attendant risk of fragmentation, but that these concerns have not proved significant and that: "The authoritative nature of ICJ judgments is widely acknowledged. It has been gratifying for the International Court to see that these newer courts and tribunals have regularly referred, often in a manner essential to their legal reasoning, to judgments of the ICJ with respect to questions of international law and procedure".

18 Statements of President Schwebel to the 53rd and the 54th UNGA, *supra* note 6, also noting that "increase in recourse to the Court is likely to endure, at any rate if a state of relative détente in international relations endures". Note that President Schwebel's triennium (1997-2000) marked the busiest docket of unmatched 22 new cases (by comparison to 6 new cases during President Guillaume's triennium 2000-2003) in the history of the Court, which had raisen the docket to about 15 cases in total annually during the next ICJ triennia in 2000-2012. Cf. Merrills, *supra* note 12, at 289; Interview of Judge Stephen M. Schwebel on International Law and the World Court of 10 January 2001, *Harvard International Review* at: www.npwj.org/pressmon/20010110_HIR.shtml; Statements of

A similar view was expressed in the Statement of ITLOS President Chandrasekhara Rao in 2000 when he characterized the establishment of new tribunals in recent years as "a positive development" and remarked that: "The effect of more tribunals being available to litigants is that more disputes have come to be resolved by parties by means of their choice".[19] At the same time, President Schwebel appreciated the virtue – as also supported in 1997-2006 by ICJ Presidents Gilbert Guillaume and Shi Jiuyong and in 2008 once again reiterated by Former President Guillaume – in enabling other international tribunals, both those which are organs of the United Nations (such as the ICTY or the ICTR) and those which are not (such as the ITLOS or the ICC), to request advisory opinions of the ICJ on issues of international law that arise in cases before those tribunals and are of importance to the unity of international law.[20] When the ILC Study

---

President Guillaume to the 55th-57th UNGA and President Shi to the 58th-59th UNGA, *supra* note 6; 2001 Speech of President Gilbert Guillaume at Lauterpacht Research Centre for International Law, Cambridge University at: www.law.cam.ac.uk/rcil/Guillaume.doc, *reprinted in* Guillaume, *La Cour Internationale de Justice*, *supra* note 1, at 33-45; Reflections on International Adjudication by Former ICJ President Stephen M. Schwebel, in 2004 Yale Alumni Reading Materials and His 2008 UN Lecture, *supra* note 13; 2006 IWPR Interview with ICJ President Rosalyn Higgins, *supra* note 13, followed by her Statements to the 61st-63rd UNGA, *supra* note 6; Merills (2007) and The Revitalization of the PCA (2007), *supra* note 12; Schwebel, *The International Judge* (2008), *supra* note 1; Alain Pellet at www.law.cam.ac.uk/faculty-resources/summary/the-function-of-law-in-the-international-community-tribute--professor-alain-pellet/6185, in Crawford and Young eds., *The Function of Law in the International Community* (2008), *supra* note 3.

19 Statement of ITLOS President Chandrasekhara Rao to the 55th General Assembly, UN Doc. A/55/PV.44, 1, 2, 30 October 2000, also noting that the exhortation of the UN Millennium Declaration to ensure compliance with the decisions of the ICJ, pursuant to the UN Charter, is equally relevant to decisions of all international courts and tribunals. See also Statement of ITLOS President Jose Luis Jesus to the 63rd General Assembly of 5 December 2008 and Gilberto Amado Memorial Lecture of President Jesus at the 61st ILC of 15 July 2009 at www.itlos.org/news/statements/news_president_en.shtml.

20 Statements of President Schwebel to the 54th UNGA and of President Guillaume to the 55th-57th UNGA, *supra* note 6; and 2001 Cambridge Speech of President Guillaume, *supra* note 15; Statement of Judge Shi Jiuyong, President of the International Court of Justice, to the 6th Committee of the 59th UNGA of 5 November 2004, pp.5-6 at http://www.un.org/News/Press/docs/2004/gal3266.doc.htm. Cf., e.g., Hans Corell, The Feasibility of Implementing The Hague/St. Petersburg Centennial Recommendations Under the UN System, in *Peaceful Resolution*, *supra* note 5, at 31; Rosenne, An Introduction to International Litigation, *supra* note 14; Statement of President Jacques Chirac of France,

Group Report under Prof. Martti Koskenniemi's Chair misinterpreted contrast between the 1986 ICJ *Nicaragua v. United States (Merits)* Judgment and the 1999 ICTY *Prosecutor v. Tadic* Judgment as an example of a "normative conflict" between "the effective control" and "an overall control" respectively, the then Court's President Rosalyn Higgins carefully clarified the occurred confusion by explaining that during consideration of attribution of the genocide at Srebrenica to the Respondent on the basis of direction or control, the 2007 *Bosnia and Herzegovina v. Serbia and Montenegro (Jurisdiction and Merits)* Judgment authoritatively showed that the two standards in question (of which 2007 Judgment applied the *Nicaragua* standard of "the effective control") were distinctly different and did not justify any concern over "normative conflict".[21]

ICJ Press Release No.2000/36, 26 October 2000 at www.icj-cij.org; 57th UNGA Statement on the ICJ by Russia, UN Doc.A/57/37, *supra* note 6, at 5; Kwiatkowska, Peaceful Settlement, *supra* note 5; Oxman, *supra* note 17; T. Gill, *Rosenne's The World Court: What It Is and How It Works* 240-241 (6th Ed. 2003); B. Kwiatkowska, The World Court and Peaceful Settlement of Oceans Disputes – Some Reflections, in R. Barnes and D. Freestone eds., *The Law of the Sea: Progress and Prospects* 433, 439-440 (Oxford 2006) at www.oup.com/uk/catalogue/?ci=9780199299614; Rosenne, *The Law and Practice* (2006), *supra* note 9, at 39-40; *Bosnia & Herzegovina v. Serbia & Montenegro Application of the Convention on the Prevention and Punishment of the Crime of Genocide (Jurisdiction and Merits)* Judgment, 46 ILM 185 (2007); ICJ Reports 2007, 238-239, *dispositif* para.471(8), requesting Serbia to transfer individuals accused of genocide for trial by the ICTY and to cooperate fully with that Tribunal; Former ICJ President Gilbert Guillaume, The International Judicial Function, at 2 & 7 at www.lcil.cam.ac.uk/Media/25_anniversary/Judicial_Function_paper.pdf, in *The Function of Law in the International Community* (2008), *supra* note 3. See also Article 119 of the 1998 UN Rome Statute of the International Criminal Court [in force: 1 July 2002, 2187 UNTS 3; 37 ILM 999 (1998); www.un.org/icc] and on its signing by the United States on 31 December 2000, see M. Leigh, The United States and the Statute of Rome, 95 AJIL 124-131, 397-400, 967-969 (2001); review by Judge Schwebel [*supra* note 4], 95 AJIL 465, and T.M. Franck, Judge Schwebel, A.V. Rovine *et al.*, ASIL Presidents' Memorandum on the ICC, *id.*, at 967-969 & http://www.amicc.org/docs/ASIL_ICC_memo.pdf; 41 ILM 1014 (2002); 97 AJIL 132-147, 710-711 (2003); US Ambassador Cunningham's Statement of 23 June 2004 at http://www.un.int/usa/04_111.htm; D. Akande, International Law Immunities and the ICC, 98 AJIL 407-433 (2004); USA and the ICC, 100 AJIL 477 (2006); ASIL Task Force (including Former ICJ President Stephen M. Schwebel) on the ICC of 6 February 2009 at www.asil.org/pdfs/pressreleases/pr090202.pdf & www.asil.org/ilib090206.cfm.

21 See *Bosnia and Herzegovina v. Serbia and Montenegro Application of the Convention on the Prevention and Punishment of the Crime of Genocide (Jurisdiction and Merits)*

* * *

As this *Reference Guide* was prepared in response to the then President Schwebel's belief that it is important for the Court, basing itself on the "intrinsic" authority and the consistency of its decisions, to continue to play and to further explore throughout the first century of the Third Millennium its pre-eminently unique role as the principal judicial organ of the United Nations,[22] the *Reference Guide* was dedicated to his outstanding commitment to "the strictly judicial tradition of the Court".[23]

Judgment, ICJ Reports 2007, 206-211, paras 396-407: The Question of Attribution of the Srebrenica Genocide to the Respondent on the Basis of Direction or Control, as presented in Speech of ICJ President Rosalyn Higgins to the 59th ILC (2007), *supra* note 6, at 8-9, in the context of the Report of ILC Study Group of Prof. Koskenniemi, UN Doc. A/CN.4/L.682, paras 49-51, at 31-32 (13 April 2006); *UNSG Report* A/62/62, ILC Articles on State Responsibility – Art.8, at 34-40 (2007), *infra* note 32; and *supra* notes 16-17. Nevertheless, Former ICJ President Guillaume, The International Judicial Function, *supra* note 20, at 5, continues to classify these cases as "conflicting jurisprudence".

22 Statement of President Schwebel to the 54th UNGA, *supra* note 6; and main text accompanying *supra* note 3.

23 Hudson, *supra* note 9, at 344; Manley O. Hudson, 43 AJIL 339 (1949), remarking: "The President is far more than the director of the public proceedings devoted to hearing agents or counsel appearing in cases before the Court. He is the guardian of the strictly judicial tradition of the Court. Upon him falls the delicate task of threading the deliberations of the judges to conclusions which will command the world's assent". Cf. also Rosenne, *The Law and Practice*, *supra* note 9, at 401-407. For President Schwebel's Bibliography, see Arthur Eyffinger, *The International Court of Justice 1946-1996* 323 (Kluwer 1996); *ICJ Yearbook 1997-1998* 20-21 (No.52); *ICJ Yearbook 1998-1999* 22-23 (No.53); the Court's website at http://www.icj-cij.org/icjwww/igeneralinformation/icvjudge/Schwebel.html & www.icj-cij.org/court/index.php?p1=1&p2=3; Cambridge Squire Law Library – Eminent Scholars Archive Gallery of H.E. Former ICJ President Stephen M. Schwebel at www.squire.law.cam.ac.uk/eminent_scholars/judge_stephen_m_schwebel.php & www.law.cam.ac.uk/faculty-resources/gallery/judge-stephen-m-schwebel/42; Who's Who Legal at http://www.whoswholegal.com/home.cfm; Wikipedia and Essex Chambers at http://en.wikipedia.org/wiki/Stephen_M._Schwebel, http://viswiki.com/en/Stephen_M._Schwebel & www.chambersandpartners.com/PersonProfile.aspx?CPK=221342&ssid=30382; Carnegie Council at www.cceia.org/people/data/stephen_m__schwebel.html; Johns Hopkins University at www.sais-jhu.edu/academics/functional-studies/international-law-orgs/index.htm & www.willamette.edu/wucl/news/2003_04/16.htm; UN Audiovisual Library at http://untreaty.un.org/cod/avl/faculty/Schwebel.html, *supra* note 13. On the Manley O. Hudson Medal and University of Miami's *Honoris Causa* awarded unanimously to Judge Schwebel in 2000 and 2002, see http://www.law.miami.edu/pdf/summer02.pdf, http://www.miami.edu/veritas/may2002/frontpage.html

Whereas the format of specific entries covered by this *Reference Guide* largely corresponds to the Parts and Annexes of the 1982 United Nations Law of the Sea Convention (UNCLOS) and the 1994 Agreement Relating to the Implementation of its Part XI, the heading of each entry also contains, as appropriate, references to the preceding provisions of the Report of the Second Committee (Territorial Sea) of the 1930 League of Nations Hague Conference for the Codification of International Law (Hague Draft) and the four 1958 United Nations Conventions and Optional Protocol.[24] This will enable the reader to identify the origin of various UNCLOS provisions in those of the 1958 Conventions, of which the Territorial Sea and Contiguous Zone Convention (TSC) drew heavily – as a result of *travaux préparatoires* of the International Law Commission – on the 1930 Hague Draft.[25] By contrast to the 1994 Part XI Agreement, the 1995 United Nations Fish Stocks Agreement, which was adopted in a follow-up

---

& http://www.asil.org/awardarchives.cfm#HudsonAwards; and on his TDM Board's Membership, see www.transnational-dispute-management.com/editors/content.htm and www.transnational-dispute-management.com/samples/toc.asp?key=10. See also particular appreciation expressed with respect to the dedication of this *Reference Guide* to Former ICJ President Stephen M. Schwebel in the *Guide*'s reviews by Sir Elihu Lauterpacht, Giuliana Ziccardi Capaldo, Said Mahmoudi and Jean-Pierre Queneudec, listed *infra* note 47.

24 For detailed surveys, taking due account of the impacts of these stages in the development of the modern international law of the sea, see Myron H. Nordquist, Editor-in-Chief, Satya N. Nandan, Shabtai Rosenne and Alexander Yankov, General Editors, *United Nations Convention on the Law of the Sea 1982 – A Commentary*, Vol.I (1985), Vol.II (1993), Vol.III (1995), Vol.IV (1991), Vol.V (1989), Vol.VI (2002) (Martinus Nijhoff). Cf. Jean-Pierre Lévy, The United Nations Convention on the Law of the Sea, in *Continental Shelf Limits – The Scientific and Legal Interface* 8-16 (Oxford 2000); David Freestone, Twenty-Five Years of the Law of the Sea Convention, 1982-2007, 22 IJMCL 1-6 (2007).

25 Cf. Sir Arthur Watts, *The International Law Commission 1949-1998*, Vol.I, 23-137, esp. 24 (Oxford 1999); Robin R. Churchill and A. Vaughan Lowe, *The Law of the Sea* 13-22, esp. 15 (Manchester 1999). Note that the 1930 Hague Draft was extensively discussed by the parties in the pleadings of the *Corfu Channel* and the *Anglo/Norwegian Fisheries* cases. Cf. the *Anglo/Norwegian* Pleadings, Vol.I, 395-6 (Counter-Memorial of Norway), invoking the *Corfu* Pleadings [Vol.III, 269-71 (11 November 1948, Agent Sir Eric Beckett)] to the effect that international conventions, referred to under Article 38(1)(a) of the ICJ Statute, "are finally agreed and ratified conventions," and that the Court is not entitled to apply as law in cases before it conventions which are only signed, and still less a mere 1930 Draft; Vol.II, 432-9 (Reply of UK), Vol.III, 301-2 (Rejoinder of Norway).

to the 1992 United Nations Conference on Environment and Development (UNCED), does not form a part of the Law of the Sea Convention. However, since the 1995 Agreement significantly promotes the implementation of the fisheries provisions of the UNCLOS, as partly originated from the 1958 High Seas and the High Seas Fishing Conventions (HSC and HSFC),[26] the Agreement's provisions are also referred to at this *Guide*'s specific entries, as appropriate. In addition, although the 1972 UN Stockholm Declaration and Action Plan and 1992 UNCED Rio Declaration and Agenda 21, reaffirmed by the 2002 Johannesburg World Summit on Sustainable Development (WSSD) and 2005 UN World Summit, are of a non-binding nature, the importance of collaborative frameworks provided by these instruments for the codification and progressive development of the law of the sea justified their inclusion in the headings of entries concerned as well.[27]

---

[26] Cf. Churchill and Lowe, *supra* note 21, at 279-327; Dolliver Nelson, The Development of the Legal Regime of High Seas Fisheries, in Alan Boyle and David Freestone eds, *International Law and Sustainable Development: Past Achievements and Future Challenges* 113-134 (Oxford 1999); Moritaka Hayashi, The 1995 UN Fish Stocks Agreement and the Law of the Sea, in Davor Vidas and Willy Ostreng eds, *Order for the Oceans at the Turn of the Century* 37-53 (Kluwer 1999); William Edeson, Closing the Gap: The Role of "Soft" International Instruments to Control Fishing, 20 *Australian Yearbook of International Law 1999* 83-104 (2000); Andrew Serdy, How Long Has the UN Fish Stocks Agreement Been in Force? 34 *Ocean Development and International Law* (ODIL) 29-39 (2003); M.W. Lodge and Satya N. Nandan, Some Suggestions Towards Better Implementation of the 1995 UN Fish Stocks Agreement, 20 IJMCL 345-379 (2005); UN Fish Stocks Agreement: 2006 Review Conference, 21 IJMCL 551-600 (2006); D. Freestone, Principles Applicable to Modern Oceans Governance, 23 IJMCL 385-391 (2008).

[27] See the recognition in the 2000 United Nations Millennium Declaration, *supra* note 7, of "respect for nature" as one of the fundamental values which are "essential to international relations in the Twenty-First Century" (para.6) and this Declaration's express reaffirmation of "support for the principles of sustainable development", including those set in the UNCED Agenda 21 (para.22). For reaffirmation of commitments to the United Nations Charter and Millennium Declaration, see 2002 WSSD Johannesburg Declaration, paras 8, 32, and Plan of Implementation, paras 1, 121(e), 124-125 at http://www.iisd.ca/wssd/portal.html and UN Doc. A/CONF.199/2002), endorsed by UNGA Resolutions A/57/141 (paras 7-8) and A/57/253 of 12 and 20 December 2002; and the 2005 UN World Summit at www.un.org/summit2005 & www.un.org/ga/59/hl60_plenarymeeting.html. Cf. Keynote Address of United Nations Legal Counsel Hans Corell on UN Stockholm Declaration of 25 May 2002 at http://www.un.org/law/counsel/english/stockholm.pdf and UNSG Kofi Annan's Message on Sustainable Management of Oceans and Seas of 12 May 2004 at: www.un.org/News/Press/docs/2004/sgsm9302.doc.htm; 2005 UN World

Consequently, the reader will be able to easily relate each judicial, arbitral or other third party decision to the respective stage of codification and progressive development of the law of the sea on a particular issue. For instance, whereas the 1927 *France v. Turkey S.S. Lotus* Judgment was rendered during the *travaux* of the League of Nations Committee of Experts for the Progressive Codification of International Law, the Judgment's pronouncement that "vessels on the high seas are subject to no authority except that of the State whose flag they fly", as recognized by all six dissenting Judges, and as reflected in the 1949 *Corfu Channel (Merits)* Judgment, was subsequently codified in Article 6(1) of the 1958 HSC, as restated in Article 92(1) of the 1982 UNCLOS.[28] It will also be apparent from the global treaties and instruments listed in the heading of each entry that, for instance, the pair of the 1973-1974 *Australia v. France; New Zealand v. France Nuclear Tests* cases were settled shortly after the 1972 UN Stockholm Conference had initiated a global impetus for protection and preservation of the natural, including marine, environment,[29] and that the proceedings of the 1995-1998 *Spain v. Canada Fisheries (Jurisdiction)* case overlapped with the final stage of *travaux* of the 1995 UN Fish Stocks Agreement, which had not yet during these proceedings entered into force (this took place only on 11 December 2001).[30] The appreciation of such relationships between global framework instruments referred to above

---

Summit Outcome, *supra* note 7; 2005 UN Millennium Ecosystem Assessment at www.un.org/News/Press/docs/2005/sgsm9789.doc.htm; UN Law of the Sea Convention 26 Years Later of 4 December 2008 at www.un.org/News/Press/docs//2008/ga10793.doc.htm; Assessment of Assessments, UN Doc.A/64/88 of 11 June 2009; UNGA Adopts Two Oceans Resolutions of 4 December 2009 at www.un.org/News/Press/docs//2009/ga10899.doc.htm.

28 See *A Reference Guide*: High Seas – Status of Ships/Criminal Jurisdiction *infra*.

29 See *A Reference Guide*: Peaceful Uses of the Sea – Nuclear (Atmospheric and Underground) Weapon Tests *infra*. Cf. Barbara Kwiatkowska, *New Zealand v. France Nuclear Tests*: The Dismissed Case of Lasting Significance, 37 *Virginia Journal of International Law* 107-190 (1996); Alain Pellet, A Tribute to Sir Elihu Lauterpacht, in *The Function of Law in the International Community* (2008), *supra* note 3.

30 See *A Reference Guide:* Fisheries *infra*. Cf. Barbara Kwiatkowska, The *Spain v. Canada Fisheries (Jurisdiction)* Judgment, 93 AJIL 502-507 (1999); Robin R. Churchill, *Fisheries Jurisdiction (Spain v. Canada)* Case, 12 LJIL 597-611 (1999). On Canada's ratification of the UN Law of the Sea Convention, see UN Secretary-General Kofi A. Annan's Statement of 7 November 2003 at: www.un.org/apps/sg/sgstats.asp?nid=616.

and decisions of various third party dispute settlement fora is a *conditio sine qua non* of adequate assessment of the contributions made by each of those decisions to the development of the law of the sea as part of general international law.

A Reference Guide covers not only decisions on the merits, but all other relevant decisions of the ICJ and other third party fora as well. This is because the impacts of decisions by international courts and tribunals on the development of rules of law can – like the impacts between the parties to the disputes concerned – be achieved as much by the decisions settling the merits of the disputes as by those rendered during various procedural phases.[31] Consequently, all the decisions of the ICJ, ITLOS and Arbitral Tribunals are being regularly reported upon in the annual *Oceans and the Law of the Sea* Reports of the UN Secretary-General and covered by the UN and ICJ *Bibliographies* and *Digest of International Cases on the Law of the Sea*.[32] In view of their accepted contributions, this *Reference Guide* covers, moreover, individual Opinions appended by Judges and Arbitrators

---

31 See, e.g., references to the 1998 *Spain v. Canada Fisheries (Jurisdiction)* Judgment, in *A Reference Guide*: Exclusive Economic (/Fishery) Zone, and those to the 1999 *Southern Bluefin Tuna (Provisional Measures)* Order, *id.*, Protection and Preservation of the Marine Environment – Precautionary Approach *infra*.

32 See, e.g., UN Docs A/56/58, *supra* note 14, at 77-80, and Add.1, at 19-20 (2001), A/58/65/Add.1 (2003) at 31-33, A/61/63/Add.1, paras 175-176 (2006), *infra* note 35, A/62/66, paras 337-341, A/62/66/Add.1, paras 242-246 (2007), A/63/63, paras 365-374 (2008); A/64/66 and Add.1 (2009) at www.un.org/Depts/los/. See also *infra* note 43. The Reports – along with other documents – were in the years 1985-2002 reproduced and indexed annually, in Editor-in-Chief Barbara Kwiatkowska, Co-Editors Harm Dotinga, Erik Molenaar, Alex Oude Elferink and Alfred Soons, *International Organizations and the Law of the Sea – Documentary Yearbook*, Vols 1-1985/17-2001, Vol.18-2002 (2005) at http://www.brill.nl/product_id 18776.htm [discontinued due to financial crisis of Utrecht Faculty of Law]. The case-law concerned and the pertaining literature are analyzed in Series listed *supra* notes 8, 15; they are inventarized, in *Digest of International Cases on the Law of the Sea* (UN-New York 2007); *Responsibility of States for Internationally Wrongful Acts – Part I: Compilation of Decisions of International Courts, Tribunals and Other Bodies*, UN Docs A/62/62 (1 February 2007) and *Part II: Comments and Information Received from Governments*, A/62/63 (9 March 2007); and they are also annually listed and indexed in *The Law of the Sea – A Select Bibliography* (UN-New York) and *Bibliography of the International Court of Justice* (UN-ICJ).

to the decisions concerned,[33] and primarily in cases before the PCIJ and ICJ, but also in some cases before the ITLOS – the written and oral pleadings.[34] In addition, the *Guide* covers valuable pleadings in the 2000 *Southern Bluefin Tuna (Jurisdiction and Admissibility)* Award, which was unprecedented in departing from the previously fundamental principle of the privacy of arbitration proceedings and was followed by inaugural accessibility of boundary delimitation pleadings in the 2006 *Barbados/Trinidad and Tobago (Jurisdiction and Merits)* Award, which both Awards were rendered by the Annex VII Arbitral Tribunals presided over by Former ICJ President Stephen M. Schwebel.[35] The *North-South Sudan*

---

[33] For assessments of individual Opinions, see especially Sir Robert Jennings, The Internal Judicial Practice of the International Court of Justice, 59 BYIL 31-47 (1988); R. Jennings, The Collegiate Responsibility and Authority of the International Court of Justice, in *International Law at a Time of Perplexity – Essays in Honour of Shabtai Rosenne* 343-353 (Martinus Nijhoff 1989); Rosenne, *The Law and Practice* (1997), at 1579-1585 and (2006), at 1526-1531, *supra* note 9; and Schwebel, The Inter-Active Influence, *supra* note 1, at 482, 485-488, 504-505.

[34] On the value of pleadings as important evidence of state practice, see especially Schwebel, The Inter-Active Influence, *supra* note 1, at 483, 487-488 and 504-505. Coverage by this *Reference Guide* of not only Judgments and Awards but also Separate and Dissenting Opinions of Judges and Arbitrators, as well as the pleadings was appreciated in reviews of Sir Elihu Lauterpacht, 48 AFDI 887 (2002), Jean-Pierre Queneudec and Ziccardi Capaldo, listed *infra* note 47.

[35] Not only were the Award and its written and oral pleadings placed on the Internet, but also public access was allowed to the Oral Hearings. See *supra* note 14; Barbara Kwiatkowska, The *Australia and New Zealand v. Japan Southern Bluefin Tuna (Jurisdiction and Admissibility)* Award of the First Annex VII Arbitral Tribunal, 16 IJMCL 239-294 (2001) at http://www.brill.nl/product.asp?ID=18253 & http://www.uu.nl/nilos/onlinepapers; Stephen M. Schwebel, The *Southern Bluefin Tuna* Case, in *Liber Amicorum Judge Shigeru Oda* 743-748 (Kluwer 2002), and essays by this author, Y. Otani and Ambassador Chusei Yamada, *id.*, at 697, 731, 763; B. Kwiatkowska, The *Southern Bluefin Tuna* Arbitral Tribunal Did Get It Right: A Commentary and Reply to the Article by David A. Colson and Dr. Peggy Hoyle, 34 ODIL 369-395 (2003); remarks of President Higgins, The ICJ, the ECJ (2003), *supra* note 14; T.L. McDorman *et al., International Ocean Law* 413-423 (2005) at: www.cap-press.com/books/1247. For 2006 *Barbados/Trinidad and Tobago* Award, including its written and oral pleadings (which were made public upon the Award's delivery), President Stephen M. Schwebel, see PCA at http://www.pca-cpa.org/; 45 ILM 800 (2006) at http://www.asil.org/resources/ilm.html; XXVII UNRIAA 147 at www.un.org/law/riaa & http://untreaty.un.org/cod/riaa/cases/vol_XXVII/147-251.pdf; *PCA Awards Series*, Vol.V (2007), *summarized in ASIL/ILIB* of 28 April 2006 at http://www.asil.org/ilib060428.htm and *UN Secretary-General Report on Oceans and the*

Abyei Boundary Arbitral Tribunal, of which Judge Schwebel was a member too, went one step further than the *Barbados/Trinidad and Tobago* Award by making all written and oral pleadings available on Internet (PCA) not upon rendering the 2009 Final *Abyei* Award, but based on the ICJ and *Southern Bluefin Tuna* practice – already upon holding of the *Abyei* Oral Hearings, which in addition were opened to the public access.[36]

Law of the Sea, Doc. A/61/63/Add.1, paras 175-176 (2006) at: http://www.un.org/Depts/los/; and other references to the 2006 Award listed, in *A Reference Guide*: Equitable Maritime Boundary Delimitation *infra*. For the 2006 Award's analysis, see Session 4 on "From *Jan Mayen* Judgment to *Barbados/Trinidad and Tobago* Award" (26 June 2006), IBRU Workshop on Options for Unlocking Maritime Boundary Disputes, Paris, 26-28 June 2006 at http://www-ibru.dur.ac.uk/workshops/2006/maritime.html; Lectures of B. Kwiatkowska on "The 2006 *Barbados/Trinidad and Tobago* Award" (11 July 2006) at the 11th Rhodes Academy of Oceans Law and Policy, Rhodes, Greece, 2-21 July 2006 at: http://www.virginia.edu/colp/; B. Kwiatkowska, The 2006 *Barbados/Trinidad and Tobago* Case Report, 101 AJIL 149-157 (2007) and her Tribute in Remembrance of Louis B. Sohn at the ASIL Symposium on The Law of the Sea in the Twenty-First Century, George Washington University Law School, Washington D.C., 24 October 2006 at http://www.asil.org/pdfs/sohnprogram1.pdf, *reprinted in* 39 *George Washington International Law Review* 573-620 (2007 No.3) available at www.allbusiness.com/government/government-bodies-offices-law-courts/8896208-1.html; Yoshifumi Tanaka, The *Barbados/Trinidad and Tobago* Case Report, 21 *International Journal of Marine and Coastal Law* (2006 No.4) and B. Kwiatkowska, The 2006 *Barbados/Trinidad and Tobago* Award: A Landmark in Compulsory Jurisdiction and Equitable Maritime Boundary Delimitation, 22 IJMCL 7-60 (2007), *reprinted* at NILOS at www.uu.nl/nilos/onlinepapers; Robin Churchill, Dispute Settlement Under the UNCLOS: Survey for 2006, 22 IJMCL 463, 470-483 (2007) at www.brill.nl/product.asp?ID=18253; Bernard H. Oxman, *Commentary on the 2006 Barbados/Trinidad and Tobago Award* (Cambridge 2010) at www.cambridge.org/us/catalogue/catalogue.asp?isbn=9067043214.

36 *North/South Sudan Abyei Boundary* Award at PCA at www.pca-cpa.org; 31 October 2008 at www.globalarbitrationreview.com/news/article/14904/dupuy-preside-sudan-dispute/; 17 April 2009, www.globalarbitrationreview.com/news/article/15231; Final *Abyei Boundary* Award of 22 July 2009 and *Press Release*, PCA *supra*, UNSG Ban Ki-Moon's Statement Welcomes the *Abyei* Award as a Major Contribution to Peace of 22 July 2009 at www.un.org/apps/news/story.asp?NewsID=31544&Cr=Abyei&Cr1; Joint SPLM-NPC Statement on Implementation of the Final Abyei Award at www.gossmission.org/goss/index.php?option=com_content&task=view&id=928&Itemid=1; EU-USA Declaration on the *Abyei* Award of 22 July 2009 at www.consilium.europa.eu/uedocs/cms_data/docs/pressdata/en/cfsp/109304.pdf; *ASIL Insights* by John R. Crook at www.asil.org/insights090916.cfm; Hague Border Ruling Raises Big Peace Hopes in Sudan of 22 July 2009 at http://news.bbc.co.uk/2/hi/africa/8162690.stm, www

Under each entry covered by this *Reference Guide*, the relevant Judgments and Orders of the PCIJ and the ICJ are first listed chronologically, followed by a separate listing of Awards of the Arbitral Tribunals and other third party decisions (e.g., of various United Nations bodies, conciliation commissions or the WTO Appellate Body), as well as by Judgments and Orders of the ITLOS. In the case of sub-entries, all the Judgments, Awards and other decisions are jointly listed chronologically.[37]

All Judgments and Orders, including Opinions of Judges, rendered in various phases of particular cases are jointly listed with reference to their sources (PCIJ Series and ICJ Reports), specification of names of the Court's Presidents and the results of voting, under entries where they effected the principal contribution to the development of law.[38] The same applies to Awards of the Arbitral Tribunals and other third party decisions[39] and

---

.globalarbitrationreview.com/news/article/18363 & www.voanews.com/english/2009-07-22-voa40.cfm; *Abyei* Homepage, www.sudantribune.com/spip.php?mot99.

37 See, e.g., *A Reference Guide*: Equitable Maritime Boundary Delimitation -1982 LOSC, Articles 74(1)/83(1) to Articles 74(4)/83(4) *infra*.

38 E.g., for the *Wimbledon* case (*supra* note 2), see *A Reference Guide*: Inter-Oceanic Canals; for the *Corfu Channel* case, see *id.*, Straits Used for International Navigation; and for *Spain v. Canada Fisheries* case, see *id.*, Fisheries *infra*; for *Romania v. Ukraine Maritime Delimitation in the Black Sea* case, see *id.*, Equitable Maritime Boundary Delimitation *infra*.

39 See, e.g., *A Reference Guide*: Equitable Maritime Boundary Delimitation, and Regime of Islands *infra*, which along with Awards cover, e.g., the 1981 *Iceland/Norway (Jan Mayen)* Conciliation Commmission, the 1993 *UN Iraq/Kuwait Boundary Demarcation* Commission and the 2002-2008 *UN Eritrea/Ethiopia Boundary* Commission. Both these major entries list decisions on sovereignty over the land and insular territory which are closely inter-related with maritime delimitation and other oceans disputes and which are covered by the *Oceans and the Law of the Sea* Reports. See, e.g., UN Doc. A/56/58, *supra* note 14, at 78; Sir Elihu Lauterpacht CBE QC, Judge Stephen M. Schwebel, Shabtai Rosenne & Francisco Orrego Vicuna, *Joint Legal Opinion on Guatemala's Territorial Claim to Belize* at www.belize-guatemala.gov.bz/library/legal_opinion/welcome.html & http://vandeplaspublishing.com; Belize/Guatemala Territorial Differendum Proposals (with Maps) from the OAS Facilitators of 30 August 2002 and Belize/Guatemala Agreement to Establish a Transition Process and Confidence Building Measures of 7 February 2003, www.belize-guatemala.gov.bz/; OAS Press Releaseof 18 April 2007 at www.oas.org/OASpage/press_releases/press_release.asp?sCodigo=E-106/07; OAS Documents, http://oas.org/documents/eng/belizeguatemala.asp; John G. Merrills, The *Belize-Guatemala Territorial* Dispute and the Legal Opinion, 2 YILJ 2002, at 77-95 (2003) at: http://wwww.oceanalaw.com/main_product_details.asp?ID=298 and Vols 1-6 (2001-2006) www.us.oup.com/us/catalog/general/subject/Law/?view=usa&ci=037921475X; Belize/

Judgments and Orders of the ITLOS.[40] Subsequently, only specific decisions of a given case are referred to elsewhere under the various entries and sub-entries to which they apply. Under each main entry, treaties implementing the PCIJ and ICJ Judgments[41] and/or their other major impacts as between the parties[42] are also specified. Similar specification is made with respect to various decisions of other fora, including the 2000 *Southern Bluefin Tuna* Award, which marked the first instance of application of the UNCLOS Annex VII, followed by *Ireland v. United Kingdom Mox Plant*, *Malaysia v. Singapore*, *Barbados/Trinidad and Tobago*, *Guyana/Suriname* and newly instituted *Bay of Bengal* Arbitrations.[43] Whereas the multiple contributions

---

Guatemala Sign at OAS in Washington D.C. a Historic Special Agreement (*Compromis*) on Submitting Their Territorial and Maritime Dispute to the ICJ of 8 December 2008 at www.oas.org/OASpage/press_releases/press_release.asp?sCodigo=E-463/08 & 48 ILM 250 (2009). See also remarks on the relation between the maritime and land boundary questions, in *Cameroon v. Nigeria; Equatorial Guinea Intervening (Merits)* Oral Hearings, CR 2002/12, 61-64 [Counsel Crawford, 6 March], CR 2002/17, 41-43 [Counsel Sir Ian Sinclair, 12 March 2002] at: www.icj-cij.org.

For the 1986-1990 *New Zealand v. France The Rainbow Warrior* case, comprising a Ruling by the UN Secretary-General and two Awards, see *A Reference Guide*: Access to, Jurisdiction and Treatment in Ports; Kwiatkowska, *supra* note 29, at 120-121; *supra* note 12.

40 See, e.g., *A Reference Guide*: Settlement of Disputes – Prompt Release of Vessels and Crews *infra*. Cf. *supra* note 15.

41 E.g., for treaties implementing the *Corfu Channel* case, see *A Reference Guide*: Straits Used for International Navigation; and for those implementing many maritime boundary related decisions of the PCIJ and ICJ, see *id.*, Equitable Maritime Boundary Delimitation *infra*.

42 For the impacts of the 1998 *Spain v. Canada Fisheries (Jurisdiction)* Judgment in terms of Canada's ratification on 3 August 1999 of the 1995 UN Fish Stocks Agreements and initiation of work aimed at developing specific dispute settlement procedures of the NAFO, see *A Reference Guide*: Fisheries; and for the 1956 *Greece v. UK Ambatielos Claim* Award, which followed the 1952-1953 *Ambatielos* Judgments, see *id.*, High Seas *infra*.

43 For the impacts of the 2000 *Southern Bluefin Tuna* Award (*supra* notes 14 and 35) in terms of resolution of the dispute on 29 May 2001, as well as New Zealand's ratification on 18 April 2001 of the 1995 UN Fish Stocks Agreement, see *A Reference Guide*: Settlement of Disputes – Preventive Diplomacy A) and D). Cf. William R. Mansfield, The *Southern Bluefin Tuna* Arbitration: Comments on Professor Barbara Kwiatkowska's Article, 16 IJMCL 361-366 (2001) at http://www.brill.nl/product.asp?ID=18253; also available at: http://www.mft.govt.nz/. On the second instance of an Annex VII Arbitral Tribunal in the *Ireland v. UK Mox Plant* case, coupled with the 2003 OSPAR *Ireland v. UK Mox Plant* Award and the 2006 ECJ *EC Commission v. Ireland* Judgment, see

of the PCIJ and the older ICJ cases are briefly summarized in this *Reference Guide*, this is not done with respect to the current cases of the Court, of which texts and related literature, especially AJIL case reports under longstanding editorship of Bernard H. Oxman, Daniel Bodansky, and most recently of David J. Bederman, as well as the annual AJIL Judicial Activity of the ICJ by John R. Crook and Stephen Mathias – like those concerning the ITLOS, Arbitral Tribunals and other third party fora – are easily available on and/or can be traced through the Internet.

Each entry and sub-entry covered by *A Reference Guide* commences with a listing – in the manner explained above – of the "Relevant Jurisprudence", and includes cross-references to other entries and sub-entries, as appropriate. In the cases of broad entries, such as Internal Waters, Territorial Sea and Baselines, Equitable Maritime Boundary Delimitation, Regime of Islands, Protection and Preservation of the Marine Environment or Peaceful Uses of the Sea, the specific sub-entries are followed by the chronological lists of references to the major Awards and some decisions of national courts,[44] as well as bilateral, regional and

---

supra note 15. On the third instance, see Annex VII 2005 *Malaysia v. Singapore* Award, including Settlement Agreement, President M.C.W. Pinto at: www.pca-cpa.org/. On the fourth and fifth instances, see the 2006 Annex VII *Barbados/Trinidad and Tobago (Jurisdiction and Merits)* Award, *supra* note 35 and *Guyana/Suriname* Arbitration, President L.D.M. Nelson, *id.*; D. Dzurek, 9 March 2004 at http://www.boundaries.com/bits and Th.W. Donovan, April 2004 at http://www.asil.org/insights/insigh131.htm; *UNSG Oceans Report*, UN Docs A/59/62, paras 38-39 and A/59/62/Add.1, paras 46-48 (2004) at http://www.un.org/Depts/los/; 2007 *Guyana v. Suriname (Jurisdiction and Merits)* Award of 17 September 2007 at www.pca-cpa.org/, ASIL/ILIB at www.asil.org/ilib071214.htm & http://cgxenergy.ca/news.html; UN Court Settles Border Dispute of 20 September 2007 at www.iht.com/articles/ap/2007/09/20/business/CB-FIN-Suriname-Guyana-Border-Dispute.php & http://cgxenergy.ca/News_Sep20_2007.html; 21 September 2007 at http://cgxenergy.ca/News_Sep21_20071.html & http://cgxenergy.ca/News_Sep21_20072.html; 22 September 2007, http://cgxenergy.ca/News_Sep22_20071.html; 23 September 2007, www.trinidadexpress.com/index.pl/article_news?id=161206967; Suriname Parliament Rejects Motion to Challenge Maritime Boundary Award and Former ICJ President Stephen M. Schwebel Speaks in Support of the *Guyana/Suriname* Award's Maritime Delimitation Resolution of 15 October 2007 at www.rigzone.com/news/article.asp?a_id=51473 & http://cgxenergy.ca/News_Oct12_2007.html. See also The Revitalization of the PCA (2007), *supra* note 12; *A Reference Guide*: Equitable Maritime Boundary Delimitation – newly instituted Annex VII *Bay of Bengal* and the EU *Croatia/Slovenia* Arbitrations *infra*.

44 Cf. *supra* notes 9 and 34.

global treaties in the decisions (including their individual Opinions and pleadings) of the PCIJ and ICJ as well as other third party fora. The listing of treaties reflects jurisprudential recognition of the fact that the particular density of "treaties implementing or relating to provisions of that great law-making treaty", the Law of the Sea Convention,[45] forms a remarkable part of the modern law of the sea.[46]

* * *

I wish to express my gratitude to the Publishing Director of International Law, Mr. Hans van der Meij and his assistant Ms. Ingeborg van der Laan as well as to editor Ms. Birgitta Poelmans of Brill-Martinus Nijhoff Publishers for their excellent cooperation in the publication of the presently revised and updated second edition of *A Reference Guide*. Special words of thanks are due to Professor Alfred H.A. Soons, Director of Public International Law and the Netherlands Institute for the Law of the Sea (NILOS) at Utrecht University Faculty of Law, Economics and Governance, as well as to other NILOS staff members, Dr. Alex Oude Elferink, Dr. Erik Molenaar and Mr Harm Dotinga, for their friendship and collaborative

---

45 See 2000 *Southern Bluefin Tuna* Award, *supra* note 14, para.44. On the significance of the Award's holdings for special treaties implementing the UNCLOS, see literature on the 2000 Award listed *supra* note 35; and on important interpretation made in this respect in the 2006 Award, para.200, see Kwiatkowska, The 2006 *Barbados/Trinidad and Tobago* Award, 22 IJMCL, 21-27 (2007), *supra* note 35.

46 For indexes of such numerous global and regional treaties, see *A Reference Guide*: Relation to Other Conventions *infra*. The growing importance of those treaties is shown by the annual *United Nations Oceans and the Law of the Sea* Reports, *supra* note 32, and it was stressed in a Statement of the UN Legal Counsel, Dr. Hans Corell, UN Doc. A/55/274 (2000), referring to over 400 treaties existing in the field of ocean affairs at www.un.org/Depts/los/; UN OLA at http://untreaty.un.org/ola; UN Treaties at http://treaties.un.org; UN Law at www.un.org/law/lindex.htm.

Cf. Dr. Corell's Foreword, in *Treaty Handbook* iv-v (United Nations 2001), noting in the context of the implementation of commitment expressed in the 2000 United Nations Millennium Declaration to advancing the international rule of law (*supra* notes 7 and 27), that treaties are a primary source of international law. For an appraisal of the Court's jurisprudence concerning the law of treaties in the context of its inter-action with the ILC's work, see Schwebel, The Inter-Active Influence, *supra* note 1, at 488-492; Sir Arthur Watts, The International Court and the Continuing Customary International Law of Treaties, in *Liber Amicorum Judge Shigeru Oda*, *supra* note 35, at 251-266; and for detailed surveys, see Thirlway, *supra* note 8; and annual Statements of the ICJ Presidents – initiated by then President Schwebel – to the ILC, *supra* note 6.

spirit which enabled the carrying out and completing of *A Reference Guide* along with multiple other NILOS activities.

It is to be hoped that this *Guide* will fulfill its intended purpose to benefit further development of the law of the sea by the International Court of Justice and other courts and tribunals, as a part of general international law and as a part of the global system of peace and security throughout the first century of the Third Millennium.[47] It is also hoped that this *Guide*'s publication will perhaps lead to its further extended revision in the future.

Prof. Dr. Barbara Kwiatkowska
Deputy Director NILOS (1985-2009)
Professor of International Law of the Sea (1991-)
Faculty of Law, Economics and Governance
Utrecht University
Achter Sint Pieter 200
3512 HT Utrecht – The Netherlands
E-mail: B.Kwiatkowska@uu.nl
http://www.uu.nl/nilos
9 March 2010

---

[47] See main text accompanying *supra* notes 1-23. For reviews of B. Kwiatkowska, *Decisions of the World Court Relevant to the UN Convention on the Law of the Sea: A Reference Guide* (2002) at: http://www.brill.nl/product_id20709.htm, see Sir Elihu Lauterpacht, QC CBE, 1 *The Law and Practice of International Courts and Tribunals* 651 (2002); Jean-Pierre Queneudec, 106 *Revue Générale de Droit International Public* 728-729 (2002); 48 *Annuaire Francais de Droit International* 887 (2002); Giuliana Ziccardi Capaldo, 50 *Netherlands International Law Review* 88-93 (2003); David Freestone, 19 *International Journal of Marine and Coastal Law* 201-202 (2004); Said Mahmoudi, Faculty of Law, Stockholm University at: http://www.intfish.net/announcements/publicity/review.htm.

TABLE OF CASES
(chronologically)

Permanent Court of International Justice and International Court of Justice

Pending Cases

Inter-State Arbitral Tribunals

Pending Cases

International Tribunal for the Law of the Sea

Pending Cases

Other Third-Party Fora

Pending Cases

National Courts

TABLE OF TREATIES
(chronologically)

Multilateral Treaties

Bilateral Treaties

TABLE OF STATES AND SELECTED GEOGRAPHICAL NAMES
(alphabetically)*

* ***Editors Note***: Page numbers listed in this Table are other than pages of Cases and Treaties which can be found in their respective Tables *supra*. In the case of multi-phase cases, reference is only made to the main (not all) decision, e.g., Hawar Islands 2001 Qatar v. Bahrian Judgment (with 1994-1995 Jurisdiction Judgments, which also apply to Hawars, not being listed in the present Table). References to Cases and Treaties at each entry below follow the order in which they appear in the respective Tables. Cases are listed not only under their respective parties, but also under states which were particularly involved in the respective proceedings [e.g., 1949 ICJ Reparation Advisory Opinion is listed under: Israel, Palestine and Egypt, while 1995 Nuclear ICJ Tests is apart from its parties, also listed under Australia]. All Cases of the ICJ and ITLOS are covered by the present Table, while Arbitral and Other Cases as well as Treaties are – given their intensity – only listed selectively below.

A

B

C

Cambodia 1962 ICJ Temple of Preah Vihear

Cameroon xix n.6, 2002 ICJ Cameroon v. Nigeria; Equatorial Guinea Intervening & 2002-2009 UN Cameroon/Nigeria Commission; 2006 Cameroon/Nigeria Agreement

Canada xix n.6; 53, 58, 136, 138, 171, 208, 229, 235 & 244, 265, 296, 1970 ICJ Barcelona Traction; 1984 ICJ Canada/USA Gulf of Maine; 1998 ICJ Spain v. Canada Fisheries; 2004 ICJ Legality of Use of Force; 1798 UK/USA St. Croix River; 1837 Canada/USA Caroline; 1935 Canada/USA I'm Alone; 1938-1941 Trail Smelter; 1992 Canada/France (St. Pierre & Miquelon); 1986 Canada/France Filleting; 1998 WTO EC Hormones; 1914 Attorney-General for British Columbia; 1967 Reference Re Ownership; 1970 Arrow; 1977 Re Ownership of the Bed; 1984 Reference Re the Seabed; 1989 Rubin v. Canada; 1997 Dagg v. Canada; 1998 Occam Marine Technologies; 2001-2002 Newfoundland & Labrador/Nova Scotia (Phases I-II); 2004 Colville Tribes v. Teck Cominco; 1952 & 1993 North Pacific Anadromous Stocks Conventions; 1953 USA/Canada Convention; 1995 EC/Canada Fisheries Agreement; 1955 Canada/USA Great Lake Fisheries Treaty; 1930 and 1985 Canada/USA Salmon Treaties; 1984 Canada/USA Skagit River Treaty; 1989 Canada/Denmark (Greenland) Whales Memorandum; 1990 Canada/USA Fisheries Agreement; 2007-2012 Canada/USA Gulf of Maine Action Plan

Canary Islands 77

Cape Race Lighthouse 24

Cape Spartel 1865 Cape Spartel Lighthouse Convention

Caribbean Sea (see **Latin America & Caribbean**)

Caroline Islands 1885 Germany/Spain Caroline Islands

Caspian Sea 225

Castellorizo Island 1933 PCIJ Castellorizo; 1932 Italy/Turkey Ankara Agreement

Chad 1994 ICJ Libya/Chad; 2009 ICJ Belgium v. Senegal President Habre and pending Merits

Chad Lake 2002 ICJ Cameroon v. Nigeria; Equatorial Guinea Intervening & 2002-2009 UN Cameroon/Nigeria Commission; 1964 Chad Lake Convention

Chamizal 1911 USA/Mexico Chamizal

D

E

F

G

H

I

J

K

L

M

N

O

P

S

T

U

V

TABLE OF UN CONVENTION ON THE LAW OF THE SEA

Part XIII and 1994 Agreement

Part XIV and Final Act Annex VI

Part XV, Annexes V-VIII and 1994 Agreement

TABLE OF ABBREVIATIONS

A.C.	Law Reports (Third Series) Appeal Cases 1891- (UK)
AFDI	*Annuaire Francais de Droit International*
African JICL	*African Journal of International and Comparative Law*
AJIL	*American Journal of International Law*
Annuaire IDI	*Annuaire de l'Institut de Droit International – Yearbook of the Institute of International Law*
App. Cas.	Law Reports (Second Series) Appeal Cases 1875-1890 (UK)
AU	African Union
Australian YIL	*Australian Yearbook of International Law*
Bell C.C.	Bell's Crown Cases 1856-1860 (UK)
BIT	Bilateral Investment Treaties
BFSP	British and Foreign State Papers (UK)
BYIL	*British Yearbook of International Law*
Can. S.Ct.	Canadian Supreme Court Reports 1876-1922 (Canada)
Canadian YIL	*Canadian Yearbook of International Law*
Charney/ASIL	J.I. Charney and L.M. Alexander eds, *International Maritime Boundaries*, Vols I-II (ASIL/Martinus Nijhoff 1993), Vol.III (1998); J.I. Charney and R.W. Smith eds, Vol.IV (2002)
Colson/ASIL	D.A. Colson and R.W. Smith eds, *International Maritime Boundaries*, Vol.V (2005)
CLCS	Commission on the Limits of the Continental Shelf
Clunet	*Journal du Droit International* (Edouard Clunet) 1874- (France)
Cox C.C.	Cox's Criminal Cases 1843-1941 (UK)
C.P.D.	Law Reports (Common Pleas Division) 1875-1890 (UK)
CR	Verbatim Record of Oral Pleadings (ICJ)
Cranch	Cranch's United States Supreme Court Reports 1801-1841 (USA)

C. Rob	Christopher Robinson's Admiralty Reports 1799-1808 (UK)
CTS	Consolidated Treaty Series (C. Parry ed.)
DLR	Dominion Law Reports (Canada)
EPL	*Environmental Policy and Law*
E.R.	English Reports 1220-1865 (UK)
Exchequer D.	Law Reports Exchequer Division 1875-1880 (UK)
F. (Ct. of Sess.)	Fraser's Sessions Cases 1898-1906 (UK)
Fed.	Federal Reporter 1880-1924 (USA)
Fed. 2nd	Federal Reporter Second Series 1924- (USA)
Fed. Cas.	Federal Cases 1789-1880 (USA)
Fla.	Florida Reports (USA)
ICJ Rep.	*Reports of Judgments, Advisory Opinions and Orders* (ICJ)
ICLQ	*International Comparative Law Quarterly*
ICSID	International Centre for Settlement of Investment Disputes (World Bank)
ILM	*International Legal Materials*
ILR	*International Law Reports*
ITLOS Rep.	*Reports of Judgments, Advisory Opinions and Orders* (ITLOS)
Journal DI	*Journal de Droit International*
K.B.	Law Reports (Second Series) King's Bench 1891- (UK)
Limits in the Seas	*Limits in the Seas – United States Department of State, Bureau of Oceans and International Environmental and Scientific Affairs* (USA) <www.state.gov/g/oes/ocns/opa/convention/c16065.htm>
L.J.P.	Law Journal Reports, New Series, Probate, Divorce & Admiralty 1831-1949 (UK)
LNTS	*League of Nations Treaty Series*
L.R. Mad.	Indian Law Reports (Madras Series)
Netherlands ILR	*Netherlands International Law Review*
OAU	Organization of African Unity (superseded by AU)
Ocean Dev. & Int'l L.	*Ocean Development and International Law*
OJEC	*Official Journal of Economic Communities*
P.	Law Reports (Third Session) Probate Division 1891- (UK)

Pleadings	*Pleadings, Oral Arguments, Documents* (ICJ)
PCA 1999	P. Hamilton, H.C. Requena, L. van Scheltinga and B. Shifman eds, *The Permanent Court of Arbitration: International Arbitration and Dispute Resolution – Summaries of Awards, Settlement Agreements and Reports* (Kluwer 1999)
RGDIP	*Revue Générale de Droit International Public*
RIAA	*Reports of International Arbitral Awards* (UN) <http://www.un.org/law/riaa>
Scott	Scott's *Cases on International Law* 1885
S.L.R.	Scottish Law Review 1886-1963 (UK)
S.L.T.	Scots Law Times (UK)
Stuyt	A.M. Stuyt, *Survey of International Arbitrations 1794-1989* (Martinus Nijhoff 1990)
Simmonds	K.R. Simmonds ed., *Cases on the Law of the Sea*, Vol.I (Oceana 1976), Vol.II (1977), Vol.III (1980) and Vol.IV (1984)
TIAS	US Treaties and Other International Acts (USA)
T.L.R.	Times Law Reports (UK)
UNCITRAL	United Nations Commission on International Trade Law
UNCLOS III Off. Rec.	*Third United Nations Conference on the Law of the Sea, Official Records, United Nations*, Vols I-XVI
UNCLOS	United Nations Convention on the Law of the Sea
UNGA	United Nations General Assembly
UN LOS Bull.	*United Nations Law of the Sea Bulletin*
UN LOSIC	*United Nations Law of the Sea Information Circular*
UNTS	*United Nations Treaty Series*
US	US Supreme Court Reports 1754- (USA)
UST	US Treaties and Other International Agreements (USA)
USTS	US Treaty Series (USA)
W.L.R.	Weekly Law Reports 1953- (UK)

GLOBAL FRAMEWORK INSTRUMENTS

1930 Hague Draft – Report of the Second Committee (Territorial Sea) of the League of Nations Conference for the Codification of International Law, The Hague, 13 March-12 April 1930 [24 AJIL Supp. 169, 234-258 (1930); *Anglo/Norwegian Fisheries* Pleadings, Vol.II, 174-189]

1958 TSC – United Nations Convention on the Territorial Sea and the Contiguous Zone, Geneva, 29 April 1958 [in force: 10 September 1964, 516 UNTS 205]

1958 HSC – United Nations Convention on the High Seas, Geneva, 29 April 1958 [in force: 30 September 1962, 450 UNTS 11]

1958 HSFC – United Nations Convention on Fishing and Conservation of the Living Resources of the High Seas, Geneva, 29 April 1958 [in force: 20 March 1966, 559 UNTS 285]

1958 CSC – United Nations Convention on the Continental Shelf, Geneva, 29 April 1958 [in force: 10 June 1964, 499 UNTS 311]

1958 DSP – United Nations Optional Protocol of Signature Concerning the Compulsory Settlement of Disputes, Geneva, 29 April 1958 [in force: 30 September 1962, 450 UNTS 169]

1972 UN Stockholm Declaration and Action Plan – United Nations Conference on the Human Environment, 16 June 1972: Stockholm Declaration on the Human Environment [11 ILM 1416 (1972)] and Action Plan [UN Doc. A/CONF.48/14/Rev.1 (1972)]; available online <www.unep .org/Documents/>

1982 UNCLOS – United Nations Convention on the Law of the Sea, Montego Bay, 10 December 1982 [in force: 16 November 1994, 1833 UNTS 3 (Arabic), 203 (Chinese), 397 (English) and 1834 UNTS 4 (French), 179

(Russian), 371 (Spanish); 21 ILM 1245 (1982)] and 1994 Agreement – Agreement Relating to the Implementation of Part XI of the United Nations Convention on the Law of the Sea of 10 December 1982, New York, 28 July 1994 [in force: 28 July 1996, 1836 UNTS 3; 33 ILM 1309 (1994); 34 ILM 1393 (1995)]; both texts in English and their status available online <www.un.org/Depts/los/>; Canada's Ratification on 7 November 2003 <www.un.org/apps/sg/sgstats.asp?nid=616>; US Senate Committee on Foreign Relations Hearings of 14 and 21 October 2003 <http://foreign.senate.gov/hearings/2003/hrg031014a.html> and <http://foreign.senate.gov/hearings/2003/hrg031021a.html>; 25 February 2004 <http://lugar.senate.gov/pressapp/record.cfm?id=218386>; U.S. Ocean Action Plan of 17 December 2004 <www.state.gov/r/pa/prs/ps/2004/39924.htm> and <www.ocean.ceq.gov>; 98 AJIL 173-175, 307-308, 590-591 (2004); 99 AJIL 498-500 (2005); M.A. Browne, The Law of the Sea Convention and U.S. Policy, CRS Issue Brief for U.S. Congress of 4 August 2005 at <www.ncseonline.org/NLE/CRSreports/05aug/IB95010.pdf>; Roundtable Discussion: Should the United States Join the Convention? If Not, Why Not? If So, What Are the Prospects?, chaired by Former ICJ President Stephen M. Schwebel, with participation of U.S. Ambassador David A. Balton, John Noyes and Edwin Willamson at the ASIL Symposium in Remembrance of Louis Sohn: The Law of the Sea in the Twenty-First Century, George Washington University Law School, Washington D.C., 24 October 2006 <www.asil.org/pdfs/sohnprogram1.pdf>, of which proceedings were published in 39 *George Washington International Law Review* (2007 No.3); as followed by President G.W. Bush's Statement on Advancing U.S. Interests in the World's Oceans of 15 May 2007, 46 ILM 886 (2007); <www.whitehouse.gov/news/releases/2007/05/20070515-2.html & www.asil.org/ilib070521.htm>; U.S. Senate Committee on Foreign Relations' Hearings of 27 Sep 2007 <http://foreign.senate.gov/hearings/2007/hrg070927p.html> and 4 Oct 2007 <http://foreign.senate.gov/hearings/2007/hrg071004a.html>; 102 AJIL 168-169 (2008); U.S. Legal Adviser John B. Bellinger, The United States and the UNCLOS of 3 Nov 2008 <www.state.gov/s/l/rls/111587.htm>; UN Law of the Sea Convention 26 Years Later of 4 Dec 2008 <www.un.org/News/Press/docs//2008/ga10793.doc.htm>; U.S. National Security Presidential Directive on Arctic of 9 Jan 2009 <www.whitehouse.gov/news/releases/2009/01/20090112-3.html>; UNGA Adopts Two Oceans Resolutions, UN Doc.GA/10899 of 4 December 2009 <www.un.org/News/

Press/docs//2009/ga10899.doc.htm>; U.S. Leadership in the World and the Law of the Sea <http://lugar.senate.gov/sfrc/sea.html>

1995 SSA – United Nations Agreement for the Implementation of the Provisions of the United Nations Convention on the Law of the Sea of 10 December 1982 Relating to the Conservation and Management of Straddling Fish Stocks and Highly Migratory Fish Stocks, New York, 4 August 1995 [in force: 11 December 2001, 2167 UNTS 3; 34 ILM 1542 (1995); 90 AJIL 270 (1996)]; text and status available online <www.un.org/Depts/los/>. See also FAO Agreement on Port State Measures to Prevent, Deter and Eliminate Illegal, Unreported and Unregulated Fishing of 25 November 2009 <www.un.org/apps/news/story.asp?NewsID=33064&Cr=fishing&Cr1 & www.fao.org/news/story/en/item/37627/icode/>

1992 UNCED Rio Declaration and Agenda 21 – United Nations Conference on Environment and Development (UNCED), Rio de Janeiro, Brazil, 3-14 June 1992, UN Doc. A/CONF.151/26, Vols I-IV (1992): Rio Declaration on Environment and Development [31 ILM 874 (1992)] and Agenda 21, 1997-2000 Programme for Further Implementation of Agenda 21, UNGA Resolution S-19/2 of 28 June 1997 [36 ILM 1639 (1997)]; available online <www.un.org/documents/ga/conf151> and <www.un.org/esa/sustdev/agreed. htm>; reaffirmed by the 2002 Johannesburg World Summit on Sustainable Development (WSSD), Johannesburg, South Africa, 26 August-4 September 2002: Johannesburg Declaration on Sustainable Development and Plan of Implementation, UN Doc. A/CONF.199/20 (2002), available online <www.iisd.ca/wssd/portal.html> and by the 2005 UN World Summit Outcome <www.un.org/ga/59/hl60_plenarymeeting.html> & <www.un.org/summit2005>; Assessment of Assessments, UN Doc. A/64/88, 11 June 2009; UNGA Adopts Two Oceans Resolutions, UN Doc.GA/10899 of 4 December 2009 <www.un.org/News/Press/docs//2009/ga10899.doc.htm>

A REFERENCE GUIDE

INTERNAL WATERS, TERRITORIAL SEA AND BASELINES

1930 Hague Draft, Annex I, Articles 1-13
1958 TSC
1982 UNCLOS, Part II, Articles 2-32

Internal Waters/Territorial Sea: Legal Status
1930 Hague Draft, Articles 1 and 2; 1958 TSC, Articles 1 and 2; 1982 UNCLOS, Article 2:

Relevant Jurisprudence

SS Lotus PCIJ Series A, No.10 (1927) – Judgment, 18-19, Dissent Weiss, 46, Dissent Moore, 75; *SS Lotus* Pleadings, PCIJ Series C, No.13-II, 59-61 [Agent Basdevant, 2 Aug 1927], 127 [Agent Bey, 6 and 8 Aug 1927], 180, 202 [France's Memorial], 271-272, 273 [France's Counter-Memorial]; *Access To, Or Anchorage In, The Port of Danzig, of Polish War Vessels* PCIJ Series A/B, No.43 (1931) – Advisory Opinion, 141, 144-145; *Legal Status of Eastern Greenland* PCIJ Series A/B, No.53 (1933) – Judgment, 33-34, 38-40, 45-46, 62, Dissents Anzilotti, 92, 93, Vogt, 109; *Eastern Greenland* Pleadings, PCIJ Series C, No.62, 31-40 [Denmark's Memorial], 174-430 [Norway's Counter-Memorial], No.63, 685-900 [Denmark's Reply], 1038-1109, 1295-1298 [Norway's Rejoinder], No.66, 2717, 2727-2732, 2768 2776-2781 [Agent Steglich-Petersen, 24 and 26 Nov 1932], 2940-2942, 2948-2954 [Counsel Rygh, 3 and 5 Dec 1932], No.67, 3303, 3319 [Agent Steglich-Petersen, 16 Jan 1933]; *Corfu Channel (Merits)* ICJ Rep. 1949, 4 – Individual O. Alvarez, 43, Dissents Winiarski, 53-54, Badawi Pascha, 64; *Anglo/Norwegian Fisheries* ICJ Rep. 1951, 116 – Judgment, 128, 132-133, 135, 142-143, Individual O. Alvarez, 147, 150-152, Dissents Sir Arnold McNair, 160-163, Read, 189; *Anglo/Norwegian* Pleadings, Vol.I, 56, 59 [UK Memorial], 372-373, 388-402 [Norway's Counter-Memorial], Vol.II, 439-440, 574 [UK Reply]; *Minquiers and Ecrehos* ICJ Rep. 1953, 47 – Judgment, 51, 57, 66, Individual O. Basdevant, 82; Pleadings, Vol.I, 114 [UK Memorial], 452-455 [UK Reply], Vol.II, 351-353 [Counsel Fitzmaurice, 5 October 1953]; *Antarctica* Pleadings, 17-18, 27, 57-58 [UK Applications].

North Sea Continental Shelf Judgment, ICJ Rep. 1969, 22, para.19, 29, para.39, 31, para.43, 51, para.95, 53, para.101(C)(1), Separate Os Jessup, 78-79, Ammoun, 116, 118, 150-151, Dissents Koretsky, 159-161, Morelli, 201-202; *North Sea* Pleadings, Vol.II, 20 [Agent Jaenicke, 23 Oct 1968], 92-93 [Counsel Sir Humphrey Waldock, 29 Oct] 125 [Agent Jaenicke, 30 Oct 1968]; *Fisheries Jurisdiction (Jurisdiction)* Separate Os Fitzmaurice, ICJ Rep. 1973, 24-25, 27-28, 68-69, 71-72, *(Merits)* Judgments, ICJ Rep. 1974, 27, 196, Separate Os de Castro, 81-82, 225; *Nuclear Tests (Interim Measures)* Orders, ICJ Rep. 1973, 99, 135, Dissents Ignacio-Pinto, 129, 131-133, 163; *Nuclear Tests* Dissents Petren, ICJ Rep. 1974, 304, 488, Joint Dissents, 361, 369, 513, 521, Dissent Barwick, 431-434; Pleadings (Australia), 335-336 [Memorial]; *Aegean Sea Continental Shelf (Jurisdiction)* Judgment, ICJ Rep. 1978, 31-34, 37, Dissent de Castro, 64-67; Pleadings, 251-254 [Greece's Memorial (Jurisdiction)], 341-346 [Counsel O'Connell, 10 Oct 1978], 414-425 [Counsel Weil, 13 Oct], 426-439 [Counsel Economides, 13 and 16 Oct 1978], 441-460 [O'Connell], 552-554 [treaty list]; *Tunisia/Libya Continental Shelf (Merits)* Judgment, ICJ Rep. 1982, 71, 76, Dissent Evensen, 313-314; *Canada/USA Gulf of Maine* Judgment, ICJ Rep. 1984, 296; Pleadings, Vol.II, 64-65 [US Memorial], Vol.VII, 199 [Counsel Stevenson, 9 May 1984]; *Libya/Malta (Merits)* Judgment, ICJ Rep. 1985, 41, Joint Separate O., 83; *Nicaragua v. USA Military and Paramilitary Activities (Provisional Measures)* Order, ICJ Rep. 1984, 170, para.1(b) and (e), 181, para.28, 187, para.41(B)(1), Dissent Schwebel, 190, 199, *Nicaragua v. USA (Jurisdiction and Admissibility)* Judgment, ICJ Rep. 1984, 424, para.73, *as reaffirmed* by *Nicaragua v. USA (Merits)* Judgment, ICJ Rep. 1986, 93, para.174, also *id.* 46-53, paras 76-92, and 111-112, para.213, Dissent Schwebel, 259; *Great Belt* Pleadings, 570 [Denmark's Counter-Memorial]; *Gulf of Fonseca* Judgment, ICJ Rep. 1992, 592, 604-605, Dissent Oda, 745; *Qatar v. Bahrain (Merits)* Judgment, ICJ Rep. 2001, 91, 101, paras 169, 204; Hearings, CR 2000/6, 44-45 [Counsel Sir Ian Sinclair, 30 May 2000] <www.icj-cij.org>; 2003 *Malaysia v. Singapore (Provisional Measures)* Order, Case No.12, paras 31, 70, Separate O. Rao, para.5; Hearings, ITLOS/PV.03/02/Corr.1, 18 [Counsel Schrijver, 25 Sep 2003] <www.itlos.org>; 2006 *Barbados/Trinidad & Tobago* Award, para.60, Maps I-II, paras 170, 356 <www.pca-cpa.org>; RIAA XXVII, 147; 45 ILM 800 (2006); 2007 *Guyana/Suriname* Award, paras 283, 307-309, Map 2 <www.pca-cpa.org>; *Nicaragua v. Honduras (Merits)* Judgment, ICJ Rep. 2007, paras 262-263 <www.icj-cij.org>.

See also Regime of Islands *infra*.

Land-Dominates-the-Sea (*La terre domine la mer*) Principle

For reliance on the finding of the 1909 *Norway v. Sweden Grisbadarna Maritime Frontier* Award that "the maritime territory is essentially an appurtenance of a land territory" [RIAA XI, 155, 159; 4 AJIL 186, 226 (1910); No.288/Stuyt; Charney/ASIL Report No.9-14 (Anderson)], see *North Sea* Dissent Vice-President Koretsky, ICJ Rep. 1969, 160 n.1; *Gulf of Maine* Judgment, ICJ Rep. 1984, 312, para.157, 338, para.226; Pleadings, Vol.II, 67-68, 93 n.2 [US Memorial], Vol.V, 49 [Reply of Canada].

"It is the land which confers upon the coastal State a right to the waters off its coasts" – *Anglo/Norwegian Fisheries* Judgment, ICJ Rep. 1951, 133, also: 128, Separate O. Hsu Mo, 154; Pleadings, Vol.I, 532 [Norway's Counter-Memorial], Vol.II, 659 [UK Reply], Vol.IV, 397-398 [Counsel Waldock, 18 Oct 1951]; *Minquiers and Ecrehos* Pleadings, Vol.II, 200 [Agent Gros, 28 Sep 1953]; *North Sea* Judgment, ICJ Rep. 1969, 31, para.43, 51, paras 95-96, Separate O. Ammoun, 117, 146, Dissent Koretsky, 159-160, 164; Pleadings, Vol.I, 63 [FRG Memorial], 373 [NL Counter-Memorial], Vol.II, 124, 222 [Agent Riphagen, 30 Oct and 7 Nov 1968], 271 [Counsel Sir Humphrey Waldock, 11 Nov 1968]; *Fisheries Jurisdiction (Jurisdiction)* Separate Os Sir Gerald Fitzmaurice, ICJ Rep. 1973, 28 n.9, 72 n.9, *(Merits)* Separate Os de Castro, ICJ Rep. 1974, 98, 225; Pleadings (UK), 63 [Iceland]; *Aegean Sea (Jurisdiction)* Judgment, ICJ Rep. 1978, 36, Dissent de Castro, 66; Pleadings, 99 [Counsel O'Connell, 26 Aug 1976], 441 [O'Connell, 16 Oct 1978]; *Tunisia/Libya (Merits)* Judgment, ICJ Rep. 1982, 61, Separate O. de Arechaga, 132; Pleadings, Vol.I, 161 [Tunisia's Memorial]; *Gulf of Maine* Judgment, ICJ Rep. 1984, 312, 338; *Gulf of Maine* Pleadings, Vol.I, 119, 126, 145 [Canada's Memorial], Vol.II, 93 n.2 [US Memorial], Vol.III, 210 [Canada's Counter-Memorial], Vol.IV, 4, 15 n.2, 60, 74-75, 83, 123, 125-126 [US Counter-Memorial], Vol.V, 5, 49, 51-52, 54 [Canada's Reply], Vol.VI, 39, 40 [2 April 1984, Agent Legault], 255, 268 [11 and 12 April, Counsel Stevenson], Vol. VII, 198 [9 May 1984, Stevenson]; and all subsequent maritime delimitation decisions of the Court and other courts and tribunals, including *Cameroon v. Nigeria* Hearings, CR 98/4 [trans.], 43 [Adviser Bipoun Woum, 6 March 1998]; *Qatar v. Bahrain (Merits)* Judgment, ICJ Rep. 2001, 97, para.185, Joint Dissent Bedjaoui, Ranjeva, Koroma, 149, 202, paras 2, 181, Separate O. Kooymans, 226, para.3, Dissent Torres Bernardez, 431-432, 435, paras 505, 520; Hearings, CR 2000/15, 28 [Counsel Weil, 14 June 2000] <www.icj-cij.org>; 2006 *Barbados/Trinidad & Tobago (Jurisdiction and Merits)* Award, President S.M. Schwebel, para.316 <www.pca-cpa.org>; 2007 *Guyana/Suriname (Jurisdiction and Merits)* Award, President L.D.M. Nelson, para.344 <www.pca-cpa.org>; *Nicaragua v. Honduras (Merits)* Judgment, President R. Higgins, ICJ Rep. 2007, paras 113, 126, 135; Hearings, CR 2007/6, 15, para.8 [Counsel Greenwood, 12 March 2007], CR 2007/8, 51, para.52 [Counsel Dupuy, 14 March 2007] <www.icj-cij.org>; *Romania v. Ukraine* Judgment, President R. Higgins, ICJ Rep. 2009, paras 77, 99 <www.icj-cij.org>.

Historic Titles

Anglo/Norwegian Fisheries ICJ Rep. 1951, 116 – Judgment, 120-123, 124, 130-131, 132, 133, 138-139, 142, Declaration Hackworth, 144, Individual O. Alvarez, 151-153, Separate O. Hsu Mo, 154, 156-157, Dissent Sir Arnold McNair, 183-185, Dissent Read, 194-196; *Anglo/Norwegian* Pleadings, Vol.I, 24, 94-97 [UK Memorial], 547-573 [Norway's Counter-Memorial], Vol.II, 580-581, 587-590, 605, 606-681 [UK Reply], Vol.III, 438-492 [Norway's Rejoinder], Vol.IV, 27-29, 98-143 [Counsel Sir Frank Soskice, 25, 28 and 29 Sep 1951], 307-325 [Counsel Bourquin, 12 Oct], 419-459 [Agent Sir Eric Beckett, 19 and 20 Oct 1951], relying on extensive jurisprudence; *Minquiers and Ecrehos* Declaration Alvarez, ICJ Rep. 1953, 73; Pleadings, Vol.I, 88-98 [UK Memorial]; *Antarctica* Pleadings, 33, 71 [UK Applications]; *North Sea* Separate O. Jessup, ICJ Rep. 1969, 80, Separate O. Ammoun, 106, 112, 113-114; Pleadings, Vol.I, 316, 364 [NL Counter-Memorial], 472, 484-485 [Common Rejoinder of Denmark/NL], Vol.II, 90, 281 [Counsel Sir Humphrey Waldock, 28 Oct and 11 Nov 1968]; *Tunisia/Libya (Merits)* Judgment, ICJ Rep. 1982, 35, 62-65, 67-68, 70-77, 80, 84, 86, 92, Separate Os Ago, 95-98, de Arechaga, 122-132, 136, 139-140, Dissents Gros, 153-155, Oda, 197-211, 241, 248; Pleadings, Vol.I, 73-105 [Tunisia's Memorial], Vol.IV, 427-475 [Counsel Abi-Saab, 17 Sep 1981]; *Gulf of Maine* Judgment, ICJ Rep. 1984, 341; Pleadings, Vol.I, 129 [Canada's Memorial], Vol.II, 68-69 [US Memorial], Vol.III, 224-225 [Canada's Counter-Memorial], Vol.IV, 49, 79-80 [US Counter-Memorial], Vol.VII, 88 [Counsel Binnie, 4 May 1984]; *Gulf of Fonseca (Intervention)* Judgment, ICJ Rep. 1990, 103-106, 120-122, *(Merits)* Judgment, ICJ Rep. 1992, 586-610, 616-618, para.432, Separate Os Valticos, 628, Torres Bernardez, 712-730, Dissent Oda, 733-757; *Denmark v. Norway* Separate O. Weeramantry, ICJ Rep. 1993, 262; *Qatar v. Bahrain (Merits)* Judgment, ICJ Rep. 2001, 40, Joint Dissent Bedjaoui, Ranjeva, Koroma, 145, Separate O. Kooymans, 225, Dissent Torres Bernardez, 257; *Cameroon v. Nigeria; Equatorial Guinea Intervening (Merits)* Judgment, ICJ Rep. 2002, 352, para.65, Dissents Koroma, 484-485, paras 25-27, Ajibola, 581, para.134, Separate O. Mbaye, 516, para.53; *Indonesia/Malaysia (Intervention)* and *(Merits)* Judgments, ICJ Rep. 2001, 575 and 2002, 625; *El Salvador v. Honduras (Revision)* Judgment, ICJ Rep 2003 <www.icj-cij.org>.

1998 *Eritrea/Yemen Territorial Sovereignty and Scope of the Dispute (Phase I)* Award <www.pca-cpa.org>, 40 ILM 900 (2001); 114 ILR 1; RIAA XXII, 211; 2005 *Belgium/Netherlands Iron Rhine* Award <www.pca-cpa.rg>.

See also Historic Bays *infra*; Straits Used for International Navigation – Longstanding International Conventions in Force; Regime of Islands – Sovereignty Over Island Territory *infra*.

Treaties of Friendship, Commerce and Navigation (FCN)

Greece v. United Kingdom Ambatielos (Preliminary Objection) Judgment, Vice-President J.G. Guerrero, Acting President concurring, ICJ Rep. 1952, 28, Dissent President Sir Arnold McNair, 58, *(Merits: Obligation to Arbitrate)* Judgment, ICJ Rep. 1953, 10, Dissent President McNair and Judges Basdevant, Klaestad and Read, 25; *Greece v. UK Ambatielos Claim* Award, President R.J. Alfaro [RIAA XII, 83; 23 ILR 306 and 24 ILR 291; No.422/Stuyt]; *IMCO* Pleadings, 93-98 [Liberia/ Extracts from FCN Treaties], 137 n.1 [USA]; *Western Sahara* Advisory Opinion, ICJ Rep. 1975, 51-53; *Nicaragua v. USA (Jurisdiction and Admissibility)* Judgment, President T.O. Elias concurring, ICJ Rep. 1984, 392, 397-398, para.12, 426-429, paras 79-83, 442, para.113(1)(b), Dissent Schwebel, 562, para.3, and 628-637, paras 117-129, *(Merits)* Judgment, President Nagendra Singh concurring, ICJ Rep. 1986, 14, 115-117, paras 221-225, Dissent Schwebel, 306-311, paras 100-106; *USA v. Italy Eletronica Sicula S.p.A. (ELSI)* Judgment, Chamber's President M. Ruda concurring, ICJ Rep. 1989, 15, Separate O. Oda, 83, Dissent Schwebel, 94; *Iran v. USA Oil Platforms (Preliminary Objection)* Judgment, President Bedjaoui concurring, ICJ Rep. 1996, 803, Dissent Vice-President Schwebel, 874, Dissent Oda, 890, *(Counter-Claim)* Order, Vice-President Weeramantry, Acting President and President Schwebel concurring, ICJ Rep. 1998, 190, *(Merits)* Judgment, President Shi Jiuyong concurring, ICJ Rep. 2003 (in press); Hearings, CR 2003/5-19, 17 Feb-7 March 2003; *Guinea v. DR Congo (Preliminary Objections)* Judgment, ICJ Rep. 2007, para.87, also referring to BITs in para.88; *Djibouti v. France Certain Questions of Mutual Assistance in Criminal Matters (Jurisdiction and Merits)* Judgment, paras 107-114, ICJ Rep. 2008; *Kosovo* Hearings, CR 2009/30, 23, para.2 [Agent Harold H. Koh, 8 Dec 2009] <www.icj-cij.org>.

The FCN Treaties have in recent years been discontinued by the United Sates in favour of more modern bilateral investment treaties (BIT) <www.worldbank .org/icsid/treaties/treaties.htm>.

Breadth and Outer Limit of the Territorial Sea
1958 TSC, Article 6; 1982 UNCLOS, Articles 3-4:

SS Lotus PCIJ Series A, No.10 (1927) – Dissent Moore, 84; *Legal Status of Eastern Greenland* PCIJ Series A/B, No.53 (1933) – Judgment, 33, 53-54; Pleadings, PCIJ Series C, No.62, 34 [Denmark's Memorial], 198, 528 [Norway's Counter-Memorial], No.63, 799-800, 801 [Denmark's Reply], 1039, 1294 [Norway's Rejoinder], No.64, 1541 [Annex], No.66, 2951, 2953 [Counsel Rygh, 5 Dec 1932], No.67, 3570 [Counsel Rygh, 3 Feb 1933], 3658 [Rygh, 7 Feb 1933].

Anglo/Norwegian Fisheries ICJ Rep. 1951, 116 – Judgment, 119, 120, 121, 124, 125-126 [noting that although Norway's 4-mile TS is not the subject of the present dispute, that limit was acknowledged by the UK in the course of the proceedings], 128, 135, 138, Individual O. Alvarez, 147, 150, 152-153, Separate O. Hsu Mo, 156, Dissent Sir Arnold McNair, 159-161, 168-169, 171, 179, Dissent Read, 186-187, 189-190, 192, 196, 198, 202-203; *Anglo/Norwegian* Pleadings, Vol.I, 18, 22-23, 29, 38-37 [UK Memorial], 345-357, 373-374, 393-402, 539 [Norway's Counter-Memorial], Vol.II, 304, 421-424, 595, 643, 681-683 [UK Reply], Vol.IV, 60 [Agent Sir Eric Beckett, 26 Sep 1951]. Cf. *id.* Vol.I, 345-368 [Norway's Counter-Memorial], 394-402, 415-420, 462-463, 465 [UK Reply], Vol.III, 231-278 [Norway's Rejoinder]; *Fisheries Jurisdiction (Merits)* Separate Os Waldock, ICJ Rep. 1974, 107, 227.

For reliance on the *Anglo/Norwegian Fisheries* Judgment as binding authority with respect to Norway's 4-mile limit (wider than then customary 3-mile limit), see 1953 *Rex v. Cooper* Judgment of the Norwegian Supreme Court [20 ILR 166].

On the methods of the *tracé parallèle* and the *courbe tangente* (envelopes of arcs-of circles) [UNCLCS Scientific & Technical Guidelines, Doc.CLCS/11, paras 3.4.6-3.410 (1999) <www.un.org/Depts/los>], see *Anglo/Norwegian Fisheries* ICJ Rep. 1951, 116 – Judgment, 128-129, 135; Pleadings, Vol.I, 402-405 [Norway's Counter-Memorial], Vol.II, 441-444, 752-753 [UK Reply], Vol.III, 209-213 [Norway's Rejoinder], Vol.IV, 62-71 [Agent Sir Eric Beckett, 26 Sep 1951], 258-265 [Counsel Bourquin, 10 Oct], 407-409 [Counsel Waldock, 18 Oct 1951]; *North Sea* Pleadings, Vol.I, 47-48 [FRG Memorial].

For reliance on the *Anglo/Norwegian* findings of the Court, see *Libya/Malta* Pleadings, Vol.III, 171-173, 179 [Malta's Reply]; *Gulf of Maine* Pleadings, Vol. III, 213 [Canada's Counter-Memorial]; 2002 *Eritrea/Ethiopia Boundary* Decision, para.6.20-6.22 <www.pca-cpa.org>, 41 ILM 1057 (2002).

On the 1951 Egypt's Royal Decree on the Territorial Waters [*Anglo/Norwegian* Pleadings, Vol.III, 676], as protested by the United Kingdom and the United States [*id.* Vol.IV, 578], see *Anglo/Norwegian Fisheries* Pleadings, Vol.III, 630, 634, 641, 650 [Norway's Rejoinder]. The historic Bay of El-Arab claim under that Decree was rolled back by Egypt upon promulgation of its straight baselines in 1990.

Minquiers and Ecrehos ICJ Rep. 1953, 47 – Judgment, 51, 57, 66; Pleadings, Vol.I, 51-52, 54, 56-58, 60, 62, 114-117 [UK Memorial], 555, 588 [UK Reply], Vol.II, 78, 83 [Counsel Fitzmaurice, 19 Sep 1953], 252-256 [Agent Gros, 30 Sep 1953]; *North Sea* Judgment, ICJ Rep. 1969, 18, 34, 37, 45, Separate O.

President Bustamante y Rivero, 59-60, 65, Separate O. Ammoun, 108, 124-126, 128, 144, Dissents Koretsky, 159-161, 164-165, 170, Morelli, 203-204, Sorensen, 249-252; *North Sea* Pleadings, Vol.I, 62 [FRG Memorial], 201-202 [Denmark's Counter-Memorial], 354-355 [NL Counter-Memorial], Vol.II, 92-93 [Counsel Sir Humphrey Waldock, 29 Oct 1968], 138 [Agent Riphagen, 31 Oct], 193 [Counsel Shigeru Oda, 5 Nov 1968]; *Fisheries Jurisdiction (Interim Measures)* Dissents Padilla Nervo, ICJ Rep. 1972, 23, 40, *(Jurisdiction)* Judgments, 16-17, 61, Separate Os Fitzmaurice, ICJ Rep. 1973, 25, 29, 69, 73, Dissents Padilla Nervo, 39, 41, 84, 86, *(Merits)* Judgments, ICJ Rep. 1974, 22-23, 25, 191-192, 194, Joint Separate Os, 45-47, 217-219, Separate O. Dillard, 56-59, Separate Os de Castro, 78-94, 97, 225, Separate Os Waldock, 106-115, 119-122, 227, Dissents Onyeama, 165-167, 245; *Fisheries Jurisdiction* Pleadings (UK), 458-461 [Counsel Silkin, 25 March 1974], (FRG), 219-229 [Memorial (Merits)]; *Aegean Sea (Jurisdiction)* Judgment, ICJ Rep. 1978, 37, para.89.

Tunisia/Libya (Merits) Judgment, ICJ Rep. 1982, 35, 67, 74, 83, Separate Os Ago, 96-98, de Arechaga, 117, Dissents Gros, 154, Oda, 185-187, 199, 223-224, 227, 267, Evensen, 283, 295, 310; *Gulf of Maine* Judgment, ICJ Rep. 1984, 287, Separate O. Schwebel, 355, Dissent Gros, 366, 371, 381; Pleadings Vol.I, 186-187 [Canada's Memorial], Vol.II, 64 [US Memorial], Vol.III, 216 [Canada's Counter-Memorial], Vol.V, 26, 55 [Canada's Reply], 386, 411, 514, 532 [US Reply]; *Libya/Malta (Intervention)* Judgment, ICJ Rep. 1984, 24; *Libya/Malta (Merits)* Separate Os Vice-President Sette-Camara, ICJ Rep. 1985, 69, Mbaye, 100; Pleadings, Vol. II, 73 [Libya's Counter-Memorial], Vol.III, 440-441 [Counsel Brownlie, 3 Dec 1984]; *Gulf of Fonseca* Judgment, ICJ Rep. 1992, 592, 604-608, Separate O. Bernardez, 721, Dissent Oda, 735, 742-744, 753-754, 757-758; Hearings, C 4/CR 91/46, 35 [Counsel Lauterpacht, 11 June 1991]; *Denmark v. Norway* Separate O. Vice-President Oda, ICJ Rep. 1993, 93-94, 102; Hearings, CR 93/3, 9-10 [Agent Magid, 13 Jan 1993]; *Cameroon v. Nigeria* Hearings, CR 94/2, 44-45 [Counsel Crawford, 3 March 1998], CR 98/4, 55 [Counsel Highet, 6 March 1998]; *Qatar v. Bahrain (Merits)* Judgment, ICJ Rep. 2001, 93, paras 171-172, Separate O. Oda, 124-125, 130-132, paras 7-8, 19-21, Joint Dissent Bedjaoui, Ranjeva, Koroma, 195, para.165, Dissent Torres Bernardez, 426, para.482; Hearings, CR 2000/11, 28-29 [Counsel Lauterpacht, 8 June 2000], CR 2000/15, 17 [Counsel Weil, 14 June 2000]; *Cameroon v. Nigeria; Equatorial Guinea Intervening (Merits)* Judgment, ICJ Rep. 2002, 352, 425, paras 65, 250-251, Dissents Koroma, 484-485, paras 25-27, Ajibola, 581, para.134, Separate O. Mbaye, 516, para.53; Hearings, CR 2002/5, 41 [Counsel Bipoun Woum, 22 Feb 2002]; *Indonesia/Malaysia (Merits)* Judgment, ICJ Rep. 2002, 625, paras 20, 35, 75, 103-108, 113, 118, 130, 142; Hearings, CR 2002/28, 36-37, 39-42 [Counsel Soons, 3 June], CR 2002/29, 12-13 [Counsel Bundy, 4 June], 55 [Counsel Pellet], CR 2002/30, 57 [Counsel Crawford,

6 June], CR 2002/31, 61-63 [Counsel Schrijver, 7 June], CR 2002/32, 36-38 [Crawford], CR 2002/33, 41-43 [Soons, 10 June], CR 2002/34, 17 [Counsel Malintoppi], CR 2002/35, 24-25 [Schrijver, 12 June 2002]; *Yugoslavia v. Bosnia & Herzegovina (Revision of 1996 Judgment)* Separate O. Mahiou, ICJ Rep. 2003, 73, para.9 <www.icj-cij.org>.

2006 *Barbados/Trinidad & Tobago (Jurisdiction and Merits)* Award, para.60, Maps I-II, paras 170, 356; Hearings Day-4, 45-46 [Counsel Greenwood, 21 Oct 2005]; 2007 *Guyana/Suriname (Jurisdiction and Merits)* Award, paras 212, 252, 290, 316, Map 2 <www.pca-cpa.org>; *Nicaragua v. Honduras (Merits)* Judgment, ICJ Rep. 2007, paras 101-103, 262-264, 300-302, Dissent Torres Bernardez, para.146; Hearings, CR 2007/6, 35, paras 81-82 [Counsel Greenwood, 12 March 2007], CR 2007/12, 37, para.22 [Counsel Pellet, 20 March], 44, paras 26-27 [Counsel Brownlie], 54 [Judge Simma's Question], CR 2007/14, 24, para.54, referring to Simma's Question [Counsel Colson, 23 March 2007], 33, para.9 [Greenwood] <www.icj-cij.org>; *Malaysia/Singapore Pedra Branca/Pulau Batu Puteh (Merits)* Judgment, ICJ Rep. 2008, paras 28, 30, 173, 181, 192, 197-200, 204, 221, 225, 231-234, 238, 242, 254-257, 259, 264, 286-287, 293-297, Separate Os Parra Aranguren, paras 3, 21-22, Rao, paras 40-41, Dissent Dugard, paras 1, 6, 21, 23, 27; Hearings, CR 2007/20, 31, paras 33-34 [Counsel Chao, 6 Nov 2007], CR 2007/22, 39, paras 6-8 [Counsel Malintoppi, 8 Nov], 43-45, paras 23-26 and at 49, para.41, CR 2007/24, 16, para.34 [Agent Kadir, 13 Nov], 26, para.23 [Co-Agent Fadir], CR 2007/26, 70, para.49 and at 72, para.56 [Counsel Crawford, 15 Nov], CR 2007/30, 36, para.29 [Counsel Schrijver, 22 Nov 2007]; *Romania v. Ukraine* Judgment [12-mile TS around Serpents Island], ICJ Reports 2009, paras 23, 26-30, 43-66, 71-76, 150, 182, 188, 203, 206, 218 and *dispositif* para.219; Hearings, CR 2008/18, 24, para.28 [Agent Aurescu, 2 Sep 2008], 62, para.8 [Counsel Crawford], CR 2008/19, 21-52 [Crawford, 3 Sep], CR 2008/20, 37, para.62 [Counsel Pellet, 4 Sep], CR 2008/21, 35-42, paras 1-20 [Crawford, 5 Sep], 67, para.79 [Counsel Lowe], CR 2008/24, 14, para.17 [Agent Vassylenko, 9 Sep], 26-27, paras 30-33 [Counsel Bundy], 38, para.9 [Counsel Sir Michael Wood], CR 2008/26, 24, para.19 [Bundy, 10 Sep], 53-55 [Wood], CR 2008/28, 18-20, paras 32-40 [Wood, 11 Sep], 49, para.61 [Bundy], CR 2008/29, 11, para.31 [Counsel Malintoppi, 12 Sep], 49, para.30 [Counsel Bundy], CR 2008/30, 10-15, paras 4-15 [Agent Aurescu, 15 Sep], 39-40, paras 20-24 [Co-Agent Dinescu], CR 2008/31, 13, para.16 [Counsel Lowe, 16 Sep], 55, para.2(b) [Agent Aurescu], CR 2008/32, 13, para.13 [Agent Vassylenko, 18 Sep], 21-22, paras 19-23 [Counsel Sir Michael Wood] <www.icj-cij.org>.

Normal Baselines (Low-Water Line)

1930 Hague Draft, Annex II: Base Line; 1958 TSC, Article 3; 1982 UNCLOS, Part II, Article 5:

SS Lotus PCIJ Series A, No.10 (1927) - Dissent Moore, 75; *Eastern Greenland* Pleadings, PCIJ Series C, No.64, 1546 [Annex]; *Anglo/Norwegian Fisheries* ICJ Rep. 1951, 116 - Judgment, 121, 128-129, 137, Separate O. Hsu Mo, 154, Dissent Sir Arnold McNair, 161-163, 168-169, 179, Dissent Read, 186, 203-204; Pleadings, Vol.I, 54-60, 87 [UK Memorial], 399-402 [Norway's Counter-Memorial], Vol.II, 439-440, 452-453, 574 [UK Reply]; *Minquiers and Ecrehos* ICJ Rep. 1953, 47 - Judgment, 58; Pleadings, Vol.I, 51, 54, 56, 58, 73, 286 [UK Memorial], 555, 556 [UK Reply]; *North Sea* Judgment, ICJ Rep. 1969, 24, para.26, Separate O. President Bustamante y Rivero, 59, Separate O. Ammoun, 143, Dissents Koretsky, 162, 165, Tanaka, 184, Morelli, 203-204; *North Sea* Pleadings, Vol.I, 359 [NL Counter-Memorial], Vol.II, 92-93 [Counsel Sir Humphrey Waldock, 29 Oct 1968], 150 [Agent Jacobsen, 31 Oct], 212 [Request Mosler, 7 Nov], 273 [Waldock, 11 Nov 1968]; *Aegean Sea (Jurisdiction)* Dissent de Castro, ICJ Rep. 1978, 66-67; Pleadings, 142 [Counsel O'Connell, 27 Aug 1976]; *Tunisia/Libya (Intervention)* Judgment, ICJ Rep. 1981, 9, 17, *(Merits)* Judgment, ICJ Rep. 1982, 48, 71, 74-76, 87, 91, 94, para.133 C(2), Separate O. de Arechaga, 135, Dissent Oda, 261-267, *(Revision)* Judgment, ICJ Rep. 1985, 224-225, Separate O. Bastid, 252; *Gulf of Maine* Judgment, ICJ Rep. 1984, 270, 287, 332, 336; Pleadings, Vol.I, 105, 134-137 [Canada's Memorial], Vol.III, 254-255 [Canada's Counter-Memorial], Vol.V, 46 [Canada's Reply]; *Libya/Malta (Merits)* Judgment, ICJ Rep. 1985, 48, 57, para.79C, Dissent Oda, 161; *Guinea-Bissau v. Senegal Arbitral Award* Judgment, ICJ Rep. 1991, 57, 74, Separate O. Vice-President Oda, 82; *Gulf of Fonseca* Judgment, ICJ Rep. 1992, 608, Dissent Oda, 745; *Denmark v. Norway* Judgment, ICJ Rep. 1993, 78; *Qatar v. Bahrain (Merits)* Judgment, ICJ Rep. 2001, 40, paras 179-180, 184, 216, 245, Joint Dissent Bedjaoui, Ranjeva, Koroma, 202-203, para.185, Dissent Torres Bernardez, 434, para.515; Hearings, CR 2000/6, 40-41 [Counsel Ian Sinclair, 30 May 2000], CR 2000/9 [trans.], 35 [Counsel Queneudec, 5 June], CR 2000/14, 35-37 [Counsel Reisman, 13 June 2000]; *Cameroon v. Nigeria; Equatorial Guinea Intervening (Merits)* Judgment, ICJ Rep. 2002, 443, para.292; *Nicaragua v. Honduras* Hearings, CR 2007/6, 35, para.82 [Counsel Greenwood, 12 March 2007], CR 2007/12, 44, para.26 [Counsel Brownlie, 20 March], CR 2007/14, 34, para.9 [Greenwood, 23 March 2007]; *Romania v. Ukraine* Judgment, ICJ Rep. 2009, paras 124-126, 136-137, 183; Hearings, CR 2008/20, 25, para.36 [Counsel Pellet, 4 Sep 2008], CR 2008/24, 32, para.55 [Counsel Bundy, 9 Sep], CR 2008/26, 25, para.23 [Bundy, 10 Sep 2008] <www.icj-cij.org>.

1999 *Eritrea/Yemen Maritime Delimitation (Phase II)* Award, President R.Y. Jennings, paras 133-135, 146 [40 ILM 983 (2001)]; 2006 *Barbados/Trinidad & Tobago* Award, President S.M. Schwebel, paras 94, 114, 329-331, 334, 356, 381, 383, Maps V-VII, Technical Report [RIAA XXVII, 147; 45 ILM 800 (2006)]; 2007 *Guyana/Suriname* Award, President L.D.M. Nelson, paras 215, 240, 393-396 <www.pca-cpa.org>.

See also Fisheries, 1882 North Sea Convention, *infra*.

Reefs
1982 UNCLOS, Article 6:

Anglo/Norwegian Fisheries Judgment, ICJ Rep. 1951, 127, Dissent Sir Arnold McNair, 182; Pleadings, Vol.I, 491 [Norway's Counter-Memorial], Vol.II, 511, 660, 761-762 [UK Reply], Vol.III, 377 [Norway's Rejoinder]; *Tunisia/Libya (Merits)* Dissent Evensen, ICJ Rep. 1982, 302, 315; *Libya/Malta* Pleadings, Vol.II, 129 [Libya's Counter-Memorial], Vol.III, 248 [Malta's Reply]; *New Zealand v. France* Hearings, CR 95/19, 71 [Counsel Lauterpacht, 11 Sep 1995]; *Qatar v. Bahrain (Merits)* Hearings, CR 2000/15, 53 [Counsel Weil, 14 June 2000]; *Indonesia/Malaysia (Merits)* Judgment, ICJ Rep. 2002, 634, 650, paras 14, 47; Hearings, CR 2002/27, 20 (Ligitan Reef) [Agent Wirajuda, 3 June], CR 2002/30, 24 [Co-Agent Ariffin, 6 June], CR 2002/33, 13-14 [Counsel Watts, 10 June 2002]; *Nicaragua v. Honduras (Merits)* Judgment, ICJ Rep. 2007, para.136; Hearings, CR 2007/12, 44, para.26 [Counsel Brownlie, 20 March 2007], CR 2007/14, 34, para.9 [Counsel Greenwood, 23 March 2007] <www.icj-cij.org>; *Nicaragua v. Colombia* [Equitable Maritime Boundary Delimitation *infra*].

1909 *Norway v. Sweden Grisbadarna* Award [Equitable Maritime Boundary Delimitation *infra*]; 1977 *Anglo/French* Decision [18 ILM 397 (1979)], para.126; 1999 *Eritrea/Yemen Maritime Delimitation (Phase II)* Award, paras 143-145, 40 ILM 983 (2001) <www.pca-cpa.org>.

Straight Baselines
1958 TSC, Articles 4 and 5(2); 1982 UNCLOS, Articles 7 and 8(2):

1958 TSC, Article 4(1); 1982 UNCLOS, Article 7(1): *Anglo/Norwegian Fisheries* Judgment, ICJ Rep. 1951, 139, 143 (*dispositif*); *Tunisia/Libya (Merits)* Dissent Evensen, ICJ Rep. 1982, 315; *Qatar v. Bahrain (Merits)* Judgment, ICJ Rep. 2001, 103-104, paras 211-215; *Romania v. Ukraine* Judgment, ICJ Rep. 2009, paras 124-129, 136-137; Hearings, CR 2008/20, 20, para.25 and at 22, para.28 [Counsel Pellet, 4 Sep 2008], CR 2008/24, 32, para.55 [Counsel Bundy, 9 Sep], CR 2008/26, 13, para.53 [Counsel Queneudec, 10 Sep], 23, para.13 and at 25-26, paras 22-29 [Bundy], CR 2008/31, 13, para.15 [Counsel Lowe, 16 Sep 2008] <www.icj-cij.org>.

1982 UNCLOS, Article 7(2): *Nicaragua v. Honduras (Merits)* Judgment, ICJ Rep. 2007, para.7, Dissent Torres Bernardez, para.161.

1958 TSC, Article 4(2); 1982 UNCLOS, Article 7(3) and Article 47(3) – general direction of the coast and link to the land domain: *Anglo/Norwegian Fisheries* ICJ Rep. 1951, 116 – Judgment, 133, 135, 140-142, Separate O. Hsu Mo, 154-155, 156; *North Sea* Pleadings, Vol.II, 92 [Counsel Sir Humphrey Waldock, 29 Oct 1968], 221 [Agent Riphagen, 7 Nov], 272 [Waldock, 11 Nov 1968]; *Tunisia/Libya (Merits)* Separate O. de Arechaga, ICJ Rep. 1982, 138; *Gulf of Maine* Pleadings, Vol.V, 479 [US Reply], Vol.VII, 223 [Counsel Colson, 10 May 1984]; *Indonesia/Malaysia (Merits)* Judgment, ICJ Rep. 2002, 679, 683, paras 130, 137; Hearings, CR 2002/29, 54-55 [Counsel Pellet, 4 June], CR 2002/32, 28 n.36 [Counsel Crawford, 7 June 2002] <www.icj-cij.org>; 2002 *Russia v. Australia Volga* Separate O. Cot, para.17 <www.itlos.org>.

1958 TSC, Article 4(3); 1982 UNCLOS, Article 7(4) & Article 47(4) – low-tide elevations: *Anglo/Norwegian Fisheries* Judgment, ICJ Rep. 1951, 137-138, 140; *Tunisia/Libya (Merits)* Separate O. de Arechaga, ICJ Rep. 1982, 139, Dissent Evensen, 302, 316; 1999 *Eritrea/Yemen Maritime Delimitation (Phase II)* Award, para.144 <www.pca-cpa.org>; *Qatar v. Bahrain (Merits)* Judgment, ICJ Rep. 2001, 100, 102, paras 201, 208.

See also Low-Tide Elevations *infra*.

1958 TSC, Article 4(4); 1982 UNCLOS, Article 7(5) and Article 47(6) – economic interests: *Anglo/Norwegian Fisheries* Judgment, ICJ Rep. 1951, 133.

See also Equitable Maritime Boundary Delimitation – Economic Factors *infra*.

1958 TSC, Article 4(5); 1982 UNCLOS, Article 7(6) – another State's TS's cutt off from the HS/EEZ: *Anglo/Norwegian Fisheries* Pleadings, Vol.I, 95 [UK Memorial], 396, 470, 609 [UK Reply]; *Gulf of Fonseca* Oral Hearings, C 4/CR 91/45, 28 [Counsel Bowett, 10 June 1991]; 2002 *Belize/Guatemala* OAS Facilitators' Proposals, B-para.5 <www.belize-guatemala.gov.bz/>.

Cf. *UNCLOS III Off. Rec.* Vol.XVI, Statement of Rosenne (Israel), 56, para.49, 31 March 1982 (1984).

1958 TSC, Article 5(2); 1982 UNCLOS, Article 8(2) – preservation of IP: *Fisheries Jurisdiction* Pleadings (UK), 475 [Counsel Silkin, 25 March 1974]; *Great Belt* Pleadings, 540 [Denmark's Counter-Memorial].

United Kingdom v. Norway Fisheries (*Anglo/Norwegian Fisheries*) ICJ Rep. 1951, President J. Basdevant – Judgment, 116, Declaration Hackworth, 144, Individual O. Alvarez, 145, Separate O. Hsu Mo, 154, Dissents Sir Arnold McNair, 158, Read, 186; Orders, ICJ Rep. 1949, 233, 1950, 263, 1951, 8; *Anglo/Norwegian* Pleadings, Vol.I, 25-55, 87-101 [UK Memorial], 406-412, 524-547 [Norway's

Counter-Memorial], Vol.II, 316-453, 580-606, 681-721 [UK Reply], Vol.III, 162-203, 303-317 [Norway's Rejoinder], Vol.IV, 72-81 [Agent Sir Eric Beckett, 27 Sep 1951].

After the Court upheld the validity in international law of Norway's Royal Decree of 12 July 1935, as amended by a Decree of 10 December 1937, which applied straight baselines to the areas northward of latitude 66°28.8' North, i.e., north of the Arctic circle [*Anglo/Norwegian Fisheries* Pleadings, Vol.I, 14 (text), 199 (basepoints in blue line of the Decree)], a Decree of 18 July 1952 enclosed by 74 straight baselines also the areas situated to the south of this latitude, whereas Decrees of 30 June 1955 and 25 September 1970 applied straight baselines around the Jan Mayen Island and Spitzbergen (Svalbard) Archipelago respectively [*The Law of the Sea – Baselines: National Legislation with Illustrative Maps* 235-246 (UN 1989)].

See also *ILC Yearbook* 1956-II, 267-268; Sir Arthur Watts, *The International Law Commission 1949-1998*, Vol.I, 34-38 (Oxford 1999); *Malaysia/Singapore (Merits)* Judgment, ICJ Reports 2008, para.225, Separate O. Parra Aranguren, para.21, Dissent Dugard, para.26 <www.icj-cij.org>.

On 1927 *The Deutschland* Judgment of the Norwegian Supreme Court, Judge Bonnevie [28 BYIL 123-124 (1951); *Anglo/Norwegian* Pleadings, Vol.I, 162-170], see *Anglo/Norwegian Fisheries* Dissent Sir Arnold McNair, ICJ Rep. 1951, 181-183; Pleadings, Vol.I, 37-41, 44, 48 [UK Memorial], 174, 316-321 [Norway's Counter-Memorial], Vol.II, 190-208, 325-324, 377-380, 599, 732-738 [UK Reply], Vol.III, 150-155 [Norway's Rejoinder], Vol.IV, 69 [Agent Sir Eric Beckett, 26 Sep 1951], 100, 127 [Counsel Sir Frank Soskice, 28 Sep], 334-346 [Agent Arntzen, 13 Oct], 409 [Counsel Waldock, 18 Oct], 436 [Agent Beckett, 19 Oct 1951]; *Tunisia/Libya* Pleadings, Vol.IV, 326 [Libya's Reply].

On 1934 *The St. Just* Judgment of the Norwegian Supreme Court as final authority for application of the straight baselines, see *Anglo/Norwegian Fisheries* ICJ Rep. 1951, 116 – Judgment, 134, 135, Dissents McNair, 181-183, Read, 195, 196, 205; Pleadings, Vol.I, 47-49 [UK Memorial], 173-181 [text of Judgment], 321-323, 543 [Norway's Counter-Memorial], Vol.II, 208-222, 380, 600 [UK Reply], Vol.III, 147, 155 [Norway's Rejoinder], Vol.IV, 149, 454 [Agent Sir Eric Beckett, 1 and 20 Oct 1951].

On British suggestion made after enactment of the Norwegian Royal Decree of 12 July 1935 to refer the dispute to the PCIJ, see *Anglo/Norwegian Fisheries* Judgment, ICJ Rep. 1951, 124; Pleadings, Vol.I, 52 [UK Memorial].

On the protests of the UK, the Netherlands, Belgium and the FRG against Iceland's Regulations No.56 of 22 April 1950 which were deliberately modelled on the Norwegian system of straight baselines, see *Anglo/Norwegian Fisheries*

Pleadings, Vol.III, 317, 384 [Norway's Rejoinder], 631, 700 [text of Regulations], Vol.IV, 37, 79-81 [Agent Sir Eric Beckett, 25 and 27 Sep 1951], 400-404 [Counsel Waldock, 18 Oct 1951], 576-578 [1950 UK Notes], 606-609 [1951 NL Note and Iceland's Reply].

Three months after the delivery of the *Anglo/Norwegian Fisheries* Judgment, Iceland replaced Regulations No.56 by the new Regulations No.21 of 19 March 1952 establishing a 4-mile fishery zone measured from straight baselines where all foreign fishing was prohibited [UN Doc. ST/LEG/SER.B/6, 516 (1957)]. The *UK v. Iceland Fisheries Jurisdiction (Merits)* Judgment, ICJ Rep. 1974, 11, indicated that Regulations No.21 were protested by the United Kingdom (on 2 May and 18 June 1952). See also Separate Os Sir Humphrey Waldock, ICJ Rep. 1974, 107-108, 227-228; *Fisheries Jurisdiction* Pleadings (UK), 271 [Memorial (Merits)], and (FRG), 152 [Memorial (Merits)]. The United Kingdom proposed on 20 January 1953 to submit to the Court the validity of Icelandic straight baselines in the Bay of Foxa, but Iceland did not agree.

Iceland's Regulations No.21 were superseded by the new Regulations No.70 of 30 June as supplemented on 29 August 1958, which provided for a 12-mile exclusive fisheries zone measured from the modified straight baselines [UN Doc. ST/LEG/SER.B/8, 11 (1959)], and which were again protested by the FRG and the United Kingdom on 16 July and 23 August 1958, as well as by France on 11 July and Spain on 1 September 1958. See *Fisheries Jurisdiction (Merits)* Judgments, ICJ Rep. 1974, 12, 183-184, Separate Os Waldock, 110-111, 227. On British suggestion, declined by Iceland, to bring the dispute to the ICJ, see *Fisheries Jurisdiction* Pleadings (UK), 129, 153-156 [Memorial (Jurisd)]. Under the UK/Iceland and the FRG/Iceland Exchange of Notes Constituting Agreements Settling the Fisheries Dispute of 11 March and 19 July 1961 [397 UNTS 275 and 409 UNTS 47], Britain and the FRG ultimately recognized Icelandic baselines, subject to the modification of four specified points. Cf. *Fisheries Jurisdiction (Jurisdiction)* Judgment, ICJ Rep. 1973, 17, Separate Os Fitzmaurice, 29 n.11, 32, 73 n.11, 76, *(Merits)* Judgments, ICJ Rep. 1974, 12-13, 184-185, Separate Os Waldock, 113-114, 227; Pleadings (UK), 171-172 [Iceland's Memorandum of 28 Feb 1961].

North Sea Judgment, ICJ Rep. 1969, 21, para.15, 52, para.98, Separate O. President Bustamante y Rivero, 59, Separate O. Ammoun, 145, 148, 150-151, 152; *North Sea* Pleadings, Vol.I, 39 [FRG Memorial], Vol.II, 125, 138 [Agent Riphagen, 30 and 31 Oct], 193-195 [Counsel Oda, 5 Nov], 271-272 [Counsel Sir Humphrey Waldock, 11 Nov 1968]; *Fisheries Jurisdiction (Merits)* Separate Os Waldock, ICJ Rep. 1974, 107-114, 227; *Aegean Sea (Jurisdiction)* Judgment, ICJ Rep. 1978, 37, para.89; Pleadings, 89, 142 [Counsel O'Connell, 25 and 27 Aug 1976]; *Tunisia/Libya (Merits)* Judgment, ICJ Rep. 1982, 74-76, Dissents Oda, 210, Evensen, 285,

301, 314-317, *(Revision)* Judgment, ICJ Rep. 1985, 225; *Gulf of Maine* Judgment, ICJ Rep. 1984, 309; Pleadings, Vol.I, 166-167, 200-201 [Canada's Memorial], Vol.II, 69, 109 [US Memorial], Vol.III, 50 [Canada's Counter-Memorial], Vol.IV, 74-75 [US Counter-Memorial], Vol.V, 55 [Canada's Reply], 383-384, 447, 487, 513, 521 [US Reply], Vol.VI, 382, 384 [Counsel Feldman, 16 April 1984]; *Libya/Malta (Merits)* Judgment, ICJ Rep. 1985, 22; Pleadings, Vol.I, 128 [Libya's Memorial], Vol.II, 363 [Malta's Counter-Memorial], Vol.III, 48 [Libya's Reply], 247 [Malta's Reply]; *Libya/Chad Territorial Dispute* Separate O. Ajibola, ICJ Rep. 1994, 79-80; *Gulf of Fonseca* Judgment, ICJ Rep. 1992, 593, Dissent Oda, 745, 755; *Qatar v. Bahrain (Merits)* Judgment, ICJ Rep. 2001, 40, paras 201, 208, 210-215, 223, Dissent Torres Bernardez, paras 479, 507; Hearings, CR 2000/9 [trans.], 35 [Counsel Queneudec, 5 June 2000], CR 2000/18, 22 [Counsel Sinclair, 21 June], CR 2000/25, 12-14 [Counsel Weil, 29 June 2000]; *Cameroon v. Nigeria; Equatorial Guinea Intervening (Merits)* Judgment, ICJ Rep. 2002, 352, para.65, Dissents Koroma, 484-485, paras 25-27, Ajibola, 581, para.134; *Romania v. Ukraine* Judgment, ICJ Rep. 2009, paras 124-129, 136-137; *Nicaragua v. Colombia* Nicaragua's Memorial, 203-204, 214-215 <www.icj-cij.org>.

1977 *Anglo/French* Decision [18 ILM 397 (1979)], paras 50-51, 71; 1999 *Eritrea/Yemen (Phase II)* Award, paras 50, 140-145, 151, Annex II: Eritrea's Answer to Judge Schwebel's Question <www.pca-cpa.org>; 2002 *Newfoundland/Nova Scotia (Phase II)* Award, para.5.16 <www.boundary-dispute.ca>; 2002 *Belize/Guatemala* OAS Facilitators' Proposals, B-paras 4-6 <www.belize-guatemala.gov.bz/>; 2006 *Barbados/Trinidad & Tobago* Award, paras 329-331, 334 <www.pca-cpa.org>.

See also Regime of Islands *infra*.

Mouth of Rivers

1930 Hague Draft, Annex II, Appendix A: US Proposal, Appendix B: French Proposal; 1958 TSC, Article 13; 1982 UNCLOS, Article 9:

Honduras v. Nicaragua Arbitral Award of 23 December 1906 Judgment, ICJ Rep. 1960, 202-203, 212, 216-217; *Tunisia v. Libya (Revision)* Judgment, ICJ Rep. 1985, 224-225, Separate O. Oda, 243-245; *Gulf of Fonseca (Merits)* Judgment, ICJ Rep. 1992, 543-553, 615, para.430, Dissent Oda, 759; Hearings, C 4/CR 91/44, 26 [Counsel Lauterpacht, 4 June 1991], CR 91/46, 41-43 [11 June 1991]; *(Revision)* Judgment, ICJ Rep. 2003, 392; *Cameroon v. Nigeria (Preliminary Objections)* Judgment, ICJ Rep. 1998, 283, 302, Separate O. Oda, 335-336, *Cameroon v. Nigeria; Equatorial Guinea Intervening (Merits)* Judgment, ICJ Rep. 2002, 303, paras 40, 52, 54-61, 73, 248-250, 261, 325.IV(B), Dissents Koroma, 478, para.11, Ajibola, 589, para.155, Separate O. Mbaye, 517-518, 522, paras 60-64, 79; Hearings, CR 2002/10, 45-49 [Counsel Watts, 4 March 2002]; *Indonesia/Malaysia (Merits)*

Judgment, ICJ Rep. 2002, 659, paras 68, 71; *El Salvador v. Honduras Gulf of Fonseca (Revision)* and *Nicaragua v. Honduras* cases – see Equitable Maritime Boundary Delimitation *infra*; *Romania v. Ukraine* Judgment, ICJ Rep. 2009, para.137; Hearings, CR 2008/26, 25, para.24 [Counsel Bundy, 10 Sep 2008]; *Costa Rica v. Nicaragua San Juan River* Judgment, ICJ Rep. 2009, paras 15-16, Declaration Guillaume, para.5 <www.icj-cij.org>.

1906 *Honduras/Nicaragua Boundary Question*, 1911 *Mexico/USA Chamizal* and 1914 *Costa Rica/Panama Boundary* Awards – see Equitable Maritime Boundary Delimitation *infra*; 1910 *USA/Venezuela Orinoco Steamship Company* Award – see Settlement of Disputes – Interpretation or Application *infra*; 1985 *Guinea/Guinea-Bissau* Award, paras 73, 97 [25 ILM 285, 292 (1986)]; 2007 *Guyana/Suriname* Award, paras 170-171, 181, 279-280, 307-309 – see Equitable Maritime Boundary Delimitation *infra*; Sir Creek – see 1968 *India/Pakistan Rann of Kutch* Award, Equitable Maritime Boundary Delimitation *infra*.

Bays

1930 Hague Draft, Annex II: Base Line (10-mile closing line); 1958 TSC, Article 7 (24-mile line); 1982 UNCLOS, Article 10 (24-mile line):

Relevant Jurisprudence

Anglo/Norwegian Fisheries ICJ Rep. 1951, 116 – Judgment, 127, 129, 130-131, 132, 133, 139, 141, Individual O. Alvarez, 151, Separate O. Hsu Mo, 155-156, Dissent Sir Arnold McNair, 163-166, 168, Dissent Read, 188; *North Sea* Pleadings, Vol.II, 222 [Agent Riphagen, 7 Nov 1968], 246, 260-261, 264 [Reply by Counsel Waldock to Questions Fitzmaurice, 8 Nov 1968]; *Fisheries Jurisdiction (Merits)* Joint Separate Os, ICJ Rep. 1974, 51, 223; *Tunisia/Libya (Merits)* Judgment, ICJ Rep. 1982, 74; *Gulf of Maine* Judgment, ICJ Rep. 1984, 268-271, 322-325, 336, 354, Separate O. Schwebel, 354-359 [incl. Map]; Pleadings, Vol.III, 45-47, 247 [Canada's Counter-Memorial], Vol.IV, 16, 127-130 [US Counter-Memorial], Vol.V, 50-51, 55, 71-72, 128, 143-147 [Canada's Reply], 443-445, 448-451, 484-486, 508 [US Reply], Vol. VI, 49 [Agent Legault, 3 April 1984], 74-86 [Deputy Agent Hankey, 4 April], 206, 213-219 [Counsel Malintoppi, 10 April], 293-295 [Counsel Colson, 12 April], 310-315 [Colson, 13 April], 328-336 [Counsel Feldman, 13 April], 464 [Question 2 of Judge Schwebel, 19 April], Vol.VII, 126-134 [Malintoppi's Reply to Schwebel, 5 May, with err. at 377], 215, 234-235 [Colson's Reply, 10 May 1984], Vol.VIII, 55 [Fig.13], 76 [Fig.51], 117 [Fig.36], 118 [Fig.39], 256 [Fig.171]; *Libya/Malta (Merits)* Joint Separate O., ICJ Rep. 1985, 92; *Gulf of Fonseca* Judgment, ICJ Rep. 1992, 588, 593, Dissent Oda, 735-747; *Indonesia/Malaysia (Merits)* Hearings, CR 2002/28, 40 [Counsel Soons, 3 June], CR 2002/33, 41 [Soons, 10 June 2002], 45

[Counsel Bundy] <www.icj-cij.org>; 2007 *Guyana/Suriname* Award, paras 171, 181 <www.pca-cpa.org>; *Romania v. Ukraine* Judgment, ICJ Rep. 2009, paras 130, 137; Hearings, CR 2008/26, 25, para.24 [Counsel Bundy, 10 Sep 2008]; *Costa Rica v. Nicaragua San Juan River* Hearings, CR 2009/4, 17, para.35: Bay of San Juan del Norte and Salinas Bay [Agent Arguello, 5 March 2009], CR 2009/6, 38, para.7 [Counsel Caflisch, 9 March 2009], 67, para.9 [Agent Ugalde-Alvarez] <www.icj-cij.org>.

See also *ILC Yearbook* 1956-II, 269 (para.1); Sir Arthur Watts, *The International Law Commission 1949-1998*, Vol.I, 39 (Oxford 1999).

On USSR closure of the Peter the Great Bay in 1957, see *Nuclear Tests* Pleadings (Australia), 340 [Memorial].

An inarticulate premise of Libya in the *Libya/Malta Continental Shelf* case [see Equitable Maritime Boundary Delimitation *infra*] was to obtain recognition for its some 300 miles long closing straight line drawn in the Gulf of Sirt (Sidra/Surt), protested by the USA in 1974, 1979 and 1985 [Libya's Information of 19 October 1973, *The Law of the Sea: National Legislation on the Territorial Sea* 198 (UN 1995); *UN LOS Bull.* 40 (1985 No.6); *US Responses to Excessive National Claims, Limits in the Seas* No.112, 11-13 (1992)]. For references to Gulf of Sirt, see UN Doc. S/PV.2246th Meeting-4 September 1980, para.33 (Malta); *Tunisia/Libya (Intervention)* Judgment, ICJ Rep. 1981, 9, 17, Separate O. Schwebel, 37, *(Merits)* Judgment, ICJ Rep. 1982, 34, 53, Dissent Evensen, 316; Pleadings, Vol.II, 48 [Tunisia's Counter-Memorial], Vol.III, 447 [Counsel Lauterpacht, 23 March 1981]; *Libya/Malta (Intervention)* Judgment, ICJ Rep. 1984, 11, Separate O. de Arechaga, 65, *(Merits)* Judgment, ICJ Rep. 1985, 22; Pleadings, Vol.I, 167 [Libya's Memorial], Vol.II, 44, 56 [Libya's Counter-Memorial], Vol.IV, 157 [Counsel Bowett, 13 Dec 1984], Vol.V, 42 [Fig.11].

On 1977/1978 *Anglo/French* Decisions and 1988 *Taba* Award, see Equitable Maritime Boundary Delimitation *infra*.

On 1992 *Canada/France* Award [Equitable Maritime Boundary Delimitation *infra*], para.29, see *Qatar v. Bahrain (Merits)* Hearings, CR 2000/9 [trans.], 40-41 [Counsel Queneudec, 5 June 2000].

10-Mile Closing Line

Eastern Greenland Pleadings, PCIJ Series C, No.62, 34 [Memorial of Denmark], No.63, 1295 [Rejoinder of Norway], No.64, 1541 [Annex]; *Anglo/Norwegian Fisheries* ICJ Rep. 1951, 116 – Judgment, 120, 121-122, 131 [stating that although the 10-mile rule was applied in the legislative and treaty practice of states and in certain arbitral decisions (without specifying the *Washington* and the *North Atlantic Coast Fisheries* Awards), it "has not acquired the authority of a general rule of international law"], 136, Individual O. Alvarez, 150, Dissents McNair, 163-165, Read, 188; *Anglo/Norwegian* Pleadings (invoking extensive jurisprudence of arbitral tribunals and national courts), Vol.I, 24-25, 31, 60-71, 83-84, 86, 89-93 [UK Memorial], 422-451 [Norway's Counter-Memorial], Vol.II, 444-451, 467-503, 576-577, 580-581, 585, 596, 610-640 [UK Reply], Vol.III, 317-361, 436, 633-647 [Norway's Rejoinder], Vol.IV, 81-90 [Agent Sir Eric Beckett, 27 Sep 1951], 265-279, 507 [Counsel Bourquin, 10, 11 and 26 Oct 1951], 402-405, 411-412 [Counsel Waldock, 18 Oct 1951]; *Minquiers and Ecrehos* Pleadings, Vol.I, 54 [UK Memorial].

For reliance on the *Anglo/Norwegian Fisheries* findings of the Court, see *Minquiers and Ecrehos* Pleadings, Vol.II, 200 [Agent Gros, 28 Sep 1953]; *North Sea* Separate O. Ammoun, ICJ Rep. 1969, 151, Dissent Sorensen, 247; Pleadings, Vol.I, 60 [FRG Memorial], 400 [FRG Reply], 509 [Common Rejoinder of D/NL]; *Fisheries Jurisdiction (Merits)* Separate O. Dillard, ICJ Rep. 1974, 58; Pleadings (UK), 322, 350-351 [Memorial (Merits)], 468-469 [Counsel Silkin, 25 March 1974]; *Gulf of Fonseca* Judgment, ICJ Rep. 1992, 588.

On 1853 *UK/USA The Washington (The Julia*; Bay of Fundy) Award [6 AJIL 434 (1912); No.47/Stuyt], see *Anglo/Norwegian Fisheries* Dissent McNair, ICJ Rep. 1951, 165, 168; Pleadings, Vol.I, 61-62 [UK Memorial], 429-430, 450, 476-477 [Norway's Counter-Memorial], Vol.II, 475-476, 525-526 [UK Reply], Vol.IV, 86-87 [Agent Sir Eric Beckett, 27 Sep 1951]; *Gulf of Maine* Pleadings, Vol.I, 187-189 [Canada's Memorial], Vol.VI, 218-219 [Counsel Malintoppi, 10 April 1984], Vol.VII 215 [Counsel Colson, 10 May 1984].

On 1910 *UK/USA North Atlantic Coast Fisheries* Award [RIAA XI, 167; PCA Awards <www.haguejusticeportal.net>; No.291/Stuyt], see *Anglo/Norwegian Fisheries* Dissent Read, ICJ Rep. 1951, 188; Pleadings, Vol.I, 63-64, 67, 69, 90 [UK Memorial], 423-424, 427-437, 443, 444, 450 [Norway's Counter-Memorial], Vol.II, 263-278 (excerpts of *North Atlantic Fisheries* arguments of Britain), 468, 471-473, 475-477, 479-488, 576, 617-619, 622, 629 [UK Reply], Vol.III, 318, 322-328, 341, 356 [Norway's Rejoinder], Vol.IV, 82-85, 87 [Agent Sir Eric Beckett, 27 Sep 1951], 268, 272-275, 507 [Counsel Bourquin, 10, 11 and 26 Oct 1951]; *Gulf of Maine* Pleadings, Vol.V, 509 [US Reply]; *Gulf of Fonseca* Judgment, ICJ Rep. 1992, 591-592, Dissent Oda, 736, 738, 747, 750-751.

On 1882 North Sea Fisheries Convention, see Fisheries *infra*.

Historic Bays
1958 TSC, Article 7(6); 1982 UNCLOS, Article 10(6) and Article 298(1)(a):

Eastern Greenland Pleadings, PCIJ Series C, No.63, 766 [Reply of Denmark], 1218 [Rejoinder of Norway]; *Corfu Channel (Merits)* Dissent Azevedo, ICJ Rep. 1949, 103; *Anglo/Norwegian Fisheries* Dissents McNair, ICJ Reports 1951, 164, Read, 188; Pleadings, Vol.I, 92 [UK Memorial], 548-556, 568-571 [Norway's Counter-Memorial], Vol.II, 445-446, 456, 566, 644 [UK Reply], Vol.III, 336 [Norway's Rejoinder]; *Aegean Sea (Jurisdiction)* Dissent de Castro, ICJ Rep. 1978, 66-67; *Tunisia/Libya (Merits)* Judgment, ICJ Rep. 1982, 73-74, Dissents Oda, 209-210, Evensen, 316-317; Pleadings, Vol.I, 74 [Tunisia's Memorial], 505-506 [Libya's Memorial], Vol.IV, 113-124 [Libya's Reply]; *Gulf of Maine* Separate O. Schwebel, ICJ Rep. 1984, 354; Pleadings, Vol.V, 484, 508 [US Reply]; *Gulf of Fonseca* case – see Equitable Maritime Boundary Delimitation *infra*; *Qatar v. Bahrain (Merits)* Dissent Torres Bernardez, para.470, ICJ Rep. 2001, 422; *Romania v. Ukraine* Hearings, CR 2008/26, 25, para.24 [Counsel Bundy, 10 Sep 2008] <www.icj-cij.org>.

On 1877 *Direct United States Cable Co. v. Anglo-American Telegraph Co.* (The Conception Bay) Judgment, see the end of this section *infra*.

On 1885 *Stetson v. USA (The Alleganean)* Judgment, see Straits Used for International Navigation *infra*.

On 1917 *El Salvador v. Nicaragua Gulf of Fonseca* Judgment, see Equitable Maritime Boundary Delimitation *infra*.

On 1951 Egypt's Royal Decree, see TS Breadth and Outer Limit *supra*.

Ports and Roadsteads
1930 Hague Draft, Annex II, Appendix B: Compromisory Proposal of the French Delegation, 250-251; 1958 TSC, Articles 8-9; 1982 UNCLOS, Articles 11-12:

Anglo/Norwegian Fisheries Pleadings, Vol.I, 416, 452 [Norway's Counter-Memorial], Vol.II, 455, 505 [UK Reply]; 1981 *Dubai/Sharjah* Award [91 ILM 660-663]; *Great Belt* Pleadings, 250-251 [Finland's Memorial]; *Gulf of Fonseca* Dissent Oda, ICJ Rep. 1992, 755; *Malaysia v. Singapore (Provisional Measures)* Hearings, ITLOS/PV.03/02/Corr.1, 7 [Counsel Crawford, 25 Sep 2003] <www.itlos.org>; *Romania v. Ukraine* Judgment [Romania's Sulina Dyke], ICJ Rep. 2009, paras 81, 123, 125, 130-144, 151, 199-201, 206, 218 and Sketch-maps Nos 1-9; Hearings, CR 2008/21, 43-46, paras 21-35, quoting at 45, para.31 *Dubai/Sharjah* Award [Counsel Crawford, 5 Sep 2008], CR 2008/24, 15, para.22 [Agent Vassylenko, 9 Sep], 30-33, paras 48-61 [Counsel Bundy], CR 2008/26, 26, para.28 and at 28, para.35 [10 Sep], CR 2008/28, 37-38, paras 11-17, quoting *Dubai/Sharjah* Award [Bundy, 11 Sep], 44, para.44 and at 48, para.57 [Bundy], CR 2008/29, 34-36 [Counsel Queneudec, 12 Sep], CR 2008/30, 18, para.23 [Agent Aurescu, 15 Sep], 65-72 [Counsel Muller], CR 2008/31, 18-22 [Counsel Lowe, 16 Sep], CR 2008/32, 44-47, quoting *Dubai/Sharjah* Award [Bundy, 18 Sep 2008] <www.icj-cij.org>.

Low-Tide Elevations
1930 Hague Draft, Annex II: Base Line; 1958 TSC, Article 11; 1982 UNCLOS, Article 13:

Anglo/Norwegian Fisheries ICJ Rep. 1951, 116 – Judgment, 120, 121, 128; Pleadings, Vol.I, 75-78, 84 [UK Memorial], Vol.II, 510-511 [UK Reply], Vol.IV, 91 [Agent Sir Eric Beckett, 27 Sep 1951]; *Minquiers and Ecrehos* Judgment, ICJ Rep. 1953, 53; Pleadings, Vol.I, 21-26, 58-59 [UK Memorial], 424-425, 432-433 [UK Reply]; *North Sea* Pleadings, Vol.I, 211-212 [Denmark's Counter-Memorial], 364-365 [NL Counter-Memorial], Vol.II, 72-73 [Agent Riphagen, 28 Oct 1968], 85 [Counsel Sir Humphrey Waldock], 190 [Agent Jaenicke, 4 Nov, referring to Hohe Riff], 277 [Waldock, 11 Nove 1968]; *Tunisia/Libya (Merits)* Judgment, ICJ Rep. 1982, 62-64, 88-89, Separate O. de Arechaga, 135, 138-139, Dissents Oda, 266-267, 269, 271, Evensen, 285, 299-304; *Gulf of Maine* Judgment, ICJ Rep. 1984, 287, 329, 332; Pleadings, Vol.V, 485 n.3 [US Reply]; *Gulf of Fonseca* Judgment, ICJ Rep. 1992, 570, para.356; *Qatar v. Bahrain (Merits)* Judgment, ICJ Rep. 2001, 40, paras 33-34, 61, 179, 187-209, 218, 220, 222, 247-248, Separate Os Oda, 123-125, 131, paras 5-9, 20, Parra-Aranguren, 224, para.7, Dissent Torres Bernardez, 257, paras 474, 490, 507, 509, 513, 518, 522-533, 550-551; Hearings, CR 2000/9 [trans.], 33, 35, 41-48 [Counsel Queneudec, 5 June 2000], CR 2000/14, 38-45, 49 [Counsel Reisman, 13 June], CR 2000/15, 12 [14 June], 51-52 [Counsel Weil], CR 2000/16, 41, 47 [Reisman, 15 June], CR 2000/25, 6-10 [29 June 2000], 12-14 [Weil]; *Nicaragua v. Honduras (Merits)* Judgment, ICJ Rep. 2007, paras 136-145; *Malaysia/Singapore (Merits)* Judgment, ICJ Rep. 2008, paras 18-19, 278, 291-299, Separate Os Parra Aranguren, paras 27-29, Rao, paras 40-41; Hearings, CR 2007/20, 18, paras 9-10 [Agent Koh, 6 Nov 2007], 26-27, para.12 [Counsel Chao], CR 2007/22, 18, para.28 [Counsel Bundy, 8 Nov], 65, para.8 [Bundy], CR 2007/23 [transl.], 42-43, paras 12-15 [Counsel Pellet, 9 Nov], CR 2007/26, 34, para.38 [Counsel Sir Elihu Lauterpacht, 15 Nov], CR 2007/28, 22, para.16 [Counsel Chao, 19 Nov 2007] <www.icj-cij.org>; *Nicaragua v. Colombia (Preliminary Objections)* Judgment, paras 12, 26, ICJ Rep. 2007; *Romania v. Ukraine* Hearings, CR 2008/26, 24, para.18 [Counsel Bundy, 10 Sep 2008] <www.icj-cij.org>.

1977 *Anglo/French* Decision [18 ILM 397 (1979)], paras 125-127, 136-138, 1978 Decision [*id.* 462]; *Canada/France* Award, para.69 [31 ILM 1170 (1992)];

1998 *Eritrea/Yemen Territorial Sovereignty (Phase I)* Award, paras 30, 75, 475, 482, 527 [40 ILM 900 (2001) <www.pca-cpa.org>].

See also Straight Baselines *supra*; Regime of Islands – Nature of a High-Tide Elevation, and Rocks Which Cannot Sustain Human Habitation or Economic Life of Their Own

The Right and Meaning of Innocent Passage

1930 Hague Draft, Articles 3-6; 1958 TSC, Articles 5(2) and 14-17; 1982 UNCLOS Part II, Articles 8(2) and 17-21, Part IV, Article 52, Part XII, Article 211(3)-(4):

Corfu Channel (Merits) ICJ Rep. 1949, 4 – Judgment, 28, 30-31, 35, Dissents Krylov, 75, Azevedo, 108-109, Ecer 129-130; *Corfu* Pleadings, Vol.I, 42-46 [UK Memorial], Vol.II, 112-115 [Albania's Counter-Memorial], 259-260 [UK Reply], Vol.III, 290-293 [Agent Sir Eric Beckett, 12 Nov 1948], Vol.IV, 553-554 [Beckett, 18 Jan 1949], 672-675 [Counsel Cot, 22 Jan 1949]; *Anglo/Norwegian Fisheries* ICJ Rep. 1951, 116 – Judgment, 137, 142, Individual O. Alvarez, 150, 153, Dissents Sir Arnold McNair, 171-178, Read, 190-192, 197-198; *Anglo/Norwegian* Pleadings, Vol.I, 361, 476 [Norway's Counter-Memorial], Vol.II, 412 [UK Reply]; *North Sea* Dissent Vice-President Koretsky, ICJ Rep. 1969, 161; Pleadings, Vol.II, 193 [Counsel Shigeru Oda, 5 Nov 1968]; *Fisheries Jurisdiction (Interim Measures)* Orders, ICJ Rep. 1972, 13, 31, *(Jurisdiction)* Separate Os Fitzmaurice, ICJ Rep. 1973, 28 n.8, 72 n.8; *Gulf of Maine* Pleadings, Vol.V, 514 [US Reply], Vol.VII, 199-200 [Counsel Stevenson, 9 May 1984]; *Libya/Malta* Pleadings, Vol.IV, 137 [Counsel Lucchini, 12 Dec 1984]; *Nicaragua v. USA (Provisional Measures)* Order, ICJ Rep. 1984, 170, para.1(b) and (e), 181, para.28, 187, para.41(B)(1), Dissent Schwebel, 190, 199, *(Jurisdiction and Admissibility)* Judgment, ICJ Rep. 1984, 424, para.73, *as reaffirmed* by *(Merits)* Judgment, ICJ Rep. 1986, 93, para.174, also *id.* 46-53, paras 76-92, and 111-112, paras 213-214, Dissent Schwebel, 259; *Great Belt* Pleadings, 146-154 [Counsel Jimenez de Arechaga, 2 July 1991], 155-156 [Counsel Fergo], 193-194 [Counsel Treves, 4 July 1991], 333-336 [Finland's Memorial], 613-619 [Denmark's Counter-Memorial]; *Gulf of Fonseca* Judgment, ICJ Rep. 1992, 379, 590, 592-593, 605, 616, para.432(1), Dissent Oda, 742, 745, 760; Hearings, C 4/CR 91/43, 35 [Agent Arguello, 7 June 1991], CR 91/45, 23 [Counsel Bowett, 10 June 1991]; *Qatar v. Bahrain (Merits)* Judgment, ICJ Rep. 2001, 110, 117, paras 223, 252(2)(b), Joint Dissent Bedjaoui, Ranjeva, Koroma, 196-201, paras 169-180, Declaration Herczegh, 216, Separate O. Parra-Aranguren, 223, paras 2-3, Dissent Torres Bernardez, 420, 443-445, paras 462, 543-545, 550; Hearings, CR 2000/14, 36 [Counsel Reisman, 13 June 2000], CR 2000/16, 49-50 [15 June 2000]; *Oil Platforms (Merits)* Hearings, CR 2003/12, 12-13 [Counsel

Weil, 26 Feb 2003], 2003/13, 24 [Counsel Murphy], CR 2003/17, 32 [Murphy, 5 March], CR 2003/19, 10-13 [Counsel Sellers, 7 March 2003], 30 [Counsel Pellet]; *Nicaragua v. Honduras* Hearings, CR 2007/14, 14, para.12 [Counsel Colson, 23 March 2007]; *Romania v. Ukraine* Hearings, CR 2008/28, 20-21, para.40 [Counsel Sir Michael Wood, 11 Sep 2008] <www.icj-cij.org>.

See also *ILC Yearbook* 1956-II, 273; UNGA Adopts Two Oceans Resolutions, UN Doc.GA/10899 of 4 Dec 2009, Statements of EU-Sweden and Thailand, at 5 & 15 <www.un.org/News/Press/docs//2009/ga10899.doc.htm>.

1992 ECJ *Anklagemyndigheden v. Poulsen* Judgment, para.10, Case C-286/90, 1992 ECR 1-6019 <http://eur-lex.europa.eu> & 103 AJIL 555 (2009); 1993 *UN Iraq/Kuwait Boundary Demarcation* Report, paras 96-97 [32 ILM 1448 (1993)]; 1999 *Eritrea/Yemen (Phase II)* Award, paras 107-111 <www.pca-cpa.org>; *M/V Saiga* Separate O. Laing [38 ILM 1323 (1999)], paras 49-50; 2002 *Russia v. Australia Volga* Judgment, ITLOS Case No.11, para.78 <www.itlos.org>; 2006 *Barbados/Trinidad & Tobago (Jurisdiction and Merits)* Award, para.282 [<www .pca-cpa.org; 45 ILM 800 (2006); RIAA XXVII, 147 <www.un.org/law/riaa & http://untreaty.un.org/cod/riaa/cases/vol_XXVII/147-251.pdf>]; 2007 *Guyana/ Suriname (Jurisdiction and Merits)* Award, para.316 <www.pca-cpa.org>; ECJ Grand Chamber *International Association of Independent Tank Owners (Intertanko) v. Secretary of State for Transport*, Case C-308/06 of 3 June 2008 <http://eur-lex.europa.eu> & 103 AJIL 555 (2009).

Innocent Passage of Warships

1930 Hague Draft, Articles 3 and 12-13; 1958 TSC, Articles 14-17 and 23; 1982 UNCLOS, Articles 17-26 and 29-32:

SS Wimbledon Pleadings, PCIJ Series C, No.3-Additional Volume, 154 [Rejoinder of Germany]; *Polish War Vessels* Pleadings, PCIJ Series C, No.55, 136 [Report Naval Subcommission], 151 [LN Council], 173 [Memorial of Poland]; *Corfu Channel (Merits)* ICJ Rep. 1949, 4 – Judgment, 12, 14, 19, 27-31, 33-34, Individual O. Alvarez, 41, 46-47, Dissents Winiarski, 55-56, Badawi Pascha, 65-66, Krylov, 73-75, Azevedo, 98, 99-106, Ecer, 121, 130; *Corfu* Pleadings, Vol.I, 29-30, 43-47 [UK Memorial], Vol.II, 112-115, 128-138, 142-143 [Albania's Counter-Memorial], 256-257, 285-286, 288-295, 297 [UK Reply], 355-357 [Albania's Rejoinder], Vol.III, 267-288 [Agent Sir Eric Beckett, 11 Nov 1948], 376-405 [Counsel Cot, 18 Nov 1948], Vol.IV, 542-546 [Beckett, 18 Jan 1949], 669-689 [Counsel Cot, 22 Jan 1949]; *Anglo/Norwegian Fisheries* Dissent Sir Arnold McNair, ICJ Rep. 1951, 162-163; *Gulf of Maine* Pleadings, Vol.VII, 199 [Counsel Stevenson, 9 May 1984]; *Great Belt* Pleadings, 149 [Counsel de Arechaga, 2 July 1991], 250-252, 327-329, 331 [Finland's Memorial], 576 [Denmark's Counter-Memorial]; *Qatar v. Bahrain*

(Merits) Separate O. Oda, para.19, ICJ Rep. 2001, 130; *Romania v. Ukraine* Hearings, CR 2008/28, 20-21, para.40 [Counsel Sir Michael Wood, 11 Sep 2008]; Romania's Memorial, Annex 81 (Article 8) <www.icj-cij.org>.

For reliance on Elihu Root's aphorism (amounting to an unconsidered *obiter dictum*) from his oral argument in the *UK/USA North Atlantic Coast Fisheries* Proceedings that, "Warships may not pass without consent into this zone [territorial waters], because they threaten; merchantmen may pass and repass because they do not threaten" [Vol.XI, 2007 (1912)], see *Corfu Channel (Merits)* Dissents Krylov, ICJ Rep. 1949, 74, Azevedo, 101; Pleadings, Vol.II, 137 [Albania's Counter-Memorial], 293 [UK Reply], Vol.III, 273-5 and 276 [Agent Sir Eric Beckett, 11 Nov 1948], 377, 382 and 386 [Counsel Cot, 18 Nov 1948], Vol.IV, 543 and 553 [Agent Beckett, 18 Jan 1949], 673 [Counsel Cot, 22 Jan 1949].

1977 *Anglo/French* Decision [18 ILM 397 (1979)], paras 161-162, 175-176, 188; 2002 *Belize/Guatemala* OAS Facilitators' Proposals, B-para.5 <www.belize-guatemala.gov.bz/>; Annex VII *Mox Plant* UK Counter-Memorial, 149 <www.pca-cpa.org>.

See also *ILC Yearbook* 1956-II, 277 (paras 3-4); USA/USSR Wyoming Joint Statement on Uniform Interpretation of Rules of International Law Governing Innocent Passage of 23 Sep 1989, 28 ILM 1444 (1989); *Oceans and the Law of the Sea*, UN Docs A/56/58, para.23(b) (2002), A/57/57, para.22(b) (2002), A/59/62, para.12 (2004), classifying Declarations that request notification or authorization for the IP of warships as not conforming with the LOSC <www.un.org/Depts/los/>.

On passage of warships through international rivers, see *Costa Rica v. Nicaragua San Juan River* Judgment, ICJ Rep. 2009, paras 23-26, 49; Hearings, CR 2009/3, 9-12, paras 7-19 [Counsel Crawford, 3 March 2009], CR 2009/5, 30-36, paras 8-26 [Counsel McCaffrey, 6 March], CR 2009/6, 52-64, paras 7-33 [Crawford, 9 March], CR 2009/7, 33-34, paras 6-9 [Counsel McCaffrey, 12 March 2009] <www.icj-cij.org>.

Sea Lanes and Traffic Separation Schemes
1982 UNCLOS, Article 22:

North Sea Pleadings, Vol.II, 139 [Agent Riphagen, 31 Oct 1968]; *Great Belt* Pleadings, 336 [Finland's Memorial], 493, 608, 616, 623 [Denmark's Counter-Memorial].

See also Straits Used for International Navigation – Safety Passage Regulations *infra*.

Criminal Jurisdiction
1930 Hague Draft, Article 8; 1958 TSC, Article 19; 1982 UNCLOS, Article 27:

SS Lotus PCIJ Series A, No.10 (1927) – Dissent Moore, 74-78, 87-88; *Anglo/Norwegian Fisheries* Pleadings, Vol.II, 417-419 [UK Reply]; *Malaysia/Singapore (Merits)* Judgment, ICJ Rep. 2008, paras 231-234 <www.icj-cij.org>.

M/V Saiga Separate O. Laing [38 ILM 1323 (1999)], para.15; 2007 *Guyana/Suriname* Award, para.316 <www.pca-cpa.org>.

See also High Seas – Status of Ships/Criminal Jurisdiction *infra*.

Maintenance of Navigational Aids and Territorial Sovereignty

For reliance on the holding of the 1909 *Norway v. Sweden Grisbadarna Maritime Frontier* Award [RIAA XI, 155; 4 AJIL 186, 226 (1910); No.288/Stuyt] that the placing of beacons and navigational aids was not sufficient evidence substantiating Swedish title based on the use of the disputed area for fisheries, see *Eastern Greenland* Pleadings, PCIJ Series C, No.63, 817-818 [Reply of Denmark], 1314-1315 [Rejoinder of Norway]; *Minquiers and Ecrehos* Judgment, ICJ Rep. 1953, 66, 69, 70, 71 (rejecting validity of France's title to the Minquiers on this basis); *Minquiers and Ecrehos* Pleadings, Vol.I, 64-66, 69, 73, 112-113, 122-123, 272-285, 296, 332 [UK Memorial], 554-558 [UK Reply], Vol.II, 27 [Counsel Heald, 17 Sep 1953], 177-178, 184 [Counsel Harrison, 24 Sep], 274-275 [Agent Gros, 30 Sep], 339-343 [Harrison, 5 Oct], 406 [Gros, 8 Oct 1953], 436-450; *Antarctica* Pleadings, 12 [UK Application]; *Gulf of Maine* Pleadings, Vol.III, 225-226 [Canada's Counter-Memorial], Vol.IV, 76 [US Counter-Memorial], Vol. VI, 137 [Counsel Bowett, 5 April 1984], 352 [Counsel Rashkov, 16 April 1984]; *Gulf of Fonseca* Hearings, C 4/CR 91/33, 80 [Counsel Highet, 29 May 1991].

1998 *Eritrea/Yemen Territorial Sovereignty and Scope of the Dispute (Phase I)* Award [40 ILM 900 (2001)], paras 20, 43, 72, 112, 174-175, 200-238, 237, noting that "the erection and maintenance of lights...had certain implications", paras 282-283, 327-328, noting that "the operation or maintenance of lighthouses and navigational aids is...not normally taken as a test of sovereignty", paras 332, 334-335, 341-345, 478, 483, 485, 491-492, 510, 513-514, 516 <www.pca-cpa.org>.

For reversal of the *Minquiers and Ecrehos* holdings, see *Qatar v. Bahrain (Merits)* Judgment, ICJ Rep. 2001, 99-100, paras 196-198, asserting that the construction of navigational aids "can be legally relevant in the case of very small islands", and paras 104, 128, 155-156, 159, 162, Separate Os Parra-Aranguren, para.6, Kooymans, para.88, Dissent Torres Bernardez, paras 361, 403; Hearings, CR 2000/5 [trans.], 33-34 [Counsel Salmon, 29 May 2000], CR 2000/6, 38 [Counsel Sinclair, 30 May], CR 2000/8, 38 [5 June], CR 2000/9 [trans.], 50, 51-52 [Counsel

Queneudec], CR 2000/10, 48-49 [6 June], CR 2000/14, 48 [Counsel Reisman, 13 June], CR 2000/15, 13-14 [14 June 2000] <www.icj-cij.org>.

For reaffirmation of the *Qatar v. Bahrain (Merits)* holdings, see *Indonesia/ Malaysia (Merits)* Judgment, ICJ Rep. 2002, 625, para.147, and *id.*, paras 132, 146, 148, Dissent Franck, 696-697, paras 18, 21; Hearings, CR 2002/29, 15-16 [Counsel Bundy, 4 June], 30-32, 57-59 [Counsel Pellet], CR 2002/30, 20-21, 24 [Co-Agent Ariffin, 6 June], CR 2002/32, 19 [Counsel Lauterpacht, 7 June], 40 [Counsel Crawford], CR 2002/33, 14-15 [Counsel Watts, 10 June], CR 2002/34, 24, 34, 35 [Pellet], CR 2002/35, 55-56 [Lauterpacht, 12 June 2002]; *Malaysia/ Singapore* Hearings, CR 2007/24, 50-51, paras 54-56 and at 56, para.71 [Counsel Sir Elihu Lauterpacht, 13 Nov 2007, CR 2007/26, 35-36, para.1 and at 39-40, paras 13-14 [Sir Elihu, 15 Nov 2007] <www.icj-cij.org>.

Nicaragua v. Honduras Hearings, CR 2007/8, 48, para.39, at 58, para.75 [Counsel Dupuy, 14 March 2007], CR 2007/13, 49, para.32 [Counsel Sands, 22 March 2007] <www.icj-cij.org>.

Nicaragua v. Colombia (Preliminary Objections) Judgment, ICJ Rep. 2007, para.19; Nicaragua's Memorial, 128-142, 253; Colombia's Preliminary Objections, 53-56 <www.icj-cij.org>.

Malaysia/Singapore Pedra Branca/Pulau Batu Puteh (Merits) Judgment, ICJ Rep. 2008, paras 17, 25, 37-69, 118-163, Dissent Dugard; Hearings, CR 2007/20, 17-18, paras 7-11 and at 21, paras 25-26 [Agent Koh, 6 Nov 2007], 24, paras 2-3 and at 26-36, paras 9-47 [Counsel Chao], CR 2007/21, 60-62, paras 120-128 [Counsel Brownlie, 7 Nov], CR 2007/22, 12-37, paras 1-97 and at 62-66, paras 1-12 [Counsel Bundy, 8 Nov], CR 2007/23 [transl.], 40-42, paras 6-11 [Counsel Pellet, 9 Nov], CR 2007/24, 12-19, paras 1-45 [Agent Kadir, 13 Nov], 32-57, paras 1-73 [Counsel Sir Elihu Lauterpacht], CR 2007/26, 12-55, paras 1-66 [Sir Elihu, 15 Nov], 55-73, paras 1-59 [Counsel Crawford], CR 2007/29, 57-61, paras 1-21 [Agent Koh, 20 Nov], CR 2007/30, 49-58 [Counsel Sir Elihu Lauterpacht, 22 Nov], CR 2007/31, 40-45, paras 1-13 [Counsel Nevill, 23 Nov 2007], 45-55, paras 1-26 [Crawford], 55-60, paras 1-12 [Agent Kadir] <www.icj-cij.org>.

On Cape Spartel Lighthouse Convention of 31 May 1865, see *Malaysia/ Singapore (Merits)* Judgment, ICJ Rep. 2008, paras 143, 166; Hearings, CR 2007/23, 15, paras 23-24 [Counsel Bundy, 9 Nov 2007], CR 2007/26, 38, para.9 [Counsel Sir Elihu Lauterpacht, 15 Nov 2007] <www.icj-cij.org>.

On Eddystone Lighthouse, see Regime of Islands – Rocks Which Cannot Sustain Human Habitation or Economic Life of Their Own *infra*.

On MENAS in the Persian Gulf, see *Malaysia/Singapore* Hearings, CR 2007/26, 37-38, paras 6-7 and at 47, paras 39, 42 [Counsel Sir Elihu Lauterpacht, 15 Nov 2007] <www.icj-cij.org>.

On Cape Race Lighthouse in Newfoundland, see *Malaysia/Singapore* Hearings, CR 2007/23, 15-16, para.25 [Counsel Bundy, 9 Nov 2007] <www.icj-cij.org>.

On Sombrero Lighthouse in Anguilla, see *Malaysia/Singapore* Hearings, CR 2007/26, 38, para.8 [Counsel Sir Elihu Lauterpacht, 15 Nov 2007] <www.icj-cij.org>.

For reliance on 1998 *Eritrea/Yemen* Award in *Malaysia/Singapore*, see Equitable Maritime Boundary Delimitation – 1998 *Eritrea/Yemen* Award *infra*.

On 1793 *The Grange (The Embuscade*; Delaware Bay) Opinion of the US Attorney General Randolph, see *Anglo/Norwegian Fisheries* Pleadings, Vol.I, 550-551 [Norway's Counter-Memorial], Vol.II, 610-611 [UK Reply]; *Tunisia/Libya* Pleadings, Vol.IV, 330 [Libya's Reply]; *Gulf of Fonseca* Dissent Oda, ICJ Rep. 1992, 737.

On 1800/1 *Twee Gebroeders (The Espiegle* and four Dutch vessels) [3 C. Rob. 162 & 336; 165 E.R. 422 & 485; Nos 1-2/Simmonds], see *Anglo/Norwegian Fisheries* Dissent Sir Arnold McNair, ICJ Rep. 1951, 183-184; Pleadings, Vol.I, 346 [Norway's Counter-Memorial].

On 1804 *Church v. Hubbart (The Aurora)* [6 US (2 Cranch) 187; 20 AJIL 115 (1926); No.4/Simmonds], see *Gulf of Maine* Pleadings, Vol.V, 649 n.7, 650-651 [US Reply]; *M/V Saiga* Separate O. Laing [38 ILM 1323 (1999)], para.13 n.8 <www.itlos.org>.

On 1805 *The Anna*, see Regime of Islands *infra*.

On 1812 *Schooner Exchange (The Balaou) v. McFaddon* Judgment [11 US (7 Cranch) 116; 3 AJIL 227 (1909); No.10/Simmonds], see *SS Lotus* Dissent Moore, PCIJ Series A, No.10 (1927), 68; *Pakistan v. India Right of Passage (Preliminary Objections)* Dissent Chagla, ICJ Rep. 1957, 176; *Congo v. France (Provisional Measures)* Dissent de Cara, ICJ Rep. 2003, 123 n.18 <www.icj-cij.org>.

On 1859 *R. v. Cunningham (The Gleaner*; Bristol Channel) Judgment [Bell C.C.72; 169 E.R. 1171; No.29/Simmonds], see *Anglo/Norwegian Fisheries* Pleadings Vol.I, 65, 91 [UK Memorial], 430-431, 442, 551-552 [Norway's Counter-Memorial], Vol.II, 477, 491-492, 493, 612 [UK Reply], Vol.III, 448 [Norway's Rejoinder]; *Gulf of Fonseca* Dissent Oda, ICJ Rep. 1992, 737.

On 1868 *Les Quatre-Frères*, see *Anglo/Norwegian Fisheries* Dissent McNair, ICJ Rep. 1951, 175; Pleadings, Vol.I, 257-258 [Norway's Counter-Memorial], Vol.II, 53 [texts] 331 [UK Reply], Vol.III, 470, 481-482 [Norway's Rejoinder], Vol.IV, 138 [Counsel Soskice, 29 Sep 1951], 303 [Counsel Bourquin, 11 Oct 1951], 437 [Agent Sir Eric Beckett, 19 Oct 1951]; *Tunisia/Libya* Pleadings, Vol.IV, 325 [Libya's Reply].

On the 1876 *R. v. Keyn (The Franconia, The Strathclyde)* Judgment of Lord Chief Justice Cockburn [L.R. 2 Ex.D. 63; 13 Cox C.C. 403; No.37/Simmonds; and the 1877 *Harris v. Owners of the Steamship Franconia*, 2 C.P.D. 173; No.38/Simmonds], see *SS Lotus* PCIJ Series A, No.10 (1927) – Judgment, 28, Dissents Weiss, 47-48, Lord Finlay, 53-54, Moore, 73-76, 80, 87-88, Altamira, 97; *SS Lotus*

Pleadings, PCIJ Series C, No.13-II, 58-63, 66, 74 [Agent Basdevant, 2 and 3 Aug 1927], 126-129 [Agent Bey, 8 Aug], 158, 161-162, 163-164 [Basdevant, 9 Aug], 168 [Bey, 10 Aug 1927], 201, 251, 254, 263 [France's Memorial], 315 [Turkey's Counter-Memorial], 325 [Observations of Diena]; *Anglo/Norwegian Fisheries* Pleadings, Vol.I, 91-92 [UK Memorial], Vol.II, 270, 417 [UK Reply], Vol.III, 299 [Norway's Rejoinder]; *IMCO* Pleadings, 45 [Liberia]; *Fisheries Jurisdiction* Pleadings (UK), 323 [Memorial (Merits)].

See also High Seas, Status of Ships/Criminal Jurisdiction *infra.*

On 1877 *Direct United States Cable Co. v. Anglo-American Telegraph Co.* (The Conception Bay) Judgment of Justice Lord Blackburn [2 App. Cas. 394; 46 L.J.P. 71; No.39/Simmonds], see *Anglo/Norwegian Fisheries* Dissent Sir Arnold McNair, ICJ Reports 1951, 164; Pleadings, Vol.I, 430-431, 442, 444, 552 [Norway's Counter-Memorial], Vol.II, 477, 478, 492, 612-615, 616, 617, 618, 622, [UK Reply], Vol.III, 446-447, 456 [Norway's Rejoinder]; *Tunisia/Libya* Pleadings, Vol.IV, 327-328, 330, 331 [Libya's Reply]; *Gulf of Maine* Pleadings, Vol.V, 508 [US Reply]; *Gulf of Fonseca* Dissent Oda, ICJ Rep. 1992, 737.

On 1891 *Manchester v. Commonwealth* Judgment [139 US 240; 1890 *Commonwealth v. Manchester*, 152 Mass. 230; No.45/Simmonds], see *Anglo/Norwegian Fisheries* Pleadings, Vol.I, 357 [Norway's Counter-Memorial]; *Tunisia/Libya* Pleadings, Vol.IV, 331 [Libya's Reply].

On 1893 *UK/USA Behring Sea Fur Seal* Award [1 AJIL 742 (1907); 6 AJIL 233, and Supp. 72, 162 (1912); 37 AJIL 562 (1943); No.170/Stuyt], see *Anglo/Norwegian Fisheries* Pleadings, Vol.I, 269-270, 352 [Norway's Counter-Memorial], Vol.II, 79-80, Vol.III, 479, 485-486 [Norway's Rejoinder].

See also Fisheries *infra.*

On 1897 *UK/Netherlands The Costa Rica Packet* Award of Frederic Martens [No.188/Stuyt], see *Anglo/Norwegian Fisheries* Pleadings, Vol.I, 346 [UK Memorial].

See also High Seas, Status of Ships/Criminal Jurisdiction *infra.*

On 1903 *UK/USA Alaska Boundary* Award [RIAA XV, 481; No.251/Stuyt], see *Anglo/Norwegian Fisheries* Pleadings, Vol.I, 431-432, 554 [Norway's Counter-Memorial], Vol.II, 477, 478-479, 617 [UK Reply].

See also Equitable Maritime Boundary Delimitation and Regime of Islands *infra.*

On 1904 *Annakumaru Pillai v. Muthupayal* Judgment of the Supreme Court of Madras [1 L.R. 27 Mad.551; *Anglo/Norwegian* Pleadings, Vol.III, 695; *Tunisia/Libya* Pleadings, Vol.II, 488], see *Anglo/Norwegian Fisheries* Pleadings, Vol.III, 254-255, 448, 456 [Norway's Rejoinder], Vol.IV, 123 [Counsel Sir Franklin Soskice, 29 Sep 1951]; *Tunisia/Libya* Pleadings, Vol.II, 211 n.2 [Libya's Counter-Memorial], Vol.IV, 335 [Libya's Reply].

On 1906 *Mortensen v. Peters (The Niobe*; Moray Firth) Judgment, see Fisheries *infra.*

On 1909 *Norway v. Sweden Grisbadarna Maritime Frontier* Award, see Equitable Maritime Boundary Delimitation *infra.*

On 1910 *UK/USA North Atlantic Coast Fisheries* Award, see Fisheries *infra.* See also Bays *supra*, and Regime of Islands, and Good Faith *infra.*

On 1914 *Attorney-General for British Columbia v. Attorney-General for Canada* Judgment [A.C. 153/No.74/Simmonds], see *Anglo/Norwegian Fisheries* Pleadings, Vol.II, 492-493 [UK Reply].

On 1918 *The Loekken (The Calliope)* Judgment of Sir Samuel Evans [34 T.L.R. 594; No.81/Simmonds], see *Anglo/Norwegian Fisheries* Pleadings, Vol.I, 441 [Norway's Counter-Memorial], Vol.II, 114-116 489, 765-772 (text of Judgment) [UK Reply].

On 1927 *The Fagerness (The Cornish Coast*; Bristol Channel) Judgment of Lord Justice Bankes [P. 311; 9 BYIL 120 (1928)], see *Anglo/Norwegian Fisheries* Pleadings, Vol.I, 64-65, 92 [UK Memorial], 442-443 [Norway's Counter-Memorial], Vol.II, 491-493 [UK Reply], Vol.III, 338-342 [Norway's Rejoinder], Vol.IV, 267, 276-277 [Counsel Bourquin, 10 and 11 Oct 1951]; *Tunisia/Libya* Pleadings, Vol.IV, 337-338 [Libya's Reply]; *Malaysia/Singapore* Hearings, CR 2007/30, 50-51, para.7 [Counsel Sir Elihu Lauterpacht, 22 Nov 2007] <www.icj-cij.org>.

On 1927 *Ocean Industries, Inc. v. Green et al.* (Monterey Bay) Judgment [200 Cal. 235, 252 Pac. 722], see *Anglo/Norwegian Fisheries* Pleadings, Vol.I, 424 [Norway's Counter-Memorial], Vol.II, 469 [UK Reply], Vol.III, 337, 356, 358, 449 [Norway's Rejoinder], 742-744 [text of Judgment].

On 1927 *The Heinrich-Augustin (The Svensksund*; Laholm Bay) Judgment of the Swedish Supreme Court [24 AJIL 776-83 (1930); 26 AJIL 59, 63 (1932); Case No.90, upheld by Case No.60 1931/2], see *Anglo/Norwegian Fisheries* Pleadings, Vol.I, 441-442 [Norway's Counter-Memorial], Vol.II, 490-491 [UK Reply], 753, Vol.III, 321, 343 [Norway's Rejoinder]; *Tunisia/Libya* Pleadings, Vol.IV, 328 [Libya's Reply].

On 1935 *US v. Carillo* (San Pedro Bay) Judgment, see *Anglo/Norwegian Fisheries* Pleadings, Vol.III, 334 n.1, 337, 356, 357, 449 [Norway's Rejoinder], 744-745 [text of Judgment], Vol.IV, 85-86, 88-89 [Agent Sir Eric Beckett, 27 Sep 1951].

On 1939 *The People v. Stralla and Adams* (Santa Monica Bay) Judgment [34 AJIL 143 (1940)], see *Anglo/Norwegian Fisheries* Pleadings, Vol.III, 357, 457 [Norway's Rejoinder], 745-747 [text of Judgment], Vol.IV, 85 [Agent Sir Eric Beckett, 27 Sep 1951].

On 1947 *US v. California* Judgment [332 US 19; 42 AJIL 209 (1948)], *reaffirmed* by the 1950 *US v. Texas* Judgment [70 S.Ct. 918; 339 US 707; 44 AJIL 770 (1950)], see *Anglo/Norwegian Fisheries* Dissent McNair, ICJ Rep. 1951, 160; Pleadings,

Vol.II, 536 [UK Reply]; *Gulf of Maine* Pleadings, Vol.IV, 106 n.3 [US Counter-Memorial]; 2001 *Newfoundland and Labrador/Nova Scotia Limits of Their Offshore Areas (Phase I)* Award, para.3.5 <www.bissettmatheson.com/arbitration/>.

On 1967 *Reference Re Ownership and Jurisdiction Over Offshore Mineral Rights of British Columbia* Judgment [65 DLR (2d) 353], see *Aegean Sea* Pleadings, 258-259 n.1 [Greece's Memorial (Jurisd.)]; 2001 *Newfoundland /Nova Scotia (Phase I)* Award, paras 5.1 n.71, 5.8 n.73, 5.9 <www.bissettmatheson.com/arbitration/> and 2002 *(Phase II)*, para.1.7 <www.boundary-dispute.ca>.

On 1968 *Post Office v. Estuary Radio* (Thames Estuary) Judgment [2 Q.B. 740], see *Tunisia/Libya* Pleadings, Vol.II, 54 n.44 [Tunisia's Counter-Memorial], Vol.IV, 117 n.3 [Libya's Reply], Vol.V, 110 [Counsel Colliard, 2 Oct 1981], 271-272 [Counsel Sir Robert Jennings, 13 Oct 1981].

On 1974/5 *US v. Maine et al.* Judgments [420 US 515; 423 US 1; 69 AJIL 432, 683 (1975)], see *Aegean Sea* Pleadings, 139 [Reply, 27 Aug 1976], 258-259 n.1 Greece's [Memorial (Jurisd.)]; 2001 *Newfoundland and Labrador/Nova Scotia Limits of Their Offshore Areas (Phase I)* Award, para.3.5 <www.bissettmatheson.com/arbitration/>.

On 1975 *New South Wales v. The Commonwealth (Australia) Seas and Submerged Lands* Judgment [51 ILR 89], see *Aegean Sea* Pleadings, 139 [Reply, 27 Aug 1976], 258-259 n.1 [Greece's Memorial (Jurisd.)], 458 [Counsel O'Connell, 16 Oct 1978]; 2001 *Newfoundland and Labrador/Nova Scotia Limits of Their Offshore Areas (Phase I)* Award, para.3.5 <www.bissettmatheson.com/arbitration/>.

ACCESS TO, JURISDICTION AND TREATMENT IN PORTS

1958 TSC, Articles 5, 14(2) and 16(2); 1958 HSC, Articles 3, 6(1) and 12(1)(c)
1982 UNCLOS, Part II, Articles 8, 18(1) and 25(2), Part VII, Articles 92(1) and 98(1)(c), Part X, Articles 129 and 131, Part XII, Articles 211(3), 218-220 and 225, Part XIII, Article 255
1995 SSA, Article 23

Danzig Port (one of the former protectorates in Europe):

SS Wimbledon PCIJ Series A, No.1 (1923) – Judgment, 19, Dissent Schücking, 47 [The *Wimbledon* was on its way to Polish Naval Base at Danzig when it was refused passage through the Kiel Canal].

Access To, Or Anchorage In, The Port of Danzig, of Polish War Vessels Advisory Opinion, PCIJ Series A/B, No.43 (1931), President M. Adatci concurring –

Part III, Section XI of the Treaty of Peace, Versailles, 28 June 1919 [in force: 10 January 1920, 13 AJIL Supp. 151, 359-361 (1919)]; Poland/Danzig Convention of Paris of 9 November 1920.

PCIJ Series E, No.8, 221; *League of Nations Official Journal* 1932, 489; Poland/Danzig Protocol of 13 August 1932, *id.* 1933, 142.

Other five advisory cases which were litigated between Poland and the Free City of Danzig with respect to the international and constitutional position of Danzig (Gdansk) were: *Polish Postal Service in Danzig*, PCIJ Series B, No.11 (1925), *Jurisdiction of the Courts of Danzig Over Pecuniary Claims of Danzig Railway Officials Who Have Passed Into the Polish Service Against the Polish Railways Administration*, PCIJ Series B, No.15 (1928), *Free City of Danzig and International Labour Organization*, PCIJ Series B, No.18 (1930), *Treatment of Polish Nationals and Other Persons of Polish Origin or Speech in the Danzig Territory*, PCIJ Series A/B, No.44 (1932), and *Consistency of Certain Danzig Legislative Decrees With the Constitution of the Free City*, PCIJ Series A/B, No.65 (1935), Advisory Opinions. Cf. S.M. Schwebel, National Judges, 48 ICLQ 889, 898 (1999); *Congo v. Belgium Arrest Warrant of 11 April 2000* Separate O. President Guillaume, ICJ Rep. 2002, 44-45, para.17 <www.icj-cij.org>.

For reliance on the *Polish War Vessels* Advisory Opinion, see *Corfu Channel (Merits)* Dissent Azevedo, ICJ Rep. 1949, 100; *Guinea-Bissau v. Senegal Arbitral Award of 31 July 1989* Dissent Weeramantry, ICJ Rep. 1991, 146.

On status of the Free City of Danzig, see also *Aegean Sea* Pleadings, 445 [Counsel O'Connell, 16 Oct 1978], 601 [Turkey's Letter].

Relevant Jurisprudence

SS Lotus Dissent Moore, PCIJ Series A, No.10 (1927), 87, Dissent Altamira, 101; *SS Lotus* Pleadings, PCIJ Series C, No.13-II, 53, 75 [Agent Basdevant, 2 and 3 Aug 1927], 180 [France's Memorial], 232-235 [Turkey's Memorial], 259, 273 [France's Counter-Memorial], 418 [Consultation Mercier]; *Eastern Greenland* Pleadings, PCIJ Series C, No.62, 36 [Denmark's Memorial], 285, 421 [Norway's Counter-Memorial], No.63, 784-785 [Denmark's Reply]. No.64, 1541, No.65, 2456, No.66, 3150 [Counsel Sunde, 10 Dec 1932]; *Corfu Channel (Merits)* Judgment, ICJ Rep. 1949, 29, Dissents Winiarski, 50, 54, Badawi Pacha, 59, 63, Azevedo, 99, 101, 107, 109, 111; *Corfu Channel* Pleadings, Vol.I, 38, 42 [UK Memorial], Vol.II, 243, 293 [UK Reply], 356 [Albania's Rejoinder], Vol.III, 273-275, 279 [Agent Sir Eric Beckett, 11 Nov 1948], Vol.IV, 543, 571 [Beckett, 18 and 19 Jan 1949]; *Minquiers and Ecrehos* Judgment, ICJ Rep 1953, 65, 66; *Minquiers and Ecrehos* Pleadings, Vol.I, 119 [UK Memorial], 549, 555 [UK Reply], Vol.II, 184, 336 [Counsel Harrison, 24 Sep and 5 Oct 1953]; *Antarctica* Pleadings, 19, 21, 31, 58, 60, 67

[UK Applications]; *IMCO* Pleadings, 184 [Panama], 208-209 [P, *The Savannah*]; *Fisheries Jurisdiction (Interim Measures)* Orders, ICJ Rep. 1972, 13, 31, *(Merits)* Judgments, ICJ Rep. 1974, 28, 197; *Fisheries Jurisdiction* Pleadings (UK), 74, 77 [Request], 375, 420 [Memorial (Merits)]; *Western Sahara* Separate O. Vice-President Ammoun, ICJ Rep. 1975, 93; *Aegean Sea (Interim Measures)* Order, ICJ Rep. 1976, 8, para.19, *(Jurisdiction)* Judgment, ICJ Rep. 1978, 20-37, Dissent Stassinopoulos, 76, 78-80, 341-346 [Counsel O'Connell, 10 Oct 1978], 421 [Counsel Weil, 13 Oct], 426-439 [Counsel Economides, 13 and 16 Oct 1978]; *Gulf of Maine* Judgment, ICJ Rep. 1984, 277, 343; Pleadings, Vol.I, 196 [Canada's Memorial], Vol.III, 56-57, 226 [Canada's Counter-Memorial], Vol.V, 46 [Canada's Reply], 636 [US Reply]; *Libya/Malta* Pleadings, Vol.I, 128 [Libya's Memorial], Vol.II, 70 [Libya's Counter-Memorial], 251 [Malta's Counter-Memorial], Vol.IV, 438 [Counsel Jaenicke, 21 Feb 1985]; *Nicaragua v. USA (Provisional Measures)* Order, ICJ Rep. 1984, 170, para.1(b), 181, para.28, 187, para.41(B)(1), Dissent Schwebel, 190, 199, *(Merits)* Judgment, ICJ Rep. 1986, at 46-53, paras 76-92, at 111-112, paras 213-214, at 147, operative para.292(8), Dissent Schwebel, 259, 378-381, paras 234-241; *Great Belt (Provisional Measures)* Order, ICJ Rep. 1991, 14, 16, 18-19; Pleadings, 114 [Co-Agent Koskenniemi, 1 July 1991], 138 [Counsel Gimsing, 2 July 1991], 463, 542, 549 [Denmark's Counter-Memorial]; *Gulf of Fonseca* Judgment, ICJ Rep. 1992, 605, Separate O. Bernardez, 691, 697; *Nuclear Tests* Dissent Palmer, ICJ Rep. 1995, 387-388; *Spain v. Canada Fisheries (Jurisdiction)* Judgment, ICJ Rep. 1998, 443-446, paras 19-22, Torres Bernardez, 598, para.47; Pleadings, 434 [Counsel Rodriguez, 9 June 1998], 463 [Counsel Highet, 10 June], 512 [Co-Agent Hankey, 11 June 1998]; *Qatar v. Bahrain (Merits)* Judgment, para.37, ICJ Rep. 2001, 54, Dissent Torres Bernardez, 291, 435, paras 89, 91. 519; *Nicaragua v. Honduras* Hearings, CR 2007/1, 26, para.38 [Agent Arguello, 5 March 2007], CR 2007/9, 44, para.21 [Counsel Colson, 15 March], CR 2007/11, 25, paras 57-59 [Arguello, 19 March], CR 2007/14, 14-15, paras 13-15, at 19, para.35 [Colson, 23 March 2007]; *Romania v. Ukraine* Judgment, ICJ Rep.2009, para.134 <www.icj-cij.org>.

See also High Seas – Nationality of Ships (*Oil Platforms* Case) *infra*.

1977 *Anglo/French* Decision [18 ILM 397 (1979)], paras 161-162, 175-176, 188; 1985 *Guinea-Guinea/Bissau* Award [25 ILM 301 (1986)], para.121; *Canada/France* Dissent Weil, para.31 [31 ILM 1209 (1992)]; 1998 *Eritrea/Yemen (Phase I)* Award, paras 143, 285, and 1999 *(Phase II)* Award, paras 107-111 [40 ILM 900, 983 (2001) <www.pca-cpa.org>]; 2001 *EC/Chile Swordfish*, ITLOS Case No.7 and WTO Panel [Fisheries *infra*; <www.itlos.org> and <www.europa.eu.int/comm/trade/miti/dispute/swordfish.htm>]; 2002 *Belize/Guatemala* OAS Facilitators' Proposals, D-para.2 <www.belize-guatemala. gov.bz/>; 2003 *Malaysia v. Singapore (Provisional Measures)* Order, Case No.12, paras 22(2)-(3)(e), 61, 77, Separate O.

Rao, paras 18, 26 <www.itlos.org> and 2005 Annex VII *Malasia v. Singapore* Award and Settlement Agreement, para.8 <www.pca-cpa.org>.

Deepwater Ports

Aegean Sea Pleadings, 456 [Counsel O'Connell, 16 Oct 1978], noting the 1974 US Deepwater Port Act. For 1982-1983 Agreements on Jurisdiction over Vessels Utilizing the Louisiana Offshore Oil Port, see 1750 UNTS 418, 1871 UNTS 166, 2000 UNTS 452, 2011 UNTS 122, 2015 UNTS 20, 118 and 2174 UNTS 187, 199.

Ports/Oil and Gas Development

North Sea Continental Shelf Separate O. Jessup, ICJ Rep. 1969, 68; Pleadings, Vol.I, 203 [Denmark's Counter-Memorial], 355 [NL Counter-Memorial]; *Tunisia/ Libya (Merits)* Separate O. de Arechaga, ICJ Rep. 1982, 121-122; *Gulf of Maine* Pleadings, Vol.III, 57 [Canada's Counter-Memorial]; *Iran v. USA Oil Platforms* – see High Seas, Freedom of the High Seas *infra*.

On the Convention and Statute on the International Regime of Maritime Ports, Geneva, 9 Dec 1923 [in force: 26 July 1926, 58 LNTS 287; 38 *Canadian YIL* 355-357 (2000)], see *Corfu Channel* Pleadings, Vol.III, 274-275 [Agent Sir Eric Beckett, 11 Nov 1948]; *IMCO* Pleadings, 51 [Liberia]; *Great Belt* Pleadings, 344 n.3 [Finland's Memorial]; *M/V Saiga* Separate O. Laing [38 ILM 1323 (1999)], para.24.

On 1887 *US v. Wildenhus (The Noorland)* Judgment [120 US 1; No.44/ Simmonds], see *SS Lotus* Dissent Moore, PCIJ Series A, No. 10 (1927), 68-69; *IMCO* Pleadings, 184 [Panama].

On 1891 *The August* Judgment [C.A. 328], see *IMCO* Pleadings, 257 [India].

On 1911 *France/UK Savarkar (The Morea)* Award [RIAA XI, 252; 5 AJIL 208, 520 and Supp.37 (1911); No.304/Stuyt; PCA 1999, 73], see *SS Lotus* Pleadings, PCIJ Series C, No.13-II, 249 n.2 [France's Counter-Memorial], 368 [Consultation Diena]; *Cameroon v. Nigeria (Merits)* Hearings, CR 2002/14, 61 [Counsel Crawford, 8 March 2002] <www.icj-cij.org>.

On 1917 *El Salvador v. Nicaragua Gulf of Fonseca* Judgment, see Equitable Maritime Boundary Delimitation *infra*.

On 1923 *Cunard SS Co. v. Mellon* Judgment [262 US 100; 285 F. 516 (2d Cir. 1922); 17 AJIL 563 (1923)], see *Anglo/Norwegian Fisheries* Pleadings, Vol.II, 537 [UK Reply].

On 1986/90 *New Zealand v. France The Rainbow Warrior* [*NZ v. France* Ruling by UN Secretary-General Javier Perez de Cuellar of 6 July 1986 – 74 ILR 241; 26 ILM 1341 (1987); 81 AJIL 325 (1987); 90 RGDIP 216-225, 993-996 (1986); No.446/

Stuyt; *Greenpeace v. France* Award of 2 October 1987 – 74 ILR 274; 33 AFDI 923-924 (1987); 34 AFDI 896-897 (1988); 92 RGDIP 395 (1988); No.447/Stuyt; *NZ v. France (Treatment of Mafart and Prieur)* Award of 30 April 1990, President Eduardo Jimenez de Arechaga (Uruguay/ICJ), Jean-Denis Bredin (France), Sir Kenneth Keith (New Zealand) – 82 ILR 449; 93 RGDIP 444 (1989); 94 RGDIP 806-847, 1069-1070 (1990); No.448/Stuyt], see *Nuclear Tests* Dissent Palmer, ICJ Rep. 1995, 388; *Cameroon v. Nigeria; Equatorial Guinea Intervening (Merits)* Hearings, CR 2002/7, 39 n.54 [Counsel Corten, 26 Feb 2002]; *Oil Platforms (Merits)* Hearings, CR 2003/12, 16-17 [Counsel Weil, 26 Feb], CR 2003/14, 51 [Counsel Crawford] <www.icj-cij.org>.

The *Rainbow Warrior* was the first and as of 2009 the only arbitration between a state and a non-governmental organization (Greenpeace). Cf. <www.greenpeace .org /international> & <www.nzherald.co.nz/index.cfm?c_id=1500930>; Vingt ans apres le *Rainbow-Warrior*: le rapport secret de l'admiral Lacoste, *Le Monde*, 9 July 2005 <www.lemonde.fr/web/article/0,1-0@2-3226,36-671207,0.html>; 10 July <www.abc.net.au/news/newsitems/200507/s1410724.htm>; 11 July 2005 <www.iht .com/articles/2005/07/10/news/green.php> & <http://news.bbc.co.uk/1/hi/world/ europe/4672495.stm>; NZ Court of Appeal Permits TVNZ to Show the Footage of Guilty Pleas by Alain Mafart and Dominique Prieur of 7 August 2006 <www .stuff.co.nz/stuff/0,2106,3757394a10,00.html & www.nzherald.co.nz/feature/story .cfm?c_id=1500930&ObjectID=10395084>; Court of Appeal Stops Showing the Footage of 11 August 2006 <www.nzherald.co.nz/feature/story.cfm?c_id=150 0930&ObjectID=10395657>; and NZ Supreme Court Upholds Appeal Court's Judgment of 26 Sep 2006 <www.stuff.co.nz/stuff/0,2106,3809691a1860,00.html & http://tvnz.co.nz/view/page/411366/836279>.

See also references to the *Rainbow Warrior* case, in *UNSG Report on Responsibility of States for Internationally Wrongful Acts: Decisions of International Courts, Tribunals and Other Bodies*, UN Doc. A/62/62, paras 75, 87, 90, 101 (2007) and UK Comments-Table, in UN Doc. A/62/63, at 18-23 (2007) <www .un.org/law>.

On 1998 *Sellers v. Maritime Safety Inspector* Judgment of the New Zealand Court of Appeal [120 ILR 585], see *Southern Bluefin Tuna (Jurisdiction)* Hearings, Vol.III [Lauterpacht, 10 May 2000] <www.worldbank.org/icsid>.

See also Internal Waters, Territorial Sea and Baselines – FCN Treaties, and Ports and Roadsteads, *supra*; Protection and Preservation of the Marine Environment – Pollution from Vessels/Port State Jurisdiction; Right of Access of Land-Locked States to and from the Sea and Freedom of Transit; Settlement of Disputes – Prompt Release of Vessels and Crews *infra*.

CONTIGUOUS ZONE

1958 TSC, Article 24
1982 UNCLOS, Part II, Article 33, and Part XVI, Article 303(2):

Corfu Channel (Merits) Dissent Azevedo, ICJ Rep. 1949, 99-100; *Anglo/Norwegian Fisheries* ICJ Rep. 1951, 116 – Individual O. Alvarez, 150, Dissent Sir Arnold McNair, 159; *Anglo/Norwegian* Pleadings, Vol.I, 38, 50 [UK Memorial], 277-279, 352-354 [Norway's Counter-Memorial], Vol.II, 86-89 [texts], 412, 582 [UK Reply], Vol.III, 647 [texts]; *Minquiers and Ecrehos* Individual O. Basdevant, ICJ Rep. 1953, 82; *North Sea* Judgment, ICJ Rep. 1969, 51, para.96, Separate O. Ammoun, 108, 124, 128, Dissent Vice-President Koretsky, 159, 161, Dissent Sorensen, 249-252; *North Sea* Pleadings, Vol.I, 364 [NL Counter-Memorial], 461 [Common Rejoinder of Denmark/NL], Vol.II, 92-93, 97 [Counsel Sir Humphrey Waldock, 29 Oct 1968], 125-126, 138 [Agent Riphagen, 30 and 31 Oct], 193 [Counsel Shigeru Oda, 5 Nov], 264 [Reply by Waldock to Questions Fitzmaurice, 8 Nov 1968]; *Fisheries Jurisdiction (Jurisdiction)* Separate Os Fitzmaurice, ICJ Rep. 1973, 25, 29 n.10, 69, 73 n.10, *(Merits)* Judgments, ICJ Rep. 1974, 22, 191, Joint Separate Os, 46, 218, Separate Os de Castro, 92, 93, 225, Separate Os Waldock, 109, 227, Dissent Gros 135; *Fisheries Jurisdiction* Pleadings (UK), 459 [Counsel Silkin, 25 March 1974]; *Aegean Sea* Pleadings, 99 [Counsel O'Connell, 26 Aug], 140 [27 Aug 1976], 442, 454 [16 Oct 1978]; *Tunisia/Libya (Merits)* Judgment, ICJ Rep. 1982, 65, 69, Dissent Oda, 227; *Gulf of Maine* Judgment, ICJ Rep. 1984, 302, Dissent Gros, 365, 381; Pleadings, Vol.IV, 83 [US Counter-Memorial], Vol.V, 411, 512, 536 [US Reply]; *Libya/Malta* Pleadings, Vol.I, 66, 69 [Libya's Memorial], Vol.II, 73, 115 [Libya's Counter-Memorial], Vol.III, 440-441 [Counsel Brownlie, 3 Dec 1984], Vol.IV, 437 [Counsel Jaenicke, 21 Feb 1985]; *Guinea-Bissau v. Senegal (Provisional Measures)* Order, ICJ Rep. 1990, 68, Dissent Thierry, 82-83, *Arbitral Award* Judgment, ICJ Rep. 1991, 57, 59, 64, 66, Separate Os Vice-President Oda, 81-82, 85, 86, Ni, 96-97, 101, Shahabuddeen, 116. Dissents Weeramantry, 131, 150, 170, Thierry, 177, 181; *Gulf of Fonseca* Judgment, ICJ Rep. 1992, 608; *Denmark v. Norway* Separate O. Oda, ICJ Rep. 1993, 102; Hearings, CR 93/1Corr., 28 [Agent Lehmann, 11 Jan 1993], CR 93/3, 50 [13 Jan], CR 93/9 [trans.], 26-27 [Counsel Weil, 21 Jan 1993]; *Romania v. Ukraine* Hearings, CR 2008/29, 51 [Judge Oxman's Question 2, 12 Sep 2008], CR 2008/31, 42-43, paras 2-7 [Counsel Lowe's Reply to Question 2], 55, para.2(g) [Agent Aurescu's Corrig. to Lowe's Reply, 16 Sep], CR 2008/32, 18, para.14 [Counsel Sir Michael Wood, 18 Sep 2008] <www.icj-cij.org>.

1985 *Guinea/Guinea-Bissau* Award, para.29 [25 ILM 268 (1986)]; 1989 *Guinea-Bissau/Senegal* Award [94 RGDIP 270 (1990)], para.85; *Canada/France* Award, para.69 [31 ILM 1170 (1992)], Dissent Gotlieb, para.61 [*id.* 1195], Dissent

Weil, paras 3-4 [*id.* 1198]; 1997 *M/V Saiga (Prompt Release)* Judgment, ITLOS Case No.1 [37 ILM 360 (1998)], paras 54, 60-61, 70, Dissents President Mensah, Anderson, Joint Dissent; *M/V Saiga* Judgment, ITLOS Case No.2 [38 ILM 1323 (1999)], paras 28-30, 110-127, 151-152, Separate Os Vukas, para.20, Laing, paras 5-16, 51 <www.itlos.org>; 2007 *Guyana/Suriname* Award, para.317 n.370, paras 320-321; Guyana's Memorial, para.7.12 <www.pca-cpa.org>.

On Convention for the Suppression of the Contraband Traffic in Alcoholic Liquors, Helsinki, 19 August 1925 [in force: 24 Dec 1925, 42 LNTS 75], see *Eastern Greenland* Pleadings, PCIJ Series C, No.62, 35 [Denmark's Memorial]; *Anglo/Norwegian Fisheries* Pleadings, Vol.I, 278-279, 483 [Norway's Counter-Memorial], Vol.II, 88-89 [excerpts], 346, 539, 541-542 [UK Reply], Vol.III, 383 [Norway's Rejoinder].

On 1804 *Church v. Hubbart (The Aurora)*, see Internal Waters, Territorial Sea and Baselines *supra.*

On 1888 *The Araunah*, see Fisheries *infra.*

On 1893 *UK/USA Behring Sea Fur Seal*, see Fisheries *infra.*

On 1922 *The Grace and Ruby* [283 Fed. 475 (D. Mass.); 19 AJIL 157 (1925); *Gulf of Maine* Pleadings, Vol.V, 639-645], see *Gulf of Maine* Pleadings, Vol.V, 471 n.3, 635, 648-653 [US Reply], citing Jessup 1927 [*id.* 647-653].

On 1927 *Deutschland*, see Internal Waters, Territorial Sea and Baselines *supra.*

On 1935 *Canada/USA I'm Alone (The Wolcott, The Dexter)* Award, see Use of Force in Enforcement at Sea *infra.*

See also High Seas – Hot Pursuit; Archaeological and Historical Objects *infra.*

INTER-OCEANIC CANALS

France, Britain, Italy, Japan v. Germany SS Wimbledon PCIJ Series A, No.1 (1923) – *(Question of Intervention by Poland)* Judgment [unanimous], 11, President B.C.J. Loder; *(Merits)* Judgment, 15, President B.C.J. Loder concurring – Kiel Canal, Article 380 of the Treaty of Peace, Versailles, 28 June 1919 [in force: 10 January 1920, 13 AJIL Supp. 151, 359-361 (1919)].

PCIJ Series E, No.1, 163.

For reference to passage through canals, see *Corfu Channel (Merits)* ICJ Reports 1949, 4 – Dissent Azevedo, 99.

Nicaragua v. Colombia (Preliminary Objections) Hearings, CR 2007/17, 9, para.8 [Agent Arguello, 5 June 2007], CR 2007/19, 11, para.14 [Arguello, 8 June 2007]; Nicaragua's Memorial, 3-5, 52-54, 61-77, 93-96; Colombia's Preliminary Objections, 32-33, 47, 63; *Costa Rica v. Nicaragua San Juan River* Judgment, President Hisashi Owada concurring, ICJ Rep. 2009; Hearings, CR 2009/4, 9-11, paras 6-4, at 15, para.28 [Agent Arguello, 5 March 2009], CR 2009/6, 14, para.27 [Counsel Crawford, 9 March 2009], 38, para.7 [Counsel Caflisch] <www.icj-cij .org>.

On 1888 *Costa Rica/Nicaragua* Award of U.S. President Grover Cleveland and 1916 CAC *Costa Rica v. Nicaragua* Judgment, see Individual Canals *infra*.

Definition of an Inter-Oceanic Canal

Great Belt Pleadings, 541-542 [Denmark's Counter-Memorial].

Concept of International Servitudes

SS Wimbledon Judgment, 24-25, Dissent Schücking, 43-45.

This concept was earlier also rejected (in accordance with the British contention) by the 1910 *UK/USA North Atlantic Coast Fisheries* Award [RIAA XI, 167; No.291/ Stuyt]. However, Germany might have been encouraged by the 1914 *Dutch State Servitude in Prussia* Judgment [8 AJIL 858-860, 907-913 (1914)], in which the Supreme Court of Cologne decided that the right claimed by Holland was not a mining concession subject to Prussian law, but an international servitude created by the 1816 Prussia/Netherlands Boundary Treaty.

For reliance on rejection of servitudes in the 1910 Award, see *Rights of Nationals of the USA in Morocco* Pleadings, Vol.I, 66 [France's Memorial], Vol.II, 173 [Agent Gros, 16 July 1952]; *Minquiers and Ecrehos* Pleadings, Vol.II, 88 [Counsel Fitzmaurice, 21 Sep 1953].

On the concept of servitudes, see also the *Corfu Channel (Merits)* Dissent Azevedo, ICJ Rep. 1949, 104; *Minquiers and Ecrehos* Pleadings, Vol.I, 473, 477, 487 [UK Reply], 716 [France's Rejoinder]; *Rights of Passage over Indian Territory (Preliminary Objections)* and *(Merits)* Judgment, ICJ Rep. 1957, 125 and 1960, 6; *Aegean Sea (Jurisdiction)* Dissent de Castro, ICJ Rep. 1978, 65; *Great Belt* Pleadings, 154 [Counsel Jimenez de Arechaga, 2 July 1991], 397 [Denmark's Counter-Memorial]; *Guinea-Bissau v. Senegal Arbitral Award* Dissent Weeramantry, ICJ Rep. 1991, 153; *Gabcikovo* Oral Hearings, CR 97/6, 46 [Counsel Sands, 7 March 1997]; 1998 *Eritrea/Yemen (Phase I)* Award, para.126 and 1999 *(Phase II)* Award, paras 27, 38 [40 ILM 900, 983 (2001) <www.pca-cpa.org>]; *Qatar v. Bahrain (Merits)* Joint Dissent Bedjaoui, Ranjeva, Koroma, paras 172, 175, ICJ Rep. 2001, 197, 199; *Indonesia/Malaysia (Merits)* Hearings, CR 2002/33, 21 [Counsel Watts, 10 June 2002] <www.icj-cij.org>; 2009 *Abyei Boundary* Award, para.754 n.1255 <www.pca-cpa.org>, *reaffirming* 1998 *Eritrea/Yemen (Phase I)* Award, para.126, *supra*.

Individual Canals

On Suez Canal and Panama Canal <http://en.wikipedia.org/wiki/Suez_Canal & http://en.wikipedia.org/wiki/Panama_Canal>, see *SS Wimbledon* Judgment, 25-28, Dissent Anzilotti and Huber, 39, 40, Dissent Schücking, 43-44, 46; *SS Wimbledon* Pleadings, PCIJ Series C, No.3-Additional Volume, 47-48 [Germany's Counter-Memorial], 69-71, 84-85, 88, 99, 101-102, 108 [Reply of Four Powers], 146-147, 155 [Germany's Rejoinder]; *SS Lotus* Pleadings, PCIJ Series C, No.13-II, 162-163 [Agent Basdevant, 9 Aug 1927]; *Eastern Greenland* Pleadings, PCIJ Series C, No.67, 3592 [Counsel Rygh, 3 Feb 1933]; *Corfu Channel (Merits)* Dissent Azevedo, ICJ Rep. 1949, 105; *Anglo/Norwegian Fisheries* Pleadings, Vol.II, 427 [UK Reply], Vol.III, 290 [Norway's Rejoinder]; *IMCO* Pleadings, 61 [Liberia]; *Nuclear Tests* Pleadings (New Zealand), 58 [Request]; *Tunisia/Libya* Pleadings, Vol.I, 483 [Libya's Memorial], Vol.II, 48 [Tunisia's Counter-Memorial]; *Taba* Award, paras 22, 30, 38, 69 [27 ILM 1436, 1438-1439, 1447 (1988)]; *Great Belt* Pleadings, 59 [Denmark's Observations], 312-314 [Finland's Memorial], 547-548 [Denmark's Counter-Memorial]; 1998 *Eritrea/Yemen (Phase I)* Award, paras 93, 125 <www.pca-cpa.org>; 2001 *Ireland v. UK Mox Plant* Ireland's Request & Statement, paras 33, 36 <www.itlos.org>; *Nicaragua v. Colombia* Nicaragua's Memorial, 67-68, 74, 95, 122-123; Colombia's Preliminary Objections, 56 n.65 <www.icj-cij.org>.

On Convention Respecting the Free Navigation of the Suez Canal, Constantinople, 29 Oct 1888 [in force: 22 Dec 1888, 171 CTS 241; <http://en.wikipedia.org/wiki/Suez_Canal>], see *Great Belt* Pleadings, 313 [Finland's Memorial]; Suez: End of Empire of 24 July 2006 <http://news.bbc.co.uk/2/hi/middle_east/5199392.stm> and Suez Canal Maps <http://news.bbc.co.uk/2/hi/middle_east/5195068.stm>

On Panama/USA Panama Canal Treaty and Treaty on the Permanent Neutrality and Operation of the Panama Canal, both of 7 Sep 1977 [in force: 1 Oct 1979, 1280 UNTS 3; 16 ILM 1022, 1040 (1977); <www.pancanal.com & http://en.wikipedia.org/wiki/Panama_Canal>] and Panama/USA Alternatives to the Panama Canal Agreement of 26 Sep 1985 [2231 UNTS 265], see *Great Belt* Pleadings, 313, 351 n.3 [Finland's Memorial]; *Nicaragua v. Colombia (Preliminary Objections)* Hearings, CR 2007/17, 10, para.15 [Agent Arguello, 5 June 2007] <www.icj-cij.org>. The Panama Canal's transfer from the USA to Panama was completed in Dec 1999 <www.pancal.com & www.acp.gob.pa/eng/index.html>; 25 April 2006 <http://news.bbc.co.uk/1/hi/americas/4941126.stm>; Panama Ports, 30 *Marine Policy* 483-495 (2006) <www.elsevier.com/locate/marpol>; First Russian Warship Uses Panama Canal Since 1944 of 6 Dec 2008 <http://news .bbc.co.uk/2/hi/americas/7768743.stm & www.telegraph.co.uk/news/worldnews/

europe/russia/3628867/First-Russian-warship-uses-Panama-Canal-since-1944.html>.

On the 1920 *The Dorrit* incident – Kiel Canal, see *SS Wimbledon* Pleadings, 4, 5-6, 20-31 [Memorial of Four Powers], 40-41 [Germany's Counter-Memorial], 62-63 [Reply of Four Powers], 140 [Germany's Rejoinder]; *Tunisia/Libya* Pleadings, Vol.III, 451-452 [Counsel Bathurst, 23 March 1981].

For reference to the Kiel Canal, see *SS Wimbledon* [*supra*]; *SS Lotus* Pleadings, PCIJ Series C, No.13-II, 163 [Agent Basdevant, 9 August 1927]; *Corfu Channel (Merits)* Dissent Azevedo, ICJ Rep. 1949, 108; *Nuclear Tests* Pleadings (Australia), 326 [Memorial]; *Tunisia/Libya (Intervention)* Judgment, ICJ Rep. 1981, 15, Separate O. Oda, 28; Pleadings, Vol.III, 378-379 [Counsel Vallat, 20 March 1981]; *Libya/Malta (Intervention)* Dissents Sette-Camara, ICJ Rep. 1984, 74, Oda, 99; *Great Belt (Provisional Measures)* Order, ICJ Rep. 1991, 16; Pleadings, 59 [Denmark's Observations], 138 [Counsel Gimsing, 2 July 1991], 239, 241-242, 311-313 [Finland's Memorial], 546-547 [Denmark's Counter-Memorial]; *M/V Saiga* Separate O. Laing [38 ILM 1323 (1999)], paras 24-25; *Oil Platforms (Merits)* Hearings, CR 2003/12, 18 [Counsel Weil, 26 Feb], CR 2003/14, 59 [Counsel Crawford, 28 Feb 2003]; *Costa Rica v. Nicaragua San Juan River* Hearings, CR 2009/6, 9-10, paras 3, 7 [Counsel Crawford, 9 March 2009], CR 2009/7, 12, para.29 [Counsel Brownlie, 12 March 2009] <www.icj-cij.org>.

German state practice since the 1950s, has likely terminated the validity of the Versailles provisions with respect to warships by requiring foreign warships to notify and to obtain authorization from the Foreign Office to pass through the Kiel Canal. For NATO warships this has meant merely registering with local German naval units. Even if the Versailles Treaty is no longer applicable, the multitude of bilateral treaties, the European Community law and the status of the Baltic Sea as a cooperation zone support the customary norm of free passage of the merchant shipping through the Kiel Canal as the most used man-made waterway, which shortens sea travel into the Baltic by a maximum (Hamburg/Möen route) of 440 miles.

On 1888 *Costa Rica/Nicaragua* Award of U.S. President Grover Cleveland [10 AJIL 346 (1916); No.147/Stuyt; RIAA, XXVIII, 189], see *Nicaragua v. Colombia (Preliminary Objections)* Declaration Tomka, ICJ Rep. 2007, paras 6-15 n.1; Hearings, CR 2007/19, 43, para.27 [Counsel Bretons, 8 June 2007]; *Costa Rica v. Nicaragua San Juan River* Judgment, ICJ Rep. 2009, President Hisashi Owada concurring, paras 12-13, 14, 20-22, 39, 41, 49, 56, 82-83, 86, 94, 155; *Costa Rica v. Nicaragua* Hearings, CR 2009/2, 13, para.3 [Agent Ugalde-Alvarez, 2 March 2009], 37-46, paras 24-49 [Counsel Caflisch], 64, paras 57-58 [Counsel Kohen], CR 2009/3, 9-16, paras 6-29, at 21, para.48 [Counsel Crawford, 3 March], 45, para.8 [Counsel Parlett], CR 2009/4, 11, paras 13-14, at 14-15, paras 27-28 [Agent Arguello, 5 March], 19, para.5, at 32-49, paras 59-67 [Counsel Brownlie], 58-60, paras 19-23 [Counsel Pellet], CR 2009/5, 27-56, paras 1-30 [Counsel McCaffrey, 6 March], CR 2009/6, 11, paras 14-15, at 15-16, paras 29-32 [Crawford, 9 March], 38, para.5, at 50, para.22 [Caflisch], 50-57, paras 1-17 [Crawford], 66, paras 7-8, at 68, para.10 (g)-(h) [Ugalde-Alvarez], CR 2009/7, 31-37, paras 1-16 [Counsel McCaffrey, 12 March 2009], 55, para.4, at 58-61, paras 12-23 [Agent Arguello] <www.icj-cij.org>.

On 1916 *Costa Rica v. Nicaragua* Judgment of the Central American Court of Justice (construction of an inter-oceanic canal under the 1914 Bryan-Chamorro Treaty) [11 AJIL 181 (1917); 17 AJIL 309 (1923); 25 AJIL 328 (1931)], see *Anglo/Norwegian Fisheries* Pleadings, Vol.I, 447 [Norway's Counter-Memorial], Vol.III, 644 [Norway's Rejoinder]; *Gulf of Fonseca (Intervention)* Judgment, ICJ Rep. 1990, 104, *(Merits)* Judgment, ICJ Rep. 1992, 590, 600-601, Separate O. Bernardez, 725; Oral Hearings, C 4/CR 91/43, 41 [Agent Arguello, 7 June 1991]; *East Timor* Separate O. Shahabuddeen, ICJ Rep. 1995, 124 n.3, Dissent Skubiszewski, 253; Hearings [trans.], CR 95/6, 29 [Co-Agent Teles, 3 Feb 1995], CR 95/8, 55 [Counsel Crawford, 7 Feb], CR 95/13, 62 [Teles, 13 Feb 1995]; *Nicaragua v. Colombia (Preliminary Objections)* Hearings, CR 2007/19, 10-11, para.12 [Agent Arguello, 8 June 2007]; Nicaragua's Memorial, 75; Colombia's Preliminary Objections, at 33 n.26, at 61; *Costa Rica v. Nicaragua San Juan River* Judgment, ICJ Rep. 2009, paras 22, 41, 49; Hearings, CR 2009/2, 13, para.3 [Agent Ugalde-Alvarez, 2 March 2009], 37-41, paras 24-47 [Counsel Caflisch], 64-65, paras 59-60 [Counsel Cohen], CR 2009/3, 15, para.26, at 20, para.44 [Counsel Crawford, 3 March], CR 2009/4, 15, para.28 [Agent Arguello, 5 March], 60-61, paras 23-25 [Counsel Pellet], CR 2009/6, 8, para.2 [Crawford, 9 March], 50, para.22 [Caflisch], 66, para.8 [Ugalde-Alvarez] <www.icj-cij.org>.

On 1917 *El Salvador v. Nicaragua Gulf of Fonseca* Judgment, see Equitable Maritime Boundary Delimitation *infra*.

On the Nicaragua Canal Proposal, see *Nicaragua v. Colombia (Preliminary Objections)* Hearings, CR 2007/17, 9, para.8 [Agent Arguello, 5 June 2007], CR 2007/19, 11, para.14 [Arguello, 8 June 2007]; Nicaragua's Memorial, 3-5, 52-54, 61-77, 93-96; Colombia's Preliminary Objections, 32-33, 47, 63 <www.icj-cij.org>; and <www.american.edu/projects/mandala/TED/niccanal.htm>; *Costa Rica v. Nicaragua San Juan River* Judgment, ICJ Rep. 2009, paras 22, 41; Hearings, CR 2009/4, 9-11, paras 6-4, at 15, para.28 [Agent Arguello, 5 March 2009], CR 2009/6, 14, para.27 [Counsel Crawford, 9 March 2009], 38, para.7 [Counsel Caflisch] <www.icj-cij.org>.

STRAITS USED FOR INTERNATIONAL NAVIGATION

1930 Hague Draft, Article 12, and Annex II, Appendix B: Compromise-Proposal of the French Delegation (Straits), 252
1958 TSC, Article 16(4)
1982 UNCLOS, Part III, Articles 34-45, Part V/VI, Articles 60(7)/80, Part XII, Article 233

Relevant Jurisprudence

Corfu Channel (Preliminary Objection) Judgment, ICJ Rep. 1947/1948, 15, President J.G. Guerrero concurring; *Corfu Channel (Merits)* Judgment, ICJ Rep. 1949, 4, Acting President Guerrero concurring; *Corfu Channel (Assessment of the Amount of Compensation Due From the People's Republic of Albania to the United Kingdom of Great Britain and Northern Ireland)* Judgment, *id.* 244; Orders, ICJ Rep. 1947, 4, 7, 1948, 53, 124 (*An Expert Opinion*), 1949, 171, 222, 237.

1953 *France, UK, USA v. Italy Monetary Gold Looted by Germany From Rome* Arbitral Advice of G. Sauser-Hall [20 ILR 441; RIAA XII,19; No.415/Stuyt]; *Italy v. France, UK and USA Monetary Gold Removed From Rome in 1943 (Preliminary Question)* Judgment, ICJ Reports 1954, 19, Vice-President J.G. Guerrero, Acting President.

UK/Albania Rome Agreement of 8 May 1992 [on the file with the author], referred to in, Speech of President Sir Robert Jennings to the UNCED, Rio de Janeiro, 3-14 June 1992, *ICJ Yearbook 1991-1992* 212, 217 (No.46); USA/Albania Tirana Agreement on the Settlement of Certain Outstanding Claims and Financial Issues of 10 March 1995 [in force: 18 April 1995, 34 ILM 595 (1995)]; France/Albania Agreement on the Settlement of the Question of Monetary Gold Matter and Other Public or Private Claims of 22 February 1996 [1941 UNTS 358].

The Corfu Channel exemplifies geographical location of straits [*Corfu Channel* Pleadings, Vol.I, 21 (UK Memorial)] covered presently by the 1982 UNCLOS, Article 38(1) referred to under Innocent Passage Through Straits *infra.*

Anglo/Norwegian Fisheries ICJ Rep. 1951, 116 – Judgment, 123, 127, 130, 132, 142, Separate O. Hsu Mo, 156; *Anglo/Norwegian Fisheries* Pleadings, Vol.I, 517-520 [Norway's Counter-Memorial], Vol.II, 402, 573, 579, 683 [UK Reply], Vol.III, 22-27, 402-406, 409, 429-446 [Norway's Rejoinder], Vol.IV, 293-295, 300-307 [Counsel Bourquin, 11 Oct 1951], 413-414 [Counsel Waldock, 18 Oct 1951].

It was of greatest importance to Norway that the Indreleia Strait, stretching along almost the whole of the coast of southern, western and northern Norway, and passing straight through the naval base in the port of Tromsoe, was acknowledged by the Court to be not strait but international waterway of Norway.

Finland v. Denmark Passage Through the Great Belt (Request for the Indication of Provisional Measures) Order, ICJ Rep. 1991, 12 [unanimous], President Sir Robert Jennings, Declaration Tarassov, 22, Separate O. Vice-President Oda, 25, Separate Os Shahabuddeen, 28, Broms, 37; Order, *id.* 40; *(Discontinuance)* Order of President Jennings, ICJ Rep. 1992, 348.

Press Release No.281 of Finland's Ministry of Foreign Affairs and Press Release No.88 of Denmark's Ministry of Foreign Affairs, both of 3 September 1992 [27 *Ocean Dev. & Int'l L.* 288 (1996)].

Statement of President Stephen M. Schwebel to the 52nd UNGA [UN Doc. A/52/PV.36, 3 (27 October 1997) <www.icj-cij.org>, *reprinted in ICJ Yearbook 1997-1998* 288-300 (No.52) and 92 AJIL 614 (1998); Statement of President Schwebel on the Occasion of Visit of President Martti Ahtisaari of Finland to the Court on 20 January 1999, *ICJ Communiqué* No.99/1. Cf. *Mexico v. USA Avena and other Mexican Nationals (Provisional Measures)* Hearings, CR 2003/1, 38 [Counsel Donovan, 21 January 2003], CR 2003/2, 13 [Counsel Matias], 29 [Co-Agent Thessin], 38 [Counsel Sir Elihu Lauterpacht], CR 2003/4, 23 [Lauterpacht] <www.icj-cij.org>; Annex VII *Mox Plant (Provisional Measures)* Hearings, 9 [Counsel Crawford & Sands, 18 June 2003], 79 [Counsel Bethlehem, 21 June] <www.pca-cpa.org>; *Malaysia v. Singapore (Provisional Measures)* Singapore's Response, paras 84-85; Hearings, ITLOS/PV.03/02/Corr.1, 24-25 [Counsel Crawford, 25 Sep], ITLOS/PV.03/04, 9-10 [Counsel Reisman, 26 Sep 2003] <www.itlos.org>; *Argentina v. Uruguay (Provisional Measures)* Order, paras 62, 77, ICJ Rep. 2006, 113, Dissent Vanuesa, 148, 152.

See also Settlement of Disputes – Preventive Diplomacy, B) *infra*.

Had the *Great Belt* case proceeded to the phase of merits, it would have been the second (after *Corfu*) case contributing to the critical regime of international straits, including the issues pertaining to Transit Passage, bridges over straits and mobile offshore drilling units (MODU – drill ships and drill rigs), as well as the IMO involvement in those matters. See Pleadings, 88-93 [Agent Gronberg, 1 July 1991], 116 [Co-Agent Koskenniemi], 146-154 [Counsel Jimenez de Arechaga, 2 July], 156-160 [Agent Fergo], 181-184 [Gronberg, 4 July], 202 [Judge Schwebel's Questions], 204-205 [Gronberg's Reply to Schwebel, 5 July 1991], 210-215 [Agent Magid], 215-216 [his Reply to Schwebel], 224 [Agent Lehmann], 234, 242, 256, 275-292, 335-340 [Finland's Memorial], 463-465, 470-509, 574, 589-596 [Denmark's Counter-Memorial]; UN Docs IMO LEG 83/14, paras 159-161, and NAV 47/13, paras 4.1/13 (2001).

On two bridges erected over the Turkish Straits in 1973 and 1988, and on the Kanmon, Seto and Akasi Kaikyo Bridges constructed by Japan in 1971, 1973 and 1998, see *Gret Belt* Pleadings, 126 [Agent Lehmann, 2 July 1991], 140-142 [Counsel Gimsing]; on bridges over the Kiel Canal, see *id.* 138; also *id.* 139

(Golden Gate and Verrazano Narrows Bridges), 183-184 [Agent Gronberg, 4 July 1991]; Turkish Tunnel under Bosphorus Strait of 18 February 2005 <www.turkishpress.com/news.asp?ID=37489>.

On Eurotunnel, consisting of a fixed twin-bored tunnel rail link under the English Channel, a service tunnel and terminal areas at Coquelles in the French Pas de Calais Department and Cheriton in the County of Kent, and constructed under the UK/France Canterbury Treaty of 12 Feb 1986 [in force: 29 July 1987, 1497 UNTS 334; 1509 UNTS 199; 39 AFDI 833 (1993)] and opened on 6 May 1994 [1747 UNTS 109; 1892 UNTS 335; 2226 UNTS 197 & 203; 2007 *Eurotunnel* Award, *infra*, para.52], see *Great Belt* Pleadings, 314 [Finland's Memorial], 488, 552-555 [Denmark's Counter-Memorial]; 31 March 2005 <http://news.bbc.co.uk/1/hi/business/4396083.stm>; 24 May 2006 <http://news.bbc.co.uk/2/hi/business/5011974.stm>; *The Channel Tunnel Group Ltd & France-Manche S.A./United Kingdom/France Construction and Operation by Private Concessionaires of a Channel Fixed Link (Eurotunnel)* Partial Award of 30 Jan 2007 <www.pca-cpa.org/PDF/ET_PAen.pdf>, President James Crawford SC, Arbitrators: L. Yves Fortier CC QC, Judge Gilbert Guillaume, Jan Paulsson, Dissent Lord Millett <www.pca-cpa.org/PDF/ETMillettDOen.pdf> & <www.eurotunnel.com/ukcP3Main/ukcCorporate/ukpP3CorporateHome.htm>, <http://news.bbc.co.uk/2/hi/business/6396599.stm>.

On Africa-Europe Tunnel Link under the Strait of Gibraltar, see 20 Oct 2006 <www.guardian.co.uk/international/story/0,,1926685,00.html>; 13 March 2007 <http://news.bbc.co.uk/2/hi/africa/6442697.stm> and UN Doc. E/2007/21 (23 March 2007); 19 July 2008 <http://news.bbc.co.uk/2/hi/europe/7515125.stm>.

On Yemen/Djibouti "Bridge of the Horns" Joining the African Continent to the Arabian Peninsula Across the Red Sea, see 29 July 2008 <http://yementimes.com/article.shtml?i=1177&p=local&a=5 & www.zawya.com/Story.cfm/sidZAWYA20080730035034>.

On these and other bridges and tunnels, see also *Great Belt* Pleadings, 59-60, 71 [Denmark's Observations], 311-317, 339 [Finland's Memorial], 543-577 [Denmark's Counter-Memorial].

On Denmark/Sweden Oresund Bridge, see 14 Sep 2006 <http://news.bbc.co.uk/2/hi/europe/5339726.stm> and Denmark/Germany Bridge of 5 Sep 2008 <http://news.bbc.co.uk/2/hi/europe/7598090.stm>.

On the World's longest Messina Bridge linking Sicily to the mainland of Italy, see 6 March 2009 <http://news.bbc.co.uk/2/hi/europe/7928949.stm & http://en.wikipedia.org/wiki/Sicily_Bridge>.

On road tunnels, see 20 March 2007 <http://news.bbc.co.uk/2/hi/europe/6471241.stm>.

On bridges over international watercourses, see *Benin/Niger* Judgment, ICJ Rep. 2005, 141-142, paras 119-124, Dissent Bennouna, 163, para.48; *Argentina v. Uruguay Pulp Mills on the River Uruguay (Provisional Measures)* Orders, ICJ Rep. 2006, 113 and 2007, 3; *Costa Rica v. Nicaragua San Juan River* Hearings, CR 2009/5, 18-19, para.30 [Counsel Reichler, 6 March 2009] <www.icj-cij.org>.

2003 *Malaysia v. Singapore Land Reclamation by Singapore In and Around the Straits of Johor (Provisional Measures)* Order, President L.D.M. Nelson, ITLOS Case No.12, paras 22(2)-(3)(e), 61, 77, 106, Separate Os Rao, paras 18, 26, 32-33, Cot, para.2 <www.itlos.org>; 2005 Annex VII *Malaysia v. Singapore* Award, President Ch. Pinto and Settlement Agreement, para.8 <www.pca-cpa .org>, <http://internet-stg1.mfa.gov.sg/internet/press/land/frm_main_land.htm> & <www.asil.org/ilib050929.htm>. See also Protection and Preservation of the Marine Environment *infra*.

Definition of Strait Used for International Navigation
1930 Hague Draft, Article 12, and Annex II, Appendix B: Compromise-Proposal of the French Delegation (Straits), 252; 1958 TSC, Article 16(4); 1982 UNCLOS, Article 37:

Corfu Channel (Merits) ICJ Rep. 1949, 4 – Judgment, 27, 28-29, Individual O. Alvarez, 46, Dissent Azevedo, 105-107; *Corfu* Pleadings, Vol.I, 21, 24, 40, 42 [UK Memorial], Vol.II, 130-131 [Albania's Counter-Memorial], 242-243, 295-296, 298 [UK Reply], Vol.II, 356 [Albania's Rejoinder], Vol.III, 200-201 [Counsel Shawcross, 9 Nov 1948], 268, 278, 287-288 [Agent Sir Eric Beckett, 11 and 12 Nov], 382-383 [Counsel Cot, 18 Nov 1948], Vol.IV, 547-551 [Agent Beckett, 18 Jan 1949]; *Anglo/Norwegian Fisheries* Judgment, ICJ Reports 1951, 120, 122, 132; Pleadings, Vol.I, 77-79, 84, 86 [UK Memorial], 495-520 [Norway's Counter-Memorial], Vol.II, 554-579 [UK Reply]; *IMCO* Pleadings, 132 [USA], 179 [Panama], 334 [Italy]; *Gulf of Maine* Pleadings, Vol.V, 533 [US Reply]; *Great Belt (Provisional Measures)* Order, ICJ Rep. 1991, 13, para.5, Declaration Tarassov, 22; Pleadings, 7 [Finland's Application, para.24], 88 [Agent Gronberg, 1 July 1991], 147 [Counsel de Arechaga, 2 July 1991], 253 [Finland's Memorial], 541 [Denmark's Counter-Memorial].

See also *ILC Yearbook* 1956-II, 273, 277; Sir Arthur Watts, *The International Law Commission 1949-1998*, Vol.I, 48-49, 55-57 (Oxford 1999).

Transit Passage
1958 HSC; 1982 UNCLOS, Part III, Articles 37-44, Part XII, Article 233:

Corfu Channel (Merits) ICJ Rep. 1949, 4 – Judgment, 10, 27-31 (esp.28, 29). The Court expounded the right of non-suspendable Innocent Passage as then envisaged in the 1930 Hague Draft to straits such as the Corfu Channel, because navigation through all strategically important straits was at the time of a 3-mile TS limit governed by the high seas freedom of navigation. But the underlying concern of the *Corfu Channel (Merits)* Judgment with preserving the free passage of warships and commercial ships through straits is the same as in the case of non-suspendable Transit Passage laid down in the 1982 UNCLOS as a result of a 12-mile TS limit. See also UNGA Adopts Two Oceans Resolutions, UN Doc. GA/10899 of 4 Dec 2009, Statements of EU-Sweden, Singapore and Thailand at 5, 13-14 & 15 <www.un.org/News/Press/docs//2009/ga10899.doc.htm>.

Tunisia/Libya (Merits) Dissent Oda, ICJ Rep. 1982, 223-224; *Gulf of Maine* Pleadings, Vol.V, 386 [US Reply]; *Great Belt (Provisional Measures)* Order, ICJ Rep. 1991, 13-14, Declaration Tarassov, 22-24, Separate O. Broms, 37-38; Pleadings, 7-9 [Finland's Application, paras 25-33], 67 [Denmark's Observations], 88-91 [Agent Gronberg, 1 July 1991], 147-154 [Counsel de Arechaga, 2 July], 155-156 [Agent Fergo], 193-194 [Counsel Treves, 4 July], 224 [Agent Lehmann, 5 July 1991], 235, 328-329, 334-335 [Finland's Memorial], 554, 601-602, 615-628, 645 [Denmark's Counter-Memorial]; *Botswana/Namibia* Dissent Vice-President Weeramantry, para.110 n.92, ICJ Rep. 1999, 1192 <www.icj-cij.org>.

On transit passage through the Strait of Hormuz [*Limits in the Seas No.114 – Iran's Maritime Claims* (U.S. Department of State 1994)], see *Oil Platforms (Merits)* Judgment, ICJ Rep. 2003, 188, para.54; Hearings, CR 2003/5, 37 [Counsel Crawford, 17 Feb 2003], 46 [Counsel Momtaz], CR 2003/6, 60 [Counsel Sellers, 18 Feb], CR 2003/7, 20 [Counsel Bundy, 19 Feb], CR 2003/8, 45 [Crawford], CR 2003/10, 16, 17, 18 [Counsel Mattler, 24 Feb], CR 2003/13, 41 [Counsel Murphy, 26 Feb], CR 2003/14, 51-52 [Crawford, 28 Feb], CR 2003/15, 26 [Sellers, 3 March], 36 [Bundy], CR 2003/17, 16 [Co-Agent Bettauer, 5 March 2003] <www.icj-cij .org>.

On Straits of Malacca and Singapore [1982 Statements on Transit Passage Through the Straits of Malacca and Singapore, UN Doc. A/CONF.62/L.145 and Add.1-Add.8, in *UNCLOS III Off. Rec.* Vol.XVI, 250-251 (UN 1984)], see *Malaysia/ Singapore Pedra Branca/Pulau Batu Puteh (Merits)* Judgment, ICJ Rep. 2008, paras 16-19, 29, 61, 166-180, 260; Hearings, CR 2007/29, 17-18, para.8 [Agent Koh, 6 Nov 2007], 26-27, paras 9-15 [Counsel Chao], CR 2007/22 [transl.], 45-46, paras 9-10 [Counsel Pellet, 8 Nov], CR 2007/24, 12-13, paras 5-10 and at 16-17, paras 28-30, 37 [Agent Kadir, 13 Nov], CR 2007/26, 40-43, paras 15-24 [Counsel Sir Elihu Lauterpacht, 15 Nov], CR 2007/27, 27-28, paras 55-59 [Counsel Schrijver, 16 Nov], CR 2007/28, 24-25, paras 21-25 [Counsel Chao, 19 Nov 2007] <www .icj-cij.org>. See also Singapore Statement of Indonesia, Malaysia and Singapre on the Straits of Malacca and Singapore, UN Doc. A/62/518 (22 Oct 2007); UNGA Adopts Two Oceans Resolutions, UN Doc.GA/10899 of 4 Dec 2009, Statement of Singapore at 13-14 <www.un.org/News/Press/docs//2009/ga10899.doc.htm>.

On maritime accidents and shipwrecks in territorial sea surrounding Pedra Brance in 1920-2005, see *Malaysia/Singapore (Merits)* Judgment, ICJ Rep. 2008, paras 167, 231-234; Hearings, CR 2007/22, 25-26, paras 56-60 [Counsel Bundy, 8 Nov 2007], CR 2007/22 [transl.], 46, para.10 [Counsel Pellet], CR 2007/26, 47-51, paras 39-53 [Counsel Sir Elihu Lauterpacht, 15 Nov 2007], 64, para.33 and at 66-67, paras 39-43 [Counsel Crawford] <www.icj-cij.org>.

See also Statements of Greece and Turkey under the *Aegean Sea* case in Equitable Maritime Boundary Delimitation *infra*.

Innocent Passage through Straits

1930 Hague Draft, Article 12, and Annex II, Appendix B: Compromise-Proposal of the French Delegation (Straits), 252; 1958 TSC, Article 16(4); 1982 UNCLOS, Part III, Articles 38(1) and 45:

SS Wimbledon PCIJ Series A, No.1 (1923) – Judgment, 28, Dissent Schücking, 45-46; *SS Wimbledon* Pleadings, PCIJ Series C, No.3-Additional Volume, 42 [Counter-Memorial of Germany]; *Legal Status of Eastern Greenland* PCIJ Series A/B, No.53 (1933) – Dissent Vogt, 107, 109, 117; *Eastern Greenland* Pleadings, PCIJ Series C, No.62, 414-416, 418 [Norway's Counter-Memorial], No.63, 766, 783-784 [Denmark's Reply], 1066-1070 [Norway's Rejoinder], No.66, 2779-2781 [Agent Steglich-Petersen, 26 Nov 1932]; *Corfu Channel (Merits)* ICJ Rep. 1949, 4 – Judgment, 10, 27-31 (esp.28, 29), Individual O. Alvarez, 46-47, Dissents Winiarski, 55-56, Krylov, 73-75, Azevedo, 97-98, 103-109, Ecer, 128-130; *Corfu* Pleadings, Vol.I, 24, 42-47, 51, [UK Memorial], Vol.II, 128-133, 142-143 [Albania's Counter-Memorial], 242-243, 256-257, 281, 295-299 [UK Reply], 354-358 [Albania's Rejoinder], Vol.III, 267-288 [Agent Sir Eric Beckett, 11 Nov 1948], 376-405 [Counsel Cot, 18 Nov 1948], Vol.IV, 546-565 [Agent Beckett, 18 Jan 1949], 669-689 [Counsel Cot, 22 Jan 1949]; *Anglo/Norwegian Fisheries* Judgment, ICJ Rep. 1951, 132; *Anglo/Norwegian* Pleadings, Vol.I, 77-79, 86 [UK Memorial], 495-520 [Norway's Counter-Memorial], Vol.II, 407, 434, 437, 554-573, 579, 683 [UK Reply], Vol.III, 22-27, 395-434, 437 [Norway's Rejoinder], Vol.IV, 39 [Agent Sir Eric Beckett, 25 Sep 1951], 251-252, 291-306 [Counsel Bourquin, 9 and 11 Oct 1951]; *Nuclear Tests* Pleadings (Australia), 329 [Memorial]; *Great Belt (Provisional Measures)* Order, ICJ Rep. 1991, 13; Pleadings, 7 [Finland's Application, para.25], 88 [Agent Gronberg, 1 July 1991], CR 91/11, 148-151 [Counsel de Arechaga, 2 July], 193-194 [Counsel Treves, 4 July 1991]; *Gulf of Fonseca* Oral Hearings, C 4/CR 91/40, 26 [Counsel Lauterpacht, 5 June 1991], CR 91/43, 78 [Counsel Brownlie, 7 June 1991]; *Oil Platforms (Merits)* Hearings, CR 2003/13, 25-26 [Counsel Murphy, 26 Feb 2003] <www.icj-cij.org>.

See also *ILC Yearbook* 1956-II, 273, 277; Sir Arthur Watts, *The International Law Commission 1949-1998*, Vol.I, 48-49, 55-57 (Oxford 1999).

Longstanding International Conventions in Force
1982 UNCLOS, Article 35(c):

SS Wimbledon Pleadings, PCIJ Series C, No.3-Additional Volume, 42-43 [Germany's Counter-Memorial]; *Corfu Channel (Merits)* ICJ Rep. 1949, 4 – Judgment, 28, Dissents Krylov, 74, Azevedo, 104, 105, 107; *Corfu* Pleadings, Vol.II, 242, 297 [UK Reply], Vol.III, 383-384 [Counsel Cot, 18 November 1948], Vol.IV, 549, 550-565 [Agent Sir Eric Beckett, 18 Jan 1949], 670 [Counsel Cot, 22 Jan 1949]; *Anglo/Norwegian Fisheries* Pleadings, Vol.I, 499 [Norway's Counter-Memorial]; *Great Belt* Pleadings, 147-148, 152-154 [Counsel de Arechaga, 2 July 1991], 155 [Counsel Fergo], 326, 329-331 [Finland's Memorial], 601, 603, 619-624 [Denmark's Counter-Memorial].

On special regime of the Sound (Oresund) and the Belts under the Copenhagen Treaty on the Abolition of the Sound Dues of 14 March 1857 [in force: 31 March 1857, 116 CTS 357; 47 BFSP 24] and the US/Denmark Convention on Discontinuance of Sound Dues of 11 April 1857 [11 Stat.719, T.S.67; 7 Bevans 11], see *Corfu (Merits)* Dissent Azevedo, ICJ Rep. 1949, 107; Pleadings, Vol.II, 242 [UK Reply], Vol.IV, 549 [Agent Sir Eric Beckett, 18 Jan 1949]; *Anglo/Norwegian Fisheries* Pleadings, Vol.I, 514 [Norway's Counter-Memorial], Vol.II, 569 [UK Reply], Vol.IV, 299-300 [Counsel Bourquin, 11 Oct 1951]; *North Sea* Pleadings, Vol.I, 518 [Common Rejoinder of Denmark/NL]; *Great Belt (Provisional Measures)* Order, ICJ Rep. 1991, 13-14; Pleadings, 7-9 [Finland's Application, paras 25-33], 68-71 [Denmark's Observations], 88-89 [Agent Gronberg, 1 July 1991], 147-148, 152-154 [Counsel de Arechaga, 2 July], 155-156 [Agent Fergo], 175 [Gronberg, 4 July], 193-194 [Counsel Treves], 225 [Agent Lehmann, 5 July 1991], 244-254, 322-332 [Finland's Memorial], 570-588, 603-628 [Denmark's Counter-Memorial].

On the US position, see Pleadings, 245 [Finland's Memorial], 604 [Denmark's Counter-Memorial]. Cf. *United States Responses to Excessive National Claims, Limits in the Seas* 73 (No.112, 1992). On Russian position, see Pleadings, 181-182 [Agent Gronberg, 4 July 1991], 127 [Agent Lehmann, 2 July], 213 [Agent Magid, 5 July 1991], 246-248, 261-263 [Finland's Memorial].

See also Inter-Oceanic Canals, 1920 *The Dorrit* incident, *supra*.

On special regime of Ahvenanrauma Strait (between the Aalands and Sweden) under Convention on the Non-Fortification and Neutralization of the Aaland Islands of 20 October 1921 [in force: 6 April 1922, 9 LNTS 212], see *Anglo/Norwegian Fisheries* Pleadings, Vol.I, 458 [Norway's Counter-Memorial]; *Aegean Sea* Pleadings, 252 [Greece's Memorial (Juris)], 445 [Counsel O'Connell, 16 Oct 1978]; *Libya/Malta* Pleadings, Vol.IV, 121-122 [Counsel Colliard, 12 Dec 1984], 312-313 [Counsel Brownlie, 8 Feb 1985]; *Great Belt* Pleadings, 147 [Counsel de Arechaga, 2 July 1991], 323-324 [Finland's Memorial], 611-512, 619-620 [Denmark's Counter-Memorial]; *Kosovo* Hearings, CR 2009/30, 55-56, para.10 [Finland's Agent Kaukoranta, 8 Dec 2009]; CR 2009/32, 49, para.12 [UK Counsel Crawford, 10 Dec 2009] <www.icj-cij.org>.

See also Finland's and Sweden's Declarations made with respect to Ahvenanrauma Strait upon their signing the UNCLOS on 10 December 1982 and ratifying the UNCLOS and Part XI Agreement on 21 and 25 June 1996 [*UN LOS Bull.* 7, 11 (1996 No.32)]. For the US position, see *Limits in the Seas* 64 (No.112, 1992); *id.* 52 ns 73-75, and at 59.

For Report of the International Committee of Jurists Entrusted by the Council of the League of Nations with the Task of Giving an Advisory Opinion upon the Legal Aspects of the Aaland Islands Questions, see *League of Nations O.J., Spec. Supp. No.3*, 5-6 (1920) and The Aaland Islands Question: Report Submitted to the Council of the League of Nations by the Commission of Rapporteurs, League of Nations Doc. 57/21/68/106 (1921); 101 AJIL 812 .18 & at 823 n.87 (2006); 150th UN Aaland Islands Demilitarization Anniversary of 14 August 2006 <www.un.org/News/Press/docs/2006/sgsm10591.doc.htm & www.un.org/apps/news/story.asp?NewsID=19503&Cr=Finland&Cr1=Sweden>; Aaland Islands and the EU Lisbon Treaty of 26 August 2008 <http://news.bbc.co.uk/2/hi/europe/7582077.stm>.

Safety of Passage Regulations
1982 UNCLOS, Articles 41-44:

Great Belt (Provisional Measures) Order, ICJ Rep. 1991, 17-18, Declaration Tarassov, 24, Separate Os Vice-President Oda, 25-26, Broms, 38-39; Pleadings, 5-6 [Finland's Application, paras 14-20], 88 [Agent Gronberg, 1 July 1991], 113-121 [Co-Agent Koskenniemi], 143 [Counsel Gimsing, 2 July], 149-151 [Counsel de Arechaga], 157 [Agent Fergo], 181-182 [Gronberg, 4 July], 202 [Judge Schwebel's Questions], 204-205 [Agent Gronberg's Reply to Schwebel, 5 July 1991], 210-215 [Agent Magid], 215-216 [his Reply to Schwebel].

See also references to the IMO involvement in *Great Belt*, and those to the Strait of Hormuz and Straits of Malacca and Singapore in Transit Passage *supra*.

1977 *Anglo/French* Decision [18 ILM 397 (1979)], paras 161-163, 175-176, 188; *M/V Saiga* Separate O. Laing [38 ILM 1323 (1999)], para.50 n.49; 2005 Settlement Agreement and 2005 Annex VII *Malaysia v. Singapore* Award <www.pca-cpa.org>.

On Morocco/Spain Agreement on the Strait of Gibraltar of 20 March 1967, see *North Sea* Separate O. Ammoun, ICJ Rep. 1969, 129.

On 1866 *Mahler v. Norwich and New York Transportation Company* (Long Island Sound) Judgment [Scott, Cases on International Law 219 (1885)], see *Anglo/Norwegian Fisheries* Pleadings, Vol.I, 516 [Norway's Counter-Memorial], Vol.II, 570 [UK Reply], Vol.III, 420-421 [Norway's Rejoinder]; *Tunisia/Libya* Pleadings, Vol.IV, 331 [Libya's Reply].

On 1872 *UK/USA San Juan River Boundary* (Haro Channel, Rosario Strait) Award [No.95/Stuyt; <www.infoplease.com/ce6/history/A0843485.html], see *Anglo/Norwegian Fisheries* Pleadings, Vol.I, 516 [Norway's Counter-Memorial]. The 1977 *Re Ownership of the Bed of the Strait of Georgia and Related Areas* Judgment [Canada, 73 ILR 186] took into account the *San Juan River* Award.

On 1885 *Stetson v. US (The Alleganean*; Chespeake Bay) Judgment [Scott, 232], see *Anglo/Norwegian Fisheries* Dissent McNair, ICJ Rep. 1951, 168; *Anglo/Norwegian* Pleadings, Vol.I, 553-554, 569 [Norway's Counter-Memorial], Vol.II, 566, 615-617 [UK Reply], Vol.III, 447, 456 [Norway's Rejoinder]; *Tunisia/Libya* Pleadings, Vol.I, 74 [Tunisia's Memorial], Vol.IV, 330 [Libya's Reply]; *Gulf of Fonseca* Dissent Oda, ICJ Rep. 1992, 737.

On 1910 *North Atlantic Coast Fisheries* Award [RIAA XI, 167; No.291/Stuyt], see *Anglo/Norwegian Fisheries* Pleadings, Vol.I, 504-506 [Norway's Counter-Memorial], Vol.II, 562-564 [UK Reply].

On 1926 *The J. Duffy (US v. 2802 Cases Scotch Whisky, etc.*; Long Island Sound) Judgment [14 F. 2nd 426 (DC Conn.)], see *Anglo/Norwegian Fisheries* Pleadings, Vol.III, 420 [Norway's Rejoinder].

On 1939 *The City of Flint* (Indreleia Strait) Judgment [Hyde, 34 AJIL 89-95 (1940)], see *Anglo/Norwegian Fisheries* Pleadings, Vol.II, 572 [UK Reply], Vol.III, 25-26 [Norway's Rejoinder].

On 1977/1984 *Argentina/Chile Beagle Channel* case, see Equitable Maritime Boundary Delimitation *infra*.

See also Internal Waters and Territorial Sea, Innocent Passage of Warships; Inter-Oceanic Canals, Concept of International Servitudes, *supra*.

ARCHIPELAGIC STATES

1982 UNCLOS, Part II, Article 2(1), Part IV, Articles 46-54

Archipelagic State: Definition
1982 UNCLOS, Article 46:

Theory of the Unity of (Coastal) Archipelagos

Anglo/Norwegian Fisheries Pleadings, Vol.I, 480-495 [Norway's Counter-Memorial], Vol.II, 578, 660-662 [UK Reply], Vol.IV, 283-284 [Counsel Bourquin,

11 Oct 1951]; *Minquiers and Ecrehos* ICJ Rep. 1953, 47 – Judgment, 55, Separate Os Basdevant, 78, Carneiro, 97-102; Pleadings, Vol.II, 196-197 [Agent Gros, 28 Sep 1953]; *Gulf of Fonseca* Judgment, ICJ Rep. 1992, 570, para.356, Separate O. Bernardez, 710.

Libya/Malta Pleadings, Vol.II, 68 [Libya's Counter-Memorial], 349 [Malta's Counter-Memorial], Vol.IV, 137 [Counsel Lucchini, 12 Dec 1984]; *Qatar v. Bahrain (Merits)* Judgment, ICJ Rep. 2001 (in press), para.180-183, 214, Dissent Torres Bernardez, paras 45-58, 223-226, 248, 251, 362, 463-466, 473-479, 511; Hearings, CR 2000/14, 34-38 [Counsel Reisman, 13 June 2000], CR 2000/15, 15-16 [14 June], CR 2000/25, 10 [29 June 2000]; *Indonesia/Malaysia (Merits)* Hearings, CR 2002/30, 14 [Agent Mohamad, 6 June], 24, 26 [Co-Agent Ariffin], 29-30 [Counsel Lauterpacht], CR 2002/32, 17 [7 June], CR 2002/33, 15-16 [Counsel Watts, 10 June], CR 2002/34, 31 [Counsel Pellet], CR 2002/35, 51 [Lauterpacht, 12 June 2002] <www.icj-cij.org>; 2006 *Barbados/Trinidad & Tobago* Award, para.44 <www.pca-cpa.org>; *Nicaragua v. Colombia* Nicaragua's POs Written Statement, para.1.33 <www.icj-cij.org>.

On Svalbard Archipelago, see Equitable Maritime Boundary Delimitation – *Denmark v. Norway* case *infra*.

On 1977/1978 *Anglo/French Continental Shelf*, 1977/1984 *Argentina /Chile Beagle Channel*, 1985 *Guinea/Guinea-Bissau*, 1989 *Guinea-Bissau /Senegal*, 1998 *Eritrea/Yemen (Phase I)* and 2006 *Barbados/Trinidad & Tobago* Awards, see Equitable Maritime Boundary Delimitation *infra*.

Archipelagic Baselines
1982 UNCLOS, Article 47-48:

Libya/Malta Pleadings, Vol.I, 129 [Libya's Memorial]; *Gulf of Fonseca* Judgment, ICJ Rep. 1992, 593, para.393; Hearings, C 4/CR 91/45, 28 [Counsel Bowett, 10 June 1991]; *Qatar v. Bahrain (Merits)* Judgment, ICJ Rep. 2001 (in press) – see Bahrain *infra*; Oral Hearings, CR 2000/14, 36-37 [Counsel Reisman, 13 June 2000], CR 2000/16, 48-50 [15 June 2000]; *Cameroon v. Nigeria; Equatorial Guinea Intervening (Merits)* Hearings, CR 2002/12, 65-6 [Counsel Crawford, 6 March], CR 2002/13, 28 [7 March 2002]; *Indonesia/Malaysia* – see Indonesia and the Philippines *infra*.

For Malta's 1971 Territorial Waters and Contiguous Zone Act No.13, as Amended in 1975, 1978 and 1981, see *Libya/Malta* Pleadings, Vol.V, 14 [Map 2], 42 [Fig.11]; *The Law of the Sea – Baselines: National Legislation with Illustrative Maps* 217-218 (UN 1989); *The Law of the Sea – National Legislation on the Territorial Sea* 208-209 (UN 1995). The water to land ratio of Malta (comprising islands of Malta, Gozo, Comino and Cominotto, as well as Fifla of 500 by 250 metres) is 0.64:1 (204 square km:320 square km). The *Libya/Malta (Merits)* Judgment, ICJ Rep. 1985, 20, 48, 50-52, 57, para.79C, Dissent Mosler, 120-121, Oda, 135, 169, Schwebel, 179, did not express any opinion on whether inclusion of tiny uninhabited rock – Fifla Island into the Maltese baselines was legally justified; Pleadings, Vol.I, 35, 65-66, 155, 175 [Libya's Memorial], 413-414 [Malta's Memorial], Vol.II, 37, 41 [Libya's Counter-Memorial], Vol.III, 137 [Malta's Reply], 278, 281 [Agent Mizzi, 26 Nov 1984]. Cf. *Denmark v. Norway* Hearings, CR 93/5, 35 [Agent Tresselt, 15 Jan 1993]; *Qatar v. Bahrain (Merits)* Joint Dissent Bedjaoui, Ranjeva, Koroma, para.188, ICJ Rep. 2001, 203-204; *Nicaragua v. Honduras* Hearings, CR 2007/1, 20, para.18 [Agent Arguello, 5 March 2007], 61, para.43, at 63, para.47 [Counsel Oude Elferink], CR 2007/11, 59, para.21 [Oude Elferink, 19 March 2007]; *Romania v. Ukraine* Judgment, ICJ Rep. 2009, paras 149, 182, 185; Hearings, CR 2008/18, 67, para.18 [Counsel Crawford, 2 Sep 2008], CR 2008/19, 55, para.11 and at 57, para.15 [Agent Aurescu, 3 Sep], CR 2008/28, 49, para.64 and at 52, para.76 [Counsel Bundy, 11 Sep 2008] <www.icj-cij.org>. For Declaration made by Malta on 20 May 1993 upon ratification of the 1982 LOSC, that its baselines are fully compatible with the Convention, see *UN LOS Bull.* 15 (1994, No.25).

Bahrain, including the Hawar Islands which were attributed by the 2001 Judgment to its sovereignty, satisfies the water to land ratio of 1:1. Cf. *Qatar v. Bahrain (Jurisdiction and Admissibility)* Judgment, ICJ Rep. 1994, 118, Dissent Oda, 144-145, 147, *(Jurisdiction and Admissibility)* Judgment, ICJ Rep. 1995, 9-10, 12, 25, Dissent Oda, 42, *(Merits)* Judgment, ICJ Rep. 2001, 40, paras 32-34, 109, 180-183, 214, Dissent Torres Bernardez, 257, paras 45-58, 223-226, 248, 251, 362, 462-479, 507, 511; Hearings, CR 94/4, 45 [Counsel Bowett, 4 March 1994], CR 94/5, 43 [Counsel de Arechaga, 7 March 1994], CR 2000/5, 19 [Agent Al-Muslemani, 29 May 2000], CR 2000/10, 15-16 [Counsel Queneudec, 6 June], CR 2000/14, 33-38 [Counsel Reisman, 13 June], CR 2000/15, 8, 14-16 [14 June], 37 [Counsel Weil], CR 2000/16, 41-42, 45-46, 48-50 [Reisman, 15 June], CR 2000/19, 17-19 [Queneudec, 22 June], CR 2000/25, 7 [Reisman, 29 June 2000] <www.icj-cij.org>.

On Baselines Act No.4 of Indonesia of 18 February 1960 (without Ligitan and Sipadan) [*The Law of the Sea – Baselines* 187-193 (UN 1989); *The Law of the Sea – Practice of Archipelagic States* 45-53 (UN 1992)], see *Indonesia/Malaysia (Merits)* Judgment, ICJ Rep. 2002, 625, paras 84, 130-131, 137; Hearings, CR 2002/29, 51, 53-56 [Counsel Pellet, 4 June], CR 2002/32, 27-29 [Counsel Crawford, 7 June], CR 2002/34, 33 [Pellet, 10 June 2002].

On the Indonesian archipelagic regime and baselines, see also *Indonesia/ Malaysia (Merits)* Hearings, CR 2002/27, 15 [Agent Wirajuda, 3 June], CR

2002/30, 13 [Agent Mohamad, 6 June 2002], 22 [Co-Agent Ariffin] <www.icj-cij.org>; 2004 Archipelagic Baselines Act No.38, in *MIMA Bull.* 26-36 (Kuala Lumpur 2004 No.11); 2002 Archipelagic Baselines Regulation No.38, as Amended by 2008 Regulation No.37, in *LOS Bull.* 81 (2009 No.69); 2009 *Abyei Boundary* Award, para.762 <www.pca-cpa.org>.

See also Equitable Maritime Boundary Delimitation – Mineral Resource Factor, *Portugal v. Australia East Timor* Judgment, ICJ Rep. 1995, 90, *infra*; *Malaysia/Singapore (Merits)* Judgment, ICJ Rep. 2008, para.225, Separate O. Parra Aranguren, para.21, Dissent Dugard, para.26.

On Baselines Act No. 3046 of the Philippines of 17 June 1961, as Amended by Act No.5446 of 18 September 1968 [*The Law of the Sea – Baselines* 250-259 (UN 1989); *The Law of the Sea – Practice of Archipelagic States* 75-83 (UN 1992)], as Amended by Act No. 9522 of 10 March 2009 [<www.op.gov.ph/directives/RA9522.pdf>; UN LOS Bull. 32 (2009 No. 70) and China's Protest, *id.* 58 <www.un.org/Depts/los>] see *Indonesia/Malaysia (Intervention)* Hearings, CR 2001/1, 17-18 [Co-Agent Magallona, 25 June], CR 2001/2, 31 [Counsel Lauterpacht, 26 June], CR 2001/3, 19 [Magallona, 28 June 2001].

On the Philippine archipelago, see also *Indonesia/Malaysia (Merits)* Judgment, ICJ Rep. 2002, 625, paras 24, 28, 102-105, 115-119; Hearings, CR 2002/28, 50, 53-54 [Counsel Bundy, 3 June], CR 2002/29, 14 [Bundy, 4 June], 48 [Counsel Malintoppi], CR 2002/31, 44-45 [Counsel Crawford, 7 June 2002], CR 2002/32, 24 [Crawford] <www.icj-cij.org>; 50th Anniversary of the Archipelagic Doctrine of the Philippines 7 March 2005 <www.dfa.gov.ph/news/pr/pr2005/mar/pr134.htm>; 12 August 2008 <www.manilastandardtoday.con/?page=politics2_aug12_2008>; *Romania v. Ukraine* Hearings, CR 2008/31, 17, para.31 [Counsel Lowe, 16 Sep 2008] <www.icj-cij.org>.

On archipelagic baselines of Papua New Guinea, see Equitable Maritime Boundary Delimitation – Fishery Resource Factors, 1978 Australia/PNG Torres Strait Treaty *infra.*

On Archipelagic Waters and EEZ Act No.24 of Trinidad and Tobago of 18 August 1986 [*UN LOS Bull.* 6 (1987 No.9); *The Law of the Sea – Practice of Archipelagic States* 112 (UN 1992)], Continental Shelf (Amendment) Act No.23 of 7 Nov 1986 [*UN LOS Bull.* 125 (2005 No.56)] and 2004 Maritime Zone Baselines Notification M.Z.N.49 of 14 May 2004 [*UN LOS Bull.* 29 (2004 No.55); *UN LOSIC* 41-42 (2004 No.20)], see 2006 *Barbados/Trinidad & Tobago (Jurisdiction and Merits)* Award, President S.M. Schwebel, para.49, Maps I-II, paras 95, 114, 161, Map III, paras 326, 332-334, 356, 373, 381-382, Maps VI-VII, Technical Report; Trinidad's Counter-Memorial, paras 190-198 [<www.pca-cpa.org>; RIAA XXVII, 147; 45 ILM 800 (2006)].

Archipelagic Waters
1982 UNCLOS, Article 2(1) and Articles 49-54:

Tunisia/Libya (Merits) Dissent Evensen, ICJ Rep. 1982, 283; *Gulf of Fonseca* Judgment, ICJ Rep. 1992, 593, para.393, Dissent Oda, 734 n.1, 745 n.1, 746, 756; *Qatar v. Bahrain (Merits)* Hearings, CR 2000/14, 36 [Counsel Reisman, 13 June 2000] <www.icj-cij.org>; *Barbados/Trinidad & Tobago* Award, para.44, Maps I-II, paras 138, 266, 288, 302 <www.pca-cpa.org>; 2009 *Abyei Boundary* Award, para.762 <www.pca-cpa.org>.

See also Internal Waters, Territorial Sea and Baselines – The Right and Meaning of Innocent Passage *supra*.

Archipelagic Sea Lanes Passage
1982 UNCLOS, Articles 53-54:

Qatar v. Bahrain (Merits) Dissent Torres Bernardez, para.462, ICJ Rep. 2001, 419-420; Oral Hearings, CR 2000/14, 36 [Counsel Reisman, 13 June 2000]; *Indonesia/Malaysia (Merits)* Hearings, CR 2002/34, 33 [Counsel Pellet, 10 June 2002] <www.icj-cij.org>.

M/V Saiga Separate O. Laing [38 ILM 1323 (1999)], para.50 n.49 <www.itlos.org>.

See also references to Article 47 under Internal Waters, Territorial Sea and Baselines – Straight Baselines *supra*; and pronouncements listed under the Regime of Islands – Coastal Archipelago *infra*, which provided an important incentive for early archipelagic practice of Indonesia and the Philippines.

EXCLUSIVE ECONOMIC (/FISHERY) ZONE

1958 HSFC, Article 7
1982 UNCLOS, Part V, Articles 55-75, Part VI, Articles 77-85, Part VII
1992 UNCED Rio Agenda 21, Chapter 17
1995 SSA

Evolution

Anglo/Norwegian Fisheries Individual O. Alvarez, ICJ Rep. 1951, 150; *North Sea* Separate O. Ammoun, ICJ Rep. 1969, 107-118; *Tunisia/Libya (Merits)* Dissent Oda, ICJ Rep. 1982, 224-226; *M/V Saiga* Judgment, [38 ILM 1323 (1999)], Separate O. Vukas, para.16; 2002 *Russia v. Australia* Declaration Vice-President Vukas, paras 3-5 <www.itlos.org>.

On 100-mile zone sought in the Behring Sea by the Russian Ukase of 1821, as protested by Britain and the USA, see *Nuclear Tests* Pleadings (Australia),

339-340 [Memorial]; 1985 *Guinea/Guinea-Bissau* Award, para.80 [25 ILM 287 (1986)].

On Declaration of Panama of 3 October 1939 which proclaimed a 300-Mile Zone around the American Continent [34 AJIL Supp. 1, 17 (1940)], see *Anglo/Norwegian Fisheries* Pleadings, Vol.I, 355 [Norway's Counter-Memorial], Vol.II, 403, 744-747 [UK Reply]; *Fisheries Jurisdiction (Merits)* Separate Os de Castro, ICJ Rep. 1974, 82, 225; *Fisheries Jurisdiction* Pleadings (UK), 327 [Memorial (Merits)], (FRG), 214 [Memorial (Merits)].

On Truman Proclamations on the Continental Shelf and on Coastal Fisheries in Certain Areas of the High Seas of 28 September 1945 [40 AJIL 45-47 (1946); *Anglo/Norwegian* Pleadings, Vol.II, 252, Vol.III, 747; *Gulf of Maine* Pleadings, Vol.II, 133-147], see *Anglo/Norwegian Fisheries* Dissent McNair, ICJ Rep. 1951, 159; Pleadings, Vol.I, 357 [Norway's Counter-Memorial], Vol.II, 403-405, 748 [UK Reply]; *Fisheries Jurisdiction (Merits)* Declarations Nagendra Singh, ICJ Rep. 1974, 43, 216, Separate Os de Castro, 74, 82-84, 87, 88, 91, 98, 225, Separate Os Sir Humphrey Waldock, 106-107, 109, 227; Pleadings (FRG), 215-216 [Memorial (Merits)], 292-293 [Agent Jaenicke, 28 March 1974]; *Aegean Sea (Jurisdiction)* Separate O. Tarazi, ICJ Rep. 1978, 57, Dissent de Castro, 63-64; Pleadings, 258 [Greece's Memorial (Jurisd.)], 453, 457 [Counsel O'Connell, 16 Oct 1978]; *Gulf of Maine* Judgment, ICJ Rep. 1984, 278-279; Pleadings, Vol.II, 33, 70, 77, 95 [US Memorial], Vol.III, 146-147, 172-173 [Canada's Counter-Memorial], Vol.IV, 115, 118 [US Counter-Memorial]; *Libya/Malta (Merits)* Judgment, ICJ Rep. 1985, 42, Separate Os Sette-Camara, 62, 70, Mbaye, 94; Pleadings, Vol.I, 446 [Malta's Memorial], Vol.II, 360 [Malta's Counter-Memorial], Vol.III, 151 [Malta's Reply], 441 [Counsel Brownlie, 3 Dec 1984]; *Gulf of Fonseca* Separate O. Bernardez, ICJ Rep. 1992, 632; *Denmark v. Norway* Separate O. Oda, ICJ Rep. 1993, 97; *Spain v. Canada* Separate O. Oda, para.12, ICJ Rep. 1998, 480; *Qatar v. Bahrain (Merits)* Separate O. Oda, ICJ Rep. 2001, 128, 136-137, paras 14, 31; *Romania v. Ukraine* Judgment, ICJ Rep. 2009, para.70.

See also Equitable Maritime Boundary Delimitation, Truman Proclamation *infra*.

On Iceland's Law No.44 Concerning the Scientific Conservation of the Continental Shelf Fisheries of 5 April 1948 [UN Doc. ST/LEG/SER.B/1, 12 (1951), SER.B/6, 513 (1957); *Anglo/Norwegian Fisheries* Pleadings, Vol.III, 696; as Amended by Law No.81 of 1952, SER.B/8, 10 (1959); *Fisheries Jurisdiction* Pleadings (UK), 45], see *North Sea* Separate O. Ammoun, ICJ Rep. 1969, 104; *Fisheries Jurisdiction (Interim Measures)* Dissents Padilla Nervo, ICJ Rep. 1972, 27, 43, *(Jurisdiction)* Judgments, ICJ Rep. 1973, 8, 55, Dissents Nervo, 40, 85, *(Merits)* Judgments, ICJ Rep. 1974, 10-11, 182-183, Separate O. Dillard, 64, Separate Os de Castro, 72-75, 84, 103, 225, Separate Os Waldock, 106-111, 122-123, 227, Dissent

Petren, 247; *Fisheries Jurisdiction* Pleadings (UK), 27-28 [Iceland's Memorandum], 462 [Counsel Silkin, 25 March 1974], 490-491 [Counsel Slynn, 29 March 1974], (FRG), 3-4 [Application], 242 [Memorial (Merits)].

For references to early practice of Iceland, see *Eastern Greenland* Pleadings, PCIJ Series C, No.62, 52-53, 107, 117 [Denmark's Memorial], 210, 226-229, 447 [Norway's Counter-Memorial]; PCIJ Series C, No.63, 637-643, 671 [Denmark's Reply], 1208 [Norway's Reply].

See also Internal Waters, Territorial Sea and Baselines – Straight Baselines *supra*.

On 1954 *In Re Sauger et al. (The Olympic Challenger, The Olympic Victor, The Olympic Lightning, The Olympic Fighter, The Olympic Conqueror)* Judgment of Peru's Tribunal of Paita [49 AJIL 575 (1955)], see *North Sea* Separate O. Ammoun, ICJ Rep. 1969, 107 n.4. Cf. M.M. Whiteman's *Digest*, Vol.4, 1060-1070 (1965), also noting (1200-1201), that by three identical Aide Memoires to Chile, Ecuador and Peru (CEP) of 13 May 1955, the United States proposed adjudication by the ICJ of the "basic legal controversy" with respect to the 200-mile zone claimed by CEP which, however, replied that such a referral had to be deferred as it involved "aspects of international law not yet defined".

On Canada's Act of 26 June 1970 [9 ILM 553 (1970)] and Order-in-Council P.C. 1971-366 of 25 February 1971, extending its EFZ beyond 12 miles, see *Gulf of Maine* Pleadings, Vol.I, 100, 201 [Canada's Memorial], Vol.V, 384, 484 n.4, 516, 529 [US Reply], Vol.VI, 294 [Counsel Colson, 12 April 1984].

On Canada's 1970 Arctic Waters Act, see Protection and Preservation of the Marine Environment in this section *infra*.

On Canada's reservation of 7 April 1970 to its Optional Clause Declaration, under Article 36(2) of the ICJ Statute, which excluded from the ICJ jurisdiction "disputes arising out of or concerning jurisdiction or rights claimed or exercised by Canada in respect of the conservation, management or exploitation of the living resources of the sea, or in respect of the prevention or control of pollution or contamination of the marine environment" [9 ILM 598-615 (1970)], see *Gulf of Maine* Pleadings, Vol.V, 382-385, 515, 529-537 [US Reply], Vol.VI, 368 [Counsel Rashkow, 16 April 1984]; *Nicaragua v. USA (Jurisdiction and Admissibility)* Separate Os Oda, ICJ Rep. 1984, 494, Sir Robert Jennings, 551-552; *Spain v. Canada Fisheries (Jurisdiction)* Separate O. Kooymans, paras 8-9, ICJ Rep. 1998, 491-492, Dissents Bedjaoui, 516-517, paras 2-4, 67, Torres Bernardez, 689-691, paras 288-293, at 696, paras 309-310, at 720, para.383, at 733-735, paras 423, 430; Pleadings, 277 [Canada's Counter-Memorial], 432 [Counsel Rodriguez, 9 June 1998], 447, 456 [Counsel Brotons, 9 and 10 June], 524 [Counsel Willis, 12 June 1998] <http://www.icj-cij.org>.

On special/preferential rights under the 1958 HSFC based upon exceptional dependence on coastal fisheries, see *North Sea* Pleadings, Vol.II, 94 [Counsel

Sir Humphrey Waldock, 29 Oct 1968], 126 [Agent Riphagen, 30 Oct], 198-199 [Counsel Shigeru Oda, 5 Nov], 248 [Reply by Waldock to Questions Fitzmaurice, 8 Nov 1968]; *Fisheries Jurisdiction (Interim Measures)* Orders, ICJ Rep. 1972, 16, 34, Dissents Padilla Nervo, 23-24, 26-27, 40-41, 43-44, *(Jurisdiction)* Judgments, ICJ Rep. 1973, 7, 19-20, 52, 63-65, Dissents Padilla Nervo, 38, 83, *(Merits)* Judgments, ICJ Rep. 1974, 7, 12-13, 14, 16, 20-22, 23-32, 34 (para.79), 179, 184-185, 188, 189-201, 205 (para.77), Declarations Ignacio-Pinto, 35, 38, 208, 211, Declarations Nagendra Singh, 40, 43, 213, 216, Joint Separate Os of Forster, Bengzon, Jiménez de Aréchaga, Nagendra Singh and Ruda, 50-52, 222-224, Separate O. Dillard, 53-54, 63-66, Separate Os de Castro, 72-76, 84-85, 98-100, 225, Separate Os Waldock, 109-115, 120-125, 227-229; *Fisheries Jurisdiction* Pleadings (UK), 331-344, 357-359 [Memorial (Merits)], 457-476 [Counsel Silkin, 25 March 1974], 477 [Questions of Judge Waldock], 494-505 [Replies Counsel Slynn, 29 March 1974], (FRG), 219-229, 249-257 [Memorial (Merits)], 350-351 [Questions of Jiménez de Aréchaga and Waldock, 28 March 1974], 352-366 [Replies by Agent Jaenicke, 2 April 1974], 367 [Question Waldock], 480 [Reply]; *Tunisia/Libya (Merits)* Dissent Oda, ICJ Rep. 1982, 223-224; *Gulf of Maine* Pleadings, Vol.II, 71-72 [US Memorial], Vol.III, 196, 207-208, 218 n.25, 220 [Canada's Counter-Memorial], Vol.IV, 67-68, 73, 76 [US Counter-Memorial], Vol.VI, 46 [Agent Legault, 3 April 1984], 91, 94 [Counsel Binnie, 4 April], 380-385 [Counsel Feldman, 16 April], Vol.VII, 84 [Binnie, 4 May], 174 [Feldman, 9 May 1984]; *Libya/Malta* Pleadings, Vol.I, 443-444, 479 [Malta's Memorial], Vol.II [Libya's Counter-Memorial], 281, 366-367 [Malta's Counter-Memorial], Vol.III, 362 [Counsel Weil, 28 Nov 1984]; *Denmark v. Norway* Dissent Fischer, ICJ Rep, 1993, 310, 312; Denmark's Memorial, para.305, Denmark's Reply, para.82; *Spain v. Canada* Separate O. Oda, ICJ Rep. 1998, 482, para.14; 2002 *Russia v. Australia* Declaration Vice-President Vukas, paras 3-4 <www.itlos.org>.

On denunciation by Senegal in 1971 of the 1958 TSC and HSFC, see *Aegean Sea* Pleadings, 482 n.1 [Counsel Pinto, 16 Oct 1978].

See also Continental Shelf – Evolution *infra*.

Customary Law Status

Fisheries Jurisdiction (Interim Measures) Orders, ICJ Rep. 1972, 15, 33, Joint Declarations Vice-President Ammoun and Judges Forster and Jiménez de Aréchaga, 18, 36, Dissents Padilla Nervo, 23, 27, 40, 44, *(Jurisdiction)* Judgments, ICJ Rep. 1973, 5-6, 7, 9, 17-18, 20, 51-52, 54, 55, 61-62, 64, Declarations President Sir Muhammad Zafrulla Khan, 23, 67, Separate Os Sir Gerald Fitzmaurice, 24-30, 68-74, Dissents Padilla Nervo, 39, 41, 43-44, 46, 84, 86, 88, 91, *(Merits)* Judgments, ICJ Rep. 1974, 6-7, 14, 21-22, 23-24, 29, 33, 178-179, 186, 190, 192,

198, 203, Declarations Ignacio-Pinto, 36-38, 209-211, Declarations Nagendra Singh, 39, 43, 212, 216, Joint Separate Os, 45-52, 217-224, Separate O. Dillard, 55-61, Separate O. de Castro, 72-104, 225, Separate Os Waldock, 116-125, 227-229, Dissents Gros, 126-147, 234-235, Dissents Petren, 150-163, 240-242, Dissents Onyeama, 171-173, 246; *Fisheries Jurisdiction* Pleadings (UK), 353-357, 366-372 [Memorial (Merits)], 451 [Questions of Judges Jiménez de Aréchaga and Dillard, 25 March 1974], 457-476 [Counsel Silkin], 479-493 [Replies Counsel Slynn, 29 March 1974], (FRG), 233-241, 255-256 [Memorial (Merits)], 292, 297-302, 310 [Agent Jaenicke, 28 March 1974].

For reliance on the *Fisheries Jurisdiction* Judgments, see *UNCLOS III Off. Rec.*, Vol.II, Statements of: Goerner (GDR), 22nd Meeting-31 July 1974, 173; Rosenne (Israel), 178; Jaenicke (FRG), 24th Meeting-1 August, 191-192; Sir Roger Jackling (UK), 25th Meeting-5 August, 200; Ogiso (Japan, 28th Meeting-6 August, 217-218; Andersen (Iceland), 30th Meeting-7 August 1974, 229 (1975).

The inclusion by the *Aegean Sea (Jurisdiction)* Judgment, ICJ Rep. 1978, 29-37, of the continental shelf (as now extending beyond 200 miles) into the notion of "territorial status" of state, may lead logically to the same propensity in the case of the 200-mile zone. Cf. *Aegean Sea* Pleadings, 458-459 [Counsel O'Connell, 16 Oct 1978]. But see 1978 Dissents de Castro, 63-71, and Stassinopoulos, 78-80. Cf. also *Libya/Malta* Pleadings, Vol.I, 443 [Malta's Memorial], Vol.II, 360 [Malta's Counter-Memorial], Vol.III, 445 [Counsel Brownlie, 3 Dec 1984]; *Gulf of Fonseca* Oral Hearings, C 4/CR 91/4 [trans.], 44 [Counsel Weil, 18 April 1991]; *Spain v. Canada* Pleadings, 239-240, 250, 256, 273 [Canada's Counter-Memorial]; *Oil Platforms (Merits)* Hearings, CR 2003/15, 48-49 [Counsel Pellet, 3 March 2003], quoting ICJ Rep. 1978, 32 <www.icj-cij.org>; 2005 *Belgium/Netherlands Iron Rhine* Award, para.79 <www.pca-cpa.org>; *Nicaragua v. Colombia (Preliminary Objections)* Hearings, CR 2007/16, 39, paras 22-23 [Counsel Weil, 4 June 2007] <www.icj-cij.org>; *Costa Rica v. Nicaragua San Juan River* Judgment, ICJ Rep. 2009, para.65, Separate O. Skotnikov, para.6 <www.icj-cij.org>.

Nuclear Tests (Interim Measures) Dissents Gros, ICJ Rep. 1973, 122, 156; *Nuclear Tests* Joint Dissents Onyeama, Dillard, Jiménez de Aréchaga and Sir Humphrey Waldock, ICJ Rep. 1974, 367, 519; *Aegean Sea* Pleadings, 337-338 [Counsel O'Connell, 10 Oct 1978], 423 [Counsel Weil, 13 Oct 1978]; *Tunisia/Libya (Merits)* Judgment, ICJ Rep. 1982, 37, 74, Separate O. de Arechaga, 114-116, Dissents Oda, 157, 172, 215-216, 222-234, 248-249, Evensen, 283-288, 296-297, 319-320; Pleadings, Vol.IV, 420-421 [Counsel Sir Robert Jennings, 16 Sep 1981]; *Gulf of Maine* Judgment, ICJ Rep. 1984, 278, 282-283, 291, 294, Dissent Gros, 361, 364, 367-369, 371-375; Pleadings, Vol.I, 118, 129 [Canada's Memorial], Vol.II, 53-54 [US Memorial], Vol.III, 174, 192, 224 [Canada's Counter-Memorial], Vol.IV, 67-68, 87-88 [US Counter-Memorial], Vol.V, 403-404, 407 [US Reply],

Vol.VI, 91 [Counsel Binnie, 4 April 1984], Vol.VI, 245-246 [Agent Robinson, 11 April], Vol.VII, 88 [Binnie, 4 May 1984], 147-149 [Agent Robinson, 9 May 1984]; *Libya/Malta (Merits)* Judgment, ICJ Rep. 1985, 32-33, Separate Os Valticos, 104-105, 113, Mbaye, 98-99, Dissents Mosler, 119, Oda, 126, 128-129, 153, 155-157; Pleadings, Vol.I, 490-491 [Malta's Memorial], Vol.II, 282, 362 [Malta's Counter-Memorial], Vol.III, 151-152 [Malta's Reply], 363, 413-415 [Counsel Weil, 28 and 30 Nov 1984], Vol.IV, 77-89 [Counsel Queneudec, 10 and 11 Dec 1984], 354-356, 370-373 [Weil, 12 Feb 1985], 443-445 [Qeuneudec, 21 Feb 1985]; *Guinea-Bissau v. Senegal (Provisional Measures)* Separate O. Shahabuddeen, ICJ Rep. 1990, 76-77, *Arbitral Award* Judgment, ICJ Rep. 1991, 59, 64, 66, 73, Separate Os Oda, 81-85, 86-87, 89. Ni, 96-97, 104, Dissents Weeramantry, 150, 171-173, Thierry, 177-178; *Nauru v. Australia (Preliminary Objections)* Judgment, ICJ Rep. 1992, 30, para.67; *Gulf of Fonseca* Judgment, ICJ Rep. 1992, 608, 617, para.432(3), Dissent Oda, 735, 760-761; *Denmark v. Norway* Judgment, ICJ Rep. 1993, 46, 54-55, 59, 61, 69, Separate Os Oda, 92-101, 110, Shahabuddeen, 198-199, Weeramantry, 257; Hearings, CR 93/6, 38 [Agent Haug, 18 Jan 1993]; *Nuclear Weapons (WHO Request)* Dissent Koroma, ICJ Rep. 1996, 223; *Spain v. Canada* Separate O. Oda, ICJ Rep. 1998, 482, para.14, Dissent Torres Bernardez, 609, para.77, at 683, para.271, at 714, para.366; *Cameroon v. Nigeria* Hearings, CR 94/2, 44-45 [Counsel Crawford, 3 March 1998], CR 98/4, 55-56 [Counsel Highet, 6 March 1998].

1977 *Anglo/French Continental Shelf* Decision [18 ILM 397 (1979)], paras 6, 45-46; *Iceland/Norway* Conciliation [20 ILM 804-805 (1981)]; 1985 *Guinea/Guinea-Bissau* Award [25 ILM 251 (1986)]; 1986 *Canada/France* Award, para.59 [see Fisheries *infra*]; 1989 *Guinea-Bissau/Senegal* Award [94 RGDIP 268-271 (1990)], paras 83-85; 1992 ECJ *Anklagemyndigheden v. Poulsen* Judgment, para.10, Case C-286/90, 1992 ECR 1-6019 <http://eur-lex.europa.eu> & 103 AJIL 555 (2009); 1992 *Canada/France* Award, paras 14-15 [see Equitable Maritime Boundary Delimitation *infra*].

Coastal State's Rights over Resources
1982 UNCLOS, Article 56(1):

Fisheries Jurisdiction (Interim Measures) Joint Declarations, ICJ Rep. 1972, 18, 36, Dissents Padilla Nervo, 22-27, 39-44, *(Jurisdiction)* Judgments, ICJ Rep. 1973, 9, 55, Dissents Padilla Nervo, 37-46, 82-91, *(Merits)* Judgments, ICJ Rep. 1974, 14-15, 186-187, Separate O. Dillard, 59, 64-65, Separate Os de Castro, 73-74, 88, 225; Pleadings (UK), 465 [Counsel Silkin, 25 March 1974], (FRG), 235-237 [Memorial (Merits)]; *Tunisia/Libya (Merits)* Dissents Oda, ICJ Rep. 1982, 223-234, 249, Evensen, 284-287; *Gulf of Maine* Judgment, ICJ Rep. 1984, 282-283, 294, 302, Dissent Gros, 367-381; Pleadings, Vol.I, 118-119 [Canada's Memorial],

Vol.III, 54, 172-177, 218, 224 [Canada's Counter-Memorial], Vol.V, 386-391, 412, 416 [US Reply], Vol.VI, 88 [Counsel Binnie, 4 April 1984], Vol.VII, 190, 200 [Counsel Stevenson, 9 May 1984]; *Libya/Malta (Merits)* Judgment, ICJ Rep. 1985, 30-33, 55, Separate Os Sette-Camara, 69-71, Mbaye, 98, Dissent Oda, 156-157; Pleadings, Vol.I, 490-491 [Malta's Memorial], Vol.III, 151-152 [Malta's Reply]; *Guinea-Bissau v. Senegal (Provisional Measures)* Dissent Thierry, ICJ Rep. 1990, 82-83, *Arbitral Award* Separate O. Vice-President Oda, ICJ Rep. 1991, 86, 89-90; *Gulf of Fonseca* Hearings, C 4/CR 91/7 [trans.], 5-6 [Counsel Weil, 23 April 1991], CR 91/46, 35 [Counsel Lauterpacht, 11 June 1991]; *Denmark v. Norway* Judgment, ICJ Rep. 1993, 46, 54-55, 59, Separate Os Shahabuddeen, 198-199, Ajibola, 287-289; Norway's Counter-Memorial, paras 206-244; Hearings, CR 93/9, 83 [Question 1 Oda, 21 Jan 1993], GJM 93/5 [Denmark's Reply, 27 Jan 1993]; *Qatar v. Bahrain (Merits)* Judgment, ICJ Rep. 2001, 93, para.170 <www.icj-cij.org>.

1986 *Canada/France* Award – see Fisheries *infra*; *United States – Import Prohibition of Certain Shrimp and Shrimp Products* Report AB-1998-4, WTO Appellate Body, President F. Feliciano, WT/DS58/AB/R, 12 Oct 1998, paras 130-131 [AB]; 1997 *M/V Saiga (Prompt Release)* Judgment [37 ILM 360 (1998)], paras 56-59, 63-73 – included bunkering (refuelling) of fishing vessels into the coastal state's rights; *M/V Saiga (Provisional Measures)* Separate O. Laing [37 ILM 1218 (1998)], para.19; *M/V Saiga* Judgment, [38 ILM 1323 (1999)], paras 110-138, 151, Separate Os Zhao, Nelson, Anderson; 2002 *Russia v. Australia* Judgment, paras 76, 79, Declaration Vice-President Vukas, para.5, Separate O. Cot, para.11, Dissent Anderson, para.2 [42 ILM 159 (2003)]; 2006 *Barbados/Trinidad & Tobago (Jurisdiction and Merits)* Award, President S.M. Schwebel, paras 82, 88-93, 144, 179, 181-183, 262; Hearings Day-4, 47 [Counsel Greenwood, 21 Oct 2005]; Day-8, 42-43 [Questions of the President and Lowe, 28 Oct 2005], 32-59 [Counsel Crawford] <www.pca-cpa.org>.

Production of Energy from the Waters, Currents and Winds
1982 UNCLOS, Article 56(1):

UK/France Minquiers and Ecrehos ICJ Rep. 1953, 47 – Judgment, 71, Individual O. Carneiro, 89, 109; Pleadings, Vol.I, 729-735, including map [France's Rejoinder], Vol.II, 186-188 [Counsel Harrison, 24 Sep 1953], 407-409 [Agent Gros, 8 Oct 1953]; *Tunisia/Libya (Merits)* Dissents Oda, ICJ Rep. 1982, 228, Evensen, 284; *Gulf of Maine* Pleadings, Vol.III, 224-225 [Canada's Counter-Memorial], Vol.IV, 153 n.1 [US Counter-Memorial], Vol.V, 71-72, 345 [Canada's Reply]; *M/V Saiga* Separate O. Laing [38 ILM 1323 (1999)], para.38.

Cf. 26 *Marine Policy* 471-479 (2002).

Protection and Preservation of the Marine Environment
1982 UNCLOS, Article 56(1)(b)(iii):

Aegean Sea Pleadings, 442 [Counsel O'Connell, 16 Oct 1978]; *Tunisia/Libya (Merits)* Dissent Oda, ICJ Rep. 1982, 224-225, 228; *Gulf of Maine* Judgment, ICJ Rep. 1984, 279, 344; Pleadings, Vol.I, 35 n.7, 106-107 [Canada's Memorial], Vol.II, 34-38 [US Memorial], Vol.III, 58, 137 n.26, 170, 352-357 [Canada's Counter-Memorial], Vol.IV, 152-153, 166, 259-271 [US Counter-Memorial], Vol.V, 64-65, 342-343 [Canada's Reply], 381 [US Reply], Vol.VI, 450-455 [Counsel Colson, 19 April 1984], Vol.VII, 117, 123-124 [Counsel Fortier, 5 May], 154, 269 [Agent Robinson, 9 and 11 May 1984].

The Queen v. The Secretary of State for Trade and Industry Ex Parte Greenpeace Ltd. Judgment, Justice Maurice Kay, Case No. CO/1336/1999 [120 ILR 617]; *M/V Saiga* Judgment, [38 ILM 1323 (1999)], para.130, 133-134, Separate O. Laing, paras 38, 45; *Ireland v. UK Mox Plant (Provisional Measures)* Hearings, ITLOS/PV.01/07, 25-26 [Counsel Goldsmith, 19 Nov 2001]; 2002 *Russia v. Australia (Prompt Release)* Judgment, paras 67, 76, 79, Declarations Vice-President Vukas, para.7, Marsit, Separate O. Cot <www.itlos.org>; *Barbados/Trinidad & Tobago* Hearings Day-8, 102, 118 [Counsel Greenwood, 28 Oct 2005] <www.pca-cpa.org>.

On Canada's Arctic Waters Pollution Prevention Act of 26 June 1970 [9 ILM 543 (1970)], see *Gulf of Maine* Pleadings, Vol.III, 358 [Canada's Counter-Memorial], Vol.IV, 115 [US Counter-Memorial], Vol.V, 384, 514-515, 518, 523, 529-537 [US Reply], Vol.VI, 368 [Counsel Rashkow, 16 April 1984], Vol.VII, 204 [Counsel Stevenson, 9 May 1984]. On 1970 *The Arrow* (which prompted this Act), see Vol.III, 359-360.

On Canada's 1970 Optional Clause Declaration, see *supra*.

On Iceland's Policy Statement of 14 July 1971, announcing a 50-mile EFZ as of 1 September 1972 and a 100-mile pollution prevention zone (based on Canada's 1970 Arctic Waters Pollution Prevention Act), see *Fisheries Jurisdiction (UK v. Iceland)* Separate O. Onyeama, ICJ Rep. 1974, 168, 169; Pleadings (UK), 6, 13, 25 [Application], (FRG), 6 [Application]; *Denmark v. Norway* Separate O. Oda, ICJ Rep. 1993, 94.

Rights over the Sea-Bed and Subsoil
1982 UNCLOS, Part V, Article 56(1)(3) cross-referring to Part VI:

Barbados/Trinidad & Tobago Award, para.182; Barbados' Reply, para.157; Hearings Day-1, 33 [Counsel Sir Elihu Lauterpacht, 17 Oct 2005], Day-4, 82-88 [Counsel Greenwood, 21 Oct 2005], D-6, 55-56, 59 [Lauterpacht, 25 Oct], Day-7, 32-33 [President Schwebel's Question, Counsel Greenwood, 27 Oct], 34-36 [Arbitrator Lowe's Questions, Greenwood], Day-8, 50-52 [Counsel Crawford, 28

Oct 2005]; *Guyana/Suriname* Guyana's Memorial, para.7.26 <www.pca-cpa.org>; *Romania v. Ukraine* Hearings, CR 2008/31, 21, para.44 [Counsel Lowe, 16 Sep 2008] <www.icj-cij.org>.

See also Continental Shelf *infra*.

Outer Limit
1982 UNCLOS, Article 57:

Fisheries Jurisdiction (Interim Measures) Dissents Padilla Nervo, ICJ Rep. 1972, 27, 44; *(Merits)* Separate Os de Castro, 88, 225; *Tunisia/Libya (Merits)* Separate O. de Arechaga, ICJ Rep. 1982, 114-116, Dissents Oda, 222, 227, 233-234, 249, 253, 270, Evensen, 284-287, 296-297, 315; *Gulf of Maine* Judgment, ICJ Rep. 1984, 282-283; Pleadings, Vol.I, 118, 124 [Canada's Memorial], Vol.III, 54, 148-149, 175, 210-211 [Canada's Counter-Memorial], Vol.V, 22-23, 27 [Canada's Reply], 407-408, 410 [US Reply], Vol.VI, 17 [Counsel McGuigan, 2 April 1984], Vol. VII, 196 [Counsel Stevenson, 9 May 1984]; *Libya/Malta (Merits)* Judgment, ICJ Rep. 1985, 32, 35, 46, Separate O. Sette-Camara, 69-71; Pleadings, Vol.I, 105-106 [Libya's Memorial], 490-491 [Malta's Memorial], Vol.II, 100-101 [Libya's Counter-Memorial], 371 [Malta's Counter-Memorial], Vol.III, 170 [Malta's Reply]; *Denmark v. Norway* Judgment, ICJ Rep. 1993, 59, 69; Norway's Rejoinder, paras 365-368; Hearings, CR 93/4, 14, 30 [Counsel Bowett, 14 Jan 1993]; *East Timor* Hearings [trans.], CR 95/3, 74-77 and map [Co-Agent Teles, 31 Jan 1995]; *Spain v. Canada (Jurisdiction)* Judgment, ICJ Rep. 1998, 445, para.21, Dissent Torres Bernardez, 609, para.77 <www.icj-cij.org>; *Barbados/Trinidad & Tobago* Award, paras 6, 8, 40, Maps I-II, paras 93-94, 103, 171, Map III, paras 224-227; Hearings Day-8, 37-38 [Counsel Crawford, 28 Oct 2005] <www.pca-cpa.org>; *Romania v. Ukraine* Judgment, ICJ Rep. 2009, paras 132, 136.

Jus Communicationis
1982 UNCLOS, Part V, Article 58, Part VII, Articles 87-115:

Aegean Sea Pleadings, 458-459 [Counsel O'Connell, 16 Oct 1978]; *Tunisia/Libya (Merits)* Dissent Oda, ICJ Rep. 1982, 225-227; *Gulf of Maine* Pleadings, Vol.V, 386-387, 412 [US Reply], Vol.VII, 200, 204 [Counsel Stevenson, 9 May 1984]; *Libya/Malta (Merits)* Separate O. Sette-Camara, ICJ Rep. 1985, 69; *Nicaragua v. USA Military and Paramilitary Activities (Merits)* Judgment, ICJ Rep. 1986, 111-112, para.213; *Gulf of Fonseca* Dissent Oda, ICJ Rep. 1992, 761; *Nicaragua v. Honduras* Hearings, CR 2007/14, 14, para.12 [Counsel Colson, 23 March 2007] <www.icj-cij.org>.

Canada/France Award [31 ILM 1175 (1992)], para.88, Dissent Weil [*id.* 1219], paras 51-52; *M/V Saiga (Prompt Release)* Judgment [ITLOS Rep. 1997, 16; 37

ILM 360 (1998)], para.58 – suggested inclusion of bunkering (refuelling) of fishing vessels into the freedom of navigation, Dissents President Mensah, paras 6, 21-22, Wolfrum and Yamamoto, Anderson, Joint Dissent (Park, Nelson, Rao, Vukas and Ndiaye); *M/V Saiga* Judgment, [ITLOS Rep. 1999, 10; 38 ILM 1323 (1999)], paras 28-30, 91, 93, 97, 123-136, 137-138 (declined to hold whether bunkering falls within the freedom of navigation), Separate Os Anderson, Vukas, Laing; 2001 *Ireland v. UK Mox Plant (Provisional Measures)* Separate O. Anderson, para.4; Ireland's Request, paras 36-38; 2004 *Saint Vincent v. Guinea-Bissau Juno Trader (Prompt Release)* Declaration Kolodkin, para.4 <www.itlos.org>.

See also High Seas *infra*; UNGA Adopts Two Oceans Resolutions, UN Doc. GA/10899 of 4 Dec 2009, Statements of EU-Sweden and Thailand at 5, 15 <www.un.org/News/Press/docs//2009/ga10899.doc.htm>.

Equality-of-Uses Principle

1958 HSC, Article 2; 1982 UNCLOS, Part V, Articles 56(2) and 58(3), Part VII, Article 87(2):

North Sea Pleadings, Vol.II, 66 [Agent Jaenicke, 25 Oct 1968, referring to "reconciling the different uses of the North Sea"], 129-130 [Agent Riphagen, 30 Oct 1968]; *Fisheries Jurisdiction (Merits)* Judgments, ICJ Rep. 1974, 29-31, 34 (para.79(4)(c)), 198-199, 206 (para.77(4)(c)), Declarations Nagendra Singh, 40, 213, Separate O. Dillard, 56-57, 69-70; Pleadings (UK), 497-499 [Counsel Slynn, 29 March 1974]; *Nuclear Tests* Joint Dissents, ICJ Rep. 1974, 370, 522, Dissent de Castro, 390; Pleadings (Australia), 338-339 [Memorial], (NZ), 430-431 [Replies Agent to Questions by Waldock, 15 July 1974]; *Aegean Sea* Pleadings, 459 [Counsel O'Connell, 16 Oct 1978]; *Tunisia/Libya (Merits)* Separate O. de Arechaga, ICJ Rep. 1982, 130, Dissent Oda, 178.

M/V Saiga Judgment [ITLOS Rep. 1999, 10; 38 ILM 1323 (1999)], paras 121, 131, Separate Os Vukas, paras 6, 14, Laing, paras 3, 18, 37-38, 55.

Cf. *Seychelles v. France Monte Canfurco* Judgment, paras 70-72 [ITLOS Rep. 2000, 86]; 2002 *Russia v. Australia Volga* Judgment, paras 79-83, Separate O. Cot, para.26, Dissents Anderson, paras 20-21, 24, Shearer, para.19 [42 ILM 159 (2003)].

Residual Rights

1982 UNCLOS, Part V, Article 59:

M/V Saiga Judgment [38 ILM 1323 (1999)], paras 125, 137, Separate Os Vukas, paras 16, 21. Laing, para.55.

Artificial Islands, Installations and Structures
1958 CSC, Article 5; 1982 UNCLOS, Part V/VI, Articles 60/80, Part XIII, Articles 258-262:

Corfu Channel (Merits) ICJ Rep. 1949, 4 – Individual O. Alvarez, 43; *North Sea* Pleadings, Vol.II, 96-97 [Counsel Sir Humphrey Waldock, 29 Oct 1968], 130 [Agent Riphagen, 30 Oct 1968]; *Aegean Sea (Interim Measures)* Order, ICJ Rep. 1976, 10, para.30; Pleadings, 455-457 [Counsel O'Connell, 16 Oct 1978]; *Tunisia/Libya (Merits)* Separate O. de Arechaga, ICJ Rep. 1982, 115, 120-121, Dissent Oda, 228; *Libya/Malta* Pleadings, Vol.I, 81, 128 [Libya's Memorial]; *M/V Saiga* Judgment [ITLOS Rep. 1999, 10; 38 ILM 1323 (1999)], para.127, Separate Os Nelson, Laing, paras 38, 50; *Oil Platforms* – see High Seas, Freedom of the High Seas *infra*; 2006 *Barbados/Trinidad & Tobago* Award, President S.M. Schwebel, paras 178, 182; Barbados' Reply, paras 157-158; Hearings Day-4, 60-61, 104 [Counsel Crawford, 21 Oct 2005] <www.pca-cpa.org>.

On MODU (drill ships and drill rigs, including semi-submersible rigs and jack-up rigs), see *Great Belt* case – Straits Used for International Navigation *supra*; High Seas – Status of Ships/Criminal Jurisdiction (Definition of Ships) *infra*.

On the World's biggest artificial island Palm Jumeirah in Dubai, UAE, see 4 Jan 2009 <www.telegraph.co.uk/finance/4093544/Owner-of-Dubai-landmarks-eyes-float.html>.

See also Internal Waters, Territorial Sea and Baselines – Ports and Roadsteds *supra*.

Artificial Islands, Installations and Structures Used for Military Purposes

1977 *Anglo/French* Decision [18 ILM 397 (1979)], para.161; *Aegean Sea* Pleadings, 455-456 [Counsel O'Connell, 16 Oct 1978]; *Oil Platforms (Preliminary Objection)* Hearings, CR 96/14, 20 [Zeinoddin, 19 Sep 1996], CR 96/16, 10 [Agent Matheson, 23 Sep 1996]; *Oil Platforms (Merits)* Judgment, ICJ Rep. 2003, 161, paras 25-26, 46-53, 76-85, 125; Hearings, CR 2003/5, 20, 24 [Agent Zahedin-Labbaf, 17 Feb 2003], 37 [Counsel Crawford], CR 2003/6, 39-48 [Counsel Zeinoddin, 18 Feb], CR 2003/7, 12-29 [Counsel Bundy, 19 Feb], 2003/9, 13-17 [Agent Taft, 21 Feb], 22-24 [Counsel Beaver], CR 2003/10, 31 [24 Feb], 34-51 [Co-Agent Bettauer], 56-58 [Counsel Matheson], CR 2003/11, 41-43, specifying CS/EEZ location of platforms [Counsel Murphy, 25 Feb], 57-58 [Co-Agent Bettauer], CR 2003/12, 41-54 [Matheson, 26 Feb], CR 2003/13, 46, 49 [Agent Taft], CR 2003/15, 29-33 [Counsel Sellers, 3 March], 37-40 [Bundy], CR 2003/17, 23-28 [Bettauer, 5 March 2003], CR 2003/18, 31-33, 35 [Taft], 35 [Question 2 of Judge Al-Khasawneh], 36 [Question 1 of Judge *ad hoc* Rigaux] <www.icj-cij.org>.

On the 2005 IMO SUA Convention and Protocol, see Peaceful Uses of the Sea – Maritime Terrorism *infra*.

Rational Conservation and Optimum Utilization of Fisheries
1958 HSC and HFSC; 1982 UNCLOS, Part V, Articles 61-62, Part VII, Articles 116-120:

Fisheries Jurisdiction (Merits) Judgments, ICJ Rep. 1974, 31, 34 (para.79(4)(d)), 200, 206 (para.77(4)(d)), Declarations Nagendra Singh, 40, 213, Separate O. Dillard, 68-69; Pleadings (UK), 359-366 [Memorial (Merits)]; *Tunisia/Libya (Merits)* Dissents Oda, ICJ Rep. 1982, 226, 228-231, Evensen, 284; *Gulf of Maine* Judgment, ICJ Rep. 1984, 278, 340-344; Pleadings, Vol.I, 90, 99-103, 118 [Canada's Memorial], Vol.II, 23, 52-61, 72-76 [US Memorial], Vol.III, 83-89, 141-146, 150-162, 186-198 [Canada's Counter-Memorial], Vol.IV, 45, 134-151 [US Counter-Memorial], Vol.V, 74-76, 99-126 [Canada's Reply], 416, 432-439 [US Reply], Vol.VI, 91, 95 [Counsel Binnie, 4 April 1984], 104 [Counsel Bowett, 5 April], 174 [Counsel Feldman, 9 May 1984], 203 [Counsel Stevenson]; *Libya/ Malta* Pleadings, Vol.III, 327-328 [Counsel Lauterpacht, 27 Nov 1984], Vol.IV, 139 [Counsel Lucchini, 12 Dec], Vol.VII, 245-263 [Counsel Colson, 11 May 1984]; *Guinea-Bissau v. Senegal (Provisional Measures)* Order, ICJ Rep.1990, 65, 67-68, Separate O. Evensen, 73, Dissent Thierry, 80-83; Hearings, CR 90/1, 43 [Questions 1/2 Judge Oda, 12 Feb 1990], 44 [Questions Judges Schwebel, Guillaume], CR 90/2, 13, 18 and Annex (map) [Co-Agent Bowett], CR 91/3, 81-83 [Counsel Highet, 4 April 1991]; *Denmark v. Norway* Judgment, ICJ Rep. 1993, 46, 54-55, 70-72; *Spain v. Canada Fisheries (Jurisdiction)* Judgment, ICJ Rep. 1998, 458-466, paras 62-84, Separate Os President Schwebel, 470-473, Oda, 474-485, Dissents Vice-President Weeramantry, 506, para.39, Bedjaoui, 540-552, paras 62-97, Ranjeva, 561-568, paras 22-38, Vereshchetin, 577-580, paras 14-21, Torres Bernardez, 683-685, paras 272-278, at 693-706, paras 302-340, at 715-717, paras 372-376; Pleadings, 95-99 [Spain's Memorial], 248-258, 274-279 [Canada's Counter-Memorial], 490-500 [Agent Kirsch, 11 June 1998], 522-526 [Counsel Willis], 527-537 [12 June], 616-624 [17 June 1998]; *Peru v. Chile* – see Equitable Maritime Boundary Delimitation *infra*.

On Canada's 1970 Optional Clause Declaration, see *supra*; and on its 1994 Declaration, see Settlement of Disputes – Automatic Exemption of Fishery Disputes *infra*.

1986 *Canada/France* Award – see Fisheries *infra*; *US – Import Prohibition of Certain Shrimp and Shrimp Products* Report AB-1998-4 – see Protection and Preservation of the Marine Environment, Obligation to Protect and Preserve the Marine Environment *infra*; *Panama v. France Camuco, Seychelles v. France M/V Monte Confurco, Belize v. France Grand Prince, Russia v. Australia Volga, Saint Vincent v. Guinea-Bissau Juno Trader* and *Japan v. Russia Hoshinmaru* and *Tomimaru* Judgments, ITLOS Cases Nos 5, 6, 8, 11, 13 and 14-15 – see Settlement of Disputes, Prompt Release of Vessels and Crews *infra*; 2006 *Barbados/Trinidad & Tobago* Award – see Equitable Maritime Boundary Delimitation *infra*; *EC/Chile Swordfish* – see Presential Sea *infra*.

Traditional Fishing Rights
1982 UNCLOS, Part V, Article 62(3):

Fisheries Jurisdiction (Merits) Judgments, ICJ Rep. 1974, 24, 27-33, 34 (para.79), 192-193, 196-203, 205 (para.77), Joint Separate Os, 50-51, 222-223, Separate O. Dillard, 53-54; *Gulf of Maine* Judgment, ICJ Rep. 1984, 278, 341-342; Pleadings, Vol.III, 196, 220 [Canada's Counter-Memorial], Vol.IV, 135-136 [US Counter-Memorial], Vol.V, 114-115, 119 [Canada's Reply], 386, 422 [US Reply], Vol.VI, 92, 95, 100 [Counsel Binnie, 4 April 1984].

1986 *Canada/France* Award, Dissent Weil – see Fisheries *infra*; 1992 *Canada/France* and 2006 *Barbados/Trinidad & Tobago* Awards – see Equitable Maritime Boundary Delimitation *infra*.

Rights of Land-Locked and Geographically Disadvantaged States (GDS)
1982 UNCLOS, Part V, Articles 69-72:

Fisheries Jurisdiction (Merits) Separate O. Dillard, ICJ Rep. 1974, 57; Pleadings (FRG), 232 [Memorial (Merits)], 303-305, 309, 310 [Agent Jaenicke, 28 March 1974]; *Tunisia/Libya (Merits)* Dissent Oda, ICJ Rep. 1982, 226, 228, 256; *Gulf of Maine* Pleadings, Vol.VI, 255 [11 April 1984]; *Libya/Malta (Merits)* Judgment, ICJ Rep. 1985, 41, Separate O. Sette-Camara, 71, Dissent Oda, 155; Pleadings, Vol.I, 480-482, 554-569 [Malta's Memorial], Vol.II, 68-71 [Libya's Counter-Memorial], Vol.III, 147-148, 166 [Malta's Reply]; *Gulf of Fonseca* Dissent Oda, ICJ Rep. 1992, 761.

1999 *Eritrea/Yemen (Phase II)* Award, para.72 n.6 [40 ILM 983 (2001)]; *M/V Saiga* Separate O. Laing [38 ILM 1323 (1999)], paras 38-39; *Guyana/Suriname* Guyana's Reply, paras 5.29/5.31 <www.pca-cpa.org>.

Definition of GDS
1982 UNCLOS, Part V, Article 70(2):

North Sea Pleadings, Vol.II, 160 [Agent Jacobsen, 1 Nov 1968]; *Fisheries Jurisdiction* Pleadings (FRG), 303 [Agent Jaenicke, 28 March 1974]; *Gulf of Fonseca* Dissent Oda, ICJ Rep. 1992, 761; *Guyana/Suriname* Guyana's Reply, para.5.30 <www.pca-cpa.org>.

See also Continental Shelf – Revenue Sharing; Enclosed or Semi-Enclosed Seas *infra*.

Coastal State's Fisheries Enforcement
1982 UNCLOS, Part V, Article 73:

See Use of Force in Enforcement at Sea *infra*; Settlement of Disputes – Prompt Release of Vessels and Crews and Military Activities and Law Enforcement Disputes *infra*.

***Presential Sea* (Mar Presencial):**

On Argentina's Act No.23.968 of 14 August 1991 [*UN LOS Bull.* 20 (1992 No.20)] and Chile's General Law (Decree No.430) on Fishing and Acquaculture of 28 September 1991 as well as Fisheries Laws Nos 19.079 and 19.080 of 1991 (amending its General Law) and Decree No.598 of 1999 [*Diario Oficial de la Republica de Chile* of 6 September 1991 and 25 November 1999], see *Spain v. Canada* Pleadings, 44-45 [Spain's Memorial]; *Peru v. Chile* – see Equitable Maritime Boundary Delimitation *infra*.

On Chile's Decree No.598, see *EC/Chile Swordfish* <www.europa.eu.int/comm/trade/miti/dispute/swordfish.htm> [Fisheries *infra*].

See also Continental Shelf; Equitable Maritime Boundary Delimitation; Fisheries; Charts and Geographical Coordinates; High Seas; Fisheries; Enclosed or Semi-Enclosed Seas; Protection and Preservation of the Marine Environment; Use of Force in Enforcement at Sea; Marine Scientific Research; Participation by International Organizations; and other relevant sections *infra*.

CONTINENTAL SHELF

1958 CSC
1982 UNCLOS, Part V, Articles 56(3) and 68, Part VI, Articles 76-85, Part VII and Annex II; Final Act Annex II; CLCS Rules of Procedure

Evolution

Anglo/Norwegian Fisheries Individual O. Alvarez, ICJ Rep. 1951, 150; Pleadings, Vol.I, 357-361, 366-367 [Norway's Counter-Memorial], Vol.II, 252-262 [texts], 402-407, 580-581, 747-752 [UK Reply], Vol.III, 257-262, 647 [Norway's Rejoinder], Vol.IV, 56-57 [Agent Sir Eric Beckett, 26 Sep 1951], 581 [texts]; *Minquiers and Ecrehos* Pleadings, Vol.II, 255-256 [Agent Gros, 30 Sep 1953], 353-354 [Counsel Fitzmaurice, 5 Oct 1953]; *North Sea* Pleadings, Vol.II, 242 [Reply by Counsel Waldock to Questions Fitzmaurice]; *Fisheries Jurisdiction* Pleadings (UK), 328-329 [Memorial (Merits)]; *Tunisia/Libya (Merits)* Separate O. de Arechaga, ICJ Rep. 1982, 110-113, 120-121, Dissent Oda, 172-211; *Romania v. Ukraine* Judgment,

ICJ Rep. 2009, para.70; Hearings, CR 2008/26, 56-57, paras 48-49 [Counsel Sir Michael Wood, 10 Sep 2008], CR 2008/30, 52, para.31 [Counsel Crawford, 15 Sep 2008] <www.icj-cij.org>.

1951 *Petroleum Development (Trucial Coast) Ltd. v. Sheikh of Abu Dhabi* Award, *as reaffirmed* by 1989 *Guinea-Bissau/Senegal* Award – see Equitable Maritime Boundary Delimitation *infra.*

See also Exclusive Economic (/Fishery) Zone – Evolution *supra*; Equitable Maritime Boundary Delimitation – Truman Proclamation *infra.*

Definition of the Outer Limit

1958 CSC, Article 1; 1982 UNCLOS, Article 76, Final Act, Annex II and CLCS Rules of Procedure:

North Sea ICJ Rep. 169, 3 – Judgment, 40, para.67, 49, para.89(b), Separate O. Padilla Nervo, 95-96, Separate O. Ammoun, 103, 106, 110-112, 123, Dissents Koretsky, 154, Tanaka, 179-181, 187, Morelli, 201, Sorensen, 249; *North Sea* Pleadings, Vol.I, 17, 61 [FRG Memorial], 201 [Counter-Memorial of Denmark], 351, 353 [NL Counter-Memorial], 393, 402, 409 [FRG Reply], 464, 512 [Common Rejoinder of Denmark/NL], Vol.II, 19 [Agent Jaenicke, 23 Oct 1968], 92-95, 99, 104-111 [Counsel Sir Humphrey Waldock, 29 Oct], 138 [Agent Riphagen, 31 Oct 1968], 162 [Questions Sir Gerald Fitzmaurice, 1 Nov], 172-174 [Jaenicke, 4 Nov], 197 [Counsel Oda, 5 Nov], 216 [Riphagen, 7 Nov], 244 [Reply by Waldock to Questions Fitzmaurice, 8 Nov], 273-274, 278 [Waldock, 11 Nov 1968]; *Fisheries Jurisdiction (Jurisdiction)* Dissents Padilla Nervo, ICJ Rep. 1973, 45, 89-90, *(Merits)* Separate Os Waldock, ICJ Rep. 1974, 108, 227, Dissent Gros, 135; *Aegean Sea* Pleadings, 337-338 [Counsel O'Connell, 10 Oct 1978]; *Tunisia/Libya (Merits)* Judgment, ICJ Rep. 1982, 46-49, Separate O. de Arechaga, 110-115, Dissents Oda, 165-166, 174, 179-184, 192; *Gulf of Maine* Judgment, ICJ Rep. 1984, 279, 311, Dissent Gros, 371-377; Pleadings, Vol.I, 47-56 [Canada's Memorial], Vol.II, 10-15, 78-79 [US Memorial], Vol.V, 392-421 [US Reply]; *Libya/Malta* Pleadings, Vol.I, 450 [Malta's Memorial]; 1989 *Guinea-Bissau/Senegal* Award [94 RGDIP 271 (1990)], para.85; *Denmark v. Norway* Judgment, President R.Y. Jennings, ICJ Rep. 1993, 50, Separate O. Oda, 97-99, 102-103 <www.icj-cij.org>; 2006 *Barbados/Trinidad & Tobago (Jurisdiction and Merits)* Award, President S.M. Schwebel, paras 63-65 and Map II, paras 80-87, 103, 155, 157, Map III, paras 174-187, 189-190, 196, 213-215, 217, 297, 367-368, para.384(1)(ii); Trinidad's Counter-Memorial, paras 265-269, 287-288; Barbados' Reply, paras 125-145; Trinidad's Rejoinder, paras 157, 219; Hearings Day-1, 85-87 [Counsel Reisman, 17 Oct 2005], 94-95, 105 [Counsel Volterra], Day-4, 77-87 [Counsel Greenwood, 21 Oct], 88-109 [Counsel Crawford], Day-6, 39-49 [Reisman, 25 Oct], Day-8, 32-59 [Crawford, 28 Oct 2005], 42-43 [Questions of the President and Lowe] <www.pca-cpa.org>.

1982 UNCLOS, Article 76(1)

Tunisia/Libya (Intervention) Separate O. Schwebel, ICJ Rep. 1981, 37, *(Merits)* Judgment, ICJ Rep. 1982, 47-49, 65, 73-74, Separate O. de Arechaga, 113-115, Dissents Oda, 211-222, 247-248, 253, Evensen, 284-287, 296, 315; Pleadings, Vol.I, 163-165 [Tunisia's Memorial], Vol.V, 58-60 [Counsel Vallat, 1 Oct 1981], 244 [Judge Mosler's Questions, 9 Oct], 261-262 [Counsel Sir Robert Jennings, 13 Oct], 362-363 [Vallat, 19 Oct], 502, 504 [Replies to Mosler, 21 Oct 1981]; *Gulf of Maine* Judgment, ICJ Rep. 1984, 266, 273-274, Dissent Gros, 367, 374, 376; Pleadings, Vol.I, 47, 122-124 [Canada's Memorial], Vol.III, 210 n.9, 214-215 [Canada's Counter-Memorial], Vol.V, 22-23 [Canada's Reply], 415-416 [US Reply], Vol.VI, 173 [Counsel Weil, 5 April 1984], Vol.VII, 191, 196, 198 [Counsel Stevenson, 9 May 1984]; *Libya/Malta (Intervention)* Judgment, ICJ Rep. 1984, 11, Dissent Sette-Camara, 78, 82, *(Merits)* Judgment, ICJ Rep. 1985, 30-33, 55, Separate Os Sette-Camara, 64-65, 68-71, Mbaye, 94-97, 99, Valticos, 104-105, Dissents Mosler, 119, Oda, 128, 151-157; Pleadings, Vol.I, 100-101, 105-108 [Libya's Memorial], 489-490 [Malta's Memorial], Vol.II, 101-102 [Libya's Counter-Memorial], 280-282, 289, 299 [Malta's Counter-Memorial], Vol.III, 150, 153-156, 161-163, 170 [Malta's Reply], 294-295 [Agent Mizzi, 26 Nov 1984], 363, 365, 388, 411-413 [Counsel Weil, 28-30 Nov], Vol.IV, 14 [Counsel Vallat, 6 Dec], 35-39 [Counsel Briggs, 7 Dec], 76-77, 86 [Counsel Queneudec, 10 and 11 Dec 1984], 362-368 [Weil, 12 Feb 1985], 428 [Counsel Jaenicke, 21 Feb 1985], 445 [Counsel Qeuneudec]; 1985 *Guinea/Guinea-Bissau* Award, paras 96, 113-115 [20 ILM 292, 299 (1986)]; *Gulf of Fonseca* Hearings, C 4/CR 91/46, 31 [Counsel Lauterpacht, 11 June 1991]; *Canada/France* Award, paras 23, 75-82 [31 ILM 1160, 1171-1172 (1992)]; *Denmark v. Norway* Separate Os Oda, ICJ Rep. 1993, 99, Shahabuddeen, 134-135; Hearings, CR 93/6, 12 [Agent Haug, 18 Jan 1993], CR 93/7, 23-24 [Counsel Brownlie, 19 Jan 1993]; *East Timor* Hearings [trans.], CR 95/3, 75 [Co-Agent Teles, 31 Jan 1995], CR 95/11, 39-40 [Counsel Bowett, 11 Feb 1995]; *Spain v. Canada (Jurisdiction)* Dissent Torres Bernardez, ICJ Rep. 1998, 650 para.181; *Cameroon v. Nigeria; Equatorial Guinea Intervening (Merits)* Hearings, CR 2002/13, 60-61 [Counsel Crawford, 7 March 2002] <www.icj-cij.org>; 2002 *Newfoundland /Nova Scotia (Phase II)* Award, paras 2.22, 2.29/33, 4.10, 4.18, 4.27, 5.18 <www.gov.ns.ca/>; 2006 *Barbados/Trinidad & Tobago* Award, paras 224-227; Hearings Day-6, 44 [Counsel Reisman, 25 Oct 2005, Day-8, 44 [Counsel Crawford, 28 Oct 2005] <www.pca-cpa.org>; *Nicaragua v. Honduras* Hearings, CR 2007/2, 22, para.59 [Counsel Brownlie, 6 March 2007] <www.icj-cij.org>; 2007 *Guyana/Suriname* Award, para.212; Guyana's Memorial, para.7.24 <www.pca-cpa.org>; *Romania v. Ukraine* Judgment, ICJ Rep. 2009, paras 132, 136.

1982 UNCLOS, Article 76(2)

Libya/Malta Pleadings, Vol.I, 106 [Libya's Memorial].

1982 UNCLOS, Article 76(3)

Tunisia/Libya (Merits) Judgment, ICJ Rep. 1982, 56-57, Dissents Oda, 219-220, Evensen, 286, 289-290; *Libya/Malta* Pleadings, Vol.I, 106 [Libya's Memorial], Vol.II, 101 [Libya's Counter-Memorial]; 2002 *Newfoundland /Nova Scotia (Phase II)* Award, para.2.30 <www.boundary-dispute.ca/>; *Barbados/Trinidad & Tobago* Hearings Day-6, 44 [Counsel Reisman, 25 Oct 2005] <www.pca-cpa.org>.

1982 UNCLOS, Article 76(4)

Tunisia/Libya (Merits) Dissent Evensen, ICJ Rep. 1982, 284, 286, 290; *Libya/Malta* Pleadings, Vol.I, 106 [Libya's Memorial]; *Canada/France* Award, paras 23, 75, 81-82 [31 ILM 1160, 1171-1173 (1992)], Dissent Gotlieb, paras 63-64 [*id.* 1195-1196], Dissent Weil, para.42 [*id.* 1215]. See also Article 76(4)-(6) *infra.*

1982 UNCLOS, Article 76(5)

Tunisia/Libya (Merits) Dissent Evensen, ICJ Rep. 1982, 284, 286, 290; Pleadings, Vol.V, 59 [Counsel Vallat, 1 Oct 1981]; *Libya/Malta (Merits)* Separate O. Sette-Camara, ICJ Rep. 1985, 70; Pleadings, Vol.I, 106 [Libya's Memorial], Vol.III, 412 [Counsel Weil, 30 Nov 1984], Vol.IV, 35 [Counsel Briggs, 7 Dec 1984].

1982 UNCLOS, Article 76(6)

Tunisia/Libya (Merits) Dissent Evensen, ICJ Rep. 1982, 290; *Libya/Malta* Pleadings, Vol.I, 106 [Libya's Memorial]; *Cameroon v. Nigeria; Equatorial Guinea Intervening (Merits)* Hearings, CR 2002/13, 61 [Counsel Crawford, 7 March 2002] <www.icj-cij.org>.

1982 UNCLOS, Article 76(4)-(6)

2006 *Barbados/Trinidad & Tobago* Award, President S.M. Schwebel, paras 63-65 and Map II, paras 80-87, 103, 155, 157, Map III, paras 174-187, 189-190, 196, 213-215, 217, 297, 367-368, para.384(ii); Trinidad's Counter-Memorial, paras 265-269, 287-288; Barbados' Reply, paras 125-145; Trinidad's Rejoinder, paras 157, 219; Hearings Day-1, 85-87 [Counsel Reisman, 17 Oct 2005], 94-95, 105 [Counsel Volterra], Day-4, 77-87 [Counsel Greenwood, 21 Oct], 88-109 [Counsel Crawford], Day-6, 39-49 [Reisman, 25 Oct], Day-8, 32-59 [Crawford, 28 Oct 2005],

42-43 [Questions of the President and Lowe]; 2007 *Guyana/Suriname* Award, paras 246, 353; Guyana's Memorial, para.7.24 <www.pca-cpa.org>; *Nicaragua v. Honduras (Merits)* Judgment, ICJ Rep. 2007, para.319.

1982 UNCLOS, Article 76(7)

Tunisia/Libya (Merits) Dissent Evensen, ICJ Rep. 1982, 286, 290; *Libya/Malta* Pleadings, Vol.I, 106 [Libya's Memorial].

1982 UNCLOS, Article 76(8), Annex II and CLCS Rules of Procedure <www.un.org/Depts/los/>

Gulf of Maine Pleadings, Vol.VII, 191 [Counsel Stevenson, 9 May 1984]; *Libya/Malta* Pleadings, Vol.IV, 365 [Counsel Weil, 12 Feb 1985]; *Canada/France* Award, President E. Jimenez de Arechaga, paras 23, 79 [31 ILM 1160, 1172 (1992)]; 2006 *Barbados/Trinidad & Tobago (Jurisdiction and Merits)* Award, President S.M. Schwebel, paras 82-87, 103 *in fine*, 213-215, 217, 367-368, para.384(ii); Trinidad's Counter-Memorial, paras 265-269, 287-288; Barbados' Reply, paras 56, 132-145; Trinidad's Rejoinder, paras 157, 219; Hearings Day-1, 85-87 [Counsel Reisman, 17 Oct 2005], 94-95, 105 [Co-Agent Volterra], Day-4, 89-90, 94, 98-100, 107-108 [Counsel Crawford, 21 Oct], Day-5, 27-31 [Volterra, 24 Oct], Day-6, 44-46 [Reisman, 25 Oct], Day-7, 38-40 [Counsel Greenwood, 27 Oct], 82-83 [Counsel Wordsworth], Day-8, 39-40, 58 [Crawford, 28 Oct 2005] <www.pca-cpa.org>; *Nicaragua v. Honduras (Merits)* Judgment, ICJ Rep. 2007, para.319.

On Barbados' Submission to the CLCS of 8 May 2008 <www.un.org/Depts/los>, see 2006 *Barbados/Trinidad & Tobago* Award, Map II, paras 103, 157; Barbados' Reply, para.56; Hearings Day-1, 94-95, 105 [Co-Agent Volterra, 17 Oct 2005], Day-5, 27-29 [Volterra, 24 Oct], Day-7, 82-83 [Counsel Wordsworth, 27 Oct 2005] <www.pca-cpa.org>; 26 April 2006 <www.barbadosadvocate.com/NewViewNewsleft.cfm?Record=25617>; 6 July 2008 <www.barbadosadvocate.com/NewViewNewsleft.cfm?Record=35901>; 22nd CLCS Session, 18 August-12 Sep 2008, *Press Release SEA/1908* of 12 Sep 2008 <www.un.org/News/Press/docs//2008/sea1908.doc.htm>; Barbados/Guyana/Venezuela Notes <http://notesfromthemargin.wordpress.com/>; Barbados Co-Agent R. Volterra, The 2006 Award and International Law (2008) <www.energy.gov.bb>.

On intended Trinidad and Tobago's Submission to the CLCS, see Day-4, 89-90 [Counsel Crawford, 21 Oct], Day-5, 28-31 [Co-Agent Volterra, 24 Oct], Day-7, 38-40 [Counsel Greenwood, 27 Oct 2005], 82 [Wordsworth] <www.pca-cpa.org>; Trinidad's Letter of 11 August 2008 on Barbados' Submission of 8 May 2008 <www.un.org/Depts/los>.

1982 UNCLOS, Article 76(10) and Annex II, Article 9

Tunisia/Libya (Merits) Judgment, ICJ Rep. 1982, 48, Dissent Evensen, 285, 290; Pleadings, Vol.V, 60 [Counsel Vallat, 1 Oct 1981], 262 [Counsel Jennings, 13 Oct], 502, 504 [Replies to Mosler, 21 OSct 1981]; *Gulf of Maine* Pleadings, Vol.V, 417 n.1 [US Reply], Vol.VII, 191 [Counsel Stevenson, 9 May 1984]; *Libya/Malta (Merits)* Judgment, ICJ Rep. 1985, 30, Separate O. Sette-Camara, 68; Pleadings, Vol.I, 100 n.4 [Libya's Memorial], Vol.II, 103 n.1 [Libya's Counter-Memorial], Vol.III, 97 [Libya's Reply], Vol.IV, 86 [Counsel Queneudec, 11 Dec 1984], 437 [Counsel Jaenicke, 21 Feb 1985] <www.icj-cij.org>; 2006 *Barbados/Trinidad & Tobago* Award, para.87; Hearings Day-4, 97-100 [Counsel Crawford, 21 Oct 2005] <www.pca-cpa.org>; *Nicaragua v. Colombia* case – see Equitable Maritime Boundary Delimitation *infra*. See also the CLCS Rules of Procedure, UN Doc. CLCS/40, CLCS/40/Rev.1, Rule 46 and Annex I, 17 April 2008 <www.un.org/Depts/los>.

Coastal State's Rights
1958 CSC, Article 2; 1982 UNCLOS, Article 77:

North Sea ICJ Rep. 1969, 3 – Judgment, 22, para.19, 29, para.39, 31, para.43, 32-33, paras 47-48, 39, para.63, 40, para.67, 51, para.95, Declaration Sir Muhammad Zafrulla Khan, 55, Separate O. President Bustamante y Rivero, 57, 60, Separate Os Padilla Nervo, 95-97, Ammoun, 102-106, 114-118, 123-124, Dissents Koretsky, 154, Tanaka, 172, 179-181, 187, Morelli, 198-199, 201, 205, Lachs, 221, Sorensen, 245, 246; *North Sea* Pleadings, Vol.I, 17, 61, 63 [FRG Memorial], 351 [NL Counter-Memorial], 393, 402, 409 [FRG Reply], 464, 466-467, 508, 512 [Common Rejoinder of Denmark/NL], Vol.II, 19 [Agent Jaenicke, 23 Oct 1968], 55-56 [Counsel Shigeru Oda, 25 Oct], 92-97, 99, 104-111 [Counsel Sir Humphrey Waldock, 29 Oct], 137 [Agent Riphagen, 31 Oct], 169-170, 173-174 [Jaenicke, 4 Nov], 197 [Oda, 5 Nov], 213-216 [Riphagen, 7 Nov], 242-244, 246-248, 258 [Reply by Waldock to Questions Fitzmaurice, 8 Nov], 273-274, 278 [Waldock, 11 Nov 1968]; *Fisheries Jurisdiction (Interim Measures)* Joint Declarations, ICJ Rep. 1972, 18, 36, Dissents Padilla Nervo, 22-27, 39-44, *(Jurisdiction)* Separate Os Fitzmaurice, ICJ Rep. 1973, 27-28, 71-72, Dissents Padilla Nervo, 38, 83, *(Merits)* Separate Os Waldock, 108, 227, Dissent Gros, 135; *Fisheries Jurisdiction* Pleadings (UK), 149 [Memorial (Jurisdiction)], 462 [Counsel Silkin, 25 March 1974], (FRG), 216-217, 231 [Memorial (Merits)]; *Aegean Sea (Interim Measures)* Order, ICJ Rep. 1976, 4, 6-11, Separate Os Mosler, 25-26, Elias, 27-30, Dissent Stassinopoulos, 35-40, *(Jurisdiction)* Judgment, ICJ Rep. 1978, 6-8, 20-37, Dissents de Castro, 63-71, Stassinopoulos, 76, 78-80; 1976 Observations of Turkey; *Aegean Sea* Pleadings, 3-11 [Greece's Application], 63-66 [Request], 107-110 [Counsel

O'Connell, 25 Aug 1976], 118 (Question Ruda], 128-131 [Counsel Pinto, 26 Aug], 139-140 [Reply O'Connell to Ruda, 27 Aug 1976], 251-259 [Memorial of Greece (Jurisdiction)], 341-346 [O'Connell, 10 Oct 1978], 421-425 [Counsel Weil, 13 Oct], 433-440 [Counsel Economides, 13 and 16 Oct 1978], 441, 453-460 [O'Connell], 467 [Question by President de Aréchaga], 495 [Reply Economides], 604 [Turkey's Letter], 560-568 and 621-622 [Written Reply to Question by Mosler, 26 Oct 1978].

Tunisia/Libya (Merits) Judgment, ICJ Rep. 1982, 61, Separate O. de Arechaga, 123-124, Dissents Oda, 176-182, 190-192, 221-222, 231-234, 247, 249, 253-254, Evensen, 284-287; *Gulf of Maine* Judgment, ICJ Rep. 1984, 279-283, 305-308, Dissent Gros, 371-381; Pleadings, Vol.I, 129 [Canada's Memorial], Vol.II, 34-38 [US Memorial], Vol.III, 342-351 [Canada's Counter-Memorial], Vol.IV, 65 [US Counter-Memorial], Vol.V, 392-399, 415-416 [US Reply], Vol.VII, 200 [Counsel Stevenson, 9 May 1984]; *Libya/Malta (Intervention)* Judgment, ICJ Rep. 1984, 11, Dissents Sette-Camara, 87-88, Oda, 108, Sir Robert Jennings, 155, 159, *(Merits)* Judgment, ICJ Rep. 1985, 30-33, 43, 56, Separate O. Sette-Camara, 63-64, 69-71, Joint Separate O., 83, Dissent Oda, 156-157; Pleadings, Vol.I, 63-84 [Libya's Memorial], 442-443 [Malta's Memorial], Vol.II, 16-23, 72-73 [Libya's Counter-Memorial], 555-556 [Counsel Virally, 26 Jan 1984], Vol. III, 12-19 [Libya's Reply]; *Great Belt* Pleadings, 308-310 [Finland's Memorial], 510-511 [Denmark's Counter-Memorial]; *Guinea-Bissau v. Senegal Arbitral Award* Separate O. Vice-President Oda, ICJ Rep. 1991, 89; *Gulf of Fonseca* Hearings, C 4/CR 91/7 [trans.], 5-6 [Counsel Weil, 23 April 1991]; *Denmark v. Norway* Separate Os Schwebel, ICJ Rep. 1993, 118, Ajibola, 292, 294; *Qatar v. Bahrain (Merits)* Judgment, ICJ Rep. 2001, 93, para.170; *Cameroon v. Nigeria; Equatorial Guinea Intervening (Merits)* Hearings, CR 2002/6, 42 [Co-Agent Kamto, 25 Feb 2002], 2002/7, 25 [Kamto, 26 Feb 2002]; *Oil Platforms (Merits)* Judgment, ICJ Rep. 2003, 200, para.82; Hearings, CR 2003/15, 48-49 [Counsel Pellet, 3 March 2003] <www.icj-cij.org>; 2006 *Barbados/Trinidad & Tobago* Award, paras 175, 182; Hearings Day-4, 47 [Counsel Greenwood, 21 Oct 2005]; *Guyana/Suriname* Guyana's Memorial, para.7.25 <www.pca-cpa.org>; *Peru v. Chile* – see Equitable Maritime Boundary Delimitation *infra*.

On covering by the "freedom of commerce and navigation" clause contained in the FCN Treaties of oil platforms located within the EEZ/CS, see High Seas – Freedom of the High Seas, *Iran v. USA Oil Platforms* case *infra*.

See also Equitable Maritime Boundary Delimitation – Natural Prolongation *infra*.

Sedentary Species
1958 CSC, Article 2(4); 1982 UNCLOS, Articles 68 and 77(4):

Anglo/Norwegian Fisheries Pleadings, Vol.I, 352, 368-370 [Counter-Memorial of Norway], II, 413-414, 584 [UK Reply], Vol.III, 253-259 [Norway's Rejoinder]; *Minquiers and Ecrehos* Pleadings, Vol.II, 255 [Agent Gros, 30 Sep 1953], 353-354 [Counsel Fitzmaurice, 5 Oct 1953]; *North Sea* Separate O. Ammoun, ICJ Rep. 1969, 112-113, 126; *North Sea* Pleadings, Volume I, 467 [Common Rejoinder of Denmark/NL]; *Fisheries Jurisdiction (Jurisdiction)* Separate Os Fitzmaurice, ICJ Rep. 1973, 27-28, 71-72, *(Merits)* Separate Os de Castro, 85, 225; Pleadings (FRG), 217 [Memorial (Merits)]; *Tunisia/Libya (Merits)* Judgment, ICJ Rep. 1982, 67-68, 70, 72-73, 75, 77, Separate O. de Arechaga, 122-132, 136, Dissents Gros, 154-155, Oda, 197-211, 248; Pleadings, Vol.I, 73-105 [Tunisia's Memorial]; *Gulf of Maine* Judgment, ICJ Rep. 1984, 281-282, 343; Pleadings, Vol.II, 51-52 [US Memorial], Vol.III, 160-161 [Canada's Counter-Memorial], Vol.V, 416 [US Reply]; 2006 *Barbados/Trinidad & Tobago* Award, paras 175, 182; Hearings Day-4, 94 [Counsel Crawford, 21 Oct 2005], Day-8, 48 [Counsel Crawford, 28 Oct 2005] <www.pca-cpa.org>.

Superjacent Waters and Air Space
1958 CSC, Articles 3 and 5(1); 1982 UNCLOS, Part VI, Article 78 and Part VII:

North Sea Judgment, ICJ Rep. 1969, 31, para.43, 37, para.59, 39, para.63, Separate O. Ammoun, 101, 110, 143, 150, Dissents Koretsky, 154, Tanaka, 179-181, 187; *North Sea* Pleadings, Vol.I, 61 [FRG Memorial], 409 [FRG Reply], 464, 512 [Common Rejoinder of Denmark/NL], Vol.II, 97, 98, 107-110 [Counsel Sir Humphrey Waldock, 29 Oct 1968], 129-130, 137, 139 [Agent Riphagen, 30 and 31 Oct], 174 [Agent Jaenicke, 4 Nov], 244 [Reply by Waldock to Questions Fitzmaurice, 8 Nov 1968]; *Fisheries Jurisdiction (Jurisdiction)* Separate Os Fitzmaurice, ICJ Rep. 1973, 27-28, 72, *(Merits)* Joint Separate Os, 46, 218, Separate Os de Castro, 85, 93, 225, Separate Os Waldock, 108, 227, Dissent Gros, 135, Dissents Petren, 150, 161, 240, Dissent Onyeama, 171; *Fisheries Jurisdiction* Pleadings (UK), 349, 373 [Memorial (Merits)], (FRG), 217, 232 [Memorial (Merits)]; *Tunisia/Libya (Merits)* Judgment, ICJ Rep. 1982, 69, Dissent Oda, 178, 192, 231; *Gulf of Maine* Dissent Gros, ICJ Rep. 1984, 374; Pleadings, Vol.VII, 200 [Counsel Stevenson, 9 May 1984]; *Libya/Malta (Merits)* Judgment, ICJ Rep. 1985, 33.

1951 *Petroleum Development (Trucial Coast) Ltd. v. Sheikh of Abu Dhabi* Award – see Equitable Maritime Boundary Delimitation *infra*; *Barbados/Trinidad & Tobago* Hearings Day-8, 44-45 [Counsel Crawford, 28 Oct 2005] <www.pca-cpa.org>.

Revenue Sharing
1982 UNCLOS, Article 82:

Tunisia/Libya (Merits) Dissents Oda, ICJ Rep. 1982, 166, 215-219, 248, Evensen, 285; *Libya/Malta (Merits)* Separate O. Sette-Camara, ICJ Rep. 1985, 71, Dissent Oda, 155; Pleadings, Vol.IV, 365 [Counsel Weil, 12 Feb 1985] <www.icj-cij.org>; *Barbados/Trinidad & Tobago* Hearings Day-6, 45 [Counsel Reisman, 25 Oct 2005], Day-8, 47 [Counsel Crawford, 28 Oct 2005] <www.pca-cpa.org>.

Tunnelling
1958 CSC, Article 7; 1982 UNCLOS, Article 85:

Tunisia/Libya (Merits) Dissent Oda, ICJ Rep. 1982, 175-176, paras 31-32; *Gabcikovo* Oral Pleadings, CR 97/5, 66 [Counsel Sands, 6 March 1997].

On bridges and tunnels across straits, including 2007 *Eurotunnel* Award, see Straits Used for International Navigation – Relevant Jurisprudence, *Great Belt* case *supra*.

On 1856/8 *Cornwall Submarine Mines (First)* Arbitration, Sir John Patteson, see *Tunisia/Libya (Merits)* Dissent Oda, ICJ Rep. 1982, 175.

On 1964 *L'ile de la REM,* see High Seas – Unauthorized Broadcasting *infra*.

On 1967 *Atlantis Development Co. v. US* [379 F 2d 818; 63 AJIL 642 (1969); *Tunisia/Libya* Pleadings, Vol.III, 482], see *Tunisia/Libya* Pleadings, Vol.III, 343 [Counsel Lalive, 20 March 1981]; *Indonesia/Malaysia* Separate O. Weeramantry, para.20 n.17, ICJ Rep. 2001 <www.icj-cij.org>.

On 1970 *Ministre d'Etat chargé de la défense nationale v. Starr (The Johmo)* Judgment of Conseil d'Etat, President Odent [99 *Journal DI* 572 (1972)], see *Aegean Sea* Pleadings, 139 [Reply, 27 Aug 1976], 256 [Greece's Memorial (Jurisd.)], 456 [Counsel O'Connell, 16 Oct 1978].

On 1978 *Treasure Salvors*, see High Seas *infra*.

On 1984 *Reference Re the Seabed and Subsoil of the Continental Shelf Offshore Newfoundland* Judgment of Supreme Court of Canada [23 ILM 288 (1984); 79 AJIL 139 (1985)], see 2002 *Newfoundland/Nova Scotia (Phase II)* Award, paras 1.14, 1.16, 3.10 <www.gov.ns.ca/>.

See also Access to and Jurisdiction and Treatment in Ports – Ports/Oil and Gas Development; Exclusive Economic (/Fishery) Zone *supra*; Equitable Maritime Boundary Delimitation; Charts and Geographical Coordinates; High Seas; Submarine Cables and Pipelines; Enclosed or Semi-Enclosed Seas; Protection and Preservation of the Marine Environment; Use of Force in Enforcement at Sea; Marine Scientific Research; Peaceful Uses of the Sea – Prohibition of Threat or Use of Force (2007 *Guyana/Suriname* Award); Participation by International Organizations; and other relevant sections *infra*.

EQUITABLE MARITIME BOUNDARY DELIMITATION

1958 TSC, Articles 12 and 24(3); 1958 HSFC, Article 7(5); 1958 CSC, Article 6
1982 UNCLOS, Part II, Article 15, Parts V/VI, Articles 60(8), 74/83, 76(10), Part XV, UNCLOS Annex II, Article 9 and CLCS Rules of Procedure

Relevant Jurisprudence

Italy/Turkey Delimitation of the Territorial Waters Between the Island of Castellorizo and the Coast of Anatolia Order, PCIJ Series A/B, No.51 (1933), President M. Adatci – Treaty of Peace of Lausanne of 24 July 1923 [28 LNTS 11; 18 AJIL Suppl., 1, 6-12 (1924)]; Orders of 1931/1932, *Castellorizo* Pleadings, PCIJ Series C, No.61, 33-36.

The case was discontinued as a result of conclusion of Italy/Turkey Ankara Agreement of 4 Jan 1932 [in force: 10 May 1933, 138 LNTS 243; Registered with the LN Secretariat, No.3191, 24 May 1933]. See *supra* and eight *Legality of Use of Force (Preliminary Objections)* Separate Os Higgins, para.5 and Kreca, para.35 n.7, ICJ Rep. 2004 <www.icj-cij.org>.

For references to the 1932 Ankara Agreement, see *North Sea* Separate O. Ammoun, ICJ Rep. 1969, 126; *North Sea* Pleadings, Vol.I, 263-264 [Denmark's Counter-Memorial, Annex 13, B.Territorial Waters: Equidistance Principle], 388 [NL Counter-Memorial, Annex 15], 450 [FRG Reply, Annex, B.Territorial Waters], 489 [Common Rejoinder of Denmark/NL]; *Aegean Sea* Pleadings, 44 [Turkey's Note Verbale of 15 March 1976], 88 [Counsel O'Connell, 25 Aug 1976].

The *Aegean Sea (Jurisdiction)* Judgment, ICJ Rep. 1978, 33, para.78 noted that at the time of accession by Greece on 14 Sep 1931 to the 1928 Geneva General Act for the Pacific Settlement of International Disputes, the Dodecanese Group was not in Greece's possession, for those islands were ceded to Greece by Italy only in the Treaty of Peace of Paris of 10 Feb 1947 [49 UNTS 126; Article 14, in UN Doc. S/1976/12176]. Cf. *North Sea* Separate O. Ammoun, ICJ Rep. 1969, 127; Pleadings, Vol.I, 263, 342 [NL Counter-Memorial]; *Qatar v. Bahrain (Merits)* Hearings, CR 2000/18, 21-22 [Counsel Sinclair, 21 June 2000].

In tension arisen in January 1996 over the islet (rock) of Imia (Kardak), Turkey based its claim on the 1932 Ankara Agreement, while Greece invoked the 1947 Treaty of Peace of Paris as the basis of its title. See Aegean Dispute, <www.american.edu/TED/ice/aegean.htm>; The 82nd Anniversary of Lausanne Treaty of 25 July 2005 <www.turkishpress.com/news.asp?id=62129>.

Anglo/Norwegian Fisheries Judgment, ICJ Rep. 1951, 116, 128-129, 132-133, took first step towards creating a concept of equity as part of international law applicable to maritime boundary delimitation; as referred to in *North Sea* Separate O. Ammoun, 145; *North Sea* Pleadings, Vol.II, 179-180 [Agent Jaenicke, 4 Nov 1968], 194-195 [Counsel Oda, 5 Nov], 271-272 [Counsel Sir Humphrey Waldock, 11 Nov 1968]; *Gulf of Maine* Pleadings, Vol.IV, 69-70 [US Counter-Memorial], Vol.VII, 31 [Counsel Weil, 3 May 1984]; *Denmark v. Norway* Separate O. Weeramantry, ICJ Rep. 1993, 238-239, 258-259.

FRG/Denmark; FRG/Netherlands North Sea Continental Shelf ICJ Rep. 1969, President J.L. Bustamante y Rivero concurring – Judgment, 3, 46-54, Declaration Sir Muhammad Zafrulla Khan, 54, Declaration (dissenting) Bengzon, 56, Separate O. President Bustamante y Rivero, 57, Separate Os Jessup, 67, Padilla Nervo, 85, Ammoun, 100, Dissent Vice-President Koretsky, 154, Dissents Tanaka, 171, Morelli, 197, Lachs, 218, Sorensen, 241; Orders, ICJ Rep. 1967, 3, 6, 1968, 3, 6, 9.

FRG/Denmark Agreement on Remainder of Boundary [UN Doc. ST/LEG/SER. B/16, 424 (1974); *Gulf of Maine* Pleadings, Vol.IV, 444; Charney/ASIL Report No.9-8 (Anderson)] and FRG/Netherlands Treaty on the Continental Shelf Delimitation [857 UNTS 131; *Gulf of Maine* Pleadings, Vol.IV, 445; Charney/ ASIL Report No.9-11 (Anderson)], both of 28 Jan 1971 [both in force: 7 Dec 1972], implemented the 1969 Judgment by boundaries which were drawn to the center of the North Sea on the basis of equitable principles, and which completed the partial boundaries under the 1964 FRG/Netherlands [in force: 18 Sep 1965, 550 UNTS 123] and the 1965 FRG/Denmark [in force: 27 May 1966, 570 UNTS 91] Agreements. Cf. *Gulf of Maine* Pleadings, Vol.IV, 154-157, 161, 166, 444-445 [US Counter-Memorial], State Practice Vol.I, 195, 201; *Libya/Malta* Pleadings, Vol.II, 108 [Libya's Counter-Memorial], Vol.III, 297 [Agent Mizzi, 26 Nov 1984], Vol.IV, 107 [Counsel Colliard, 11 Dec 1984], 464 [Counsel Bowett, 22 Feb 1985]; *Denmark v. Norway* Hearings, CR 93/6, 60 [Agent Haug, 18 Jan 1993].

The new boundaries also necessitated amendment of the 1965 UK/Netherlands Agreement [in force: 23 Dec 1966, 595 UNTS 105] by a Protocol of 25 Nov 1971 [861 UNTS 224; Charney/ASIL Report No.9-13 (Anderson)], as further amended by the 2004 UK/Netherlands Exchange of Notes [in force: 10 Jan 2006, *UN LOS Bull.* 79 (2007 No.63); 94 (2008 No.66)] and replacement of the 1966 UK/Denmark Agreement [in force: 6 February 1967, 592 UNTS 207] by the new UK/Denmark Agreement on the Continental Shelf Delimitation of 25 Nov 1971 [11 ILM 723 (1972); ASIL/Charney Report No.9-10 (Anderson)] [both in force: 7 Dec 1972]. Cf. *Libya/Malta (Merits)* Joint Separate O., ICJ Rep. 1985, 80; Pleadings, Vol.II, 125 n.1 [Libya's Counter-Memorial], 344, 356 [Malta's Counter-Memorial], Vol.III, 45, 47 [Libya's Reply], Vol.IV, 464 [Counsel Bowett, 22 Feb 1985].

The northernmost part of the initial UK/Netherlands boundary, and the southernmost part of the initial UK/Denmark boundary became the boundary between the United Kingdom and Germany [Charney/ASIL Report No.9-13 (Anderson)]. The subsequently concluded UK/Netherlands Agreement on the

Exploitation of the Markham Field Reservoirs of 26 May 1992 [1731 UNTS 155] applies to the area extending across the dividing line as defined in the 1965/1971 Agreement between the two states [63 *British YIL* 750 (1992)].

For reliance on the *North Sea* Judgment, see *UNCLOS III Off. Rec.*, Vol.II, Statements of: Orion (Israel), 16th Meeting-26 July 1974, 144; Herrera Caceres (Honduras), 145; Galindo Pohl (El Salvador), 18th Meeting-29 July, 149; Kelly de Guibourg (Argentina), 150; Chao (Singapore), 151; Lupinacci (Uruguay), 153; Mircea (Romania), 19th Meeting-30 July, 156; Caflisch (Switzerland), 157; Yolga (Turkey), 158; Araim (Iraq), 159; Panupong (Thailand), 159-60; Kedadi (Tunisia), 20th Meeting-30 July, 163; Gayan (Mauritius), 163; Jacovides (Cyprus), 163; Lysaght (Ireland), 165; Sobarzo (Mexico), 166; Robinson (Jamaica), 167-168; Bellizzi (Malta), 168-169; Al-Nimer (Bahrain), 22nd Meeting-31 July 1974, 171 (1975). Cf. also Vol.V, Guney (Turkey), 61st Meeting-6 April 1976, 30, and Vol. XIV, Yolga (Turkey), 140th Meeting-27 August 1980, 79 (1982); *Libya/Malta* Pleadings, Vol.I, 105-107 [Memorial of Libya]. The Netherlands Draft of 19 July 1974 was amongst the first attempts to combine the application of equitable principles with equidistance [Doc. A/CONF.62/C.2/L.14, in Vol.III, 190 (1975), and Statement of Riphagen (NL), 28th Meeting-6 August 1974, Vol.II, 218. Cf. Statement of Kiaer (Denmark), 20th Meeting-30 July 1974, Vol.II, 162.

During the *North Sea* proceedings, Germany claimed that the principle of a "just and equitable share" belonged to the realm of the general principles of law to which the international judge was authorized to recur in order to avoid a *non liquet*. Denmark and the Netherlands – which countered the validity of the "just and equitable share" principle within the meaning of Article 38(1)(c) of the ICJ Statute – alleged that the FRG was virtually asking the Court to pronounce a *non liquet* or "a thinly disguised *non liquet*", and to remand the cases back to the parties for another round of negotiations. Germany found this criticism as not being justified and as putting the legal issue before the Court into a wrong perspective. See *North Sea* Pleadings, Vol.I, 393 [FRG Reply], 456, 468, 521-522 [Common Rejoinder of Denmark/NL], and Vol.II, 9-10 [Agent Jaenicke, 23 Oct 1968], 98, 117 [Counsel Sir Humphrey Waldock, 29 and 30 Oct 1968]. Cf. also *Corfu Channel (Merits)* Dissent Azevedo, ICJ Rep. 1949, 83; 1988 *Taba* Award [*infra*], paras 216-225, 239, Dissent Lapidoth, paras 150-165; *Great Belt* Oral Hearings, CR 91/13, 62 [Counsel Treves, 4 July 1991]. The unprecedented instance of a *non liquet* formula was subsequently provided by the paramount holding 105.2.E, narrowly adopted in the *Nuclear Weapons (UNGA Request)* Advisory Opinion by seven to seven votes, by the President's casting vote. See *Nuclear Weapons* Declaration Vereshchetin, ICJ Rep. 1996, 279, Dissents Vice-President Schwebel, 322-323, Shahabuddeen, 389-390, Higgins, 590-592.

Western Sahara Advisory Opinion, ICJ Rep. 1975, 3, President M. Lachs concurring, Declarations Gros, 69, Ignacio-Pinto, 78, Nagendra Singh, 78,

Separate Os Vice-President Ammoun, 83, Forster, 103, Petren, 104, Dillard, 116, de Castro, 127, Boni, 173, Dissent Ruda, 175; Order, ICJ Rep. 1975, 3. Cf. Statement of ICJ President Guillaume to the Sixth Committee, 30 October 2002 <www.un.org/News/Press/docs/2002/gal3221.doc.htm>.

For other decisions involving Morocco prior to its acquiring of independence, see *Nationality Decrees Issued in Tunis and Morocco* Advisory Opinion, PCIJ Series B, No.4 (1923); *Phosphates in Morocco* Judgment, PCIJ Series A/B, No.74 (1938); and *France v. USA Rights of Nationals of the United States of America in Morocco* Judgment, ICJ Rep. 1952, 176. On status of Morocco as a protectorate in its treaty relations with France, see *Cameroon v. Nigeria; Equatorial Guinea Intervening (Merits)* Judgment, ICJ Rep. 2002, 405, para.205, Separate O. Al-Khasawneh, 503-504, paras 18-19, Dissent Ajibola, 570, para.117 <www.icj-cij.org>.

On the dispute over the future of the Western Saharan territory, formerly the Spanish colony of Rio de Oro and Sakiet El Hamra and the current Sahrawi Arab Democratic Republic, possessing 1,062 km long sea coast [<www.mbendi.co.za/land/af/ws/p0005.htm>; <www.cia.gov/cia/publications/factbook/geos/wi.html>], see 70 AJIL 694 (1976); 49 BYIL 119 (1978); Joint Statement of East Timor and Sahrawi Republic of 24 May 2002 <http://iiasnt.leidenuniv.nl:8080/DR/2002/05/DR_2002_05_27/29>; Oil Deals Cause Concern, 6 Feb 2002 <http://allafrica.com/stories/200202060354.html>; Protests Against "Illegal" Oil Exploration off Western Sahara, 28 Oct 2001, linking to news of 25 and 27 May and 11 June 2002 <www.afrol.com/News2001/wsa013_oil_illegal. htm>; UNGA Resolutions 56/69 and 57/135 on Question of Western Sahara of 10 Dec 2001 and 11 Dec 2002; Letter of 29 Jan 2002 from the Under-Secretary-General for Legal Affairs to the President of the Security Council, UN Doc. S/2002/161, 12 Feb 2002 (analyzing the legality of the offering and signing by Morocco of contracts with foreign oil companies for the exploration of mineral resources off the coast of Western Sahara); *Reports of the Secretary-General on the Situation concerning Western Sahara*, UN Docs S/2002/178 and S/2002/467, A/57/206 (2002), S/2004/325, S/2007/202; UNSC Resolutions S/RES/1495 (2003) & S/RES/1541 (2004); A/59/134 (2004); S/2005/645 & S/RES/1634 (2005), S/RES/1754 (2007); UN-Led Western Sahara Talks, 18-19 June 2007 <www.un.org/apps/news/story.asp?NewsID=22961&Cr=western&Cr1=sahara>, <http://news.bbc.co.uk/2/hi/africa/6220630.stm> & <www.suntimes.co.za/News/Article.aspx?id=495497>; S/2007/385; 10-11 August 2007 <www.un.org/apps/news/story.asp?NewsID=23494&Cr=western&Cr1=sahara & www.washingtontimes.com/article/20070810/FOREIGN/108100049/1003>; UN Docs S/2007/619 and S/RES/1783 (2007); S/2008/45; 7-9 Jan 2008 <www.un.org/apps/news/story.asp?NewsID=25251&Cr=western&Cr1=sahara>; 11-13 March 2008 <www.un.org/apps/news/story.asp?NewsID=2543

7&Cr=western&Cr1 =sahara>; 63rd UNGA Debates on Western Sahara Status of 7/8 Oct 2008 <www.un.org/News/Press/docs//2008/gaspd397.doc.htm & *id.* gaspd398.doc.htm> and 10 Oct 2008 <www.un.org/News/Press/docs//2008/gaspd 400.doc.htm>; 12 August 2009 <www.un.org/apps/news/story.asp?NewsID=3174 9&Cr=Western+Sahara&Cr1>.

United Nations and Western Sahara <www.arso.org/06-0.htm>; UNSC – Western Sahara <www.globalpolicy.org/security/issues/wsahara/wsindex.htm & www.un.org/Docs/sc/> and MINURSO <www.un.org/Depts/dpko/missions/ minurso/index.html>; US Report on the Middle East <www.usrom.com/ Countries/usa.htm>; Western Sahara Dispute and Chronology <www.alertnet. org/thefacts/reliefresources/114044949191.htm & www.alertnet.org/thenews/ newsdesk/L18811909.htm>; <www.alertnet.org/db/crisisprofiles/WS_DIS.htm> & <http://en.wikipedia.org/wiki/Western_Sahara>.

On Morocco's Exclusive Economic Zone Act No.1-81 of 18 Dec 1980 [*The Law of the Sea – National Legislation on the Exclusive Economic Zone* 195 (UN 1986)], see *Libya/Malta* Pleadings, Vol.IV, 84-85 [Counsel Queneudec, 11 Dec 1984].

For Morocco/Mauritania Maritime Boundary Agreement of 14 April 1976 [in force: 10 Nov 1976], see *Gulf of Maine* Canada's Reply, Annexes, Vol.I-No.52; Charney/ASIL No.4-6 (Adede). On maritime delimitation dispute between Morocco and Spain (Canary Islands), see <www.afrol.com/News2002/mor015_ oil_spain.htm>.

On 1988 EC/Morocco Fisheries Agreements, see Participation by International Organizations *infra.*

Greece v. Turkey Aegean Sea Continental Shelf (Request for the Indication of Interim Measures of Protection) Order, ICJ Rep. 1976, 3, President E. Jiménez de Aréchaga concurring, Separate O. President de Aréchaga, 15, Separate O. Vice-President Nagendra Singh, 17, Separate Os Lachs, 19, Morozov, 21, Ruda, 23, Mosler, 24, Elias, 27, Tarazi, 31, Dissent Stassinopoulos, 35, *(Jurisdiction)* Judgment, ICJ Rep. 1978, 3, Declarations Gros, 49, Morozov, 54, Separate Os Nagendra Singh, 46, Lachs, 50, Tarazi, 55, Dissents de Castro, 62, Stassinopoulos, 72; Orders, ICJ Rep. 1976, 42, 1977, 3.

See also 1933 *Castellorizo* Order *supra.*

The Court's reliance, ICJ Rep. 1978, 29-37, on the "territorial status" clause in Greece's reservation to the 1928 General Act for the Pacific Settlement of International Disputes [93 LNTS 344] provided, by analogy, a significant contribution to the interpretation that a "territorial status/disputes" reservation in the Optional Clause declarations covers the continental shelf. But see Dissents de Castro, 63-71, and Stassinopoulos, 78-80. See also Exclusive Economic (/Fishery) Zone – Customary Law Status *supra.*

Cf. UN Doc. A/CONF.62/WS/26 of 4 May 1982 (Greece), in *UNCLOS III Off. Rec.*, Vol.XVI, 266 (1984), and A/CONF.62/WS/34 of 15 November 1982 (Turkey), Vol.XVII, 226 (1984); Montego Bay Statements of Kirca (Turkey), 189th Meeting-8 December 1982, and Papoulias (Greece), 191st Meeting-9 December 1982, Vol.XVII, 76-78, 110 (1984); Greece's Declaration upon signing the LOSC on 10 December 1982, *UN LOS Bull.* 29 (1994 No.25), as responded by Tukey's Statement of 24 February 1983, Vol.XVII *supra*, 242-243; UN Docs S/18759 and S/18766 (1987); A/46/87-S/22243 and A/46/98-S/22297 (1991); A/50/216-S/1995/476, A/50/256-S/1995/505, A/50/264-S/1005/526, A/50/279-S/1995/568 and A/50/300-S/1995/603; Greece's Declaration upon ratifying the LOSC and Part XI Agreement on 21 July 1995, *UN LOS Bull.* 6-7 (1995 No.29), as responded by Turkey's Note of 19 December 1995, *id.* 9 (1996 No.30), as rejoined by Greece's Note of 30 June 1997, *id.* 11 (1997 No.35); UN Docs S/1998/167, S/1998/235, A/57/641 (2002); Turkey/Greece Ties of 16 December 2004 <http://news.bbc.co.uk/1/hi/world/europe/4100871.stm> and Exchange on Imia Island of 12 January 2005 <www.turkishpress.com/news.asp?ID=35869>; Greece/Turkey Defuse Crash Row (of collision of their F-16 jets near Karpathos, about 270 miles southeast of Athens) of 23 May 2006 <http://news.bbc.co.uk/2/hi/europe/5010736.stm> and Former Greek President Stephanopoulos' Suggestion on the "Package Solution" Should Be Evaluated of 2 June 2006 <www.turkishpress.com/news.asp?id=126450>; First Russian Military Exercises in the Southeast Aegean on 3-4 and 8-11 Jan 2009 <http://en.rian.ru/russia/20090102/119334382.html>; Greece to Inform EU of Turkey's Violations of 28 July 2009 <www.chinadaily.com.cn/world/2009-07/28/content_8478989.htm>.

Tunisia/Libya Continental Shelf (Application of Malta for Permission to Intervene) Judgment [unanimous], ICJ Rep. 1981, 3, President Sir Humphrey Waldock, Separate O. Morozov, 22, Separate O. Oda, 23, Separate O. Schwebel, 35, *(Merits)* Judgment, ICJ Rep. 1982, 18, Acting President T.O. Elias concurring, Separate Os Ago, 95, Schwebel, 99, Jiménez de Aréchaga, 100, Dissents Gros, 143, Oda, 157, Evensen, 278, *Tunisia v. Libya (Application for Revision and Interpretation)* Judgment [unanimous], ICJ Rep. 1985, 192, President Nagendra Singh, Separate Os Ruda, 232, Oda, 236, Schwebel, 246, de Bastid, 247; Orders, ICJ Rep. 1979, 3, 1980, 70, 1981, 42.

Tunisia/Libya Benghazi Agreement of 8 August 1988 to Implement the Judgment of the International Court of Justice in the *Tunisia/Libya Continental Shelf* Case [in force: 11 April 1989, Charney/ASIL Report No.8-9 (Scovazzi); Francalanci/Scovazzi No.111] literally followed the geographical coordinates and elements suggested by the Court with respect to the first and second (giving a half effect to the Tunisian Kerkennahs) sectors of the boundary line. On the same day, the parties also concluded two other Agreements [*id.*] – one concerning their

Joint Development Zone in the Gulf of Gabes (El Bouri Field), with this zone being divided in two parts by the boundary, and another Agreement concerning the financing of joint projects by a percentage of oil revenues. Thus, the parties, motivated primarily throughout the long course of their dispute by their concerns with petroleum exploitation, opted ultimately for a solution of joint development, as originally envisaged in Communiqué of Presidents Habib Bourguiba and Muammar Ghadaffi of 18 December 1972 [*Tunisia/Libya* Pleadings, Vol.I, 233-237; cf. *id.* 469-470 (Libya's Memorial); Libya became an independent state in 1951 and Tunisia in 1956], and as suggested in Dissent of Judge *ad hoc* Evensen (former UNCLOS III Vice-President and *Iceland/Norway* Conciliator), ICJ Rep.1982, 317-323.

Tunisia's Declaration made upon ratifying the UNCLOS on 24 April 1985, *UN LOS Bull.* 19 (1994 No.25); Tunisia's Communication of 27 May 1994 (which might claim a CS entitlement vis-a-vis Malta), objecting to interpretation of Articles 74/83 contained in Malta's Declaration made upon ratifying the UNCLOS on 20 May 1993 [*id.* 15], *id.* 4 (No.26); 2005 Tunisia's EEZ Act, *id.* 19 (2005 No.58) and 2005 Libya's Fisheries Protection Zone, *id.* 14 and UN Doc. A/60/68 (2005); Libya's 2005 Straight Baselines and Outer EFZ Limits Decisions Nos.104-105, *UN LOS Bull.* 15, 19 (2006 No.59).

Canada/USA Delimitation of the Maritime Boundary in the Gulf of Maine Area (Constitution of Chamber) Order, electing Judges Gros, Ruda, Mosler, Ago and Schwebel to the *ad hoc* Chamber in pursuance of Article 26(2) of the Statute, ICJ Rep. 1982, 3, Acting President T.O. Elias concurring, Declaration Oda, 10, Dissents Morozov, 11, El-Khani, 12 [President Sir Humphrey Waldock, whom the parties intended to elect as the Chamber's President, died on 15 August 1981; cf. Pleadings, Vol.VII, 289]; *(Merits)* Judgment, ICJ Rep. 1984, 246, Chamber's President Ago concurring, Technical Report Cmdr. Beazley, 347, Separate O. Schwebel, 353, Dissent Gros, 360; Orders, ICJ Rep. 1982, 557, 1983, 6, 1984, 165.

The Canadian/US boundary determined by the *Gulf of Maine* Judgment has continued to impact and shape the course of post-adjudicative fisheries relations, management and conditions in the Gulf of Maine region. On Canada/USA Agreement on Fisheries Enforcement of 26 September 1990 [in force: 16 December 1991, 30 ILM 419 (1991)] and the 1991-2000 Action Plan on the Marine Environment in the Gulf of Maine Region (including Georges Bank and the Bay of Fundy), see 19 *Marine Policy* 301-323 (1995). On the US decision to establish marine protected area in the Gulf of Maine, see *Secretary-General Law of the Sea Report*, UN Doc. A/53/456, para.263 (1998); Canada/US Boundary Commission <www.internationalboundarycommission.org>. On the Northeast Consortium – U.S. Congressional policy response (since 1999) in the Gulf of

Maine and Georges Bank fisheries, see 30 *Marine Policy* 580-592 (2006) <www.elsevier.com/locate/marpol>; Gulf of Maine Action Plan 2007-2012 <www.gulfofmaine.org/actionplan/>.

On Canada/USA Machias Seal Island and North Rock dispute, see Regime of Islands – Sovereignty over Island Territory *infra*.

On possible extension of the outer continental shelf in the Gulf of Maine, see 79 AJIL 578, 585 (1985); 97 AJIL 91, 104 (2003); *Barbados/Trinidad & Tobago* Hearings, President S.M. Schwebel, Day-4, 99 [Counsel Crawford, 21 Oct 2005], Day-8, 40 [Crawford, 28 Oct 2005] <www.pca-cpa.org>; U.S. Considers Seismic Testing on the Georges Bank for the First Time in 30 years of 28 Jan 2010 <www.cbc.ca/canada/nova-scotia/story/2010/01/28/ns-georges-bank-seismic.html>.

On *Gulf of Maine* boundary, see also, e.g., *Romania v. Ukraine* Hearings, CR 2008/26, 34-36, paras 63-71 [Counsel Bundy, 10 Sep 2008], CR 2008/28, 53, paras 81-82 [Bundy, 11 Sep], CR 2008/29, 50, paras 33-35 [12 Sep 2008] <www.icj-cij.org>.

Libya/Malta Continental Shelf (Application of Italy for Permission to Intervene) Judgment, ICJ Rep. 1984, 3, President T.O. Elias concurring, Separate Os Morozov, 30, Nagendra Singh, 31, Mbaye, 35, Jiménez de Aréchaga, 55, Dissent Vice-President Sette-Camara, 71, Dissents Oda, 90, Ago, 115, Schwebel, 131, Sir Robert Jennings, 148; *(Merits)* Judgment, ICJ Rep. 1985, 13, Declaration El-Khani, 59, Separate O. Vice-President Sette-Camara, 60, Separate O. Ruda, Bedjaoui, Jiménez de Aréchaga, 76, Separate Os Mbaye, 93, Valticos, 104, Dissents Mosler, 114, Oda, 123, Schwebel, 172; Orders, ICJ Rep. 1982, 554, 1983, 3, 1984, 162.

Libya/Malta Valetta Agreement of 10 November 1986 [in force: 11 December 1987, Charney/ASIL Report No.8-8 (Scovazzi)] determined a 10-segment line precisely following the Court's Judgment.

On Malta's 1993 UNCLOS Declaration, see *Tunisia/Libya*; and on its archipelagic status, see Archipelagic State – Archipelagic Baselines *supra*. On Libya's claim to some 300 miles long closing line in the Gulf of Sidra, see Internal Waters, Territorial Sea and Baselines – Bays *supra*; 2005 Libya's Fisheries Zone, see *Tunisia/Libya supra*.

On *Libya/Malta* boundary, see also, e.g., *Romania v. Ukraine* Hearings, CR 2008/26, 36-37, paras 72-74 [Counsel Bundy, 10 Sep 2008] <www.icj-cij.org>; *Libya/Malta* Demarcation Problems of 28 Feb. 2010 <www.maltatoday.com.mt/2010/02/28/t11.html>.

Guinea-Bissau v. Senegal Arbitral Award of 31 July 1989 (Request for the Indication of Provisional Measures) Order, ICJ Rep. 1990, 64, President J.M. Ruda concurring, Separate Os Evensen, 72, Shahabuddeen, 74, Dissent Thierry, 79; *Guinea-Bissau v. Senegal* Judgment, ICJ Rep. 1991, 53, President Sir Robert

Jennings concurring, Declarations Tarassov, 77, Mbaye, 80, Separate O. Vice-President Oda, 81, Separate Os Lachs, 92, Ni, 96, Shahabuddeen, 106, Joint Dissent Aguilar Mawdsley and Ranjeva, 120, Dissents Weeramantry, 130, Thierry, 175; Order, ICJ Rep. 1989, 126. Whereas the Judgment concerned the procedural question of the validity of the 1989 Award (which it upheld), it was of direct relevance to future delimitation in that it reaffirmed the Award's findings on the validity of the 1960 Franco/Portuguese Agreement with respect to delimitation of the TS, CZ and the CS between the parties.

For Notes Verbales of Guinea-Bissau and Senegal of 14 Nov 1991 to the UN Secretariat concerning the Court's Judgment, see *UN LOS Bull.* 52, 53 (1992 No.20).

Guinea-Bissau v. Senegal Maritime Delimitation (Discontinuance) Order, ICJ Rep. 1995, 423, President M. Bedjaoui. The case was discontinued in a follow-up to conclusion of the Guinea-Bissau/Senegal Dakar Management and Cooperation Agreement of 14 October 1993 and Bissau Protocol on the Establishment and Functioning of the International Agency of 12 June 1995 [both in force: 21 Dec 1995], *UN LOS Bull.* 40, 42 (1996 No.31); *ICJ Communiqué* No.95/36; Charney/ASIL No.4-4(4) & (5) (Prescott); Guinea-Bissau/Senegal Joint Development Zone, 21 Oct 2003 <www.rigzone.com/news/article _pf.asp?a_id=9025>. Cf. *Arbitral Award* Judgment, ICJ Rep. 1991, 74-75, Declaration Tarassov, 79, Separate O. Vice-President Oda, 91, Joint Dissent Aguilar and Ranjeva, 120, Dissent Thierry, 185.

On France/Portugal Agreement concerning Senegal and the French implementing Decree of 25 May 1960 [*North Sea* Pleadings, Vol.I, 267], see *North Sea* Separate O. Ammoun, ICJ Rep. 1969, 126; *North Sea* Pleadings, Vol.II, 59-60 [Counsel Shigeru Oda, 25 Oct 1968], 112-113 [Counsel Sir Humphrey Waldock, 30 Oct 1968]; *Tunisia/Libya* Pleadings, Vol.I, 493 [Libya's Memorial], Vol.II, 108, 313, 315 [Libya's Counter-Memorial]; *Gulf of Maine* Pleadings, Vol.II, 101-102 [US Memorial], Vol.IV, 446 [US Counter-Memorial], State Practice Vol.I, 89; 1989 *Guinea-Bissau/Senegal* Award [*infra*]; *Guinea-Bissau v. Senegal (Provisional Measures)* Order, ICJ Rep. 1990, 66-68, Dissent Thierry, 83, *Arbitral Award* Judgment, ICJ Rep. 1991, 57-61, 64-66, 68-69, 71-74, Declaration Tarassov, 77-79, Separate Os Vice-President Oda, 81-85, 86-88, Ni, 96-97, 101-104, Shahabuddeen, 114-117, Joint Dissent Aguilar and Ranjeva, 124, Dissents Weeramantry, 131-134, 143-145, 150-151, Thierry, 177-178, 180-181; *Barbados/Trinidad & Tobago* Hearings Day-2, 77-80 [Counsel Reisman, 18 Oct 2005] <www.pca-cpa.org>; *Nicaragua v. Honduras* Hearings, CR 2007/2, 14, para.21 [Counsel Brownlie, 6 March 2007], CR 2007/10, 17, para.99 [Counsel Colson, 16 March 2007]; *Nicaragua v. Colombia* Nicaragua's Memorial, 172-173; Colombia's Preliminary Objections, 97 <www.icj-cij.org>; *Guyana/Suriname* Suriname's Counter-Memorial, paras 4.68/4.71 <www.pca-cpa.org>; *Romania v.*

Ukraine Hearings, CR 2008/26, 56, paras 47-49 [Counsel Sir Michael Wood, 10 Sep 2008] <www.icj-cij.org>.

On 1989 *Guinea-Bissau/Senegal Maritime Boundary* Award, see *infra*.

On Guinea-Bissau's Declaration made upon ratifying the 1982 UNCLOS on 25 August 1986 [*UN LOS Bull.* 14 (1994 No.25)], see *Arbitral Award (Provisional Measures)* Separate O. Evensen, ICJ Rep. 1990, 72; and on its Optional Clause Declaration of 7 August 1989, see *id.*, Order, 68-69, *Arbitral Award* Judgment, ICJ Rep. 1991, 61-62, Declaration Mbaye, 80, *Guinea-Bissau v. Senegal* Order, ICJ Rep. 1995, 424.

See also Settlement of Disputes – Preventive Diplomacy, C) *infra*.

El Salvador/Honduras Land, Island and Maritime Frontier Dispute (Composition of Chamber) Order [unanimous], electing Judges Sette-Camara, Oda and Sir Robert Jennings, and Judges *ad hoc* Valticos and Torres Bernardez to the *ad hoc* Chamber in pursuance of Article 26(2) of the Statute, ICJ Rep. 1989, 162, President M. Ruda, Separate O. Shahabuddeen, 165; *(Application by Nicaragua for Permission to Intervene)* Order, ICJ Rep. 1990, 3, President Ruda concurring, Declaration Oda, 7, Dissents Elias, 9, Tarassov, 11, Shahabuddeen, 18, and Chamber's Judgment [unanimous], 92, Separate O. Oda, 138;

El Salvador/Honduras; Nicaragua Intervening (Merits) Judgment, ICJ Rep. 1992, 351, Chamber's President J. Sette-Camara concurring, Declaration Oda, 619, Separate Os Valticos, 621, Torres Bernardez, 629, Dissent Oda, 732; Orders, ICJ Rep. 1987, 10, 176, 1989, 3, 129;

El Salvador v. Honduras (Revision of the 1992 Judgment – Formation of Chamber) Order, President G. Guillaume, ICJ Rep. 2002, 618, Declaration Oda, 621, *El Salvador v. Honduras (Revision of the 1992 Judgment)* Judgment, ICJ Rep. 2003, 392, Dissent Paolillo, 413 <www.icj-cij.org>, *reprinted in* UN Doc. S/2004/9, 16 January 2004.

Request of the Ministry of Foreign Affairs of Honduras to the President of the UN Security Council of 20 January 2002, in pursuance of Article 94(2) of the UN Charter, that the SC intervene and assist in execution of and faithful compliance with the 1992 Judgment, UN Doc.S/2002/108; as referred to, in *El Salvador v. Honduras (Revision)* Hearings, C6/CR 2003/3, at 8, para.1.3, at 11, para.1.16 [Agent Lopez Contreras, 9 Sep 2003] <www.icj-cij.org>. See also 2002-2003 UN Docs *infra*.

Joint Communiqué of the Presidents of Honduras and El Salvador of 29 September 1992 stated that they will comply with the Chamber's Judgment, as was quoted and reaffirmed on behalf of both states by Mr. Castaneda Cornejo of El Salvador in his Statement to the 47th UNGA, UN Doc. A/47/PV.43, 17, 21-25 (1992). In its Diplomatic Note Circulated by the Permanent Mission of Nicaragua to Other Missions Accredited to the UN in October 1993, Nicaragua declared that this Judgment "has not altered nor can it alter Nicaragua's rights in the Gulf of Fonseca or in the maritime spaces in the Pacific Ocean", and reiterated "its willingness to reach bilateral or multilateral agreements with its neighbours". See also Map <www.sovereigngeographic.com/central_america.html>; Nicaragua/ Honduras Memorandum on Gulf of Fonseca & the Caribbean of 24 September 1997; OAS Communiqué of 30 December 1999 <www.summit-americas.org/ASG/ Honduras-Nicaragua/Communique-DEC30-99.htm>; Nicaragua's Declaration made upon ratifying the UNCLOS on 3 May 2000 and Honduras's Decree No.7, Article 1.B, in *UN LOS Bull.* 13, 96 (2000 No.43) and its Executive Decree No.17 of 28 August 2000, *id.* 25 (2003 No.50); 2002 Nicaragua's Bidding Round <www .ine.gob.ni>; 98 AJIL 437-439 (2004); 1998 and 2006 El Salvador/Honduras Demarcation Treaties [*infra*].

UN Docs S/2002/251, A/57/299 and A/57/337 (2002), S/2002/1088, S/2002/1102, S/2002/1194, S/2003/306, S/2003/430, S/2003/561 – *OAS Press Release* E-095 of 30 April 2003 <www.oas.org/OASpage/press_releases/press_release.asp?sCodigo= E-095/03>; Managua Declaration on the Gulf of Fonseca of El Salvador, Honduras and Nicaragua of 4 Oct 2007, A/62/486 (2007).

On 1916 *Costa Rica v. Nicaragua* Judgment, see Inter-Oceanic Canals *supra.*

On 1917 *El Salvador v. Nicaragua Gulf of Fonseca* Judgment and 1933 *Guatemala/Honduras* Award, see *infra.*

On 1949 Declaration of Nicaragua, see *North Sea* Pleadings, Vol.I, 31 [FRG Memorial]. On 1950 Constitution of Honduras [*Anglo/Norwegian Fisheries* Pleadings, Vol.III, 693, Vol.IV, 581], see *Anglo/Norwegian* Pleadings, Vol.II, 525 [UK Reply], Vol.III, 651; *Gulf of Fonseca* Hearings, C 4/CR 91/45, 14-15 [Counsel Bowett, 10 June 1991], CR 91/46, 24-26 [Counsel Lauterpacht, 11 June 1991]. On also 1957, 1965, 1980 and 1982 Constitutions of Honduras [*Law of the Sea – National Legislation on the Territorial Sea, the Right of Innocent Passage and the Contiguous Zone* 156 (UN 1995)], see *id.* 27-29, CR 91/47, 10-12 [Bowett, 12 June], CR 91/48, 10-15 [Lauterpacht, 13 June 1991], CR 91/49, 21-24 [Agent Arguello], 38-39 [Counsel Brownlie].

On 1950 Constitution of El Salvador [*Anglo/Norwegian Fisheries* Pleadings, Vol.IV, 596, 600; *National Legislation on the Territorial Sea* 118 (UN 1995) *supra*], see *Gulf of Fonseca* Hearings, C 4/CR 91/45, 22-23 [Counsel Bowett, 10 June 1991], CR 91/46, 24-26 [Counsel Lauterpacht, 11 June 1991].

On El Salvador/Honduras Land Boundary Demarcation Treaty concluded on 19 January 1998 in implementation of the 1992 *Gulf of Fonseca (Merits)* Judgment, see BBC/CIA Notice, 21 Oct 2002 <www.americas.org/news/ nir/20021021_finding_renews _border_dispute.asp>; *El Salvador v. Honduras (Revision)* Hearings, C6/CR 2003/3, 9-11, paras 1.7/1.16 [Agent Lopez Contreras, 9 Sep], C6/CR 2003/5, 24-25, paras 3/5 [Lopez, 12 Sep 2003] <www.icj-cij.org>; 2002-2003 UN Docs *supra*; El Salvador/Honduras Demarcation Treaty, OAS

Press Release E-095/06 of 19 April 2006 <www.oas.org/OASpage/press_releases/press_release.asp?sCodigo=E-095/06>.

Denmark v. Norway Maritime Delimitation in the Area Between Greenland and Jan Mayen Judgment, ICJ Rep. 1993, 38, President Sir Robert Jennings concurring, Declaration and Separate O. Vice-President Oda, 83 and 89, Declarations Evensen, 84, Aguilar Mawdsley, 86, Ranjeva, 87, Separate Os Schwebel, 118, Shahabuddeen, 130, Weeramantry, 211, Ajibola, 280, Dissent Fischer, 304; Orders, ICJ Rep. 1988, 66, 1990, 89.

Denmark/Norway Oslo Agreement on Delimitation of the Continental Shelf in the Area Between Jan Mayen and Greenland and on the Boundary Between the Fishery Zones in the Area of 18 Dec 1995 [in force: upon signature, *UN LOS Bull.* 59 (1996 No.31)], Denmark (Greenland)/Iceland Delimitation Agreement and Additional Denmark /Norway Protocol of 11 Nov 1997 [in force: 27 May 1998, *id.* 35, 37 (1999 No.39); 111 (2000 No.43); 2074 UNTS 58, 61; 2100 UNTS 180], Iceland/Norway Protocol of 11 Nov 1997 [in force: 27 May 1998, *UN LOS Bull.* 38 (1999 No.39)] implemented the Court's Judgment and fixed the tripoint; Charney/ASIL Reports Nos 9-4(2), 9-19, 9-19(2), 9-22 (D.H. Anderson). See also 1996 Norway's Optional Clause Declaration [1928 UNTS 85]; Denmark/Norway/Sweden Agreement, Stockholm, 25 Jan 1994 [in force: 9 April 1995, 2090 UNTS 229] amending 1983 North Sea Pollution Agreement. Cf. 13 IJMCL 607 (1998); Regime of Islands – Kolbeinsey rock *infra*.

On discovery of Jan Mayen Island in 1614 by Dutch after whom it was named, see *Eastern Greenland* Pleadings, PCIJ Series C, No.63, 744-745, 755 [Denmark's Reply]. On establishment in 1922 and early operation of meteorological station on the Jan Mayen Island, see *Eastern Greenland* Pleadings, PCIJ Series C, No.62, 226-229 [Norway's Counter-Memorial]; PCIJ Series C, No.63, 1073-1077 [Norway's Rejoinder]; *Denmark v. Norway* Judgment, ICJ Rep. 1993, 44. On the island's present LORAN-C station, see *id.* 46, 73-74, Separate O. Ajibola, 299, Dissent Fischer, 310; Denmark's Memorial, paras 194-207, Norway's Counter-Memorial, paras 78-109, 586-594, Appendixes 1-2, Denmark's Reply, paras 52-71; GJM 92/2 Add., Annex 95 (25 Nov 1992); Hearings, CR 93/1Corr., 27 [Agent Lehmann, 11 Jan 1993], 37 [Counsel Thomsborg], CR 93/4, 24 [Counsel Bowett, 14 Jan], CR 93/5, 33-39 [Agent Tresselt, 15 Jan 1993].

On Svalbard Archipelago (Spitzbergen, Bear and Hopen Islands), including Spitzbergen Treaty of 9 February 1920 [in force: 1925, 2 LNTS 7; Denmark's Reply, Annexes 79-80] and the EEZ claim, see *Legal Status of Eastern Greenland* Judgment, PCIJ Series A/B, No.53 (1933) – Judgment, 36, 47, 60, 69-70, Dissent Anzilotti, 86-87, 115; Pleadings, PCIJ Series C, No.62, 41-42 [Denmark's Memorial], 385, 388, 397, 406-407, 412-413 [Norway's Counter-Memorial], No.63, 663-664, 756, 908 [Denmark's Reply], 1194-1195 [Norway's Rejoinder],

No.64, 1871, No.66, 2871 [Counsel de Visscher, 29 Nov 1932]; *Anglo/Norwegian Fisheries* Pleadings, Vol.I, 241 [Norway's Counter-Memorial]; *Denmark v. Norway* Judgment, ICJ Rep. 1993, 75, 76, Dissent Fischer, 313; Denmark's Reply, paras 52-71, 277-298, 433, Norway's Rejoinder, paras 633-641; Hearings, CR 93/1Corr., 38 [Counsel Thomsborg, 11 Jan 1993], CR 93/3, 30-37 [Agent Magid, 13 Jan], CR 93/4, 23-24 [Counsel Bowett, 14 Jan], CR 93/5, 24 [Agent Haug, 15 Jan], 39 [Agent Tresselt], CR 93/10, 45-47 [Magid, 25 Jan 1993]; 1996 *Public Prosecutor v. Haraldsson et al. (Abel Island)* Judgment of Norway's Supreme Court, 11 IJMCL 576-580 (1996); D.H. Anderson, 40 ODIL 373-384 (2009).

On Denmark/Norway Agreement on the Continental Shelf Delimitation of 8 December 1965 [in force: 22 June 1966], as Amended on 24 April 1968 [634 UNTS 71, 414; Charney/ASIL Report No.9-9 (Anderson)], see *North Sea* Separate O. Ammoun, 129, Dissent Tanaka, 174; *North Sea* Pleadings, Vol.I, 23 [FRG Memorial], 194 [Denmark's Counter-Memorial], 325, 347 [NL Counter-Memorial]; *Tunisia/Libya (Merits)* Separate O. de Arechaga, ICJ Rep. 1982, 111-112; *Gulf of Maine* Pleadings, Vol.IV, 437 [US Counter-Memorial], State Practice Vol.I, 129; *Libya/Malta* Pleadings, Vol.I, 119 [Libya's Memorial], Vol.II, 343-344, 356 [Malta's Counter-Memorial], Vol.III, 43 [Libya's Reply], 262 [Malta's Reply]; *Denmark v. Norway* Judgment, ICJ Rep. 1993, 48-56, Separate Os Oda, 104, Weeramantry, 263, Ajibola, 282, 283-284, Dissent Fischer, 304; Norway's Counter-Memorial, paras 337-339, 539, Denmark's Reply, paras 336-350, Norway's Rejoinder, paras 172-194, 213-218; Hearings, CR 93/2, 60-62, 70-71 [Counsel de Arechaga, 12 Jan 1993], CR 93/5, 21-24 [Agent Haug, 15 Jan], CR 95/6, 8-37, 59 [18 Jan], CR 93/10, 35-42 [Agent Magid, 25 Jan], CR 93/11, 36-37 [Haug, 27 Jan 1993]; *Libya/Chad* Separate O. Ajibola, ICJ Rep. 1994, 58.

On Denmark(Faroes)/Norway Maritime Boundary Agreement of 15 June 1979 [in force: 3 June 1980; Charney/ASIL Report No.9-1 (Anderson)], see *Gulf of Maine* Pleadings, Vol.IV, 437 [US Counter-Memorial], State Practice Vol.I, 603; *Libya/Malta* Pleadings, Vol.I, 436, 466, 497 [Malta's Memorial], Vol.II, 127, 157 [Libya's Counter-Memorial], Vol.IV, 121 [Counsel Colliard, 12 Dec 1984]; *Denmark v. Norway* Judgment, ICJ Rep. 1993, 51, 55; Denmark's Memorial, para.289, Norway's Counter-Memorial, paras 354, 541, Denmark's Reply, paras 342-344, 381, Norway's Rejoinder, paras 195-199; Hearings, CR 93/2, 62-65 [Counsel de Arechaga, 12 Jan 1993], CR 93/6, 59 [Agent Haug, 18 Jan], CR 93/7, 80 [Counsel Brownlie, 19 Jan], CR 93/10, 38-40 [Agent Magid, 25 Jan], CR 93/11, 32 [Haug, 27 Jan 1993].

On 1981 *Iceland/Norway (Jan Mayen)* Conciliation, see *infra*.

For Norway's Declaration made upon ratifying the UNCLOS and Part XI Agreement on 24 June 1996, see *UN LOS Bull.* 10 (1996 No.32). For Norway's Maritime Zone Notifications Nos 39/40 (mainland & Jan Mayen) of 20 June 2002, see *UN LOSIC* 24, 34, 36 (2002 No.16), 57 (2004 No.19); for its Royal Decree of

30 August and Denmark's Executive Order No.613 of 19 July 2002, see *UN LOS Bull.* 21, 22 (2003 No.50), Norway's 2003 TS/CZ Act, *id.* 29 (2004 No.54), and Denmark (Greenland)'s 2004 Decree, *id.* 126 (2005 No.56) and its 2005 CZ Act, *id.* 17 (2005 No.58). On Jan Mayen's straight baselines, see also Baselines *supra.*

Portugal v. Australia East Timor Judgment – see Economic Factors/Mineral Resource Factors *infra.*

Qatar v. Bahrain Maritime Delimitation and Territorial Questions (Jurisdiction and Admissibility) Judgment, ICJ Rep. 1994, 112, President M. Bedjaoui concurring, Declaration Shahabuddeen, 129, Separate O. Vice-President Schwebel, 130, Separate O. Valticos, 132, Dissent Oda, 133, and Judgment, ICJ Rep. 1995, 6, Dissent Vice-President Schwebel, 27, Dissents Oda, 40, Shahabuddeen, 51, Koroma, 67, Valticos, 74; Orders, ICJ Rep. 1991, 50, 1992, 237, 1995, 83, 1996, 6, 800;

Orders, ICJ Rep.1998, 243, and 1999, 3, President S.M. Schwebel, on 82 Qatar's documents challenged by Bahrain. Cf. *Qatar v. Bahrain (Merits)* Judgment, paras 15-25, Separate O. Fortier, paras 1-11; 71 BYIL 357-373 (2000);

Qatar v. Bahrain (Merits) Judgment, ICJ Rep. 2001, 40, President G. Guillaume concurring, Separate O. Oda, 119, Joint Dissent Bedjaoui, Ranjeva, Koroma, 145, Declarations Herczegh, 216, Vereshchetin, 217, Higgins, 222, Separate Os Parra-Aranguren, 223, Kooymans, 225, Al-Khasawneh, 248, Dissent Torres Bernardez, 257, Separate O. Fortier, 451 <www.icj-cij.org>; Charney/ASIL Report No.7-13 (D.Colson).

Statement of UN Secretary-General Kofi Annan of 23 March 2001, UN Doc. SG/SM/7751, 40 ILM 897 (2001); Letters of Bahrain and Qatar to the ICJ Registrar of 19 and 27 March 2001, 40 ILM 898, 899 (2001); and <www.gna .gov.bh/bahrain-qatar/news /title-e1.html>; Bahrain/Qatar Joint Committee of 24 February 2004 <www.gulf-news.com/Articles/news.asp?ArticleID=111910>; Gulf Haven of 11 June 2005 <http://news.bbc.co.uk/1/hi/programmes/from_our_own_correspondent/4080452.stm>.

On Proclamation No.37/1368 of 5 June 1949 of Bahrain [*Tunisia/Libya* Pleadings, Vol.II, 490], see *North Sea* Pleadings, Vol.I, 31 [FRG Memorial]; *Tunisia/Libya* Pleadings, Vol.II, 213 [Libya's Counter-Memorial]; *Libya/Malta* Pleadings, Vol.I, 446, 449, 456 [Malta's Memorial]. On archipelagic status of Bahrain, see Archipelagic States – Archipelagic Baselines *supra.*

Cameroon v. Nigeria Land and Maritime Boundary (Request for the Indication of Provisional Measures) Order, ICJ Rep. 1996, 13, President M. Bedjaoui and Vice-President S.M. Schwebel concurring, Declarations Oda, 26, Shahabuddeen, 28,

Ranjeva, 29, Koroma, 30, Joint Declaration Weeramantry, Shi and Vereshchetin, 31, Declaration Mbaye, 32, Separate O. Ajibola (dissenting), 35;

Cameroon v. Nigeria (Preliminary Objections) Judgment, ICJ Rep. 1998, 275, President S.M. Schwebel concurring, Separate Os Oda, 328, Vereshchetin, 342, Higgins, 345, Kooymans, 354, Dissent Vice-President Weeramantry, 362, Dissents Koroma, 377, Ajibola, 392;

Nigeria v. Cameroon Land and Maritime Boundary (Request for Interpretation of the Cameroon v. Nigeria Judgment of 11 June 1988) Judgment, President S.M. Schwebel concurring, ICJ Rep. 1999, 31, Dissent Vice-President Weeramantry, 42, Dissents Koroma, 49, Ajibola, 54 <www.icj.law.gla.ac.uk/idocket/inc/inccontent.htm>;

Cameroon v. Nigeria (Counter-Claims) Orders, Presidents S.M. Schwebel and G. Guillaume concurring, ICJ Rep. 1999, 983 and 2001, 9;

Cameroon v. Nigeria (Application of Equatorial Guinea for Permission to Intervene) Order [unanimous], President S.M. Schwebel, ICJ Rep. 1999, 1029 [*Indonesia/Malaysia (Intervention)* Judgment, President G. Guillaume, ICJ Rep. 2001, 588-589, 596, 606 paras 35, 48, 88];

Cameroon v. Nigeria; Equatorial Guinea Intervening (Merits) Judgment, ICJ Rep. 2002, 303, President G. Guillaume concurring, Declarations Oda, 459, Herczegh, 472, Rezek, 489. Separate Os Ranjeva, 469, Parra-Aranguren, 488, Al-Khasawneh, 492, Mbaye, 506, Dissents Koroma, 474, Ajibola, 538 <www.icj-cij.org>; and Hearings, *id.* and at <www.crtv.cm/actualite_det.php?code=563>;Colson/ASIL Rep No.4-1 Add.2 (T.Daniel);

Orders, ICJ Rep. 1994, 105, 1996, 3, 1998, 420, 1999, 24, 983; France/Nigeria Forum for Dialogue Agreement of 7 Feb 2000 [in force: *id.*, 2141 UNTS 455].

Agreement expressed by President Obasanjo of Nigeria and President Biya of Cameroon at their *First UN Summit* held with UNSG Kofi Annan in Paris on 5 September 2002 that they will implement the Court's Judgment of 10 Oct 2002 <www.un.org/apps/news/story.asp?NewsID=4627&Cr=Bakassi&Cr1> and <www.un.org/News/Press/docs/2002/sgsm8368.doc.htm>; UN Doc. A/57/380-S/2002/988, at 4-5; Statements of UN Secretary-General Kofi Annan of 10 Oct and 1 Nov <www.un.org/apps/news/story.asp?NewsID=5000&Cr=nigeria&Cr1=cameroon>, <www.un.org/News/Press/docs/2002/sgsm8474.doc.htm> and at the *Second UN Summit* on 15 Nov 2002 <www.un.org/News/Press/docs/2002/sgsm8495.doc.htm>, <www.unwire.org/UNWire/20021011/29567_story.asp & *id.* /20021118/30427_story. asp>; Nigeria's Statement Rejecting ICJ Judgment <www.nigeriaembassyusa.org/110 802_1.shtml> <http://news.bbc.co.uk/2/hi/africa/2356923.stm>; UN *Cameroon/Nigeria* Mixed Commission, *1st Meeting*: 2-3 Dec 2002 <www.un.org/apps/news/story.asp?NewsID=5537&Cr=bakassi&Cr1>, Bakassi Conflict <www.spm.gov.cm/gouv/grands_dossiers/bakassi/commissions_a.htm>;

20 Jan 2003 <http://allafrica.com/stories/200301200654.html>; *2nd Meeting*: 4-5 Feb <http://allafrica.com/stories/200302050225.html, *id.*, /200302050451 .html & *id.*, /200302060092.html>; Bakassi Conflict, *supra*; *3rd Meeting*: 2-3 April <http://allafrica.com/stories/200304040092.html & *id.*, /200304070204.html>; Statement of the UN Secretary-General, 2 April <www.un.org /apps/sg/sgstats .asp?nid=300>; Bakassi Conflict, *supra*; *4th Meeting*: 13 June 2003 <http:// allafrica.com/stories /200306140001.html>, <www.nigeriafirst.org/article_651 .shtml> and <www.afrol.com/News2003; UN Doc. A/58/177, at 3 (2003); *5th Meeting*: 6-7 August <http://allafrica.com/stories/200308040654.html>, <http:// icicemac.com/nouvelle/cm /affiche_nouvelle.php3?nid=481> & <http://news.bbc .co.uk/2/hi/africa/3131809.stm>; *6th Meeting*: 29-30 Oct <http://news.bbc.co.uk/2/ hi/africa/3224729.stm>, <http://allafrica.com/stories/200310290805.html, *id.* /200310300650.html, /200310300775. html, /200310310285.html, /200310310468 .html & /200310310814.html>; *id.* </200311140466.html, /200311170168.html, /200311190703.html & /200311210804.html>; *7th Meeting*: 2-3 Dec 2003 <www .un.org/apps/news/story.asp?NewsID=9072&Cr=cameroon&Cr1=nigeria>, <www.unwire.org/UNWire/20031205/449_11060. asp>, <http://allafrica. com/stories/200312020603.html, *id.* /200312030365.html, /200312040445.html, /200312040804.html, /200312110322.html, 200312151008.html, /200312180559 .html, /200312180592.html, /200312190357.html, /200312240232.html & /200312240289.html>; *Third UN Summit* held with UNSG Kofi Annan in Geneva on 31 Jan 2004 <www.un.org/apps/news/story.asp?NewsID=9597&Cr=Bakassi& Cr1>, <www.unwire.org/UNWire/20040202/449_12650.asp>, <http://news.bbc.co .uk/2/hi/africa/3446833.stm> and Nigeria/Cameroon Friendship and Non-Aggression Treaty <http://aol.countrywatch.com/aol_wire.asp?vCOUNTRY=31 &UID=994931>; *8th Meeting*: 10-11 Feb <http://allafrica.com/stories/ 200402161273 .html>, Nigeria's renewed boycott of the 2002 Judgment, *id.* </200402160326.html>, <www.unwire.org/UNWire/20040211/449_13018.asp>; UN Mixed Commission's Visit to Bakassi of 13 Feb <www.unwire.org/ UNWire/20040213/449_13102.asp> <www.scoop.co.nz/mason/stories/WO0402/ S00113.htm>; Resettlement of Nigerians of 17 February <http://allafrica.com/ stories/200402170235.html>; Pro-Nigerian Protesters Meet UN Commision of 26/27 February <www.rigzone.com/news/article.asp?a_id=11266>, <www .irinnews.org/report.asp? ReportID=39701&SelectRegion=West_Africa&SelectC ountry=CAMEROON-NIGERIA>, <http://allafrica.com/stories/200402270174 .html>; Press Conference of 12 March 2004 <www.un.org/News/briefings/ docs/2004/mixedcommission PC.doc.htm>; UN Docs S/2004/298 & 299; *9th Meeting – 6-7 April* <www.unwire.org/UNWire/20040409/449 _22649. asp>; Local Nigerian Leader of 21 May <www.unwire.org/UNWire/20040521 /449_24129.asp>; *10th Meeting – 1-2 June* <www.rigzone.com/news/article. asp?a_id =13588>, <www.unwire.org/UNWire/20040602/449_24449.asp>, *id.*

</20040604/449 _24515.asp>, US Navy Exercise of 4 June <http://news.bbc .co.uk/2/hi/africa/3778479. stm>; UN Doc. S/2004/612 of 29 July; *11th Meeting – 18-19 August*; Handling over Bakassi Delayed of 13 September <www.irinnews .org/report.asp?ReportID=43158& SelectRegion=West_Africa&SelectCountry= CAMEROON-NIGERIA; *12th Meeting – 21-22 Oct* <www.irinnews.org/report.as p?ReportID=43820&SelectRegion=West_Africa &SelectCountry=CAMEROON-NIGERIA>; *Fourth UN Summit* in Geneva, 11 May 2005 <www.un.org/apps/ sg/offthecuff.asp?nid=727>; *13th Meeting – 28-29 July*; *14 Meeting – 13-14 Oct 2005*; Partial UN Border Demarcation of 29 Dec 2005 <http://allfrica.com/ stories/200512290316.html>;

Fifth UN Summit held with UNSG Kofi Annan <www.un.org/sg/> in New York and Cameroon/Nigeria Agreement on Nigeria's Withdrawal from Bakassi Peninsula and Other Measures Completing Implementation of the 2002 ICJ Judgment [*supra*] of 12 June 2006 <www.un.org/apps/news/story.asp?NewsID=188 25&Cr=cameroon&Cr1=nigeria> and the Agreement's text <www.cameroon-info .net/cmi_show_news.php?id=17737>, UNSG Kofi Annan's Statement <www.un .org/News/Press/docs/2006/afr1397.doc.htm>, <www.un.org/News/Press/docs/ 2006/sgsm10511.doc.htm> & <www.un.org/apps/sg/sgstats.asp?nid=2083> and his Press Conference <www.un.org/apps/sg/offthecuff.asp?nid=884>, Cameroon/ Nigeria Joint Communique of 12 June 2006 <www.un.org/News/Press/docs/2006/ sg2113.doc.htm> and British FCO Minister Lord Triesman's Statement <www .gnn.gov.uk/Content/Detail.asp?ReleaseID=207343&NewsAreaID=2>; Niger ia Hands Cameroon Formal Control of Bakassi Peninsula of 14 August 2006 <www.un.org/apps/news/story.asp?NewsID=19509&Cr=cameroon&Cr1= nigeria & http://news.bbc.co.uk/2/hi/africa/4789647.stm>; *15th Meeting – 6-7 Sept 2006*; UNSG Letter to the UNSC President, UN Doc.S/2006/778 and UNSG Kofi Annan Hails Steady Cameroon/Nigeria Demarcation Progress of 6 Oct 2006 <www.un.org/apps/news/story.asp?NewsID=20163&Cr=Nigeria&Cr1=Ca meroon>; *16th Meeting – 6-7 Nov 2006*; *17th Meeting – 25-26 Jan 2007*; *18th Meeting – 5-6 April; 5th Special Meeting – 10-11 May 2007*, which completed maritime delimitation by finalizing the conversion of the British Admiralty Chart 3433 (1994 Edition) into WGS84 Datum and adopting the Map together with the corresponding geographical coordinates <www.un.org/unowa/cnmc/preleas/ fifthsm.htm>; *19th Meeting – 5-6 July 2007* Completing Implementation of the 2002 ICJ Judgment; *20th Meeting – 16 Nov 2007; 21st Meeting – 13 March 2008; 22nd Meeting – 20 June 2008* <www.un.org/unowa/cnmc/preleas/pr.htm>; *UNSG Ban Ki-Moon: Nigeria-Cameroon Peninsula Transfer of 14 August 2008* <www. un.org/apps/news/story.asp?NewsID=27706&Cr=cameroon&Cr1=bakassi, www .un.org/News/Press/docs/2008/sgsm11745.doc.htm, http://news.bbc.co.uk/2/hi/ africa/7559895.stm & www.voanews.con/english/2008-08-14-voa19.cfm>; End of *Cameroon/Nigeria* Dispute by 2011 of 10 Jan 2010 <http://www1.voanews

.com/english/news/africa/central/cameroon-nigeria-boundary-demarcation-voa-81094267.html>. For Communiques of all Summits and Meetings, see UNOWA <www.un.org/unowa/index.htm>; 98 AJIL 449-452 (2004); Map <www.sovereigngeographic.com>; News <http://allafrica.com/cameroon>.

On Equatorial Guinea/Sao Tome & Principe Maritime Boundary Delimitation Treaty of 26 June 1999 [*UN LOS Bull.* 39 (2001 No.47), see *Cameroon v. Nigeria; Equatorial Guinea Intervening (Merits)* Hearings, CR 2002/13, 26, 28 [Crawford, 7 March 2002]; Charney/ASIL Report No.4-8 (D.A. Colson).

On Nigeria/Equatorial Guinea Maritime Boundary Treaty of 23 September 2000 [in force: 3 April 2002, 2205 UNTS 325; *UN LOS Bull.* 68 (2001 No.45)] and Protocol of 3 April 2002 [in force: 29 June 2002], see *Cameroon v. Nigeria; Equatorial Guinea Intervening (Merits)* Judgment, ICJ Rep. 2002, 423, 440, paras 243, 284, Separate O. Mbaye, para.136; Hearings, CR 2002/6, 58-60, 62, 64-65 [Deputy Agent Pellet, 25 Feb], CR 2002/13, 26-28, 63-65 [Counsel Crawford, 7 March], CR 2002/20, 53 [15 March], CR 2002/21, 32-33 [Counsel Colson, 18 March], CR 2002/22, 33 [Counsel Cot, 19 March], CR 2002/23, 27-30, 33 [Crawford], CR 2002/26, 20-21 [21 March 2002]; Charney/ASIL Report Nos 4-9, 4-9 Add.1 & 4-9(2) (D.A. Colson).

On Nigeria/Sao Tome & Principe Joint Development Zone Treaty of 21 February 2001 [in force: 16 Jan 2003, *UN LOS Bull.* 42 (2003 No.50); Colson/ASIL No.4-10 (T. Daniel); <www.nigeriasaotomejda.com/>], see *Cameroon v. Nigeria; Equatorial Guinea Intervening (Merits)* Hearings, CR 2002/6, 58-62 [Deputy Agent Pellet, 25 Feb], CR 2002/13, 28-29 [Counsel Crawford, 7 March], CR 2002/20, 55 [15 March], CR 2002/22, 33-34 [Counsel Cot, 19 March 2002], CR 2002/23, 30-33 [Crawford] <www.icj-cij.org>; 21 May and 18 June 2003 <www.gulf-news.com/Articles/news.asp?ArticleID=88242> and <www.rigzone.com/news/article.asp?a_id=7049>, 28 Oct 2003 <http://news.bbc.co.uk/2/hi/africa/3219409.stm>; 16 Dec 2004 <www.rigzone.com/news/article.asp?a_id=18809>; 15 March 2006 <www.rigzone.com/news/article.asp?a_id=30307>; 14/16 July 2008 <www.guardian.co.uk/business/2008/jul/14/oil.internationalaidanddevelopment & www.rigzone.com/news/article.asp?a_id=64261>; 25/28 Nov 2008 <www.rigzone.com/news/article.asp?a_id=70007 & www.globalarbitrationreview.com/news/article/4953/energy-company-claims-against-west-african-states>; 15 Jan 2009 <www.rigzone.com/news/article.asp?a_id=71740>.

Indonesia/Malaysia Pulau Ligitan and Pulau Sipadan – see Regime of Islands *infra*.

Nicaragua v. Honduras Territorial and Maritime Dispute in the Caribbean Sea; Orders, ICJ Rep. 2000, 6, 2002, 216; *Nicaragua v. Honduras (Merits)* Judgment, ICJ Rep. 2007, President Higgins concurring, Separate Os Ranjeva, Koroma,

Declarations Parra-Aranguren and Gaja, Dissent Torres Berbardez <www.icj-cij.org>; UN Court Awards Honduras Sovereignty of Four Cays in Dispute with Nicaragua of 8 Oct 2007 <www.un.org/apps/sg/sgstats.asp?nid=2786, www.un.org/apps/news/story.asp?NewsID=24223&Cr=nicaragua&Cr1=honduras & www.un.org/News/Press/docs/2007/sgsm11210.doc.htm>; <http://news.bbc.co.uk/2/hi/americas/7033987.stm>; ASIL/ILIB and Insight <www.asil.org/ilib071023.cfm and ASIL Insight & www.asil.org/insights/2007/10/insights071017.html>; ICJ President Rosalyn Higgins' Statement (63rd UNGA) of 30 Oct 2008 <www.icj-cij.org & www.un.org/News/Press/docs//2008/ga10774.doc.htm>.

On 1906 *Honduras/Nicaragua Boundary Question* Award, see *infra.*

On 1992 *El Salvador/Honduras; Nicaragua Intervening* Judgment, see *supra.*

Nicaragua v. Colombia Territorial and Maritime Dispute; Orders, ICJ Rep. 2002, 189, 2003, 158; Withdrawal of 1937 Colombia's Optional Clause [2166 UNTS 3] on 5 Dec 2001, with immediate effect, in 2166 UNTS 3; 2167 UNTS 549; *ICJ Yearbook 2001-2002* 117 (No.56); *Nicaragua v. Colombia (Preliminary Objections)* Judgment, ICJ Rep. 2007, President Rosalyn Higgins concurring, Declarations Tomka, Keith, Parra-Aranguren, Simma and Gaja, Separate Os Ranjeva, Abraham, Dissents Vice-President Al-Khasawneh and Bennouna; Hearings, CR 2007/16, 47-52 [Counsel Stephen M. Schwebel, 4 June 2007], CR 2007/18, 13-15 [Counsel Schwebel, 6 June], 32-33 [Agent Paredes] <www.icj-cij.org>; *UNSG Oceans Report*, A/62/66/Add.1, para.242 (2007) <www.un.org/Depts/los/>; UN Court Rules Disputed Islands in Caribbean Sea Belong to Colombia of 13 Dec 2007 <www.colombiaemb.nl/communicadomre13dic.htm>, <www.un.org/apps/news/story.asp?NewsID=25046&Cr=icj&Cr1>, <http://news.bbc.co.uk/2/hi/americas/7142890.stm> and Colombia President Uribe's Speech <http://web.presidencia.gov.co/sp/2007/diciembre/13/22132007.html & www.eltiempo.com/politica/2007-12-14/ARTICULO-WEB-NOTA_INTERIOR-3859454.html> and Colombia MFA Press Release of 13 December 2007 <http://web.presidencia.gov.co/sp/2007/diciembre/13/02132007.html>; *Nicaragua v. Colombia* Order, ICJ Rep. 2008, 3; ICJ President Rosalyn Higgins' Statement (63rd UNGA) of 30 Oct 2008 <www.un.org/News/Press/docs//2008/ga10774.doc.htm & www.icj-cij.org> and 6th UN Legal Committee of 31 Oct 2008 <www.un.org/News/Press/docs//2008/gal3355.doc.htm>; Application of Costa Rica to Intervene under Art. 62 of the ICJ Statute of 25 Feb 2010 <www.icj-cij.org>.

On applicability to Colombia's reservation *ratione temporis* of the 2005 *Liechtenstein v. Germany (Preliminary Objections)* conclusions that the critical issue is the date of the facts or situations that are the source of the dispute, its real cause, see *Nicaragua v. Colombia (Preliminary Objections)* Hearings, CR 2007/16, 54-56, paras 33-39, 41 [Counsel Stephen M. Schwebel, 4 June 2007], CR 2007/18, 17-19, paras 23-28 [Counsel Schwebel, 6 June], 20, para.9 [Counsel Sir Arthur

Watts], 32, para.2 [Agent Paredes]; Judgment, ICJ Rep. 2007, paras 127, 131, 138-140 <www.icj-cij.org>.

See also 23 AJIL 155 (1929); 25 AJIL 328 (1931); Nicaragua/Honduras Memorandum on the Caribbean of 24 Sep 1997; <www.american.edu/TED/ice/nicaragua-honduras.htm>; Technical Report of the 2001 OAS International Verification Mission to Honduras and Nicaragua, OEA/Ser.G, CP/doc.3540/02 rev.1, 23 Jan 2002 <www.summit-americas.org/ASG/Honduras-Nicaragua/VerificationMissionReport-ENG. htm>; UN Docs A/57/219 and 261 (2002) and <www.ine.gob.ni>, 2002 Bidding Round; San Andres and Providencia <http://en.wikipedia.org/wiki/San_Andres_and_Providencia>; Colombia's President Tours Providencia of 31 Oct 2005 <http://newsfromrussia.com/world/2005/10/31/66561.html>.

Copies of the *Nicaragua v. Honduras* pleadings were – upon the parties' agreement – furnished to Colombia and Jamaica but refused to El Salvador, as referred to, in *Nicaragua v. Honduras (Merits)* Judgment, ICJ Rep. 2007, paras 9-11, 21-23, 222-225, 246, 249-251, 255-258, 312-319, *dispositif* para.321(3) *in fine*, Dissent Torres Bernardez, paras 63, 154-157; Hearings CR 2007/1, 13 [President Rosalyn Higgins, 5 March 2007], 49, para.6 [Counsel Oude Elferink], CR 2007/3, 47-49, paras 28-30, 33 [Oude Elferink, 7 March], CR 2007/5, 24-25, paras 72-74 [Counsel Pellet, 9 March], CR 2007/11, 37, para.19 [Pellet, 19 March 2007], 61, para.28, at 63, para.33 [Oude Elferink] <www.icj-cij.org>.

Copies of the *Nicaragua v. Colombia* pleadings were – upon the parties' agreement – furnished to Honduras, Jamaica, Chile, Ecuador, Peru and Venezuela, as referred to, in *Nicaragua v. Colombia (Preliminary Objections)* Judgment, para.7; Hearings, CR 2007/16, 10 *in fine* [President Rosalyn Higgins, 4 June 2007] <www.icj-cij.org>.

On *Nicaragua v. Colombia* case, see *Nicaragua v. Honduras (Merits)* Judgment, ICJ Rep. 2007, paras 9, 18, 21-23, 59-71, 222-225, 246, 251, 255, 312-319, *dispositif* para.321(3) *in fine*, Dissent Torres Bernardez, paras 34-35, 63, 154-157, 162; Hearings, CR 2007/3, 26, para.44 [Counsel Brotons, 7 March 2007], CR 2007/5, 23, paras 67-69 [Counsel Pellet, 9 March], CR 2007/6, 54-55, paras 33-34, at 57, para.39, at 58, para.41 [Counsel Sanchez, 12 March], CR 2007/11, 19, paras 34-36 (preceding paras 25-27 concern *Nicaragua v. USA* case) [Agent Arguello, 19 March], CR 2007/13, 48, para.28 [Counsel Sands, 22 March 2007].

On *Nicaragua v. Honduras (Provisional Measures)* Order of Central American Court of Justice of 30 Nov 1999 and *(Merits)* Judgment of 27 Nov 2001 <www.ccj.org/ni/ resolnes/resol42.htm>, see *Nicaragua v. Honduras (Merits)* Judgment, ICJ Rep. 2007, paras 68-70, 222.

See also Signature, Ratification and Accession – Unratified Treaties; and Reservations and Declarations *infra*.

Romania v. Ukraine Maritime Delimitation in the Black Sea Judgment, President Rosalyn Higgins concurring, ICJ Rep. 2009; Orders, ICJ Rep. 2004, 273, 2006, 110, 2007, 650 <www.icj-cij.org>.

Snake (Serpents) Island <www.korrespondent.net/main/84164> & <http://en.wikipedia.org/wiki/Snake_Island_%28Black_Sea%29 & http://en.wikipedia.org/wiki/Serpents_Island>.

UN Court Splits Waters of Black Sea Between Ukraine and Romania of 3 Feb 2009 <www.un.org/apps/news/story.asp?NewsID=29760&Cr=icj&Cr1> and Video <http://euronews.net/en/article/03/02/2009/court-settles-snake-island-black-sea-row>; World Court Opens New Era of Cooperation <http://news.bbc.co.uk/1/hi/world/europe/7867683.stm & www.forbes.com/feeds/afx/2009/02/03/afx5999663.html>; <www.rferl.org/content/World_Court_Decides_Ukraine_Romania_Sea_Border_Dispute_/13786 & www.iht.com/articles/ap/2009/02/03/europe/EU-World-Court-Romania-Ukraine.php>; <www.financiarul.ro/2009/02/03/romanian-political-class-hails-the-hague-court-ruling-round-up>; ICJ Judgment Helps to Exploit Oil Near Serpents Island of 4 Feb 2009 <www.kyivpost.com/nation/34771>; EU Welcomes ICJ Judgment <www.euractiv.com/en/enlargement/romania-resolves-snake-island-conflict-ukraine/article-179141>; Russia Considers that Ukraine Lost to Romania of 4 Feb 2009 <http://english.hotnews.ro/stiri-regional_europe-5388047-ukrainian-analyst-the-decision-the-hague-court-opens-romanias-way-for-new-territorial-demands.htm & www.regnum.ru/english/1119970.html>; Ukraine and Romania Will Duly Implement the ICJ Judgment of 4 Feb 2009 <www.nineoclock.ro/index.php?page=detalii&categorie=homenews&id=20090204-10408>.

Chile v. Peru Maritime Boundary Case; Orders, ICJ Rep. 2008, 6.

Peru Takes Chile to the World Court over Maritime Dispute of 16 Jan 2008 <www.un.org/apps/news/story.asp?NewsID=25314&Cr=ICJ&Cr1>, <www.ft.com/cms/s/0/f7c33aa6-c47a-11dc-a474-0000779fd2ac.html>, <http://edition.cnn.com/2008/WORLD/americas/01/16/peru.chile.ap/index.html> & with Map at <www.dur.ac.uk/ibru/news/>; Chile Recalls Its Ambassador from Peru of 17 Jan 2008 <www.dailycomet.com/article/20080117/API/801170699>, <http://news.bbc.co.uk/2/hi/americas/7194854.stm> & <www.eltiempo.com/internacional/latinoamericas/noticias/ARTICULO-WEB-NOTA_INTERIOR-3923549.html>; Peru ICJ Team <www.peru.com/noticias/especiales/2008/diferendo_maritimo/index.asp>.

On 1925 *Chile/Peru Tacna-Arica* Award [RIAA II, 921; 19 AJIL 303, 633 (1925); 20 AJIL 605 (1926); 21 AJIL Supp. 39 (1927); 23 AJIL Supp. 183 (1929); No.349/Stuyt], see *infra*.

On 1954 *In Re Sanger et al.* Judgment of Peru's Tribunal of Paita, see Exclusive Economic (Fishery) Zone – Evolution *supra*.

On the practice of Chile, Ecuador and Peru (CEP) regarding delimitation (by parallel of geographical latitude, and not equidistance) of their CS/EEZ, see *North Sea* Separate O. Ammoun, ICJ Rep. 1969, 126; *North Sea* Pleadings, Vol.I, 437-438 [FRG Reply], 496 [Common Rejoinder of Denmark/NL], Vol.II, 58 [Counsel Oda, 25 Oct 1968], 101, 112 [Counsel Sir Humphrey Waldock, 29 and 30 Oct], 258 [Waldock, 8 Nov 1968]; *Tunisia/Libya (Merits)* Dissent Evensen, ICJ Rep. 1982, 308; *Gulf of Maine* Pleadings, Vol.II, 101 [US Memorial], Vol.III, 239 [Canada's Counter-Memorial], Vol.IV, 444-445 [US Counter-Memorial], Vol. VII, 219 [Counsel Colson, 10 May 1984], Vol.VIII, 265 [Figures], State Practice Vol.I, 69, 73; *Libya/Malta* Pleadings, Vol.II, 110 n.5, 111 [Libya's Counter-Memorial], 298 [Malta's Counter-Memorial]; *Denmark v. Norway* Hearings, CR 93/4, 15 [Counsel Bowett, 14 Jan 1993]; *Guyana/Suriname* Hearings Day 6, 872-878 [Counsel Oxman, 14 Dec 2006] <www.pca-cpa.org>; *Nicaragua v. Honduras* Hearings, CR 2007/10, 32, para.154 [Counsel Colson, 16 March 2007] <www.icj-cij.org>.

On providing CEP – along with Honduras, Jamaica and Venezuela – with copies of the written pleadings, see *Nicaragua v. Colombia (Preliminary Objections)* Judgment, para.7; Hearings, CR 2007/16, 10 *in fine* [President Rosalyn Higgins, 4 June 2007] <www.icj-cij.org>.

1909 *Norway v. Sweden Grisbadarna Maritime Frontier* Award, PCA/ Arbitrators: President J.A. Loeff (Netherlands), F.V.N. Beichmann (Norway), K.Hj.L. Hammarskjold (Sweden); RIAA XI, 147; 4 AJIL 186, 226 (1910); No.288/ Stuyt; *Gulf of Maine* Pleadings, Vol.II, 148-169; Charney/ASIL Report No.9-14 (Anderson); PCA 1999, 51; PCA Awards <www.haguejusticeportal.net>. See also *infra*.

1951 *Petroleum Development (Trucial Coast) Ltd. v. Sheikh of Abu Dhabi* Award of Lord Asquith of Bishopstone; (1951)ILR 144; 1 ICLQ 247 (1952); 46 AJIL 512 (1952); 47 AJIL 156 (1953); *Tunisia/Libya* Pleadings, Vol.II, 469-470; No.A 1.28/Stuyt.

See also *infra*.

1977 and 1978 *Anglo/French Continental Shelf Delimitation* Decisions, Court of Arbitration: President Erik Castren, Herbert Briggs, Andre Gros (France/ICJ), Endre Ustor, Sir Humphrey Waldock (UK/ICJ); 18 ILM 397, 463 (1979); 54 ILR 139, 213; RIAA XVIII, 3, 271; No.437/Stuyt; Charney/ASIL Reports Nos 9-3, 9-3(1)-(4) & (4)Corr. (D.H. Anderson).

See also *infra*.

1977 *Argentina/Chile Beagle Channel* Award, President Sir Gerald Fitzmaurice (UK/ICJ), Andre Gros (France/ICJ), Sture Petren (Sweden/ICJ), Charles Onyeama (Nigeria/ICJ), Hardy C. Dillard (USA/ICJ); 17 ILM 634 (1978); 52 ILR 93; RIAA

XXI, 55; 2244 UNTS 83 & 2246 UNTS 71; No.435/Stuyt. The 1977 Award was rejected by Argentina in 1978 [17 ILM 738, 750 (1978); followed by Proposal of H.H. Pope John Paul II of 1980 and final settlement of 1984, 24 ILM 1 (1985); No. D 2/Stuyt; RIAA XXI, 240; Charney/ASIL Report No.3-1 (Jiménez de Aréchaga).

See also *infra*.

1981 *Dubai/Sharjah Boundary* Award, Court of Arbitration: President Philippe Cahier (France), John L. Simpson (UK), Kenneth R. Simmonds (UK); 91 ILR 543; No.438/Stuyt; Charney/ASIL Report No.7-4 (Petrovski) & Add.1 (Charney). See also *infra*.

1981 *Iceland/Norway (Jan Mayen) Continental Shelf* Commision, Conciliators: Chairman Elliot L. Richardson (USA), Hans G. Andersen (Iceland), Jens Evensen (Norway/ICJ); 20 ILM 797 (1981); No.B 18/Stuyt; Charney/ASIL Report No.9-4 (Anderson); 1981 Agreement, 21 ILM 1222 (1982); 2124 UNTS 247 and 1997 Protocol, 2127 UNTS 227, 237; Colson/ASIL Report No.9-4(2).

See also *infra*.

1985 *Guinea/Guinea-Bissau Delimitation of the Maritime Boundary* Award, Arbitration Tribunal: Manfred Lachs (Poland/ICJ), Keba Mbaye (Senegal/ICJ), Mohammed Bedjaoui (Algeria/ICJ); 89 RGDIP 484 (1985); 25 ILM 251 (1986); No.441/Stuyt; Charney/ASIL Reports Nos 4-3 (Adede) & 4-3 Add.1/Corr1.

See also *infra*.

1988 *Egypt/Israel Taba Beachfront Boundary* Award, Arbitral Tribunal: President Gunnar Lagergren (Sweden), Pierre Bellet, Dietrich Schindler, Hamed Sultan (Egypt), Ruth Lapidoth (Israel); 80 ILR 226; 27 ILM 1421 (1988); 28 ILM 611 (1989); No.449/Stuyt.

See also *infra*.

1989 *Guinea-Bissau/Senegal Maritime Boundary* Award, Arbitral Tribunal: President Julio A. Barberis (Argentina), Mohammed Bedjaoui (Algeria/ICJ), Andres Gros (France/ICJ); 94 RGDIP 204 (1990); 83 ILR 1; No.443/Stuyt; Charney/ASIL Report No.4-4 (Adede) & (4)/(5) (Prescott).

See also *infra*.

1992 *Canada/France (St. Pierre & Miquelon) Delimitation of the Maritime Areas* Award, Arbitral Tribunal: President Eduardo Jimenez de Arechaga (Uruguay/ICJ), Allan E. Gotlieb (Canada), Prosper Weil (France), Gaetano Arangio-Ruiz (Italy), Oscar Schachter (USA); 31 ILM 1165 (1992); 96 RGDIP 673 (1992); No.450/Stuyt; RIAA XXI, 267; Charney/ASIL Report No.1-2 (Smith) & Add.2 (Schneider).

France's continental shelf beyond 200 miles <www.extraplac.fr/FR/extensions/StPierre.php>; Saint Pierre et Miquelon <http://en.wikipedia.org/wiki/Saint-Pierre_and_Miquelon>. See also *infra*.

Cf. 2001/2002 *Newfoundland and Labrador/Nova Scotia* Awards *infra.*

1993 UN *Iraq/Kuwait Boundary Demarcation* Commission, Members: Chairman Nicolas Valticos (Switzerland), Riyadh Al-Qaysi (Iraq), Tarek A. Razzouki (Kuwait), Ian Brook (Sweden), William Robertson (New Zealand); UN Security Council Resolution 833 of 27 May 1993; 32 ILM 1425 (1993); Charney/ASIL Report No.7-11 (L.M. Alexander); UNCC <www.uncc.ch> & 29 Oct 2009 <www.un.org/apps/news/story.asp?NewsID =32766&Cr=kuwait&Cr1>. See also *infra.*

1998 *Eritrea/Yemen Territorial Sovereignty and Scope of the Dispute (Phase I)* Award and 1999 *Eritrea/Yemen Maritime Delimitation (Phase II)* Award, PCA 1999, 196; 114 ILR 1; 119 ILR 417; 40 ILM 900, 983 (2001); RIAA XXII, 211, 335; Arbitrators: President Sir Robert Jennings (UK/ICJ), Rosalyn Higgins (UK/ICJ), Stephen M. Schwebel (USA/ICJ), Ahmed S. El-Kosheri (Egypt), Keith Highet (USA) <www.pca-cpa.org>; <www.al-bab.com/yemen/pol/int.htm>; the Awards' texts in English and French with Introduction by J.-P. Queneudec, in *PCA Awards Series,* Vol.I <www.asserpress.nl & www.pca-cpa.org/showpage.asp?pag_id=1056>; Charney/ASIL Report No.6-14. See also *infra.*

Press Statement of U.S. Department of State of 19 October 1998 <http://secretary. state.gov/www/briefings/statements/1998/ps981019c.html>; Statement of Eritrea's Ministry of Foreign Affairs of 20 December 1999, UN Doc. S/1999/1265, and Interview with Yemen's Vice-Minister of Foreign Affairs <www.y.net.ye/yementimes/99/iss51/interview. html>. On Eritrea/Yemen Meeting on 27 March 2002, see <http://globalarchive.ft.com /globalarchive/article.html?id=020329004725&query=eritrea>; and on their Meeting on 8-10 May 2002, see <www.yementimes.com/02/iss20/In.htm>; Military Stalks Terrorists in Africa/HOA of 31 Dec 2003 <http://washingtontimes.com/world/20031231-083517-2847r.htm>; Eritrean President's Message to Yemen's President of 4 January 2004 <www.shabait.com/articles/publish/article_1387.html> & <www.ethioindex.com/medrek/viewtopic.php?t=4566>; Eritrea/Hardman MOU on Offshore Massawa Block (Dahlaks) Exploration of 5 Jan 2004 <www.rigzone.com/news/article.asp?a_id=10237>; Counter-Terrorism in the Horn of Africa <www.usip.org/pubs/specialreports/sr113.html>; May 2006 <www.iht.com/articles/2006/05/29/opinion/edhorn.php>; 23 May 2007 <www.navytimes.com/news/2007/05/navy_africa_admiral_070523w/> and 3 Oct 2008 <www.navytimes.com/news/2008/10/military_africacommand_100108w/>; Eritrea's Oil Exploration Agreements of 6 Oct 2008 <www.rigzone.com/news/article.asp?a_id=67506 & http://usinfo.state.gov/af>.

On 1994 Eritrea/Yemen Memorandum and 1998 Joint Committee for Bilateral Cooperation Treaty, see Protection of the Marine Environment *infra.*

2002 UN *Eritrea/Ethiopia Delimitation of the Border (Merits)* Decision of 13 April (S/2002/423; 41 ILM 1057 (2002)), *(Interpretation)* Decision of 24 June (dismissing Ethiopia's Request), as well as *(Interim Measures)* and *(Demarcation)* Orders of 17 July (S/2002/853) as revised by *(Demarcation)* Directions of 7 November 2002, March & July 2003 (Encl.2, in S/2005/142), *Eritrea/Ethiopia Boundary (Demarcation)* Observations of 21 March 2003 (S/2003/257/Add.1; 42 ILM 1010 (2003)), Article 15B Decision of 7 July 2003 (S/2003/752) and Instructions of 21 March & 23 August 2003 (Encl.3-4, in S/2005/142), all of them published, in RIAA XXV, 83 <http://untreaty.un.org/cod/riaa/vol_XXV.htm>; *Eritrea/Ethiopia Boundary (Demarcation)* Statement of 27 Nov 2006 and PRs of 29-30 Nov 2006 (46 ILM 155 (2007)) and Statement of 12 Sep 2007 and Press Release of 30 Nov 2007; Commission's Members: President Sir Elihu Lauterpacht CBE QC (UK), Stephen M. Schwebel (USA), Bola Ajibola (Nigeria), Sir Arthur Watts KCMG QC (UK), W. Michael Reisman (USA) <www.waltainfo.com/Boundary/Ethio_Eritrea/Boundary_Decision.asp>, <www.pca-cpa.org> & <www.un.org/NewLinks/eebcarbitration/>; 101 AJIL 616-627 (2007). See also *infra*.

Statements of UN Secretary-General Kofi A. Annan and Security Council of 13 April 2002 <www.un.org/NewLinks/eebcarbitration/>; Statements of Governments of Eritrea and Ethiopia of 13 April 2002 <http://dehai.org/archives/dehai_news_archive /0221.html>, <www.nitesoft.com/border/> and <www.waltainfo.com/Boundary/Ethio_ Eritrea/Boundary/Latest_Statement.htm>.

UN Security Council Resolution 1320 of 15 Sept 2000; Algiers Peace Agreement of 12 Dec 2000 (Article 4) [in force: 26 February 2001, UN Doc. A/55/686-S/2000/1183; 40 ILM 260 (2001); 2138 UNTS 85, 93]; UN/Ethiopia Agreement on UNMEE, New York, 23 March 2001 [in force: *id.*, 2141 UNTS 23]; UNSG Reports, Docs S/2001/45, paras 4-6; S/2001/1194; A/56/1, para.53 (2001); A/57/1, para.39 (2002); S/2002/129, /205 & /245; UN SC Resolution 1398 of 15 March 2002; S/2002/744; UNSC Resolutions 1430 and 1434 of 14 August and 6 Sept 2002; S/2002/977 & /1393; UNSC President Statement of 7 Jan 2003 <www.un.org/News/Press/docs/2003/afr539.doc.htm>; UNSC Resolution 1466 of 14 March 2003; S/2003/257 & Add.1; ACP-EU Joint Parliamentary Assembly Resolution on the Situation in East Africa of 3 April 2003, preambular paras B-D and paras 1/4 <www.europarl.eu.int/intcoop/acp/60_05/pdf/resolution_17_en.pdf> and <www.biddho.com/portal/article3338.html>; UNSC President Statement of 17 July 2003 <www.un.org/News/Press/docs/2003/sc7817.doc.htm>; UN Docs S/2003/665 and Add.1, /752 & /858; UN SC Resolution 1507 of 12 Sep 2003; EU Declaration of 23 Sep 2003, CFSP Press 279 <http://ue.eu.int/cms3_fo/showPage.asp?id=339&lang=en> and 19 Dec <www.irinnews.org/report.asp?ReportID=38518&SelectRegion=Horn_of_Africa&Select Country=ERITREA-ETHIOPIA>, <http://eri24.com/news4150.htm>; S/2003/1186 and UNSC President Statement of 7 Jan 2004 <www.un.org/News/Press/docs/2004/sc7972. doc.htm>; S/2004/116, S/2004/180, S/2004/543, S/2004/708; UNSC Resolutions 1531 & 1560 of 12 March & 14 Sep; A/59/2, at 6, 129-130 (2004); EU Declaration of 17 Dec <http://ue.eu.int/ueDocs/cms_Data/docs/pressData/en/cfsp/83198.pdf>; UNSC Press Statement of 21 Dec 2004 <www.un.org/News/Press/docs/2004/sc8276.doc.htm>; S/2005/142; UNSC Resolutions 1586 of 14 March and 1622 of 13 Sep 2005 <www.un.org/News/Press/docs/2005/sc8494.doc.htm>; S/2005/553; UNSC Welcomes Algiers Agreement Meeting of 24 Feb 2006 <www.un.org/News/Press/docs/2006/sc8651.doc.htm> and EU Statement <http://ue.eu.int/ueDocs/cms_Data/docs/pressData/en/er/88497.pdf>; S/2006/140; UNEEBC PR of 13 March 2006 <http://eri24.com/news8495.htm; UNSC Resolution 1681 of 31 May 2006 <www.un.org/News/Press/docs/2006/sc8736.doc.htm>; S/2006/749 and UNSC Resolution 1710 of 29 Sep 2006 <www.un.org/News/Press/docs/2006/sc8842.doc.htm>; UNEEBC Statement of 27 Nov and PRs of 29-30 Nov 2006 and S/2007/33, at 11-16: Annex II with Enclosure (2007), 46 ILM 155 (2007) & <www.un.org/Docs/journal/asp/ws.asp?m=s/2007/33>; UNSC Resolution 1741 of 30 Jan 2007 <www.un.org/News/Press/docs/2007/sc8944.doc.htm>; S/2007/250, S/2007/440 and UNSC Resolution 1767 of 31 July 2007 <www.un.org/News/Press/docs/2007/sc9086.doc.htm>; UNEEBC Statement of 12 Sep 2007 and S/2007/645, Annex II [President Lauterpacht's 25th Report] (2007) <www.un.org/Docs/journal/asp/ws.asp?m=s/2007/645> and PCA Press Release of 30 Nov 2007; S/2008/40, at 13-23, Annex II [President Lauterpacht's 26th Report] (2008) <www.un.org/Docs/journal/asp/ws.asp?m=s/2008/40>; UNSC Resolutions 1798 of 30 Jan 2008 <www.un.org/News/Press/docs/2008/sc9237.doc.htm> and 1827 of 30 July 2008, terminating UNMEE <www.un.org/News/Press/docs/2008/sc9410.doc.htm & www.unmeeonline.org>; UNSG Letter to the UNSC President, S/2008/630 [President Lauterpacht's 27th Final Report] (2008) <www.un.org/Docs/journal/asp/ws.asp?m=s/2008/630 & www.un.org/apps/news/story.asp?NewsID=28548&Cr=ethiopia&Cr1=eritrea> and PCA <www.pca-cpa.org>.

For texts of colonial treaties of 1900, 1902 and 1908, see <www.geocities.com / CollegePark/Quad/6460/hf/98_6/index.html>; and for current events, see <http://eri24.com/bottom.htm>, <www.whitehouse.gov/infocus/africa/>, <www.alertnet.org/thenews/emergency/EE_BOR.htm> & <www.alertnet.org/db/crisisprofiles/EE_BOR.htm>.

See also *infra* as well as Right of Access of Land-Locked States to and from the Sea and Freedom of Transit *infra*.

2001 *Newfoundland and Labrador/Nova Scotia Limits of Their Offshore Areas (Phase I)* Award <www.gov.ns.ca/petro/documents/TribunalAwardPhaseI.pdf> and 2002 *(Phase II)* Award <http://law.unb.ca/library/boundaryarbitration/>,

<www.gov.ns.ca/ & www.nr.gov.nl.ca>, Arbitrators: President Gerard V. La Forest (Canada), Leonard H. Legault (Canada), James R. Crawford (UK).

Press Statement of Newfoundland and Labrador of 2 April 2002, including Maps <www.releases.gov.nl.ca/releases/2002/mines&en/0402n01.htm>, <www.worldcat.org/oclc/50523575> & <www.cbc.ca/canada/story/2002/04/02/seabed020402.html>.

See also *infra*.

2002 Sir Elihu Lauterpacht CBE QC, Judge Stephen M. Schwebel, Shabtai Rosenne and Francisco Orrego Vicuna, *Joint Legal Opinion on Guatemala's Territorial Claims to Belize* <www.centralamericaweekly.net/180/english/inter.html>, <www.belize-guatemala.gov.bz & http://vandeplaspublishing.com/>; *Belize/Guatemala* Territorial Differendum Proposals from the OAS Facilitators of 30 August 2002 <*id*.>, <www.caricom.org/belize-guatemala.htm>; Belize/Guatemala Agreement to Establish a Transition Process and Confidence Building Measures of 7 Feb <www.belize-guatemala.gov.bz> and OAS Permanent Council Resolution CP/RES.836 (1353/03) of 12 Feb 2003 on Support for the Peaceful Resolution of the Belize/Guatemala Territorial Differendum <www.oas.org/consejo/resolutions/res836.htm>; *OAS Press Releases* E-168/03 of 29 August <www.oas.org/OASpage/press_releases/press_release.asp?sCodigo=E-168/03>, E-193/03 of 7 Oct 2003 <www.oas.org/OASpage/press_releases/press_release.asp?s Codigo=E-193/03>, E-82/04 of 10 May 2004 <www.oas.org/OASpage/press_releases /press_release.asp?sCodigo=E-082/04> and OAS *Belize/Guatemala* Documents <www.oas.org/documents/eng/belizeguatemala.asp>; PRs of 15 Nov 2005 <www.belize-guatemala.gov.bz/press_releases/14-15-nov-2005.html> & E-023/06 of 10 Feb 2006 <www.oas.org/OASpage/press_releases/press_release.asp?sCodigo=E-023/06>; PR of 29 March 2006 <www.belize-guatemala.gov.bz/press_releases/2006/29_march.html> & E-106/07 of 18 April 2007 <www.oas.org/OASpage/press_releases/press_release.asp?sCodigo=E-106/07>. See also *Nicaragua v. Honduras* Hearings, CR 2007/1, 22, paras 24-25, at 41, para.90 [Agent Arguello, 5 March 2007], CR 2007/3, 25-29, paras 42-54 [Counsel Brotons, 7 March 2007] <www.icj-cij.org>; Interview of Sir Elihu Lauterpacht CBE QC on Preparation of *Belize/Guatemala Compromis* for Submission to the ICJ of 22 July 2008 <www.amandala.com.bz/index.php?id=7217>; 12 August 2008 <www.amandala.com.bz/index.php?id=7309>; 11 Nov <www.amandala.com.bz/index.php?id=7691>; 18 Nov 2008 <www.amandala.com.bz/index.php?id=7728>; Foreign Ministers Elrington and Rodas to Sign ICJ *Compromis* in Washington D.C. on 8 Dec 2008 of 5 Dec <www.amandala.com.bz/index.php?id=7831>; Belize/Guatemala Sign at OAS in Washington D.C. a Historic Special Agreement (*Compromis*) on Submitting Their Territorial and Maritime

Dispute to the ICJ of 8 Dec 2008, 48 ILM 250 (2009); <www.oas.org/OASpage/press_releases/press_release.asp?sCodigo=E-463/08, www.oas.org/OASpage/videosondemand/home_eng/videos_query.asp?sCodigo=08-0382 & www.oas.org/Photos/2008/12Dec/07/index.htm>; U.S. and U.K. Congratulations <www.state.gov/r/pa/prs/ps/2008/dec/112975.htm & www.fco.gov.uk/en/newsroom/latest-news/?view=PressR&id=10383921>; A *Compromis* for Christmas of 8 Dec 2008 <www.amandala.com.bz/index.php?id=7839> and 11 Dec 2008 <www.caribbeannetnews.com/belize/belize.php?news_id=12840&start=0&category_id=27>; OAS Adjacency Zone and *Belize/Guatemala Compromis* of 25 Feb 2009 <www.oas.org/OASpage/press_releases/press_release.asp?sCodigo=E-058/09>.

2003 *Malaysia v. Singapore (Provisional Measures)* Order, Case No.12, President L.D.M. Nelson, paras 22(1)-(3)(e), 23(a), 82, Separate O. Rao, paras 7, 17 <www.itlos.org>; 2005 Annex VII *Malaysia v. Singapore* Award, para.23 and Settlement Agreement, preamble & para.13 <www.pca-cpa.org>. See also 1982 UNCLOS, Article 15 *infra*.

2004-2006 Annex VII *Barbados/Trinidad and Tobago Maritime Delimitation (Jurisdiction and Merits)* Award, Arbitrators: President Stephen M. Schwebel (USA), Ian Brownlie CBE QC (UK), Vaughan Lowe (UK), Francisco Orrego Vicuna (Chile), Sir Arthur Watts KCMG QC (UK), PCA <www.pca-cpa.org>, including: Rules of Procedure of 23 August 2004, Orders No.1 of 7 June and No.2 of 23 August 2004, Orders No.3 of 17 September and No.4 of 26 Oct 2004, President's Statement on Confidentiality of the Proceedings of 21 Oct 2005, Written Pleadings and Oral Hearings at IDRC-London, 17-28 Oct 2005; and see also 18 Oct 2005 <www.barbadosadvocate.com/NewViewNewsleft.cfm?Record=23172>, 31 Oct <www.barbadosadvocate.com/NewViewNewsleft.cfm?Record=23314> & 7 Nov 2005 <www.caribbeannetnews.com/2005/11/07/dispute.shtml>;

Award of 11 April 2006, RIAA XXVII, 147 <www.un.org/law/riaa & http://untreaty.un.org/cod/riaa/cases/vol_XXVII/147-251.pdf>, PCA <www.pca-cpa.org/upload/files/Final%20Award.pdf.pdf>; 45 ILM 800 (2006) <www.asil.org/resources/ilm.html>, including excellent appraisal in Chapter V, paras 219-245 of the process and law of Equitable Maritime Boundary Delimitation, combining the need for predictability and stability within the rule of law and the need for flexibility in the outcome, as developed in accordance with the UNCLOS and state practice by the ICJ and Arbitral Tribunals, having – within equity *infra legem* – both the right and the duty to exercise judicial discretion in order to achieve an equitable result; *Press Releases* of 10-11 April 2006 <www.pca-cpa.org> & ASIL/ILIB of 28 April 2006 <www.asil.org/ilib060428.cfm>; *UNSG Report on Oceans and the Law of the Sea*, Doc. A/61/63/Add.1, paras 175-176 (2006) and Award's *dispositif* with Maps, in *UN LOS Bull.* 99-106 (2006 No.61) <www.un.org/Depts/

los/>; Award's text in English and French with Introduction by B.H. Oxman, in *PCA Awards Series*, Vol.V (2007) <www.asserpress.nl & www.pca-cpa.org/showpage.asp?pag_id=1056> and Cambridge (2010) <www.cambridge.org/us/catalogue.asp?isbn=9067043214>.

Statements issued by Barbados and Trinidad and Tobago upon the Award's delivery – 11 April 2006 <www.barbados.gov.bb/Docs/FISHERIES_DISPUTE.pdf> & <www.ttparliament.org/hansard/senate/2006/hs20060411.pdf>; 12 April 2006 <www.barbadosadvocate.com/NewViewNewsleft.cfm?Record=25419>, <www.caribbeannetnews.com/cgi-script/csArticles/articles/000012/001234.htm>, <www.barbadosadvocate.com/NewViewNewsleft.cfm?Record=25408> & <www.barbadosadvocate.com/NewViewNewsleft.cfm?Record=25411>; 13 April <www.caribbeannetnews.com/cgi-script/csArticles/articles/000012/001253.htm>; 17 April <www.thetobagonews.com/index.pl/article?id=6536490>, <www.trinidadexpress.com/index.pl/article_opinion?id=151428558> & <www.thetobagonews.com/index.pl/article?id=6536488>; 19 April <www.trinidadexpress.com/index.pl/article_opinion?id=152112164>; 26 April 2006 <www.barbadosadvocate.com/NewViewNewsleft.cfm?Record=25617> & <www.acutevision.com/web/gismedia/index.php?categoryid=1&p2_articleid=11>.

On Barbados/Trinidad and Tobago Fishing Agreement of Nov 1990, see 2006 *Barbados/Trinidad and Tobago* Award, paras 48, 52-56, Map I, paras 89-98, 129, 260-262, 270; Hearings Day-5, 18-21 [Co-Agent Volterra, 24 Oct 2005] <www.pca-cpa.org>. On Barbados/Trinidad and Tobago negotiations on the new Fisheries Agreement carried out pursuant to the Award's paras 284-293 and *dispositif* para.385(3) and commitments made by the Agents, in Hearings Day-1, 12-14 [Agent Mottley, 17 Oct 2005], Day-8, 128, 130 [Agent Jeremie, 28 Oct 2005], see Statements *supra*; 24 April 2006 <www.barbadosadvocate.com/NewViewNewsleft.cfm?Record=25583>; 28 April <www.barbadosadvocate.com/NewViewNewsleft.cfm?Record=25630>; 13 June <www.barbadosadvocate.com/NewViewNewsleft.cfm?Record=26369>; 29 June 2006 <www.barbadosadvocate.com/NewViewNewsleft.cfm?Record=26599>; 28 July 2007 <www.trinidadexpress.com/index.pl/article_news?id=161182551>; 3 August <www.tobagonews.com/index.pl/article?id=12870444> & 10 August 2007 <www.tobagonews.com/index.pl/article?id=12978214>.

On CARICOM Common Fisheries Policy, see 10 August 2007 <www.barbadosadvocate.com/NewViewNewsleft.cfm?Record=32361>. See also Fishery Resource Factors *infra*.

On Trinidad and Tobago's ratification in a follow-up to the 2006 Award [*supra*] of the 1995 UN Fish Stocks Agreement, see 25 Sep 2006 <www.un.org/News/Press/docs/2006/lt4399.doc.htm>, as preceded by Barbados' ratification on 22 Sep 2000 <www.un.org/Depts/los>.

On Barbados/France (Guadeloupe and Martinique) negotiations on the Outer Continental Shelf Delimitation Agreement, see 18 June 2006 <www.barbadosadvocate.com/NewViewNewsleft.cfm?Record=26431>; France's 1978 EEZ French Guyana Decree No.77-276/170; 2009 France's Partial Submission (Antilles & Kerguelens) to the CLCS <www.un.org/Depts/los/> and France's Extraplac continental shelf beyond 200 miles <www.extraplac.fr/FR/extensions/Guyane.php>; Barbados/France Agreement of 17 October 2009 <www.caribbeannetnews.com/article.php?news_id=19370; France's d'outre mer <http://en.wikipedia.org/wiki/Administrative_divisions_of_France>.

On United Kingdom (Trinidad and Tobago)/Venezuela Gulf of Paria Treaty of 26 Feb 1942 [205 LNTS 221; Whiteman Vol.4, 789-973; *Gulf of Maine* Canada's Reply, Annexes Vol.I, 63 (No.1); termination, in 1654 UNTS 614; Charney/ASIL Report No.2-13(1) (Nweihed)], which preceded the 1945 Truman Proclamation, and which was superseded by the 1990 Treaty and 1991 Exchange of Notes [*infra*], see *North Sea* Pleadings Vol.I, 437 [F.R.G.'s Reply]; *Fisheries Jurisdiction* Pleadings Vol.I, 357 [Norway's Counter-Memorial]; *Minquiers* Pleadings Vol.II, 256 [Agent Gros, 30 Sep 1953], 353-254 [Sir Gerald Fitzmaurice, 5 Oct 1953] <www.icj-cij.org>; *Barbados/Trinidad and Tobago* Trinidad's Counter-Memorial, para.275; Hearings Day-3, 5 [Agent Jeremie], 20 Oct 2005] <www.pca-cpa.org>; *Romania v. Ukraine* Hearings, CR 2008/30, 52, para.31(3) [Counsel Crawford, 15 Sep 2008], CR 2008/32, 24-25, para.28 [Counsel Sir Michael Wood, 18 Sep 2008] <www.icj-cij.org>.

On Trinidad and Tobago/Venezuela Delimitation of Submarine Areas Treaty of 18 April 1990 and Exchange of Notes of 23 July 1991 [in force: 23 July and 8 November 1991, 1654 UNTS 293, 614 & attached Map; Charney/ASIL Reports Nos 2-13(2)-(3) (Nweihed); identical Notes Verbales of Guyana to Trinidad and Venezuela of 7 Feb 2002, *UN LOS Bull.* 62 (2002 No.48) and Trinidad's Note to Guyana of 27 March 2002, *id.* 63], see 2006 *Barbados/Trinidad and Tobago* Award, paras 51, 64, Map II, paras 85-86, 117, 163-164, 168, Map III, paras 340-341, 343, 345-348, 371, 374, 381-383, Maps V-VII, Technical Report; Barbados' Reply, paras 25, 32, 74, 193-206; Trinidad's Rejoinder, paras 196-197; Hearings Day-2, 30-52 [Co-Agent Volterra, 18 Oct 2005], Day-4, 71-73 [Counsel Crawford, 21 Oct], Day-6, 10-15 [Volterra, 25 Oct], Day-8, 131-133 [Agent Jeremie, 28 Oct 2005] <www.pca-cpa.org>. See also Trinidad/Venezuela Resume Oil and Boundary Talks of 14 Dec 2005 <www.vheadline.com/readnews.esp?id=47415> and 19 July 2006 <www.caribbeannetnews.com/cgi-script/csArticles/articles/000024/002413.htm>; Barbados/Guyana/Venezuela Notes (2008) <http://notesfromthemargin.wordpress.com/>; 2009 ICSID *RSM Petroleum Corporation (Jack J. Grynberg) v. Grenada* Award <www.globalarbitrationreview.com/news/article/5196/icsid-tribunal-criticises-oil-investor & http://icsid.worldbank.org/ICSID/Index.

jsp> and *(Annulment)* of 7 Sep 2009 <www.globalarbitrationreview.com/news/article/18758/mclachlan-griffith-appointed-rsm-annulment> and Grynberg's Video <http://video.yahoo.com/watch/3876339/10565846>.

On Dominica/France (Guadeloupe and Martinique) Maritime Delimitation Agreement of 7 Sept 1987 [Charney/ASIL Report No.2-15 (Nweihed); France's 1978 EEZ Decrees Nos 78-276/277 and 1979 Decree No.324 on Straight Baselines of Marinique and Guadeloupe, *UN LOS Bull.* 27 (2003 No.50)], see 2006 *Barbados/Trinidad and Tobago* Award, paras 163, 177, 180, 340, 342-344; Barbados' Reply, para.186; Hearings Day-4, 69-71, 102-104 [Counsel Crawford, 21 Oct 2005], Day-6, 40 [Counsel Reisman, 25 Oct 2005] <www.pca-cpa.org>. See also 2009 France's Partial Submission (Antilles & Kerguelens) to the CLCS <www.un.org/Depts/los/> and France's Extraplac continental shelf beyond 200 miles <www.extraplac.fr/FR/extensions/Guadeloupe.php>.

On Barbados/Guyana EEZ Cooperation Treaty of 2 Dec 2003 [in force: 5 May 2004, 2277 UNTS 201; *UN LOS Bull.* 36 (2004 No.55); Colson/ASIL Report No. 2-27 (Dundas); <www.stabroeknews.com/index.pl/article_affairs?id=6402111>], see 2006 *Barbados/Trinidad and Tobago* Award, paras 10, 40, Map I, paras 103, 164, 171, Map III, 349, 358; Barbados' Memorial, paras 22-24, 92; Trinidad's Counter-Memorial, paras 26-27, 188; Barbados' Reply, paras 203-204; Hearings Day-5, 35-36 [Questions Lowe, 24 Oct 2005], Day-6, 11-12 [Co-Agent Volterra, 25 Oct], Day-8, 14-15 [Counsel Crawford, 28 Oct 2005] <www.pca-cpa.org>; Barbados Oil Hopes and Submission to the CLCS of 6 July 2008 <www.barbadosadvocate.com/NewViewNewsleft.cfm?Record=35901>; Barbados/Guyana/Venezuela Notes (2008) <http://notesfromthemargin.wordpress.com/>.

Barbados Oil Bidding and Drilling in 2006-2009 of 22 April 2006 <www.barbadosadvocate.com/NewViewNewsleft.cfm?Record=25567>, 25 August 2006 <www.barbadosadvocate.com/NewViewNewsleft.cfm?Record=27517>, 28 March 2007 <www.rigzone.com/news/article.asp?a_id=43140>, 6 July 2008 <www.barbadosadvocate.com/NewViewNewsleft.cfm?Record=35901>. Trinidad Oil of 28 April 2006 <www.thetobagonews.com/index.pl/article?id=6706022> & 9 April 2007 <www.rigzone.com/news/article.asp?a_id=43622>; Barbados/Guyana/Venezuela Notes (2008) <http://notesfromthemargin.wordpress.com/>; Barbados Co-Agent R. Volterra, The 2006 Award and International Law (2008) <www.energy.gov.bb>. See also Mineral Resource Factors *infra*.

On Barbados' Submission to the CLCS, see Continental Shelf – 1982 UNCLOS, Article 76(8), Annex II and CLCS Rules of Procedure *supra*.

On archipelagic status, baselines and waters of Trinidad and Tobago, see Archipelagic States *supra*.

See also *infra*.

2004-2007 Annex VII *Guyana/Suriname Maritime Delimitation (Jurisdiction and Merits)* Award, Arbitrators: President Dolliver Nelson (Grenada), Thomas Franck (USA), Kamal Hossain (Malaysia), Hans Smit (USA) and Ivan Shearer (Australia), PCA <www.pca-cpa.org>, including: Rules of Procedure of 24 Feb 2004, Orders 1-6, Written Pleadings and Oral Hearings at OAS-Washington D.C., 7-20 December 2006; and see also Award Due in August 2007 of 7 Jan 2006 <http://cgxenergy.ca/News_Jan7_06_Stabroek.html> & <http://cgxenergy.ca/News_Jan7_06_GuyanaChronicle.html>; 4 May 2007 <http://cgxenergy.ca/News_May4_2007_Chronicle.html> and CGX News <http://cgxenergy.ca/news.html>.

Award of 17 Sep 2007 and *Press Release* of 20 Sep 2007 <www.pca-cpa.org> and ASIL/ILIB of 14 Dec 2007 <www.asil.org/ilib071214.htm>.

Access of Guyana to documents contained in the archives of the Netherlands Ministry of Foreign Affairs – *Guyana/Suriname* Award, paras 17-102; Hearings on 6 July 2005; Tribunal's Orders No.1 of 18 July 2005, Nos 3 and 4 of 12 Oct 2005 and No.5 of 16 Feb 2006.

Statements issued by Guyana and Suriname upon the Award's delivery – 20 Sep 2007 <www.iht.com/articles/ap/2007/09/20/business/CB-FIN-Suriname-Guyana-Border-Dispute.php & http://cgxenergy.ca/News_Sep20_2007.html>; 21 Sep <http://cgxenergy.ca/News_Sep21_20071.html & http://cgxenergy.ca/News_Sep21_20072.html>; 22 Sep <http://cgxenergy.ca/News_Sep22_20071.html & www.trinidadexpress.com/index.pl/article_news?id=161206967>; Guyana's Reply of 22 Sep to Suriname's Statement of 20 Sep <http://cgxenergy.ca/News_Sep22_20072.html>; 62nd UNGA <www.un.org/webcast/ga/62/> Statements of Guyana of 2 Oct 2007, pp.7-8 and Suriname of 3 Oct 2007 p.4 <www.un.org/webcast/ga/62/2007/pdfs/guyana-en.pdf & www.un.org/webcast/ga/62/2007/pdfs/suriname-eng.pdf>; Suriname Parliament Rejects Motion to Challenge the Award of 11 Oct 2007 <http://cgxenergy.ca/News_Oct12_2007.html & www.rigzone.com/news/article.asp?a_id=51473> [On 2001 *Bouterse* Judgment of the NL Supreme Court, see *DR Congo v. Belgium* Separate O. President Guillaume, ICJ Rep. 2002, 41, para.12 <www.icj-cij.org>].

Agreement for Establishment of Surinam/Guyana Commission of 18 Aug 1971, 1971 UNTS 194.

See also 1990 Trinidad and Tobago/Venezuela Treaty, 2003 Barbados/Guyana EEZ Treaty and 2009 ICSID *Jack J. Grynberg v. Grenada* Award under 2006 *Barbados/Trinidad and Tobago* Award *supra*.

On Guyana/Suriname dispute, see *North Sea* Pleadings, Vol.II, 46-49, incl. Map [Agent Jaenicke, 23 Oct 1968], 73-75, incl. Map [Agent Riphagen, 28 Oct 1968], 298-299 [Surinamese S.E. Werner's article in English], 386-387 [Agents' Letters to ICJ Registrar on Guyana/Suriname article of 17 & 22 October 1968].

On Suriname/France (French Guyana) Delimitation Negotiations, see 2007 *Guyana/Suriname* Award, paras 132, 226 and 391; France's Extraplac Submission to the CLCS <www.extraplac.fr/FR/extensions/geographie.php>; 2007 France's Submission (French Guyana) to the CLCS and Suriname's Letter of 17 August 2007 and 2008 Suriname's Submission to the CLCS <www.un.org/Depts/los/clcs_new/clcs_home.htm>; French Guyana Oil of 11 Nov 2009 <www.rigzone.com/news/article.asp?a_id=82325 & www.guardian.co.uk/business/marketforceslive/2009/nov/11/tullowoil>.

2008-2009 *The Government of Sudan/The Sudan People's Liberation Movement Army (North/South Sudan) Abyei Boundary* Arbitral Tribunal, comprising President Pierre-Marie Dupuy (France), Stephen M. Schwebel (USA), Awn Al-Khasawneh (Jordan), Gerhard Hafner (Austria) and W. Michael Reisman (USA), PCA <www.pca-cpa.org>, including Arbitration Agreement of 7 July 2008, Terms of Appointment of 24 Nov 2008, Preliminary Procedural Meeting – Hearings at PCA, 24 Nov 2008, Written Pleadings and Oral Hearings at PCA, 18-23 April 2009; Abyei Road Map Agreement of 8 June 2008 <www.sudantribune.com/spip.php?article27519 & http://news.bbc.co.uk/2/shared/bsp/hi/pdfs/08_06_08_abyei.pdf> and 2005 Abyei Boundaries Commission <www.sudantribune.con/spip.php?article25125 & www.sudanarchive.net/cgi-bin/sudan?a=d&d=Dl1d18>; U.S. GOSS Press Release <www.gossmission.org/goss/index.php?option=con_content&task=view&id=534&Itemid =1> and PILPG <www.pilpg.org/sudan/>; 1 Sep 2008 <www.globalarbitrationreview.com/news/article/4740/panel-nearly-completed-sudan-pca-arbitration>; 31 Oct 2008 <www.globalarbitrationreview.com/news/article/14904/dupuy-preside-sudan-dispute/>; 17 April 2009 <www.globalarbitrationreview.com/news/article/15231>.

Final *Abyei Boundary* Award of 22 July 2009 and *Press Release* <www.pca-cpa.org>; *Abyei* Homepage <www.sudantribune.com/spip.php?mot99>; UNSG Ban Ki-Moon's Statement Welcomes the *Abyei* Award as Major Contribution to Peace of 22 July 2009 <www.un.org/apps/news/story.asp?NewsID=31544&Cr=Abyei&Cr1 & www.un.org/apps/sg/sgstats.asp?nid=3990>; An International Court Affirms Northern Boundary and Redefines the Eastern and Western Boundaries of Abyei ("Kashmir" of Sudan) of 22 July 2009 <www.nation.co.ke/News/africa/-/1066/627998/-/138pi99z/-/index.html, www.globalarbitrationreview.com/news/article/18363 & www.voanews.com/english/2009-07-22-voa40.cfm>; Joint SPLM-NPC Statement on Implementation of the Final Abyei Award of 22 July 2009 <www.gossmission.org/goss/index.php?option=com_content&task=view&id=928&Itemid=1>; Hague Border Ruling Raises Big Peace Hopes in Sudan of 22 July 2009 <http://news.bbc.co.uk/2/hi/africa/8162690.stm, www.haguejusticeportal

.net/eCache/DEF/10/881.TGFuZz1FTg.html, www.alertnet.org/thenews/newsdesk/LM233012.htm, www.euronews.net/2009/07/22/north-and-south-sudan-agree-oil-region-deal/ & www.sudantribune.com/spip.php?article31901, *id.* 31902, *id.* 31903>; ASIL Insights on the *Abyei Boundary* Award by John R. Crook of 16 Sep 2009 <www.asil.org/insights090916.cfm> and 21 Nov 2009 at BIICL <www.biicl.org/events/view/-/id/462>.

2003- *Gabon/Equatorial Guinea Sovereignty over Islands in the Corisco Bay* Good Offices of the UN Secretary-General/Judge L. Yves Fortier CC, QC of 23 Jan 2004 <www.un.org/apps/news/story.asp?NewsID=9499&Cr=gabon&Cr1=guinea>; 19 March <http://aol.countrywatch.com/aol_wire.asp?vCOUNTRY=62&UID=1044031>; 6/7 July 2004 <www.un.org/News/Press/docs/2004/sgsm9407.doc.htm & www.irinnews.org/report.aspx?reportid=50522>; Gabon/Equatorial Guinea Convention Demarcating the Land and Maritime Frontiers of 12 Sep 1974, 2248 UNTS 93 and Equatorial Guinea's Second and Third Objections of 7 and 26 April 2004, 2261 UNTS 308, 319; UNSG Kofi Annan Reopens Talks of 28 Feb 2006 <www.irinnews.org/Report.aspx?ReportID=58282>; UNSG Kofi Annan's Visit on 23-24 March 2006 <www.un.org/apps/news/story.asp?NewsID=17932&Cr=annan&Cr1=travel & www.scoop.co.nz/stories/WO0603/S00457.htm>; UNSG Ban Ki-Moon Resumes UN Equatorial Guinea/Gabon Mediation of 11 June 2008 <www.un.org/apps/news/story.asp?NewsID=26979&Cr=gabon&Cr1, www.un.org/News/Press/docs/2008/sgsm11633.doc.htm, www.un.org/News/Press/docs//2008/sgsm11634.doc.htm, www.un.org/apps/sg/sgstats.asp?nid=3226 & www.unmultimedia.org/photo/detail/180/0180512.html>; UN *Equatorial Guinea/Gabon Corisco Bay* Will Be ReChannelled Into the ICJ of 22 July 2008 <www.un.org/apps/news/story.asp?NewsID=27446&Cr=Gabon&Cr1> and 17 Sep 2008 <www.un.org/apps/news/story.asp?NewsID=28087&Cr=gabon&Cr1>; Declarations under UNCLOS Article 298(1)(a) of Equatorial Guinea of 21 July 1997, in *UN LOS Bull.* 14 (2002 No.49) and Gabon of 23 Jan 2009, in *UN LOS Bull.* 13 (2009 No.69) <www.un.org/Depts/los/>; Gabon Oil of 8 July 2008 <www.rigzone.com/news/article.asp?a_id=63821>; Equatorial Guinea Oil of 1 Sep 2008 <www.rigzone.com/news/article.asp?a_id=66071 with Map at www.rigzone.com/news/image_detail.asp?img_id=3993&a_id=66071> and Oil Maps <www.rigzone.com/news/image_results.asp?ctry_id=73>; Profiles of Gabon & Equatorial Guinea <www.eia.doe.gov/emeu/cabs/gabon.html, www.state.gov/r/pa/ei/bgn/7221.htm> & <http://news.bbc.co.uk/2/hi/africa/country_profiles>.

1999- *Guyana/Venezuela* Good Offices of the UN Secretary-General, Venezuela <www.mre.gov.ve/metadot/index.pl?iid=3136&isa=Category>; Guyana <www.guyana.org/spanish/Guyana_mycountry.html>; Map <www.sovereigngeographic.htm>; Ambassador Odeen Ishmael, The Guyana Story (1998-2003) <www.guyana.org/features/guyanastory/guyana_story.html>; *CARICOM Press*

Releases Nos 109/1999, 91/2000, 36/2001, 78/2001, 98/2001, 61/2002, 91/2002, 36/2003, 71/2003 <www.caricom.org>; Venezuelan President's Rafael Cardela's Visit to the ICJ, *ICJ Press Release* No.1998/09 of 16 March 1998 <www.icj-cij.org/icjwww/ipresscom/iPress1998/ipr9809.htm & www.icj-cij.org/icjwww/ipresscom/ipreven.htm>; UN Secretary-General Kofi A. Annan's Good Offices, 29 Sep 2003 <www.un.org/apps/news/story.asp?NewsID=8402&Cr=venezuela &Cr1 & www.un.org/News/briefings/docs/2003/db092903.doc.htm>, <www.scoop.co.nz/mason/stories/WO0309/S00353.htm>; 30 Sep 2004 <http://cgxenergy.ca/news/News_Sep30_04.html>; 12 Jan 2006 <www.stabroeknews.com/index.pl/article_editorial?id=41278928> & <www.vheadline.com/readnews.asp?id=47689>; 5 Feb 2006 <http://cgxenergy.ca/GuyanaChronicle-Feb5_06.html>; 26 Jan 2007 <www.un.org/News/Press/docs/2007/sgsm10854.doc.htm & www.un.org/apps/news/story.asp?NewsID=21351&Cr=Guyana&Cr1=venezuela>; 4 May 2007 <http://cgxenergy.ca/News_May4_2007_Chronicle.html>; 31 July 2007 <http://cgxenergy.ca/News_July_31_2007.html>; UN *Guyana/Venezuela* Mediation to Be Re-activated, 17 & 25 Nov 2007 <http://news.bbc.co.uk/2/hi/americas/7099476.stm> & <www.stabroeknews.com/index.pl/article_general_news?id=56533840>; 17 Dec 2007, www.caribbeannetnews.com/venezuela/venezuela.php?news_id=5031&start=0&cat_id=12; Venezuela-Guyana-Suriname Gas Pipeline Proposal, 8 July 2008 <www.caribbeannetnews.com/venezuela/venezuela.php?news_id=9013>; Barbados/Guyana/Venezuela Notes (2008) <http://notesfromthemargin.wordpress.com/>.

See also *infra* and the 1899 *UK(Guyana)/Venezuela Boundary* Award *infra.*

2009- Annex VII *Bangladesh/India Bay of Bengal Territorial and Maritime Dispute* Arbitral Tribunal, comprising P. Sreenivasa Rao (India), Vaughan Lowe (UK), Tullio Treves (ITLOS-Italy), Ivan A. Shearer (Australia) and President R. Wolfrum (ITLOS-Germany); *Bangladesh/India* and *Bangladesh/Myanmar* Applications of Bangladesh Instituting the UNCLOS Annex VII Arbitrations against India and Myanmar of 8 Oct 2009 <http://finance.yahoo.com/news/Foley-Hoag-Retained-by-prnews-3825507638.html?x=0&.v=1, www.bangladesh-web.com/view.php?hidRecord=289186, www.rigzone.com/news/article.asp?a_id=81254 & http://english.people.com.cn/90001/90777/90851/6778140.html>; as referred to in Bangladesh's Note Verbale of 29 Oct 2009, para.2(a) on India's Submission to the CLCS of 11 May 2009, as preceded by Bangladesh's Note Verbale of 23 July 2009 on Myanmar's Submission of 16 Dec 2008 <www.un.org/Depts/los/clcs_new/commission_submissions. htm>; UNGA Adopts Two Oceans Resolutions, UN Doc.GA/10899 of 4 Dec 2009, Statements of Bangladesh and India, at 21-22 <www.un.org/News/Press/docs//2009/ga10899.doc.htm>; Establishing *Bangladesh/India Bay of Bengal* Tribunal of 13 Dec 2009 <www.newkerala.com/news/fullnews-10186.html>; 1 March 2010 <www.malaysianews.net/story/607142>.

2009- *Bangladesh/Myanmar Bay of Bengal Maritime Delimitation*, ITLOS Case No. 16, ITLOS Press Releases No. 140 of 16 Dec 2009 and No. 142 of 29 Jan 2010 <www.itlos.org>.

2009- *Croatia/Slovenia Land and Maritime Boundary Delimitation* Arbitration Agreement, concluded by Croatia's and Slovenia's Prime Ministers under Sweden's EU Presidency of 4 Nov 2009, with the Tribunal to be established in the year 2011 <www.mzz.gov.si/fileadmin/pageuploads/Novinarsko_sredisce/Sporocila_za_javnost? Sporazum-angl.pdf & www.mzz.gov.si/nc/si/splosno/cns/novica/article/6/26200/91b077d5f6 and Slovenia's MFA <www.mzz.gov.si/en/ministry_of_foreign_affairs/>; Slovenia's White Paper on Border with Croatia of 19 June 2006 <www.csees.net/?page=news&news_id=53452&country_id=7 & www.mzz.gov.si/fileadmin/pageuploads/Novinarsko_sredisce/Sporocila_za_javnost/AIDE_MEMOIRE-ang.pdf>; Slovenia-Croatia Border Row Heats Up of 18 Feb 2009 <http://news.bbc.co.uk/2/hi/europe/7896040.stm>; Croatia/Slovenia Arbitration Deal of 4 Nov 2009 <www.thelocal.se/23076/20091104, www.eubusiness.com/news-eu/slovenia-croatia.1as, www.dw-world.de/dw/article/0,,4860710,00.html, www.euronews.net/2009/11/04/slovenia-croatia-border-arbitration-deal/, http://edition.cnn.com/2009/WORLD/europe/11/04/croatia.slovenia.agreement, www.euractiv.com/en/enlargement/slovenia-croatia-pms-sign-border-arbitration-deal/article-187031 & http://news.bbc.co.uk/2/hi/europe/8342733.stm>; U.S. Statement Welcoming Croatia/Slovenia Agreement <www.state.gov/r/pa/prs/ps/2009/nov/131336.htm> and Statement by the EC Commissioner Olli Rehn of 4 Nov 2009 <http://ec/europa.eu/commission_barroso/rehn/index_el.html>; UK Statement of 5 Nov 2009 <www.fco.gov.uk/en/news/latest-news/?view=News&id=21136388>.

See also Signature, Ratification and Accession – Unratified Treaties: 2001 Croatia/Slovenia Maritime Delimitation (Bay of Piran) Treaty.

See also Settlement of Disputes – Definition of Obligation to Negotiate; and Equity *infra.*

"The delimitation of sea areas has always an international aspect"

Anglo/Norwegian Fisheries Judgment, ICJ Rep. 1951, 132; Pleadings, Vol.II, 429 [UK Reply], Vol.IV, 395-397 [Counsel Waldock, 18 October 1951]; *North Sea* Judgment, ICJ Rep. 1969, 46, Separate O. Padilla Nervo, 91; Pleadings, Vol.I, 177 [Denmark's Counter-Memorial], 331 [NL Counter-Memorial], 505 [D/NL Common Rejoinder], Vol.II, 104 [Counsel Sir Humphrey Waldock, 29 Oct 1968], 172-173 [Agent Jaenicke, 4 Nov 1968]; *Fisheries Jurisdiction (Merits)* Judgments, ICJ Rep. 1974, 22, 24, 191, 193, Separate O. de Castro, 80, 95, 96; Pleadings (UK), 318 [Memorial (Merits)], 458 [Counsel Silkin, 25 March 1974], (FRG),

105 [Memorial (Jurisdiction)], 230 [Memorial (Merits)]; *Aegean Sea (Jurisdiction)* Dissent Stassinopoulos, ICJ Rep. 1978, 77-79; Pleadings, 244 [Greece's Memorial (Jurisd.)], 421 [Counsel Weil, 13 Oct 1978]; *Tunisia/Libya (Merits)* Judgment, ICJ Rep. 1982, 67; *Gulf of Fonseca* Hearings, C 4/CR 91/7 [trans.], 5-6 [Counsel Weil, 23 April 1991]; *Denmark v. Norway* Separate O. Shahabuddeen, ICJ Rep. 1993, 150-151; Hearings, CR 93/3, 8 [Agent Magid, 13 Jan 1993]; *Cameroon v. Nigeria* Hearings, CR 98/4, 38 [Adviser Bipoun Woum, 6 March 1998] <www .icj-cij.org>; *M/V Saiga (Merits)* Reply of Saint Vincent and the Grenadines, para.19, and Hearings, ITLOS/PV.99/7, 9 [Counsel Thiam, 11 March 1999] <www .itlos.org>; 2006 *Barbados/Trinidad & Tobago* Award, para.365 <www.pca-cpa .org>; *Romania v. Ukraine* Judgment, ICJ Rep. 2009, para.137 <www.icj-cij.org>.

Truman Proclamation

On reference to "equitable principles" in Truman Proclamation on the Continental Shelf of 28 September 1945 [40 AJIL 45 (1946)], see *North Sea* Judgment, ICJ Rep. 1969, 32-33, 47, 51, 53, Separate O. President Bustamante y Rivero, 58, Separate Os Padilla Nervo, 95, 96, 97, Ammoun, 104, 105-106, 126, 128, 146, Dissent Vice-President Koretsky, 157, 158, 166, Dissents Tanaka, 171, 174, Sorensen, 245; *North Sea* Pleadings, Vol.I, 31 [FRG Memorial], Vol.II, 55 [Counsel Shigeru Oda, 25 Oct 1968], 97-98 [Counsel Sir Humphrey Waldock, 29 Oct], referring to "self-protection" concept, 258 [Reply by Waldock to Questions Fitzmaurice, 8 Nov], 280 [Waldock, 11 Nov 1968]; *Fisheries Jurisdiction* Pleadings (UK), 328 [Memorial (Merits)]; *Tunisia/Libya (Merits)* Judgment, ICJ Rep. 1982, 43, 92, Separate O. de Arechaga, 111, 121, 123-124, Dissent Oda, 174, 176, 184, 191, 255; *Gulf of Maine* Judgment, ICJ Rep. 1984, 293, 306, Dissent Gros, 367-368; Pleadings, Vol.II, 48 [US Memorial], Vol.V, 393 [US Reply], Vol.VI, 233, 245 [Agent Robinson, 11 April 1984], Vol.VII, 17 [Agent Legault, 3 May 1984]; *Libya/Malta (Merits)* Dissent Oda, ICJ Rep. 1985, 159; Pleadings, Vol.I, 99, 103, 111, 112 [Libya's Memorial], Vol.II, 107 [Libya's Counter-Memorial], Vol.III, 97-98 [Libya's Reply]; *Denmark v. Norway* Separate Os Weeramantry, ICJ Rep. 1993, 258, Ajibola, 293-294; Denmark's Reply, para.443; *Qatar v. Bahrain (Merits)* Separate O. Oda, ICJ Rep. 2001, 136-137, 140, paras 31, 36; *Barbados/Trinidad & Tobago* Trinidad's Counter-Memorial, para.142; Hearings Day-4, 57 [Counsel Crawford, 21 Oct 2005], 80 [Counsel Greenwood], 93 [Crawford], Day-8, 55 [Crawford, 28 Oct 2005] <www.pca-cpa.org>; *Romania v. Ukraine* Hearings, CR 2008/19, 51, para.115 [Counsel Crawford, 3 Sep 2008], CR 2008/26, 57, paras 50-51 [Counsel Sir Michael Wood, 10 Sep], CR 2008/30, 52, para.31(1) [Crawford, 15 Sep 2008] <www.icj-cij.org>.

Delimitation and Demarcation

1993 UN *Iraq/Kuwait* Final Report, 32 ILM 1425 (1993), paras 8-13, 22-26, 111-114; *Libya/Chad Territorial Dispute* Judgment, ICJ Rep. 1994, 28, para.56, *as reaffirmed* by *Cameroon v. Nigeria; Equatorial Guinea Intervening (Merits)* Judgment, ICJ Rep. 2002, 303, paras 53, 55, 80, 84, Dissent Ajibola, 555, paras 46-47; UN Mixed *Cameroon/Nigeria* Commission [*supra*]; 1998 El Salvador/ Honduras Treaty [*Gulf of Fonseca* case *supra*]; 2002 UN *Eritrea/Ethiopia Delimitation of the Border (Merits)* Decision, paras 1.2, 3.37, 41 ILM 1057 (2002), *(Interpretation)* Decision, as well as *(Interim Measures)* and *(Demarcation)* Orders and *(Determinations)* Decision, 2003 *(Demarcation)* Observations, Article 15B Decision & Instructions, all of them published, in RIAA XXV, 83 <http://untreaty.un.org/cod/riaa/vol_XXV.htm>; S/2005/142 and *Eritrea/Ethiopia Boundary (Demarcation)* Statement of 27 Nov 2006, PRs of 29-30 Nov 2006, 46 ILM 155 (2007), S/2007/33, at 11-16: Annex II with Enclosure (2007) <www.un.org/Docs/journal/asp/ws.asp?m=s/2007/33>, PCA Press Release of 30 Nov 2007, S/2008/40, at 13-23, Annex II [President Lauterpacht's 26th Report] (2008) <www.un.org/Docs/journal/asp/ws.asp?m=s/2008/40> [<www.pca-cpa.org> *supra*]; *Romania v. Ukraine* Hearings, CR 2008/19, 45-46, paras 86-91 [Counsel Crawford, 3 Sep 2008] <www.icj-cij.org>; 2009 *Abyei Boundary* Award, paras 477-482, 769 [*supra*].

Geographical Factors

Anglo/Norwegian Fisheries Judgment, ICJ Rep. 1951, 133, 139; *North Sea* ICJ Rep. 1969, 3 – Judgment, 29-32, 35, 36-37, 45, 49-51, 54, para.101(D), Separate O. President Bustamante y Rivero, 61-62, 65, Separate Os Jessup, 76, Padilla Nervo, 92-94, Ammoun, 150-151, Dissents Koretsky, 155, Morelli, 199-200, 208-210, Lachs, 239, Sorensen, 249-256; *Aegean Sea (Jurisdiction)* Dissent de Castro, ICJ Rep. 1978, 65-66; *Tunisia/Libya (Intervention)* Judgment, ICJ Rep. 1981, 9, 12-13, 16-18, Separate Os Oda, 33-34, Schwebel, 36-39, *(Merits)* Judgment, ICJ Rep. 1982, 34-35, 47, 61-64, 82-83, 86-87, 92-93, Separate O. de Arechaga, 132-137; *Gulf of Maine* Judgment, ICJ Rep. 1984, 268-273, 296-303, 318-320, 327-334, Separate O. Schwebel, 353-359, Dissent Gros, 374-381; Pleadings, Vols I-VIII; *Libya/Malta (Intervention)* Judgment, ICJ Rep. 1984, 11, Dissents Sette-Camara, 78, 81-83, Schwebel, 133, Sir Robert Jennings, 151, 155; *Gulf of Fonseca (Intervention)* Judgment, ICJ Rep. 1990, 100-101, 124-128, *(Merits)* Judgment, ICJ Rep. 1992, 586-588; *Denmark v. Norway* Judgment, ICJ Rep. 1993, 64, Separate O. Weeramantry, 262-263; and all subsequent Judgments and Awards.

See also Equidistant Line, Natural Prolongation, Islands and Proportionality *infra*; Internal Waters, Territorial Sea and Baselines – Land Dominates the Sea Principle *supra*; Enclosed or Semi-Enclosed Seas *infra*.

Equidistant (Median) Line/Special (Relevant) Circumstances

North Sea ICJ Rep. 1969, 3 – Judgment, 17-18, 20-21, 23-27, 31-46, 47, 49-50, 53, para.101(A), Declarations Sir Muhammad Zafrulla Khan, 54-56, Bengzon, 56, Separate O. President Bustamante y Rivero, 62-65, Separate Os Padilla Nervo, 85-99, Ammoun, 120-131, 143-145, 148-152, Dissent Vice-President Koretsky, 154-170, Dissents Tanaka, 171-196, Morelli, 197-217, Lachs, 218-240, Sorensen, 241-257; *North Sea* Pleadings, Vol.I, 37-75 [FRG Memorial], 178-221 [Denmark's Counter-Memorial], 330-375 [NL Counter-Memorial], 396-416 [FRG Reply], 474-535 [Common Rejoinder of Denmark/NL], Vol.II, 11-36 [Agent Jaenicke, 23 and 24 Oct 1968], 138-139 [Agent Riphagen, 31 Oct], 153-162 [Agent Jacobsen, 31 Oct and 1 Nov], 163 [Questions Sir Gerald Fitzmaurice], 166-177 [Jaenicke, 4 Nov], 249-266 [Reply by Counsel Waldock to Questions Fitzmaurice, 8 Nov], 278-283 [Waldock, 11 Nov], 283-284 [Riphagen]; *Fisheries Jurisdiction (Merits)* Separate Os de Castro, ICJ Rep. 1974, 99, 225; *Aegean Sea (Jurisdiction)* Judgment, ICJ Rep. 1978, 8; Pleadings, 10 [Greece's Application], 170-173 [Grisel's Draft]; *Tunisia/Libya (Intervention)* Judgment, ICJ Rep. 1981, 9, 17, *(Merits)* Judgment, ICJ Rep. 1982, 49, 78-82, 84, 87-88, Separate O. de Arechaga, 104-109, 116, 132-137, Dissents Gros, 148-151, Oda, 157, 185-190, 193-197, 210-211, 234-247, 257, 260-274, Evensen, 280, 282, 285, 291-297, 309-310, 319; *Gulf of Maine* Judgment, ICJ Rep. 1984, 279-281, 284-289, 291, 297, 300-311, 313, 321-325, 331-332, 335, 338, Separate O. Schwebel, 353, Dissent Gros, 365-366, 375, 385-388, 390 [Map]; Pleadings, Vol.I, 134-146 [Canada's Memorial], Vol.II, 102-106, 117-124 [US Memorial], Vol.III, 207-208, 258 [Canada's Counter-Memorial], Vol.IV, 84-96 [US Counter-Memorial], Vol.V, 6, 19-27, 129-135 [Canada's Reply], 400-427, 452-462 [US Reply], Vol.VI, 22-28 [Agent Legault, 2 April 1984], 283-286 [Counsel Stevenson, 12 April], Vol.VII, 7-13 [Agent Legault, 3 May 1984]; *Libya/Malta (Intervention)* Dissent Sette-Camara, ICJ Rep. 1984, 78, *(Merits)* Judgment, ICJ Rep. 1985, 23-24, 37-38, 44-48, 51-52, 56, 57, para.79C, Separate O. Sette-Camara, 66-67, 74-75, Joint Separate O., 82-92, Separate O. Valticos, 105-110, Dissents Mosler, 119-120, Oda, 125-170, Schwebel, 179-187; Pleadings, Vol.I, 111-115 [Libya's Memorial], 431-433, 456-476, 486-499 [Malta's Memorial], Vol.II, 104-119, 153 [Libya's Counter-Memorial], 307-316, 350, 362-364, 370-378 [Malta's Counter-Memorial], 646 [Question Judge Oda, 30 Jan 1984], Vol.III, 176-181 [Malta's Reply], 421-436 [Counsel Weil, 30 Nov 1984], Vol.IV, 406 [Agent Mizzi, 13 Feb 1985], 503-506 [Replies to Judge Oda, 6 Feb 1984].

Gulf of Fonseca Judgment, ICJ Rep. 1992, 367-368, 371, 569, 578, 601-602, Separate O. Bernardez, 664, Dissent Oda, 759; *Denmark v. Norway* Judgment, ICJ Rep. 1993, 45-69, 72, 76-82, Separate Os Oda, 98, 102-109, 115-117, Schwebel, 121-128, Shahabuddeen, 130-159, Weeramantry, 222-225, 259-267, Ajibola, 295, 299, Dissent Fisscher, 304-309, 313; *East Timor* Hearings, CR 95/3 [trans.],

70-72 [Co-Agent Teles, 31 Jan. 1995]; *Cameroon v. Nigeria* Hearings, CR 98/2, 40 [Counsel Crawford, 3 March 1998]; *Qatar v. Bahrain* Judgment, ICJ Rep. 2001, 40, paras 61, 175-179, 209, 217, 227-233, 249-251, 252(6), Separate O. Oda, 126-143, paras 10-41, Joint Dissent Bedjaoui, Ranjeva, Koroma, 205-213, paras 191-210, Dissent Torres Bernardez, 422-444, paras 474-549; Hearings, CR 94/1, 19 [Agent Al-Nauimi, 28 Feb 1994], CR 2000/10, 41-55 [Counsel Queneudec, 6 June 2000]; *Cameroon v. Nigeria; Equatorial Guinea Intervening (Merits)* Judgment, ICJ Rep. 2002, 303, paras 255-256, 269-307, 325.IV(C)-(D), Separate O. Mbaye, 532-534, paras 127-137; Hearings, CR 2002/5, 43-52 [Co-Agent Pellet, 22 Feb 2002], CR 2002/6, 27-44 [Co-Agent Kamto, 25 Feb], CR 2002/7, 28 [Co-Agent Kamto, 26 Feb], CR 2002/13, 53-72 [Counsel Crawford, 7 March], CR 2002/17, 58-60 [Kamto, 12 March], CR 2002/22, 28-35 [Counsel Cot, 19 March], 35-37 [Kamto], CR 2002/24, 30-39 [Counsel Colson, 20 March 2002]; *Nicaragua v. Honduras*, *Nicaragua v. Colombia* and *Romania v. Ukraine* cases <www.icj-cij.org>.

1977/1978 *Anglo/French Continental Shelf* Decisions; 1977/1984 *Argentina/Chile Beagle Channel* case; 1981 *Dubai/Sharjah* Award; 1985 *Guinea/Guinea Bissau* Award; 1989 *Guinea-Bissau/Senegal* Award; 1992 *Canada/France* Award; 1998 *Eritrea/Yemen (Phase I)* Award, paras 110-113, 404, 486, 509, and 1999 *(Phase II)* Award [*infra*]; 2002 *Newfoundland/Nova Scotia (Phase II)* Award [*supra*]; 2002 *Belize/Guatemala* OAS Facilitators' Proposals, B-paras 4-5 <www.belize-guatemala.gov.bz/>; 2006 *Barbados/Trinidad & Tobago* Award and 2007 *Guyana/Suriname* Award [*supra*].

Bisector Method/Special (Relevant) Circumstances

Nicaragua v. Honduras (Merits) Judgment, ICJ Rep. 2007, paras 83-85, 102, 283-298, Dissent Torres Bernardez, paras 111-115; *Romania v. Ukraine* Judgment, ICJ Rep. 2009, para.116, *reaffirming Nicaragua v. Honduras* Judgment, ICJ Rep. 2007, para.281; *Romania v. Ukraine* Hearings, CR 2008/18, 61, para.7 and at 69-70, para.26 [Counsel Crawford, 2 Sep 2008] <www.icj-cij.org>.

Natural Prolongation

North Sea ICJ Rep. 1969, 3 – Judgment, 22, 30, 31-32, 36, 47, 53, para.101(C)(1), Separate O. President Bustamante y Rivero, 58, 62, Separate Os Padilla Nervo, 97, Ammoun, 114-116, 146, 148, 150, Dissents Koretsky, 158-159, Morelli, 215; Pleadings, Vol.I, 461 [Common Rejoinder of Denmark/NL]; Vol.II, 104, 247 [Counsel Sir Humphrey Waldock, 29 Oct and 8 Nov 1968], 137, 217-218 [Agent Riphagen, 31 Oct and 7 Nov 1968], 155 [Agent Jacobsen]; *Aegean Sea (Jurisdiction)* Judgment, ICJ Rep. 1978, 36, Dissent de Castro, 66; Pleadings, 95-99 [Counsel O'Connell, 26 Aug 1976], 441 [16 Oct 1978], 602-604 [Turkey's Letter]; *Tunisia/Libya (Merits)* Judgment, ICJ Rep. 1982, 43-47, 52-59, 73, 80,

92, para.133 A(2), Separate O. de Arechaga, 103-104, 109-122, Dissents Oda, 191-195, 216-221, 248, 256, 270, Evensen, 284, 286-289; Pleadings, Vol.IV, 403-411, 416-419, 425 [Counsel Sir Robert Jennings, 16 Sep 1981], Vol.V, 260-262, 277-278, 345-348 [Jennings, 13 and 15 Oct 1981]; *Gulf of Maine* Judgment, ICJ Rep. 1984, 296; Pleadings, Vol.I, 120-127 [Canada's Memorial], Vol.III, 60-64, 178-182, 209-212 [Canada's Counter-Memorial], Vol.IV, 87 [US Counter-Memorial], Vol.V, 21 [Canada's Reply], 417-421 [US Reply], Vol.VI, 29-30 [Agent Legault, 2 April 1984]; *Libya/Malta (Intervention)* Dissent Sette-Camara, ICJ Rep. 1984, 78, 82, *(Merits)* Judgment, ICJ Rep. 1985, 31-37, 45, 55-56, 57, para.79A(2), Separate Os Sette-Camara, 63-65, Mbaye, 93-95; Pleadings, Vol.I, 115-122, 145-151, 172 [Libya's Memorial], 444-445 [Malta's Memorial], Vol.II, 253-257, 296-307, 353-355 [Malta's Counter-Memorial], Vol.III, 158-164 [Malta's Reply], Vol.IV, 427-438 [Counsel Jaenicke, 21 Feb 1985]; *Denmark v. Norway* Separate Os Oda, ICJ Rep. 1993, 104-105, Schwebel, 124, Shahabuddeen, 161-168; *Cameroon v. Nigeria; Equatorial Guinea Intervening (Merits)* Judgment, ICJ Rep. 2002, 433-434, paras 272-273 <www.icj-cij.org>; 2006 *Barbados/Trinidad & Tobago* Award, paras 153, 224-227, 232; Hearings Day-4, 79-80 [Counsel Greenwood, 21 Oct 2005], Day-7, 32-33 [President Schwebel's Question, Counsel Greenwood, 27 Oct], Day-8, 29 [Counsel Crawford, 28 Oct 2005] <www.pca-cpa.org>.

1982 UNCLOS, Article 15

Iceland/Norway Conciliation [20 ILM 824 (1981)]; *Tunisia/Libya (Merits)* Dissents Oda, ICJ Rep. 1982, 211, Evensen, 295; *Gulf of Maine* Pleadings, Vol.V, 411 [US Reply], Vol.VII, 200 [Counsel Stevenson, 9 May 1984]; *Libya/Malta (Merits)* Separate O. Vice-President Sette-Camara, ICJ Rep. 1985, 61; Pleadings, Vol.III, 440 [Counsel Brownlie, 3 Dec 1984], Vol.IV, 437-438 [Counsel Jaenicke, 21 Feb 1985]; *Gulf of Fonseca* Dissent Oda, ICJ Rep. 1992, 758-759; Oral Hearings, C 4/CR 91/43, 81 [Counsel Brownlie, 7 June 1991], CR 91/45, 27-28 [Counsel Bowett, 10 June], CR 91/49, 47, 59 [Brownlie, 13 June 1991]; 1999 *Eritrea/Yemen (Phase II)* Award [*supra*], paras 24-25, 41, 125, 133, 158, 161; 2000 *Southern Bluefin Tuna (Jurisdiction)* Award, para.61 [39 ILM 1359 (2000) <www.worldbank.org/icsid>]; *Qatar v. Bahrain (Merits)* Judgment, ICJ Rep. 2001, 93-94, paras 175-176, Separate O. Oda, 128-130, paras 16-19, Declaration Herczegh, 216, Dissent Torres Bernardez, 257, paras 483-484, 487-488, 494, 496, 513; Hearings, CR 2000/15, 18-20 [Counsel Weil, 14 June 2000], CR 2000/16, 42 [Counsel Reisman, 15 June], CR 2000/25, 7 [29 June 2000]; *Cameroon v. Nigeria; Equatorial Guinea Intervening (Merits)* Judgment, ICJ Rep. 2002, 435, para.278; Hearings, CR 2002/5, 40 [Counsel Bipoun Woum, 22 Feb 2002], 43 [Co-Agent Pellet], CR 2002/13, 32 [Counsel Abi-Saab, 7 March 2002] <www.icj-cij.org>; 2003 *Malaysia v. Singapore (Provisional Measures)* Order, paras 31, 70, Separate O. Rao, para.5; Hearings, ITLOS/PV.03/02/Corr.1, 9-10 [Counsel Crawford, 25

Sep], PV.03/03, 27 [Agent Koh, 26 Sep 2003] <www.itlos.org>; 2006 *Barbados/Trinidad & Tobago* Award, para.305; Barbados' Memorial, para.108 <www.pca-cpa.org>; 2007 *Guyana/Suriname* Award, paras 164, 168, 175, 212, 214, 237-245, 282-298, 313, 352; Guyana's Memorial, para.7.23 <www.pca-cpa.org>; *Nicaragua v. Honduras (Merits)* Judgment, ICJ Rep. 2007, paras 102-103, 265-277, 280-282, Separate O. Ranjeva, Dissent Torres Bernardez, paras 67, 131, 146, 161; Hearings, CR 2007/8, 40, para.14 [Counsel Dupuy, 14 March 2007], CR 2007/9, 39-40, paras 2-4 [Counsel Colson, 15 March], CR 2007/10, 11-12, para.76, at 29, para.146 [16 March], CR 2007/11, 36, para.17 [Counsel Pellet, 19 March], CR 2007/12, 37, paras 22-23 [20 March], 39. para.1, at 44, para.26 [Counsel Brownlie], CR 2007/13, 18, para.24 [Dupuy, 22 March], CR 2007/14, 26, para.11 [Counsel Queneudec, 23 March 2007], 33, para.8 [Counsel Greenwood] <www.icj-cij.org>; *Romania v. Ukraine* Judgment, ICJ Rep. 2009, para.137; Hearings, CR 2008/19, 11-12, para.7 [Counsel Crawford, 3 Sep 2008], CR 2008/24, 30, para.46 [Counsel Bundy, 9 Sep], CR 2008/26, 13, para.54 [Counsel Queneudec, 10 Sep], 30, para.49 [Bundy], CR 2008/28, 50, para.69 [Bundy, 11 Sep], CR 2008/31, 24, para.4 [Counsel Pellet, 16 Sep 2008] <www.icj-cij.org>.

1982 UNCLOS, Articles 74(1)/83(1)

1977 *Anglo/French* Decision [18 ILM 397 (1979)], paras 91, 96; *Iceland/Norway* Conciliation [20 ILM 804, 823-824 (1981)]; *Tunisia/Libya (Merits)* Judgment, ICJ Rep. 1982, 48-49, Separate Os Ago, 95, de Arechaga, 104, 107-108, Dissents Oda, 234-247, 255, 257, 260, Evensen, 280-281, 282, 285; *Gulf of Maine* Judgment, ICJ Rep. 1984, 294-295, Dissent Gros, 365-367, 372, 374, 377-379, 382; Pleadings, Vol.I, 119, 143 [Canada's Memorial], Vol.II, 105-106 [US Memorial], Vol.III, 16, 208-209 [Canada's Counter-Memorial], Vol.IV, 70, 88-91 [US Counter-Memorial], Vol.V, 20 [Canada's Reply], 411-414 [US Reply], Vol.VI, 173-174 [Counsel Weil, 5 April 1984], 227 [Agent Legault, 10 April], 270 [Counsel Stevenson, 12 April 1984], Vol.VII, 148 [Agent Robinson, 9 May], 189 [Stevenson, 9 May 1984]; *Libya/Malta (Intervention)* Dissent Oda, ICJ Rep. 1984, 112, *(Merits)* Judgment, ICJ Rep. 1985, 30-31, 48, 55, Separate Os Sette-Camara, 61, 68, 75, Mbaye, 95-96, Dissent Oda, 127, 140-141, 148-150; Pleadings, Vol.I, 115, 141-142 [Libya's Memorial], Vol.II, 99, 113-114, 119, 153 [Libya's Counter-Memorial], 280, 312 [Malta's Counter-Memorial], 498 [Counsel Arangio-Ruiz, 25 Jan 1984], 554, 557 [Counsel Virally, 26 Jan], Vol.III, 48 [Libya's Reply], 147, 176-177 [Malta's Reply], 366 [Weil, 28 Nov], Vol.IV, 15 [Counsel Vallat, 6 Dec], 38 [Counsel Briggs, 7 Dec], 45, 47 [Counsel Jaenicke], 95-97 [Counsel Colliard, 11 Dec 1984], 349, 363 [Weil, 12 Feb 1985], 438 [Jaenicke, 21 Feb 1985]; 1985 *Guinea/Guinea-Bissau* Award, para.88 [25 ILM 289 (1986)]; 1989 *Guinea-Bissau/Senegal* Award [94 RGDIP 265 (1990)], para.79; *Guinea-Bissau v. Senegal (Provisional Measures)*

Separate O. Evensen, ICJ Rep.1990, 72, *Arbitral Award* Separate O. Vice-President Oda, ICJ Rep. 1991, 90.

Gulf of Fonseca Dissent Oda, ICJ Rep. 1992, 759; *Denmark v. Norway* Judgment, ICJ Rep. 1993, 59, Separate Os Oda, 106-109, 111, 113, Schwebel, 127-128, Shahabuddeen, 132, 151, 183, Weeramantry, 222-224, 234, 259-261, 265, Ajibola, 282-283, 287; Denmark's Memorial, paras 226-234, Norway's Counter-Memorial, paras 310-312, 345-353, Denmark's Reply, para.443-444, Norway's Rejoinder, paras 264-266, 387; Hearings, CR 93/1Corr., 29-30 [Agent Lehmann, 11 Jan 1993], CR 93/2, 69, 73-74 [Counsel de Arechaga, 12 Jan], CR 93/4, 10 [Counsel Bowett, 14 Jan], CR 93/6, 48-49 [Agent Haug, 18 Jan 1993]; *East Timor* Separate O. Oda, ICJ Rep. 1995, 110, Dissent Weeramantry, 203; Hearings, CR 95/15, 11 [Counsel Pellet, 16 Feb 1995]; *Cameroon v. Nigeria (Preliminary Objections)* Judgment, ICJ Rep. 1998, 321-322, Separate Os Oda, 336, Higgins, 346, Kooymans, 355, Dissent Ajibola, 413-414; Hearings, CR 98/2, 48 [Counsel Crawford, 3 March 1998], CR 98/4 [trans.], 37-39 [Adviser Bipoun Woum, 6 March 1998]; 1999 *Eritrea/Yemen (Phase II)* Award [*supra*], paras 23, 116, 124, 131; 2000 *Southern Bluefin Tuna (Jurisdiction)* Award, para.61 [39 ILM 1359 (2000) <www.worldbank.org/icsid>]; *Qatar v. Bahrain (Merits)* Judgment, ICJ Rep. 2001, 94, 110-111, paras 176, 224-230, Separate O. Oda, 138-140, paras 33-36, Dissent Torres Bernardez, 257, paras 483, 485, 487; 2001 *Newfoundland and Labrador/Nova Scotia (Phase I)* Award, para.3.12 <www.gov.ns.ca/> and 2002 *(Phase II)* Award, paras 1.24, 2.26/27, 5.2 <www.boundary-dispute.ca/>; *Cameroon v. Nigeria; Equatorial Guinea Intervening (Merits)* Judgment, ICJ Rep. 2002, 303, paras 26, 27, 239-245, 270, 278, 285, Declaration Oda, paras 25-27, Dissent Ajibola, paras 170-172; Hearings, CR 2002/5, 40 [Counsel Bipoun Woum, 22 Feb 2002], 44 [Co-Agent Pellet], CR 2002/6, 28-29, 30-32, 42 [Co-Agent Kamto, 25 Feb], 68 [Pellet], CR 2002/12, 58-59 [Counsel Crawford, 6 March], CR 2002/13, 32 [Counsel Abi-Saab, 7 March], CR 2002/22, 32 [Counsel Cot, 19 March], CR 2002/26, 38 [Crawford, 21 March 2002] <www.icj-cij.org>; 2002 *Belize/Guatemala* OAS Facilitators' Proposals, B-paras 2, 7 <www.belize-guatemala.gov.bz/>; *Indonesia/Malaysia (Merits)* Declaration Oda, ICJ Rep. 2002, 690; *Malaysia v. Singapore (Provisional Measures)* Hearings, ITLOS/PV.03/03, 27 [Agent Koh, 26 Sep 2003] <www.itlos .org>; 2006 *Barbados/Trinidad & Tobago* Award, President S.M. Schwebel, paras 57, 62, 75-77, 193, 197, 200-202, 205-206, 212, 215, 221, 229, 243, 299, 305, 315, 335, 370-372 <www.pca-cpa.org>; 2007 *Guyana/Suriname* Award, President L.D.M. Nelson, paras 164, 168, 172, 175, 214, 246-273, 331-342 <www.pca-cpa. org>; *Nicaragua v. Honduras (Merits)* Judgment, ICJ Rep. 2007, paras 270, 294, Dissent Torres Bernardez, paras 121, 159; Hearings, CR 2007/8, 40, para.14 [Counsel Dupuy, 14 March 2007], CR 2007/9, 39-40, paras 2-4 [Counsel Colson, 15 March], CR 2007/11, 36, para.17 [Counsel Pellet, 19 March], CR 2007/12, 39.

para.1 [Counsel Brownlie], CR 2007/14, 33, para.8 [Counsel Greenwood, 23 March 2007] <www.icj-cij.org>; *Romania v. Ukraine* Judgment, ICJ Rep. 2009, paras 31, 35, 69-70, 120, 155, 185; Hearings, CR 2008/18, 28, para.40 [Agent Aurescu, 2 Sep 2008], 43-44, paras 26-28 [Counsel Pellet], CR 2008/19, 11-12, paras 7-8 [Counsel Crawford, 3 Sep], CR 2008/20, 53, para.73 [Counsel Lowe, 4 Sep], CR 2008/26, 30, para.49 [Counsel Bundy, 10 Sep], CR 2008/28, 55, para.8 [Counsel Malintoppi, 11 Sep], CR 2008/29, 19, para.61 [Malintoppi, 12 Sep 2008], 27, para.27 [Counsel Queneudec], 44, para.1 [Counsel Bundy] <www.icj-cij.org>; 2009 *Abyei Boundary* Award, paras 203-207, referring to decision *ex aequo et bono* <www.pca-cpa.org>.

1982 UNCLOS, Articles 74(2)/83(2) and Part XV

Gulf of Maine Judgment, ICJ Rep. 1984, 299; *Qatar v. Bahrain (Merits)* Separate O. Oda, para.36, ICJ Rep. 2001, 140; *Cameroon v. Nigeria (Preliminary Objections)* Judgment, ICJ Rep. 1998, 320-322, Separate Os Higgins, 346, Kooymans, 355, Dissent Ajibola, 413-414; Hearings, CR 98/2, 48-49, 51 [Counsel Crawford, 3 March 1998], CR 98/4 [trans.], 38-39, 41 [Adviser Bipoun Woum, 6 March 1998]; *Cameroon v. Nigeria; Equatorial Guinea Intervening (Merits)* Judgment, ICJ Rep. 2002, 422-423, paras 239, 242, Declaration Oda, 467, paras 27-28 <www.icj-cij.org>; 2006 *Barbados/Trinidad & Tobago* Award, President S.M. Schwebel, paras 67, 71, 73, 195, 199-202, 207; Hearings Day-1, 66-79 [Counsel Reisman, 17 Oct 2005], Day-7, 51-55, 71 [Counsel Wordsworth, 27 Oct], Day-8, 48-49 [Counsel Crawford, 28 Oct 2005] <www.pca-cpa.org>.

See also Settlement of Disputes – 1982 LOSC, Articles 281 and 283 (No Settlement Reached) *infra*.

1982 UNCLOS, Articles 74(3)/83(3)

Tunisia/Libya (Merits) Dissent Evensen, ICJ Rep. 1982, 318; *Guinea-Bissau v. Senegal (Provisional Measures)* Separate O. Evensen, ICJ Rep.1990, 73; *East Timor* Hearings, CR 95/11, 42-43 [Counsel Bowett, 10 Feb 1995]; *Cameroon v. Nigeria* Hearings, CR 98/2, 48 [Counsel Crawford, 3 March 1998]; 1998 *Eritrea/Yemen (Phase I)* Award [*supra*], paras 65, 71; *Southern Bluefin Tuna (Jurisdiction)*, Japan's Memorial, para.119, A/NZ Reply, para.159, Hearings, Vol.I [Counsel Lauterpacht, 7 May 2000], Vol.III [Lauterpacht, 10 May 2000] <www.worldbank.org/icsid>; 2006 *Barbados/Trinidad & Tobago* Award, President S.M. Schwebel, paras 71, 75-77, 201-202, 205-207; 2007 *Guyana/Suriname* Award, President L.D.M. Nelson, paras 184, 267, 272-278, 406, 453-486, *dispositif* paras 487(iii), 488(3) <www.pca-cpa.org>.

See also Peaceful Uses of the Sea – Prohibition of Threat or Use of Force (2007 *Guyana/Suriname* Award) *infra*.

1982 UNCLOS, Articles 74(4)/83(4)

Guinea-Bissau v. Senegal Hearings, CR 90/3, 73, 79 [Counsel Highet, 4 April 1991]; *Cameroon v. Nigeria* Hearings, CR 98/2, 48 [Counsel Crawford, 3 March 1998]; 2001 *Newfoundland and Labrador/Nova Scotia (Phase I)* Award, paras 3.12/13 <www.bissettmatheson.com/arbitration/>; *Cameroon v. Nigeria; Equatorial Guinea Intervening (Merits)* Hearings, CR 2002/13, 59 [Counsel Crawford, 7 March 2002] <www.icj-cij.org>; *Romania v. Ukraine* Judgment, ICJ Rep. 2009, paras 32, 40, 41, 69; Hearings, CR 2008/18, 44-45, paras 29, 31 [Counsel Pellet, 2 Sep 2008], CR 2008/19, 44-45, para.79 [Counsel Crawford, 3 Sep], CR 2008/28, 11, paras 6-7 [Counsel Sir Michael Wood, 11 Sep], CR 2008/30, 55, para.39 [Counsel Crawford, 15 Sep 2008] <www.icj-cij.org>.

See also Settlement of Disputes – Maritime Boundary Disputes *infra*.

Single Boundary Line

Tunisia/Libya (Merits) Separate O. Jimenez de Arechaga, ICJ Rep. 1982, 115-116, Dissents Oda, 231-232, 249, Evensen, 287, 296-297; *Gulf of Maine* Judgment, ICJ Rep. 1984, 267, 276, 288-291, 294-295, 300-303, 312, 314-318, 321, 326-330, 344-346, 347-352 (citing, at 314, Pleadings, Vol.VI, 461 [Question of President Ago, 19 April 1984], Vol.VII, 139-142 [Agent Legault's Reply, 5 May], 186-189 [Counsel Stevenson's Reply, 9 May 1984]), Separate O. Schwebel, 353, Dissent Gros, 360-381; and Pleadings, Vol.I, 116-132 [Canada's Memorial], Vol.II, 64, 92-106 [US Memorial], Vol.III, 14-20, 172-177 [Canada's Counter-Memorial], Vol.IV, 59-64 [US Counter-Memorial], Vol.V, 421-424 [US Reply], Vol.VI, 227-229 [Agent Legault, 10 April 1984], 462 [Question IV of Judge Gros, 19 April], Vol.VII, 181-182 [Counsel Stevenson's Reply, 9 May]; and Vol. VI, 226-229 [Agent Legault, 10 April], 464 [Question 1 of Judge Cohen, 19 April], Vol.VII, 39-40 [Counsel Weil's Reply, 4 May], 185-186 [Counsel Stevenson's Reply, 9 May 1984]; *Libya/Malta* Pleadings, Vol.III, 320 [Counsel Lauterpacht, 27 Nov 1984], 414 [Counsel Weil, 30 Nov], Vol.IV, 132 [Counsel Lucchini, 12 Dec 1984]; *Guinea-Bissau v. Senegal (Provisional Measures)* Order, ICJ Rep. 1990, 67, *Arbitral Award* Judgment, ICJ Rep. 1991, 65, 71-72, 74, Declaration Tarassov, 78, Separate Os Vice-President Oda, 84, 87, 89-91, Ni, 99, 103-104, Shahabuddeen, 114-116, Joint Dissent Aguilar and Ranjeva, 129, Dissents Weeramantry, 138, 144-145, 170-173, Thierry, 177-178, 180; Hearings, CR 90/3, 57-59 [Counsel Highet, 4 April 1991]; *Gulf of Fonseca (Intervention)* Judgment, ICJ Rep. 1990, 106, 126, Separate O. Oda, 143-144, *(Merits)* Judgment, ICJ Rep. 1992, 367-368, 371; *Denmark v. Norway* Judgment, ICJ Rep. 1993, 47, 56-58, 68, 71, 79, Separate Os Oda, 91, 96, 100, 109-110, 117, Schwebel, 120-121, 127-128, Shahabuddeen, 131-132, 197-202, Ajibola, 285-290, Dissent Fischer, 304-305; Hearings, CR 93/2, 65-69 [Counsel de Arechaga, 12 Jan 1993], CR 93/9, 47-82 [Counsel Highet, 21 Jan], CR 93/10,

12-17 [Agent Lehmann, 25 Jan], CR 93/11, 27-32 [Agent Haug, 27 Jan 1993]; *Qatar v. Bahrain (Jurisdiction and Admissibility)* Judgment, ICJ Rep. 1994, 118, 123-125, Dissent Oda, 144-146, *(Jurisdiction and Admissibility)* Judgment, ICJ Rep. 1995, 25, Dissent Oda, 41-42, 47, *(Merits)* Judgment, ICJ Rep. 2001, 40, paras 31-34, 67, 168-174, 217, 221-230, 249-251, 252(6), Separate O. Oda, 119, paras 5, 10-41, Joint Dissent Bedjaoui, Ranjeva, Koroma, 194-211, paras 163-205, Dissent Torres Bernardez, 422-446, paras 474-553; Hearings, CR 94/6, 49 [Counsel Highet, 8 March 1994], CR 2000/9 [trans.], 31-32 [Counsel Queneudec, 5 June 2000], CR 2000/19, 21-22 [Queneudec, 22 June 2000]; *Cameroon v. Nigeria; Equatorial Guinea Intervening (Merits)* Judgment, ICJ Rep. 2002, 303, paras 38, 214, 226, 247, 268-307, 325.IV, Separate O. Mbaye, 532-534, paras 127-137; *Nicaragua v. Honduras*, *Nicaragua v. Colombia* and *Romania v. Ukraine* cases – see *supra*.

1985 *Guinea/Guinea-Bissau*, 1989 *Guinea-Bissau/Senegal* and 1992 *Canada/France* Awards [*infra*]; 1993 *UN Iraq/Kuwait* Commission [*supra*]; 1999 *Eritrea/Yemen (II)* Award [*infra*]; 2002 *Newfoundland/Nova Scotia (Phase II)* Award, 2006 *Barbados/Trinidad and Tobago* Award and 2007 *Guyana/Suriname* Award [*supra*].

Economic Factors

Anglo/Norwegian Fisheries ICJ Rep. 1951, 116 – Judgment, 133, Dissents McNair, 161, 169, 171, Read, 186, 194; Pleadings, Vol.I, 534, 572-573 [Norway's Counter-Memorial], invoking the doctrine of "legitimate interests", Vol.II, 414-416, 586-588, 597-598, 659, 662-664, 675, 676, 679 [UK Reply]; *North Sea* Dissents Koretsky, ICJ Rep. 1969, 155, Tanaka, 184, Lachs, 239, Sorensen, 256; Pleadings, Vol.I, 461 [Common Rejoinder of Denmark/NL], Vol.II, 138 [Agent Riphagen, 31 Oct], 276-277 [Counsel Sir Humphrey Waldock, 11 Nov 1968]; *Tunisia/Libya (Merits)* Judgment, ICJ Rep. 1982, 62, 77-78, Dissent Oda, 255-256; Pleadings, Vol.I, 67-72 [Tunisia's Memorial], Vol.II, 153-154 [Libya's Counter-Memorial]; *Gulf of Maine* Judgment, ICJ Rep. 1984, 340-344; Pleadings, Vol.I, 43-46, 128-132, 150 [Canada's Memorial], Vol.III, 186-204, 209, 217-221 [Canada's Counter-Memorial], Vol.IV, 62-63, 72-84 [US Counter-Memorial], Vol.V, 18-19 [Canada's Reply], 421-424, 432-439 [US Reply], Vol.VI, 87-105 [Counsel Binnie, 4 April 1984], 261-273 [Counsel Stevenson, 12 April 1984]; *Libya/Malta (Merits)* Judgment, ICJ Rep. 1985, 41, Separate O. Valticos, 112, Dissent Oda, 159; Pleadings, Vol.I, 131-132 [Libya's Memorial], 414-418, 479-485, 498-499 [Malta's Memorial], Vol.II, 59-71 [Libya's Counter-Memorial], 365-369 [Malta's Counter-Memorial], Vol.III, 52 [Libya's Reply], 141-148 [Malta's Reply], 326-330 [Counsel Lauterpacht, 27

Nov 1984], Vol.IV, 405 [Agent Mizzi, 13 Feb 1985]; *Arbitral Award* Dissent Weeramantry, ICJ Rep. 1991, 169; *Gulf of Fonseca* Judgment, ICJ Rep. 1992, 396; *Denmark v. Norway* Judgment, ICJ Rep. 1993, 44, 73-74, Separate Os Oda, 116-117, Schwebel, 118-120, Weeramantry, 224, 262-263, 267-270, Dissent Fischer, 309-310; Hearings, CR 93/1Corr., 28-29 [Agent Lehmann, 11 Jan 1993], CR 93/7, 8-21 [Counsel Brownlie, 19 Jan], CR 93/9 [trans.], 26-29 [Counsel Weil, 21 Jan 1993]; *Qatar v. Bahrain (Merits)* Separate O. Oda, para.37, ICJ Rep. 2001 (in press); Hearings, CR 2000/5 [trans.], 39 [Counsel Salmon, 29 May 2000].

For reliance on the *Anglo/Norwegian Fisheries* pronouncement as to "economic interests... evidenced by a long usage," ICJ Reports 1951, 133 [1958 TSC, Article 4(4); 1982 LOSC, Articles 7(5) and 47(6)], see *North Sea* Pleadings, Vol.II, 179-180 [Agent Jaenicke, 4 Nov 1968]; *Fisheries Jurisdiction (Merits)* Separate Os de Castro, ICJ Rep. 1974, 96, 225; *Tunisia/Libya (Merits)* Dissent Evensen, ICJ Rep. 1982, 302, 316-317; Pleadings, Vol.I, 74, 76 [Tunisia's Memorial], Vol.V, 103-104 [Counsel Colliard, 2 Oct 1981], 293-294 [Counsel R.-J. Dupuy, 14 Oct], 382-390 [Colliard, 20 Oct 1981]; *Gulf of Maine* Dissent Gros, ICJ Rep. 1984, 360-361, 371, 388; Pleadings, Vol.I, 129 [Canada's Memorial], Vol.II, 69-70, 109 [US Memorial], Vol.III, 203, 219 [Canada's Counter-Memorial], Vol.IV, 69-70, 75 [US Counter-Memorial], Vol.V, 30-32, 50 n.51, 119 [Canada's Reply], 447 [US Reply], Vol.VI, 46 [Agent Legault, 3 April 1984], 91, 98, 100 [Counsel Binnie, 4 April], 380-385 [Counsel Feldman, 16 April], Vol.VII, 31 [Counsel Weil, 3 May], 88-91 [Binnie, 4 May], 174 [Feldman, 9 May 1984]; *Libya/Malta* Pleadings, Vol.I, 443 [Malta's Memorial]; *1989 Arbitral Award* Dissent Weeramantry, ICJ Rep. 1991, 137; *Denmark v. Norway* Hearings, CR 93/1Corr., 17 [Agent Lehmann, 11 Jan 1993]; 1998 *Eritrea/Yemen (Phase I)* Award, para.357, and 1999 *(Phase II)* Award, para.50 [*supra*]; *Qatar v. Bahrain (Merits)* Hearings, CR 2000/11, 24 [Sir Elihu Lauterpacht, 8 June 2000]; *Cameroon v. Nigeria; Equatorial Guinea Intervening (Merits)* Hearings, CR 2002/9, 64 [Counsel Brownlie, 1 March 2002] <www.icj-cij.org>.

Mineral Resource Factors

North Sea ICJ Rep. 1969, 3 – Judgment, 21, para.17, 51-52, paras 94, 97 and 99, and 53, para.101(C)(2), Separate O. President Bustamante y Rivero, 59-60, Separate Os Jessup, 66-84, Padilla Nervo, 93, Ammoun, 149, Dissents Koretsky, 168-169, Tanaka, 171, 191, Lachs, 239, Sorensen, 254; *North Sea* Pleadings, Vol.I, 51, 69, 79 [FRG Memorial], 211 [Denmark's Counter-Memorial], 317, 321, 364-365 [NL Counter-Memorial], Vol.II, 62 [Counsel Shigeru Oda, 25 Oct 1968], 65 [Questions of Judge Jessup], 103 [Counsel Sir Humphrey Waldock, 29 Oct], 139 [Agent Riphagen, 31 Oct], 164-165 [Reply by Agent Jaenicke to Questions Jessup,

4 Nov], 281 [Waldock, 11 Nov 1968]; 1975 *Western Sahara* Advisory Opinion [*supra*]; *Aegean Sea (Jurisdiction)* Dissent de Castro, ICJ Rep. 1978, 65; Pleadings, 98 [Counsel O'Connell, 26 Aug 1976]; *Tunisia/Libya (Intervention)* Judgment, ICJ Rep. 1981, 18, *(Merits)* Judgment, ICJ Rep. 1982, 35-37, 83-84, 68-69, 71, 77, 83-84, 87, 93, para.133 C(2), Separate O. Ago, 95, 98, Dissents Gros, 154-155, Oda, 188, 232, Evensen, 292, 304-306, 314, 317-323, *(Revision)* Judgment, ICJ Rep. 1985, 198-214, Separate Os Oda, 236-241, Schwebel, 246, Bastid, 249-251; Pleadings, Vol.I, 68-72 [Tunisia's Memorial]; *Gulf of Maine* Judgment, ICJ Rep. 1984, 246, 275, 278, 340, 342-344, Dissent Gros, 373-375; Pleadings, Vol.I, 54-55, 125-126, 150 [Canada's Memorial], Vol.II, 95-96 [US Memorial], Vol.III, 188-190, 219-220, 224, 237 [Canada's Counter-Memorial], Vol.IV, 77-79 [US Counter-Memorial], Vol.VI, 235-237 [Agent Robinson, 11 April 1984], Vol.VII, 89-90 [Counsel Binnie, 4 May], 269 [Agent Robinson, 11 May 1984], Vol.VIII, 4 [Fig.4], 61 [Fig.19], 165 [Fig.19]; *Libya/Malta (Merits)* Judgment, ICJ Rep. 1985, 22, 28-29, 41, Separate Os Sette-Camara, 72, Valticos, 112; Pleadings, Vol.I, 71-92 [Libya's Memorial], Vol.III, 328 [Counsel Lauterpacht, 27 Nov 1984]; *Gulf of Fonseca (Intervention)* Judgment, ICJ Rep. 1990, 108; *Denmark v. Norway* Judgment, ICJ Rep. 1993, 70, Separate Os Oda, 116, Schwebel, 118-120, 123.

Portugal v. Australia East Timor Judgment, ICJ Rep. 1995, 90, President M. Bedjaoui concurring, Separate Os Oda, 107, Shahabuddeen, 119, Ranjeva, 129, Vereshchetin, 135, Dissents Weeramantry, 139, Skubiszewski, 224; Orders, ICJ Rep. 1991, 9, 1992, 228, 1993, 32.

On Australia/Indonesia Treaty on the Zone of Cooperation in an Area Between the Indonesian Province of East Timor and Northern Australia of 11 Dec 1989 [Timor Gap Treaty, in force: 9 Feb 1991, 29 ILM 469 (1990); 1654 UNTS 106; Charney/ASIL Report No.6-2(5) (Prescott)], see also *Libya/Malta (Merits)* Joint Separate O., ICJ Rep. 1985, 80; *Southern Bluefin Tuna (Jurisdiction)* Hearings, Vol.I [Counsel Lauterpacht, 7 May 2000], Vol.III [Counsel Lauterpacht, 10 May 2000] <www.worldbank.org/icsid>; *Barbados/Trinidad & Tobago* Trinidad's Counter-Memorial, para.280 n.377 <www.pca-cpa.org>.

For 1994 *Horta v. Commonwealth* case, in which the three East Timorese plaintiffs challenged the validity of Australian 1990 legislation implementing the 1989 Treaty, see 123 ALR 1. For Portugal's Note Verbale to Australia of 28 August 1997, see *UN LOS Bull.* 97 (1997 No.35), and for Portugal's Declaration (para.5) upon ratifying the UNCLOS and Part XI Agreement on 3 November 1997, see *id.* 13, and 7 (1998 No.36).

On the Timor Gap Treaty ceasing to be in force as between Australia and Indonesia, and on its terms continuing to apply as between Australia and the UN Transitional Administration of East Timor (UNTAET), in pursuance of their Memorandum of Understanding [Joint Media Release <http://www.dfat.gov.au/

media/releases/downer/fa010_2000.html; 2000 ATS 9; *UN LOS Bull.* 175-178 (2000 No.42) and *id.* 45 (2001 No.47); UN Docs IMO MSC 72/23, para.10.75 and MSC 73/21, para.11.33 (2000); 17 IJMCL 79 (2002); Charney/ASIL Report No.6-15 (J.R.V. Prescott)], see *Southern Bluefin Tuna (Jurisdiction)* Hearings, Vol. II [Counsel Irwin, 8 May 2000] <www.worldbank.org/icsid>; *Barbados/Trinidad & Tobago* Trinidad's Counter-Memorial, para.280 n.377 <www.pca-cpa.org>.

On Australia/East Timor Dili Timor Sea Treaty and Exchange of Notes of 20 May 2002 [in force: 2 April 2003] and MOU on the Greater Sunrise, *UN LOS Bull.* 95 (2003 No.51); 2003 ATS 13 and <www.austlii.edu.au/au/other/dfat/special/etimor/index.html>], see *Barbados/Trinidad & Tobago* Trinidad's Counter-Memorial, para.280 n.377 <www.pca-cpa.org>. See also Australia/Timor-Leste Dili International Unitisation Agreement for Greater Sunrise of 6 March 2003 and Treaty on Certain Maritime Arrangements in the Timor Sea of 12 Jan 2006, *id.* & <www.dfat.gov.au/geo/east_timor/fs_maritime_arrangements.html>; Colson/ASIL Reports Nos 6-20(1), (2) & (3); East Timor Country Information <www.dfat.gov.au/geo/east_timor/>; East Asian & Pacific Affairs <www.state.gov/p/eap/>; and <www.petrotimor.com>. For Timor-Leste Maritime Borders Law No.7 of 20 May 2002, see *UN LOS Bull.* 35 (2003 No.50).

See also Settlement of Disputes – Article 298(1)(a) *infra*.

Botswana/Namibia Dissent Vice-President Weeramantry, paras 102-113, ICJ Rep. 1999, 1188-1194; *Qatar v. Bahrain (Merits)* Judgment, ICJ Rep. 2001 (in press), paras 49-54, 61, 102, 108, 159, 161, 237-240, Separate O. Oda, paras 14-15, 41, Joint Dissent Bedjaoui, Ranjeva, Koroma, paras 24-30, 77, 206-212, 215, Separate O. Kooymans, paras 12-13, 60, Dissent Torres Bernardez, paras 277-283, 401, 419, 491-502; Oral Hearings, CR 2000/6, 19-32 [Counsel Shankardass, 30 May 2000], CR 2000/7, 25-44 [31 May], CR 2000/10, 24-41 [Counsel Salmon, 6 June], CR 2000/14, 20-32 [Counsel Paulsson, 13 June 2000]; *Cameroon v. Nigeria; Equatorial Guinea Intervening (Merits)* Judgment, ICJ Rep. 2002, 303, paras 211, 215, 241, 256, 268, 282-284, 302-304, Dissent Ajibola, para.170; Hearings, CR 2002/7, 20-21 [Co-Agent Kamto, 26 Feb 2002], CR 2002/9, 45-47 [Counsel Brownlie, 1 March], CR 2002/12, 64 [Counsel Crawford, 6 March], CR 2002/17, 21-31 [Co-Agent Pellet, 12 March], CR 2002/13, 23-25 [Crawford, 7 March], CR 2002/20, 50-58 [15 March], CR 2002/22, 37-39 [Kamto, 19 March], CR 2002/23, 28-35 [Crawford], CR 2002/24, 35-38 [Counsel Colson, 20 March 2002]; *Indonesia/Malaysia (Merits)* Judgment, ICJ Rep. 2002, 625, paras 31, 78-79, Declaration Oda, 687-690, Dissent Franck, 702, para.35; Hearings, CR 2002/27, 24 [Agent Wirajuda, 3 June], CR 2002/29, 50, 59-63 [Counsel Pellet, 4 June], CR 2002/32, 33-34 [Counsel Crawford, 7 June], CR 2002/34, 34-36 [Pellet, 10 June 2002]; *Nicaragua v. Honduras (Merits)* Judgment, ICJ Rep. 2007, paras 80, 95, 170, 202-208, 238-239, 248, 253-258, Dissent Torres Bernardez, para.65; Hearings,

CR 2007/1, 34, para.65, at 42-45 [Agent Arguello, 5 March 2007], CR 2007/2, 43-48 [Counsel Brownlie, 6 March], CR 2007/3, 58-62 [Counsel Oude Elferink, 7 March], CR 2007/7, 29-33 [Counsel Sands, 13 March], CR 2007/9, 10-25, 38 [15 March], 40, para.6 [Counsel Colson], CR 2007/10, 20-22 [16 March], CR 2007/11, 62 [Oude Elferink, 19 March], CR 2007/12, 18-26 [Counsel Brotons, 20 March], CR 2007/13, 38, para.2, at 49-50, para.32, at 54-58 [Sands, 22 March], CR 2007/14, 12, para.7 [Colson, 23 March 2007], 30, para.37 [Counsel Queneudec] <www.icj-cij.org>; *Malaysia/Singapore Pedra Branca/Pulau Batu Puteh (Merits)* Judgment, ICJ Rep. 2008, paras 251-253, 286, Dissent Dugard, paras 21, 27-28, 41; Hearings, CR 2007/22, 39, para.6 and at 42-43, paras 17-22 [Counsel Malintoppi, 8 Nov 2007]; *Romania v. Ukraine* Judgment, ICJ Rep. 2009, paras 189-190, 193-195, 197; Hearings, CR 2008/18, 31, para.50 [Agent Aurescu, 2 Sep 2008], CR 2008/21, 14-16, paras 10-14 [Counsel Muller, 5 Sep], 25-30, paras 20-38 [Co-Agent Dinescu], CR 2008/28, 26-29, 31-35 [Counsel Malintoppi, 11 Sep], CR 2008/30, 39-42, paras 23-32 [Co-Agent Dinescu, 15 Sep], CR 2008/32, 50-53, paras 11-22 [Malintoppi, 18 Sep 2008] <www.icj-cij.org>; *Nicaragua v. Colombia (Preliminary Objections)* Judgment, ICJ Rep. 2007, paras 22, 79-82, 113; Hearings, CR 2007/16, 55-56, para.40 [Counsel Stephen M. Schwebel, 4 June 2007], CR 2007/18, 18, para.27 [Counsel Schwebel, 6 June 2007], 31, para.5 [Agent Paredes] and *Nicaragua v. Colombia (Merits)* Judgment <www.icj-cij.org>.

1981 *Iceland/Norway* Conciliation [*infra*]; 1981 *Dubai/Sharjah* Award [*infra*]; 1985 *Guinea/Guinea-Bissau* Award [*infra*]; 1989 *Guinea-Bissau/Senegal* Award [*infra*]; 1998 *Eritrea/Yemen (Phase I)* Award, paras 55-72, 110, 346, 389-439, 481, 497-506, 517-521 and 1999 *(Phase II)* Award, paras 75-86, 132, Annex II: Yemen's Answer to Judge Schwebel's Question [*supra*]; 2001 *Newfoundland and Labrador/ Nova Scotia (Phase I)* Award and 2002 *(Phase II)* Award, paras 3.4/23, 5.11 [*supra*]; 2002 *Belize/Guatemala* OAS Proposals, B-para.9 [*supra*]; 2006 *Barbados/Trinidad & Tobago* Award [*supra*], paras 11, 13, 18 & Tribunal's Order No.4, Award's paras 48, 103, 106-107, 194, 241, 259, 361-364; Barbados' Memorial, paras 74-75, 89-93; Trinidad's Counter-Memorial, paras 38-41; Barbados' Reply, paras 46, 51, 53, 322-323; Trinidad's Rejoinder, paras 171-180; Hearings Day-5, 22-31 [Counsel Volterra, 24 Oct 2005]; 2007 *Guyana/Suriname* Award, paras 197-199, 218, 231-232, 250-251, 291, 378-390 [*supra*]; 2009 *Abyei Boundary* Award, paras 212-216, referring to oilfields in the context of land boundaries [*supra*].

For reliance on Judge Jessup's analysis [ICJ Rep. 1969, 66-84], see *Fisheries Jurisdiction (Merits)* Separate O. Dillard, ICJ Rep. 1974, 70; *Tunisia/Libya (Merits)* Separate O. de Aréchaga, ICJ Rep. 1982, 121-122, Dissent Evensen, 322; *Gulf of Maine* Dissent Gros, ICJ Rep. 1984, 374; Pleadings, Vol.III, 57, 189-190, 195-197, 219-220 [Canada's Counter-Memorial], Vol.VI, 121-122 [Counsel Fortier, 4 April 1984], Vol.VII, 78 [Counsel Binnie, 4 May 1984]; *Libya/Malta* Pleadings, Vol.I,

472 [Malta's Memorial]; *Botswana/Namibia* Dissent Vice-President Weeramantry, para.108, ICJ Rep. 1999, 1190 <www.icj-cij.org>; 1999 *Eritrea/Yemen (Phase II)* Award [*supra*], para.84.

On Indonesia/Malaysia Delimitation of the Continental Shelves Agreement of 27 October 1969 [in force: 7 November 1969, 9 ILM 1173 (1970); ASIL/Charney Report No.5-9(1) (Choon-ho Park)], see *Indonesia/Malaysia (Merits)* Judgment, ICJ Rep. 2002, 625, paras 31, 123, 128, Declaration Oda, 688, Dissent Franck, 697, para.20; Hearings, CR 2002/27, 15-17, 20 [Agent Wirajuda, 3 June], CR 2002/29, 45-46 [Counsel Malintoppi, 4 June], 52-53, 55 [Counsel Pellet], CR 2002/30, 17-18 [Agent Mohamad, 6 June], 27 [Counsel Lauterpacht], CR 2002/32, 25 [Counsel Crawford, 7 June], CR 2002/34, 24, 37, 39 [Pellet, 10 June], CR 2002/35, 60 [Agent Mohamad, 12 June 2002]; *Malaysia/Singapore (Merits)* Judgment, ICJ Rep. 2008, paras 251, 257, Dissent Dugard, paras 21, 27-41; Hearings, CR 2007/20, 31, para.34 [Counsel Chao, 6 Nov 2007], CR 2007/22, 39, para.6, at 45, paras 27-28 and at 49, para.41 [Counsel Malintoppi, 8 Nov], CR 2007/22 [transl.], 50, para.19 [Counsel Pellet], CR 2007/24, 16-17, paras 34-35 [Agent Kadir, 13 Nov], CR 2007/26, 72, para.57 [Counsel Crawford, 15 Nov 2007] <www.icj-cij.org>.

On Japan/South Korea Joint Development Agreement of 30 Jan 1974 [in force: 22 June 1978, ASIL/Charney Report No.5-12 (Choon-ho Park)], which was the first bilateral scheme to follow upon the *North Sea* Judgment, see *Gulf of Maine* Pleadings, Vol.IV, 440 [US Counter-Memorial], Vol.V, 161 [Canada's Reply], State Practice Vol.I, 323; *Libya/Malta* Pleadings, Vol.II, 109, 134-135 [Libya's Counter-Memorial], Vol.III, 38 [Libya's Reply], Vol.IV, 315 [Counsel Brownlie, 8 Feb 1985]; *Denmark v. Norway* Oral Hearings, CR 93/4, 32 [Counsel Bowett, 14 Jan 1993], CR 93/7, 75-76 [Counsel Brownlie, 19 Jan], CR 93/10, 64 [Bowett, 25 Jan 1993].

On 1988 Tunisia/Libya Benghazi Joint Development (El Bouri Field) Agreements, see *Tunisia/Libya* case *supra*. On 1993 Guinea-Bissau/Senegal Dakar Agreement and its 1995 Protocol, see *Guinea-Bissau v. Senegal* case *supra*.

On 2001 Nigeria/Sao Tome & Principe Joint Development Treaty, see *Cameroon v. Nigeria; Equatorial Guinea Intervening* case *supra*.

On 2003 Barbados/Guyana EEZ Cooperation Treaty, see 2006 *Barbados/Trinidad & Tobago* Award *supra*.

See also 1982 LOSC, Articles 74(3)/83(3) *supra*; Peaceful Uses of the Sea – Prohibition of Threat or Use of Force (2007 *Guyana/Suriname* Award) *infra*.

Fishery Resource Factors

Anglo/Norwegian Fisheries ICJ Rep. 1951, 116 – Judgment, 127-128; *North Sea* Separate O. Jessup, ICJ Rep. 1969, 66, 80, 82-83, Separate O. Padilla Nervo,

93, Dissent Sorensen, 254; *North Sea* Pleadings, Vol.I, 69, 78 [FRG Memorial], 364 [NL Counter-Memorial]; *Tunisia/Libya (Merits)* Judgment, ICJ Rep. 1982, 67-68, 70, 72-73, 75, 77, 83-84, 86, 92, Separate Os Ago, 95-98, Schwebel, 99, de Arechaga, 122-132, 136, Dissents Gros, 154-155, Oda, 188, 197-211, 232, Evensen, 306-307, 317; *Gulf of Maine* Judgment, ICJ Rep. 1984, 275-278, 281-287, 298, 309, 316-317, 319, 340-344, Dissent Gros, 370, 373-374; Pleadings, Vol. I, 56-114, 128-133, 150-151 [Canada's Memorial], Vol.II, 19-33, 68-69, 75-76, 95-98, 112-114 [US Memorial], Vol.III, 83-89, 141-146, 190-198, 222-228, 237 [Canada's Counter-Memorial], Vol.IV, 30-49, 66-70, 80-84, 134-151, 166, 465-467 [US Counter-Memorial], Vol.V, 30-36, 94-126 [Canada's Reply], 401-404, 423-424, 447, 474-482 [US Reply], Vol.VI, 44-49 [Agent Legault, 3 April 1984], 380-394 [Counsel Feldman, 16 April 1984]; *Libya/Malta* Pleadings, Vol.I, 483, 485, 498 [Malta's Memorial], Vol.II, 63-67, 220-226 [Libya's Counter-Memorial], Vol.III, 146 [Malta's Reply], 327-328, 330 [Counsel Lauterpacht, 27 Nov 1984], Vol.IV, 139 [Counsel Lucchini, 12 Dec], Vol.VII, 87-93 [Counsel Binnie, 4 May], 268 [Agent Robinson, 11 May 1984]; *Denmark v. Norway* Judgment, ICJ Rep. 1993, 46, 70-73, 79-82, Declaration Evensen, 85, Separate Os Oda, 115-117, Schwebel, 118-120, 123, 126-129, Weeramantry, 268-270, Dissent Fischer, 310-313; Hearings, CR 93/4, 24-29 [Counsel Bowett, 14 Jan 1993]; *Botswana/Namibia* Dissent Vice-President Weeramantry, paras 102-113, ICJ Rep. 1999, 1184-1194; *Qatar v. Bahrain (Jurisdiction and Admissibility)* Judgment, ICJ Rep. 1994, 118, Dissent Oda, 144-145, 147, *(Jurisdiction and Admissibility)* Judgment, ICJ Rep. 1995, 10, 12, 25, Dissent Oda, 42, *(Merits)* Judgment, ICJ Rep. 2001, 40, paras 32-34, 101-102, 128, 155-156, 235-236, Dissent Torres Bernardez, 257, paras 389, 394, 399, 471; Hearings, CR 94/4, 45 [Counsel Bowett, 4 March 1994], CR 94/5, 43 [Counsel de Arechaga, 7 March 1994], CR 2000/10, 19-23 [Counsel Salmon, 6 June 2000], CR 2000/15, 14-16 [Counsel Reisman, 14 June], CR 2000/17, 30-33 [Counsel Shankardass, 20 June 2000]; *Nicaragua v. Honduras (Merits)* Judgment, ICJ Rep. 2007, paras 49, 52, 55-58, 65-66, 80, 95, 131, 162, 170-175, 186-187, 190-201, 240-243, 245, 252, 256, Dissent Torres Bernardez, para.65; Hearings, CR 2007/1, 26-29, at 32, para.58, at 36-39, at 41, para.90 [Agent Arguello, 5 March 2007], CR 2007/2, 44-46 [Counsel Brownlie, 6 March], CR 2007/3, 40-48 [Counsel Oude Elferink, 7 March], CR 2007/7, 33 [Counsel Sands, 13 March], CR 2007/9, 10, 25-39 [15 March], CR 2007/11, 12-15, 17-18 [Agent Arguello, 19 March], 64-65 [Oude Elferink], CR 2007/13, 52-53 [Sands, 22 March], CR 2007/14, 11-12, paras 5-6 [Counsel Colson, 23 March 2007], 37, paras 4-5 [Agent Flores] <www.icj-cij.org>; *Malaysia/Singapore* Hearings, CR 2007/22, 30-32, paras 75-79 [Counsel Bundy, 8 Nov 2007], 39, para.6, at 45-47, paras 29-34 and at 49, para.41 [Counsel Malintoppi], CR 2007/24, 17-18, para.38 [Agent Kadir, 13 Nov], 23-24, paras 14-16 [Co-Agent Fadir], CR 2007/26, 49-51, paras 48-53 [Counsel Sir Elihu

Lauterpacht, 15 Nov], CR 2007/29, 30, paras 17-18 [Malintoppi, 20 Nov], CR 2007/29 [transl.], 46, para.35 [Counsel Pellet], CR 2007/31, 57-58, para.6 [Agent Kadir, 23 Nov 2007]; *Romania v. Ukraine* Hearings, CR 2008/18, 31, para.50 [Agent Aurescu, 2 Sep 2008], CR 2008/21, 31-34, paras 39-51 [Co-Agent Dinescu, 5 Sep], 66, paras 72-73 [Counsel Lowe], CR 2008/28, 29-31, 33 [Counsel Malintoppi, 11 Sep 2008]; *Nicaragua v. Colombia (Preliminary Objections)* Judgment, ICJ Rep. 2007, para.31 and *Nicaragua v. Colombia (Merits)* Judgment <www.icj-cij.org>.

1909 *Norway v. Sweden Grisbadarna* Award; 1985 *Guinea/Guinea-Bissau* Award; 1992 *Canada/France* Award, Dissent Weil; 1999 *Eritrea/Yemen (Phase II)* Award [*infra*]; 2002 *Newfoundland/Nova Scotia (Phase II)* Award, paras 3.20/23 [*supra*]; 2002 *Belize/Guatemala* OAS Facilitators' Proposals, B-paras 8-10 [*supra*].

2006 *Barbados/Trinidad & Tobago* Award, paras 50, 58, 60, Map I, paras 68, 72, 75, 88-102, 109-113, 125-150, 194, 215, 241 [*reaffirming* catastrophic repercussions' exception of *Gulf of Maine* Judgment, ICJ Rep. 1984, 342, para.237], 246-293 [with para.267 rejecting applicability of this exception], 278-282 [Questions of Lowe & Orrego Vicuna], paras 384(iii) and 385(3); Hearings Day-2, 21-29 [Counsel Reisman, 18 Oct 2005], 29 [Brownlie's Question], Day-3, 25-27 [Counsel Crawford, 20 Oct], 83-84 [Counsel Wordsworth], Day-4, 29 [Vicuna's Questions, 21 Oct – Award's para.280 *supra*], 49 [Counsel Greenwood's on Brownlie's Question *supra*], 109-110 [President Schwebel's Questions], Day-5, 53-57 [Counsel Fietta replying to the President *supra*, 24 Oct], 35-36 [Lowe's Questions], 37-40 [Fietta], 40-45 [Counsel Forde], 48-57 [Fietta], 57-58 [President's Questions], 58-65 [Reisman], 63-66 [Reisman's reply to Brownlie], 72 [Lowe's Questions], Day-6, 50-53 [Counsel Sir Elihu Lauterpacht, 25 Oct], 63-67, 74 [Agent Mottley], Day-7, 73 [Orrego Vicuna's Question, 27 Oct], Day-8, 59-95 [Wordsworth replying to Questions of Day-4, 109 *supra*, 28 Oct], 101-125 [Greenwood, replying to Orrego Vicuna's and Lowe's Questions, Days-4/5 *supra*], 135-137 [Agent Jeremie, 28 Oct 2005] <www.pca-cpa.org>; 2007 *Guyana/Suriname* Award, paras 200, 218, 231-232, 236, 356 <www.pca-cpa.org>; *Romania v. Ukraine* Judgment, ICJ Rep. 2009, paras 191, 193, 196, 198, 203, *reaffirming* in para.198 catastrophic repercussions' exception of the 1984 *Gulf of Maine* Judgment and 2006 *Barbados/Trinidad and Tobago* Award, para.241 [*supra*]; 2009 *Abyei Boundary* Award, paras 748-769, *dispositif* para.770(e) [*supra*].

On Australia/Papua New Guinea Torres Strait Treaty (Joint Protected Zone) of 18 December 1978 [18 ILM 291 (1979)], see *Tunisia/Libya (Merits)* Dissent Oda, ICJ Rep. 1982, 234; Pleadings, Vol.II, 212, 268 [Libya's Counter-Memorial], Vol.V, 246 [Question II of Judge Schwebel, 9 Oct 1981], 504 [Libya's Reply to Schwebel]; *Gulf of Maine* Pleadings, Vol.IV, 443 [US Counter-Memorial], Vol.VI, 169 [Counsel Weil, 5 April 1984], State Practice Vol.I, 529; *Libya/Malta* Pleadings, Vol.II, 112 [Libya's Counter-Memorial], 344 [Malta's Counter-Memorial],

Vol.III, 45 [Libya's Reply], 256 [Malta's Reply], Vol.IV, 116 [Counsel Colliard, 11 Dec 1984]; *Great Belt* Pleadings, 329 [Finland's Memorial]; *Gulf of Fonseca* Hearings, C 4/CR 91/45, 19 [Counsel Bowett, 10 June 1991], CR 91/46, 52-53 [Counsel Lauterpacht, 11 June], CR 91/47, 27 [Bowett, 12 June], CR 91/48, 29 [Lauterpacht, 13 June 1991]; *Denmark v. Norway* Hearings, CR 93/10, 63 [Counsel Bowett, 25 Jan 1993]; *Southern Bluefin Tuna (Jurisdiction)* Japan's Memorial, para.140 <www.worldbank.org/icsid>; *Cameroon v. Nigeria; Equatorial Guinea Intervening (Merits)* Hearings, CR 2002/6, 71 [Co-Agent Pellet, 25 Feb 2002]; 2006 *Barbados/Trinidad & Tobago* Award, paras 177, 235; Trinidad's Counter-Memorial, para.380; Barbados' Reply, para.164; Trinidad's Rejoinder, para.137; Hearings Day-4, 104-105 [Counsel Crawford, 21 Oct 2005] <www.pca-cpa.org>; *Nicaragua v. Honduras* Hearings, CR 2007/14, 23, para.51, at 24, para.54 [Counsel Colson, 23 March 2007]; *Nicaragua v. Colombia* Nicaragua's Memorial, 244 <www.icj-cij.org>; 2009 *Abyei Boundary* Award, para.762 <ww.pca-cpa.org>.

For Papua New Guinea's Maritime Zone Notification No.41 of 8 October 2002, see *UN LOSIC* 38 (2002 No.16); and for its Declaration on Archipelagic Baselines of 25 July 2002, see *UN LOS Bull.* 31 (2003 No.50).

On 2003 Barbados/Guyana EEZ Cooperation Treaty, see 2006 *Barbados/Trinidad & Tobago* Award *supra.*

On 1990 Barbados/Trinidad & Tobago Fishing Agreement and on their New Fisheries Agreement, see 2006 *Barbados/Trinidad & Tobago* Award *supra.*

See also Regime of Islands *infra.*

Islands

Minquiers and Ecrehos Pleadings, Vol.I, 51 [UK Memorial]; *North Sea* Judgment, ICJ Rep. 1969, 20, para.13, and 36, para.57, referring to "an islet or small protuberance" and "islets, rocks and minor coastal projections" [They included for the FRG: Borkum, Nordstrand, Pellworm, Helgoland (outside TS), Die, Amrun, Fohr and Sylt; for Denmark: Fanö, Mandö and Röm; and for the Netherlands: Texel, Vlieland, Terschelling, Ameland and Schiermonni-Koog], Separate Os Padilla Nervo, 93-94, Ammoun, 149, 151, Dissents Morelli, 201, 206, 207, 208, Lachs, 239, Sorensen, 249, 254; *North Sea* Pleadings, Vol.I, 18, 68-71, 74, 77 [FRG Memorial], 160, 181, 203, 210-213 [Denmark's Counter-Memorial], 357, 359, 362, 363-365 [NL Counter-Memorial], 420 [FRG Reply], Vol.II, 27-28, 33, 35, 44, 46 [Agent Jaenicke, 23 and 24 Oct 1968], 72-74 [Agent Riphagen, 28 Oct], 85, 86, 103 [Counsel Sir Humphrey Waldock, 28 and 29 Oct], 141, 147, 149-150 [Agent Jacobsen, 31 Oct], 163 [Questions Sir Gerald Fitzmaurice, 1 Nov], 190, 204, 208 [Jaenicke, 4 and 5 Nov], 247, 248, 252 [Reply by Waldock to Questions Fitzmaurice, 8 Nov], 271-273 [Waldock, 11 Nov 1968], 348 [map]; *Tunisia/Libya*

(Intervention) Judgment, ICJ Rep. 1981, 17, *(Merits)* Judgment, ICJ Rep. 1982, 35-36, 41-42, 62-64, 74, 85, 88-90, 93-94, para.133 B(3) and C(3), Separate Os Schwebel, 99, de Arechaga, 122, 133, 135-136, Dissents Gros, 149-150, Oda, 185-188, 235-237, 262-267, 268-269, 270-274, Evensen, 283, 285, 293, 296-304, 310, 313-317, *(Revision)* Judgment, ICJ Rep. 1985, 210, 226-227, Separate Os Oda, 243, Bastid, 242; Pleadings, Vol.IV, 414-415 [Counsel Jennings, 16 Sep 1981]; *Gulf of Maine* Judgment, ICJ Rep. 1984, 268-273, 284-286, 322, 325, 328, 329, 332, 336-337, Dissent Gros, 380, 387; Pleadings, Vol.I, 134-137, 141 [Canada's Memorial], Vol.II, 86, 90, 111 [US Memorial], Vol.III, 140, 254-257 [Canada's Counter-Memorial], Vol.V, 454, 475 [US Reply], Vol.VI, 461 [Question I.2 of Judge Gros, 19 April 1984], 463 [Question V of Judge Mosler, 19 April], Vol. VII, 36 [Counsel Weil's Reply to Gros, 4 May], 73-74 [Deputy Agent Hankey's Reply to Mosler, 4 May], 181 [Counsel Stevenson's Reply to Gros, 9 May], 232-233 [Counsel Colson, 10 May 1984]; *Libya/Malta (Intervention)* Judgment, ICJ Rep. 1984, 17, *(Merits)* Judgment, ICJ Rep. 1985, 42-43, 47-52, Joint Separate O., 86, Separate O. Valticos, 107, Dissents Mosler, 120, Oda, 135, 139, 146-148, 163-165, 167-169, Schwebel, 178-179; Pleadings, Vol.I, 122-124, 128-131, 134, 155-161, 166-169 [Libya's Memorial], 440-475, 497-499 [Malta's Memorial], Vol.II, 26-33, 89-100, 125-135 [Libya's Counter-Memorial], 313, 329-330, 358-361 [Malta's Counter-Memorial], Vol.III, 36-40, 90 [Libya's Reply], 194-197, 205-207, 247-257 [Malta's Reply], Vol.IV, 431-432 [Counsel Jaenicke, 21 Feb 1985], 446, 450-451 [Counsel Queneudec]; *Arbitral Award* Dissent Weeramantry, ICJ Rep. 1991, 169; *Denmark v. Norway* and *Qatar v. Bahrain* cases – see *supra*; *Cameroon v. Nigeria; Equatorial Guinea Intervening (Merits)* Judgment, ICJ Rep. 2002, 303, paras 241, 272, 274, 278-280, 284, 291-299, Separate O. Mbaye, 532-533, paras 132-135; *Indonesia/Malaysia (Merits)* Judgment, ICJ Rep. 2002, 662-664, paras 75-77, Declaration Oda, 690; *Romania v. Ukraine* Judgment, ICJ Rep. 2009, paras 16, 33, 35, 39, 41, 98-129, 179-188, 206, 218, *dispositif* para.219, sketch-Maps Nos 1-9; Hearings, CR 2008/28, 49-53, paras 61-82, appraising the legal entitlement of islands [Counsel Bundy, 11 Sep 2008] <www.icj-cij.org>; *Nicaragua v. Honduras* and *Nicaragua v. Colombia* cases – see *supra*.

1909 *Norway v. Sweden Grisbadarna* Award; 1977/1978 *Anglo/French Continental Shelf* Decisions; 1977/1984 *Argentina/Chile Beagle Channel* case; 1981 *Iceland/Norway* Conciliation; 1981 *Dubai/Sharjah* Award; 1985 *Guinea/Guinea Bissau* Award; 1989 *Guinea-Bissau/Senegal* Award; 1992 *Canada/France* Award, Dissents Gotlieb, Weil; 1998 *Eritrea/Yemen (Phase I)* and *(Phase II)* Awards [*infra*]; 2002 *Newfoundland/Nova Scotia (Phase II)* Award [*supra*].

On Iran/UAE Abu Musa/Tunbs Islands, see 1981 *Dubai/Sharjah* Award, 91 ILR 672-677; *Nicaragua v. Colombia* Nicaragua's Memorial, 245-246, para.3.110 <www.icj-cij.org>; *Romania v. Ukraine* Hearings, CR 2008/19, 55, para.11 [Agent

Aurescu, 3 Sep 2008], CR 2008/20, 25, para.36 and at 33, para.53 [Counsel Pellet, 4 Sep], CR 2008/28, 49, para.63 [Counsel Bundy, 11 Sep 2008] <www.icj-cij.org>; UN Docs S/1998/2, S/1999/305 and 802, S/2000/281, S/2001/309 and 319, A/57/417-S/2002/1042, S/2002/1082, S/2004/7, S/2004/486, S/2004/530, S/2004/617 of 30 July, A/59/2, at 187-188 (2004), S/2005/5, S/2005/144, S/2005/189, S/2005/215, S/2005/232, S/2005/300, S/2005/301, S/2005/363, S/2005/386, S/2005/468, A/60/2, at 195 (2005), S/2006/108, S/2006/200, S/2008/609; Iran/UAE Joint Commission of 29 Oct 2008 <www.middle-east-online.com/english/?id=28527 & www.metimes.com/Politics/2008/10/29/iran_uae_ink_accord_despite_islands_dispute/afp/>; S/2009/89, S/2009/145 and further continuing appeals, reaffirming the UAE sovereignty over these islands and inviting Iran to bring the matter before the ICJ <www.uaeinteract.com/news/?ID=147>.

"Ignoring the Presence of Islets, Rocks and Minor Coastal Projections" Approach

North Sea Judgment, ICJ Rep. 1969, 20, para.13, and at 36, para.57 (applying to: for the FRG – Borkum, Nordstrand, Pellworm, Helgoland [outside TS], Die, Amrun, Fohr and Sylt; for Denmark – Fanö, Mandö and Röm; and for the Netherlands – Texel, Vlieland, Terschelling, Ameland and Schiermonni-Koog); as reaffirmed by the 1977 *Anglo/French* Award [*infra*], paras 237-251 [with para.244 reaffirmed by the 2001 *Qatar v. Bahrain* Judgment, para.247]; On Turkey's perception of the Greek islands as "mere protuberance", see *Aegean Sea (Jurisdiction)* Judgment, ICJ Rep. 1978, 35, 37; Pleadings, 93-94 [Counsel O'Connell, 26 Aug 1976];

Canada/USA Gulf of Maine Judgment, ICJ Rep. 1984, 329-330, 332, paras 201-203, 210; *Libya/Malta (Merits)* Judgment, ICJ Rep. 1985, 48, para.64 (Filfla); 1999 *Eritrea/Yemen (Phase II)* Award [*supra*], paras 119, 138, 147-148 (Jabal al-Tayr Island and Group of Jabal al-Zubayr); *Qatar v. Bahrain (Merits)* Judgment, ICJ Rep. 2001, 95, para.179 [reaffirming the 1984 *Gulf of Maine* Judgment, para.210], at 99-100, paras 197-198, at 104-109, paras 219-222 (Qit-at Jaradah), at 114-115, paras 246-249 (Fasht al Jarim), with both paras 219 & 246 reaffirming the 1969 *North Sea*, para.57 and the 1985 *Libya/Malta*, para.64, Judgments; 2002 *Newfoundland and Labrador/Nova Scotia (Phase II)* Award, paras 4.31, 4.35 (Sable Island); *Nicaragua v. Honduras* Judgment, ICJ Rep. 2007, para.302 *et seq*; Hearings, CR 2007/1, 20, para.18: Fifla [Agent Arguello, 5 March 2007], 60-64 [Counsel Oude Elferink], CR 2007/2, 18, para.39, at 36, paras 112-113 [Counsel Brownlie, 6 March], CR 2007/8, 37, para.7 [Counsel Dupuy, 14 March 2007]; *Romania v. Ukraine* Judgment, ICJ Rep.2009 paras 149, 182, 185 (Serpents Island) <www.icj-cij.org>.

For ignoring small river rocks and sandbanks, see *Benin/Niger* Judgment, paras 19, 78-79, ICJ Rep. 2005, 104, 127-128; Niger's Memorial, 151; Hearings, C5/CR 2005/4, 25, paras 16-17 [Counsel Salmon, 8 March 2005] <www.icj-cij.org>.

Islands on the Wrong Side of the Median Line

Aegean Sea (Interim Measures) Order, ICJ Rep. 1976, 4, 6-7, *(Jurisdiction)* Judgment, ICJ Rep. 1978, 6, 8, 33-37, Dissent de Castro, 66; Pleadings, 3-11 [Greece's Application], 92-110 [Counsel O'Connell, 25 Aug 1976], 128-131 [Counsel Pinto, 26 Aug 1976], 445-446 [16 Oct 1978]; *Libya/Malta (Merits)* Dissent Oda, ICJ Rep. 1985, 146-148; Pleadings, Vol.II, 97 [Libya's Counter-Memorial]; *Denmark v. Norway* case – see *supra*, and Norway's Counter-Memorial, para.472, Denmark's Reply, para.299, Norway's Rejoinder, paras 459-461; Oral Hearings, CR 93/8 [trans.], 56-57 [Counsel Weil, 20 Jan 1993]; *Qatar v. Bahrain (Merits)* Hearings, CR 2000/11, 34-35 [Counsel Lauterpacht, 8 June 2000]; *Cameroon v. Nigeria; Equatorial Guinea Intervening (Merits)* Judgment, ICJ Rep. 2002, 434-436, 446, paras 274-275, 279, 299; Hearings, CR 2002/6, 41-42 [Co-Agent Kamto, 25 Feb 2002], CR 2002/13, 22, 68-69 [Counsel Crawford, 7 March], CR 2002/17, 48-50 [Kamto, 12 March], CR 2002/20, 41-43 [Counsel Abi-Saab, 15 March 2002]; *Romania v. Ukraine* Hearings, CR 2008/28, 51, paras 71-74 [Counsel Bundy, 11 Sep 2008] <www.icj-cij.org>; *Nicaragua v. Honduras* and *Nicaragua v. Colombia* – see *supra*.

On 1978 Australia/Papua New Guinea Treaty, see Economic Factors *supra*.

1977/1978 *Anglo/French* and 1992 *Canada/France* Awards [*infra*]; 1985 *Guinea/Guinea-Bissau* Award, paras 103, 106-111 [*supra*]; 2002 *Newfoundland/Nova Scotia (Phase II)* Award, paras 3.16, 4.26-4.29 [*supra*].

See also Regime of Islands *infra*.

Historic Factors

– see Internal Waters, Territorial Sea and Baselines, Historic Titles and Historic Bays, *supra*.

Security Factors

Anglo/Norwegian Fisheries Pleadings, Vol.I, 534, 572 [Counter-Memorial of Norway], Vol.II, 659, 663-664, 676, 679 [UK Reply], Vol.IV, 41-42 [Agent Sir Eric Beckett, 25 Sep 1951]; *North Sea* Separate O. Padilla Nervo, ICJ Rep. 1969, 93, Dissent Koretsky, 155; Pleadings, Vol.I, 364 [NL Counter-Memorial]; *Tunisia/Libya (Merits)* Dissent Oda, ICJ Rep. 1982, 256; Pleadings, Vol.V, 276-277 [Counsel Jennings, 13 Oct 1981]; *Gulf of Maine* Judgment, ICJ Rep. 1984, 278,

340-341, 342; Pleadings, Vol.II, 46-47, 114 [US Memorial], Vol.III, 19, 168-169, 226, 374-380 [Canada's Counter-Memorial], Vol.IV, 137 [US Counter-Memorial], Vol.V, 36, 78 [Canada's Reply], 654-655, 660 [US Reply], Vol.VI, 140 [Counsel Bowett, 5 April 1984], 278-279 [Counsel Stevenson, 12 April], 351-353 [Counsel Rashkow, 16 April 1984], Vol.VIII, 28 [Fig.14], 105 [Fig.17], 106 [Fig.18]; *Libya/Malta (Merits)* Judgment, ICJ Rep. 1985, 41-42, 52, Separate O. Valticos, 112-113; Pleadings, Vol.I, 103, 128 [Libya's Memorial], 420, 483, 498-499, 514 [Malta's Memorial], Vol.II, 71-75 [Libya's Counter-Memorial], 328-329, 349, 360-361, 367, 369, 373-374, 376 [Malta's Counter-Memorial], Vol.III, 52, 67 [Libya's Reply], 325 [Counsel Lauterpacht, 27 Nov 1984], Vol.IV, 136-138 [Counsel Lucchini, 12 Dec 1984], 321-323 [Lauterpacht, 11 Feb 1985], 405 [Agent Mizzi, 13 Feb 1985]; *Denmark v. Norway* Judgment, ICJ Rep. 1993, 74-75, Separate Os Schwebel, 119, Weeramantry, 262, 271-272; Norway's Counter-Memorial, paras 74-77, 561-566, Norway's Rejoinder, para.529; Hearings, CR 93/1Corr., 28-29 [Agent Lehmann, 11 Jan 1993], CR 93/7, 11, 36 [Counsel Brownlie, 19 Jan 1993]; *Qatar v. Bahrain (Merits)* Dissent Torres Bernardez, para.519, ICJ Rep. 2001, 435; Hearings, CR 2000/5 [trans.], 39 [Counsel Salmon, 29 May 2000], CR 2000/22, 29 [Counsel Volterra, 28 June 2000]; *Nicaragua v. Honduras* Hearings, CR 2007/2, 47-48 [Counsel Brownlie, 6 March 2007], CR 2007/6, 38, para.93 [Counsel Greenwood, 12 March], CR 2007/14, 13-14, para.10 [Counsel Colson, 23 March 2007]; *Malaysia/Singapore (Merits)* Judgment, ICJ Rep. 2008, paras 247-248, Dissent Dugard, para.27; *Romania v. Ukraine* Judgment, ICJ Rep. 2009, paras 202-204; Hearings, CR 2008/21, 66, paras 72-73 [Counsel Lowe, 5 Sep 2008], CR 2008/29, 38-39, paras 81-85 [Counsel Queneudec, 12 Sep 2008], 44-45 [Counsel Bundy]; *Nicaragua v. Colombia (Merits)* Judgment; Nicaragua's Memorial, 224-226 <www.icj-cij.org>.

1917 *El Salvador v. Nicaragua Gulf of Fonseca* Judgment [*supra*]; 1977 *Anglo/French* Decision [*supra*], paras 161-163, 175-176, 188, 197; 1985 *Guinea/Guinea-Bissau* Award [*supra*], para.124; 1988 *Taba* Award [*supra*], paras 22, 30, 38, 69; 1992 *Canada/France* Dissent Weil [*supra*], paras 31-33, 35; 1999 *Eritrea/Yemen (Phase II)* Award [*supra*], para.21; 2006 *Barbados/Trinidad & Tobago* Award [*supra*], para.241.

Navigational Factors

North Sea Separate Os Padilla Nervo, ICJ Rep. 1969, 93-94, Ammoun, 149, Dissents Lachs, 239, Sorensen, 254; Pleadings, Vol.I, 68-70, 78 [FRG Memorial], 181 [Denmark's Counter-Memorial], 357, 364 [NL Counter-Memorial], 420 [FRG Reply], Vol. II, 46 [Agent Jaenicke, 24 Oct 1968], 69 [Agent Jacobsen, 28 Oct 1968]; *Tunisia/Libya (Merits)* Dissent Oda, ICJ Rep. 1982, 185-188; *Gulf of Maine*

Judgment, ICJ Rep. 1984, 340-341, 342, 343-344; Pleadings, Vol.II, 38-43, 46-47, 114 [US Memorial], Vol.III, 19, 56-58, 166-167, 225-226, 381-385 [Canada's Counter-Memorial], Vol.IV, 137 [US Counter-Memorial], Vol.V, 36, 78 [Canada's Reply], Vol.VI, 139 [Counsel Bowett, 5 April 1984], 278-279 [Counsel Stevenson, 12 April], 351-353 [Counsel Rashkow, 16 April], Vol.VII, 17 [Agent Legault, 3 May 1984], Vol.VIII, 27 [Fig.13], 104 [Fig.16]; *Libya/Malta (Merits)* Judgment, ICJ Rep. 1985, 42, 52; Pleadings, Vol.I, 128 [Libya's Memorial], 479, 483 [Malta's Memorial], Vol.II, 73 [Libya's Counter-Memorial], 251, 328-329, 367 [Malta's Counter-Memorial], Vol.IV, 321-323 [Counsel Lauterpacht, 11 Feb 1985], 438 [Counsel Jaenicke, 21 Feb 1985]; *Gulf of Fonseca (Intervention)* Judgment, ICJ Rep. 1990, 125; *Denmark v. Norway* Separate O. Schwebel, ICJ Rep. 1993, 119, 122-123; *Cameroon v. Nigeria (Preliminary Objections)* Judgment, ICJ Rep. 1998, 283; *Qatar v. Bahrain (Merits)* Separate O. Oda, para.18, ICJ Rep. 2001, 129-130; *Nicaragua v. Honduras (Merits)* Judgment, ICJ Rep. 2007, paras 80, 95, 170, 199-201, 220-221, 242, 291-292; Hearings, CR 2007/1, 26, para.38 [Agent Arguello, 5 March 2007], CR 2007/2, 48-50 [Counsel Brownlie, 6 March], CR 2007/3, 50-52 [Counsel Oude Elferink, 7 March], CR 2007/9, 44, para.21 [Counsel Colson, 15 March], CR 2007/11, 25, paras 57-59 [Arguello, 19 March], CR 2007/14, 14-15, paras 13-15 & 18, at 19, para.35 [Colson, 23 March 2007]; *Malaysia/Singapore (Merits)* Judgment, ICJ Rep. 2008, paras 19, 61, 166-167, 231-234, 240-243; *Romania v. Ukraine* Judgment, ICJ Rep. 2009, para.196 <www.icj-cij.org>.

1909 *Norway v. Sweden Grisbadarna* Award [*supra*]; 1977 *Anglo/French* Decision [*supra*], paras 161-163, 175-176, 188, 197, rejecting the French arguments based on security considerations concerning risk to French submarines based in Cherbourg and to navigational routes for merchant vessels serving French ports; 1977/1984 *Argentina/Chile Beagle Channel* case [*infra*]; 1981 *Dubai/Sharjah* Award [91 ILM 660-663]; 1985 *Guinea/Guinea-Bissau* Award, paras 25, 105, 121 [25 ILM 266, 295, 301 (1986)]; 1992 *Canada/France* Dissent Weil [*supra*], para.35; 1998 *Eritrea/Yemen (Phase I)* Award, paras 77, 93, 125, 478, and 1999 *(Phase II)* Award, paras 26, 45-46, 107-109, 124-125, 128, 155 [*supra*]; 2002 *Belize/Guatemala* OAS Facilitators' Proposals, B-para.5, D-para.2 [*supra*]; 2006 *Barbados/Trinidad & Tobago* Award, para.241 [*supra*]; 2007 *Guyana/Suriname* Award, paras 243-245, 282-285, 292-293, 300-306, 313-324; Guyana's Memorial, para.4.51, Suriname's Counter-Memorial, para.3.33, Guyana's Reply, paras 6.24/6.34, Suriname's Rejoinder, para.2.54 <www.pca-cpa.org>.

See also International Waters, Territorial Sea and Baselines – Maintenance of Navigational Aids and Territorial Sovereignty; Access to, Jurisdiction and Treatment in Ports – Ports/Oil and Gas Development *supra*.

Environmental Factors

Tunisia/Libya Pleadings, Vol.I, 77-79 (ecological unity/climate) [Tunisia's Memorial], Vol.II, 153-154 [Libya's Counter-Memorial]; *Gulf of Maine* Judgment, ICJ Rep. 1984, 275-277, 279, 286, 316-317, 319-320, 326-327, Dissent Gros, 370; Pleadings, Vol.II, 16-22, 112 [US Memorial], Vol.III, 83, 170, 352-361 [Canada's Counter-Memorial], Vol.IV, 22-23, 130-133, 152-153, 166, 259-271 [US Counter-Memorial], Vol.V, 5, 36, 64-65, 73, 342-343 [Canada's Reply], 440, 464-470, 529-537 [US Reply], Vol.VII, 112-117, 123-124 [Counsel Fortier, 5 May 1984], 250-251 [Counsel Colson, 11 May], 269-271 [Agent Robinson, 11 May 1984]; *Arbitral Award* Dissent Weeramantry, ICJ Rep. 1991, 169; *Denmark v. Norway* Judgment, ICJ Rep. 1993, 44, 72-73, Separate Os Oda, 116, Schwebel, 120, Weeramantry, 271, 276-278, Ajibola, 298, Dissent Fischer, 309; Hearings, CR 93/5, 38-39 [Agent Tresselt, 15 Jan 1993], CR 93/10, 76-77 [Counsel Lynge, 25 Jan 1993].

1977 *Anglo/French* Decision [18 ILM 397 (1979)], paras 163, 175; *Canada/France* Dissent Weil [31 ILM 1211 (1992)], para.35; 1999 *Eritrea/Yemen (Phase II)* Award, para.108 [*supra*]; 2002 *Belize/Guatemala* OAS Facilitators' Proposals (Belize-Guatemala-Honduras Ecological Park), B-paras 1, 12, C and Annex A [*supra*]; 2009 *Abyei Boundary* Award, paras 357-371, referring to environmental considerations in land boundary delimitation [*supra*].

See also Regime of Islands – Environmental Factors in Disputes Over Territorial Sovereignty *infra*.

Proportionality

North Sea Judgment, ICJ Rep. 1969, 49, para.89, at 52, para.98, at 54, para.101(D)(2), Separate O. President Bustamante y Rivero, 58-59, Separate O. Ammoun, 148, Dissents Tanaka, 188-189, Lachs, 239, Sorensen, 255-256; Pleadings, Vol.I, 468-469 [Common Rejoinder of Denmark/NL], Vol.II, 145, 150 [Agent Jacobsen, 31 Oct 1968]; *Tunisia/Libya (Intervention)* Judgment, ICJ Rep. 1981, 17, *(Merits)* Judgment, ICJ Rep. 1982, 62, 72, 75-76, 80, 91, 93, para.133 B(5), Separate O. de Arechaga, 137-139, Dissents Gros, 149-152, Oda, 258-260, 267, Evensen, 311-314, *(Revision)* Judgment, ICJ Rep. 1985, 226; *Gulf of Maine* Judgment, ICJ Rep. 1984, 318, 322-323, 335-336, Separate O. Schwebel, 354-359 [incl. Map], Dissent Gros, 381-385; Pleadings, Vol.I, 146-152 [Canada's Memorial], Vol.II, 86, 94 [US Memorial], Vol.III, 183-186, 247-251, 261-268 (264 Fig.51A) [Canada's Counter-Memorial], Vol.IV, 16-17, 127-130 [US Counter-Memorial], Vol.V, 128, 143-147 [Canada's Reply], 401, 431, 482-491 (485 Fig.51A), [US Reply], Vol.VI, 49 [Agent Legault, 3 April 1984], 74-86 [Deputy Agent Hankey, 4 April], 206-219 [Counsel Malintoppi, 10 April], 293-295 [Counsel Colson, 12 April], 310-315 [Colson, 13

April], 328-336 [Counsel Feldman, 13 April], 464 [Question 2 of Judge Schwebel, 19 April], Vol.VII, 126-134 [Malintoppi's Reply to Schwebel, 5 May, with err. at 377], 215, 216 [Fig.51A], 234-235 [Colson's Reply, 10 May 1984], Vol.VIII, 55 [Fig.13], 76 [Fig.51], 256 [Fig.171]; *Libya/Malta (Intervention)* Judgment, ICJ Rep. 1984, 24-25, *(Merits)* Judgment, ICJ Rep. 1985, 43-46, 49-50, 53-56, 57, para.79B, Separate O. Sette-Camara, 72-75, Joint Separate O., 82-92, Separate O. Valticos, 109-113, Dissents Oda, 132-134, Schwebel, 181-187; Pleadings, Vol.I, 132-134, 156-157, 173-178 [Libya's Memorial], 435-439, 492-493 [Malta's Memorial], Vol.II, 90-94, 144-152 [Libya's Counter-Memorial], 256-257, 331-345 [Malta's Counter-Memorial], Vol.III, 87-95 [Libya's Reply], 214-225 [Malta's Reply], 321 [Counsel Lauterpacht, 27 Nov 1984], 454-476 [Counsel Brownlie, 3 Dec 1984], Vol.IV, 432-434 [Counsel Jaenicke, 21 Feb 1985]; *Denmark v. Norway* Judgment, ICJ Rep. 1993, 48, 65-69, 81, Declaration Aguilar Mawdsley, 86, Separate Os Oda, 115-116, Schwebel, 120-129, Shahabuddeen, 159-191, Weeramantry, 272-273, Ajibola, 301, Dissent Fischer, 308-309; Hearings, CR 93/2, 77-80 [Counsel de Arechaga, 12 Jan 1993], CR 93/4, 41-52 [Agent Bernhard, 14 Jan], CR 93/7, 54-71 [Counsel Brownlie, 19 Jan], CR 93/9 [trans.], 2-22 [Counsel Weil, 21 Jan 1993]; *Qatar v. Bahrain (Merits)* Judgment, ICJ Rep. 2001, 114, paras 241-243, Dissent Torres Bernardez, 435-436, paras 520-522; Hearings, CR 2000/9 [trans.], 32-41 [Counsel Queneudec, 5 June 2000]; *Cameroon v. Nigeria; Equatorial Guinea Intervening (Merits)* Judgment, ICJ Rep. 2002, 303, paras 271-273, 278, 291, 300-301; *Nicaragua v. Honduras* Hearings, CR 2007/12, 51-52 [Counsel Brownlie, 20 March 2007], CR 2007/14, 19-20, paras 37-41, adhering to the 2006 *Barbados/T&T* Award's perception of proportionality *infra* [Counsel Colson, 23 March 2007] <www.icj-cij.org>; *Romania v. Ukraine* Judgment, ICJ Rep. 2009, paras 83, 87, 93, 98-149, 158-168, 210-216, sketch-Maps Nos 1-9; Hearings, CR 2008/20, 29, para.45 [Counsel Pellet, 4 Sep 2008], CR 2008/28, 52, para.76 [Counsel Bundy, 11 Sep], CR 2008/31, 38, para.33 [Pellet, 16 Sep], 44-45, paras 15-17 and at 46, para.21 n.80 [Counsel Lowe, 16 Sep], CR 2008/32, 39, para.41 [Bundy, 18 Sep], CR 2008/33, 24, para.41 [Bundy, 19 Sep 2008] <www.icj-cij.org>.

1977/1978 *Anglo/French Continental Shelf* Decisions [*infra*]; 1985 *Guinea/Guinea-Bissau* Award [*supra*], paras 118-120; 1992 *Canada/France* Award, paras 60-63, 92-93, Dissents Gotlieb, Weil [*infra*]; 1999 *Eritrea/Yemen Maritime Delimitation (Phase II)* Award [*supra*], paras 20, 39-43, 117, 165-168; 2002 *Newfoundland/Nova Scotia (Phase II)* Award [*supra*], paras 1.28, 2.34, 4.11/24, 5.14/15, 5.17/19; *Barbados/Trinidad & Tobago* Award, President S.M. Schwebel, paras 119-120, 158-161, 173, 232-233, 236-240, 320, 326-338, 350-352, 376-379; Hearings Day-1, 30-35 [Counsel Sir Elihu Lauterpacht, 17 Oct 2005], Day-4, 65-68 [Counsel Crawford, 21 Oct], Day-6, 17-31 [Counsel Paulsson, 25 Oct], Day-8,

17-31 [Crawford, 28 Oct 2005] <www.pca-cpa.org>; 2007 *Guyana/Suriname* Award, President L.D.M. Nelson, para.392; Hearings Day 8, 1179-1191 [Counsel McRae, 16 Dec 2006], 1239-1249 [Counsel Greenwood] <www.pca-cpa.org>.

On the methods of the *tracé parallèle* and the *courbe tangente* (envelopes of arcs-of circles), see Internal Waters, Territorial Sea and Baselines, TS Breadth and Outer Limit *supra*.

On the practice of Chile, Ecuador and Peru (CEP) regarding delimitation (by parallel of geographical latitude, and not equidistance) of their CS/EEZ, see *Peru v. Chile* case *supra*.

Thalweg Principle/Lakes and Rivers

Honduras v. Nicaragua Arbitral Award of 23 December 1906 Judgment, ICJ Rep. 1960, 202-203, 212, 216-217; *North Sea* Judgment, ICJ Rep. 1969, 45, para.80, Separate O. Ammoun, 124-125, 126, 128, Dissents Tanaka, 175, Lachs, 222; Pleadings, Vol.I, 34-35, 38 [FRG Memorial], 173, 187, 270-279 [Denmark's Counter-Memorial], 327, 340 [NL Counter-Memorial], 406-407 [FRG Reply], 461 [Common Rejoinder of Denmark/NL], Vol.II, 20 [Agent Jaenicke, 23 Oct 1968], 90 [Counsel Sir Humphrey Waldock, 28 Oct], 264 [Reply by Waldock to Questions Fitzmaurice, 8 Nov 1968]; *Tunisia/Libya (Merits)* Separate O. de Arechaga, ICJ Rep. 1982, 117; *Gulf of Maine* Judgment, ICJ Rep. 1984, 319, para.172; Pleadings, Vol.III, 201 [Canada's Counter-Memorial], Vol.VII, 258-259 [Counsel Colson, 11 May 1984]; *Libya/Malta* Pleadings, Vol.IV, 180-181 [Counsel Bowett, 14 Dec 1984]; *Gulf of Fonseca (Merits)* Judgment, ICJ Rep. 1992, 543-553, 615, para.430, *(Revision)* Judgment, ICJ Rep. 2003, 392; *Gabcikovo-Nagymaros Project* Judgment, President S.M. Schwebel, ICJ Rep. 1997, 18, para.16, Separate O. Bedjaoui, 126; Hearings, CR 97/2 [trans.], 36 [Counsel Kiss, 3 March 1997], CR 97/5 [trans.], 5 [6 March 1997]; *Botswana/Namibia Kasikili/Sedudu* Judgment, ICJ Rep. 1999, 1045, <www.namibian.com.na/Netstories /December99/ko.html>, President S.M. Schwebel concurring, Declarations Ranjeva, 1110, Koroma, 1111, Higgins, 1113, Separate Os Oda, 1116, Kooymans, 1144, Dissent Vice-President Weeramantry, 1153, Dissents Fleischhauer, 1196, Parra-Aranguren, 1208, Rezek, 1233; Questions of President Schwebel and Judge Fleischhauer, in Hearings, CR 99/9, 55-56 [25 Feb 1999], as relied upon in Dissent of Vice-President Weeramantry, paras 56-57; 98 AJIL 455 (2004); *Cameroon v. Nigeria; Equatorial Guinea Intervening (Merits)* Judgment, ICJ Rep. 2002, 303, paras 36, 39-102, 147-152, 200, 213-214, 250, 261, 325.III(C) and IV(B), Dissent Koroma, 477-478, 482, paras 11, 19; Hearings, CR 2002/2, 21, 43-44 [Counsel Cot, 19 Feb 2002], CR 2002/10, 47-49 [Counsel Sir Arthur Watts, 4 March], CR 2002/11, 54-58 [5 March], CR 2002/15, 40-43 [Counsel Cot, 11 March 2002]; *El Salvador v. Honduras Gulf of Fonseca (Revision)* case [*supra*]; *Benin/Niger Frontier Dispute (Formation of Chamber)* Orders, ICJ Rep. 2002, 613, 2003, 155; ICJ Trust Fund's Grant of 4 June 2004 <www.un.org/News/Press/docs/2004/sg2087.doc.htm & www.unwire .org/UNWire/20040607/449_24601.asp>, *Benin/Niger (Composition of Chamber)* Order and *(Merits)* Judgment, ICJ Rep. 2005, 84, 90 and Niger Takes Over Disputed Lete Island of 15 Feb 2007 <http://news.bbc.co.uk/2/hi/africa/6364703.stm>; *Costa Rica v. Nicaragua San Juan River* Order, ICJ Rep. 2005, 165 and Judgment, ICJ Rep. 2009, paras 18, 19, 21, Sketch-Map No.2, paras 33, 63, 77-79, Declaration Guillaume, paras 4-6, 11 <www.icj-cij.org> & Map <www.sovereigngeographic .com/central_america.html>; *Nicaragua v. Honduras Maritime Delimitation* case [*supra*] and 1906 *Honduras/Nicaragua* Award [*infra*]; Sir Creek – see 1968 *India/Pakistan Rann of Kutch* Award [*infra*].

On France/Switzerland Agreement on the Delimitation of the Lake of Léman of 25 February 1953 [*North Sea* Pleadings, Vol.I, 270], see *North Sea* Separate O. Ammoun, ICJ Rep. 1969, 127, 146.

1798 *UK/USA St. Croix River* Award [*infra*]; 1814 *UK/USA St. Lawrence River* Award [*infra*]; 1831 *UK/USA Northeastern Boundary* Award [*infra*]; 1868 Ord *Johor/Pahang Boundary* Award of Sir Harry Ord, British Governor of the Straits Settlement [*infra*]; 1888 *Costa Rica/Nicaragua* Award [Inter-Oceanic Canals *supra*]; 1892 *Iowa v. Illinois* Judgment [*infra*]; 1906 *Honduras/Nicaragua* Award [*infra*]; 1911 *Mexico/USA Chamizal* Award [*infra*]; 1914 *Netherlands/Portugal Island of Timor* Award [Regime of Islands, Sovereignty Over Island Territory *infra*]; 1916 CAC *Costa Rica v. Nicaragua* Judgment [Inter-Oceanic Canals *supra*]; 1919 *Minnesota v. Wisconsin* Judgment [*infra*]; 1929 *USA McMahan v. Mexico Rio Grande Boundary* Award [*infra*]; 1934 *New Jersey v. Delaware* and *Wisconsin v. Michigan* Judgments [*infra*]; 1947 *Sieur George v. Sieur Nadin* [*infra*]; 1966 *Argentina/Chile Frontier (Rio Palena)* Award [*infra*]; 1968 *India/Pakistan Rann of Kutch* Award [*infra*]; 1982 *Hazlett v. Presnell* [*infra*]; 1985 *Guinea/Guinea-Bissau* Award, paras 16-17, 19, 22, 32, 62, 72-74, 78, 106, 129 [*supra*]; 1994/1995 *Argentina/Chile Laguna del Desierto* Awards [*infra*]; 2002 UN *Eritrea/Ethiopia Boundary (Merits)* Decision, Chapters II, paras 2.20-2.32, IV (central sector), V (western sector), VII (the main river channel boundary), VIII (*dispositif*), Appendix A, and *(Interpretation)* Decision, 2003 *(Demarcation)* Observations <www.pca-cpa.org>; 2002 *Belize/Guatemala* OAS Facilitators' Proposals, A-para.1, D-para.2 [*supra*]; 2007 *Guyana/Suriname* Award, para.301 [*supra*]; 2009 *Abyei Boundary* Award, paras 669-672 <www.pca-cpa.org>.

See also Internal Waters, Territorial Sea and Baselines – Mouth of Rivers *supra*; Regime of Islands – Islands in the Rivers *infra*.

Sector Principle/Arctic and Antarctic

Corfu Channel (Merits) Individual O. Alvarez, ICJ Rep. 1949, 43; *North Sea* Separate O. Ammoun, ICJ Rep. 1969, 116; Pleadings, Vol.I, 80-87 [FRG Memorial], 214-217 [Denmark's Counter-Memorial], 368-373 [NL Counter-Memorial], 425-433 [FRG Reply], 471-472 [Common Rejoinder of Denmark/NL]; *Gulf of Maine* Pleadings, Vol.III, 63-64 [Canada's Counter-Memorial], Vol.V, 62 [Canada's Reply], Vol.VI, 384 [Counsel Feldman, 16 April 1984]; *Romania v. Ukraine* Hearings, CR 2008/30, 52, para.31(2) [Counsel Crawford, 15 Sep 2008] <www.icj-cij.org>.

Sector Principle has been relied upon by Russia in its negotiations since 1974 with Norway on their Barents Sea maritime delimitation. See <http://ocean-futures.com/ABOUT/Announcement-OF-Focus-North-2006-11.htm> and 2001 Russia's and 2006 Norway's Submission to the CLCS <www.un.org/Depts/los/>.

Cf. Regime of Islands – Presumption in Favour of Sovereignty over Islands within and beyond the Territorial Sea; CLCS Submissions: *Arctic* – Norway, Russia, Denmark, Iceland; *Antarctic* – Australia, NZ, France, UK, Norway, Chile, Argentina and U.S. and Russia's Notes Verbales on these Submissions <www.un.org/Depts/los/>.

On 1798 *UK/USA St. Croix River* Award [No.1/Stuyt; RIAA, XXVIII, 1], see *Gulf of Maine* Pleadings, Vol.I, 182 [Canada's Memorial], Vol.V, 52 n.58, 99 n.79 [Canada's Reply], Vol.VI, 15 [Counsel MacGuigan, 2 April 1984], 60 [Deputy-Agent Hankey, 3 April 1984]; *Denmark v. Norway* Separate Os Shahabuddeen, ICJ Rep. 1993, 194-195, Weeramantry, 248.

On 1814 *UK/USA St. Lawrence River* Award [No.13/Stuyt; RIAA, XXVIII, 11], see *Honduras v. Nicaragua* Dissent Urrutia, ICJ Rep. 1960, 223, 226.

On 1831 *UK/USA Northeastern Boundary* Award of King William I [No.27/Stuyt; RIAA, XXVIII, 33], see *Taba* Dissent Lapidoth, para.4 [27 ILM 1497 (1988)]; *Arbitral Award* Dissent Weeramantry, ICJ Rep. 1991, 153.

On 1868 Ord *Johor/Pahang Boundary* Award of Sir Harry Ord, British Governor of the Straits Settlement [Malaysia's Memorial Vol.3, Annex 86], see *Malaysia/Singapore Pedra Branca* Hearings, CR 2007/24, 26-27, paras 23-25 [Co-Agent Farida, 13 Nov 2007], CR 2007/28, 34-35, para.26 [Counsel Chan, 19 Nov], CR 2007/30, 36, para.29 and at 38-39, para.34 [Counsel Schrijver, 22 Nov], CR 2007/31, 51-52, paras 11-13 [Crawford, 23 Nov 2007] <www.icj-cij.org>.

On 1872 *UK/USA San Juan Water Boundary* Award, see Straits Used for International Navigation *supra*.

On 1888 *Costa Rica/Nicaragua* Award of U.S. President Grover Cleveland, see Inter-Oceanic Canals *supra*.

On 1891 *Colombia/Venezuela Boundary* Award of King of Spain Alphonso XII and 1918/1922 Award [RIAA I, 227, 292; 27 RGDIP 181 (1920); 28 RGDIP 107

(1921); 16 AJIL 428 (1922); Nos 121 and 320/Stuyt; Los Monjes Dispute (1988) <www.country-data.com/cgi-bin/query/r-3109.html>], see *Honduras v. Nicaragua* Dissent Urrutia, ICJ Rep. 1960, 223, 225-227, 229, 230-231, 233; *Gulf of Fonseca* Hearings, C 4/CR 91/5 [trans.], 49 [Counsel de Arechaga, 19 April 1991], CR 91/35, 43-44 [Counsel Highet, 30 May], CR 91/37, 30 [31 May 1991]; *Joint Legal Opinion on Guatemala's Territorial Claim to Belize*, Annex II, para.13 (Jan 2002) <www.belize-guatemala.gov.bz/>; *Nicaragua v. Honduras (Merits)* Judgment, ICJ Rep. 2007, para.133; *Nicaragua v. Colombia (Preliminary Objections)* Hearings, CR 2007/16, 12-13, para.7 [Agent Paredes, 4 June 2007] <www.icj-cij.org>.

On 1892 *Iowa v. Illinois* Judgment [147 US 13], see *Botswana/Namibia* Hearings, CR 99/1, 57, 59, 64 [Counsel Delbruck, 15 Feb 1999].

On 1899 *UK(Guyana)/Venezuela Boundary* Award, President Frederic Martens [No.207/Stuyt; 43 AJIL 523-530 (1949); 44 AJIL 683-693, 720-727 (1950); RIAA, XXVIII, 31], see *Eastern Greenland* Pleadings, PCIJ Series C, No.62, 393-394, 463-464, 491 [Norway's Counter-Memorial], No.63, 840 [Denmark's Reply]; *Cameroon v. Nigeria; Equatorial Guinea Intervening (Merits)* Dissent Ajibola, ICJ Rep. 2002, 541, para.9; 2007 *Guyana/Suriname* Award, paras 132, 224; Suriname's Counter-Memorial, para.6.23, Guyana's Reply, paras 5.20, 7.21 <www.pca-cpa .org>. Since 1951, the Award has been considered by Venezuela a nullity. Cf. *Arbitral Award* Joint Dissent Aguilar Mawdsley and Ranjeva, ICJ Rep. 1991, 120-129; *Botswana/Namibia* Hearings, CR 99/5 [trans.], 6 n.6, 16 [Counsel Cot, 18 Feb 1999].

See also 1999- UNSG *Guyana/Venezuela* Mediation *supra*.

On 1902 *Argentina/Chile Southern Andes Boundary* Award of King Edward VII [2246 UNTS 71; No.198/Stuyt], see *Antarctica* Pleadings, 68, 69 [UK Application]; *Arbitral Award* Dissent Weeramantry, ICJ Rep. 1991, 168; Hearings, CR 91/3, 67 [Counsel Highet, 4 April 1991]; *Qatar v. Bahrain (Merits)* Hearings, CR 2000/12, 56 [Counsel Reisman, 9 June 2000]; *Cameroon v. Nigeria; Equatorial Guinea Intervening (Merits)* Hearings, CR 2002/11, 54 [Counsel Watts, 5 March 2002]. See also 1994/5 *Argentina/Chile Laguna del Desierto* Awards *infra*.

On 1903 *UK/USA Alaska Boundary* Award [RIAA XV, 481; No.251/Stuyt; <www.internationalboundarycommission.org/ibcpg2.htm], see *Eastern Greenland* Pleadings, PCIJ Series C, No.62, 475, 492 [Norway's Counter-Memorial]; *Anglo/Norwegian Fisheries* Pleadings, Vol.I, 410, 431-432, 554 [Norway's Counter-Memorial], Vol.II, 451, 477, 478-479, 538-539, 617 [UK Reply]; Vol.III, 372 [Norway's Rejoinder]; *Minquiers and Ecrehos* Pleadings, Vol.II, 268 [Agent Gros, 30 Sep 1953]; *Gulf of Maine* Pleadings, Vol.IV, 110 [US Counter-Memorial], Vol. V, 510, 518 [US Reply], Vol.VI, 20 [Agent Legault, 2 April 1984], 376 [Counsel Rashkow, 16 April 1984]; *Libya/Chad* Separate O. Ajibola, ICJ Rep. 1994, 81; *Qatar v. Bahrain (Merits)* Joint Dissent Bedjaoui, Ranjeva, Koroma, para.94 n.27, ICJ Rep. 2001, 175; 2005 US Supreme Court's *Alaska v. US* Judgment <www

.supremecourtus.gov/opinions/opinions.html> & <www.asil.org/ilib050811 .html>; Canada/US Territorial and Maritime Beaufort Sea Dispute of 14 Sep 2009 <www.canada.com/news/press+Harper+raise+Canada+boundary+dispute +with+Obama/1997222/story.html>; 26 Nov 2009 <www.cbc.ca/canada/north/ story/2009/11/26/north-beaufort-sea.html>; 17-18 Feb 2010 <www.nationalpost. com/news/canada/politics/story.html?id=2578976 & www.vancouversun.com/ news/Beaufort+breakthrough/2579664/story.html>.

On 1904 *Brazil/UK Guiana Boundary* Award of King Victor Emmanuel III [RIAA XI, 21; No.240/Stuyt], see *Eastern Greenland* Pleadings, PCIJ Series C, No. 62, 394-395, 427 [Norway's Counter-Memorial], No.63, 777, 818 [Denmark's Reply]; *Minquiers and Ecrehos* Pleadings, Vol.II, 270 [Agent Gros, 30 Sep 1953]; *Gulf of Maine* Pleadings, Vol.III, 200 [Canada's Counter-Memorial]; *Qatar v. Bahrain (Merits)* Joint Dissent Bedjaoui, Ranjeva, Koroma, ICJ Rep. 2001, 175, para.94 n.27; Hearings, CR 2000/12, 56, 60 [Counsel Reisman, 9 June 2000]; *Joint Legal Opinion on Guatemala's Territorial Claim to Belize*, Annex II, para.23 (January 2002) <www.belize-guatemala.gov.bz/>; *Cameroon v. Nigeria; Equatorial Guinea Intervening (Merits)* Dissent Ajibola, para.9, ICJ Rep. 2002, 541.

On 1906 *Honduras/Nicaragua Boundary Question* Award of Alphons XIII, King of Spain [RIAA XI, 111 & XXVIII, 451; <www.sovereigngeographic.com/central_ america. html>; No.180/Stuyt], see *Honduras v. Nicaragua Arbitral Award Made by the King of Spain on 23 December 1906* Judgment, ICJ Rep. 1960, 192, Declaration Moreno Quintana, 217, Separate O. Sir Percy Spender, 219, Dissent Urrutia, 221 – the Judgment found the Award valid and binding and was implemented by the 1961 Decision of the Chairman of the OAS Inter-American Peace Commission and fixing by the OAS *Nicaragua/Honduras* Mixed Commission on 15 Dec 1962 of the point at the thalweg at the mouth of the Coco River as the initial point of the land boundary [30 ILR 76; *Nicaragua v. Honduras* Nicaragua's Memorial Vol.I, Chap III Sect.B & Vol.II, Annex 1]; *Aegean Sea* Pleadings, 347 [Counsel De Visscher, 10 Oct 1978]; *Tunisia v. Libya* Pleadings, 231 [Counsel Queneudec, 18 June 1985]; *Gulf of Maine* Judgment, ICJ Rep. 1984, 310; Pleadings, Vol.I, 167 [Canada's Memorial], Vol.IV, 107-109 [US Counter-Memorial], Vol.V, 82 n.12, 86 n.27, 90 n.43 [Canada's Reply], Vol.VI, 374 [Counsel Rashkow, 16 April 1984]; *Nicaragua v. USA (Jurisdiction)* Dissent Schwebel, ICJ Rep. 1984, 595-600, paras 53-61; *Great Belt* Pleadings, 369-370, 373-375, 385 [Finland's Memorial]; *Arbitral Award* Judgment, ICJ Rep. 1991, 62, Declaration Mbaye, 80 n.1, Separate O. Shahabuddeen, 111, Dissent Weeramantry, 152, 165; Hearings, CR 91/3, 49-56, 72-74 [Counsel Highet, 4 April 1991], CR 91/5, 13 [Counsel Bowett, 8 April], CR 91/49, 15 [Agent Arguello, 13 June 1991]; *Gulf of Fonseca* Judgment, ICJ Rep. 1992, 544-546, 561, Separate O. Torres Bernardez, 637-638, 670, 676, 682; Hearings, C 4/CR 91/5 [trans.], 50 [Counsel de Arechaga, 19 April 1991], CR 91/28 [trans.], 8-9, 16 [Counsel Bardonnet, 22 May], CR 91/33, 36

[Counsel Lima, 29 May], CR 91/43, 49 [Agent Arguello, 7 June 1991]; *Denmark v. Norway* Norway's Counter-Memorial, paras 395, 399, 405; *Qatar v. Bahrain (Merits)* Judgment, ICJ Rep. 2001, 76, para.111; Hearings, CR 2000/12, 46-47, 50, 52 [Counsel Reisman, 9 June 2000], CR 2000/19, 9 [Counsel David, 22 June], CR 2000/21, 35 [Reisman, 27 June 2000]; *Joint Legal Opinion on Guatemala's Territorial Claim to Belize*, para.85, Annex II, paras 24-25 (Jan 2002) <www .belize-guatemala.gov.bz/>; *Cameroon v. Nigeria; Equatorial Guinea Intervening (Merits)* Dissent Ajibola, para.9, ICJ Rep. 2002, 541; *El Salvador v. Honduras (Revision)* Hearings, C6/CR 2003/2, 17, para.28 [Co-Agent Brizuela de Avila, 8 Sep 2003]; *Nicaragua v. Honduras (Merits)* Judgment, ICJ Rep. 2007, paras 19, 38-47, 99-101, 125, 154, 229-238, 256, 260, 279, 308-311, *dispositif* para.321(4), Declaration Parra-Aranguren, Dissent Torres Bernardez, paras 25-29, 34, 38-43, 55, 64, 72-79, 148-149; Hearings, CR 2007/1, 17-21, paras 10-21, at 24-26, paras 29-38, at 30, para.52, at 40, para.88, at 45-46, paras 100-102 [Agent Arguello, 5 March 2007], 55, para.24, at 64-66, paras 52-57 [Counsel Oude Elferink], CR 2007/2, 16, para.33 [Counsel Brownlie, 6 March], CR 2007/3, 11, para.193 [7 March], 45, para.22, at 62, para.68 [Oude Elferink], CR 2007/4, 49-53, paras 4-13, at 56-58, paras 21-24, 27 [Counsel Pellet, 8 March], CR 2007/5, 26, para.75 [9 March], CR 2007/6, 12, paras 12-13 [Agent Velasquez, 12 March], 16-20, 37, para.86 [Counsel Greenwood], 43-44, paras 2-4, 55-57, 61, para.46 [Counsel Sanchez], CR 2007/9, 29 [Counsel Sands, 15 March], 41-55 [Counsel Colson], CR 2007/10, 13-14 [16 March], CR 2007/11, 25, para.59 [Counsel Arguello, 19 March], 44-45 [Pellet], 51, para.4 [Oude Elferink], CR 2007/12, 13-15 [Counsel Brotons, 20 March], 29-38 [Pellet], 53 [Arguello], CR 2007/13, 20-21, para.5 [Greenwood, 22 March], 31-32, para.8, at 35-37 [Sanchez], CR 2007/14, 14, para.15, at 16-17 [Colson, 23 March 2007], 32, paras 3-4, at 34-35, paras 12-13 [Greenwood], 37, para.3, at 38, para.8, at 39, para.11.1 [Agent Flores]; *Nicaragua v. Colombia (Preliminary Objections)* Judgment, ICJ Rep. 2007, para.76; Hearings, CR 2007/16, 22, para.32, at 25, para.45, at 26, para.47 [Counsel Sir Arthur Watts, 4 June 2007], CR 2007/17, 17, para.42 [Agent Arguello, 5 June 2007]; Colombia's Preliminary Objections, 17, 61, 81, 88 <www.icj-cij.org>; 2009 *Abyei Boundary* Award, para.527 <www.pca-cpa.org>.

On 1909 *Bolivia/Peru Boundary Question* Award of President J. Figueroa Alcorta [RIAA XI, 141; 3 AJIL 949, 1029 (1909); No.249/Stuyt], see *Honduras v. Nicaragua* Dissent Urrutia, ICJ Rep. 1960, 225, 229; *Gulf of Fonseca* Hearings, C 4/CR 91/5 [trans.], 50 [Counsel de Arechaga, 19 April 1991], CR 91/37, 30 [Counsel Highet, 31 May 1991]; *Qatar v. Bahrain (Merits)* Hearings, CR 2000/12, 47, 50, 52 [Counsel Reisman, 9 June 2000], CR 2000/21, 36 [27 June 2000].

On 1909 *Norway v. Sweden Grisbadarna Maritime Frontier* Award [*supra*], see *Eastern Greenland* Pleadings, PCIJ Series C, No.63, 817, 818 [Denmark's Reply], 1314-1315 [Norway's Rejoinder], No.67, 3553 [Counsel Gidel, 2 February

1933]; *Anglo/Norwegian Fisheries* Pleadings, Vol.I, 570-571 [Norway's Counter-Memorial], Vol.II, 655 [UK Reply]; *Minquiers and Ecrehos* Pleadings, Vol.II 177-178 [Counsel Harrison, 24 Sep 1953], 206, 266, 274 [Agent Gros, 28 and 30 Sep 1953]; *Belgium/Netherlands Certain Frontier Land* Dissent Moreno Quintana, ICJ Rep. 1959, 255; *North Sea* Separate O. Jessup, ICJ Rep. 1969, 79-80, 81, Separate O. Ammoun, 113 n.3, Dissent Koretsky 160; *North Sea* Pleadings, Vol.I, 495 [Common Rejoinder of Denmark/NL]; 1981 *Dubai/Sharjah* Award [91 ILR 622]; *Gulf of Maine* Judgment, ICJ Rep. 1984, 309; *Gulf of Maine* Pleadings, Vol.II, 64-70, 76, 93, 96-97, 99, 101, 108-109 [US Memorial], Vol.III, 16-18, 142, 190 n.25, 202, 219-220, 236-237, 244 [Canada's Counter-Memorial], Vol.IV, 69, 76-77, 83 [US Counter-Memorial], Vol.V, 32, 49 n.48, 50 n.51 [Canada's Reply], 447, 477-478, 481 [US Reply], Vol.VI 46 [Agent Legault, 3 April 1984], 63-64, 69 [Deputy Agent Hankey, 3 April 1984], 88, 91-92 [Counsel Binnie, 4 April], 137 [Counsel Bowett, 5 April], 263, 264, 275, 279-280 [Counsel Stevenson, 12 April], 338-339 [Counsel Lancaster, 16 April], 352 [Special Counsel Rashkow], 380 [Counsel Feldman], Vol.VII, 87-88, 91 [Counsel Binnie, 4 May], 101-102 [Bowett, 5 May], 114 [Counsel Fortier], 174 [Feldman, 9 May], 218 [Deputy Agent Colson, 10 May], 271 [Agent Robinson, 11 May 1984], 332, Vol.VIII, 30, [Fig.20], 74 [Fig.46]; *Great Belt* Pleadings, 373 [Finland's Memorial]; *Libya/Chad Territorial Dispute* Separate O. Ajibola, ICJ Rep. 1994, 81; *Qatar v. Bahrain (Merits)* Joint Dissent Bedjaoui, Ranjeva, Koroma, ICJ Rep. 2001, 175, para.94 n.27, Dissent Torres Bernardez, 268, 408, paras 16, 429; Hearings, CR 2000/11, 20 [Counsel Lauterpacht, 8 June 2000], CR 2000/12, 61 [Counsel Reisman, 9 June], CR 2000/15, 13 [14 June 2000] <www.icj-cij.org>; *Barbados/Trinidad & Tobago* Barbados' Reply, para.334 n.437 <www.pca-cpa.org>; *Nicaragua v. Honduras* Hearings, CR 2007/11, 37, para.20 n.39 [Counsel Pellet, 19 March 2007] <www.icj-cij.org>.

On 1911 *Mexico/USA Chamizal* Award [RIAA XI, 316; 4 AJIL 925 (1910); 5 AJIL 709, 782 and Supp. 117 (1911); 67 AJIL 423 (1973); 100 AJIL 821 (2006); No.300/Stuyt], see *Eastern Greenland* Pleadings, PCIJ Series C, No.62, 477 [Norway's Counter-Memorial], No.63, 818, 820 [Denmark's Reply]; *Minquiers and Ecrehos* Individual O. Levi Carneiro, ICJ Rep. 1953, 107-108; Pleadings, Vol.II, 267-268, 269 [Agent Gros, 30 Sep 1953]; *Honduras v. Nicaragua* Dissent Urrutia, ICJ Rep. 1960, 225; *Taba* Dissent Lapidoth, para.4 [27 ILM 1497 (1988)]; *Gulf of Fonseca* Hearings, C 4/CR 91/27 [trans.], 20, 22 [Counsel Bardonnet, 21 May 1991], CR 91/28 [trans.], 11-12 [22 May 1991]; *Botswana/Namibia* Hearings, CR 99/1, 67 [Counsel Delbruck, 15 Feb 1999], CR 99/5 [trans.], 24 [Counsel Cot, 18 Feb 1999]; *Qatar v. Bahrain (Merits)* Joint Dissent Bedjaoui, Ranjeva, Koroma, para.94 n.27, ICJ Rep. 2001, 175.

On 1911 *Germany/UK Walfish Bay Boundary* Award [3 AJIL Supp. 306 (1909); No.162/Stuyt; 1994 Namibia/South Africa Walvis Bay and Penguin

Islands Agreement, 32 ILM 1152, 1470 (1993); <www.un.org/Depts/los; http://en.wikipedia.org/wiki/Walvis_Bay & www.klausdierks.com/Walvis%20Bay>; 2004 Statement of Namibia's President <www.grnnet.gov.na/News/Archive/2004/march/independence_reintegration_rpt.htm>], see *Eastern Greenland* Pleadings, PCIJ Series C, No.62, 437-438, 463, 464 [Norway's Counter-Memorial], No.63, 733, 818 [Denmark's Reply]; *Gulf of Maine* Pleadings, Vol.II, 98 [US Memorial], Vol.III, 201 [Canada's Counter-Memorial]; *Qatar v. Bahrain (Merits)* Joint Dissent Bedjaoui, Ranjeva, Koroma, ICJ Rep. 2001, 175, para.94 n.27 <www.icj-cij.org>; 2009 *Abyei Boundary* Award, para.378 n.763 <www.pca-cpa.org>.

On 1914 *Costa Rica/Panama Boundary* Award [6 AJIL Supp.1 (1912); 8 AJIL 913 (1914); No.298/Stuyt], see *Guinea-Bissau v. Senegal* Hearings, CR 91/3, 70 [4 April 1991, Counsel Highet]; *Gulf of Fonseca* Hearings, C 4/CR 91/37, 30 [Counsel Highet, 31 May 1991].

On 1916 *Costa Rica v. Nicaragua* Judgment, see Inter-Oceanic Canals *supra.*

On 1917 *El Salvador v. Nicaragua Gulf of Fonseca* Judgment of the Central American Court of Justice [11 AJIL 674 (1917); 17 AJIL 309-313 (1923)], see *Anglo/Norwegian Fisheries* Pleadings, Vol.I, 447, 556 [Norway's Counter-Memorial], Vol.II, 619-620, 622, 644 [UK Reply], Vol.III, 447, 456, 644 [Norway's Rejoinder]; *Minquiers and Ecrehos* Pleadings, Vol.II, 255-256 [Agent Gros, 30 Sep 1953]; 1989 *Guinea-Bissau/Senegal* Award [94 RGDIP 254 (1990)], para.64; *Gulf of Fonseca (Intervention)* Judgment, ICJ Reports 1990, 102-106, 120-122, *(Merits)* Judgment, ICJ Rep. 1992, 364, 372, 381, 557, 569, 589-608, Separate O. Bernardez, 664, 708, 712-714, 725-726, Dissent Oda, 734-735, 747-758; Hearings, C 4/CR 90/1, 21 [Agent Arguello Gomez, 5 June 1990], 44 [Counsel Brownlie], CR 90/3, 9, 15 [Agent Martinez Moreno, 6 June], 44 [Counsel Weil], CR 90/4, 32-34 [Counsel Bowett, 7 June], CR 90/5, 17 [Arguello, 8 June 1990], 30-31 [Brownlie], C 4/CR 91/4 [trans.], 64 [Weil, 18 April 1991], CR 91/34, 54 [Counsel Highet, 29 May], CR 91/35, 26 [30 May], CR 91/37, 15-16 [Counsel Lima, 31 May 1991], CR 91/40, 11-32 [Counsel Lauterpacht, 5 June], CR 91/42, 10-11, 16-18, 41 [6 June], CR 91/43, 22-23, 32-50 [Arguello, 7 June], 54 [Brownlie], CR 91/44, 15-16 [Bowett, 10 June], 28-35 [Lauterpacht], CR 91/45, 21 [Bowett], CR 91/46, 22-23, 44, 51-52 [Lauterpacht, 11 June], CR 91/47, 23-25 [Bowett, 12 June], CR 91/48, 31-39 [Lauterpacht, 13 June], CR 91/49, 29 [Arguello, 13 June], CR 91/50, 21 [Martinez Moreno, 14 June 1991]; *Nauru v. Australia (Preliminary Objections)* Dissent Schwebel, ICJ Reports 1992, 336-337; *Portugal v. Australia East Timor* Separate O. Shahabuddeen, ICJ Rep. 1995, 124-125, 126, Dissents Weeramantry, 160 n.2, 169 n.1, and Skubiszewski, 253-254; Hearings, CR 95/6 [trans.], 12 [Counsel Dupuy, 3 Feb 1995], 30-31 [Co-Agent Teles], CR 95/15, 22 [Counsel Pellet, 16 Feb 1995]; *Southern Bluefin Tuna (Jurisdiction)* Hearings, Vol.II [Counsel Serdy, 8 May 2000]; *Cameroon v. Nigeria; Equatorial Guinea Intervening (Merits)* Hearings, CR 2002/24, 25 [Counsel Dupuy, 20 March

2002]; *Nicaragua v. Colombia* Nicaragua's Memorial, 75, 111-114; Colombia's Preliminary Objections, at 33 n.26, at 61 <www.icj-cij.org>.

On 1919 *Minnesota v. Wisconsin* Judgment [252 US 273], see *Botswana/Namibia* Hearings, CR 99/1, 62 [Counsel Delbruck, 15 Feb 1999].

On 1925 *Chile/Peru Tacna-Arica* Award [RIAA II, 921; 19 AJIL 303, 633 (1925); 20 AJIL 605 (1926); 21 AJIL Supp. 39 (1927); 23 AJIL Supp. 183 (1929); No.349/Stuyt], see *Aegean Sea* Pleadings, 122-123 [Counsel Pinto, 26 Aug 1976], 273 [Greece's Memorial (Jurisdiction)]; *Gabcikovo* Dissent Skubiszewski, ICJ Rep. 1997, 235; *Botswana/Namibia* Dissent Vice-President Weeramantry, para.110 n.95, ICJ Rep. 1999, 1193 <www.icj-cij.org>; *Ireland v. UK Mox Plant (Provisional Measures)* Hearings, ITLOS/PV.01/07, 18 [Counsel Lowe, 19 Nov 2001] <www.itlos.org>.

On 1929 *USA McMahan v. Mexico Rio Grande Boundary* Award of US/Mexico General Claims Commission [Nos.354-355/Stuyt], see *Costa Rica v. Nicaragua San Juan River* Hearings, CR 2009/4, 33-34, para.63 [Counsel Brownlie, 5 March 2009], CR 2009/6, 41, para.16 [Counsel Caflisch, 9 March], CR 2009/7, 9, para.6, at 12, para.31 [Brownlie, 12 March 2009] <www.icj-cij.org>.

On 1933 *Guatemala/Honduras Boundary* Award [RIAA III, 2042; 27 AJIL 403-427 (1933); No.393/Sutyt; <www.sovereigngeographic.com/central_america .html>], see *Honduras v. Nicaragua* Dissent Urrutia, ICJ Rep. 1960, 229, 231-232; *Gulf of Maine* Pleadings, Vol.I. 169 [Canada's Memorial]; *Gulf of Fonseca* Judgment, ICJ Rep. 1992, 380, 381, 397, 401-402, 408, Separate Os Valticos, 622 n.1, Bernardez, 643, 672, 713; Hearings C 4/CR 91/5 [trans.], 38-39, 49 [Counsel de Arechaga, 19 April 1991], CR 91/37, 30 [Counsel Highet, 31 May 1991]; *Libya/Chad* Separate O. Ajibola, ICJ Rep. 1994, 81; *Botswana/Namibia* Judgment, ICJ Rep. 1999, 1066, para.33; Hearings, CR 99/10, 54 [Counsel Faundez, 1 March 1999]; *Qatar v. Bahrain (Merits)* Joint Dissent Bedjaoui, Ranjeva, Koroma, para.94 n.27, ICJ Rep. 2001, 175; *Joint Legal Opinion on Guatemala's Territorial Claim to Belize*, paras 155, 157, 196, Annex II, paras 26-28 (January 2002) <www .belize-guatemala.gov.bz/>; *Cameroon v. Nigeria; Equatorial Guinea Intervening (Merits)* Hearings, CR 2002/9, 67 [Counsel Brownlie, 1 March 2002], CR 2002/18, 48 [Counsel Brownlie, 14 March 2002] <www.icj-cij.org>; *Barbados/Trinidad & Tobago* Barbados' Reply, para.334 n.437 <www.pca-cpa.org>; *Nicaragua v. Honduras (Merits)* Judgment, ICJ Rep. 2007, paras 134, 165, 213; *Costa Rica v. Nicaragua San Juan River* Declaration Guillaume, ICJ Rep. 2009, para.6 n.12 <www.icj-cij.org>.

On 1934 *New Jersey v. Delaware* Judgment (Delaware River and Bay) of Justice Cardozo [291 US 361; 29 AJIL 331 (1935)], see *Botswana/Namibia* Hearings, CR 99/1, 46 [Counsel Chayes, 15 Feb 1999], 64 [Counsel Delbruck], CR 99/5 [trans.], 33 [Counsel Cot, 18 Feb 1999].

On 1934 *Wisconsin v. Michigan* Judgment [295 US 455], see *Botswana/Namibia* Hearings, CR 99/5 [trans.], 33, 35-36 [Counsel Cot, 18 Feb 1999].

On 1944 *Spath v. Larsen* Judgment [20 Wash. 2d 500, 148 P.2d 834], see *Gulf of Maine* Pleadings, Vol.II 94 n.8 [US Memorial].

On 1947 *Sieur George v. Sieur Naudin* Judgment of Conseil d'Etat [Recueil Lebon 1947, 355], see *Benin/Niger* Hearings, C5/CR 2005/1, 46-47, paras 5.16-519 [Counsel Forteau, 7 March], C5/CR 2005/5, 21, para.3.9 [10 March 2005] <www .icj-cij.org>.

On 1950 *Petroleum Development (Qatar) Ltd. v. Ruler of Qatar* Award of Lord Radcliffe [18 ILR 161], see *Aegean Sea* Pleadings, 259 n.1 [Greece's Memorial (Jurisd.)]; *Qatar v. Bahrain (Merits)* Hearings, CR 2000/21, 36 [Counsel Reisman, 27 June 2000].

On 1951 *Petroleum Development (Trucial Coast) Ltd. v. Sheikh of Abu Dhabi* Award [*supra*], see *Aegean Sea (Jurisdiction)* Judgment, ICJ Rep. 1978, 32; Pleadings, 258-259 [Greece's Memorial (Jurisd.)]; *Tunisia/Libya (Merits)* Dissent Oda, ICJ Rep. 1982, 173; Pleadings, Vol.II, 209 n.1 [Libya's Counter-Memorial]; *Libya/Malta* Pleadings, Vol.I 448 [Malta's Memorial]; *Barbados/Trinidad & Tobago* Hearings Day-2, 86 [Counsel Reisman, 18 Oct 2005], Day-4, 92 [Counsel Crawford, 21 Oct 2005] <www.pca-cpa.org>; *Romania v. Ukraine* Hearings, CR 2008/26, 56, paras 48-49 [Counsel Wood, 10 Sep 2008], CR 2008/30, 52, para.31(1) and at 53, para.32 [Counsel Crawford, 15 Sep], CR 2008/32, 15, para.7 [Wood, 18 Sep 2008 <www.icj-cij.org>; *Costa Rica v. Nicaragua San Juan River* Hearings, CR 2009/4, 54, para.10 [Counsel Pellet, 5 March 2009] <www.icj-cij.org>.

On 1949 Proclamation of Abu-Dhabi, see *North Sea* Dissent Koretsky, ICJ Rep. 1969, 167; Pleadings, Vol.I, 31 [FRG Memorial].

On 1951 *Driesbach v. Lynch* Judgment [71 Idaho 501, 234 P.2d 446], see *Gulf of Maine* Pleadings, Vol.II, 94 n.9 [US Memorial].

On 1966 *Argentina/Chile Frontier (Rio Palena* or *Rio Encuentro)* Award [38 ILR 16; RIAA XVI, 111; *Tunisia/Libya* Pleadings Pleadings, Vol.V, 441; 2246 UNTS 71; No.432/Stuyt], see *Tunisia/Libya* Pleadings, Vol.V, 357 [Counsel Vallat, 19 Oct 1981]; *Gulf of Maine* Pleadings, Vol.I, 169, 170 [Canada's Memorial], Vol.V, 86 n.27 [Canada's Reply]; *Guinea Bissau v. Senegal Arbitral Award* Oral Hearings, CR 91/3, 47, 67-69 [Counsel Highet, 4 April 1991]; 1998 *Eritrea Yemen Territorial Sovereignty (Phase I)* Award [*infra*], para.95; *Botswana/Namibia Kasikili/Sedudu Island* Judgment, ICJ Rep. 1999, 1064, para.30, Separate O. Kooymans, 1146-1147, para.15; Hearings, CR 99/1, 41 [Counsel Chayes, 15 Feb 1999], 57-58 [Counsel Delbruck], CR 99/2, 57, 60 [Chayes, 16 Feb], CR 99/8, 41-42 [Counsel Lady Fox, 24 Feb], CR 99/11, 27 [Chayes, 2 March 1999]; *Cameroon v. Nigeria; Equatorial Guinea Intervening (Merits)* Judgment, ICJ Rep. 2002, 346, para.58; Hearings, CR 2002/2, 43-44 [Counsel Cot, 19 Feb 2002], CR 2002/10, 48 [Counsel Sir Arthur

Watts, 4 March], CR 2002/11, 27 [Counsel Macdonald, 5 March 2002], 54-55 [Watts]; *Indonesia/Malaysia (Merits)* Judgment, ICJ Rep. 2002, 682, para.135; Hearings, CR 2002/30, 27 [Counsel Sir Elihu Lauterpacht, 6 June 2002] <www.icj-cij.org>; 2002 *Eritrea/Ethiopia Boundary (Merits)* Decision, paras 3.4, 3.14 <www.un.org/NewLinks/eebcarbitration/>, Ethiopia's Request of 13 May 2002 for Interpretation of the Decision, ns 13-15 and *Eritrea/Ethiopia Boundary (Demarcation)* Statement of 27 Nov 2006, para.20 n.4 <www.pca-cpa.org>; *Guyana/Suriname* Guyana's Reply, paras 6.29/6.30 <www.pca-cpa.org>.

On 1968 *India/Pakistan Rann of Kutch* Award [50 ILR 2; 7 ILM 633 (1968); 65 AJIL 346-357 (1971); 23 ICLQ 821 (1974); No.433/Stuyt], see *Gulf of Maine* Pleadings, Vol.VII, 331 [US Agent's Letter]; *Libya/Malta* Pleadings, Vol.I, 443, 474 n.2 [Malta's Memorial], Vol.II, 72 [Libya's Counter-Memorial]; *Libya/Chad* Separate O. Ajibola, ICJ. Rep. 1994, 88; *Botswana/Namibia* Hearings, CR 99/1, 37 [Counsel Chayes, 15 Feb 1999], CR 99/5 [trans.], 14 n.25, 20-22 [Counsel Cot, 18 Feb 1999]; *Qatar v. Bahrain (Merits)* Hearings, CR 2000/5, 29 [Counsel Salmon, 29 May 2000]; *Cameroon v. Nigeria; Equatorial Guinea Intervening (Merits)* Judgment, ICJ Rep. 2002, 415, para.222, Dissent Ajibola, 541, para.9; Hearings, CR 2002/9, 64 [Counsel Brownlie, 1 March 2002]; *Nicaragua v. Honduras* Hearings, CR 2007/11, 37, para.20 n.39 [Counsel Pellet, 19 March 2007] <www.icj-cij.org>.

On the ensuing India/Pakistan Sir Creek and maritime (TS/EEZ/CS) delimitation dispute <http://en.wikipedia.org/wiki/Sir_Creek>; Point K of Pakistan's 1996 baselines, *Limits in the Seas No.118 – Pakistan's Straight Baseline Claim* (U.S. Department of State 1996); 22 Dec 2006 <http://news.bbc.co.uk/2/hi/south_asia/6202399.stm>; Pakistan's and India's Submissions to the CLCS of 30 April and 11 May 2009 <www.un.org/Depts/los/clcs_new/submissions_files/submission_pak_29_2009.htm & www.un.org/Depts/los/clcs_new/submissions_files/submission_ind_48_2009.htm>; Sir Creek Talks Resumed of 27-30 June 2009 <www.dawn.com/wps/wcm/connect/dawn-content-library/dawn/news/pakistan/12-india+pakistan+secretaries+ministers+to+meet+next+month--bi-05 & www.pakistanlink.com/Headlines/June09/30/13.htm>.

On 1977 *Argentina/Chile Beagle Channel* Award [*supra*], see *Gulf of Fonseca* Oral Hearings, C 4/CR 91/33, 67 [Counsel Highet, 29 May 1991]; *Denmark v. Norway* Separate O. Weeramantry, ICJ Rep. 1993, 259 n.2; *Botswana/Namibia* Dissent Vice-President Weeramantry, paras 4-5, ICJ Rep. 1999, 1155; Hearings, CR 99/1, 39, 41 [Counsel Chayes, 15 Feb 1999], CR 99/4, 21 [Counsel Faundez, 17 Feb 1999], 59-61, 63-64, 67-68 [Agent Kawana, 17 Feb], CR 99/10, 54 [Faundez, 1 March 1999]; *Qatar v. Bahrain* Hearings, CR 94/5 [trans.], 55 [Counsel Weil, 7 March 1994], CR 2000/7, 24 [Counsel Bundy, 31 May 2000], 2000/10, 11-12 [Counsel Queneudec, 6 June], CR 2000/14, 17 [Lauterpacht, 13 June 2000]; *Joint*

Legal Opinion on Guatemala's Territorial Claim to Belize, para.21, Annex II, para.31 (January 2002) <www.belize-guatemala.gov.bz/>; *Cameroon v. Nigeria; Equatorial Guinea Intervening (Merits)* Judgment, ICJ Rep. 2002, 415, para.222; Hearings, CR 2002/2, 36 [Counsel Cot, 19 Feb 2002], CR 2002/4, 56 [21 Feb], CR 2002/9, 57, 63 [Counsel Brownlie, 1 March 2002]; *Indonesia/Malaysia (Merits)* Hearings, CR 2002/29, 39 [Counsel Malintoppi, 4 June 2002]; *Nicaragua v. Honduras (Merits)* Dissent Torres Bernardez, ICJ Rep. 2007, para.15; Hearings, CR 2007/2, 49, paras.172, 174 [Counsel Brownlie, 6 March 2007], CR 2007/3, 55, para.46 [Counsel Oude Elferink, 7 March], CR 2007/10, 32, para.155 [Counsel Colson, 16 March 2007]; *Nicaragua v. Colombia* Nicaragua's Memorial, 258 <www.icj-cij.org>; 2007 *Guyana/Suriname* Award, paras 243, 294, 304-305 <www.pca-cpa.org>; *Malaysia/Singapore (Merits)* Separate O. Rao, para.22, ICJ Rep. 2008; Hearings, CR 2007/21, 53-54, paras 90-95 [Counsel Brownlie, 7 Nov 2007], CR 2007/28, 58, para.35 [Brownlie, 19 Nov 2007] <www.icj-cij.org>; *Romania v. Ukraine* Hearings, CR 2008/19, 39, para.57 [Counsel Crawford, 3 Sep 2008] <www.icj-cij.org>.

On 1977 and 1978 *Anglo/French Continental Shelf Delimitation* Decisions [*supra*], see *Aegean Sea* Pleadings, 337-338, 341 [Counsel O'Connell, 10 Oct 1978), 421-422 [Counsel Weil, 13 Oct 1978]; *Tunisia/Libya (Merits)* Judgment, ICJ Rep. 1982, 38, 57, 79, Separate O. Jiménez de Aréchaga, 104-107, 115, 118, 132-134, 137, Dissent Gros 150, 152, Dissent Oda, 258-260, 262, Dissent Evensen, 278, 291-292, 296-298, 312, 314; *Tunisia/Libya* Pleadings, Vol.I, 50, 162-163, 168-169, 173, 181, 486, 488-489, 492-493, 506-507, 509, 510-511, 513 [Tunisia's Memorial], Vol.II, 61, 64 [Tunisia's Counter-Memorial], 210 n.5, 215, 225, 243, 265-292, 310, 318 n.2, 325-326, 339-341 [Libya's Counter-Memorial], Vol.III, 298, 315, 316 [Counsel Lauterpacht, 19 March 1981], 410-411 [Counsel Jennings, 21 March], 434 [Agent Mizzi, 23 March 1981], 448 [Lauterpacht]; Vol.IV, 145 n.1, 151 [Libya's Reply], 403, 406, 411-415, 418 [Jennings, 16 Sep 1981], 428, 440-441, 443, 452-453 [Counsel Abi-Saab, 17 Sep], 486 [Counsel Dupuy], 494, 601-602, 615, Vol.V, 55, 62-67 [Counsel Vallat, 30 Sep and 1 Oct], 204, 207-209, 214-215, 227 [Counsel Highet, 7 Oct], 263, 265, 277 [Jennings, 13 Oct], 286 [Dupuy, 14 Oct], 356, 361 [Vallat, 19 Oct 1981], 428; *Libya/Malta (Merits)* Judgment, ICJ Rep. 1985, 42, 44, Separate O. Vice-President Sette-Camara, 60, 64, 66, 67, 72-73, 74, Joint Separate O., 81, 86, 89, Separate O. Valticos, 106, 107, 110, Dissent Mosler, 114, Dissent Oda, 139, 143, 144-148, 160, 163, 165, 168, 169, Dissent Schwebel, 185; *Libya/Malta* Pleadings: Vol.I, 96, 100, 109, 112-113, 116-117, 121-124, 128, 129-131, 132-134, 139 n.3, 140-141, 143 n.1, 145, 154, 156, 160, 172 [Libya's Memorial], 416, 420, 433-436, 438, 441, 445, 453, 457, 477 n.5, 478-479, 486-487, 492 n.2 [Malta's Memorial]; Vol.II, 26 n.4, 32, 34 n.2, 39 n.1, 44, 60, 73,

88-94, 116-118, 125, 145, 146-147, 149, 153, 154 n.8, 156-157, 158-159 [Libya's Counter-Memorial], 252, 256, 281, 290 n.2, 292-293, 295, 299, 301-302, 303, 305, 309, 311, 313, 315, 316, 329-330, 332, 334-335, 337 n.1, 339-341, 353-355, 358 n.2, 360 n.4, 365 n.1, 367, 369, 370 n.1, 371 n.1 [Malta's Counter-Memorial], 443, 446 [Malta's Observations (Intervention)], 498 [Counsel Arangio-Ruiz, 25 January 1984], 557 [Counsel Virally], 564-565 [Counsel Colliard, 27 Jan], 608 [Counsel Grisel, 27 Jan 1984], Vol.III, 8 n.3, 9, 37, 40 n.3, 49, 54, 89, 92 n.3, 101 n.2 [Libya's Reply], 156-157, 162, 166, 177, 185, 187 n.3, 188-189, 191, 195, 198, 204-210, 217 n.1, 219-221, 222 n.1, 237 n.1 [Malta's Reply], 296-297, 305 [Agent Mizzi, 26 Nov 1984], 309, 317 [Mizzi, 27 Nov], 325, 329 [Counsel Lauterpacht], 362, 364 [Counsel Weil, 28 Nov], 395, 398, 405-407, 425, 428 [Weil, 29 and 30 Nov], 442, 447, 450-452, 456-460, 462, 465, 472 [Counsel Brownlie, 3 Dec], Vol.IV, 34, 37, 38, 39 [Counsel Briggs, 7 Dec 1984], 45, 57, 65 [Counsel Jaenicke, 7 and 10 Dec], 90, 92-94, 97 [Counsel Colliard, 11 Dec], 138-139, 140 [Counsel Lucchini, 12 Dec], 158 159, 163, 168 [Counsel Bowett, 13 Dec], 184-185, 187-188 [Jaenicke, 14 Dec 1984], 289, 297-298 [Brownlie, 8 Feb 1985], 325, 326 [Lauterpacht, 11 Feb], 354, 372, 388-389 [Weil, 12 and 13 Feb], 404 [Agent Mizzi, 13 Feb], 436 [Jaenicke, 21 Feb 1985], 504.

Gulf of Maine Judgment, ICJ Rep. 1984, 267, 274, 284, 293, 301, 302-303, 324, Separate O. Schwebel, 357, Dissent Gros, 360, 361, 365, 367, 374, 375, 378, 380, 383, 385-386, 387; *Gulf of Maine* Pleadings, Vol.I, 105-106, 116-118, 121 n.21, 128, 134, 135, 138-141, 144-145, 148-149 [Canada's Memorial], Vol.II, 57, 79, 83-87, 89, 94-95, 98-101, 103-104, 110, 115, 122 [US Memorial], Vol.III, 40-41, 51-53, 140, 181, 183-185, 207 n.4, 208, 210 ns 10 & 11, 226, 232-233, 253 n.2, 254 n.5, 256, 262 [Canada's Counter-Memorial], Vol.IV, 14, 66, 77, 83, 86-87, 94, 95, 128, 130 n.1, 446, 453 [US Counter-Memorial], Vol.V, 20, 25 n.42, 29, 44 n.26, 45-46, 53, 55-56, 133 n.16, 158 n.3 [Canada's Reply], 389, 394, 399 n.1, 404, 409, 420, 426-427, 430 n.2, 446-447, 452, 454, 456-459, 480, 538-539 [US Reply], Vol.VI, 17 [Counsel MacGuigan, 2 April 1984], 24, 30-31, 35, 38, 40, 47, 53 [Agent Legault, 2 and 3 April], 62, 66, 70-71, 84-85 [Deputy Agent Hankey, 3 and 4 April], 170, 174, 203 [Counsel Weil, 6 and 10 April], 207-213 [Counsel Malintoppi, 10 April], 227 [Legault], 238-239 [Agent Robinson, 11 April], 252, 261, 278-279, 284-285 [Counsel Stevenson, 11 and 12 April], 313, 315-316 [Counsel Colson, 12 and 13 April], 334 [Counsel Feldman, 13 April], 352 [Counsel Rashkow]; Vol.VII, 7, 11, 18 [Agent Legault, 3 May], 31, 38 [Weil], 44, 51-52 [Counsel Jaenicke, 4 May], 67 [Hankey], 115 [Counsel Fortier, 5 May], 126, 128, 136 [Malintoppi], 140 [Legault], 182-183 [Stevenson, 9 May], 226-227, 231-233 [Colson, 10 May], 264-265 [Robinson, 11 May 1984]; Vol.VIII, 56 [Fig. 14]; 1985 *Guinea/Guinea-Bissau* Award, paras 102, 116 [25 ILM 294, 300 (1986)]; *Guinea-Bissau v. Senegal Arbitral Award* Oral Hearings, CR 91/3, 75 [Counsel Highet, 4 April 1991]; *Gulf of Fonseca* Judgment, ICJ Rep. 1992, 586; Hearings, C 4/CR

90/3 [Counsel Weil, 6 June 1990], CR 90/4, 38 [Counsel Bowett, 7 June 1990], C 4/CR 91/4 [trans.], 35, 57 [Counsel Weil, 18 April 1991], CR 91/5 [trans.], 3, 5-6 [19 April], CR 91/43, 77 [Counsel Brownlie, 7 June], CR 91/44, 19-20 [Bowett, 10 June], CR 91/45, 16-17, CR 91/46, 32, 36, 49-51 [Lauterpacht, 11 June], CR 91/47, 19, 28-29 [Bowett, 12 June], CR 91/48, 28-29 [Lauterpacht, 13 June 1991], CR 91/49, 54-56 [Brownlie]; *Canada/France* Award, paras 24, 41-42, 51-52, 90 [31 ILM 1160, 1163-1165, 1175 (1992)], Dissent Gotlieb, paras 5, 56-57, 61, 65 [*id.* 1181, 1193-1195, 1196], Dissent Weil, paras 21, 28-29, 37 [*id.* 1204, 1208, 1213]; *Denmark v. Norway* Judgment, ICJ Rep. 1993, 58, 60-63, 67, Separate Os Shahabuddeen, 131, 132 n.1, 133, 134, 136, 142, 145-146, 156, 157, 165-166, 169, 171 n.1, 180-182, 189, Weeramantry, 230 n.2, 248, 259 n.2, 260, 263, 265-267, 268, 271, 273, Ajibola, 285, 302, 303, Dissent Fischer, 306, 307, 308; Denmark's Memorial, paras 215, 239, 244, 249, 252, 255, 278-282, 323-324, Norway's Counter-Memorial, paras 420, 425, 429, 433, 448-449, 452, 454-456, 472-473, 488, 501, 515-522, 567-568, 595, Denmark's Reply, para.457, Norway's Rejoinder, paras 380-383, 398-399, 410, 455-461, 500, 506-507, 521-523, 528-529, 531, 544, 573, 584, 599, 608; Hearings, CR 93/1Corr., 24, 26 [Agent Lehmann, 11 Jan 1993], CR 93/2, 69 [Counsel de Arechaga, 12 Jan], CR 93/4, 12, 13 [Counsel Bowett, 14 Jan], 42, 50 [Agent Bernhard], CR 93/6, 44-45 [Agent Haug, 18 Jan], CR 93/7, 10, 13-15, 28-29, 35-36, 50, 54-56 [Counsel Brownlie, 19 Jan], CR 93/8 [trans.], 28, 46, 52, 56-57 [Counsel Weil, 20 Jan], CR 93/9 [trans.], 13, 18 [21 Jan], CR 93/9, 62 [Counsel Highet], CR 93/10, 20, 28 [Lehmann, 25 Jan], 61 [Bowett], CR 93/11 [trans.], 42 [Weil, 27 Jan 1993].

1999 *Eritrea/Yemen (Phase II)* Award, paras 39, 165 [*supra*]; *Qatar v. Bahrain* Judgment, ICJ Rep. 2001, 115, para.247, Joint Dissent Bedjaoui, Ranjeva, Koroma, 198, para.173, Dissent Torres Bernardez, 441-443, paras 537-541; Hearings, CR 94/6, 4 [Counsel Weil, 8 March 1994], CR 2000/10, 46 [Counsel Queneudec, 6 June 2000], CR 2000/15, 30-31, 35, 42-43 [Weil, 14 June], CR 2000/16, 51-52 [Counsel Reisman, 15 June 2000]; 2002 *Newfoundland/Nova Scotia (Phase II)* Award, para.2.27 n.85, para.4.21 n.143, paras 4.31, 5.6 n.161, para.5.9 <www.gov.ns.ca/>; *Cameroon v. Nigeria; Equatorial Guinea Intervening (Merits)* Judgment, ICJ Rep. 2002, 432, 434, 436, 446, paras 270, 274, 279, 299; Hearings, CR 2002/6, 41 [Co-Agent Kamto, 25 Feb 2002], 51 [Counsel Mendelson], 68, 71 [Co-Agent Pellet], CR 2002/13, 35 [Counsel Abi-Saab, 7 March], CR 2002/17, 49-50, 61 [Co-Agent Kamto, 12 March], CR 2002/20, 40, 42, 45 [Abi-Saab, 15 March], CR 2002/22, 29 [Counsel Cot, 19 March 2002], 44 [Kamto], 54 [Mendelson], CR 2002/23, 19 [Abi-Saab], 34 [Counsel Crawford]; *Indonesia/Malaysia (Merits)* Hearings, CR 2002/33, 12 [Counsel Watts, 10 June 2002] <www.icj-cij.org>; *Barbados/Trinidad & Tobago* Award, paras 122, 124, 154, 310, 313; Barbados' Memorial, para.106; Trinidad's Counter-Memorial, paras 170, 177-179; Barbados' Reply, paras 213-217, 255-258; Hearings Day-6, 24-25 [Paulsson, 25 Oct 2005]

<www.pca-cpa.org>; 2007 *Guyana/Suriname* Award, paras 302, 305 <www.pca-cpa.org>; *Nicaragua v. Honduras (Merits)* Separate O. Ranjeva, ICJ Rep. 2007, para.16; Hearings, CR 2007/2, 21, para.54, at 25-26, paras 70-72, at 29, paras 83-84, at 30, para.89, at 35, para.111, at 49, paras 173-174 [Counsel Brownlie, 6 March 2007], CR 2007/5, 20, para.60 [Counsel Pellet, 9 March], 2007/8, 23, para.29 [Counsel Queneudec, 14 March], 41, para.16 [Counsel Dupuy], CR 2007/11, 43, para.31 [Pellet, 19 March], 59, para.22 [Counsel Oude Elferink], CR 2007/13, 15, para.16 [Dupuy, 22 March], CR 2007/14, 12, para.8, at 14, para.10, at 22, para.50, at 24, para.54 [Counsel Colson, 23 March 2007], 27, para.18 [Counsel Queneudec] <www.icj-cij.org>; *Romania v. Ukraine* Judgment, ICJ Rep. 2009, para.210; Hearings, CR 2008/18, 36, para.10 [Counsel Pellet, 2 Sep 2008], CR 2008/19, 12, para.7 [Crawford, 3 Sep], CR 2008/20, 33, para.53 [Pellet, 4 Sep], CR 2008/21, 63, para.60 [Counsel Lowe, 5 Sep], CR 2008/26, 17, para.75 [Counsel Queneudec, 10 Sep], 32-33, paras 56-57 [Counsel Bundy], 49, para.21 [Counsel Wood], CR 2008/28, 49, paras 62-63 and at 51, paras 71-74 [Bundy, 11 Sep], CR 2008/29, 26, para.21, at 31, para.47 and at 38-39, paras 82-84 [Queneudec, 12 Sep], CR 2008/30, 55, para.37 [Crawford, 15 Sep], CR 2008/31, 31-32, para.21(2) and para.22 n.50 [Pellet, 16 Sep], CR 2008/32, 35, para.22 [Bundy, 18 Sep], CR 2008/33, 14, para.19 [Queneudec, 19 Sep 2008]; *Nicaragua v. Colombia* Nicaragua's Memorial, 190, 196, 209, 240-241, 244, 246 <www.icj-cij.org>.

On specifically the 1978 *Anglo/French* Decision [*supra*], see *Tunisia v. Libya (Revision and Interpretation)* Pleadings, 70 n.2, 75 n.4 [Libya's Observations], 143 [Counsel Virally, 13 June 1985], 187 [Counsel Dupuy, 14 June 1985]; *Libya/Malta (Intervention)* Separate O. Jiménez de Aréchaga, ICJ Rep. 1984, 69-70; *Denmark v. Norway* Separate O. Ajibola, ICJ Rep. 1993, 285; 1994 *Laguna del Desierto* Award, paras 70, 75 [113 ILR 44-45]; 2002 UN *Eritrea/Ethiopia Boundary (Interpretation)* Decision, para.16 <www.pca-cpa.org>.

The 1978 Decision resolved the issues of the meaning and scope of the 1977 Decision [*supra*] which were referred to the *Anglo/French* Court of Arbitration by the United Kingdom. The Court, *inter alia*, rectified the *dispositif* of its 1977 Decision concerning the basepoints of Guernsey by using all these basepoints.

On 1981 *Dubai/Sharjah Boundary* Award [*supra*], see *Gulf of Maine* Pleadings, Vol.IV, 446 [US Counter-Memorial], Vol.V, 158 n.3 [Canada's Reply]; *Denmark v. Norway*, Denmark's Reply, para.276, Annex 78, Norway's Rejoinder, paras 409, 448; *Botswana/Namibia* Hearings, CR 99/5 [trans.], 20 [Counsel Cot, 18 Feb 1999]; *Qatar v. Bahrain (Merits)* Judgment, ICJ Rep. 2001, 76-77, paras 111, 113, 117, Joint Dissent Bedjaoui, Ranjeva, Koroma, 158, para.36, Separate Os Kooymans, 225, paras 12-13, 15 n.3, 28, 48-49, 61, Al-Khasawneh, 250-251, paras 6, 9, Dissent Torres Bernardez, 330, 374, 410, 414, paras 209, 326, 434, 445, Separate O. Fortier, para.26; Hearings, CR 2000/5 [trans.], 24 [Counsel

Salmon, 29 May 2000], CR 2000/7, 46 [Counsel Bundy, 31 May], CR 2000/8, 16 [Counsel Sinclair, 5 June], CR 2000/9 [trans.], 14-15 [Counsel David], CR 2000/17, 11 [Salmon, 20 June], CR 2000/18, 7 [Bundy, 21 June], 28-29 [David], CR 2000/19, 9-10, 12-13 [Sinclair, 22 June], CR 2000/21, 37 [Counsel Reisman, 27 June 2000]; *Malaysia/Singapore* Hearings, CR 2007/22 [transl.], 49, para.17 [Counsel Pellet, 8 Nov 2007]; *Romania v. Ukraine* Hearings, CR 2008/19, 55, para.11 [Agent Aurescu, 3 Sep 2008], CR 2008/20, 25, para.36 and at 33, para.53 [Counsel Pellet, 4 Sep], CR 2008/21, 45, para.31 [Counsel Crawford, 5 Sep], CR 2008/28, 38, paras 14-17 and at 49, para.63 [Counsel Bundy, 11 Sep], CR 2008/30, 70, para.15 [Counseo Muller, 15 Sep], CR 2008/31, 32, para.22 n.51 [Pellet, 16 Sep], CR 2008/32, 44, paras 69-71 [Bundy, 18 Sep 2008] <www.icj-cij.org>; *Nicaragua v. Colombia* Nicaragua's Memorial, 245-246 <www.icj-cij.org>; 2009 *Abyei Boundary* Award, paras 430-431 <www.pca-cpa.org>.

On 1949 Proclamations of Dubai and Sharjah, see *North Sea* Pleadings, Vol.I, 31 [FRG Memorial].

On 1981 *Iceland/Norway (Jan Mayen) Continental Shelf* Conciliation [*supra*], see *Tunisia/Libya* Pleadings, Vol.V, 246 [Question IV Judge Oda & Question II Judge Schwebel, 9 Oct 1981], 503-504 [Libya's Replies, 21 Oct 1981]; *Libya/Malta* Pleadings, Vol.I, 440 n.1 [Malta's Memorial], Vol.II, 110, 135 (I/N Agr) [Libya's Counter-Memorial], Vol.III, 38 (I/N Agr), 40 n.3 (I/N Agr) [Libya's Reply], 328-329 [Counsel Lauterpacht, 27 Nov 1984], Vol.IV, 105, 135 [Counsel Colliard, 11 Dec 1984], 320 [Counsel Lauterpacht, 11 Feb 1985]; *Gulf of Maine* Pleadings, Vol.VI, 168-169 [Counsel Weil, 6 April 1984]; *Gulf of Fonseca (Intervention)* Judgment, ICJ Rep. 1990, 108, Separate O. Oda, 139; Hearings, C 4/CR 90/4, 37 [Counsel Bowett, 7 June 1990]; *Denmark v. Norway* Judgment, ICJ Rep. 1993, 75-76, Dissent Fischer, 312; Denmark's Memorial, paras 78, 289, Denmark's Reply, paras 212, 314, 328; Hearings, CR 93/3, 39, 46-48 [Agent Lehmann, 13 Jan 1993], CR 93/5, 48 [Agent Tresselt, 15 Jan], CR 93/6, 66 [Agent Haug, 18 Jan], CR 93/10, 22-24 [Lehmann, 25 Jan], CR 93/11, 16 [Tresselt, 27 Jan 1993]; *Barbados/Trinidad & Tobago* Hearings Day-4, 83, 106 [Counsel Greenwood, 21 Oct 2005] <www.pca-cpa.org>; *Romania v. Ukraine* Hearings, CR 2008/32, 59, para.41 [Counsel Malintoppi, 18 Sep 2008] <www.icj-cij.org>.

On 1982 *Hazlett v. Presnell* Judgment of the Australian High Court [91 ILR 194], see *Benin/Niger* Hearings, C5/CR 2005/1, 46-47, paras 5.16-519 [Counsel Forteau, 7 March 2005], C5/CR 2005/5, 21, para.3.9 [10 March 2005] <www.icj-cij.org>.

On 1985 *Guinea/Guinea-Bissau Delimitation of the Maritime Boundary* Award [*supra*], see *Libya/Malta (Merits)* Separate O. Vice-President Sette-Camara, ICJ Rep. 1985, 73-74, Joint Separate O., 88, 90, Dissent Mosler 114, 115; 1989 *Guinea-Bissau/Senegal* Award [94 RGDIP 256 (1990)], para.66; *Arbitral Award* Judgment, ICJ Rep. 1991, 70-71; Hearings, CR 91/3, 59, 69, 76 [Counsel Highet, 4 April

1991]; *Gulf of Fonseca* Hearings, C 4/CR 91/45, 39 [Counsel Bowett, 10 June 1991], CR 91/46, 32-33 [Counsel Lauterpacht, 11 June 1991]; *Canada/France* Dissent Weil, para.23 n.18, paras 30, 32, 35, 44, 46 [31 ILM 1206, 1209-1210, 1212, 1216 (1992)]; *Denmark v. Norway* Separate Os Weeramantry, ICJ Rep. 1993, 230 n.2, 257, 266, Ajibola, 298, Dissent Fischer, 307, 308; Denmark's Memorial, paras 268, 339, Norway's Counter-Memorial, paras 415, 425, Denmark's Reply, para.457, Norway's Rejoinder, paras 518-519, 536, 545; Hearings, CR 93/4, 27 [Counsel Bowett, 14 Jan 1993], CR 93/7, 11, 55 [Counsel Brownlie, 19 Jan], CR 93/8 [trans.], 16 [Counsel Weil, 20 Jan], CR 93/9 [trans.], 19, 25 [21 Jan 1993]; *M/V Saiga* Separate O. Laing [38 ILM 1323 (1999)], para.1 n.1, paras 36, 48; Memorial (Merits) of St.Vincents, para.16, Counter-Memorial (Merits) of Guinea, para.121; 1999 *Eritrea/Yemen (Phase II)* Award [*infra*], para.157; *Qatar v. Bahrain (Merits)* Hearings, CR 2000/10, 24 [Counsel Queneudec, 6 June 2000], CR 2000/16, 17 [Counsel Weil, 15 June], CR 2000/19, 17 [Queneudec, 22 June 2000]; 2002 *Newfoundland/Nova Scotia (Phase II)* Award, para.3.5 n.108 <www.gov.ns.ca/>; *Cameroon v. Nigeria; Equatorial Guinea Intervening (Merits)* Judgment, ICJ Rep. 2002, 433, 445, 447, paras 272-273, 297, 304; Hearings, CR 2002/5, 44, 49 [Co-Agent Pellet, 22 Feb 2002], CR 2002/6, 38-40 [Co-Agent Kamto, 25 Feb], 51-52 [Counsel Mendelson], CR 2002/17, 25 [Pellet, 12 March], CR 2002/20, 45 [Counsel Abi-Saab, 15 March], CR 2002/21, 40 [Counsel Colson, 18 March 2002]; *Indonesia/Malaysia (Merits)* Hearings, CR 2002/31, 18, 19-20, 23 [Counsel Cot, 7 June], CR 2002/35, 24 [Counsel Schrijver, 12 June 2002]; 2006 *Barbados/Trinidad & Tobago (Jurisdiction and Merits)* Award, paras 117, 120, 162, 235, 340, 343; Barbados' Reply, paras 1790185; Trinidad's Rejoinder, paras 194-195; Hearings Day-2, 77-80 [Counsel Reisman, 18 Oct 2005], Day-4, 68-69 [Counsel Crawford, 21 Oct], Day-6, 35-39 [Reisman, 25 Oct 2005] <www.pca-cpa .org>; *Nicaragua v. Honduras (Merits)* Judgment, ICJ Rep. 2007, paras 288, 311, Separate Os Ranjeva, para.12, Koroma, paras 7, 17; Hearings, CR 2007/2, 19, para.43, at 24, para.66, at 40, para.134, at 47, para.164, at 49, para.174 [Counsel Brownlie, 6 March 2007] <www.icj-cij.org>; *Romania v. Ukraine* Judgment, ICJ Rep. 2009, para.211; Hearings, CR 2008/21, 15, para.11 and at 19, para.19 n.21 [Counsel Muller, 5 Sep 2008], CR 2008/26, 19, para.83 [Counsel Queneudec, 10 Sep], CR 2008/29, 29, para.40 [Queneudec, 12 Sep], CR 2008/31, 30, para.17 and at 34, para.25 [Counsel Pellet, 16 Sep], CR 2008/33, 16, para.25 [Queneudec, 19 Sep 2008]; *Nicaragua v. Colombia (Preliminary Objections)* Hearings, CR 2007/16, 38, para.16 [Counsel Weil, 4 June 2007], CR 2007/17, 18, para.46 [Agent Arguello, 5 June 2007]; Nicaragua's Memorial, 156, 166-170, 210, 217-224, 257; Colombia's Preliminary Objections, 99-100 <www.icj-cij.org>.

On 1988 *Egypt/Israel Taba Beachfront Boundary* Award [*supra*], see *Arbitral Award* Dissent Aguilar and Ranjeva, ICJ Rep. 1991, 124-125; *Gulf of Fonseca*

Hearings, C 4/CR 91/40, 37 [Counsel Lauterpacht, 5 June 1991]; *Botswana/Namibia* Hearings, CR 99/1, 39 [Counsel Chayes, 15 Feb 1999], CR 99/5 [trans.], 16 [Counsel Cot, 18 Feb 1999]; *Qatar v. Bahrain (Merits)* Hearings, CR 2000/5, 24 [Agent Al-Muslemani, 29 May 2000], 29 [Counsel Salmon], CR 2000/11, 42 [Counsel Lauterpacht, 8 June 2000]; *Joint Legal Opinion on Guatemala's Territorial Claim to Belize*, para.87 (Jan 2002) <www.belize-guatemala.gov.bz/>; 2002 *Eritrea/Ethiopia Boundary* Decision, paras 3.10-3.11 <www.pca-cpa.org>; *Malaysia/Singapore* Hearings, CR 2007/29, 21, para.56 [Counsel Bundy, 20 Nov 2007], CR 2007/31, 43, para.7 [Counsel Nevill, 23 Nov 2007] <www.icj-cij.org>; 2009 *Abyei Boundary* Award, paras 453, 459 <www.pca-cpa.org>.

On 1989 *Guinea-Bissau/Senegal Maritime Boundary* Award [*supra*], see *Arbitral Award (Provisional Measures)* Order and *Arbitral Award* Judgment, ICJ Rep. 1990, 64, and 1991, 53; and *Guinea-Bissau v. Senegal Maritime Delimitation (Discontinuance)* Order, ICJ Rep. 1995, 423; *Denmark v. Norway* Separate O. Shahabuddeen, ICJ Rep. 1993, 201; *East Timor* Hearings, CR 95/3 [trans.], 73-74 [Co-Agent Teles, 31 Jan. 1995], CR 95/4 [trans.], 68 [1 Feb], CR 95/8, 81 [Co-Agent Burmester, 7 Feb], CR 95/10, 13-15 [9 Feb], CR 95/11, 22-23, 26 [Counsel Pellet, 10 Feb 1995]; *Cameroon v. Nigeria* Hearings, CR 98/4 [trans.], 5 [Counsel Cot, 6 March 1998]; *Qatar v. Bahrain (Merits)* Hearings, CR 2000/12, 47 [Counsel Reisman, 9 June 2000], CR 2000/15, 36 [Counsel Weil, 14 June], CR 2000/19, 9 [Counsel Sinclair, 22 June], CR 2000/21, 7 [Counsel Paulsson, 27 June 2000], 17 [Counsel Kemicha], 21 [Paulsson], 35 [Reisman]; *Benin/Niger* Hearings, C5/CR 2005/1, 33, para.3.32 n.23 [Counsel Dossou, 7 March], C5/CR 2005/5, 18, para.2.21 [10 March 2005]; *Argentina v. Uruguay (Provisional Measures)* Hearings, CR 2006/55, 22 [Counsel Kohen, 18 Dec 2006]; *Nicaragua v. Honduras* Hearings, CR 2007/3, 34, para.76 [Counsel Brotons, 7 March 2007], CR 2007/7, 47, para.13 [Counsel Sanchez, 13 March 2007]; *Nicaragua v. Colombia* Nicaragua's Memorial, 171-172; Colombia's Preliminary Objections, 97 <www.icj-cij.org>; *Guyana/Suriname* Award, para.311; Suriname's Counter-Memorial, paras 4.68/4.71, Suriname's Rejoinder, para.3.73 <www.pca-cpa.org>; *Romania v. Ukraine* Hearings, CR 2008/20, 28, para.43 n.44 [Counsel Pellet, 4 Sep 2008], CR 2008/26, 55-56, paras 47-48 [Counsel Wood, 10 Sep 2008] <www.icj-cij.org>; *Costa Rica v. Nicaragua San Juan River* Declaration Guillaume, ICJ Rep. 2009, para.13 n.32 <www.icj-cij.org>; 2009 *Abyei Boundary* Award, paras 417, 505-510 <www.pca-cpa.org>.

On 1992 *Canada/France (St. Pierre & Miquelon) Delimitation of the Maritime Areas* Award [*supra*], see *North Sea* Pleadings, Vol.II, 33 [Agent Jaenicke, 24 Oct 1968]; 1977 *Anglo/French* Decision [*supra*], paras 46, 177, 200; *Aegean Sea* Pleadings, 94 [Counsel O'Connell, 26 Aug 1976], 338 [10 Oct 1978]; *Gulf of Maine* Pleadings, Vol.II, 9, 102 [US Memorial], Vol.IV, 94 [US Counter-Memorial],

Vol.V, 516-517, 520, 545-547 [US Reply], Vol.VII, 220 [Counsel Colson, 10 May 1984]; *Libya/Malta* Pleadings, Vol.I, 154 [Libya's Memorial]; *Denmark v. Norway* Separate O. Shahabuddeen, 131, 132, 133, 146-147, 171 n.1, 200, Dissent Fischer, 307, 308; Hearings, CR 93/1Corr., 15, 31 [Agent Lehmann, 11 Jan 1993], CR 93/3, 21 [Agent Magid, 13 Jan], CR 93/4, 28 [Counsel Bowett, 14 Jan], 44, 50 [Agent Bernhard], CR 93/5, 19 [Agent Haug, 15 Jan], CR 93/8 [trans.], 21 [Counsel Weil, 20 Jan], CR 93/9, 62 [Counsel Highet, 21 Jan], CR 93/10, 20 [Lehmann, 25 Jan], 49-50, 61 [Bowett], CR 93/11, 29 [Haug, 27 Jan 1993]; *Qatar v. Bahrain (Merits)* Joint Dissent Bedjaoui, Ranjeva, Koroma, para.174, ICJ Rep. 2001, 199; Hearings, CR 2000/9 [trans.], 40-41 [Counsel Queneudec, 5 June 2000], CR 2000/18, 21 [Counsel Sinclair, 21 June 2000]; 2001 *Newfoundland and Labrador/Nova Scotia (Phase I)* Award, para.2.11 <www.bissettmatheson.com/arbitration/> and 2002 *(Phase II)* Award, paras 1.12, 1.19, 1.28/30, 2.28 n.88, paras 2.31, 3.3 n.100, para.3.5 n.108, paras 3.10, 3.16, 3.22, 4.5, 4.7/10 ns 137-140, paras 4.12, 4.26/29, 4.32 n.155, para.5.1 n.158 <www.gov.ns.ca>; *Cameroon v. Nigeria; Equatorial Guinea Intervening (Merits)* Judgment, ICJ Rep. 2002, 303, paras 273, 274, 281, 304; Hearings, CR 2002/5, 44 [Co-Agent Pellet, 22 Feb 2002], CR 2002/6, 41 [Co-Agent Kamto, 25 Feb], 50 [Counsel Mendelson], CR 2002/13, 47-48 [Counsel Abi-Saab, 7 March], 62 [Counsel Crawford], CR 2002/17, 25 [Pellet, 12 March], CR 2002/20, 44 [Abi-Saab, 15 March], 56, 61 [Crawford], CR 2002/21, 40 [Counsel Colson, 18 March], CR 2002/22, 29 [Counsel Cot, 19 March 2002], 44 [Kamto] <www.icj-cij.org>; 2006 *Barbados/Trinidad & Tobago (Jurisdiction and Merits)* Award, paras 82, 141, 171, 321; Trinidad's Counter-Memorial, paras 153, 265-269; Barbados' Reply, paras 139, 141-142; Trinidad's Rejoinder, para.157; Hearings Day-1, 85-87 [Counsel Reisman, 17 Oct 2005], Day-2, 23, 26 [Reisman, 18 Oct], Day-4, 98-99 [Counsel Crawford, 21 Oct], Day-8, 40 [Crawford, 28 Oct 2005] <www.pca-cpa.org>; 2007 *Guyana/Suriname (Jurisdiction and Merits)* Award, paras 370, 387; Guyana's Memorial, para.7.24, Suriname's Counter-Memorial, para.4.9; Hearings, Day 6, 885 [Counsel Oxman, 14 Dec 2006] <www.pca-cpa.org>; *Nicaragua v. Honduras (Merits)* Separate O. Koroma, ICJ Rep. 2007, para.5; Hearings, CR 2007/2, 45, para.154, at 46, para.159 [Counsel Brownlie, 6 March 2007], CR 2007/12, 46, para.37 [20 March], CR 2007/14, 13, para.9 [Counsel Colson, 23 March 2007] <www.icj-cij.org>; *Romania v. Ukraine* Hearings, CR 2008/21, 15, para.11 [Counsel Muller, 5 Sep 2008], CR 2008/33, 27, para.59 [Counsel Bundy, 19 Sep 2008] <www.icj-cij.org>.

See also 2002 *Newfoundland/Labrador and Nova Scotia (Phase II)* Award *infra*; France's Preliminary Partial (St. Pierre et Miquelon – zone-locked in Canada Newfoundland EEZ) Submission to the CLCS of 8 May 2009 and Canada's Protest of 9 November 2009 against this Submission <www.un.org/Depts/los/clcs_new/commission_preliminary.htm>.

On 1993 UN *Iraq/Kuwait Boundary Demarcation* Decision [*supra*], see Statement of the UN *Eritrea/Ethiopia Boundary* Commission of 27 November 2006, paras 23-25 <www.pca-cpa.org>; 2009 *Abyei Boundary* Award, para.461 <www.pca-cpa.org>.

On 1994/1995 *Argentina/Chile Laguna del Desierto* Awards [1664 UNTS 296; 113 ILR 1, 17, 194; RIAA XXII, 3, 153; 100 RGDIP 520 (1996)], see *Botswana/ Namibia* Judgment, ICJ Rep. 1999, 1060, para.20, Declaration Higgins, 1113 para.2; Oral Hearings, CR 99/2, 60 [Counsel Chayes, 16 Feb 1999], CR 99/8, 41-42 [Counsel Lady Fox, 24 Feb], CR 99/11, 27, 47 [Chayes, 2 March 1999]; *Qatar v. Bahrain (Merits)* Hearings, CR 2000/13, 64 [Counsel Kemicha, 13 June 2000]; *Cameroon v. Nigeria; Equatorial Guinea Intervening (Merits)* Hearings, CR 2002/2, 36 [Counsel Cot, 19 Feb 2002]; *Indonesia/Malaysia (Merits)* Hearings, CR 2002/29, 42 [Counsel Malintoppi, 4 June 2002]; *Costa Rica v. Nicaragua San Juan River* Declaration Guillaume, ICJ Rep. 2009, para.11 n.24 <www.icj-cij.org>.

On 1998 *Eritrea/Yemen Territorial Sovereignty and Scope of the Dispute (Phase I)* Award [*supra*], see *Qatar v. Bahrain (Merits)* Judgment, ICJ Rep. 2001, 70, para.99, Joint Dissent Bedjaoui, Ranjeva, Koroma, 145, paras 82, 94 n.27, 137, 139-140, 144, Declaration Higgins, 222, Separate Os Kooymans, 228, 242, paras 9, 66, Al-Khasawneh, 251, para.10, Dissent Torres Bernardez, 257, paras 37, 210, 244, 366, 380, 428; Hearings, CR 2000/6, 47-48 [Counsel Sinclair, 30 May 2000], CR 2000/7, 17, 24 [Counsel Bundy, 31 May], CR 2000/8, 33 [Counsel Sir Ian Sinclair, 5 June], CR 2000/9 [trans.], 45-46, 52 [Counsel Queneudec], CR 2000/11, 19, 23-25, 29-30, 38 [Counsel Sir Elihu Lauterpacht, 8 June], CR 2000/13, 42 [Counsel Volterra, 13 June], CR 2000/14, 10, 15 [Lauterpacht, 13 June], CR 2000/15, 12-14 [Counsel Reisman, 14 June], CR 2000/15, 29, 45-48, 55-56 [Counsel Weil], CR 2000/17, 30-31, 33, 36-38 [Shankardass, 20 June], 52 [Bundy], CR 2000/18, 7-8 [21 June], 19-21, 23 [Sinclair], 29 [Counsel David], CR 2000/21 [Counsel Paulsson, 27 June], CR 2000/22, 16-17 [Lauterpacht, 28 June], CR 2000/25, 10 [Reisman, 29 June 2000], 14 [Weil]; *Indonesia/Malaysia (Intervention)* Hearings, CR 2001/1, 10 [Counsel Reisman, 25 June 2001];*Joint Legal Opinion on Guatemala's Territorial Claim to Belize*, paras 76-77, 185 (January 2002) <www.belize-guatemala.gov .bz/>; *Cameroon v. Nigeria; Equatorial Guinea Intervening (Merits)* Hearings, CR 2002/16, 31-32 [Counsel Shaw, 11 March 2002], CR 2002/18, 54 [Counsel Brownlie, 14 March 2002]; *Indonesia/Malaysia (Merits)* Dissent Franck, ICJ Rep. 2002, 96-697, para.18; Hearings, CR 2002/27, 40, 41 [Counsel Pellet, 3 June], CR 2002/29, 31 [4 June], 42 [Counsel Malintoppi], CR 2002/31, 20 [Counsel Cot, 7 June 2002], CR 2002/32, 34 [Counsel Crawford], CR 2002/33, 16 [Counsel Sir Arthur Watts, 10 June], CR 2002/34, 22, 26, 36 [Pellet], CR 2002/35, 24 [Counsel Schrijver, 12 June 2002] <www.icj-cij.org>; 2006 *Barbados/Trinidad & Tobago (Jurisdiction and Merits)* Award, paras 140, 278 n.24, 279; Barbados' Reply, para.411; Hearings Day-5, 66-67 [Counsel Reisman, 24 Oct 2005], Day-8, 122 [Counsel Greenwood, 28 Oct 2005] <www.pca-cpa.org>; *Nicaragua v. Honduras* Hearings, CR 2007/3, 55, para.46, at 59-61, paras 59-61 & 63-64 [Counsel Oude Elferink, 7 March 2007], CR 2007/11, 37, para.20 n.39, at 41, para.28 [Counsel Pellet, 19 March 2007]; *Nicaragua v. Colombia (Preliminary Objections)* Hearings, CR 2007/19, 9, para.8 [Agent Arguello, 8 June 2007] <www.icj-cij.org>; *Malaysia/Singapore (Merits) Pedra Branca/Pulau Batu Puteh, Middle Rocks and South Ledge (Merits)* Judgment, ICJ Rep. 2008, para.222, Dissent Dugard, paras 10, 30, para.42, Separate O. Rao, paras 5, 17; Hearings, CR 2007/21, 61-62, paras 123-125 [Counsel Brownlie, 7 Nov 2007], CR 2007/22, 28, para.68 and at 30, para.72 [Counsel Bundy, 8 Nov], 40, para.11 [Counsel Malintoppi], CR 2007/22 [transl.], 16, para.26 [Counsel Pellet], CR 2007/23 [transl.], 44, para.15 [Pellet, 9 Nov], CR 2007/24, 50, paras 54-56 [Counsel Sir Elihu Lauterpacht, 13 Nov], CR 2007/26, 35, para.1, at 39, para.12 and at 54, para.64 [Sir Elihu, 15 Nov], CR 2007/28, 23, paras 18-19 [Counsel Chao, 19 Nov], 53, para.8 and at 65, para.15 [Bundy], CR 2007/29, 36, paras 34-35 [Malintoppi, 20 Nov 2007], CR 2007/29 [transl.], 37, para.10 [Counsel Pellet] <www.icj-cij.org>; 2009 *Abyei Boundary* Award, para.754 n.1255, para.760 <www.pca-cpa.org>.

Cf. *Gulf of Fonseca* Hearings, C 4/CR 91/43, 79 [Counsel Brownlie, 7 June 1991], CR 91/44, 20 [Counsel Bowett, 10 June 1991].

On 1999 *Eritrea/Yemen Maritime Delimitation (Phase II)* Award [*supra*], see *Qatar v. Bahrain (Merits)* Oral Hearings, CR 2000/6, 41 [Counsel Sinclair, 30 May 2000], CR 2000/10, 12 [Counsel Queneudec, 6 June], CR 2000/15, 19, 29, 36-38, 51, 53 [Counsel Weil, 14 June 2000]; 2002 *Newfoundland/Nova Scotia (Phase II)* Award, para.2.28 n.88, para.2.31 n.90, para.3.5 n.108 <www.gov.ns.ca/>; *Cameroon v. Nigeria; Equatorial Guinea Intervening (Merits)* Judgment, ICJ Rep. 2002, 417, para.228; Hearings, CR 2002/7, 20-21, 28 [Co-Agent Kamto, 26 Feb 2002], CR 2002/9, 46 [Counsel Brownlie, 1 March], CR 2002/12, 64 [Counsel Crawford, 6 March], CR 2002/13, 54 [7 March], CR 2002/17, 23-24, 27-28 [Co-Agent Pellet, 12 March], CR 2002/20, 56 [Crawford, 15 March], CR 2002/21, 39 [Counsel Colson, 18 March], CR 2002/22, 47 [Counsel Mendelson, 19 March 2002], CR 2002/23, 19 [Counsel Abi-Saab]; *Indonesia/Malaysia (Merits)* Hearings, CR 2002/34, 36 [Counsel Pellet, 10 June 2002] <www.icj-cij.org>; 2006 *Barbados/Trinidad & Tobago (Jurisdiction and Merits)* Award, paras 72, 86 n.13, 140-141, 149, 158, 183, 278 n.24, 279; Barbados' Memorial, paras 107, 133, 134 n.173, para.136 n.179; Trinidad's Counter-Memorial, paras 49, 170, 241, 244, 266 n.261; Barbados' Reply, paras 406, 408-409, 412-414; Trinidad's Rejoinder, paras 134-136; Hearings Day-2, 21-29 [Counsel Reisman, 18 Oct 2005], Day-4, 46-48 [Counsel Greenwood, 21 Oct], Day-5, 52 [Counsel Fietta, 24 Oct], 66-67 [Reisman], Day-8, 115,122 [Greenwood, 28 Oct], replying to Orrego Vicuna's and Lowe's Questions, Day-4, 29 [21 Oct] & Day-5, 35-36 [24 Oct 2005] <www.pca-cpa.org>; 2007 *Guyana/Suriname* Award, para.339 n.388, para.463; Hearings Day 2, 263 [Counsel Schrijver, 8 Dec 2006] <www.pca-cpa.org>; *Nicaragua v. Honduras (Merits)* Declaration Gaja, ICJ Rep. 2007; Hearings, CR 2007/5, 20, para.60 [Counsel Pellet, 9 March 2007], CR 2007/10, 11, para.74 [Counsel Colson, 16 March 2007]; *Nicaragua v. Colombia (Preliminary Objections)* Hearings, CR 2007/19, 9, para.8 [Agent Arguello, 8 June 2007] <www.icj-cij.org>; *Romania v. Ukraine* Judgment, ICJ Rep. 2009, para.149; Hearings, CR 2008/20, 25, para.36 and at 34, para.54 [Counsel Pellet, 4 Sep 2008], CR 2008/21, 64-65, paras 62 & 66 [Counsel Lowe, 5 Sep], CR 2008/31, 32, para.22 ns 50-51 and at 37, para.31 n.70 [Pellet, 16 Sep 2008], 44-45, paras 15-17 and at 46, para.21 n.80 [Counsel Lowe] <www.icj-cij.org>; 2009 *Abyei Boundary* Award, para.760 <www.pca-cpa.org>.

On 2002 *Eritrea/Ethiopia Delimitation of the Border* Decision [*supra*], see *Cameroon v. Nigeria; Equatorial Guinea Intervening (Merits)* Separate O. Al-Khasawneh, ICJ Rep. 2002, 497-498, para.7, Dissent Ajibola, 540-541, para.8; *Indonesia/Malaysia (Merits)* Dissent Franck, ICJ Rep. 2002, 699, para.26; Hearings, CR 2002/29, 42-43 [Counsel Malintoppi, 4 June 2002] <www.icj-cij.org>; 2006 *Barbados/Trinidad & Tobago (Jurisdiction and Merits)* Award, paras 278 n.24, 281; Hearings Day-8, 123-124 [Counsel Greenwood, 28 Oct 2005] referring to Barbados' Written Reply to Day-5, 72 [Lowe's Question, 24 Oct 2005]; *Guyana/Suriname* Guyana's Reply, para.8.11, Suriname's Rejoinder, para.4.63; Hearings Day 9, 1456 [Co-Agent Akhavan, 18 Dec 2006], Day 10, 1616-1617 [Counsel McRae, 20 Dec 2006] <www.pca-cpa.org>; *Malaysia/Singapore (Merits)* Judgment, ICJ Rep. 2008, para.271; Hearings, CR 2007/29, 38, para.45 [Counsel Malintoppi, 20 Nov 2007], CR 2007/31, 44, para.10 [Counsel Nevill, 23 Nov 2007] <www.icj-cij.org>; *Romania v. Ukraine* Hearings, CR 2008/19, 38-39, para.54 [Counsel Crawford, 3 Sep 2008], CR 2008/30, 60, para.20 [Counsel Olleson, 15 Sep], CR 2008/31, 18, para.33 [Counsel Lowe, 16 Sep], CR 2008/32, 29, para.36 [Counsel Wood, 18 Sep 2008]; *Costa Rica v. Nicaragua San Juan River* Declaration Guillaume, ICJ Rep. 2009, para.11 n.26; Hearings, CR 2009/4, 52, para.8 n.73 [Counsel Pellet, 5 March 2009] <www.icj-cij.org>; 2009 *Abyei Boundary* Award, para.457 <www.pca-cpa.org>.

On 2002 *Newfoundland/Labrador and Nova Scotia (Phase II)* Award [*supra*], see 2006 *Barbados/Trinidad & Tobago (Jurisdiction and Merits)* Award, para.86 n.13, paras 160, 306; Barbados' Memorial, para.109; Trinidad's Counter-Memorial, paras 153, 266 n.262, para.287; Barbados' Reply, paras 141-143; Hearings Day-4, 100, 107-108 [Counsel Crawford, 21 Oct 2005], Day-8, 39-40, 58 [Crawford, 28 Oct 2005] <www.pca-cpa.org>; *Nicaragua v. Honduras* Hearings, CR 2007/2, 40, para.134, at 45, paras 154-155 [Counsel Brownlie, 6 March 2007], CR 2007/5, 34, para.31, at 34, para.31, at 37-38, para.54, at 39, para.61 [Brownlie, 9 March], CR

2007/14, 12, para.7 [Counsel Colson, 23 March 2007] <www.icj-cij.org>; 2007 *Guyana/Suriname* Award, paras 339, 352 n.402, para.388 <www.pca-cpa.org>; *Romania v. Ukraine* Hearings, CR 2008/20, 25-26, para.36, at 32, para.52 and at 35, para.54 [Counsel Pellet, 4 Sep 2008], CR 2008/21, 18, para.18 [Counsel Muller, 5 Sep], CR 2008/31, 24, para.5, at 37, para.31 n.70 and at 40, para.33 [Pellet, 16 Sep 2008] <www.icj-cij.org>.

See also 1992 *Canada/France (St. Pierre & Miquelon) Delimitation of the Maritime Areas* Award *supra*; France's Preliminary Partial (St. Pierre et Miquelon – zone-locked in Canada Newfoundland EEZ) Submission to the CLCS of 8 May 2009 and Canada's Protest of 9 November 2009 against this Preliminary Submission <www.un.org/Depts/los/clcs_new/commission_preliminary.htm>.

On 2006 *Barbados/Trinidad and Tobago* Award [*supra*], see *Nicaragua v. Honduras* Hearings, CR 2007/1, 68, para.64 [Counsel Oude Elferink, 5 March 2007], CR 2007/2, 23, para.61 [Counsel Brownlie, 6 March], CR 2007/5, 20, para.60 [Counsel Pellet, 9 March], CR 2007/8, 46-47, para.35, at 53, para.59, at 55-56, para.67, at 59, para.77 *in fine* [Counsel Dupuy, 14 March], CR 2007/10, 24, para.124 [Colson, 16 March], CR 2007/12, 44, para.25 [Brownlie, 20 March], CR 2007/14, 19-20, paras 37-41, supporting the proportionality *a posteriori* in close reliance on the 2006 *Barbados/T&T* Award, paras 240, 337, 376-379 [Counsel Colson, 23 March 2007], 36, para.22, referring to "the popular tactic of advancing a maximalist claim in the hope that the Court will split the difference" (alluding to Trinidad's "maximalist claim" to vector approach which was rejected by the 2006 *Barbados/T&T* Award, paras 359-360) [Counsel Greenwood] <www.icj-cij .org>; 2007 *Guyana/Suriname* Award, paras 132, 220, 224 and 228, para.333 [*reaffirming Barbados/T&T* Award, para.222], paras 334 and 341 [*reaffirming Barbados/T&T* Award, para.244], para.340 [*reaffirming Barbados/T&T* Award, para.242], para.356 [*reaffirming Barbados/T&T* Award, para.228], para.389 [*reaffirming Barbados/T&T* Award, paras 364 and 366] and paras 410 and 457 [*reaffirming Barbados/T&T* Award, paras 201-202 and 205-207]; Suriname's Rejoinder, paras 2.74/2.75, 3.8/3.25, 3.39, 3.52, 3.131, 3.148, 3.166, 3.181/3.182, 3.277; *Guyana/Suriname* Hearings, 45 [Counsel Rosenne, 8 July 2005], 57 [Counsel Sands]; Day 1, at 9 [President Nelson, 7 Dec 2006], Day 2, 160 [Co-Agent Reichler, 8 Dec], 263-264, quoting *Barbados/T&T* Award, paras 242 and 306 [Counsel Schrijver], Day 5, 635-636, 641, 771-772 [quoting *Barbados/ T&T* Award, para.40], 803 [Counsel Greenwood, 13 Dec], Day 6, 881, 886 [Counsel Oxman, 14 Dec], 935 [Counsel McRae], Day 7, 1022 [Counsel Colson, 15 Dec], 1134-1135 [Counsel Murphy], Day 8, 1176 [McRae, 16 Dec], Day 9, 1269-1271, 1323 [quoting *Barbados/T&T* Award, para.306], 1325-1327 [quoting *Barbados/T&T* Award, paras 242, 306 and 315], 1348 [Sands, 18 Dec], 1419-1420 [quoting *Barbados/T&T* Award, paras 220-223], 1422, 1428 [Schrijver], Day 10,

1533-1537 [quoting *Barbados/T&T* Award, para.306], 1556 [Oxman, 20 Dec 2006], 1588 [McRae] <www.pca-cpa.org>; *Romania v. Ukraine* Judgment, ICJ Rep. 2009, para.198 [*reaffirming Barbados/T&T* Award, para.241]; Hearings, CR 2008/20, 29, para.45 and at 30, para.47(2) [Counsel Pellet, 4 Sep 2008], CR 2008/21, 15, para.11 ns 12-13 and at 16, para.14 n.18 [Counsel Muller, 5 Sep], CR 2008/24, 28, para.40 [Counsel Bundy, 9 Sep], CR 2008/26, 11, paras 44-46, at 15, paras 61, 64 and at 17, para.72 [Counsel Queneudec, 10 Sep], 33, para.58 [Bundy], CR 2008/28, 52, para.76 [Bundy, 11 Sep], CR 2008/29, 23, para.3 and at 27, para.26 [Queneudec, 12 Sep], CR 2008/30, 33, para.48 [Counsel Crawford, 15 Sep], CR 2008/31, 30 n.42 and at 32 n.50 and at 38, para.33 [Pellet, 16 Sep], CR 2008/32, 39, para.41 [Bundy, 18 Sep], CR 2008/33, 24, para.41 [Bundy, 19 Sep 2008] <www.icj-cij.org>; 2009 *Abyei Boundary* Award, para.754 n.1252 <www.pca-cpa.org>.

On 2007 *Guyana/Suriname* Award [*supra*], see *Romania v. Ukraine* Hearings, CR 2008/21, 14, para.11 and at 16, para.14 n.18 [Counsel Muller, 5 Sep 2008], CR 2008/24, 28, para.40 [Counsel Bundy, 9 Sep], CR 2008/26, 17, para.73 [Counsel Queneudec, 10 Sep 2008] <www.icj-cij.org>.

On UNSG *Guyana/Venezuela* Mediation [*supra*], see 2006 *Barbados/Trinidad & Tobago* Award, paras 345-346; Barbados' Reply, paras 26, 74 n.130, para.87 n.173; Trinidad's Rejoinder, para.197; Hearings Day-3, 103 [Counsel Crawford, 20 Oct 2005], Day-6, 14-15 [President Schwebel's Question, Co-Agent Volterra, 25 Oct], Day-7, 27 [Counsel Greenwood, 27 Oct], Day-8, 10, 26-27 [Crawford, 28 Oct 2005], 132-133 [Agent Jeremie] <www.pca-cpa.org>; *Guyana/Suriname* Suriname's Counter-Memorial, para.6.23, Guyana's Reply, paras 5.20, 7.21, Suriname's Rejoinder, para.3.170 <www.pca-cpa.org>.

CHARTS AND LISTS OF GEOGRAPHICAL COORDINATES DEPOSITED WITH THE UNITED NATIONS SECRETARY-GENERAL

1958 TSC, Article 12(2); 1958 CSC, Article 6(3)
1982 UNCLOS, Part II, Articles 5-6 and 16, Part IV, Article 47(8)-(9), Part V, Articles 75 and 76(9), Part VI, Article 84, Part XI, Article 134(3)

North Sea Pleadings, Vol.I, 518-519 [Common Rejoinder of Denmark/NL], Vol.II, 25 [Agent Jaenicke, 23 Oct 1968], 88-89 [Sir Humphrey Waldock, 28 Oct 1968]; *Denmark v. Norway* Hearings, CR 93/2, 62 [Counsel de Arechaga, 12 Jan 1993], CR 93/10, 39 [Agent Magid, 25 Jan 1993]; *Botswana/Namibia* Hearings, CR 99/4, 52-53, 63, 67 [Agent Kawana, 17 Feb 1999], CR 99/5, 61 [Counsel Chayes, 18 Feb 1999]; *Qatar v. Bahrain (Merits)* Dissent Torres Bernardez, paras 55, 514-515, ICJ Rep. 2001, 279, 434; Hearings, CR 2000/14, 44 [Counsel Reisman, 13 June

2000]; *Cameroon v. Nigeria; Equatorial Guinea Intervening (Merits)* Judgment, ICJ Rep. 2002, 410, 426, paras 213, 253; Hearings, CR 2002/16, 31-32 [Counsel Shaw, 11 March 2002]; *Indonesia/Malaysia (Merits)* Hearings, CR 2002/29, 42-43 [Counsel Malintoppi, 4 June], CR 2002/32, 37 [Counsel Crawford, 7 June 2002]; *Nicaragua v. Honduras (Merits)* Judgment, ICJ Rep. 2007, para.278; *Malaysia/Singapore (Merits)* Judgment, ICJ Rep. 2008, para.271; Hearings, CR 2007/29, 38-39, para.45 [Counsel Malintoppi, 20 Nov 2007], CR 2007/31, 44, para.10 [Counsel Nevill, 23 Nov 2007]; *Romania v. Ukraine* Judgment, ICJ Rep. 2009, paras 124, 129, 135-136; Hearings, CR 2008/19, 12, para.8 and at 38-39, paras 54-58 [Counsel Crawford, 3 Sep 2008], CR 2008/20, 18, para.21 [Counsel Pellet, 4 Sep], CR 2008/26, 23-26, paras 15-29 [Counsel Bundy, 10 Sep], CR 2008/28, 11-14, paras 8-15 [Counsel Sir Michael Wood, 11 Sep], CR 2008/29, 32, para.51 and at 34-35, paras 58, 63 [Counsel Queneudec, 12 Sep], CR 2008/30, 59-60, paras 16-20 [Counsel Olleson, 15 Sep], CR 2008/32, 18, para.14 and at 25-31 [Wood, 18 Sep 2008] <www.icj-cij.org>.

1978 *Anglo/French Continental Shelf* Decision – see Equitable Maritime Boundary Delimitation *supra*; 1996 *Public Prosecutor v. Haraldsson et al. (Abel Island)* Judgment of Norway's Supreme Court, 11 IJMCL 576-580 (1996); 1998 *Eritrea/Yemen (Phase I)* Award, paras 51, 376-379 [40 ILM 900 (2001) <www.pca-cpa.org>]; 2002 *Belize/Guatemala* OAS Facilitators' Proposals, B-para.6 <www.belize-guatemala.gov.bz>; 2002 *Eritrea/Ethiopia Delimitation of the Border (Merits)* Decision, paras 3.26-3.28 and Appendix A, paras A26-A32, 41 ILM 1057 (2002); RIAA XXV, 83 <http://untreaty.un.org/cod/riaa/vol_XXV.htm>; and *(Demarcation)* Statement of 27 Nov 2006, para.26, 46 ILM 155 (2007), PCA Press Release of 30 Nov 2007 and UN Doc. S/2008/40, at 13-23, Annex II [President Lauterpacht's 26th Report] (2008) <www.un.org/Docs/journal/asp/ws.asp?m=s/2008/40> & <www.pca-cpa.org>.

REGIME OF ISLANDS

1930 Hague Draft, Annex II, Appendix A: Proposal of the Delegation of the USA, 250, and Appendix B: Compromise-Proposal of the French Delegation (Islands), 251-252
1958 TSC, Article 10; 1958 CSC, Article 1(b)
1982 UNCLOS, Part VIII, Article 121

Relevant Jurisprudence

On islands, islets, rocks, banks and reefs, known as the "skjaergaard" ("rock rampart") see *Anglo/Norwegian Fisheries* ICJ Rep. 1951, 116 – Judgment, 121, 122, 123, 127, 128, 129, 130, 135, 140, 141, Separate O. Hsu Mo, 155-156,

Dissent McNair, 166-167, 170, 182, 184-185, Dissent Read, 193, 194, 199; *Anglo/Norwegian Fisheries* Pleadings, Vol.I, 71-77, 84, 88 [UK Memorial], 450-465 [Norway's Counter-Memorial], Vol.II, 324-325, 503-517, 577-578, 594-596, 660 [UK Reply], Vol.III, 361-366, 436 [Norway's Rejoinder], Vol.IV, 90-97 [Agent Beckett, 27 Sep 1951].

On 1951 Egypt's Royal Decree, see Internal Waters, Territorial Sea and Baselines, TS Breadth and Outer Limit *supra*.

On the coastal archipelago, including survey of state practice and case law, see *Anglo/Norwegian Fisheries* ICJ Rep. 1951, 116 – Judgment, 129, 131, 136, Dissent Read, 193; Pleadings, Vol.I, 79-83 [UK Memorial], 465-495 [Norway's Counter-Memorial], Vol.II, 460-461, 517-553, 578, 638, 660 [UK Reply], Vol.III, 366-394 [Norway's Reply], Vol.IV, 279-282 [Counsel Bourquin, 11 Oct 1951]; *Antarctica* Pleadings, 9, 10, 50, 52 [UK Applications]; *Tunisia/Libya (Merits)* Dissent Evensen, ICJ Rep. 1982, 301, 303-304.

1953 *France/United Kingdom Minquiers and Ecrehos* Judgment – see Fisheries *infra*; *North Sea* Judgment, ICJ Rep. 1969, 32, para.46; *Aegean Sea (Interim Measures)* Dissent Stassinopoulos, ICJ Rep. 1976, 35, *(Jurisdiction)* Judgment, ICJ Rep. 1978, 6, 8, 33-37, Dissents de Castro, 65-66, Stassinopoulos, 81, para.21; Pleadings, 3-11 [Greece's Application], 63-66 [Request], 96-99 [Counsel O'Connell, 26 Aug 1976], 467 [Question President de Aréchaga, 16 Oct 1978], 495 [Reply Counsel Economides]; *Tunisia/Libya (Merits)* Dissents Oda, ICJ Rep. 1982, 183, 212, 251-252, 263-266, Evensen, 283, 293, 299-303; *Libya/Malta* Pleadings, Vol.I, 128-132 [Libya's Memorial], 440-455 [Malta's Memorial], Vol.II, 89-100 [Libya's Counter-Memorial], 280 [Malta's Counter-Memorial], Vol.III, 194-197 [Malta's Reply]; *Denmark v. Norway* Judgment, ICJ Rep. 1993, 46, 69, 73-74, Declaration Evensen, 84-85, Separate Os Oda, 100-101, Schwebel, 126-127, Ajibola, 290-292, 299-300, Dissent Fischer, 310-312; Denmark's Memorial, paras 271-273, Norway's Counter-Memorial, para.445, Denmark's Reply, paras 299-333, 459-465, Norway's Rejoinder, paras 386-461; Hearings, CR 93/3, 45-55 [Agent Lehmann, 13 Jan 1993], CR 93/6, 67 [Agent Haug, 18 Jan], CR 93/8 [trans.], 22-23 [Counsel Weil, 20 Jan], CR 93/9 [trans.], 26-29 [21 Jan 1993]; *New Zealand v. France* Hearings, CR 95/19, 71-74 [Counsel Lauterpacht, 11 Sep 1995]; *Qatar v. Bahrain (Merits)* Judgment, ICJ Rep. 2001, 62, 97, paras 64, 185, Joint Dissent Bedjaoui, Ranjeva, Koroma, 202, paras 182-184; Hearings, CR 2000/6, 44 [Counsel Sir Ian Sinclair, 30 May 2000], CR 2000/19, 19-21 [Counsel Queneudec, 22 June 2000]; *Nicaragua v. Honduras*, *Romania v. Ukraine* and *Nicaragua v. Colombia* – see Equitable Maritime Boundary Delimitation *supra*.

Nature of a High-Tide Elevation

1930 Hague Draft, Annex II, Appendix B: Compromise-Proposal of the French Delegation (Islands), 251; 1958 TSC, Article 10(1); 1982 UNCLOS, Article 121(1):

Anglo/Norwegian Fisheries Judgment, ICJ Rep. 1951, 127, 135, 140; Pleadings, Vol.I, 74-75, 84 [UK Memorial], 457 [Norway's Counter-Memorial], Vol.II, 325, 510-511, 516 [UK Reply], Vol.IV, 91 [Agent Sir Eric Beckett, 27 Sep 1951]; *Minquiers and Ecrehos* ICJ Rep. 1953, 47 – Judgment, 53, Individual O. Carneiro, 88; Pleadings, Vol.I, 58 [UK Memorial], 433-434, 556 [UK Reply], Vol.II, 184, 329 [Counsel Harrison, 24 Sep and 3 Oct 1953]; *Aegean Sea* Pleadings, 96-97 [Counsel O'Connell, 25 Aug 1976]; *Tunisia/Libya (Merits)* Dissent Oda, ICJ Rep. 1982, 265; *Libya/Malta* Pleadings, Vol.I, 450 [Malta's Memorial], Vol.II, 359 [Malta's Counter-Memorial]; *Denmark v. Norway* Separate O. Ajibola, ICJ Rep. 1993, 299; *Qatar v. Bahrain (Merits)* Judgment, ICJ Rep. 2001, 98-100, 115, paras 191-197, 248, Separate O. Oda, 123-125, paras 5-9, Joint Dissent Bedjaoui, Ranjeva, Koroma, 207-211, paras 194-205, Declaration Vereshchetin, 220, para.13, Separate O. Parra-Aranguren, 223, para.4, Dissent Torres Bernardez, 436-439, 445, paras 523-529, 551; Hearings, CR 2000/13, 31-32 [Counsel Volterra, 13 June 2000], CR 2000/14, 45-49 [Counsel Reisman], CR 2000/15, 8 [14 June], 50-52 [Counsel Weil], CR 2000/19, 19-20 [Counsel Queneudec, 22 June], CR 2000/25, 13-14 [Weil, 29 June 2000]; *Indonesia/Malaysia (Merits)* Judgment, ICJ Rep. 2002, 634, para. 14; Hearings, CR 2002/27, 19-20 [Agent Wirajuda, 3 June], CR 2002/30, 24 [Co-Agent Ariffin, 6 June], CR 2002/33, 13-14 [Counsel Watts, 10 June 2002] <www.icj-cij.org>; *Nicaragua v. Honduras (Merits)* Judgment, ICJ Rep. 2007, paras 28-30, 113-116, 136-145, Dissent Torres Bernardez, para.146; Hearings, CR 2007/1, 36, para.70, at 40, para.89 [Agent Arguello, 5 March 2007], 50, para.8, at 60-64 [Counsel Oude Elferink], CR 2007/6, 22-23, paras 32-34 [Counsel Greenwood, 12 March], CR 2007/7, 24-26 [Counsel Sands, 13 March], CR 2007/8, 29-30 [Counsel Queneudec, 14 March], 43-44 [Counsel Dupuy], CR 2007/11, 33-35 [Counsel Pellet, 19 March], 52-55, 59, 62 [Oude Elferink], CR 2007/12, 54 [Question of Judge Simma, 20 March], CR 2007/13, 40-44 [Sands, 22 March], CR 2007/14,33-34, paras 9-11 [Greenwood, 23 March 2007], 37, paras 4-5 [Agent Flores]; *Question of Judge Gaja*, in CR 2007/10, 37 [16 March] and CR 2007/11, 26, paras 61-64 [Agent Arguello's Reply to Gaja], also CR 2007/13, 44-45, paras 21-22 [Sands, 22 March], CR 2007/14, 35, para.14 [Greenwood, 23 March 2007]; *Malaysia/Singapore Pedra Branca/Pulau Batu Puteh, Middle Rocks and South Ledge (Merits)* Judgment, paras 18-19, 278; *Romania v. Ukraine* Hearings, CR 2008/19, 53-55 [Agent Aurescu, 3 Sep 2008], CR 2008/20, 41, paras 9-13 [Counsel Lowe, 4 Sep], CR 2008/21, 37-38, para.4 [Counsel Crawford, 5 Sep], CR 2008/29, 12, paras 34-35 [Counsel Malintoppi, 12 Sep 2009] <www.icj-cij.org>.

1977 *Anglo/French* Decision [18 ILM 397 (1979)], paras 127-138, 158; 1981 *Dubai/Sharjah* Award [91 ILR 672-677].

See also Internal Waters, Territorial Sea and Baselines – Low-Tide Elevations *supra.*

***Rocks Which Cannot Sustain Human Habitation or Economic Life of Their Own* 1982 UNCLOS, Article 121(3):**

Habitability

Legal Status of Eastern Greenland Judgment, PCIJ Series A/B, No.53 (1933), 46; *Anglo/Norwegian Fisheries* Pleadings, Vol.I, 72 [UK Memorial], 462 [Norway's Counter-Memorial], Vol.II, 507 [UK Reply]; *Minquiers and Ecrehos* ICJ Rep. 1953, 47 – Judgment, 53, 65, 69, 71-72, Individual O. Basdevant, 78, 80, Individual O. Carneiro, 88, 109; *Minquiers and Ecrehos* Judgment, ICJ Rep. 1953, 53; Pleadings, Vol.I, 64, 84, 346-348 [UK Memorial], 424 n.2, 435 [UK Reply], Vol.II, 327, 329-330, 344 [Counsel Harrison, 3 and 5 Oct 1953]; *Antarctica* Pleadings, 18 [UK Application]; *Western Sahara* Advisory Opinion, ICJ Rep. 1975, 39, para.80; *Tunisia/Libya (Merits)* Dissent Oda, ICJ Rep. 1982, 265-266; Pleadings, Vol.I, 79 [Tunisia's Memorial]; *Gulf of Maine* Judgment, ICJ Rep. 1984, 336-337; Pleadings, Vol.III, 256-257 [Canada's Counter-Memorial]; *Libya/Malta* Pleadings, Vol.I, 129, 132 [Libya's Memorial], Vol.II, 98-99 [Libya's Counter-Memorial]; *Gulf of Fonseca* Judgment, ICJ Rep. 1992, 565, 570, para.356, Separate O. Bernardez, 710-711; *New Zealand v. France* Hearings, CR 95/19, 71 [Counsel Lauterpacht, 11 Sep 1995], CR 95/20 [transl.], 66 [De Brichambaut, 12 Sep 1995]; *Denmark v. Norway* Judgment, ICJ Rep. 1993, 46, 54, 64-65, 73-74, Separate Os Evensen, 84-85, Oda, 115-116, Schwebel, 126-127, Weeramantry, 267-270, Ajibola, 291-292, 299, Dissent Fischer, 310-312; Hearings, CR 93/1/Corr., 17, 25, 27-29 [Agent Lehmann, 11 Jan 1993], CR 93/2, 70 [Counsel de Arechaga, 12 Jan], CR 93/4, 24-25, 31-34 [Counsel Bowett, 14 Jan], CR 93/7, 9-21 [Counsel Brownlie, 19 Jan], CR 93/10, 21-24 [Lehmann, 25 Jan], 44-45 [Agent Magid], 71-78 [Counsel Lynge], CR 93/11 [trans.], 43 [Counsel Weil, 27 Jan 1993]; *Qatar v. Bahrain (Merits)* Judgment, ICJ Rep. 2001, 95, 104, 114, paras 179, 219, 246, Joint Dissent Bedjaoui, Ranjeva, Koroma, 208-209, para.198, Dissent Torres Bernardez, 395, 397, para.389, 394; Hearings, CR 2000/14, 45 [Counsel Reisman, 13 June 2000]; *Cameroon v. Nigeria; Equatorial Guinea Intervening (Merits)* Hearings, CR 2002/8, 33 [Agent Abdullahi, 28 Feb 2002], CR 2002/16, 34-37 [Counsel Mendelson, 11 March 2002]; *Indonesia/Malaysia (Merits)* Judgment, ICJ Rep. 2002, 625, paras 14, 98, 134, Declaration Oda, 687 690; Hearings, CR 2002/27, 15, 17 [Agent Wirajuda, 3 June], 41 [Counsel Pellet], CR 2002/30, 23-25 [Co-Agent Ariffin, 6 June], CR 2002/33, 12 [Counsel Watts, 10 June 2002]; *Benin/*

Niger Judgment, paras 19, 78-79, ICJ Rep. 2005, 104, 127-128; Niger's Memorial, 140-183; Hearings, C5/CR 2005/4, 24-26, paras 15-19 [Counsel Salmon, 8 March 2005]; *Nicaragua v. Honduras (Merits)* Judgment, ICJ Rep. 2007, paras 49, 52, 55-58, 65-66, 80, 95, 131, 162, 170-175, 186-187, 190-201, 240-243, 245, 252, 256, Dissent Torres Bernardez, para.65; Hearings, CR 2007/1, 36, para.70, at 40, para.89 [Agent Arguello, 5 March 2007], 50, para.8, at 60-64 [Counsel Oude Elferink], CR 2007/6, 22-23, paras 32-34 [Counsel Greenwood, 12 March], CR 2007/7, 24-26 [Counsel Sands, 13 March], CR 2007/8, 29-30 [Counsel Queneudec, 14 March], 43-44 [Counsel Dupuy], CR 2007/11, 33-35 [Counsel Pellet, 19 March], 52-55, 59, 62 [Oude Elferink], CR 2007/12, 54 [Question of Judge Simma, 20 March], CR 2007/14,33-34, paras 9-11 [Greenwood, 23 March 2007], 37, paras 4-5 [Agent Flores] <www.icj-cij.org>; *Malaysia/Singapore (Merits)* Judgment, ICJ Rep. 2008, paras 18, 66, 70-75, Declaration Bennouna, para.10, Separate O. Rao, paras 17, 24; Hearings, CR 2007/20, 24, paras 2-3 [Counsel Chao, 6 Nov 2007], CR 2007/22, 19, para.33 [Counsel Bundy, 8 Nov], CR 2007/24, 20-23, paras 6-13 [Co-Agent Farida, 13 Nov], CR 2007/28 [transl.], 30-31, para.6 and at 35, para.15 [Counsel Pellet, 19 Nov], CR 2007/30, 20-22, paras 6-10 [Counsel Crawford, 22 Nov], 28-31, paras 9-18 [Counsel Schrijver], 51-52, paras 9-11 [Counsel Sir Elihu Lauterpacht] <www.icj-cij.org>; *Romania v. Ukraine Maritime Delimitation in the Black Sea* Judgment, unanimous, ICJ Rep. 2009, paras 16, 33, 35, 39, 41, 124, 180, 184, 187; Hearings, CR 2008/18, 15-16, paras 4-6, at 19, para.14, at 21, para.20, at 24, para.28 and at 28-31, paras 39-52 [Agent Aurescu, 2 Sep 2008], 62, para.9 [Counsel Crawford], CR 2008/19, 12, para.8 [Crawford, 3 Sep], 52-71, paras 1-56, esp. at 56-67 & 70-71 [Agent Aurescu, 3 Sep], CR 2008/20, 31-39 [Counsel Pellet, 4 Sep], 39-54 [Counsel Lowe], 54-66 [Aurescu], CR 2008/21, 67, para.81 [Lowe, 5 Sep], CR 2008/24, 15-16, paras 20-26 [Agent Vassylenko, 9 Sep], CR 2008/29, 10-22 [Counsel Malintoppi, 12 Sep], CR 2008/30, 10-19 [Agent Aurescu, 15 Sep], CR 2008/31, 12-22 [Counsel Lowe, 16 Sep], 30-36 [Pellet], CR 2008/32, 13, paras 11-12 [Agent Vassylenko, 18 Sep], 55-60 [Malintoppi] <www.icj-cij.org>.

On 1805 *The Anna* Judgment of Lord Stowell [5 C. Rob. 373; 165 E.R. 809; No.5/ Simmonds], see *Anglo/Norwegian Fisheries* Pleadings, Vol.I, 72 [UK Memorial], 462 [Norway's Counter-Memorial], Vol.II, 507 [UK Reply]; and references listed *infra*.

On uninhabited Maltese islet of Fifla, see Archipelagic State – Archipelagic Baselines *supra*.

1928 *USA/Netherlands Island of Palmas (Miangas)* Award [*infra*]; 1931 *France/ Mexico Clipperton Island* Award [*infra*]; 1977 *Anglo/French* Decision, paras 197, 227; 1998 *Eritrea/Yemen (Phase I)* Award, paras 93, 123-124, 128, 347-357, 446, 449, and 1999 *(Phase II)* Award, paras 32-34, 83, 143, 147 [40 ILM 900, 983

(2001) <www.pca-cpa.org>]; 2002 *Newfoundland/Nova Scotia (Phase II)* Award, paras 1.28, 4.21, 4.30/36, 5.13/15 <www.gov.ns.ca/>; *Seychelles v. France Monte Canfurco* Declaration Vukas, ITLOS Rep. 2000, 86; 2002 *Russia v. Australia Volga* Declaration Vice-President Vukas, paras 2-7, 10 [42 ILM 159 (2003]; 2006 *Barbados/Trinidad & Tobago* Award, para.146 <www.pca-cpa.org>.

Economic Life of their Own/Fisheries

Minquires and Ecrehos Judgment, ICJ Rep. 1953, 57-59, 65, Individual Os Basdevant, 79-81, Carneiro, 89, 104; Pleadings, Vol.I, 49-64, 85-88, 98-101, 109-111, 112 [UK Memorial], Vol.II, 87-93 [Counsel Fitzmaurice, 21 Sep 1953]; *Tunisia/Libya (Merits)* Dissents Oda, ICJ Rep. 1982, 265-266, Evensen, 283; Pleadings, Vol.I, 79-83 [Tunisia's Memorial]; *Libya/Malta* Pleadings, Vol.I, 129 [Libya's Memorial], 440 [Malta's Memorial], Vol.II, 98-99 [Libya's Counter-Memorial]; *Denmark v. Norway* Judgment, ICJ Rep. 1993, 46, 54, 64-65, 73-74, Separate Os Evensen, 84-85, Schwebel, 126-127, Weeramantry, 269-270, Ajibola, 291-292, 299-300, Dissent Fischer, 310-312; Hearings, CR 93/1/Corr., 25, 28 [Agent Lehmann, 11 Jan 1993], CR 93/4, 24-25 [Counsel Bowett, 14 Jan], CR 93/9, 83 [Question 2 Oda, 21 Jan], GJM 93/5 [Denmark's Reply, 27 Jan], CR 93/10, 21-24 [Lehmann, 25 Jan], 71-78 [Counsel Lynge], CR 93/11 [trans.], 43 [Counsel Weil, 27 Jan 1993]; 1996 *Public Prosecutor v. Haraldsson et al. (Abel Island)* Judgment of Norway's Supreme Court, 11 IJMCL 576-580 (1996); *Qatar v. Bahrain (Merits)* Joint Dissent Bedjaoui, Ranjeva, Koroma, para.198, ICJ Rep. 2001, 208-209; *Indonesia/Malaysia (Merits)* Judgment, ICJ Rep. 2002, 625, paras 98, 128, 130, 132-133, 140, 143-145, Declaration Oda, 687, 690, Dissent Franck, 691, paras 17-21, 33; Hearings, CR 2002/27, 15, 17 [Agent Wirajuda, 3 June], CR 2002/29, 13-14 [Counsel Bundy, 4 June], 24-30, 33-34 [Counsel Pellet], CR 2002/30, 20-21, 23-26 [Co-Agent Ariffin, 6 June], 28-29 [Counsel Lauterpacht], 54-55 [Counsel Crawford], CR 2002/31, 42-43 [7 June], CR 2002/32, 16-18 [Lauterpacht], CR 2002/34, 27 [Pellet, 10 June], CR 2002/35, 51-55 [Lauterpacht, 12 June 2002]; *Benin/Niger* Judgment, paras 19, 78-79, ICJ Rep. 2005, 104, 127-128; Niger's Memorial, 140-183; Hearings, C5/CR 2005/4, 24-26, paras 15-19 [Counsel Salmon, 8 March 2005]; *Nicaragua v. Honduras (Merits)* Judgment, ICJ Rep. 2007, paras 49, 52, 55-58, 65-66, 80, 95, 131, 162, 170-175, 186-187, 190-201, 240-243, 245, 252, 256, Dissent Torres Bernardez, para.65; Hearings, CR 2007/1, 17, para.7, 36-39 [Agent Arguello, 5 March 2007], 60-64 [Counsel Oude Elferink], CR 2007/6, 20-23 [Counsel Greenwood, 12 March], CR 2007/7, 24-26 [Counsel Sands, 13 March], CR 2007/8, 29-30 [Counsel Queneudec, 14 March], 43-44 [Counsel Dupuy], CR 2007/11, 33-35 [Counsel Pellet, 19 March], 52-55, 59 [Oude Elferink], CR 2007/12, 54 [Question of Judge Simma, 20 March], CR 2007/14, 24, para.54, referring to Simma's Question [Counsel Colson, 23 March 2007], 33-34, paras 9-11 [Greenwood], 37, paras 4-5 [Agent Flores] <www.icj-cij.org>.

Malaysia/Singapore (Merits) Judgment, ICJ Rep. 2008, paras 71, 167, 190-191, 235, 247-248, 251-253, 260, 265, 278-287, Dissent Dugard, paras 21, 27-28, 41, Separate O. Rao, para.18; Hearings, CR 2007/20, 17-18, paras 7-11 [Agent Koh, 6 Nov 2007], 26, para.9 [Counsel Chao], CR 2007/22, 19, paras 32-33, at 21-23, paras 41-47, at 25, para.58 and at 30-32, paras 75-79 [Counsel Bundy, 8 Nov], 39, para.6, at 45-47, paras 29-34 and at 47-49, paras 35-41 [Counsel Malintoppi], CR 2007/22 [transl.], 46, para.10 [Counsel Pellet], CR 2007/23, 19, paras 41-42 [Bundy, 9 Nov], CR 2007/24, 15-18, paras 25-30, 38 [Agent Kadir, 13 Nov], 20, paras 6-7 and at 23-24, paras 14-16 [Co-Agent Fadir], CR 2007/26, 13, para.9 (Rockall) and at 49-51, paras 48-53 [Counsel Sir Elihu Lauterpacht, 15 Nov], 60-66, paras 20-21 & 26-38 [Counsel Crawford], CR 2007/27, 28, para.58 [Counsel Schrijver, 16 Nov], CR 2007/29, 30, paras 17-18 [Malintoppi, 20 Nov], CR 2007/29 [transl.], 46, para.35 [Counsel Pellet], CR 2007/31, 57-58, para.6 [Agent Kadir, 23 Nov 2007]; *Romania v. Ukraine Maritime Delimitation in the Black Sea* Judgment, unanimous, ICJ Rep. 2009, paras 16, 33, 35, 39, 41, 124, 180, 184, 187; Hearings, CR 2008/18, 15-16, paras 4-6, at 19, para.14, at 21, para.20, at 24, para.28 and at 28-31, paras 39-52 [Agent Aurescu, 2 Sep 2008], 62, para.9 [Counsel Crawford], CR 2008/19, 12, para.8 [Crawford, 3 Sep], 57-60, paras 17-24 and at 67-71, paras 45-56 [Agent Aurescu, 3 Sep], CR 2008/20, 31-39 [Counsel Pellet, 4 Sep], 39-54 [Counsel Lowe], 54-66 [Aurescu], CR 2008/21, 14-16, paras 10-14 [Counsel Muller, 5 Sep], 25-34, paras 20-51 [Co-Agent Dinescu], 66-67, paras 72-73 & 81 [Lowe, 5 Sep], CR 2008/24, 15-16, paras 20-26 [Agent Vassylenko, 9 Sep], CR 2008/28, 26-35 [Counsel Malintoppi, 11 Sep], CR 2008/29, 10-22 [Counsel Malintoppi, 12 Sep], CR 2008/30, 10-19 [Agent Aurescu, 15 Sep], 39-42, paras 23-32 [Co-Agent Dinescu, 15 Sep], CR 2008/31, 12-22 [Counsel Lowe, 16 Sep], 30-36 [Pellet], CR 2008/32, 13, paras 11-12 [Agent Vassylenko, 18 Sep], 50-53, paras 11-22 and at 55-60 [Malintoppi] <www.icj-cij.org>; *Nicaragua v. Colombia* case – see Equitable Maritime Boundary Delimitation *supra*.

On Netherlands/Venezuela Delimitation (Aves Island) Treaty of 31 March 1978 [Charney/ASIL Report No.2-12 (Nweihed], see *Tunisia/Libya* Pleadings, Vol.I, 494 [Libya's Memorial]; *Gulf of Maine* Pleadings, Vol.I, 178 [Canada's Memorial], Vol.IV, 443 [US Counter-Memorial], State Practice Vol.I, 491; *Libya/Malta* Pleadings, Vol.II, 111 [Libya's Counter-Memorial], Vol.III, 255 [Malta's Reply], Vol.IV, 65 [Counsel Jaenicke, 10 Dec 1984], 431-432 [Counsel Jaenicke, 21 Feb 1985]; *Denmark v. Norway* Hearings, CR 93/4, 32 [Counsel Bowett, 14 Jan 1993], CR 93/7, 79, 82 [Counsel Brownlie, 19 Jan], CR 93/10, 64-67 [Bowett, 25 Jan 1993]; *Romania v. Ukraine* Hearings, CR 2008/20, 37, para.60 [Counsel Pellet, 4 Sep 2008] <www.icj-cij.org>.

Cf. 1997 Notes Verbales of Antigua & Barbuda, St. Kitts & Nevis, Saint Lucia and Saint Vincent & the Grenadines, *UN LOS Bull.* 97-100 (1997 No.35); 2001 of St. Kitts & Nevis, *id.* 61 (2002 No.48); OECS/Aves Island of 2 June 2004 <www.stabroeknews.com/index.pl/article_general_news?id=8656647>; 39th OECS Authority's Communique, 20-21 May 2004 <www.oecs.org/assets/39th_auth meeting _communique.pdf>; OECS and CARICOM Team Up on Aves Rock Issue of 10/12 November 2005, including Map <www.vheadline.com/readnews.asp?id=46812 & www.vheadline.com/readnews.asp?id=46851>; <http://newsfromrussia.com/world/2005/11/07/67127.html>, <www.eluniversal.com/2005/11/08en_pol_art_08A629669.shtml & www.eluniversal.com/2005/11/09en_pol_art_09A630259.shtml>; *Barbados/Trinidad & Tobago* Hearings Day-6, 16 [Counsel Volterra, 25 Oct 2005], 68-69 [Agent Mottley], Day-7, 27-28 [Counsel Greenwood, 27 Oct], Day-8, 26 [Counsel Crawford, 28 Oct 2005], 133 [Agent Jeremie] <www.pca-cpa.org>; *Guyana/Suriname* Hearings Day 10, 1574-1575 [Counsel Colson, 20 Dec 2006] <www.pca-cpa.org>; and Aves Island <http://en.wikipedia.org/wiki/Aves_Island, http://wikinfo.org/wiki.php?title=Isla_Aves> & <http://da-academy.org/birdisl.html>.

See also 1865 *Netherlands/Venezuela Aves Island* Award *infra.*

On Kolbeinsey rock [66 *Nordic JIL* 301-318 (1997)], see *Denmark v. Norway* Judgment, ICJ Rep. 1993, 45, 47, para.18, at 80, 81, para.94; Denmark's Memorial, para.31 n.2, Norway's Counter-Memorial, paras 14-15 & sketch-map in Annex 72, Denmark's Reply, paras 22, 25-30 and the sketch-map at p.13, Norway's Rejoinder, para.25; Hearings, CR 93/1Corr., 41 [Counsel Thomsborg, 11 Jan. 1993], 93/3, 42 [Agent Lehmann, 13 Jan 1993]. Cf. Equitable Maritime Boundary Delimitation – 1993 *Denmark v. Norway* Judgment *supra.*

On Eddystone rock (lighthouse) <http://en.wikipedia.org/wiki/Eddystone_Rock>, see 1977 *Anglo/French* Decision [18 ILM 397 (1979)], paras 4, 114 and 121-144; *Libya/Malta (Merits)* Dissent Oda, ICJ Rep. 1985, 146-147, para.43; 2002 *Newfoundland/Nova Scotia (Phase II)* Award, para.4.31 <www.gov.ns.ca>; *Romania v. Ukraine* Hearings, CR 2008/29, 31, para.47 [Counsel Queneudec, 12 Sep 2008], CR 2008/31, 12, paras 13-14 [Counsel Lowe, 16 Sep] and Cr 2008/33, 14-15, para.19 [Queneudec, 19 Sep 2008] <www.icj-cij.org>.

On Rockall <http://en.wikipedia.org/wiki/Rockall>, see *Malaysia/Singapore* Hearings, CR 2007/26, 13, para.9 [Counsel Sir Elihu Lauterpacht, 15 Nov 2007]; *Romania v. Ukraine* Hearings, CR 2008/20, 63, para.24 [Agent Aurescu, 4 Sep 2008], CR 2008/29, 16-17, paras 48 and 52, also noting that the United Kingdom is alone in having amended its law with respect to Rockall because of Article 121(3) [Counsel Malintoppi, 12 Sep], CR 2008/31, 11-12, paras 9 and 12 [Counsel Lowe, 16 Sep 2008] <www.icj-cij.org>.

1931 *France/Mexico Clipperton Island* Award [*infra*]; 1981 *Iceland/Norway (Jan Mayen) Continental Shelf* Conciliation [see Equitable Maritime Boundary Delimitation *supra*]; *Canada/France* Award, para.43, 49 [31 ILM 1164-1165 (1992)].

See also Internal Waters, Territorial Sea and Baselines – Maintenance of Navigational Aids and Territorial Sovereignty *supra*; Exclusive Economic /Fishery) Zone – Production of Energy From the Waters, Currents and Winds; Equitable Maritime Boundary Delimitation – Economic Factors, and Islands – "Ignoring the Presence of Islets, Rocks and Minor Coastal Projections" *supra*; and Sovereignty Over Island Territory in this section *infra*.

On 1804 *Soult v. l'Africaine* Judgment [22 Federal Cases, Circuit & District Courts, 1789/1880, Case No.13179: Bee 204], see *Anglo/Norwegian Fisheries* Pleadings, Vol.II, 514 [UK Reply].

On 1805 *The Anna* Judgment of Lord Stowell [5 C. Rob. 373; 165 E.R. 809; No.5/Simmonds], see *Anglo/Norwegian Fisheries* Pleadings, Vol.I, 72 [UK Memorial], 452, 454, 462, 466-467, 476-477, 492 [Norway's Counter-Memorial], Vol.II, 506-508, 509, 518, 522, 529, 538, 545, 577, 594-595 [UK Reply], Vol. III, 374-375 [Norway's Rejoinder]; *Minquiers and Ecrehos* Pleadings Vol.II, 198 [Agent Gros, 28 Sep 1953]; *Fisheries Jurisdiction* Pleadings (UK), 321 [Memorial (Merits)]; *Qatar v. Bahrain (Merits)* Joint Dissent Bedjaoui, Ranjeva, Koroma, ICJ Rep. 2001, 208, para.198, Dissent Torres Bernardez, 345 para.247; Hearings, CR 2000/6, 46 [Counsel Sinclair, 30 May 2000].

On the 1853 *UK/USA The Washington (The Julia*; Bay of Fundy) Award [6 AJIL 434 (1912); No.47/Stuyt], see *Anglo/Norwegian Fisheries* Pleadings, Vol.I, 476-477 [Norway's Counter-Memorial], Vol.II, 525-526 [UK Reply].

See also Internal Waters, Territorial Sea and Baselines, Bays *supra*.

On 1870 *Brazil/USA The Canada* Award [No.89/Stuyt], see *Anglo/Norwegian Fisheries* Pleadings, Vol.I, 478 [Norway's Counter-Memorial], Vol.II, 528 [UK Reply]; *Ambatielos* Pleadings, 100 [Greece's Memorial].

On 1886 *Merchants Mutual Insurance Company v. Allen* (Gulf of Mexico) Judgment [121 US 67], see *Anglo/Norwegian Fisheries* Pleadings, Vol.II, 536 [UK Reply].

On 1903 *UK/USA Alaska Boundary* Award [RIAA XV, 481; No.251/Stuyt], see *Anglo/Norwegian Fisheries* Pleadings, Vol.I, 455 [Norway's Counter-Memorial], Vol.II, 538-539 [UK Reply], Vol.III, 372 [Norway's Reply].

On 1910 *North Atlantic Coast Fisheries* Award [RIAA XI, 167; No.291/Stuyt], see *Anglo/Norwegian Fisheries* Pleadings, Vol.I, 477-478 [Norway's Counter-Memorial], Vol.II, 527-528 [UK Reply].

On 1925 *US v. Henning* Judgment [7 Fed. 2nd 488], see *Anglo/Norwegian Fisheries* Pleadings, Vol.II, 514 [UK Reply]; *Henning v. US* [13 F. 2d 74; 20 AJIL 114, 445 (1926)].

On 1929 *Middleton v. USA* (Florida Keys) Judgment [32 Fed. 2nd 239], see *Anglo/Norwegian Fisheries* Pleadings, Vol.II, 537 [UK Reply].

On 1936 *Ouled Yaneg/Ouled Gacem* (Kerkennahs) Arbitration [*Tunisia/Libya* Pleadings, Vol.I, 308], see *id.* 91-92 [Tunisia's Memorial].

On 1941 *Skiriotes v. Florida* (Gulf of Mexico, Florida Straits) Judgment [331 US 69; 35 AJIL 515, 569 (1941)], see *Anglo/Norwegian Fisheries* Pleadings, Vol. II, 536 [UK Reply].

On 1947 *US v. California* Judgment, see Internal Waters, Territorial Sea and Baselines *supra*.

On 1967 *Atlantis Development Co. v. US*, see Continental Shelf *supra*.

On 2005 *Pitcairn Island* Judgment of Pitcairn Court of Appeal (sitting in NZ) [127 ILR 232] and 2006 *Christian & Others v. The Queen* Judgment of Judicial Committee of the Pitcairn Privy Council, which dismissed the Appeal from 2005 *Pitcairn* Judgment and UK Pitcairn Courts [(2007) 2 WLR 120; (2006) UKPC 47; <www.paclii.org/databases.html#PN & http://en.wikipedia.org/wiki/Politics_of_the_Pitcairn_Islands>], see *Malaysia/Singapore* Hearings, CR 2007/21, 47, para.60 [Counsel Brownlie, 7 Nov 2007], CR 2007/26, 22, para.48 [Sir Elihu Lauterpacht, 15 Nov], CR 2007/27, 67 [Question of Judge Keith to both Parties, 16 Nov 2007], CR 2007/28, 61, para.50 [Brownlie, 19 Nov], CR 2007/30, 49-51, paras 1-8 [Lauterpacht, 22 Nov], CR 2007/31, 17, para.15 [Counsel Crawford, 23 Nov 2007] <www.icj-cij.org>.

See also Equitable Maritime Boundary Delimitation - Islands *supra*.

Sovereignty over Island Territory

Legal Status of Eastern Greenland – see Fisheries *infra*; *Lighthouses Between France and Greece* and *Lighthouses in Crete and Samos* Judgments, PCIJ Series A/B No.62, 4 (1934) and No.71, 94 (1937), 1954/1956 *France/Greece Lighthouses Claims* Awards [RIAA XII, 161; No.396b/Stuyt]; *Minquiers and Ecrehos* and *Antarctica* – see Fisheries *infra*; *North Sea* Judgment, ICJ Rep. 1969, 32, para.46; *Western Sahara* Advisory Opinion – see Equitable Maritime Boundary Delimitation *supra*; *Aegean Sea (Jurisdiction)* Judgment, ICJ Rep. 1978, 33, para.78, 37, paras 87-89 (see also Equitable Maritime Boundary Delimitation *supra*); *Tunisia/Libya (Intervention)* Separate O. Oda, ICJ Rep. 1981, 32, *(Merits)* Dissent Oda, ICJ Rep. 1982, 253; *Gulf of Maine* Pleadings, Vol.VII, 39 [Counsel Weil, 4 May 1984]; *Libya/Malta (Intervention)* Judgment, ICJ Rep. 1984, 26, Dissents Oda, 94, 109, Sir Robert Jennings, 158-159, *(Merits)* Judgment, ICJ Rep. 1985, 41, 42-43, Joint

Separate O., 83, Dissent Oda, 158; *Gulf of Fonseca (Intervention)* Judgment, ICJ Rep. 1990, 100-101, 108, 119, *(Merits)* Judgment, ICJ Rep. 1992, 351-386, 553-579, 615, para.431, Separate O. Bernardez, 658-712; *Nauru v. Australia Certain Phosphate Lands in Nauru* case (Trusteeship Agreement) – see Settlement of Disputes – Preventive Diplomacy B) *infra*; *Libya/Chad* Separate O. Ajibola, ICJ Rep. 1994, 81, 86; *East Timor* Hearings, CR 95/3, 48-50 [Co-Agent Correia, 31 Jan 1995], CR 95/10, 11-15 [Co-Agent Burmester, 9 Feb 1995]; *Denmark v. Norway* and *Qatar v. Bahrain* cases – see Equitable Maritime Boundary Delimitation *supra*; *Cameroon v. Nigeria (Preliminary Objections)* Dissent Ajibola, ICJ Rep. 1998, 411, *Cameroon v. Nigeria; Equatorial Guinea Intervening (Merits)* Judgment, ICJ Rep. 2002, 412-415, paras 218, 222, Dissent Koroma, 485, para.27 <www.icj-cij.org>.

Indonesia/Malaysia Sovereignty Over Pulau Ligitan and Pulau Sipadan (Application of the Philippines for Permission to Intervene) Judgment, ICJ Rep. 2001, 575; Hearings, CR 2001/1-4 [25-29 June 2001]; *(Merits)* Judgment, ICJ Rep. 2002, 625, President Gilbert Guillaume concurring, Declaration Oda, 687, Dissent Franck, 691 <www.icj-cij.org>.

Orders, ICJ Rep. 1998, 429, 1999, 1012, 2000, 9, 173.

For Malaysia's Declaration made upon ratifying the UNCLOS on 14 October 1996, see *UN LOS Bull.* 8 (1997 No.33).

Press Statement of Indonesia's Ministry of Foreign Affairs of 27 June 2001, <www.dfa-deplu.go.id/policy/releases/press_ind_nolak.html>, 2 July 2001 <www.dfa-deplu.go.id/others/current/2001/sipadan-ligitan-020701.htm> (in Bahasa Indonesia).

Statement of Malaysia to the 56th General Assembly, UN Doc. A/56/PV.32 (30 October 2001); Datuk Seri Abdullah Visits Sipadan of 39 June 2003 <www.utusan.com.my/utusan/content.asp?y=2003&dt=0701&pub=Utusan_Express&sec=Front_Page&pg=fp_01.htm>; Indonesia/Malaysia Negotiations of 12 Jan 2006 <www.bernama.com/bername/v3/news_lite.php?id=175163>.

On archipelagic status of Indonesia and the Philippines, see Archipelagic States – Archipelagic Baselines *supra*.

On Indonesia (NL)/Malaysia (UK) Agreement of 29 September 1915 [Hertslet, Vol. XXVII, 970, concluded under 1891 Convention, Article V], see *North Sea* Separate O. Ammoun, ICJ Rep. 1969, 126; *Indonesia/Malaysia (Merits)* Judgment, ICJ Rep. 2002, 625, paras 27, 35, 65-74, 85-91, Dissent Franck, 702, para.34; Hearings, CR 2002/28, 28-29 [Counsel Watts, 3 June], CR 2002/30, 22 [Co-Agent Ariffin, 6 June], 32-34 [Counsel Lauterpacht], CR 2002/31, 38-40 [Counsel Cot, 7 June], 58 [Counsel Schrijver], CR 2002/32, 24 [Lauterpacht], 40 [Counsel Crawford], CR 2002/33, 23-24, 30-32 [Watts, 10 June], CR 2002/34, 37 [Counsel Pellet], CR 2002/35, 18 [Cot, 12 June 2002] <www.icj-cij.org>.

See also appraisal of 2002 *Indonesia/Malaysia* Judgment, in *Malaysia/Singapore* Hearings, CR 2007/31, 49, para.8 [Counsel Crawford, 23 Nov 2007].

On 1969 Indonesia/Malaysia Delimitation Agreement, see Equitable Maritime Boundary Delimitation – Economic Factors, Mineral Resource Factors *supra*.

Israel Wall (Composition of the Court) Order, ICJ Rep. 2004, 3 and Judge Elaraby's Interview <http://weekly.ahram.org.eg/2001/547/profile.htm>; Advisory Opinion, ICJ Rep. 2004, 136, President Shi concurring <www.icj-cij.org>; Israel Security Fence <http://securityfence.mfa.gov.il/mfm/web/main/missionhome.asp?MissionID=45187>. See also Peaceful Uses of the Sea – Prohibition of Threat or Use of Force *infra*.

Nicaragua v. Honduras Maritime Delimitation in the Caribbean Sea (Merits) Judgment, ICJ Rep. 2007, paras 28-30, 74-226, Dissent Torres Bernardez, paras 1-110; Hearings, CR 2007/1, 16-17, paras 5-7, at 20, para.18, at 26, para.38 *in fine*, at 26-29, at 34-45 [Agent Arguello, 5 March 2007], 48-64 [Counsel Oude Elferink], CR 2007/3, 35-37 [Counsel Brotons, 7 March], 38-63 [Oude Elferink], CR 2007/6, 11, paras 8-9, at 16, paras 9-10, at 20-33 [Counsel Greenwood, 12 March], CR 2007/7, 19-47 [Counsel Sands, 13 March], 2007/8, 33, para.61 [Counsel Queneudec, 14 March], 35-59 [Counsel Dupuy], CR 2007/9, 10-39 [Sands, 15 March], 39-55 [Counsel Colson], CR 2007/11, 10-28 [Agent Arguello, 19 March], 28-32, 35, 38-50 [Counsel Pellet], 51-65 [Oude Elferink], CR 2007/13, 11-19 [Dupuy, 22 March], 19-28 [Greenwood], 28-37 [Counsel Sanchez], 37-51 [Sands], CR 2007/14, 32-33 [Greenwood, 23 March], 39, para.1 [Agent Flores]; *Question of Judge Keith*, in CR 2007/10, 37 [16 March] and CR 2007/11, 26-27, paras 65-70 [Agent Arguello's Reply to Keith], 41-43, paras 29-30 & 33 [Pellet's Reply to Keith], also CR 2007/14, 22-24 [Colson, 23 March 2007], 36, para.19 [Greenwood]; *Nicaragua v. Colombia* <www.icj-cij.org> – see Equitable Maritime Boundary Delimitation *supra*.

Malaysia/Singapore Sovereignty over Pedra Branca/Pulau Batu Puteh, Middle Rocks and South Ledge Judgment, ICJ Rep.2008, President Rosalyn Higgins concurring, Declarations Ranjeva, Bennouna, Separate Os Parra-Aranguren, Rao, Joint Dissent Simma and Abraham, Dissent Dugard <www.icj-cij.org>; <www.un.org/apps/news/story.asp?NewsID=26780&Cr=icj&Cr1; www.asil.org/ilib/2008/06/ilib080603.htm, http://news.bbc.co.uk/2/hi/asia-pacific/7416473.stm>; Orders, ICJ Rep. 2003, 146, 2005, 3. Transcript of 6 Feb 2003 [when Judge Shi was elected as the ICJ President 2003-2006] <www.mfa.gov.sg/press/transcript.html & www.channelnewsasia.com/cna/pedrabranca/> and Singapore/Malaysia Bilateral Issues <http://internet-stg1.mfa.gov.sg/internet/press/malaysia.htm>.

The 2008 *Malaysia/Singapore* Judgment clarifies in para.222 that while in law "ownership" is distinct from "sovereignty", the 1998 *Eritrea/Yemen* Award [RIAA XXII, 211; 114 ILR 1; 40 ILM 900], paras 19 and 474 show that in international litigation "ownership" over territory has sometimes been used as equivalent to "sovereignty"; and *Malaysia/Singapore* Dissent Dugard, paras 10, 30, para.42, stressing illustrious *Eritrea/Yemen* Membership of 3 ICJ Presidents (Jennings, Schwebel and Higgins) and relying on the 1998 *Eritrea/Yemen* Award, para.239, that: "The modern international law of the acquisition (or atribution) of territory generally requires that there be: an intentional display of power and authority over the territory, by the exercise of jurisdiction and state functions, on a continuous and peaceful basic".

On 1868 Ord *Johor/Pahang* Award of Sir Harry Ord, see Equitable Maritime Boundary Delimitation *supra.*

On 1969 Indonesia/Malaysia Delimitation Agreement, see Equitable Maritime Boundary Delimitation – Economic Factors, Mineral Resource Factors *supra.*

Malaysia/Singapore Joint Statement of 6 June 2008 <www.channelnewsasia .com/stories/singaporelocalnews/view/352331/1/.html> and Singapore MFA <www.mfa.gov.sg/pedraBranca/>; Mapping of Middle Rocks by <Malaysia (4-12 June 2008) Completed, 14 June 2008 www.bernama.com/bernama/v3/news_lite .php?id=339524 & www.bernama.com/bernama/v3/news_lite.php?id=339533>.

Singapore EEZ Claim Unlawful under UNCLOS 121(3) of 23 July 2008 <www.bernama.com/bernama/v3/news_lite.php?id=348007, www.bernama.com/ bernama/v3/news_lite.php?id=348052>; Singapore EEZ Claim Is An Act of Provocation of 24 July <www.nst.com.my/Thursday/Frontpage/2301672/Article/ index_html>; Malaysia/Singapore Will Wait for Technical Committee's Report of 24 July 2008 with Map <www.nst.com.my/Thursday/Frontpage/2301681/Article/ index_html>; Malaysia Reminds Singapore to Cease Provocative Claims for EEZ Around Pulau Batu Puteh/Pedra Branca of 18 August 2008 <www.bernama.com/ bernama/v5/newsindex.php?id=353520>; Joint Malaysia/Singapore Statement of 1 September 2008 stressing that they will abide by the ICJ Judgment <www .bernama.com/bernama/v3/news_lite.php?id=356565>.

Romania v. Ukraine Maritime Delimitation in the Black Sea Hearings, CR 2008/18, 22-24, paras 23-29 and at 27, paras 37-38 [Agent Aurescu, 2 Sep 2008], CR 2008/24, 11-13, paras 5-13 [Agent Vassylenko, 9 Sep], CR 2008/29, 13, para.39 [Counsel Malintoppi, 12 Sep], CR 2008/30, 12, para.6 and at 14-16, paras 14-19 [Aurescu, 15 Sep], CR 2008/32, 11, paras 6-9 [Agent Vassylenko, 18 Sep 2008] <www.icj-cij.org>.

On 1964 Cairo Resolution 16(I) of the OAU Assembly [<www.africa-union. org>; 100 AJIL 824 n.94 & at 827 n.109 (2006)], as reaffirmed by the 2000 AU Lomé Act [Article 4(b) *infra*], see *Tunisia/Libya (Merits)* Judgment, ICJ Rep.

1982, 66, Separate O. de Arechaga, 131; 1985 *Guinea/Guinea-Bissau* Award, para.40 [25 ILM 271 (1986)]; *Burkina Faso/Mali Frontier Dispute* Judgment, ICJ Rep. 1986, 563-567; 1989 *Guinea-Bissau/Senegal* Award [94 RGDIP 252 (1990)], para.62; *Libya/Chad Territorial Dispute* Judgment, ICJ Rep. 1994, 38, Separate O. Ajibola, 61, 82, 87-88, 90; *Botswana/Namibia* Judgment, ICJ Rep. 1999, 1059, para.19; Hearings, CR 99/1, 13 [Agent Kawana, 15 Feb 1999], CR 99/5 [trans.], 17 [Counsel Cot, 18 Feb], CR 99/6, 13 [Counsel Selepeng, 22 Feb 1999]; *Joint Legal Opinion on Guatemala's Territorial Claim to Belize*, para.58 (January 2002) <www.belize-guatemala.gov.bz/>; *Cameroon v. Nigeria; Equatorial Guinea Intervening (Merits)* Separate O. Mbaye, paras 15, 77, 91, ICJ Rep. 2002, 508, 521, 525; Hearings, CR 2002/1, 53 [Co-Agent Ntamark, 18 Feb 2002], CR 2002/2, 31 [Counsel Cot, 19 Feb], CR 2002/3, 40 [Counsel Bipoun Woum, 20 Feb], CR 2002/10, 26 [Counsel Abi-Saab,4 March], CR 2002/25, 37 [Agent Ali, 21 March 2002] <www.icj-cij.org>; 2002 *Eritrea/Ethiopia Boundary* Decision, paras 3.1-3.2, 3.31-3.36, 41 ILM 1057 (2002) <www.pca-cpa.org>.

On Constitutive Act of the African Union, Lome, 11 July 2000 [in force: 26 May 2001] which superseded the OAU Charter, 12 *African JICL* 629 (2000); 41 ILM 1029 (2002) <www.africa-union.org>, see *Congo v. France (Provisional Measures)* Hearings, CR 2003/22, 6-7 [Counsel Zorgbibe, 29 April 2003]; *Benin/Niger* Judgment, ICJ Rep. 2005, 108, para.23; Hearings, C5/CR 2005/3, 12, para.4 [Agent Mindaoudou, 8 March 2005]; *DR Congo v. Uganda (Provisional Measures)* Order, ICJ Rep. 2000, 112, 129 and *(Merits)* Judgment, ICJ Rep. 2005, 193, para.33, at 210, para.95, Declaration Koroma, 291, para.13; *Belgium v. Senegal (Provisional Measures)* Order, ICJ Rep. 2009, paras 6, 32, 63, 67, Joint Separate O. Al-Khasawneh and Skotnikov, para.12 <www.icj-cij.org>.

On US proposal of 27 June 1973 to submit (by means of a *compromis*) the sovereignty dispute with Canada over Machias Seal Island and North Rock in the Gulf of Maine to the ICJ, as rejected by Canada on 4 Jan 1977, see *Gulf of Maine* Judgment, ICJ Rep. 1984, 265-266, 332; Pleadings, Vol.III, 256, 257 n.12 [Canada's Counter-Memorial], Vol.V, 475, 488, 552-554 [US Reply]. Cf. *id.* 534, Vol.VI, 461 [Question I.2 of Judge Gros, 19 April 1984], Vol.VII, 36 [Counsel Weil's Reply, 4 May], 181 [Counsel Stevenson's Reply, 9 May]; and Vol. VI, 463 [Question V of Judge Mosler, 19 April], Vol.VII, 73-74 [Deputy Agent Hankey's Reply, 4 May 1984] <www.icj-cij.org>. See also *Nicaragua v. Honduras (Merits)* Judgment, ICJ Rep. 2007, para.279; U.S. Territorial Disputes <http://en.wikipedia.org/wiki/Category:Territorial_disputes_of_the_United_States>; Machias Seal <www.wikinfo.org/wiki.php?title=Machias_Seal_Island> & <www.siue.edu/GEOGRAPHY/ONLINE/Schmidt.htm>,

On Aaland Islands – see Straits Used for International Navigation, Longstanding Conventions in Force *supra*.

On Jan Mayen Island and Svalbard Archipelago, see Equitable Maritime Boundary Delimitation – *Denmark v. Norway* case *supra.*

On Belize's reluctance to submit its territorial/maritime dispute (including over the offshore islands under its control, with the exception of St George's Caye) with Guatemala to the PCIJ/ICJ, see Oral Presentations at the OAS Headquarters, 21-22 May 2001; Sir Elihu Lauterpacht, Judge Stephen M. Schwebel, Shabtai Rosenne and Francisco Orrego, *Joint Legal Opinion on Guatemala's Territorial Claim to Belize*, Foreword, paras 160-177, 222, 225 (January 2002) <www.belize-guatemala .gov.bz> and OAS *Belize/Guatemala* Documents <www.oas.org/documents/eng/ belizeguatemala.asp> – Equitable Maritime Boundary Delimitation *supra.*

Presumption in Favour of Sovereignty over Island within and Beyond the Territorial Sea

Implication to this effect in the *Anglo/Norwegian Fisheries* Judgment, ICJ Rep. 1951, 128, was relied upon in *Minquires and Ecrehos* Individual O. Levi Carneiro, ICJ Rep. 1953, 101-102; Pleadings, Vol.I, 424 [UK Reply]. Cf. *Anglo/Norwegian* Pleadings, Vol.I, 73 [UK Memorial, para.100] and Vol.II, 508-509 [UK Reply, para.290].

The presumption to this effect was relied upon in the 1870 *UK/Portugal Bulama Island* Award [*infra*] and it was expressly ascertained in the 1998 *Eritrea/Yemen Territorial Sovereignty (Phase I)* Award, paras 25, 97-98, 458, 463, 472-474, 478, in the process of awarding Jabal al-Tayr and Zubayr Group to the sovereignty of Yemen and the Mohabbakahs and the Haycocks to the sovereignty of Eritrea [40 ILM 900 (2001) <www.pca-cpa.org>]; as referred to in *Qatar v. Bahrain (Merits)* Judgment, ICJ Rep. 2001, 40, paras 99-100, 151-152, 201-209, 220, 252(5), Joint Dissent Bedjaoui, Ranjeva, Koroma, 145, paras 60, 137-143, 158-162, Declaration Vereshchetin, 220, paras 12-13, Separate Os Kooymans, 241-242, paras 64-66, Al-Khasawneh, 255, para.20, Dissent Torres Bernardez, 257, paras 219, 242-259, 342, 349, 362, 526; Hearings, CR 2000/6, 47-48 [Counsel Sir Ian Sinclair, 30 May 2000], CR 2000/11, 19, 29-34 [Sir Elihu Lauterpacht, 8 June], CR 2000/15, 45-46 [Counsel Weil, 14 June], CR 2000/18, 20-22 [Sinclair, 21 June], CR 2000/22, 17 [Lauterpacht, 28 June 2000] <www.icj-cij.org>; Sir Elihu Lauterpacht, Judge Stephen M. Schwebel, Shabtai Rosenne and Francisco Orrego, *Joint Legal Opinion on Guatemala's Territorial Claim to Belize*, Summary, paras 3, 13, 109, 113, 179-186, 224-225 (January 2002) and *Belize/Guatemala* OAS Facilitators' Proposals (2002) <www.belize-guatemala.gov.bz/>; *Indonesia/Malaysia (Merits)* Judgment, ICJ Rep. 2002, 678-686, paras 126-149, operative para.150; Hearings, CR 2002/30, 29-30 [Counsel Lauterpacht, 6 June], CR 2002/31, 48-49 [Counsel Crawford, 7 June], CR 2002/33, 12-13, 20 [Counsel Watts, 10 June 2002], 52 [Counsel Bundy]; *Nicaragua v. Honduras (Merits)* Judgment, ICJ Rep. 2007, paras 28-30, 75, 105-107,

113-116, 160-164, Dissent Torres Bernardez, paras 48-53; Nicaragua's Reply, paras 6.90-6.92, 6.118; Hearings, CR 2007/1, 17, para.7, at 38, para.77 [Agent Arguello, 5 March 2007], 51, para.11, at 53, para.15 [Counsel Oude Elferink], CR 2007/3, 36-37, para.89 [Counsel Brotons, 7 March], CR 2007/6, 28, para.28 [Counsel Greenwood, 12 March], CR 2007/7, 20, para.5 [Counsel Sands, 13 March], CR 2007/8, 51, para.54 [Counsel Dupuy, 14 March], CR 2007/9, 40, para.3 [Counsel Colson, 15 March], CR 2007/10, 15-17 [Colson, 16 March], CR 2007/11, 27, para.68 [Arguello, 19 March], 35, 49, para.51(1) [Counsel Pellet], 56-58 [Oude Elferink], CR 2007/12, 53 [Counsel Brownlie, 20 March], CR 2007/13, 10-12, 14-17 [Dupuy, 22 March], 19, para.1, at 21, para.7, at 23, para.13, at 17, para.20 *in fine*, at 24-25, paras 17-20, 25-26, paras 22-24 [Counsel Greenwood], 34-36, paras 15-19 [Counsel Sanchez], 38, para.3 [Sands], CR 2007/14, 32-33 [Greenwood, 23 March], 38, para.3 [Sands], 39 [Agent Flores, 23 March 2007]; *Malaysia/Singapore* Hearings, CR 2007/20, 18, para.11 [Agent Koh, 6 Nov 2007], 28, para.16 [Counsel Chao], CR 2007/24, 20, para.6 [Co-Agent Farida, 13 Nov], CR 2007/28, 19-26, paras 1-28 [Counsel Chao, 19 Nov 2007] <www.icj-cij.org>.

Cf. the concept of area constituting "organic" or "individualized" whole, in 1904 *Brazil/UK Guiana Boundary* Award [RIAA XI, 21-22]; attributing islands located on the respective sides of the Niger River (main navigable channel) boundary by *Benin/Niger Frontier Dispute* Judgment, ICJ Rep. 2005, paras 103, 115-117; Equitable Maritime Boundary Delimitation – Sector Principle/Arctic and Antarctic *supra.*

Sovereignty over Island Territory and Joint Fishery Rights

See Fisheries – *Minquiers and Ecrehos* Judgment, 1839 UK/France Convention, 1951 UK/France Agreement, and 1950 Norway/Sweden Agreement, *infra*; 1992 *Gulf of Fonseca (Merits)* Judgment – Equitable Maritime Boundary Delimitation *supra*; *Botswana/Namibia Kasikili/Sedudu* Judgment, ICJ Rep. 1999, 1106, para.102, Dissent Vice-President Weeramantry, 1192-1195, paras 110-119; Hearings, CR 99/1, 20-21 [Agent Kawana, 15 Feb 1999], 29 [Counsel Chayes], CR 99/6, 22 [Counsel Selepeng, 22 Feb], CR 99/10, 10-11 [Agent Kawana, 1 March 2000]; *Indonesia/Malaysia (Merits)* Judgment, ICJ Rep. 2002, 683, para.140; *Benin/ Niger* Judgment, ICJ Rep. 2005, 127, paras 78-79; Hearings, C5/CR 2005/3, 38-39, para.14 [Counsel Niyungeko, 8 March], C5/CR 2005/5, 31, para.4.25 [Counsel Thouvenin, 10 March 2005]; *Nicaragua v. Honduras (Merits)* Judgment, ICJ Rep. 2007, paras 49, 52, 55-58, 65-66, 80, 95, 131, 162, 170-175, 186-187, 190-201, 240-243, 245, 252, 256, Dissent Torres Bernardez, para.65; Hearings, CR 2007/1, 26-29, 36-39, 41, para.90 [Agent Arguello, 5 March 2007], CR 2007/3, 40-42 [Counsel Oude Elferink, 7 March], CR 2007/6, 32, para.69 [Counsel Greenwood, 12 March], CR 2007/7, 24, para.11, at 33 [Counsel Sands, 13 March], CR

2007/9, 10, 25-39 [Sands, 15 March], CR 2007/11, 12-15, 17-18 [Agent Arguello, 19 March], 64-65 [Oude Elferink], CR 2007/13, 52-53 [Sands, 22 March], CR 2007/14, 37, paras 4-5 [Agent Flores]; *Malaysia/Singapore (Merits)* Judgment, ICJ Rep. 2008, paras 71, 190-191, 286, Separate O. Rao, paras 18-19; Hearings, CR 2007/22, 30-32, paras 75-79 [Counsel Bundy, 8 Nov 2007], 39, para.6, at 45-47, paras 29-34 and at 49, para.41 [Counsel Malintoppi], CR 2007/24, 17-18, para.38 [Agent Kadir, 13 Nov], 23-24, paras 14-16 [Co-Agent Fadir], CR 2007/26, 49-51, paras 48-53 [Counsel Sir Elihu Lauterpacht, 15 Nov], CR 2007/29, 30, paras 17-18 [Malintoppi, 20 Nov], CR 2007/29 [transl.], 46, para.35 [Counsel Pellet], CR 2007/31, 57-58, para.6 [Agent Kadir, 23 Nov 2007] <www.icj-cij.org>.

See also *Costa Rica v. Nicaragua San Juan River* Judgment, ICJ Rep. 2009, paras 29, 134-144, *dispositif* para.156(3), Separate O. Sepulveda Amor, paras 20-36, Declaration Guillaume, para.3 <www.icj-cij.org>.

Canada/France Award, paras 53-55 [31 ILM 1166 (1992)]; 1998 *Eritrea/Yemen (Phase I)* Award, paras 20, 29, 39-40, 52-53, 67, 118, 126-129, 258-273, 302-303, 308-310, 313-316, 337-340, 347-357, 446, 495, 525-526 and operative para.527(vi), 1999 *Maritime Delimitation (Phase II)* Award, Introduction, paras 2-3, Chapter I, paras 20, 27-31, 38, Chapters II and IV, and Annex II: Yemen's Answer to Judge Schwebel's Question [40 ILM 900, 983 (2001) <www.pca-cpa.org>], and <http://globalarchive.ft.com/global archive/article.html?id=020329004725&query =eritrea>; 2006 *Barbados/Trinidad & Tobago (Jurisdiction and Merits)* Award, President S.M. Schwebel, paras 72, 136, 140-141, 145, 149, 278-282; Barbados' Memorial, paras 133, 134 n.173, para.136 n.179; Barbados' Reply, paras 391-392, 406-415; Trinidad's Rejoinder, paras 134-136; Hearings Day-2, 21-29 [Counsel Reisman, 18 Oct 2005], Day-3, 25-27 [Counsel Crawford, 20 Oct], 83-84 [Counsel Wordsworth], Day-4, 29 [Orrego Vicuna's Questions, 21 Oct], 46-48 [Counsel Greenwood], Day-5, 35-36 [Lowe's Questions, 24 Oct], 52 [Counsel Fietta], 66-67 [Reisman], Day-8, 115, 121-125 [Greenwood, 28 Oct 2005, replying to Orrego Vicuna's and Lowe's Questions, Days-4/5 *supra*] <www.pca-cpa.org>; 2009 *Abyei Boundary* Award, President P.M. Dupuy, paras 748-769 and *dispositif* para.770(e) <www.pca-cpa.org>.

Environmental Factors in Disputes over Territorial Sovereignty

Legal Status of Eastern Greenland PCIJ Series A/B, No.53 (1933) – Judgment, 26-27 (climate and character of Greenland as an Arctic country), 50-51; *Eastern Greenland* Pleadings, PCIJ Series C, No.62, 13-14 [Denmark's Memorial], No.63, 677-685 [Denmark's Reply]; *Antarctica* Pleadings, 13, 19-20, 58, 60 [UK Applications]; *Gulf of Maine* Pleadings, Vol.III, 200-201 [Canada's Counter-Memorial]; *Denmark v. Norway* Oral Hearings, CR 93/2, 8-26 [Counsel Lynge,

12 Jan 1993]; *Botswana/Namibia Kasikili/Sedudu* Judgment, ICJ Rep. 1999, 1054, 1095, 1106-1108, paras 12, 76, 102-103, Separate O. Kooymans, paras 21-38, Dissent Vice-President Weeramantry, paras 4-5, 47, 77-119; Hearings, CR 99/1, 20-22 [Agent Kawana, 15 Feb 1999], 29 [Counsel Chayes], CR 99/2, 48-49 [Counsel Richards, 16 Feb], CR 99/4, 37 [Counsel Faundez, 17 Feb], CR 99/6, 20-23 [Counsel Selepeng, 22 Feb], CR 99/7, 27-28 [Counsel Brownlie, 23 Feb], CR 99/10, 11-17 [Agent Kawana, 1 March 2000]; *Qatar v. Bahrain (Merits)* Judgment, ICJ Rep. 2001, 72-73, para.104, Dissent Torres Bernardez, 398, para.399 and Gulf Haven for Exotic Species of 11 June 2005 <http://news.bbc.co.uk/1/hi/programmes/from_our_own_correspondent/4080452.stm>; *Indonesia/Malaysia (Merits)* Judgment, ICJ Rep. 2002, 625, paras 14, 132, 143-145, Dissent Franck, 696-698, 701, paras 17-21, 33; Hearings, CR 2002/27, 19-20 [Agent Wirajuda, 3 June], CR 2002/29, 13-15 [Counsel Bundy, 4 June], 24-30, 33-35 [Counsel Pellet], CR 2002/30, 20-21, 23-26 [Co-Agent Ariffin, 6 June], 28-29 [Counsel Lauterpacht], 54-55 [Counsel Crawford], CR 2002/31, 42-43 [7 June], CR 2002/32, 16-18 [Lauterpacht], CR 2002/34, 27 [Pellet, 10 June 2002]; *Benin/Niger* Judgment, ICJ Rep. 2005, 147, para.137; Hearings, C5/CR 2005/1, 23, para.2.5 [Counsel Pellet, 7 March], C5/CR 2005/3, 14, para.9 [Agent Mindaoudou, 8 March], C5/CR 2005/6, 48-49, paras 10, 13 [Counsel Klein, 11 March] <www.icj-cij.org>, including Niger's "W" Park under the 1971 Ramsar Wetlands Convention <www.ramsar.org/profiles_niger.htm> and <http://whc.unesco.org/sites/749.htm>; *Nicaragua v. Honduras (Merits)* Judgment, ICJ Rep. 2007, paras 197-198; Hearings [turtle fisheries], CR 2007/1, 36, para.70, at 41, para.89 [Agent Arguello, 5 March 2007], CR 2007/3, 38, para.4 [Counsel Oude Elferink, 7 March], CR 2007/4, 10-13 [8 March], CR 2007/7, 41, para.49 [Counsel Sands, 13 March], CR 2007/11, 24, para.56 [Agent Arguello, 19 March], 59-61 [Oude Elferink], CR 2007/13, 48, para.27 [Sands, 22 March 2007]; *Malaysia/Singapore* Hearings, CR 2007/29 [transl.], 46-47, para.36 [Counsel Pellet, 20 Nov 2007] <www.icj-cij.org>.

1998 *Eritrea/Yemen Territorial Sovereignty (Phase I)* Award, paras 43, 312 [40 ILM 900 (2001) <www.pca-cpa.org>].

See also Equitable Maritime Boundary Delimitation, Sector Principle/Arctic and Antarctic *supra* and Protection and Preservation of the Marine Environment – Environmental Protection of Lakes and Rivers *infra*.

Islands in Lakes and Rivers

Botswana/Namibia Kasikili/Sedudu Judgment and *Benin/Niger Boundary Dispute* case – see Equitable Maritime Boundary Delimitation – Thalweg Principle/Lakes and Rivers *supra*; *Qatar v. Bahrain (Merits)* Joint Dissent Bedjaoui, Ranjeva, Koroma, ICJ Rep. 2001, 200-201, paras 177, 179, Separate O. Kooymans, 244, para.76, Dissent Torres Bernardez, 331, 393, paras 210, 380; Oral Hearings, CR 2000/5 [trans.], 32, 35-36 [Counsel Salmon, 29 May 2000], CR 2000/8, 34 [Counsel Shankardass, 5 June], CR 2000/9 [trans.], 53 [Counsel Queneudec], CR 2000/11, 23-24 [Counsel Lauterpacht, 8 June], CR 2000/15, 46-47 [Counsel Weil, 14 June], CR 2000/17, 25 [Counsel Shankardass, 20 June], CR 2000/18, 20 [Counsel Sinclair, 21 June], 28 [Counsel David], CR 2000/22, 15 [Lauterpacht, 28 June 2000]; *Cameroon v. Nigeria; Equatorial Guinea Intervening (Merits)* Judgment, ICJ Rep. 2002, 336, para.43 and 445, para.325.III(C), Separate O. Mbaye, 517, para.59, Dissent Ajibola, 581, para.134; *Indonesia/Malaysia (Merits)* Dissent Franck, ICJ Rep. 2002, 696, para.18; *Benin/Niger Frontier Dispute (Formation of Chamber)* Orders, ICJ Rep. 2002, 613, 2003, 155; ICJ Trust Fund's Grant of 4 June 2004 <www.un.org/News/Press/docs/2004/sg2087.doc.htm & www.unwire.org/UNWire/20040607/449_24601.asp>, *Benin/Niger (Composition of Chamber)* Order and *(Merits)* Judgment, President Ranjeva concurring, ICJ Rep. 2005, 84, 90 and Niger Takes Over Disputed Lete Island of 15 Feb 2007 <http://news.bbc.co.uk/2/hi/africa/6364703.stm>; *Nicaragua v. Honduras (Merits)* Judgment, ICJ Rep. 2007, paras 31-32, 145, 279-280; Hearings, CR 2007/9, 40-55 [Counsel Colson, 15 March 2007], CR 2007/12, 29-38 [Counsel Pellet, 20 March], CR 2007/14, 16-18 [Colson, 23 March 2007] <www.icj-cij.org>.

On 1202 Decision of the French Court concerning the Channel Islands, see *Minquiers and Ecrehos* ICJ Rep. 1953, 47 – Judgment, 56, 75-76, Individual O. Basdevant, 75-76, 91; Pleadings, Vol.I, 378, 383 [France's Counter-Memorial], 496-502 [UK Reply], Vol.II, 98, 110-113 [Counsel Wade, 21 Sep 1953].

On 1865 *Netherlands/Venezuela Aves Island* Award [Stuyt/No.54; RIAA, XXVIII, 115], see *Eastern Greenland* Pleadings, PCIJ Series C, No.62, 433, 462 [Norway's Counter-Memorial], No.63, 733 [Denmark's Reply]; *Minquiers and Ecrehos* Pleadings, Vol.II, 267 [Agent Gros, 30 Sep 1953]; *Arbitral Award* Dissent Weeramantry, ICJ Rep. 1991, 153; *Gulf of Fonseca* Hearings, C 4/CR 91/37, 30, 35 [Counsel Highet, 31 May 1991]; *Qatar v. Bahrain (Merits)* Dissent Torres Bernardez, para.242, ICJ Rep. 2001 343; *Nicaragua v. Honduras (Merits)* Dissent Torres Bernardez, para.33; Hearings, CR 2007/6, 62, para.48 [Counsel Sanchez, 12 March 2007], CR 2007/13, 15, para.15 [Counsel Dupuy, 22 March 2007] <www.icj-cij.org>.

See also Economic Life of Their Own/Fisheries – 1978 Netherlands/Venezuela (Aves Island) Treaty *supra.*

On 1870 *UK/Portugal Bulama Island* Award of the US President [Stuyt/No.85; RIAA, XXVIII, 131], see *Eastern Greenland* Pleadings, PCIJ Series C, No.62, 392 [Norway's Counter-Memorial]; *Qatar v. Bahrain (Merits)* Joint Dissent Bedjaoui, Ranjeva, Koroma, para.94 n.27, ICJ Rep. 2001, 175.

On 1875 UK/Portugal *Delagoa Bay* Award (East Africa, including Islands of Inyack and Elephant) of the President of France [No.100/Stuyt; RIAA, XXVIII, 157], see *Eastern Greenland* Pleadings, PCIJ Series C, No.62, 427-428 [Norway's Counter-Memorial], No.63, 733, 778 [Denmark's Reply]; *Corfu (Merits)* Dissent Azevedo, ICJ Rep. 1949, 96; *Minquiers and Ecrehos* Pleadings, Vol.II, 232 [Agent Gros, 29 Sep 1953]; *Libya/Chad Territorial Dispute* Separate O. Ajibola, ICJ Rep. 1994, 81; *Qatar v. Bahrain (Merits)* Joint Dissent Bedjaoui, Ranjeva, Koroma, ICJ Rep. 2001, 175, para.94 n.27, Dissent Torres Bernardez, 408, para.429; *Cameroon v. Nigeria; Equatorial Guinea Intervening (Merits)* Declaration Ranjeva, para.2, ICJ Rep. 2002, 469 <www.icj-cij.org>; *Barbados/Trinidad & Tobago* Barbados' Reply, para.334 n.437 <www.pca-cpa.org>; *Guinea v. DR Congo (Preliminary Objections)* Judgment, para.90, ICJ Rep. 2007; *Malaysia/Singapore (Merits)* Declaration Ranjeva, para.5, ICJ Rep. 2008.

On 1880 *Attorney General for British Honduras v. Bristowe* Judgment [6 App. Cas 143], see *Malaysia/Singapore* Hearings, CR 2007/21, 47, para.60 [Counsel Brownlie, 7 Nov 2007] <www.icj-cij.org>.

On 1885 *Germany/Spain Caroline Islands* Proposition of His Holiness Pope Leo XIII as Mediator [No.141/Stuyt], see *Eastern Greenland* Pleadings, PCIJ Series C, No.62, 434-436, 518-519 [Norway's Counter-Memorial], No.63, 733 [Denmark's Reply]; *Minquiers and Ecrehos* Pleadings, Vol.I, 545 n.1 [UK Memorial].

On 1902 *Austria/Hungary Meerauge* Award [No.206/Stuyt], see *Malaysia/ Singapore (Merits)* Judgment, ICJ Rep. 2008, para.48, Separate O. Rao, para.9; Hearings, CR 2007/22, at 38, para.4 [Counsel Malintoppi, 8 November 2007]; Malaysia's Counter-Memorial, 13, para.21 <www.icj-cij.org>.

On 1911 *Mexico/USA Chamizal* Award, see Equitable Maritime Boundary Delimitation *supra*.

On 1914 *Netherlands/Portugal Island of Timor* Award [No.275/Stuyt; 9 AJIL 240 and Supp. 107 (1915); PCA 1999, 98; PCA Awards <www.haguejusticeportal.net>], see *North Sea* Separate O. Ammoun, ICJ Rep. 1969, 138 n.5; *Gulf of Maine* Pleadings, Vol.II, 97-98 [US Memorial], Vol.III, 200, 201 n.54 [Canada's Counter-Memorial], Vol.V, 99 n.79 [Canada's Reply]; *East Timor* Dissent Skubiszewski, ICJ Rep. 1995, 226-227.

On 1917 *El Salvador v. Nicaragua* Judgment, see Equitable Maritime Boundary Delimitation *supra*.

On 1928 *USA/Netherlands Island of Palmas (Miangas)* Award, [No.366/Stuyt; PCA 1999, 118; PCA Awards <www.haguejusticeportal.net>], see *Eastern Greenland* Pleadings, PCIJ Series C, No.62, 104 [Denmark's Memorial], 389-390, 395-396, 404, 426-427, 430, 477, 509 [Norway's Counter-Memorial], No.63, 733-734, 741-744, 776-777, 906 [Denmark's Reply], 1196, 1261-1262, 1307, 1309-

1311, 1358-1360 [Norway's Rejoinder], No.66, 2866-2869, 2876-2877, 2879, 2883-2884, 2886-2888, 2906-2910 [Counsel de Visscher, 29 and 30 Nov 1932], 2921 [Counsel Per Rygh, 3 Dec], 3176 [Counsel Sunde, 12 Dec], 3231-3232, 3236-3237, 3274-3275 [Counsel Gidel, 13 Dec 1932], No.67, 3411, 3437, 3452 [de Visscher, 19 Jan 1933], 3550, 3552, 3555 [Gidel, 2 Feb 1933]; *Corfu Channel* Dissent Winiarski, ICJ Rep. 1949, 53; *US Nationals in Morocco* Pleadings, Vol.I, 67 [France's Memorial], Vol.II, 172, 175 [Agent Gros]; *Anglo/Norwegian Fisheries* Pleadings, Vol.I, 381, 568 [Norway's Counter-Memorial], Vol.II, 648-651, 657-658 [UK Reply], Vol.III 441 [Norway's Rejoinder]; *Ambatielos* Pleadings, 410 [Counsel Sir Gerald Fitzmaurice, 26 March 1953]; *Minquiers and Ecrehos* Pleadings, Vol.I, 104-108 [UK Memorial], 540-561 [UK Reply], Vol.II, 32, 47-60 [Counsel Heald, 17 and 18 Sep 1953], 94 [Counsel Fitzmaurice, 21 Sep 1953], 96 [Counsel Wade], 206, 215, 230, 234-236, 260, 265, 271 [Agent Gros, 28, 29 and 30 Sep], 284-285 [Heald, 2 Oct], 367 [Fitzmaurice, 6 Oct], 375 [Agent Gros, 7 Oct 1953]; *Antarctica* Pleadings, 33-34, 68, 71-72 [UK Applications], 99-100 [UK Letter]; *Belgium/Netherlands Certain Frontier Land* Dissent Moreno Quintana, ICJ Rep. 1959, 254, 255; *Cambodia v. Thailand Temple of Preah Vihear (Merits)* Dissent Moreno Quintana, ICJ Rep. 1962, 69-70.

North Sea Individual O. Ammoun, ICJ Rep. 1969, 115; *North Sea* Pleadings, Vol.II, 169 [Agent Jaenicke, 4 Nov 1968]; *Fisheries Jurisdiction* Pleadings (UK), 318 [Memorial (Merits)]; *Nuclear Tests* Joint Dissent, ICJ Rep. 1974, 361; *Aegean Sea* Pleadings, 422 [Counsel Weil, 13 Oct 1978]; *Western Sahara* Separate Os Dillard, ICJ Rep.1975, 123, de Castro, 168-169; *Tunisia/Libya* Pleadings, Vol.IV, 460 [Counsel Dupuy, 17 Sep 1981], Vol.V, 356 [Counsel Sir Francis Vallat, 19 Oct 1981]; 1981 *Dubai/Sharjah* Award [91 ILR 594, 622]; *Gulf of Maine* Pleadings, Vol.IV, 104, 109-110 [US Counter-Memorial], Vol.V, 81 n.8, 89 n.37 [Canada's Reply], Vol.VI, 376 [Counsel Rashkow, 16 April 1984], Vol.VII, 98 [Counsel Bowett, 5 May 1984]; *Guinea-Bissau v. Senegal Arbitral Award* Oral Hearings, CR 91/4, 33 [Counsel Bowett, 5 April 1991]; *Lockerbie (Provisional Measures)* Dissents El-Kosheri, ICJ Rep. 1992, 106, 211; *Gulf of Fonseca* Judgment, ICJ Rep. 1992, 563-564, Separate O. Bernardez, 677; Pleadings, C 4/CR 91/27 [trans.], 8 [Counsel Bardonnet, 21 May 1991], CR 91/33, 79-80 [Counsel Highet, 29 May 1991]; *Libya/Chad* Separate O. Ajibola, ICJ Rep. 1994, 81, Dissent Sette-Camara, 98; 1998 *Eritrea/Yemen (Phase I)* Award, paras 104, 450-451, 454-455, 491 [40 ILM 900 (2001) <www.pca-cpa.org>]; *Botswana/Namibia* Declaration Higgins, para.3, Separate O. Kooymans, para.14, ICJ Rep. 1999, 1114, 1146 <www.icj-cij .org>; Hearings, CR 99/1, 37-38 [Counsel Chayes, 15 Feb 1999], CR 99/4, 60 [Agent Kawana, 17 Feb], CR 99/5 [trans.], 19 [Counsel Cot, 18 Feb], CR 99/5, 56 [Chayes], CR 99/8, 17 [Counsel Lady Fox, 24 Feb 1999]; *Qatar v. Bahrain (Merits)* Judgment, ICJ Rep. 2001, 70, para.100, Joint Dissent Bedjaoui, Ranjeva, Koroma, 145, paras 62, 94 n.27, 143, Separate O. Kooymans, 225, paras 63,

65-66, 71, Dissent Torres Bernardez, 257, paras 62-63, 74, 219, 243-244, 349, 364, 429; Hearings, CR 2000/6, 46 [Counsel Sinclair, 30 May 2000], CR 2000/11, 25, 30-33, 36-37 [Sir Elihu Lauterpacht, 8 June], CR 2000/14, 8 [13 June 2000], 36 [Counsel Reisman], CR 2000/15, 11-12 [14 June], 43, 46, 48 [Counsel Weil], CR 2000/18, 7 [Counsel Bundy, 21 June], 20-21 [Sinclair], CR 2000/19, 25 [Agent Al-Muslemani, 22 June], CR 2000/21, 7 [Counsel Paulsson, 27 June], CR 2000/22, 16 [Lauterpacht, 28 June], CR 2000/25, 10 [Reisman, 29 June 2000]; *Joint Legal Opinion on Guatemala's Territorial Claim to Belize*, paras 61, 80-82 (January 2002) <www.belize-guatemala.gov.bz/>; *Congo v. Belgium Arrest Warrant of 11 April 2000* Separate O. President Guillaume, ICJ Rep. 2002, 37, para.4.

Cameroon v. Nigeria; Equatorial Guinea Intervening (Merits) Judgment, ICJ Rep. 2002, 405, para.205, Separate Os Al-Khasawneh, 495-496, 499-500, 502, paras 5-6, 8, 11, 13-14, Mbaye, 524-525, paras 86, 92, Dissent Ajibola, 539, 556, paras 5, 49; Hearings, CR 2002/3, 46 [Counsel Aurillac, 20 Feb 2002], CR 2002/4, 57, 62 [Counsel Cot, 21 Feb], CR 2002/8, 55 [Agent Abdullahi, 28 Feb], CR 2002/16, 20, 23 [Counsel Shaw, 11 March], CR 2002/18, 32-33, 51 [Counsel Brownlie, 14 March 2002]; *Indonesia/Malaysia (Merits)* Judgment, ICJ Rep. 2002, 665, para.82, Dissent Franck, 696, para.18; Hearings, CR 2002/29, 42 [Counsel Malintoppi, 4 June], CR 2002/30, 30, 35-36 [Counsel Sir Elihu Lauterpacht, 6 June], 47 [Counsel Crawford], CR 2002/32, 15 [Lauterpacht, 7 June], 35, 41 [Crawford], CR 2002/33, 46, 49, 55-57 [Counsel Bundy, 10 June], CR 2002/34, 20 [Counsel Malintoppi], CR 2002/35, 23 [Counsel Schrijver, 12 June 2002], 41 [Crawford] <www.icj-cij.org>; *Barbados/Trinidad & Tobago* Barbados' Reply, para.334 n.437 <www.pca-cpa.org>; *Nicaragua v. Honduras (Merits)* Judgment, ICJ Rep. 2007, para.214, Dissent Torres Bernardez, para.51; Hearings, CR 2007/8, 47, para.38 [Counsel Dupuy, 14 March 2007], CR 2007/11, 37, para.20 n.39, at 38, para.21 [Counsel Pellet, 19 March], CR 2007/13, 14, para.15 [Dupuy, 22 March 2007], 25-26, paras 23-24 [Counsel Greenwood], 32, para.9, at 35, paras 16-17 [Counsel Sanchez] <www.icj-cij.org>; *Malaysia/Singapore (Merits)* Judgment, ICJ Rep. 2008, paras 67, 121, 280, Declaration Ranjeva, paras 2-3, Dissent Dugard, paras 33, 42, Separate O. Rao, paras 5, 19, 30, 38; Hearings, CR 2007/21, 26, para.48 [Counsel Pellet, 7 Nov 2007], CR 2007/22, 15, para.10, at 17, para.22 and at 30, para.72 [Counsel Bundy, 8 Nov], CR 2007/23 [transl.], 42, para.10 [Pellet, 9 Nov], CR 2007/28, 64, para.9 [Bundy, 19 Nov], CR 2007/28 [transl.], 30, para.3 [Pellet], CR 2007/29, 34, para.30, at 38, para.42 [Counsel Malintoppi, 20 Nov], CR 2007/31, 46, paras 1-3 [Counsel Crawford, 23 Nov 2007] <www.icj-cij.org>.

On 1931 *France/Mexico Clipperton Island* Award [No.293/Stuyt; 26 AJIL 390 (1932); 27 AJIL 130-133 (1933)], see *Eastern Greenland* Pleadings, PCIJ Series C, No.63, 733, 904, 906 [Denmark's Reply], 1262 [Norway's Rejoinder], No.66, 2888-2890 [Counsel de Visscher, 30 Nov 1932], 2921 [Counsel Per Rygh,

3 Dec], 3176 [Counsel Sunde, 12 Dec], 3219-3220, 3224, 3230, 3236-3237, 3239, 3249, 3250, 3276, 3278-3280 [Counsel Gidel, 13 Dec 1932], No.67, 3404-3405 [de Visscher, 19 Jan 1933], 3542-3543, 3552-3555 [Gidel, 2 Feb 1933]; *Anglo/Norwegian Fisheries* Pleadings, Vol.IV, 523-524 [Counsel Bourquin, 26 Oct 1951]; *Minquiers* Pleadings, Vol.II, 215, 232, 266-267 [Agent Gros, 28, 29 and 30 Sep 1953], 284-285 [Counsel Heald, 2 Oct 1953]; *Antarctica* Pleadings, 33-34, 71-72 [UK Applications]; *Belgium/Netherlands Certain Frontier Land* Dissent Moreno Quintana, ICJ Rep. 1959, 255; *Western Sahara* Separate O. Dillard, ICJ Rep.1975, 123; *Gulf of Fonseca* Hearings, C 4/CR 91/33, 65-66, 79 [Counsel Highet, 29 May 1991]; *Qatar v. Bahrain (Merits)* Dissent Torres Bernardez, para.429, ICJ Rep. 2001, 408; Hearings, CR 2000/12, 60 [Counsel Reisman, 9 June 2000]; *Indonesia/Malaysia (Merits)* Hearings, CR 2002/30, 28-29 [Counsel Sir Elihu Lauterpacht, 6 June], CR 2002/34, 32 [Counsel Malintoppi, 10 June 2002]; *Nicaragua v. Honduras (Merits)* Dissent Torres Bernardez, ICJ Rep. 2007, paras 15, 33; *Malaysia/Singapore (Merits)* Separate O. Rao, para.38, ICJ Rep. 2008; Hearings, CR 2007/21, 52, para.86 [Counsel Brownlie, 7 Nov 2007], CR 2007/24, 46-47 [Counsel Sir Elihu Lauterpacht, 13 Nov 2007] <www.icj-cij.org>.

On 1954/1956 *France/Greece Lighthouses Claims* Award [RIAA XII, 161; No.396b/Stuyt], see *Malaysia/Singapore* Hearings, CR 2007/26, 39, para.12 [Counsel Sir Elihu Lauterpacht, 15 Nov 2007] <www.icj-cij.org>.

On 1959 *James Buchanan & Co. v. Société Hanappier-Peyrelongue et Cie and Another* Judgment, see Fisheries, *Minquires and Ecrehos* Judgment *infra*.

On 1977/1984 *Argentina/Chile Beagle Channel* case, 1981 *Dubai/Sharjah* and 1985 *Guinea/Guinea-Bissau* Awards, see Equitable Maritime Boundary Delimitation *supra*.

On 1998 and 1999 *Eritrea/Yemen* Awards as well as 2002 *Joint Legal Opinion* and *Belize/Guatemala* OAS Proposals, see Equitable Maritime Boundary Delimitation *supra*.

On 2005 *Pitcairn Island* Judgment, see Rocks Which Cannot Sustain Human Habitation or Economic Life of Their Own *supra*.

On 2005 Annex VII *Malaysia v. Singapore Land Reclamation Activities In and Around the Strait of Johor* Award, see 2003 *Malaysia v. Singapore (Provisional Measures)* Order, President L.D.M. Nelson, ITLOS Case No.12 <www.itlos.org> and Protection and Preservation of the Marine Environment *infra*.

See also Internal Waters, Territorial Sea and Baselines – Maintenance of Navigational Aids and Territorial Sovereignty *supra*.

HIGH SEAS

1958 HSC; 1958 HSFC
1982 UNCLOS, Part V, Article 58, Part VI, Articles 78-79, Part VII, Articles 86-120
1992 UNCED Rio Agenda 21, Chapter 17
1995 SSA

Freedom of the High Seas
1958 HSC, Article 2; 1982 UNCLOS, Article 87:

SS Lotus – see Status of Ships/Criminal Jurisdiction *infra*; *Eastern Greenland* Pleadings, PCIJ Series C, No.63, 767-768 [Reply of Denmark], No.67, 3346 [Agent Steglich-Petersen, 17 Jan 1933]; *Corfu Channel (Merits)* ICJ Rep. 1949, 4 – Judgment, 22, Individual O. Alvarez, 46, Dissent Azevedo, 98, 103; *Anglo/Norwegian Fisheries* ICJ Rep. 1951, 116 – Judgment, 139, Individual O. Alvarez, 146, Separate O. Hsu Mo, 157, Dissent Sir Arnold McNair, 158-159, 178, 183, 185, Dissent Read, 187, 189-190; *Anglo/Norwegian* Pleadings, Vol.I, 58, 95 [UK Memorial], 342-345, 361, 418-419, 476 [Norway's Counter-Memorial], Vol.II, 312-315, 391-393, 412-413, 428-429, 464-467, 470, 608-609, 643, 646-647, 663, 666, 677 [UK Reply], Vol.III, 262-263 [Norway's Rejoinder], Vol.IV, 395 [Counsel Waldock, 18 October 1951]; *Minquiers and Ecrehos* Pleadings, Vol.I, 70 [UK Memorial], 373, 403 [France's Counter-Memorial], 441-443, 446-448, 451, 466 [UK Reply], 726 [France's Rejoinder], Vol.II, 70-71, 73, 82-83 [Counsel Fitzmaurice, 18 and 19 Sep 1953], 254-256 [Agent Gros, 30 Sep], 354 [Fitzmaurice, 5 Oct 1953]; *IMCO* Pleadings, 44 [Liberia], 134-135, 138-141 [USA], 256 [India]; *North Sea* Judgment, ICJ Rep. 1969, 39-40, para.65, Separate O. Ammoun, 101-106, 111-112, 118, Dissent Morelli, 199, 201-202, Dissent Lachs, 224; *North Sea* Pleadings, Vol.I, 309 [NL Counter-Memorial], Vol.II, 66 [Agent Jaenicke, 25 Oct 1968], 110 [Counsel Sir Humphrey Waldock, 29 Oct], 121-123, 125-126, 137 [Agent Riphagen, 30 and 31 Oct], 162 [Questions Sir Gerald Fitzmaurice, 1 Nov], 242-244 [Reply by Waldock to Questions Fitzmaurice].

Fisheries Jurisdiction (Jurisdiction) Separate Os Fitzmaurice, ICJ Rep. 1973, 24-26, 68-70, *(Merits)* Judgments, ICJ Rep. 1974, 22, 191, Declarations Ignacio-Pinto, 37, 210, Separate O. Dillard, 56-57, 63, Separate Os de Castro, 80-83, 92-93, 96-97, 225, Separate Os Waldock, 107-108, 227, Dissents Onyeama, 171, 244; *Fisheries Jurisdiction* Pleadings (UK), 318-320, 365 [Memorial (Merits)], 461 [Counsel Silkin, 25 March 1974], 480, 497-499 [Counsel Slynn, 29 March 1974], 209-210 [Memorial (Merits)], (FRG), 217-218 [Memorial (Merits)]; *Nuclear Tests (Interim Measures)* Orders, ICJ Rep. 1973, 103-104, 139-140, Dissents Forster, 114,

148, Dissents Ignacio-Pinto, 129, 163; *Nuclear Tests* Judgments, ICJ Rep. 1974, 265, 469, Dissent Gros, 281, Joint Dissents, 314, 361-362, 370, 469, 513-514, 522, Dissent de Castro, 390, Dissent Barwick, 425-427, 434, 438; Pleadings (Australia), 13-14 [Application], 43-44, 56 [Request], 330, 331, 337-343, 363-364 [Memorial], 514-522 [Counsel Byers, 9 July 1974], (New Zealand), 6-7 [Application], 49, 53, 58 [Request], 204, 209, 245-246 [Memorial], 258-259, 267 [Counsel Finlay, 10 July 1974], 297, 429-431 [Replies Agent, 15 July 1974]; *Tunisia/Libya (Merits)* Separate O. de Arechaga, ICJ Rep. 1982, 120, Dissent Oda, 171, 178, 201-202, 206, 223-224, 231; *Gulf of Maine* Judgment, ICJ Rep. 1984, 278, 340-344; Pleadings, Vol.III, 150, 225 [Canada's Counter-Memorial]; *Libya/Malta* Pleadings, Vol.II, 251 [Malta's Counter-Memorial].

Nicaragua v. USA Military and Paramilitary Activities (Provisional Measures) Order, ICJ Rep. 1984, 170, para.1(b) and (e), 181, para.28, 187, para.41(B)(1), Dissent Schwebel, 190, 199, *(Jurisdiction and Admissibility)* Judgment, ICJ Rep. 1984, 424, para.73, Dissent Schwebel, 616, para.89, *as reaffirmed* by *Nicaragua v. USA (Merits)* Judgment, ICJ Rep. 1986, 93, para.174, also *id.* 46-53, paras 76-92, and 111-112, paras 213-214, Dissent Schwebel, 259, 303, para.91, 305, para.97; 1995 NZ Request (Examination of the Situation), para.66.

Iran v. USA Oil Platforms (Preliminary Objection) Judgment, President Bedjaoui concurring, ICJ Rep. 1996, 819-820, relying on the *Oscar Chinn* Judgment, PCIJ Series A/B, No.63, 65, 85, *as reaffirmed* by *(Counter-Claim)* Order, Vice-President Weeramantry, Acting President, and President Schwebel concurring, ICJ Rep. 1998, 204, interpreted the "freedom of commerce and navigation" clause contained in the FCN Treaties (Article X(1) of the 1955 Iran/USA Treaty) as not limited to maritime commerce, but as covering commerce in general, including oil platforms located within the EEZ/CS that are connected by pipelines to the oil terminals (ports). Dissenting Opinion of Vice-President Schwebel, ICJ Rep. 1996, 885-889, advocated alternative interpretation restricting this clause to maritime commerce and shipping and confining the term "commerce" to acts of purchase and sale, thus excluding production of goods or commodities. He considered that the *Oscar Chinn* gave the Court insufficient support, because the term there under construction was "freedom of trade" not freedom of commerce; Hearings, CR 96/13, 41-44 [Counsel Crook, 17 Sep 1996], CR 96/14, 35-40 [Counsel Bundy, 19 Sep], CR 96/15 [trans.], 24-32 [Counsel Condorelli, 20 Sep], CR 96/16, 31-34 [Crook, 23 Sep 1996]. See also *Oil Platforms (Merits)* Judgment, ICJ Rep. 2003, 199-204, paras 79-89, Separate O. Owada, 306; Hearings, CR 2003/5-19, 17 Feb-7 March 2003 <www.icj-cij.org>.

Cf. *M/V Saiga (Merits)* Counter-Memorial of Guinea, paras 100-101, relying on the *Oscar Chinn*'s distinction between freedom of trade and freedom of navigation, and Reply of Saint Vincents, para.128; *Southern Bluefin Tuna (Jurisdiction)* A/

NZ Reply, paras 47, 53 n.62, Hearings, Vol.II [Counsel Burmester, 8 May 2000] <www.worldbank.org/icsid>; *Indonesia/Malaysia (Merits)* Judgment, ICJ Rep. 2002, 639, para.21; *Argentina v. Uruguay (Provisional Measures)* Order, ICJ Rep. 2007, 8-9, para.21.

Spain v. Canada Fisheries (Jurisdiction) Judgment, ICJ Rep. 1998, 432, paras 10-12, 20-23, 53, 61, 87, Separate O. President Schwebel, 470, paras 6-7, Torres Bernardez, 582, paras 74, 317-431; Pleadings, 19-20, 123 [Spain's Memorial], 423-425 [Agent Pastor Ridruejo, 9 June 1998], 430, 435-441 [Counsel Rodriguez] <www.icj-cij.org>; 1998 *Sellers v. Maritime Safety Inspector* [120 ILR 585]; *M/V Saiga* Separate O. Laing [38 ILM 1323 (1999)], paras 17-34; 2001 *Ireland v. UK Mox Plant (Provisional Measures)* Separate O. Anderson, para.2 <www.itlos.org>; 2006 *Barbados/Trinidad & Tobago (Jurisdiction and Merits)* Award, President S.M. Schwebel, paras 133, 136, 140, 143-144, 266; Hearings Day-4, 45-47 [Counsel Greenwood, 21 Oct 2005], Day-6, 47 [Counsel Reisman, 25 Oct 2005] <www .pca-cpa.org>; RIAA XXVII, 147; 45 ILM 800 (2006); *Malaysia/Singapore (Merits)* Separate O. Rao, ICJ Rep. 2008, paras 20, 22 <www.icj-cij.org>.

Nationality of Ships - Genuine Link
1958 HSC, Articles 5 and 10; 1982 UNCLOS, Articles 91 and 94:

Reparation for Injuries Suffered in the Service of the United Nations ICJ Rep. 1949, President J. Basdevant - Advisory Opinion, 174, Dissent Hackworth, 202-203, Dissent Badawi Pasha, 206-207 n.1. For reliance on the Court's finding with respect to exceptions in which "protection may be exercised by a State on behalf of persons not having its nationality" [*id.* 181], see *Barcelona Traction (Second Phase)* Dissent Riphagen, ICJ Rep. 1970, 346, referring to cases of "functional" protection (members of the crew of a vessel flying the flag of the State).

For reliance on the 1949 Advisory Opinion and Dissents Hackworth and Badawi Pasha as well as on the 1970 Dissent Riphagen in this respect, see *M/V Saiga* Memorial of Saint Vincent and the Grenadines, para.170 n.28, its Reply, paras 84-85, and Oral Hearings, ITLOS/PV.99/1, 22-23 [Counsel Plender, 8 March 1999]; as contested by Rejoinder of Guinea, paras 67-68.

Corfu Channel (Merits) Judgment, ICJ Rep. 1949, 28-29, as relied upon in *IMCO* Pleadings, 132 [USA], 179 [Panama], 334 [Italy, 28 April 1960]; *Corfu* Pleadings, Vol.IV, 548 [Agent Sir Eric Beckett, 18 Jan 1949].

Liechtenstein v. Guatemala Nottebohm (Second Phase) ICJ Rep. 1955, 4, President G.H. Hackworth - Judgment, 23.

An attempt to set limits (by requiring a link other than that based on mere registration) to the authority of states in according their nationality to ships, was undertaken by the Institut de Droit International as early as in 1896 [15 *Annuaire IDI* 51, 52 (1896). Cf. *ILC Yearbook* 1956-II, 279; *IMCO* Pleadings, 343-344 (Italy, 28 April 1960), 367 (Norway, 29 April 1960)]. But it was only as a result of proposal of the Netherlands (which along with Britain and Norway were concerned about competition from the "flags of convenience" or "open registry" ships), which was made in express reliance on the *Nottebohm* finding with a view of opposing such fleets [*ILC Yearbook* 1956-II, 15], that the ILC applied to ships the concept of "genuine link" ("un lien substantiel") [*id.* 278-279; 1961-II, 49, 53], enunciated in the *Nottebohm* Judgment with respect to individuals in the context of the question whether Nottebohm was a naturalized citizen of Liechtenstein for the purpose of diplomatic protection vis-à-vis Guatemala. The ILC draft became Article 5 of the 1958 HSC, with some changes introduced during UNCLOS I on the initiative of the genuine link's proponents [*UNCLOS I Off. Rec.* 1958-II, 20. Cf. *Barcelona Traction (Second Phase)* Separate O. Jessup, ICJ Rep. 1970, 186-187; *M/V Saiga* Judgment, ITLOS Case No.2, 38 ILM 1323 (1999), para.80.]; *Oil Platforms (Merits)* Hearings, CR 2003/13, 34 [Counsel Murphy, 26 Feb], CR 2003/14, 36 [Counsel Pellet, 28 Feb 2003] <www.icj-cij.org>.

Constitution of the Maritime Safety Committee of the Inter-Governmental Maritime Consultative Organization (*IMCO*) ICJ Rep. 1960, President H. Klaestad – Advisory Opinion, 150, Dissent President Klaestad, 173, Dissent Moreno Quintana, 177; Order, ICJ Rep. 1959, 267.

By means of the IMCO Assembly Resolution 12(1) of 19 January 1959, the Court was requested to give an Advisory Opinion on whether the Maritime Safety Committee (MSC), which was elected on 15 January 1959 during the First Assembly, was constituted in accordance with Article 28(a) of the Convention for the Establishment of the IMCO of 6 March 1948 [in force: 17 March 1958, 289 UNTS 3, as amended, 607 UNTS 276; 649 UNTS 335; 1080 UNTS 375; 1276 UNTS 468; 1380 UNTS 268, 288; IMO Assembly Resolutions 724(17) and 735(18); see also Settlement of Disputes, Article 287(1)(d) and Annex VIII *infra*], a specialized agency of the United Nations. The case was the first instance in which the Court held to be unconstitutional action taken by an international organization. Judge Sir Hersch Lauterpacht died on 8 May 1960, before the *IMCO* Advisory Opinion, on which he was working at the time, was delivered. Cf. reliance on Sir Hersch's view, in *IMCO* Pleadings, 123 [USA]. Cf. also *Nuclear Weapons (WHO)* Separate O. Oda, ICJ Rep. 1996, 89-90; Hearings, CR 95/34, 31 [UK, 15 Nov 1995].

The *IMCO* case testified to difficulties surrounding application of the then newly transposed *Nottebohm*'s concept of genuine link to nationality of ships.

During the *IMCO* proceedings, the UK, Netherlands, France and Norway argued in support of the MSC election and in favour of the genuine link [*IMCO* Pleadings, 216 (Switzerland), 250-251, 355-359 (NL, 29 April 1960), 365-368 (Norway), 374, 383 (UK)], while Liberia, the USA, Panama and India contested the validity of election and were against application of the genuine link analogy to the open registries [*id.* 71, 83 (Liberia), 115-150 (USA), 181 (Panama), 269-279, 298-299 (L, 26 and 27 April), 317-319 (P), 404-405, 407 (L, 3 May), 425-429 (USA, 4 May 1960)]. The Court reformulated a general question put to it into a more specific question whether the Assembly, in not electing Liberia and Panama to the MSC, exercised its electoral power in accordance with Article 28(a) of the IMCO Convention. Basing itself almost exclusively on treaty interpretation, the Court answered that question in the negative. As possession of "an important interest in maritime safety" was implied under this article in relation to the eight "largest ship-owning nations", the Court could not accept the Assembly's discretion to decide which states have or do not have such interest and to deny the MSC membership to any state regardless of the size of its tonnage or any other criteria [ICJ Rep. 1960, 161]. Of two tests of the "largest ship-owning nations", i.e., the tonnage beneficially owned by the nationals of a state and the registered tonnage of a flag state regardless of its private or state ownership, the Court opted for the latter test, which was advocated by Liberia, Panama and the USA and was confirmed by a number of treaties dealing with load lines, safety at sea, salvage and marine pollution [*id.* 166-170; *IMCO* Pleadings, 48-54, 86-99, 104-113 (Liberia), 120-121, 124-127, 136-137, 149 (USA), 190-191, 201-203 (Panama), 257 (India)]. The Court found the criterion of registered tonnage to be "practical, certain and capable of easy application". In view of its findings, the Court considered that an examination of the contention based on a genuine link, under Article 5 of then unratified 1958 HSC, was irrelevant for the purpose of answering the question submitted to it [ICJ Rep. 1960, 171]. Cf. *Oil Platforms (Preliminary Objection)* Separate O. Higgins, ICJ Rep. 1996, 847-848; *Oil Platforms (Merits)* Hearings, CR 2003/13, 34 [Counsel Murphy, 26 Feb 2003] <http://www.icj-cij.org>.

The Second IMCO Assembly held on 5-14 April 1961 adopted Resolution 1(2) which provided for dissolving the MSC elected in 1959 and constituting a new MSC under Article 28 of the IMCO Convention as interpreted by the *IMCO* Advisory Opinion [12 ICLQ 42-51, 78-81 (1963)]. On 13 April 1961, while electing all MSC members anew, the Assembly elected the group of "eight" on the basis of the gross tonnage as listed in the *Lloyd's Register of Shipping* for 1961 (the USA, Britain, Norway, Liberia, Japan, Greece, Italy and France). Since an amendment of the IMO Convention of 17 October 1974 [in force: 1 April 1978, 1080 UNTS 375], the MSC is open to all members of the Organization.

Belgium v. Spain Barcelona Traction, Light and Power Company, Ltd. (Second Phase) ICJ Rep. 1970, President J.L. Bustamante y Rivero – Judgment, 3 [rejecting at 42 relevance of the *Nottebohm* analogy], Separate O. Jessup, 161, 183-191.

Judge Jessup addressed at some length the *Nottebohm* concept of genuine link with a view of applying it to the relationship between a corporation and a state involved in that case. He considered it "a general principle of law" applicable both to ships flying flags of convenience and to the diplomatic protection of corporations. Judge Jessup stressed an apparent influence of the link concept on the *IMCO* case, despite the fact that the Court declined to examine its customary law status, recognized in the *IMCO* Dissent of Judge Moreno Quintana [ICJ Rep. 1960, 178].

For the view in support of relevance of the *Nottebohm* analogy in the *Barcelona Traction* case, see also Separate O. Sir Gerald Fitzmaurice, ICJ Rep. 1970, 79-84; *ELSI* Pleadings, Vol.II, 250 n.4 [Counter-Memorial of Italy].

For reliance on *Barcelona Traction* Separate O. Jessup as "a valid statement of what international law is still requiring as a minimum standard concerning the genuine link of ships", see *M/V Saiga* Counter-Memorial of Guinea, paras 66-68. But see 1949 *Reparation* Advisory Opinion *supra*.

North Sea Continental Shelf Pleadings, Vol.II, 242 [Reply by Counsel Sir Humphrey Waldock to Questions Fitzmaurice, 8 Nov 1968], invoking a genuine link principle of Article 5 as an example of "progressive development" of the law effected by the 1958 HSC.

1986 *Canada/France Filleting in the Gulf of St. Lawrence* Award [No.444/Stuyt; 90 RGDIP 713 (1986); 91 RGDIP 707 (1987)], para.27.

Spain v. Canada Fisheries (Jurisdiction) Judgment, ICJ Rep. 1998, 432, paras 10-12, 17-20, 53, 61, 74-77, Separate O. President Schwebel, 471-472, paras 6-7, Dissents Vereshchetin, 580, para.22, Torres Bernardez, 698-703, paras 317-332, at 714, paras 369-370; Pleadings, 268-272 [Canada's Counter-Memorial], Hearings, CR 98/9 [trans.], 22 [Counsel Rodriguez, 9 June 1998], 98/10 [trans.], 7-8 [Counsel Brotons, 10 June], 46-49 [Counsel Dupuy], CR 98/12, 21-26 [Counsel Willis, 12 June 1998].

Iran v. USA Oil Platforms case reflected a novel aspect of the genuine link which arose in 1987 in the context of the Iran/Iraq War and reflagging (re-registering) of Kuwaiti tankers under the US and UK flags with a view of their protection against Iranian attacks [26 ILM 1422 (1987)] – *Oil Platforms (Preliminary Objection)* Hearings, CR 96/12, 25-39 [Cdr Neubauer, 16 Sep 1996], CR 96/14, 45-54 [Counsel Bundy, 19 Sep 1996]; *Oil Platforms (Counter-Claim)* Order, ICJ Rep. 1998, 201-202; *Oil Platforms (Merits)* Judgment, ICJ Rep. 2003, 161, paras 24, 64, 108, 120-121, Separate O. Rigaux, 362; Hearings, CR 2003/5, 23-24

[Agent Zahedin-Labbaf, 17 Feb 2003], 64-66 [Counsel Bundy], CR 2003/6, 64-65 [Counsel Sellers, 18 Feb], CR 2003/7, 31 [Counsel Bothe, 19 Feb], CR 2003/8, 20, 44 [Counsel Crawford], CR 2003/9, 15 [Agent Taft, 21 Feb], 24 [Counsel Beaver], CR 2003/10, 16-17 [Counsel Mattler, 24 Feb], CR 2003/12, 51 [Counsel Matheson, 26 Feb], CR 2003/13, 13, 31-34 [Counsel Murphy], CR 2003/14, 12-13, 16-23 [Sellers, 28 Feb], 27-38 [Counsel Pellet], 49, 55-57 [Crawford], 2003/15, 14 [Bundy, 3 March], 22 [Counsel Momtaz], 26 [Sellers], CR 2003/17, 23 [Co-Agent Bettauer, 5 March], 48-52, giving excellent reply to Iran's arguments [Murphy], CR 2003/18, 26 [Matheson], CR 2003/19, 11-12, 14-15 [Sellers, 7 March 2003], 22-27, 30 [Pellet] <www.icj-cij.org>.

Saint Vincent and the Grenadines v. Guinea M/V Saiga (Merits) Judgment, paras 55-109, ITLOS Case No.2, Separate O. President Mensah, Separate O. Vice-President Wolfrum, Separate Opinions Zhao, Nelson, Rao, Anderson, Vukas and Laing, Dissent Warioba, Dissent Ndiaye, ITLOS Rep. 1999, 10; 38 ILM 1323 (1999) <www.itlos.org>; as relied upon in *Oil Platforms (Merits)* Hearings, CR 2003/13, 33 [Counsel Murphy, 26 Feb], CR 2003/14, 34 [Counsel Pellet, 28 Feb 2003] <www.icj-cij.org>.

2000 *Southern Bluefin Tuna (Jurisdiction and Admissibility)* Award, President S.M. Schwebel, para.22, 39 ILM 1359 (2000) <www.worldbank.org/icsid>.

2000 *Panama v. France* and *Seychelles v. France*, 2001 *Belize v. France* and *Panama v. Yemen* decisions, ITLOS Cases Nos 5-6 and 8-9 – see Settlement of Disputes, Prompt Release of Vessels and Crews *infra*; 2002 *Russia v. Australia Volga (Prompt Release)* Judgment, ITLOS Case No.11, President L.D.M. Nelson, paras 30, 56, Dissents Anderson, para.17, Shearer, para.19, 42 ILM 159 (2003); 2004 *Saint Vincent & the Grenadines v. Guinea-Bissau Juno Trader (Prompt Release)* Judgment, Case No.13, President L.D.M. Nelson, Joint Separate O. Mensah and Wolfrum <www.itlos.org>.

On the whole, the developments since importation of the genuine link from the *Nottebohm* Judgment to the rules governing nationality of ships, including the scant prospects for entry into force of the 1986 UNCTAD Convention on Conditions for Registration of Ships [26 ILM 1229 (1987)], have confirmed perils inherent in such, by its very nature inappropriate, transposition and the far-reaching wisdom of the 1960 *IMCO* Advisory Opinion. On the 1986 Convention, see *Great Belt* Pleadings, 349-350, 354 [Finland's Memorial], 593 [Denmark's Counter-Memorial; *M/V Saiga* Judgment, 38 ILM 1323 (1999), para.84.

On flags of vessels navigating in international waterways, see *Costa Rica v. Nicaragua San Juan River* Judgment, ICJ Rep. 2009, paras 13, 14, 130-132 <www.icj-cij.org>.

On Brussels International Convention for the Unification of Certain Rules on Bills of Lading for the Carriage of Goods by Sea of 25 August 1924 [120 UNTS

155], see *Great Belt* Pleadings, 345 [Finland's Memorial]; *Oil Platforms (Merits)* Hearings, CR 2003/11, 47-48 [Counsel Murphy, 25 Feb 2003] <www.icj-cij.org>.

On Convention on Certain Questions Relating to the Conflict of Nationality Laws, The Hague, 12 April 1930 [in force: 1 July 1937, 179 LNTS 89], see *Nottebohm (Second Phase)* Judgment, ICJ Rep. 1955, 22, as relied upon by *North Sea* Dissent Lachs, ICJ Rep. 1969, 224-225, also citing *Italy/USA Merigé* [22 ILR 450] and *Flegenheimer* [25 ILR 149] decisions [No.B 15/Stuyt]; *Great Belt* Pleadings, 345 [Finland's Memorial].

On 1855 *Ionian Ships* Judgment of the British Admiralty Prize Court [2 Spinks 193; *British International Law Cases*, Vol.I, 635-644], see *Cameroon v. Nigeria; Equatorial Guinea Intervening (Merits)* Hearings, CR 2002/3, 45 [Counsel Aurillac, 20 Feb 2002] <www.icj-cij.org>.

On 1875 *Colombia/USA The Montijo* Award [54 AJIL 113 (1960); No.108/ Stuyt], see *IMCO* Pleadings, 404 [Liberia, 3 May 1960]; *M/V Saiga* Separate O. Anderson, n.1 [38 ILM 1323 (1999)].

On 1903 *USA/Venezuela The Alliance* Award of Mixed Claims Commission [No.258/Stuyt], see *Oil Platforms (Merits)* Hearings, CR 2003/14, 33 [Counsel Pellet, 28 Feb 2003].

On 1905 *France/UK The Muscat Dhows* Award [2 AJIL 921, 923 (1908); No.276/Stuyt; PCA 1999, 42; PCA Awards <www.haguejusticeportal.net>], see *IMCO* Pleadings, 133 n.1 [USA], 183, 317 [Panama, 27 April 1960], 404 [Liberia, 3 May 1960]; *M/V Saiga* Separate O. Anderson, n.1 [38 ILM 1323 (1999)].

On 1906 *Mortensen v. Peters (The Niobe*; Moray Firth) Judgment, see Fisheries *infra*.

On 1935 *Canada/USA I'm Alone (The Wolcott, The Dexter)* Award, see Use of Force in Enforcement at Sea *infra*.

On 1948 *Naim Molvan Owner of MV Asya v. Attorney General for Palestine (The Asya, The Chequers)* Judgment [A.C. 351 (J.C.P.C.; 81 Lloyd's List L.R. 277; 42 AJIL 953 (1948); 54 AJIL 77 (1960)], see *IMCO* Pleadings, 254 [India]; *M/V Saiga* Dissent Ndiaye [38 ILM 1323 (1999)], para.89.

On 1953 *Lauritzen v. Larsen* Judgment [345 US 571; 47 AJIL 711 (1953)], see *IMCO* Pleadings, 368 [Norway, 29 April 1960]; *M/V Saiga* Separate Os Nelson, Anderson, n.2 [38 ILM 1323 (1999)]. The 1953 Judgment was, in turn, relied upon in:

1961/3 *Incres Steamship Co. v. International Maritime Workers' Union (The Nassau, The Victoria)* Judgments [(1961) II App. Div. 2d 177, 202 N.Y.S. 2d 692, on appeal (Ct. App. 1961), 10 N.Y. 2d 218, 219 N.Y.S. 2d 21, 176 N.E. 2d 719; 1 ILM 58 (1962); 372 US 24 (1963); 34 ILR 66; 39 BYIL 245-254 (1963)].

On 1963 *McCulloh v. Sociedad Nacional de Marineros de Honduras (The Empresa)* Judgment, named *The Empresa* on account of the two cases argued, decided and reported with it, i.e., *McLeod v. Empresa Hondurena de Vapores* and *National Maritime Union v. Empresa Hondurena de Vapores* [372 US 10; 34 ILR 51; 57 AJIL 659 (1963); 39 BYIL 1963, 245-254 (1963)], see *Barcelona Traction (Second Phase)* Separate O. Jessup, ICJ Rep. 1970, 187-188 n.2. See also *Sociedad Nacional de Marineros de Honduras v. McCulloch* [(D.D.C. 1962) 201 F.Supp. 82]; *Empresa Hondurena de Vapores v. McLeod* [(S.D.N.Y. 1961) 200 F.Supp. 484, on appeal (2nd Cir. 1962) 300 F 2d 222; 57 AJIL 134 (1963)].

On 1991 *Cruz et al. v. Chesapeake Shipping* Judgment of the US Court of Appeals of the Third Circuit, see *Oil Platforms (Merits)* Hearings, CR 2003/14, 17-21 [Counsel Sellers, 28 Feb 2003], 36 [Counsel Pellet] <www.icj-cij.org>.

Status of Ships/Criminal Jurisdiction
1958 HSC, Articles 6(1) and 11; 1982 UNCLOS, Articles 92(1) and 97:

France v. Turkey SS Lotus Judgment, PCIJ Series A, No.10 (1927), President H.M. Huber's casting vote, Dissent Loder, 38-39, Dissent Weiss, 46-49, Dissent Lord Finlay, 51-55, Dissent Nyholm, 62-63, Dissent Moore 69-89, Dissent Altamira, 97, 102, 106.

The *Lotus* ruling in favour of Turkey by application of the principle of objective territorial jurisdiction (Judgment, 18-19) was based, *inter alia*, on the Court's conclusion that the existence of a rule of customary international law establishing the exclusive jurisdiction of the flag state has not been conclusively proved. None of precedents relied upon by France, including the 1897 *UK/Netherlands The Costa Rica Packet* Award of Frederic Martens (Russia) [No.188/Stuyt], related to offences affecting two ships flying the flags of two different states, whereas in many instances a state has claimed a right to prosecute for an offence committed on board a foreign ship, which it regarded as punishable under its legislation (*SS Lotus* Judgment, 26). Nor did the Court accept the French contention that the flag state jurisdiction was particularly applicable to collision cases. The Court found the decisions of the domestic tribunals inconclusive. The pronouncements in favour of the exclusive flag state jurisdiction in the celebrated 1876 *R. v. Keyn (The Franconia, The Strathclyde)* Judgment of Lord Chief Justice Cockburn [L.R. 2 Ex.D. 63; 13 Cox C.C. 403; Simmonds/No.37; the 1877 *Harris v. Owners of the Steamship Franconia*, 2 C.P.D. 173; Simmonds/No.38] and 1885 *The Ortigia, The Oncle Joseph* [1882 Court of Livourne, as confirmed by Court of Florence, as overruled by Court of Aix; Clunet 1885, 286; Sirey 1887, 2, 217] cases were opposed by 1882 *The Ortigia, The Oncle Joseph* and 1914 *The Ekbatana, The West Hinder* [Court of Bruges; Clunet 1914, 1328] decisions, whereas *Franconia*'s finding concerning the localization of an offence was abandoned in the 1884 *R. v. Nillins* [53 L.J. 157] and 1923 *R. v. Godfrey* [L.R. 1923, I K.B. 24] decisions (*SS Lotus* Judgment, 28-30).

On fiction that a ship is a floating part of the state territory, see *SS Lotus* PCIJ Series A, No.10, 25 – Judgment, 25, Dissent Weiss, 45-46; *SS Lotus* Pleadings, PCIJ Series C, No.13-II, 77 [Agent Basdevant, 3 Aug 1927], 136 [Agent Bey, 8 Aug 1927], 264-266 [France's Counter-Memorial], 310 [Turkey's Counter-Memorial]; *France v. Norway Certain Norwegian Loans (Preliminary Objections)* Separate O. Sir Hersch Lauterpacht, ICJ Rep. 1957, 52; *IMCO* Pleadings, 45 [Liberia], quoting 1876 *The Franconia* [L.R. 2 Ex.D.63, at 161]; *Aegean Sea* Pleadings, 442 [Counsel O'Connell, 16 Oct 1978]; *Spain v. Canada (Jurisdiction)* Dissent Torres Bernardez, ICJ Rep. 1998, 665, para.220 <http://www.icj-cij.org>.

For survey of the relevant case law, see especially the *Lotus* Dissent of Judge Moore [who was the author of the magnificent *History and Digest of International Arbitrations* Vols I-VI 1898]; *SS Lotus* Pleadings, PCIJ Series C, No.13-II, 44-87 [Agent Basdevant, 2 and 3 Aug 1927], 103-136 [Agent Bey, 6 and 8 Aug], 137-164 [Basdevant, 9 Aug 1927], 173-213 [France's Memorial], 245-283 [France's Counter-Memorial], 287-349 [Turkey's Counter-Memorial].

The *Lotus* decision was reversed by the Brussels International Convention for the Unification of Certain Rules Relating to Penal Jurisdiction in Matters of Collision of Other Incidents of Navigation of 10 May 1952 [in force: 20 November 1955, 439 UNTS 233; cf. *IMCO* Pleadings, 52, 93 (Liberia)] and by both HSC and LOSC. Cf. *ILC Yearbook* 1956-II, 281; Sir Arthur Watts, *The International Law Commission 1949-1998*, Vol.I, 65-66 (Oxford 1999).

But the *Lotus* pronouncement that "vessels on the high seas are subject to no authority except that of the State whose flag they fly" (Judgment, 25), as recognized by all six dissenting Judges, and as reflected in the *Corfu Channel (Merits)* Judgment [ICJ Rep. 1949, 28-29], was codified in Article 6(1) of the 1958 HSC, as restated in Article 92(1) of the 1982 LOSC. For reliance on this *Lotus* pronouncement, see *Anglo/Norwegian Fisheries* Pleadings, Vol.II, 463 [UK Reply]; *IMCO* Pleadings, 44-46 [Liberia], 132-141 [USA], 179, 182-183 [Panama], 256 [India], 317 [P, 27 April 1960]; *Spain v. Canada (Jurisdiction)* Dissent Torres Bernardez, ICJ Rep. 1998, 609, 683, paras 74 and 273; Pleadings, 488 [Agent Pastor Ridruejo, 10 June 1998]; 1998 *Sellers v. Maritime Safety Inspector* [120 ILR 585]; *M/V Saiga* Separate O. Laing [38 ILM 1323 (1999)], para.19.

For France/Turkey Maritime Agreement of 5 September 1996 [in force: 17 November 1997], see 2087 UNTS 128.

See also *Access To, Or Anchorage In, The Port of Danzig, of Polish War Vessels* Pleadings, PCIJ Series C, No.55, 231-232 [Agent Williams, 9 Nov 1931]; *Anglo/*

Norwegian Fisheries Pleadings, Vol.I. 386 [Norway's Counter-Memorial], Vol.II, 412, 426, 460-463 [UK Reply]; *Fisheries Jurisdiction* Pleadings (UK), 378 [Memorial (Merits)], (FRG), 212 [Memorial (Merits)]; *Nuclear Weapons (UNGA)* Advisory Opinion, ICJ Rep. 1996, 239, Declaration President Bedjaoui, 270-271, Separate O. Guillaume, 291, Dissents Shahabuddeen, 390-396, 409, 426, Weeramantry, 494-496.

Spain v. Canada Fisheries Jurisdiction (Jurisdiction) Judgment, President S.M. Schwebel, ICJ Rep. 1998, 432; *Congo v. Belgium Arrest Warrant of 11 April 2000* Separate O. President Guillaume, ICJ Rep. 2002, 36-37, 42-43, paras 4, 13-15, Dissent Oda, 51, para.12, Declaration Ranjeva, 57-58, paras 9-10, Joint S. Opinion Higgins, Kooymans, Buergenthal, 77, 79, paras 49, 54, Separate O. Bula-Bula, 116-117, para.49, Dissent van den Wyngaert, 145, 167-169, 172, 180, paras 13, 48-51, 56, 76 <www.icj-cij.org>.

Definition of Ships

Nicaragua v. USA (Merits) Judgment, ICJ Rep. 1986, 46, para.76, at 147, para.292(7); *Great Belt (Provisional Measures)* Order, ICJ Rep. 1991, 17-18; Hearings, CR 91/9, 18-19, 22-23, 25 [Agent Gronberg, 1 July 1991], 33 [Counsel Sir Ian Sinclair], CR 91/10, 13-17 [Co-Agent Koskenniemi], CR 91/11, 14-15 [Agent Lehmann, 2 July], 57-59 [Counsel de Arechaga], 67-80 [Counsel Fergo], CR 91/13, 17 [Agent Gronberg, 4 July], 32 [Counsel Sinclair], 68 [Judge Schwebel's Questions], CR 91/14, 8-11 [Agent Gronberg's Reply to Schwebel, 5 July 1991], 19-31 [Agent Magid], 31-33 [his Reply to Schwebel], Pleadings, 4, 8-9 [Finland's Application, paras 6, 27-30, 33], 156 [Agent Fergo, 2 July 1991], 236, 341-364 [Finland's Memorial], 589-602 [Denmark's Counter-Memorial]; *Spain v. Canada Fisheries (Jurisdiction)* Judgment, ICJ Rep. 1998, 463-465, paras 75-77; *Oil Platforms (Merits)* Hearings, CR 2003/13, 26-27 [Counsel Murphy, 26 Feb], 2003/14, 18 [Counsel Sellers, 28 Feb 2003], 37 [Counsel Pellet] <www.icj-cij .org>.

The 1921 *In the Matter of the Cessions by Germany to France Under Article 357 of the Treaty of Versailles* Award of Sole Arbitrator Walker D. Hines [17 AJIL 786, 796 (1923)] asserted that a barge with a crane upon it was within the meaning of the term vessel under Article 357 of that Treaty.

On 1876 *R. v. Keyn (The Franconia, The Strathclyde)* Judgment, see Internal Waters, Territorial Sea and Baselines *supra*.

On 1897 *UK/Netherlands The Costa Rica Packet* Award of Frederic Martens (Russia) [No.188/Stuyt], see *SS Lotus* PCIJ Series A, No.10 – Judgment, 7 and 26, Dissent Weiss, 46-47, Dissent Moore 83-84, Dissent Altamira 97; *SS Lotus* Pleadings, PCIJ Series C, No.13-II, 63, 66-67, 71, 75, 77, 84 [Agent Basdevant, 2 and 3 Aug 1927], 118, 123-125 [Agent Bey, 6 and 8 Aug], 154, 155, 160-161, 162, 163-164 [Basdevant, 9 Aug], 168-169 [Bey, 10 Aug 1927], 190, 203-205, 208, 211, 212 [France's Memorial], 248, 251, 255, 269-270, 280, 281 [France's Counter-Memorial], 309, 315-316 [Turkey's Counter-Memorial], 325, 345 [Observations of Diena], 360-362 [Consultation of Diena], 379, 385-386 [Consultation of Fedozzi], 417 [Consultation of Mercier]; *Anglo/Norwegian Fisheries* Pleadings, Vol.I, 346 [Norway's Counter-Memorial].

On 1915 *H.M.S. Hawke* Judgment of Lord Justice Vaughan Williams [28 Times L.R. 319 (P.) 49 (H.L.)], see *Ambatielos* Pleadings, 20 [Greece's Memorial], 166 [UK Counter-Memorial].

United Nations Flag
1958 HSC, Article 7; 1982 UNCLOS, Article 93:

Corfu Channel (Merits) ICJ Rep. 1949, 4 – Individual O. Alvarez, 41, 46-47, Dissent Azevedo, 91; *Oil Platforms (Merits)* Hearings, CR 2003/14, 13 [Counsel Sellers, 28 Feb 2003], CR 2003/15, 17 [Counsel Momtaz, 3 March 2003] <www.icj-cij.org>.

Salvage/Assistance
1958 HSC, Article 12; 1982 UNCLOS, Article 98:

SS Lotus PCIJ Series A, No.10 (1927) – Judgment, 10, Dissent Moore, 69, 85; *Eastern Greenland* Pleadings, PCIJ Series C, No.62, 214, 269, 282 [Norway's Counter-Memorial], No.64, 1546 [Annex], No.66, 3149-3150 [Counsel Sunde, 10 Dec 1932], No.67, 3588 [Counsel Rygh, 3 Feb 1933]; *Minquiers and Ecrehos* ICJ Rep. 1953, 47 – Judgment, 67-69, Individual Os Basdevant, 82, Carneiro, 88; *IMCO* Pleadings, 113 [Liberia]; *Western Sahara* Advisory Opinion, ICJ Rep. 1975, 51-53; *Gulf of Maine* Judgment, ICJ Rep. 1984, 340-341; Pleadings, Vol.II, 46, 114 [US Memorial], Vol.III, 19, 166-167, 225, 381-385 [Canada's Counter-Memorial], Vol.IV, 137 [US Counter-Memorial], Vol.V, 36, 78 [Canada's Reply], Vol.VI, 139-140 [Counsel Bowett, 5 April 1984], 278-279 [Counsel Stevenson, 12 April 1984], Vol.VIII, 27 [Fig.13], 104 [Fig.16]; *Great Belt* Pleadings, 353 [Finland's Memorial], 529-530 [Denmark's Counter-Memorial]; *Qatar v. Bahrain (Merits)* Judgment, ICJ Rep. 2001, 71, para.101; Hearings, CR 2000/13, 15-16, 42 [Counsel Volterra, 13 June 2000], CR 2000/17, 36 [15 June 2000]; *Nicaragua v. Honduras (Merits)* Judgment, ICJ Rep. 2007, paras 80, 220-221, 242 <www.icj-cij.org>.

On maritime accidents and shipwrecks in territorial sea surrounding Pedra Branca in 1920-2005, see *Malaysia/Singapore (Merits)* Judgment, ICJ Rep. 2008, paras 167, 231-234; Hearings, CR 2007/22, 25-26, paras 56-60 [Counsel Bundy, 8 Nov 2007], CR 2007/22 [transl.], 46, para.10 [Counsel Pellet], CR 2007/26, 47-51, paras 39-53 [Counsel Sir Elihu Lauterpacht, 15 Nov 2007], 64, para.33 and at 66-67, paras 39-43 [Counsel Crawford] <www.icj-cij.org>. See also Straits Used for International Navigation – Transit Passage: Straits of Malacca and Singapore *supra*; Shipwrecks <http://en.wikipedia.org/wiki/List_of_shipwrecks & http://en.wikipedia.org/wiki/Shipwreck>.

1977 *Anglo/French* Decision [18 ILM 397 (1979)], paras 163, 175; 1998 *Eritrea/Yemen Territorial Sovereignty (Phase I)* Award, paras 284-286, 317, 336 [40 ILM 900 (2001)]; *Guyana/Suriname* Guyana's Memorial, para.4.50 <www.pca-cpa.org>.

2007 ICSID *Malaysian Historical Salvors (MHS), SDN, BHD v. Malaysia Sunken Treasure (Jurisdiction)* Award of Sole Arbitrator Michael Hwang (Singapore), as annulled by the 2009 *MHS v. Malaysia (Annulment)* Decision, President Stephen M. Schwebel (USA), Arbitrators Mohamed Shahabuddeen (Guyana) and Peter Tomka (Slovakia) <www.globalarbitrationreview.com/news/article/15229/icsid-award-annulled/ & www.investmenttreatynews.org/cms/news/archive/2009/04/23/malaysian-historical-salvors-jurisdictional-award-annulled-committee-split-on-question-of-economic-development-as criteria-of-icsid-investments.aspx>; 48 ILM 1081 (2009); and 20- *MHS v. Malaysia Sunken Treasure (Merits)* Award <http://icsid.worldbank.org/ICSID/FrontServlet & www.arbitration.fr/5.html>.

On International Convention on Maritime Search and Rescue, London, 1 November 1979 [in force: 22 June 1985, 1986 UKTS 59], see *Gulf of Maine* Pleadings, Vol.III, 167, 384 [Canada's Counter-Memorial]; *Great Belt* Pleadings, 353 [Finland's Memorial]; Annex VII *Mox Plant (Provisional Measures)* Hearings, 29, 43-45 [Counsel Lowe, 17 June 2003]; Ireland's Memorial, I, 102, UK Counter-Memorial, 149-150 <www.pca-cpa.org>.

Piracy
1958 HSC, Articles 14-22; 1982 UNCLOS, Articles 100-107 and 110(1)(a):

SS Lotus PCIJ Series A, No.10 (1927) – Dissent Lord Finlay, 51, Dissent Moore, 69, 70-71; *SS Lotus* Pleadings, PCIJ Series C, No.13-II, 79 [Agent Basdevant, 3 Aug 1927], 153, 157 [Basdevant, 9 Aug 1927], 198 [France's Memorial], 377-378 [Consultation Fedozzi], 411-412 [Consultation Mercier]; *Legal Status of Eastern Greenland* PCIJ Series A/B, No.53 (1933) – Dissent Vogt, 108; *Eastern Greenland* Pleadings, PCIJ Series C, No.62, 116 [Norway's Counter-Memorial], No.63, 768 [Denmark's Reply], 1222 [Norway's Rejoinder]; *Corfu Channel (Merits)* ICJ Rep. 1949, 4 – Dissent Azevedo, 98; *Corfu* Pleadings, Vol.II, 282-283 [UK Reply], Vol.IV, 543 [Agent Sir Eric Beckett, 18 Jan 1949]; *Anglo/Norwegian Fisheries* Pleadings, Vol.I, 241 [Norway's Counter-Memorial]; *Minquiers and Ecrehos* Pleadings, Vol.I, 35-36 [UK Memorial]; *North Sea* Pleadings, Vol.II, 242 [Reply by Counsel Sir Humphrey Waldock to Questions Fitzmaurice, 8 Nov 1968]; *Fisheries Jurisdiction (Jurisdiction)* Separate Os Fitzmaurice, ICJ Rep. 1973, 25, 69; *Gulf of Fonseca*

Judgment, ICJ Rep. 1992, 560-561, 565, Separate O. Bernardez, 700-701; *Spain v. Canada (Jurisdiction)* Dissent Bernardez, ICJ Rep. 1998, 715, para.371; Pleadings, 47, 49, 125-126 [Spain's Memorial], 270 [Canada's Counter-Memorial], Pleadings, 434 [Counsel Rodriguez, 9 June 1998], 467 [Counsel Highet, 10 June], 623 [Counsel Willis, 17 June 1998]; *Qatar v. Bahrain (Merits)* Judgment, ICJ Rep. 2001, 54-55, 67, paras 38, 40, 83, Dissent Torres Bernardez, 291, paras 90-91, 93; *Congo v. Belgium Arrest Warrant of 11 April 2000* Separate O. President Guillaume, ICJ Rep. 2002, 37-38, paras 5, 16, Dissent Oda, 51, para.12, Declaration Ranjeva, 55-56, para.6, Joint Separate O. Higgins, Kooymans, Buergenthal, 74, 81, paras 39, 60; *Indonesia/Malaysia (Merits)* Judgment, ICJ Rep. 2002, 680, 683, paras 130, 138-139, Dissent Franck, 696-697, paras 17, 33; Hearings, CR 2002/27, 27, 33, 34 [Counsel Soons, 3 June], CR 2002/28, 33, 36, 38, CR 2002/29, 12 [Counsel Bundy, 4 June], CR 2002/31, 59-62 [Counsel Schrijver, 7 June], CR 2002/32, 13 [Counsel Lauterpacht], CR 2002/33, 40-42 [Soons, 10 June], CR 2002/35, 23 [Schrijver, 12 June 2002]; *Nicaragua v. Honduras* Hearings, CR 2007/8, 36, para.3 [Counsel Dupuy, 14 March 2007]; *Malaysia/Singapore (Merits)* Judgment, ICJ Rep. 2008, paras 57, 71, 73, 152, 155, Separate O. Rao, paras 17, 24; Hearings, CR 2007/20, 25, para.3 [Counsel Chao, 6 Nov 2007], CR 2007/24, 21, para.7 [Co-Agent Farida, 13 Nov 2007] <www.icj-cij.org>. See also UNSC Docs S/2009/80 and S/2009/146; UNSC Resolution 1897 on Piracy off the Coast of Somalia, UN Doc. S/RES/1897 (2009) of 30 Nov 2009 and *EU NAVFOR Atalanta* Report S/2009/569 <www.un.org/Docs/sc/>; UNGA Adopts Two Oceans Resolutions, UN Doc.GA/10899 of 4 Dec 2009 <www.un.org/News/Press/docs//2009/ga10899.doc.htm>.

1998 *Eritrea/Yemen (Phase I)* Award, para.15 [40 ILM 900 (2001) <www.pca-cpa.org>]; *M/V Saiga* Judgment, [38 ILM 1323 (1999)], para.105; *Guyana/Suriname* Guyana's Memorial, para.4.50 <www.pca-cpa.org>.

On 1934 *In Re Piracy Jure Gentium (The S.S. Shui Chow, The S.S. Hang Sang, The H.M.S. Somme)* Judgment [A.C. 586; 29 AJIL 140, 508 (1935)] Judgment, see *Anglo/Norwegian Fisheries* Pleadings, Vol.II, 431 [UK Reply].

On 1615, 1616, 1617, 1692, 1811 and 1817 Judgments and 1950 Inquests, see *infra*.

See also Peaceful Uses of the Sea, Maritime Terrorism *infra*.

Slaves

1958 HSC Articles 13 and 22(1)(b); 1982 UNCLOS, Articles 99 and 110(1)(b):

SS Lotus Pleadings, PCIJ Series C, No.13-II, 133 [Agent Bey, 8 Aug 1927], 162 [Agent Basdevant, 9 Aug 1927], 206 [France's Memorial], 377 [Consultation

Fedozzi]; *Corfu Channel* Pleadings, Vol.IV, 543 [Agent Sir Eric Beckett, 18 Jan 1949]; *Fisheries Jurisdiction (Jurisdiction)* Separate Os Fitzmaurice, ICJ Rep. 1973, 25, 69; *Spain v. Canada (Jurisdiction)* Dissent Bernardez, ICJ Rep. 1998, 715, para.371; Pleadings, 467 [Counsel Highet, 10 June 1998]; *Congo v. Belgium Arrest Warrant of 11 April 2000* Separate O. President Guillaume, ICJ Rep. 2002, 38, para.5; *Indonesia/Malaysia (Merits)* Hearings, CR 2002/31, 59 [Counsel Schrijver, 7 June], CR 2002/35, 21, 23 [12 June 2002]; *Costa Rica v. Nicaragua San Juan River* Hearings, CR 2009/4, 10, para.10 [Agent Arguello, 5 March 2009] <www.icj-cij.org>.

1998 *Eritrea/Yemen (Phase I)* Award, para.15 [40 ILM 900 (2001) <www.pca-cpa.org>].

On Supplementary Convention on the Abolition of Slavery, the Slave Trade and Institutions and Practices Similar to Slavery, Geneva, 7 September 1956 [in force: 30 April 1957, 266 UNTS 3], see *North Sea* Dissent Lachs, ICJ Rep. 1969, 224; *Congo v. Belgium Arrest Warrant of 11 April 2000* Separate O. President Guillaume, ICJ Rep. 2002, 38, para.5 n.8.

See also 200 Years After Abolition of Slave Trade of 2 March 2007 <www.un.org/apps/news/story.asp?NewsID=21735&Cr=slavery&Cr1>; International Day for the Remembrance of the Slave Trade and Its Abolition of 23 August 2008 <www.un.org/apps/news/story.asp?NewsID=27799&Cr=Slave&Cr1 & www.un.org/News/briefings/docs/2008/080325_Slavery.doc.htm>.

Illicit Drug Trafficking
1982 UNCLOS, Article 108:

Spain v. Canada (Jurisdiction) Dissent Bernardez, ICJ Rep. 1998, 715, para.371; *Congo v. Belgium Arrest Warrant of 11 April 2000* Separate O. President Guillaume, ICJ Rep. 2002, 37-39, paras 5-6, 8, Joint Separate O. Higgins, Kooymans, Buergenthal, 72, para.33; *Guyana/Suriname* Guyana's Memorial, para.4.50 <www.pca-cpa.org>; *Nicaragua v. Honduras (Merits)* Judgment, ICJ Rep. 2007, paras 183, 220-221; Hearings, CR 2007/7, 40, para.48 [Counsel Sands, 13 March 2007]; *Ecuador v. Colombia Alleged Aerial Spraying by Colombia of Toxic Herbicides over Ecuadorian Territory*, ICJ Rep. 2008 <www.icj-cij.org>.

On UN Convention Against Illicit Traffic in Narcotic Drugs and Psychotropic Substances, Vienna, 20 Dec 1988 [in force: 11 Nov 1990, 1582 UNTS 96; 28 ILM 493 (1989)], see *Congo v. Belgium Arrest Warrant of 11 April 2000* Separate O. President Guillaume, ICJ Rep. 2002, 37-39, para.5 n.9, para.8; *Ecuador v. Colombia Toxic Herbicides* case <www.icj-cij.org>.

See also UNSC Presidential Statement SC 9807 on Drug Trafficking of 8 Dec 2009 <www.un.org/News/Press/docs//2009/sc9807.doc>.

Unauthorized Broadcasting
1982 UNCLOS, Articles 109 and 110(1)(c):

Spain v. Canada (Jurisdiction) Dissent Bernardez, ICJ Rep. 1998, 715, para.371; *Romania v. Ukraine* Hearings, CR 2008/19, 51, para.114 [Counsel Crawford, 3 Sep 2008] <www.icj-cij.org>.

On European Agreement for the Prevention of Broadcasts Transmitted from Stations Outside National Territories, Strasbourg, 22 Jan 1965 [in force: 19 Oct 1967, 634 UNTS 239], see *Aegean Sea* Pleadings, 438 [Counsel Economides, 16 Oct 1978].

On 1964 *L'ile de la REM* [12 *Netherlands ILR* 202 (1965)], see *Aegean Sea* Pleadings, 258 [Greece's Memorial (Jurisd.)], 457-458 [Counsel O'Connell, 16 Oct 1978].

1998 *Eritrea/Yemen (Phase I)* Award, para.333 <www.pca-cpa.org>.

Hot Pursuit
1930 Hague Draft, Article 11; 1958 HSC, Article 23; 1982 UNCLOS, Article 111:

SS Lotus PCIJ Series A, No.10 (1927) – Dissent Moore, 80-81, 83; *Corfu Channel (Merits)* Dissent Azevedo, ICJ Rep. 1949, 108; Pleadings, Vol.II, 283 [UK Reply]; *Fisheries Jurisdiction (Jurisdiction)* Separate Os Fitzmaurice, ICJ Rep. 1973, 25, 69.

1997 *M/V Saiga (Prompt Release)* Judgment [37 ILM 360 (1998)], paras 54, 60-61, 70, Dissents President Mensah, Anderson, Joint Dissent; *M/V Saiga (Provisional Measures)* Separate O. Laing [37 ILM 1218 (1998)], para.19; *M/V Saiga* Judgment, [38 ILM 1323 (1999)], paras 28-29, 91-92, 97, 105, 139-152, 167-175, Separate O. Anderson.

See also Contiguous Zone *supra*.

Greece v. United Kingdom Ambatielos (Preliminary Objection) Judgment, Vice-President J.G. Guerrero, Acting President concurring, ICJ Rep. 1952, 28, Individual O. Levi Carneiro, 48, Individual O. Spiropoulos, 55, Dissent President Sir Arnold McNair, 58, Dissents Basdevant, 66, Zoricic, 74, Klaestad, 80, Hsu Mo, 85, *Greece v. UK (Merits: Obligation to Arbitrate)* Judgment, ICJ Rep. 1953, 10, Dissent President McNair and Judges Basdevant, Klaestad and Read, 25; Orders, ICJ Rep. 1951, 11, 103, 113, 1952, 7, 16, 90.

The dispute reflected some important aspects of the question of a breach by a state of a contract with an alien concerning a sale of the ships. The proceedings involved the claim relating to the rights of a Greek shipowner, Nicolas Eustache Ambatielos, alleged to have suffered considerable loss in consequence of a contract which he concluded on 17 July 1919 with the British Government (represented by Major Bryan Laing of the Ministry of Shipping) for the purchase of nine steamships which were then under construction at Hong Kong and Shanghai, and in consequence of certain adverse judicial decisions in the English Courts in connection therewith. The Court's decisions were limited to the procedural questions of the arbitrability of the dispute and the jurisdiction of the Court to decide the issue, while the merits of the claim itself were settled by the 1956 *Greece v. UK Ambatielos Claim* Award, Separate O. President R.J. Alfaro, Dissent Spiropoulos [RIAA XII, 83; 23 ILR 306 and 24 ILR 291; No.422/Stuyt].

Cf. *Oil Platforms (Preliminary Objection)* Separate Os Shahabuddeen, ICJ Rep. 1996, 824-832, Higgins, 850-852, 856, Rigaux, 869; 1997 *M/V Saiga (Prompt Release)* Judgment [37 ILM 360 (1998)], para.51, Dissenting Opinions President Mensah, para.5, Anderson, para.4.

On 1615, 1616, 1617 three shipwreck cases at Minquiers of the Jersey Court [*Minquiers and Ecrehos* Pleadings, Vol.I, 169-170], see *Minquiers and Ecrehos* Judgment, ICJ Rep. 1953, 67; Pleadings, Vol.I, 88 [UK Memorial], 398 [France's Counter-Memorial], 533 [UK Reply]; Vol.II 335-336 [Counsel Harrison, 5 Oct 1953].

On 1692 decision of Royal Court of Jersey on shipwreck at Minquiers [*Minquiers and Ecrehos* Pleadings, Vol.I, 170-172], see *Minquiers and Ecrehos* Judgment, ICJ Rep. 1953, 68; Pleadings, Vol.I, 89 [UK Memorial], 399 [France's Counter-Memorial], 534 [UK Reply]; Vol.II, 336 [Counsel Harrison, 5 Oct 1953].

On 1811 decision of Royal Court of Jersey on shipwreck at Minquiers [*Minquiers and Ecrehos* Pleadings, Vol.I, 634-635], see *Minquiers and Ecrehos* Judgment, ICJ Rep. 1953, 69; Pleadings, Vol.II, 183, 334, 336 [Counsel Harrison, 24 Sep and 5 Oct 1953].

On 1817 decision of Royal Court of Jersey on shipwreck at Minquiers [*Minquiers and Ecrehos* Pleadings, Vol.I, 636-637], see *Minquiers and Ecrehos* Judgment, ICJ Rep. 1953, 69; Pleadings, Vol.II, 183, 336 [Counsel Harrison, 24 Sep and 5 Oct 1953].

On 1850 *The Superb* Inquests [*Minquiers and Ecrehos* Pleadings, Vol.I, 642-644], see *Minquiers and Ecrehos* Pleadings, Vol.II, 274-275 [Agent Gros, 30 Sep 1953], 336 [Counsel Harrison, 5 Oct], 405 [Gros, 8 Oct 1953].

On 1863 *The Esmeralda* shipwreck recovery, see *Western Sahara* Advisory Opinion, ICJ Rep. 1975, 51-53.

On 1872 *UK/USA The Alabama (The Kaersage)* Award [No.94/Stuyt; 98th ASIL Proceedings, 31 March-3 April 2004, V.V. Veeder, 33-36 (2004) <www.asil.org/resources /proceedings.html; 54 ICLQ 1-25 (2005)], see *Nottebohm (Preliminary Objection)* Judgment, ICJ Rep. 1953, 119, *as reaffirmed* by *Guinea-Bissau v. Senegal Arbitral Award* Judgment, ICJ Rep. 1991, 68-69, Separate O. Shahabuddeen, 109. See also *Corfu Channel (Merits)* Dissent Azevedo, ICJ Rep. 1949, 96; *Anglo/*

Norwegian Fisheries Dissent Sir Arnold McNair, ICJ Rep. 1951, 181; the *Rights of Nationals of the USA in Morocco* Pleadings, Vol.II, 147 [Agent Gros]; *Interhandel (Preliminary Objections)* Dissent Armand-Ugon, ICJ Rep. 1959, 92; *Fisheries Jurisdiction* Pleadings (UK), 249 [Memorial]; *Application of the Convention on the Prevention and Punishment of the Crime of Genocide (Provisional Measures)* Separate O. Ajibola, ICJ Rep. 1993, 396; *East Timor* Dissent Weeramantry, ICJ Rep. 1995, 158-159; *Spain v. Canada* Hearings, CR 98/10 [trans.], 50 [Counsel Dupuy, 10 June 1998]; *Oil Platforms (Merits)* Hearings, CR 2003/14, 61 [Counsel Crawford, 28 Feb 2003] <www.icj-cij.org>; 2009 *Abyei Boundary* Award, para.500 <www.pca-cpa.org>.

On 1906 *Mortensen v. Peters (The Niobe*; Moray Firth) Judgment, see Fisheries *infra.*

On 1912 *Titanic* disaster [9 AJIL 336 (1915)], see *IMCO* Pleadings, 113 [Liberia]. Cf. Protection and Preservation of the Marine Environment – Ice-Covered Areas, North Atlantic Ice Patrol drawn in a follow-up to this distaster under the 1914 SOLAS.

On 1915 *The Kim and Other Vessels*, see Peaceful Uses of the Sea *infra.*

On 1913 *France/Italy The Carthage and The Manouba* Award [RIAA XI, 450, 464; PCA Awards <www.haguejusticeportal.net>; Nos 306-307/Stuyt], see *South West Africa (Preliminary Objections)* Separate O. Jessup, ICJ Rep. 1962, 425; *Nuclear Tests* Pleadings (Australia), 327 [Memorial]; 1986 *Rainbow Warrior* Memorandum of France and 1990 *Rainbow Warrior* Award [see Access to and Jurisdiction and Treatment in Ports *supra*].

On 1922 *Norway/USA Norwegian Shipowners' Claim* Award [RIAA I, 339; 1 ILR 414; 16 AJIL 81 and Suppl. 16 (1922); 17 AJIL 287, 362 (1923); No.339/Stuyt; PCA 1999, 110; PCA Awards <www.haguejusticeportal.net>], see *Anglo/Norwegian Fisheries* Pleadings, I 383 [Norway's Counter-Memorial], II 428 [UK Reply]; 1969 *North Sea* Separate O. Ammoun, ICJ Rep. 1969, 134 n.1, 135 n.2; *Aegean Sea* Pleadings, 203 n.1 [Greece's Memorial (Jurisd.)]; *Denmark v. Norway* Separate O. Weeramantry, ICJ Rep. 1993, 225.

On 1928 *Portugal v. Germany Naulilaa* Award [RIAA II, 1012; No.325/Stuyt], see *Spain v. Canada (Jurisdiction)* Dissent Torres Bernardez, ICJ Rep. 1998, 731, para.420.

On 1928 *State of California v. Tashiro* Judgment [278 US 1928, 127-128], see *Oil Platforms (Merits)* Hearings, CR 2003/6, 27 [Counsel Pellet, 18 Feb 2003].

On 1934 *Finland v. UK Finnish Ships* Award, see Settlement of Disputes, Exhaustion of Local Remedies *infra.*

On 1956 *Greece v. UK Ambatielos Claim* Award, see Settlement of Disputes, Exhaustion of Local Remedies *infra.*

On 1970 *Ministre d'Etat* Judgment, see Continental Shelf *supra.*

On 1978 *Treasure Salvors, Inc. v. Unidentified Wrecked and Abandoned Sailing Vessel (The Nuestra Senora de Atocha)* Judgment [569 F. (2d) 330; 72 AJIL 664 (1978)], see *Aegean Sea* Pleadings, 457 [Counsel O'Connell, 16 Oct 1978].

See also jurisprudence quoted in this Section *supra*.

See also Internal Waters, Territorial Sea and Baselines – FCN Treaties; Exclusive Economic Zone – *Jus Communicationis* and Equality of Uses Principle, *supra*; Fisheries – Straddling/Highly Migratory Stocks; and Peaceful Uses of the Sea *infra*.

IMMUNITIES OF WARSHIPS

1930 Hague Draft, Articles 12-13; 1958 TSC, Articles 22-23; 1982 UNCLOS, Part II, Article 32
1958 HSC, Article 8
1982 UNCLOS, Part VII, Article 95, and Part XII, Article 236

SS Wimbledon PCIJ Series A, No.1 (1923) – Judgment, 25; *SS Wimbledon* Pleadings, PCIJ Series C, No.3-Additional Volume, 154 [Germany's Rejoinder]; *SS Lotus* PCIJ Series A, No.10 (1927) – Judgment, 25, Dissent Moore, 87; *Access To, Or Anchorage In, The Port of Danzig, of Polish War Vessels* PCIJ Series A/B, No.43 (1931) – Advisory Opinion, 141; *Corfu Channel* – see Straits Used for International Navigation *supra*; *Iran v. USA Oil Platforms (Preliminary Objection)* Dissent Vice-President Schwebel, ICJ Rep. 1996, 803, 874, *(Counter-Claim)* Order, ICJ Rep. 1998, President Schwebel concurring, 201-202; Hearings, CR 96/12, 25-39 [Cdr Neubauer, 16 Sep 1996]; *Oil Platforms (Mertits)* Judgment, ICJ Rep. 2003, 161; Hearings, CR 2003/5-19, 17 Feb-7 March 2003; *Malaysia/Singapore* Hearings, CR 2007/26, 67, paras 42-43 [Counsel Crawford, 15 Nov 2007] <www.icj-cij.org>.

1879/1880 *Parlament Belge* Judgment, (1879) L.R. 4 P.D.129; (1880) 5 P.D. 179; No.40/Simmonds – The Attorney-General intervened to state that the UK High Court had no jurisdiction over the *Parlament Belge* as it was the property of the Belgian monarch and that by the 1876 Britain/Belgium political agreement, the same immunity from foreign legal process as applied to warships shall apply also to the *Parlament Belge*. The Court concluded, (1879) 4 P.D. 154, that only warships were entitled to such immunity and that such immunity could not be extended to other categories by a treaty without parliamentary consent. In the Court's view, this would be "a use of the treaty-making prerogatives of the Crown…without precedent, and in principle contrary to the law of the constitution".

1999 *US v. Havenschap Delfzijl/Eemshaven (The Cape May)* Judgment of the Netherlands Supreme Court, 47 *Netherlands ILR* 359 (2000). See also UN Convention on the Jurisdictional Immunities of States and Their Property [UNGA Resolution 59/38] of 2 Dec 2004, 44 ILM 801 (2005) <www.untreaty.un.org>.

FISHERIES

1958 TSC; 1958 HSC; 1958 HSFC
1982 UNCLOS, Parts II, IV, V and VII, and Annex I
1992 UNCED Rio Agenda 21, Chapter 17
1995 SSA
2002 WSSD Johannesburg Plan of Implementation, paras 29-31

Relevant Jurisprudence

Legal Status of the Southeastern Territory of Greenland PCIJ Series A/B, No.48 (1932) – Order (joining two suits brought by Norway and Denmark), 268, President M. Adatci; *(Request for the Indication of Interim Measures of Protection)* Order, 277, President Adatci; PCIJ Series A/B, No.55 (1933) – *(Discontinuance)* Order, 157, President Adatci; Orders of 1932/1933, *Southeastern Greenland* Pleadings, PCIJ Series C, No.69, 74, 76.

The dispute concerned territorial sovereignty, in particular the validity of a Royal Decree of Norway of 12 July 1932, which involved hunting, fishing and sealing activities of Eskimos and foreigners in Southeastern Greenland. See PCIJ Series A/B, No. 48 (1932) and No.55 (1933); and *Southeastern Greenland* Pleadings, PCIJ Series C, No.69, 20-22 [Counsel Rygh, 28 July 1932], 42-43 [Agent Steglich-Petersen, 28 July 1932].

After the delivery of the *Legal Status of Eastern Greenland* Judgment on 5 April 1933, Norway revoked on 7 April 1933 its 1932 Decree [*Southeastern Greenland* Pleadings, PCIJ Series C, No.69, 71] and the case was discontinued.

Denmark v. Norway Legal Status of Eastern Greenland PCIJ Series A/B, No.53 (1933) – Judgment, 22, President M. Adatci concurring, Dissent Anzilotti, 76, Observations Schücking and Wang, 96, Dissent Vogt, 97.

The dispute concerned territorial sovereignty, in particular the validity of a Royal Proclamation of Norway of 10 July 1931 (as preceded by the verbal Ihlen Declaration of 22 July 1919), which involved whaling, sealing, fishing, hunting and research activities in Eastern Greenland. See *Eastern Greenland* Judgment, 38-40, 42-43, 50, 62-63, 72, Dissent Anzilotti, 92, 93, Dissent Vogt, 103, 108-110; *Eastern Greenland* Pleadings, PCIJ Series C, No.62, 16, 21-23, 31-37, 51-61 [Denmark's Memorial], 174-355, 456-457 [Norway's Counter-Memorial], No.63,

685-900 [Denmark's Reply], 1038-1109, 1295-1298 [Norway's Rejoinder], No.66, 2717, 2727-2732, 2768, 2776-2781 [Agent Steglich-Petersen, 24 and 26 Nov 1932], 2940-2942, 2948-2954 [Counsel Rygh, 3 and 5 Dec 1932], No.67, 3303, 3319 [Steglich-Petersen, 16 Jan 1933], 3570-3575 [Rygh, 3 Feb 1933], 3586-3589 [Rygh].

Two days after the delivery of the *Legal Status of Eastern Greenland* Judgment, Norway, by a new Proclamation of 7 April 1933, revoked the Proclamation of 10 July 1931, annulling thereby its occupation of Eirik Raudes Land [28 AJIL 8 (1934)].

Corfu Channel Pleadings, Vol.I, 22 [UK Memorial], 161 [Albania's Counter-Memorial], Vol.II, 262, 283 [UK Reply], Vol.IV, 543 [Agent Sir Eric Beckett, 18 Jan 1949].

Anglo/Norwegian Fisheries Judgment – see Internal Waters, Territorial Sea and Baselines, Historic Titles, Straight Baselines, The Right and Meaning of Innocent Passage, *supra*.

United Kingdom/France Minquiers and Ecrehos Judgment [unanimous], ICJ Rep. 1953, 47, Vice-President J.G. Guerrero, Acting President, Declaration Alvarez, 72, Separate Os Basdevant, 74, Carneiro, 85; Orders, ICJ Rep. 1952, 4, 25, 173, 1953, 4.

See also appraisal of the 1953 *Minquiers and Ecrehos* Judgment, in *Malaysia/Singapore* Hearings, CR 2007/31, 47-48, paras 4-6 [Counsel Crawford, 23 Nov 2007] <www.icj-cij.org>.

The dispute concerned territorial sovereignty over the islets and rocks (in so far as they were capable of appropriation) of the Minquiers and Ecrehos groups, lying between the English Channel Island of Jersey and the northern French coast. Underlying the dispute were interests of the parties with respect to valuable oyster, lobster, ormer, conger and prawn fisheries in the area, as well as other economic concerns, including French plans to generate electricity from the tidal power. While concluding their *compromis* referring a case to the Court, the parties agreed in advance on the modalities for the execution of the Court's Judgment as laid down in the separate UK/France Agreement (with Two Annexed Charts) Regarding Rights of Fishery in Areas of the Ecrehos and Minquires of 30 January 1951, which provided for their equal fisheries rights, and which was ratified simultaneously with their *compromis* on 24 Sep 1951 [121 UNTS 97]. Cf. *Minquiers and Ecrehos* Individual O. Carneiro, ICJ Rep. 1953, 109; Pleadings, Vol.I, 49-50 [UK Memorial], 435-436, 437 [UK Reply], Vol.II, 62-63, 66, 76, 347 [Counsel Fitzmaurice, 18 and 19 Sep and 5 Oct 1953]; and on the 1839 UK/France Convention, see *infra*.

The party held by the Court to have sovereignty – which turned to be Britain – acquired, under the 1951 Agreement, the right to grant fishing concessions within three zones designated solely as fishery limits of maximum half a mile radius, as shown on the two charts. In direct application of the 1953 *Minquiers and Ecrehos* Judgment, the French Cour de Cassation, in 1959 *James Buchanan & Co. v. Société Hanappier-Peyrelongue et Cie and Another* Judgment [39 ILR 425 (Cass. civ. com., 20 October 1959)], although finding the islands "outside the territorial waters of the UK," accepted without question that the islands belonged to Britain.

Subsequently, Article 10 of the European Fisheries Convention of 2 March 1964 [*infra*] (which sanctioned a 12-mile fisheries zone) provided that nothing in this Convention shall prevent the maintance of a special fisheries regime, *inter alia*, as between France and the United Kingdom "in respect of Granville Bay and the Minquiers and the Ecrehos." Under its 1964 Fishery Limits Act implementing the 1964 Convention, the United Kingdom, having at that time a 3-mile TS, claimed specific 12-mile limits around a number of islets, including the Ecrehos and Minquiers. The 1964 Act was largely repealed by the Fishery Limits Act of 22 December 1976. The 1977 *Anglo/French Continental Shelf Delimitation* Decision [18 ILM 397, 463 (1979); 54 ILR 139, 213; RIAA XVIII, 3, 271; No.437/ Stuyt; Charney/ASIL Report No.9-3 (Anderson); Equitable Maritime Boundary Delimitation *supra*], while noting a 12-mile TS possessed by France since 1971 (including off Normandy and Brittany), also referred to the British submission made before the Court of Arbitration that the United Kingdom already had a 12-mile fishery limit around the Channel Islands, established in conformity with the 1964 Convention (para.14; see also paras 13-22). The United Kingdom established its 12-mile TS under the Territorial Sea Act of 1 Oct 1987. On occasion of concluding on 16 August 1994 of the UK/France Agreement on Fishing Rights in Waters Between Guernsey and French Coasts, Britain stated that the Ecrehos, which were the subject of recent action by French fishermen, were within the jurisdiction of Jersey [in force: 12 Sep 1995, 65 *British YIL* 649-651 (1994); 1892 UNTS 344]. Neither their status nor fishing rights around Ecrohos were, according to Britain, in any way affected by the 1994 Agreement. The 1839 and 1951 Agreements were superseded by UK/France Fisheries in the Bay of Granville and Delimitation Agreements of 4 July 2000 [in force: 1 Jan 2004, 2269 UNTS 88, 288; 46 AFDI 524-547, 779 (2000); 71 BYIL 601 (2000)]; Channel Islands' 60th Anniversary of 9 May 2005 <http://news.bbc.co.uk/1/hi/world/europe/4528113.stm>; Charney/ASIL Reports Nos 9-24 & 9-24/Add.1 (D.H. Anderson).

United Kingdom v. Argentina and *United Kingdom v. Chile Antarctica* Orders, ICJ Rep. 1956, 12 and 15, President G.H. Hackworth.

The two parallel cases instituted by British Applications against Argentina and against Chile concerned territorial sovereignty over islands and lands forming part of the Falkland Islands (Malvinas) Dependencies lying in the Antarctica and sub-Antarctica, referred to presently as the Southern Ocean. They included with respect to Argentina the then all Dependencies, i.e., the South Georgia, South Orkney, South Shetland and South Sandwich Islands and the Graham Land (Palmer Peninsula and Palmer Archipelago), and with respect to Chile – the South Shetlands and Graham Land. The important stimulus for exercise of "the long-continued and peaceful display of British sovereignty" in these Dependencies was provided by the development of whaling, sealing and scientific exploration from 1892 onwards. See *Antarctica* Pleadings, 13-21, 24, 27, 45-47, 53-60, 62-66, 68 [UK Applications].

The two *Antarctica* cases were but a diplomatic phase in a longstanding dispute [Sir Humphrey Waldock, 25 *British YIL* 311-353 (1948)]. Previously, the United Kingdom proposed in its two Notes of 17 December 1947 to submit the dispute to the Court, but in their Notes of 28 and 31 January 1948, Argentina and Chile declined to do so [*Antarctica* Pleadings, 35, 72]. Nor did the two states accept the offer made to this effect in the next British Notes of 1948, 1951 and 1953 [*id.* 35, 73], or that made in two British Notes of 21 December 1954 proposing a referral of the dispute to an *ad hoc* Arbitral Tribunal [*id.*]. In view of the present confirmation by both Argentina and Chile, in their Letters of 1 and 2 August 1955, of their refusal to refer the dispute to the ICJ [*id.* 89-93, 94-96], as regretted in a Letter of British Agent Sir Gerald Fitzmaurice of 31 August 1955 [*id.* 97-98; ICJ Rep. 1956, 13-14, 16-17], the Court ordered that both *Antarctica* cases be removed from its General List. The conflicting claims to the Falkland Islands (Malvinas) and South Georgia and South Sandwich Islands, have continued (as was anticipated in Sir Gerald's Letter referring to "future acts"), with a varied intensity, during over five decades since the Applications were filed, against the background of the opening of the Antarctic Treaty System, evolution of modern concepts of the law of the sea, and other developments in the region.

For references to Falkland Dependencies, see also *Eastern Greenland* Pleadings, PCIJ Series C, No.62, 390, 429, 502-504 [Norway's Counter-Memorial], No.63, 778, 907, 909 [Denmark's Reply], 1457 [Norway's Reply], No.64, 1867-1869 [G. Hatt, Terres Antarctiques], No.65, 2355-2365, No.66, 3156-3159 [Counsel Sunde, 12 Dec 1932]; *North Sea* Separate O. Ammoun, ICJ Rep. 1969, 104; *Libya/ Malta* Pleadings, Vol.I, 446, 449 [Malta's Memorial]; *East Timor* Hearings, CR 95/4, 34 [Counsel Higgings, 1 Feb 1995], CR 95/9, 72, 80-82 [Co-Agent Burmester, 8 Feb], CR 95/10, 56 [Counsel Staker, 9 Feb], CR 95/13, 14 [Counsel Higgins, 13 Feb], CR 95/14, 62 [Counsel Crawford, 16 Feb 1995]; *Qatar v. Bahrain (Merits)* Hearings, CR 2000/18, 21-22 [Counsel Sinclair, 21 June 2000]; UN Decolonization

Committee's Resolution of 15 June 2005 <www.un.org/News/Press/docs/2005/gacol3122.doc.htm>; *Guardian* Special Report: the Falklands <www.guardian.co.uk/falklands/0,11707,656744,00.html>; UN Docs A/63/719 (11 Feb 2009), A/63/759 (12 March), A/63/765 (13 March), A/63/833 (27 April), A/63/859 (21 May), A/63/923 (9 July 2009), SPLOS/202 (16 July 2009), A/64/165 (23 July 2009); A/64/466 (2 Oct), A/64/479 (6 Oct), A/64/612 (28 Dec 2009), 6/64/621 (8 Jan 2010); British Start Falklands Oil Drilling of 22 Feb 2010 <http://news.bbc.co.uk/2/hi/americas/8527307.stm & www.nytimes.com/2010/02/22/world/americas/22argentina.html>; Argentina Asks UNSG to Bring UK into Falklands Talks of 24 Feb 2010 <http://news.bbc.co.uk/2/hi/americas/8533860.stm & www.un.org/apps/news/story.asp?NewsID=33888&Cr=&Cr1>.

On 1902 *Argentina/Chile Southern Andes Boundary*, 1966 *Argentina/Chile Frontier*, 1977 *Argentina/Chile Beagle Channel* and 1994 *Argentina/Chile Laguna del Desierto* Awards, see Equitable Maritime Boundary Delimitation *supra*.

Fisheries Jurisdiction (Request for the Indication of Interim Measures of Protection) Orders, ICJ Rep. 1972, 12 [*UK v. Iceland*], 30 [*FRG v. Iceland*], President Sir Muhammad Zafrulla Khan concurring, Joint Declarations Vice-President Ammoun, Forster and Jiménez de Aréchaga, 18 and 36, Dissents Padilla Nervo, 20 and 37;

Orders (first pleadings to be addressed to the Court's jurisdiction), 181 [*UK v. Iceland*], 188 [*FRG v. Iceland*], Joint Dissents Bengzon and de Aréchaga, 184 and 191;

(Jurisdiction) Judgments, ICJ Rep. 1973, 3 [*UK v. Iceland*], 49 [*FRG v. Iceland*], Declarations President Zafrulla Khan, 22 and 66, Separate Os Sir Gerald Fitzmaurice, 24 and 68, Dissents Padilla Nervo, 36 and 81; Orders, 93 and 96;

(Continuance of Interim Measures of Protection) Orders, 302 [*UK v. Iceland*], 313 [*FRG v. Iceland*], President M. Lachs concurring, Declarations Ignacio-Pinto, 304 and 315, Dissents Gros, 306 and 317, Dissents Petrén, 310 and 318;

(Merits) Judgments, ICJ Rep. 1974, 3 [*UK v. Iceland*], 175 [*FRG v. Iceland*], Declarations President Lachs, 35 and 206, Declarations Nagendra Singh, 38 and 211, Separate O. and Declaration Dillard, 53 and 207, Joint Separate Os Forster, Bengzon, de Aréchaga, Nagendra Singh and Ruda, 45 and 217, Separate Os de Castro, 72 and 225, Separate Os Sir Humphrey Waldock, 105 and 227, Declarations Ignacio-Pinto, 35 and 208, Dissents Gros, 125 and 234, Dissents Petrén, 150 and 240, Dissents Onyeama, 164 and 244.

After nearly all states spoke at the UNCLOS III in Caracas in favour of the 200-mile EEZ/EFZ, Iceland which one month prior to this session (and two months prior to the Court's Judgments) already proclaimed, under Law No.45 of 13 May 1974, its 200-mile EFZ, issued its new Regulations No.299 on the Fishery Limits of 15 July 1975, which prohibited all foreign fishing within this limit [UN Doc. ST/LEG/SER.B/18, 331 (1976); 14 ILM 1282 (1975)] and which followed inclusion of an EEZ into ISNT [*UNCLOS III Off. Rec.* Vol.IV, 152 (1975)]. Nevertheless, Iceland concluded on 28 November 1975 Fisheries Agreements with the FRG and Belgium, permitting them to fish in its 200-mile EFZ [15 ILM 1, 43 (1976)].

After expiration on 13 Nov 1975 of the UK/Iceland Interim Agreement of 13 Nov 1973 [12 ILM 1315 (1973); cf. *Tunisia/Libya (Merits)* Dissent Evensen, ICJ Rep. 1982, 307], Iceland was unable to renew it, what led to the most violent "Third Cod War". Following no action taken by the UN Security Council [UN Doc. S/11907 (1975)] and failure of negotiations, the hostilities resumed in Feb 1976. Subsequently, Norway/Iceland Fisheries Agreement was concluded on 10 March 1976, while the UK was granted access to the Icelandic 200-mile EFZ under the Agreement of 1 June 1976 for only a phase-out period until Dec 1976 [15 ILM 875, 878 (1976)]. The EC Council's Hague Resolution of 3 Nov 1976 provided for extension by member states of 200-mile EFZs from 1 Jan 1977 [15 ILM 1425 (1976); cf. Participation by International Organizations *infra*], as followed by legislation of then Twelve, including the UK and the FRG, to this effect.

British/Icelandic Cod Wars Remembered of 10 Oct 2008 <http://news.bbc.co.uk/2/hi/uk_news/politics/7662827.stm>.

1984 *Canada/USA Gulf of Maine* Judgment – see Equitable Maritime Boundary Delimitation *supra*; 1993 *Denmark v. Norway* Judgment – *id.*

Spain v. Canada Fisheries Jurisdiction (Jurisdiction) Judgment, ICJ Rep. 1998, 432, Separate O. of President S.M. Schwebel, 470, Separate Os Oda, 474, Koroma, 486, Kooymans, 489, Dissent Vice-President Weeramantry, 496, Dissents Bedjaoui, 516, Ranjeva, 553, Vereshchetin, 570, Bernardez, 582; Orders, ICJ Rep. 1995, 87, 1996, 58 <www.icj-cij.org>.

Cf. *Legality of Use of Force (Provisional Measures)* Orders in the six cases with Belgium and the Netherlands, para.30, ICJ Rep. 1999, 135, 552, Canada and Portugal, para.29 at 269, 667, Spain and the UK, para.25 at 775, 835-836 and *(Preliminary Objections)* Judgments, ICJ Rep. 2004, 328, 474, 619, 764, 910, 1206, 1351, in the cases with Belgium, para.128, Canada, Italy and France, para.115, the UK and Germany, para.114, the Netherlands, para.127 and Portugal, para.118, and 8 Separate Os Kreca, paras 22, 41-42, 59-60, 76; *Pakistan v. India (Jurisdiction)* Judgment, President G. Guillaume, paras 38, 42, 51 and 55, ICJ. Rep. 2000, 30-31, 33-34; *Southern Bluefin Tuna (Jurisdiction and Admissibility)* Award, President S.M. Schwebel, para.48; Japan's Memorial, paras 4-7, 99, A/NZ Reply, paras 49-51, Hearings, Vol.II [Burmester, 8 May 2000] <www.worldbank.org/icsid>; *Congo v. Belgium Arrest Warrant of 11 April 2000* Judgment, ICJ Rep. 2002, 15, para.34; *Liechtenstein v. Germany (Preliminary Objections)* Dissent Owada, ICJ Rep. 2005, 50, para.9; 2007 *Guyana/Suriname* Award, paras 442-445 <www.pca-cpa.org>; *Nicaragua v. Honduras (Merits)* Judgment, ICJ Rep. 2007, para.108; *Nicaragua v. Colombia (Preliminary Objections)* Hearings, CR 2007/16, 53, para.30 and at 55, para.36 [Counsel Stephen M. Schwebel, 4 June 2007]; Colombia's Preliminary Objections, 134-136 <www.icj-cij.org>; ICJ President Higgins' Statement to the 6th Committee, 31 Oct 2008 <www.un.org/News/Press/docs//2008/gal3355.doc.htm> & <www.icj-cij.org>.

The *Spain v. Canada* Judgment led to Canada's ratification of the 1995 UN Fish Stocks Agreement [*infra*] on 3 August 1999 <www.un.org/Depts/los> and it also induced the parties and the European Community to elaborating specific dispute settlement procedures of the Northwest Atlantic Fisheries Organization. See Reports of the NAFO Working Group on Dispute Settlement Procedures, Copenhagen, 29-31 May 2000, Dartmouth, 12-14 June 2001, NAFO/GC Docs 00/4 (2000) and 01/4 (2001); Reports of the General Council, Helsingor, 29 Jan-1 Feb 2002, Santiago de Compostela, 16-20 Sep 2002, NAFO/GC Docs 02/2 and 02/4 (2002). For Spain's and Canada's Declarations under UNCLOS Article 287 of 15 Jan 1997 and 7 Nov 2003, see *UN LOS Bull.* 14 (2002 No.49) and 15 (2004 No.53); UNGA Adopts Two Oceans Resolutions, UN Doc.GA/10899 of 4 Dec 2009, Canada's Statement at 15-16 <www.un.org/News/Press/docs//2009/ga10899.doc.htm>.

Peru v. Chile Maritime Delimitation – see Equitable Maritime Boundary Delimitation *supra*.

1893 *UK/USA Behring Sea Fur Seal* Award, Arbitral Tribunal: Lord Hannen (UK), J. Thompson (UK), J.M. Harlan (USA), J.T. Morgan (USA), A. de Courcel (France), E. Visconti Venosta (Italy), Gregers Gram (Sweden); No.170/Stuyt; 1 AJIL 742 (1907); 6 AJIL 233 and Supp. 72, 162 (1912); 37 AJIL 562-585 (1943); 71 BYIL 357-373 (2000); RIAA XXVIII, 263. See also *infra*.

1910 *UK/USA North Atlantic Coast Fisheries* Award, PCA/Arbitrators: President H. Lammasch, Jonkheer A.F. de Savornin Lohman, G. Gray, Sir Ch. Fitzpatrick, L.M. Drago; RIAA XI, 167; No.291/Stuyt; 4 AJIL 567, 675, 903, 948 (1910); 5 AJIL 1, 725 and Supp. 93 (1911); 6 AJIL 178 (1912); 7 AJIL 1, 140 and Supp. 41 (1913); 19 RGDIP 421 (1912); Appendix I/Simmonds; *Anglo/Norwegian Fisheries* Pleadings, Vol.II 263-278 (excerpts); PCA 1999, 57; PCA Awards <www.haguejusticeportal.net>. See also *infra*.

1986 *Canada/France Filleting in the Gulf of St. Lawrence* Award, Arbitral Tribunal: President Paul de Visscher, Donat Pharand (Canada), Jean-Pierre Queneudec (France); RIAA XIX, 225; 82 ILR 591; No.444/Stuyt; 90 RGDIP 713 (1986); 91 RGDIP 707 (1987). See also *infra*.

1999 *Southern Bluefin Tuna (Provisional Measures)* Order, ITLOS Cases Nos 3/4 – see Settlement of Disputes – Provisional Measures, Standard of Preventing Serious Harm to the Marine Environment *infra*. Cf. *Southern Bluefin Tuna (Jurisdiction and Admissibility)* Award and Pleadings [*infra*].

2000 *Australia v. Japan; New Zealand v. Japan Southern Bluefin Tuna (Jurisdiction and Admissibility)* Award, Arbitral Tribunal: President Stephen M. Schwebel (USA/ICJ), Chusei Yamada (Japan), Sir Kenneth Keith (New Zealand), Florentino P. Feliciano (Philppines), Per Tresselt (Norway), RIAA XXIII, 1; 39 ILM 1359 (2000); 119 ILR 508 <www.worldbank.org/icsid/bluefintuna/main.htm>; NZ MFA <www.mft.govt.nz/support /legal/disputes/seapol.html>.

See also *infra* and Settlement of Disputes – Preventive Diplomacy A) & D) *infra.*

2006 *Barbados/Trinidad & Tobago (Jurisdiction and Merits)* Award, President S.M. Schwebel <www.pca-cpa.org> – see Eguitable Maritime Boundary Delimitation *supra.*

2001 *EC/Chile Conservation and Sustainable Exploitation of Swordfish Stocks in the South-Eastern Pacific Ocean*, suspended ITLOS Case No.7, President P. Chandrasekhara Rao, ITLOS Rep. 2001, 4; 40 ILM 475 (2001) <www.itlos.org> and WTO Panel, WT/DS193/3 and Add.1 of 6 and 9 April 2001 and <www.europa.eu.int/comm/trade/miti/dispute/swordfish.htm>; Orders further suspending proceedings of 16 Dec 2003 and 29 Dec 2005 until 1 Jan 2008, ITLOS Rep. 2003, 69 and 2005-2007, 3 and Order of 30 Nov 2007 until 1 Jan 2009; *EC/Chile (Discontinuance)* Order of 17 Dec 2009 <www.itlos.org>. Cf. Annex VII *Mox Plant* UK Rejoinder, 54 <www.pca-cpa.org>.

See also Settlement of Disputes – Preventive Diplomacy B) *infra.*

2000 *Panama v. France Camuco, Seychelles v. France M/V Monte Confurco*, 2001 *Belize v. France Grand Prince*, 2002 *Russia v. Australia Volga*, 2004 *Saint Vincent & the Grenadines v. Guinea-Bissau Juno Trader* and 2007 *Japan v. Russia Hoshinmaru* and *Tomimaru* Judgments, ITLOS Cases Nos 5, 6, 8, 11, 13 and 14-15 – see Settlement of Disputes, Prompt Release of Vessels *infra.*

High Seas Fisheries

1958 HSC and HSFC; 1982 UNCLOS, Part VII, Articles 116-120; 1992 UNCED Rio Agenda 21, Chapter 17; 1995 SSA; 2002 WSSD Johannesburg Plan of Implementation, paras 29-31:

Anglo/Norwegian Fisheries Pleadings, Vol.I, 20, 54 [UK Memorial]; Vol.II, 335-336, 408-414 [UK Reply]; *North Sea* Separate Os Jessup, ICJ Rep. 1969, 82-83, Ammoun, 104, 110; Pleadings, Vol.II, 122 [Agent Riphagen, 30 Oct 1968], 243 [Reply by Counsel Waldock to Questions Fitzmaurice, 8 Nov 1968]; *Fisheries Jurisdiction* cases – see *supra*; *Nuclear Tests* Joint Dissents, ICJ Rep. 1974, 370, 522, Dissent Barwick, 434; Pleadings (Australia), 337 [Memorial], 514, 518 [Counsel

Byers, 9 July 1974]; *Gulf of Maine* case – see Equitable Maritime Boundary Delimitation *supra*; *Spain v. Canada Fisheries (Jurisdiction)* Judgment [*supra*].

1999/2000 *Southern Bluefin Tuna* case [*supra*]; 2001 *EC/Chile Swordfish* case [*supra*].

Straddling/Highly Migratory Stocks

1982 UNCLOS, Part V, Articles 63-67, Part VII, Article 116(b), and Annex I; 1992 UNCED Rio Agenda 21, Chapter 17; 1995 SSA; 2002 WSSD Johannesburg Plan of Implementation, paras 29-31:

Gulf of Maine and *Denmark v. Norway* cases – see Equitable Maritime Boundary Delimitation *supra*; *New Zealand v. France* Dissent Weearamantry, ICJ Rep. 1995, 356, Dissent Palmer, 401; 1995 NZ Request (Examination of the Situation), para.24; Hearings, CR 95/19, 81 [Counsel Lauterpacht, 11 Sep 1995]; *Spain v. Canada Fisheries (Jurisdiction)* Judgment, ICJ Rep. 1998, 432 [*supra*]; *United States – Import Prohibition of Certain Shrimp and Shrimp Products* Report AB-1998-4, addressing the protection and conservation of highly migratory species of sea turtles – see Protection and Preservation of the Marine Environment, Obligation to Protect and Preserve the Marine Environment *infra*; 1999 *Southern Bluefin Tuna (Provisional Measures)* Order – see Settlement of Disputes – Provisional Measures, Standard of Preventing Serious Harm to the Marine Environment *infra*; 2000 *Southern Bluefin Tuna (Jurisdiction and Admissibility)* Award – see *supra*; 2001- *EC/Chile Swordfish* case – see *supra*; 2006 *Barbados/Trinidad & Tobago* Award, paras 285-293 & *dispositif* para.385(3) and Equitable Maritime Boundary Delimitation *supra*.

On Canada's special interest in ICNAF/NAFO stocks, see *Gulf of Maine* Pleadings, Vol.I, 90 [Canada's Memorial], Vol.III, 151-152, 160, 418 [Canada's Counter-Memorial], Vol.IV, 45, 298-300 [US Counter-Memorial], Vol.V, 99-109 [Canada's Reply], 432-439, 507-508, 510, 522-524 [US Reply], Vol.VI, 354-357 [Counsel Rashkow, 16 April 1984], Vol.VII, 81 [Counsel Binnie, 4 May], 104 [Counsel Bowett, 5 May], 174-178 [Counsel Feldman, 9 May 1984].

On whaling and sealing (1982 LOSC, Articles 65 and 120), see 1932 *Southeastern Greenland* Orders, 1933 *Eastern Greenland* Judgment and 1956 *Antarctica* Orders *supra*; *Anglo/Norwegian Fisheries* Judgment, ICJ Rep. 1951, 178; Pleadings, Vol. I, 20, 101 [UK Memorial], 242 [Norway's Counter-Memorial]; *IMCO* Pleadings, 52 [Liberia]; *Gulf of Maine* Pleadings, Vol.V, 46 [Canada's Reply]; *Denmark v. Norway* Judgment, ICJ Rep. 1993, 46, 71; Norway's Counter-Memorial, paras 119-131, 572-578, Appendixes 3-4, Denmark's Reply, paras 174-199, Norway's Rejoinder, paras 135-149; Hearings, CR 93/2, 39-40, 56-58 [Counsel Trolle, 12 Jan 1993], CR 93/5, 29-32, 53-55 [Agent Tresselt, 15 Jan 1993]; *Southern Bluefin*

Tuna (Jurisdiction) Hearings, Vol.II [Counsel Irwin, 8 May], Vol.III [Counsel Lauterpacht, 10 May 2000] <www.worldbank.org/icsid>.

On presential sea, see Exclusive Economic (/Fishery) Zone *supra*.

On UK/France Convention for Defining and Regulating the Limits of the Exclusive Right of the Oyster and Other Fishery on the Coasts of Great Britain and France of 2 August 1839 [27 BFSP 983; *Minquiers and Ecrehos* Pleadings, Vol.I, 179-186; as (slightly) modified by the Anglo/French Agreement on the Limits of French Fisheries in Granville Bay of 20 Dec 1928; as superseded by 2000 UK France Agreements *infra*], see *Anglo/Norwegian Fisheries* Pleadings, Vol.I, 61 [UK Memorial], 426-427 [Norway's Counter-Memorial], Vol.II, 476 [UK Reply]; *Minquiers and Ecrehos* ICJ Rep. 1953, 47 – Judgment, 51, 57-58, 66, Individual O. Basdevant, 79, 82; *Minquiers and Ecrehos* Pleadings, Vol.I, 49-54, 56, 58, 119-121 [UK Memorial], 437-495, 556 [UK Reply], Vol.II, 62, 66, 75-77, 80 [Counsel Fitzmaurice, 18 and 19 Sep 1953], 250-256, 262-263, 276 [Agent Gros, 30 Sep], 345 [Counsel Harrison, 5 Oct], 348-351, 354, 358-362 [Fitzmaurice, 5 Oct 1953]; *Fisheries Jurisdiction* Pleadings (UK), 322 [Memorial (Merits)].

On UK/France Fisheries Convention of 11 Nov 1867, Revising the 1839 Convention [ratified by Napoleon III on 18 Dec 1867, but never came into operation, *Minquiers and Ecrehos* Pleadings, Vol.I, 187-208], see *Minquiers and Ecrehos* Judgment, ICJ Rep. 1953, 60; Pleadings, Vol.I, 49, 55 [UK Memorial], 455-464 [UK Reply], Vol.II, 80-82 [Counsel Fitzmaurice, 19 Sep 1953].

On Convention for Regulating the Police of the North Sea Fisheries, The Hague, 6 May 1882 [73 BFSP 39; UN Doc. ST/LEG/SER.B/1, 179 (1951); superseded by the 1964 European Fisheries Convention *infra*], see *SS Lotus* Pleadings, PCIJ Series C, No.13-II, 133 [Agent Bey, 8 Aug 1927], 162 [Agent Basdevant, 9 Aug 1927], 206-207 [France's Memorial], 317 [Turkey's Counter-Memorial], 347 [Observations Fedozzi], 377 [Consultation Fedozzi]; *Access To, Or Anchorage In, The Port of Danzig, of Polish War Vessels* Advisory Opinion, PCIJ Series A/B, No.43, 141 (1931); *Anglo/Norwegian Fisheries* ICJ Rep. 1951, 116 – Judgment, 139, Dissent Sir Arnold McNair, 162, 163, 178-180; *Anglo/Norwegian* Pleadings, Vol.I, 20, 31, 62, 66-67, 172 [UK Memorial], 271-274 [Norway's Counter-Memorial], Vol.II, 96-98 272, 345, 409, 473, 511, 512, 514, 526, 756-757 [UK Reply], Vol.III, 281, 347, 348-350, 362, 364, 427-428, 460-461, 479 [Norway's Rejoinder]; *Minquiers and Ecrehos* Pleadings, Vol.I, 556 [UK Reply]; *IMCO* Pleadings, 88 [Liberia], 355 [Riphagen/NL, 29 April 1960]; *North Sea* Judgment, ICJ Rep. 1969, 13; *North Sea* Pleadings, Vol.I, 218-219 [Denmark's Counter-Memorial], Vol.II, 69 [Agent Jacobsen, 28 Oct 1968]; *Fisheries Jurisdiction (Merits)* Separate Os Waldock, ICJ Rep. 1974, 105-106, 227; Pleadings (UK), 268-269, 322-323 [Memorial (Merits)],

(FRG), 3 [Application], 149-150, 211-212, 245 [Memorial (Merits)]; *Gulf of Maine* Pleadings, Vol.II, 64, 70 [US Memorial].

On UK/Denmark Convention for Regulating the Fisheries Outside Territorial Waters in the Ocean Surrounding the Faroe Islands and Iceland of 24 June 1901 [UN Doc. ST/LEG/SER.B/1, 232 (1951); upon its denunciation by Iceland in 1949, remained partly in force, as amended by UK/Denmark (Faroes) on 27 April 1959, 337 UNTS 416; SER.B/15, 879 (1970)], see *Anglo/Norwegian Fisheries* Pleadings, Vol.I, 31, 63 [UK Memorial], Vol.III, 699; *Fisheries Jurisdiction (Merits)* Judgment, ICJ Rep. 1974, 11, Separate Os Waldock, 105-106, 107, 227; Pleadings (UK), 3 [Application], 27 [Iceland's Memorandum], 269, 340 [Memorial (Merits)], 458-459 [Counsel Silkin, 25 March 1974], 490 [Counsel Slynn, 29 March 1974], (FRG), 3 [Application], 212, 225 [Memorial (Merits)]; 1989 *Guinea-Bissau/Senegal* Award [94 RGDIP 254 (1990)], para.64.

On USA/Canada Treaty for the Protection, Preservation and Extension of the Sockeye Salmon Fisheries in the Fraser River of 26 May 1930 [in force: 28 July 1937, 184 LNTS 305], as superseded by USA/Canada Treaty on Pacific Salmon Fishery of 28 January 1985 [in force: 18 March 1985, 1469 UNTS No.24913], as Amended in 1986/1995, including Agreements of 12 June 1986 [2194 UNTS 399], 13 August 1986 [*id.* 405], 5 August 1987 [*id.* 409], 10 May 1988 [2204 UNTS 613], 19 April 1989 [2204 UNTS 574], 29 June 1990 [2213 UNTS 149] and 12 August 1991 [*id.* 192; *1994/95 Tenth Annual Report of the Pacific Salmon Commission*, 122 (1995) and *1998/99 Fourteenth Annual Report* 99 (1999)], see *Fisheries Jurisdiction* Pleadings (UK), 362 [Memorial (Merits)], (FRG), 246 [Memorial (Merits)]; *Gulf of Maine* Pleadings, Vol.I, 115 [Canada's Memorial], Vol.III, 85-86 [Canada's Counter-Memorial], Vol.V, 438 [US Reply]; *Spain v. Canada* Separate O. Oda, ICJ Rep. 1998, 480, para.12.

On London International Fishery Conference of 1943 [Cmnd 6496], see *Anglo/Norwegian Fisheries* Pleadings, Vol.I, 54 [UK Memorial], 335 [Norway's Counter-Memorial]; *IMCO* Pleadings, 91 [Liberia], 355 [Riphagen/NL, 29 April 1960]; *Gulf of Maine* Pleadings, Vol.VII, 104 [Counsel Bowett, 5 May 1984].

On International Convention for the Regulation of Whaling, Washington, 2 Dec 1946 [in force: 10 Nov 1948, 161 UNTS 72], Protocol of 19 Nov 1956 [in force: 4 May 1959, 338 UNTS 366], and related arrangements [486 UNTS 263; 3 ILM 107 (1964); 71 RGDIP 184 (1972)], see *IMCO* Pleadings, 52 [Liberia]; *Fisheries Jurisdiction* Pleadings (UK), 363, 364 [Memorial (Merits)], 463 [Counsel Silkin, 25 March 1974], (FRG), 247 [Memorial (Merits)]; *Spain v. Canada* Separate O. Oda, ICJ Rep. 1998, 480, para.12; *Southern Bluefin Tuna (Jurisdiction)* Award, para.38(i), 39 ILM 1359 (2000); Hearings, Vol.I [Counsel Lauterpacht, 7 May 2000], Vol.II [Counsel Irwin, 8 May], Vol.III [Lauterpacht, 10 May 2000] <www.worldbank.org/icsid>; Australia Seeks IWC Ban on Japanese whaling in Southern Ocean of 22 Feb 2010 <www.timesonline.co.uk/tol/news/environment/article7035601.ece>.

On Convention on the Inter-American Tropical Tuna Commission of 31 May 1949 [in force: 3 March 1950, 80 UNTS 3], as Amended by the Antigua Convention on the Strengthening of the IATTC of 14 Nov 2003 [in force: 27 August 2010 <www.iattc.org>], see *Fisheries Jurisdiction* Pleadings (UK), 363, 364 [Memorial (Merits)], (FRG), 246, 247 [Memorial (Merits)]; *Gulf of Maine* Pleadings, Vol.III, 86 [Canada's Counter-Memorial]; *Spain v. Canada* Separate O. Oda, ICJ Rep. 1998, 480, para.12.

On Norway/Sweden Fishery Agreement of 20 Dec 1950 [*Minquiers* Pleadings, Vol.I, 593-594], see *Miniquiers and Ecrehos* Pleadings, Vol.I, 478 [UK Reply].

On UK/France Agreement (with Two Annexed Charts) Regarding Rights of Fishery in Areas of the Ecrehos and Minquires of 1951, as superseded by 2000 UK/France Agreements *infra*, see *Minquiers and Ecrehos* Judgment *supra*.

On International Convention for the High Seas Fisheries of the North Pacific Ocean, Tokyo, 9 May 1952 [in force: 12 June 1953, 205 UNTS 65], Protocol of 25 April 1978 [in force: 20 Feb 1979] [superseded as of 21 Feb 1993 by Convention for the Conservation of Anadromous Stocks in the North Pacific Ocean, Moscow, 11 Feb 1992, in force: 16 Feb 1993], see *IMCO* Pleadings, 51 [Liberia]; *North Sea* Separate O. Jessup, ICJ Rep. 1969, 83; *Fisheries Jurisdiction (Merits)* Joint Separate Os, ICJ Rep. 1974, 50 n.1, 222 n.1; Pleadings 362 [Memorial (Merits)], (FRG), 246 [Memorial (Merits)]; *Gulf of Maine* Pleadings, Vol.III, 86 [Canada's Counter-Memorial]; *Spain v. Canada (Jurisdiction)* Separate O. Oda, ICJ Rep. 1998, 480, para.12.

On USA/Canada Convention for the Preservation of the Halibut Fishery of Northern Pacific Ocean of 2 March 1953 [222 UNTS 77], Protocol of 29 March 1979 [32 UST 2483] and 2003 Regulations [www.iphc.washington.edu>, see *Fisheries Jurisdiction* Pleadings (UK), 362 [Memorial (Merits)], (FRG), 246 [Memorial (Merits)]; *Gulf of Maine* Pleadings, Vol.I, 115 [Canada's Memorial], Vol.III, 85-86 [Canada's Counter-Memorial].

On USA/Canada Convention on Great Lake Fisheries of 1954 [in force: 11 October 1955, 6 UST 2837; 238 UNTS 97], as Amended on 5 April 1966 and 19 May 1967 [18 UST 1402; Canada/USA International Joint Commission <www.ijc.org/en/home/main_ accueil.htm>], see *Gulf of Maine* Pleadings, Vol.III, 85 [Canada's Counter-Memorial], Vol.VII, 258-260 [Counsel Colson, 11 May 1984]; Great Lake Biennial Conference, 9-11 June 2005 <www.ijc.org/2005biennial/about_en.php>.

On Japan/USSR Convention on High Seas Fisheries of the North-West Pacific Ocean of 14 May 1956 [AJIL 763 (1959)], see *Fisheries Jurisdiction (Merits)* Joint Separate Os, ICJ Rep. 1974, 50 n.1, 222 n.1; Pleadings (UK), 362 [Memorial (Merits)], (FRG), 246 [Memorial (Merits)].

On North Pacific Fur Seals Convention of 1957 [in force: 9 Feb 1957, 314 UNTS 105], see *Fisheries Jurisdiction* Pleadings (UK), 362 [Memorial (Merits)], (FRG),

246 [Memorial (Merits)]; *Gulf of Maine* Pleadings, Vol.III, 85 [Canada's Counter-Memorial]; *Spain v. Canada* Separate O. Oda, ICJ Rep. 1998, 480, para.12.

On USA/Cuba Shrimp Convention of 1958 [358 UNTS 63], *Fisheries Jurisdiction (Merits)* Separate O. Dillard, ICJ Rep. 1974, 68; Pleadings (UK), 362 [Memorial (Merits)], (FRG), 246 [Memorial (Merits)].

On Convention on Fishing in the Waters of Danube, Bucharest, 29 Jan 1958 [339 UNTS 23], see *Gabcikovo* Judgment, ICJ Rep. 1997, 23; Oral Hearings, CR 97/2 [trans.], 37 [Counsel Kiss, 3 March 1997], CR 97/5 [trans.], 8-9 [6 March], CR 97/11, 21 [Counsel Watts, 27 March 1997].

On Convention on Fishing in the Black Sea of 7 July 1959 [in force: 21 March 1960, 377 UNTS 203], see *Fisheries Jurisdiction* Pleadings (UK), 362 [Memorial (Merits)], (FRG), 246 [Memorial (Merits)].

On Agreement on the Protection of the Salmon Population in the Baltic Sea of 20 Dec 1962 [in force: 1 March 1966, UN Doc. ST/LEG/SER.B/15, 859], see *Fisheries Jurisdiction* Pleadings (UK), 362 [Memorial (Merits)], (FRG), 246 [Memorial (Merits)].

USSR/USA Agreement on Fishing off Alaska of 1964 [4 ILM 176 (1965)], see *Fisheries Jurisdiction* Pleadings (UK), 362 [Memorial (Merits)], (FRG), 246 [Memorial (Merits)].

On European Fisheries Convention, London, 2 March 1964 [581 UNTS 57; originated in the UK initiative and superseded the 1882 North Sea Fisheries Convention *supra*], see *North Sea* Separate O. Jessup, ICJ Rep. 1969, 80, Separate O. Ammoun, 129-130, Dissent Sorensen, 250; *North Sea* Pleadings, Vol.I, 269 [Denmark's Counter-Memorial], 407 [FRG Reply], 461, 490-491 [Common Rejoinder of Denmark/NL]; *Fisheries Jurisdiction* Pleadings (UK), 342-343 [Memorial (Merits)], 459, 475 [Counsel Silkin, 25 March 1974], 505 [Counsel Slynn, 29 March 1974], (FRG), 226-227, 254 [Memorial (Merits)], 360, 366 [Agent Jaenicke, 2 April 1974]; 1977 *Anglo/French* Decision [18 ILM 397 (1979)], paras 14, 129-130, 140, 1978 Decision [*id.* 466]; *Gulf of Maine* Pleadings, Vol.III, 140 [Canada's Counter-Memorial]; *Libya/Malta* Pleadings, Vol.II, 115 n.4 [Libya's Counter-Memorial]; *Denmark v. Norway* Separate O. Oda, ICJ Rep. 1993, 94.

On Japan/Korea Fisheries Agreement of 1965 [4 ILM 1128 (1965)], see *Fisheries Jurisdiction* Pleadings (UK), 362 [Memorial (Merits)], (FRG), 246 [Memorial (Merits)].

On International Convention for the Conservation of Atlantic Tunas, Rio de Janeiro, 14 May 1966 [in force: 21 March 1969, 673 UNTS 63; 6 ILM 293 (1967)], Protocols, Paris, 10 July 1984, and Madrid, 5 June 1992, see *Fisheries Jurisdiction (Merits)* Separate O. Dillard, ICJ Rep. 1974, 68; Pleadings (UK), 361 [Memorial (Merits)], (FRG), 246 [Memorial (Merits)]; *Gulf of Maine* Pleadings, Vol.III, 86 [Canada's Counter-Memorial]; *Spain v. Canada* Separate O. Oda, ICJ Rep. 1998, 480, para.12.

On USA/USSR Agreement on Northeast Pacific Fisheries of 13 Feb 1967 [688 UNTS 157], as extended in 1969 [8 ILM 509 (1969)], 1971 and 1973 [12 ILM 550 (1973)], see *Fisheries Jurisdiction (Merits)* Joint Separate Os, ICJ Rep. 1974, 50 n.1, 222 n.1; Pleadings (UK), 363 [Memorial (Merits)], (FRG), 246 [Memorial (Merits)].

On USA/USSR Agreement on Certain Fishery Problems on the High Seas in the Western Areas of the Middle Atlantic of 25 Nov 1967 [701 UNTS 162; 7 ILM 144 (1968); 8 ILM 502 (1969)], see *Fisheries Jurisdiction (Merits)* Joint Separate Os, ICJ Rep. 1974, 50 n.1, 222 n.1; Pleadings (UK), 362 [Memorial (Merits)], (FRG), 246 [Memorial (Merits)].

On Japan/New Zealand Fisheries Agreement of 1967 [6 ILM 736 (1967)], see *Fisheries Jurisdiction* Pleadings (UK), 363 [Memorial (Merits)], (FRG), 246 [Memorial (Merits)].

On USA/Japan Agreement on Certain Fisheries Off the US Coast and Salmon Fisheries of 23 Dec 1968 [TIAS No.6600], see *Fisheries Jurisdiction (Merits)* Joint Separate Os, ICJ Rep. 1974, 50 n.1, 222 n.1.

On USA/USSR King Crab Fisheries Agreement of 1969 [8 ILM 507 (1969)], see *Fisheries Jurisdiction (Merits)* Separate O. Dillard, 68; Pleadings (UK), 362 [Memorial (Merits)], (FRG), 246 [Memorial (Merits)].

On Convention on the Conservation of the Living Resources of the Southeast Atlantic, Rome, 3 Oct 1969 [in force: 24 October 1971, 801 UNTS 101], see *Fisheries Jurisdiction (Merits)* Separate O. Dillard, 68; Pleadings (UK), 362, 364 [Memorial (Merits)], (FRG), 246 [Memorial (Merits)].

On North American Council on Fishery Investigations (NACFI), established in 1920 by the USA, Canada and Newfoundland and joined in 1922 by France, see *Gulf of Maine* Pleadings, Vol.I, 115, 198 [Canada's Memorial], Vol.II, 28, 44 [US Memorial], Vol.III 150-155 [Canada's Counter-Memorial], Vol.IV, 22, 31, 280, 282 [US Counter-Memorial], Vol.V, 436, 466 [US Reply], Vol.VI, 142 [Counsel Bowett, 5 April 1984], 247 [Agent Robinson, 11 April], Vol.VII, 239, 245 [Counsel Colson, 10 and 11 May 1984], 314, Vol.VIII, 24 [Fig.8], 102 [Fig.14], 164 [Fig.18].

On International Convention for the Northwest Atlantic Fisheries (ICNAF), Washington DC, 8 Feb 1949 [in force: 3 July 1950, 157 UNTS 157; the ICNAF superseded the 1920 NACFI], 1964 Protocol [in force: Dec 1969, 5 ILM 718 (1966)], Protocol of 6 Oct 1970 [UN Doc. ST/LEG/SER.B/19, 481 (1980)], see *Anglo/Norwegian Fisheries* Pleadings, Vol.II, 405-406, 409, 411, 681 [UK Reply], Vol.III, 248-249 [Norway's Rejoinder]; *Fisheries Jurisdiction (Merits)* Separate O. Dillard, ICJ Rep. 1974, 68, Separate Os Waldock, 111, 227, Dissent Gros, 136, 140; *Fisheries Jurisdiction* Pleadings (UK), 74 [Request], 361, 364, 413 [Memorial (Merits)], 454, 463 [Counsel Silkin, 25 March 1974], 500-502 [Counsel Slynn,

29 March 1974], (FRG), 26-27 [Request], 245-246, 247, [Memorial (Merits)], 308-309, 311 [Agent Jaenicke, 28 March 1974]; 1977 *Anglo/French Continental Shelf* Decision [18 ILM 397 (1979)], para.33; *Gulf of Maine* Judgment, ICJ Rep. 1984, 283; *Gulf of Maine* Pleadings, Vol.I, 89-91, 115, 131, 198-199, 264-291, 299-311 [Canada's Memorial], Vol.II, 28-33, 45-46 [US Memorial], Vol.III, 150-162, 191 [Canada's Counter-Memorial], Vol.IV, 23, 30-49, 134-135, 138, 275-306 [US Counter-Memorial], Vol.V, 42, 67, 75, 78, 92, 99-109, 113, 123-124 [Canada's Reply], 436, 466, 471-472, 546, 629-632 [US Reply], Vol.VI, 95 [Counsel Binnie, 4 April 1984], 139-145 [Counsel Bowett, 5 April], 235, 237, 246-247 [Agent Robinson, 11 April], 353-358 [Counsel Rashkow, 16 April], Vol.VII, 16-17 [Agent Legault, 3 May], 79-82, 103-104 [Binnie, 4 and 5 May], 239-240, 245-258 [Counsel Colson, 10 and 11 May 1984], 311-319, Vol.VIII, 11 [Fig.22], 25 [Fig.9], 103 [Fig.15], 164 [Fig.18]; *Spain v. Canada (Jurisdiction)* Judgment, ICJ Rep. 1998, 461, para.70, Separate O. Oda, 476, 480, paras 5, 12; Pleadings, 221-222 [Canada's Counter-Memorial].

The USA withdrew from the ICNAF on 31 Dec 1976.

On Convention on Future Multilateral Cooperation in the Northwest Atlantic Fisheries (NAFO), Ottawa, 24 Oct 1978 [in force: 1 Jan 1979, OJEC L 378/1 (1978); the NAFO superseded the 1949 ICNAF], as Amended (Annex III) on 1 Jan 1980, 9 Oct 1987 and 13 Sep 1996 [*Spain v. Canada* Pleadings, 169-206], see *Gulf of Maine* Pleadings, Vol.I, 198-199, 205-210 [NAFO's Annex III], Vol.II, 73 [US Memorial], Vol.III, 151-152 [Canada's Counter-Memorial], Vol.IV, 275 n.1, 304 n.2 [US Counter-Memorial], Vol.V, 67, 73 [Reply of Canada], 436, 466 [US Reply], Vol.VII, 80 [Counsel Binnie, 4 May 1984], 239, 254, 256 [Counsel Colson, 10 and 11 May 1984], Vol.VIII, 107 [Fig.19], 164 [Fig.18]; *Denmark v. Norway* Hearings, CR 93/5, 53 [Agent Tresselt, 15 Jan 1993]; *Spain v. Canada Fisheries (Jurisdiction)* Judgment, ICJ Rep. 1998 [*supra*] and Pleadings; *Southern Bluefin Tuna (Jurisdiction)* Japan's Memorial, paras 4-7, 99, A/NZ Reply, paras 49-51, Hearings, Vol.II [Burmester, 8 May 2000] <www.worldbank.org/icsid>; 2003 OSPAR *Mox Plant* Dissent Griffith, para.24 <www.pca-cpa.org>.

On Canada/USA bilateral and other regional treaties, see *Gulf of Maine* Pleadings, Vol.I, 115 [Canada's Memorial], Vol.III, 85-87 [Canada's Counter-Memorial], Vol.V, 438, 510 [US Reply], Vol.VII, 258-263 [Counsel Colson, 11 May 1984].

On North-East Atlantic Fisheries Convention (NEAFC), London, 24 Jan 1959 [in force: 27 June 1963, 486 UNTS 157] [1959 NEAFC superseded the Convention for the Regulation of the Meshes of Fishing Nets and the Size Limits of Fish, 5 April 1946, in force: 15 April 1953, 231 UNTS 199, which superseded the International Convention for the Regulation of the Meshes of Fishing Nets and the Size Limits of Fish, 23 March 1937, Cmnd 5494; cf. *IMCO* Pleadings, 90 (Liberia)], see *Fisheries Jurisdiction (Jurisdiction)* Judgment, ICJ Rep. 1973, 6, Separate Os Fitzmaurice, 26, 70, *(Merits)* Judgments, ICJ Rep. 1974, 6-7, 16, 26, 28, 31, 35, 186, 196, 200-201, 206, Separate O. Dillard, 68-69, Separate Os Waldock, 111, 124, 227, Dissent Gros, 136, 138, 140, Dissent Petren, 169, Dissent Onyeama, 172; *Fisheries Jurisdiction* Pleadings (UK), 8, 10 [Application], 74 [Request], 149 [Memorial (Jurisd.)], 270-271, 273, 296-308, 364, 365, 373, 374, 379-381 [Memorial (Merits)], 454-456, 463, 472-476 [Counsel Silkin, 25 March 1974], 490-492, 500-504, 507 [Counsel Slynn, 29 March 1974], (FRG), 5-6, 11 [Application], 26-29 [Request], 179-190, 231, 245, 246-247 [Memorial (Merits)], 309, 311 [Agent Jaenicke, 28 March 1974], 365 [Jaenicke, 2 April 1974]; 1977 *Anglo/French Continental Shelf* Decision [18 ILM 397 (1979)], para.33; *Gulf of Maine* Pleadings, Vol.IV, 290 [US Counter-Memorial]; *Spain v. Canada (Jurisdiction)* Judgment, ICJ Rep. 1998, 461, para.70, Separate O. Oda, 480, para.12.

On Convention on Future Multilateral Cooperation in the North-East Atlantic Fisheries (NEAFC), London, 18 Nov 1980 [in force: 17 March 1982, OJEC L 227/22 (1981); the 1980 NEAFC superseded the 1959 NEAFC], see *Gulf of Maine* Pleadings, Vol.III, 154, 170 [Canada's Counter-Memorial], Vol.VII, 261-262 [Counsel Colson, 11 May 1984]; *Spain v. Canada* Pleadings, 62 n.65 [Spain's Memorial].

For NEAFC Headquarters Agreement, London, 18 Feb 1999 [in force: upon signature], see 2068 UNTS 217.

On Canada/Norway Agreement on Sealing and the Conservation of the Seal Stocks in the Northwest Atlantic of 1971, see *Fisheries Jurisdiction (Merits)* Separate O. Dillard, 68; Pleadings (UK), 362 [Memorial (Merits)], (FRG), 246 [Memorial (Merits)].

On Convention for the Conservation of Antarctic Seals, London, 1 June 1972 [in force: 11 March 1978, 11 ILM 251 (1972)], see *Southern Bluefin Tuna (Jurisdiction)* Japan's Memorial, para.176 <www.worldbank.org/icsid>.

On Protocol 6 (Article 2) to the 1972 EC/Iceland Free Trade Agreement and on the 1973 EC/Norway Agreement, see Participation by International Organizations *infra*.

On Brazil/USA Shrimp Conservation Agreement of 1972 [11 ILM 453 (1972)], see *Fisheries Jurisdiction (Merits)* Separate O. Dillard, 68; Pleadings (UK), 362 [Memorial (Merits)], (FRG), 246 [Memorial (Merits)].

On Iceland/Norway/USSR Agreement on the Regulation of the Fishing of the Atlanto-Scandian Herring of 1972, *Fisheries Jurisdiction (Merits)* Separate O. Dillard, 68; Pleadings (UK), 362 [Memorial (Merits)], 463 [Counsel Silkin, 25 March 1974], (FRG), 246 [Memorial (Merits)].

On Convention on Fishing and Conservation of the Living Resources in the Baltic Sea and the Belts, Gdansk, 13 Sep 1973 [in force: 28 July 1974, 12 ILM 1291 (1973)], see *Spain v. Canada (Jurisdiction)* Judgment, ICJ Rep. 1998, 461, para.70.

On UK/Faroes Fisheries Arrangement of 18 Dec 1973 [in force: 1 Jan 1974, 925 UNTS No.I-13185], see *Fisheries Jurisdiction (Merits)* Judgments, ICJ Rep. 1974, 26, 28, 195; Pleadings (UK), 455-456 [Counsel Silkin, 25 March 1974], 500-501, 502-503 [Counsel Slynn, 29 March 1974], (FRG), 364-365 [Agent Jaenicke, 2 April 1974].

On Agreement on the Regulation of the Fishing of North-East Arctic Cod of 15 March 1974 [(1974) UKTS No.35], see *Fisheries Jurisdiction (Merits)* Judgments, ICJ Rep. 1974, 26, 28, 195; Pleadings (UK), 503-504 [Counsel Slynn, 29 March 1974], (FRG), 365 [Agent Jaenicke, 2 April 1974].

On Convention of the Conservation of Antarctic Marine Living Resources (CCAMLR), Canberra, 20 May 1980 [in force: 7 April 1982, 19 ILM 837 (1980); 1329 UNTS 47], see *Gulf of Maine* Pleadings, Vol.IV, 132 [US Counter-Memorial], Vol.V, 447 [US Reply], Vol.VI, 277 [Counsel Stevenson, 12 April 1984]; *Gabcikovo* Oral Hearings, CR 97/2 [trans.], 12 n.11 [Agent Szenasi, 3 March 1997]; *Southern Bluefin Tuna (Jurisdiction)* Japan's Memorial, paras 37, 39-46, 137, A/NZ Reply, para.137 <www.worldbank.org/icsid>; 2000 *Panama v. France Camuco* Judgment, Dissents Anderson, Vukas and Wolfrum, and *Seychelles v. France M/V Monte Confurco* Judgment, 2001 *Belize v. France Grand Prince* Judgment and 2002 *Russia v. Australia Volga* Judgment, ITLOS Cases Nos 5, 6, 8 and 11 – see Settlement of Disputes, Prompt Release of Vessels and Crews *infra*; 2007 *Japan v. Russia Hoshinmaru (Prompt Release)* Separate O. Yanai, para.2, Case No.14 <www.itlos.org>.

On Convention for the Conservation of Salmon in the North Atlantic Ocean of 2 March 1982 [in force: 1 Oct 1983, 1338 UNTS 33], see *Gulf of Maine* Pleadings, Vol.III, 86 [Canada's Counter-Memorial]; *Spain v. Canada* Pleadings, 62 n.65 [Spain's Memorial].

On Japan/Russia Agreement on the Mutual Relations in the Field of Fisheries off the Coasts of the Two Countries of 7 Dec 1984 [1402 UNTS 272; 28 JAIL 297 (1985)] and Protocol of 14 Dec 2006, see 2007 *Japan v. Russia Hoshinmaru (Prompt Release)* Judgment <www.itlos.org>.

On Japan/Russia Agreement on Cooperation in the Field of Fisheries of 12 May 1985 [1402 UNTS 302; 29 JAIL 283 (1986)] and Protocol of 26 April 2007, see 2007 *Japan v. Russia Hoshinmaru (Prompt Release)* Judgment <www.itlos.org>.

On 1985 USA/Canada Pacific Salmon Fishery Treaty – see 1930 USA/Canada Salmon Fishery Treaty *supea*

On 1985 EC/Denmark(Greenland) Fisheries Agreement, see Participation by International Organizations *infra*.

On 1988 and 1992 EC/Morocco Fisheries Agreement, see Participation by International Organizations *infra*.

On Denmark(Greenland)/Iceland/Norway Agreement on the Capelin Stock of 12 June 1989, as extended until 30 April 1994 [Denmark's Memorial, Annex 17; GJM 92/2 Add., Annex 104 (1992)], see *Denmark v. Norway* Judgment, ICJ Rep. 1993, 71; Denmark's Memorial, paras 90-91, Denmark's Reply, paras 154-156; Hearings, CR 93/1Corr., 11 [Agent Lehmann, 11 Jan 1993], CR 93/2, 53-54 [Counsel Trolle, 12 Jan], CR 93/5, 27, 55, 64 [Agent Tresselt, 15 Jan 1993].

On Convention for the Prohibition of Fishing with Long Driftnets in the South Pacific Ocean, Wellington, 24 Nov 1989 [in force: 17 May 1991, 29 ILM 1449 (1990)], Protocols I and II, Noumea, 20 Oct 1990 [in force: 28 Feb 1992 and 5 Oct 1993, 29 ILM 1462, 1463 (1990)], see 1997 *M/V Saiga (Prompt Release)* Judgment [37 ILM 360 (1998)], para.57, Dissent Wolfrum and Yamamoto, para.23; *Southern Bluefin Tuna (Jurisdiction)* Hearings, Vol.I [Counsel Sir Elihu Lauterpacht, 7 May 2000] <www.worldbank.org/icsid>.

On Canada/Denmark(Greenland) Memorandum on Conservation of Narwhal and Beluga Whales of 7 Dec 1989 [28 *Canadian YIL* 467 (1990)], see *Denmark v. Norway* Hearings, CR 93/2, 32 [Counsel Lynge, 12 Jan 1993].

On 1990 Barbados/Trinidad & Tobago Fishing Agreement, see 2006 *Barbados/Trinidad & Tobago (Jurisdiction and Merits)* Award, President S.M. Schwebel – Equitable Maritime Boundary Delimitation *supra*.

On Agreement on Cooperation in Research, Conservation and Management of Marine Mammals in the North Atlantic (NAMMCO), Nuuk, 9 April 1992 [in force: 8 July 1992, *UM LOS Bull.* 66 (1994 No.26)], see *Denmark v. Norway* Hearings, CR 93/1Corr., 14-15 [Agent Lehmann, 11 Jan 1993], CR 93/2, 58 [Counsel Trolle, 12 Jan], CR 93/5, 27, 57 [Agent Tresselt, 15 Jan 1993].

On Treaty on Cooperation in Fisheries Surveillance and Law Enforcement in the South Pacific Region, Niue, 9 July 1992 [in force: 20 May 1993, 32 ILM 136 (1993)], see *Southern Bluefin Tuna (Jurisdiction)* Japan's Memorial, para.141, Hearings, Vol.III [Question 9 of Arbitrators, 10 May 2000], Written Answers of the Parties to Question 9 [26 May 2000] <www.worldbank.org/icsid>.

On Arrangement for the Management of the Western Pacific Purse Seine Fishery, Palau, 28 Oct 1992 [in force: 8 Dec 1995], see *Southern Bluefin Tuna (Jurisdiction)* Hearings, Vol.I [Counsel Sir Elihu Lauterpacht, 7 May 2000] <www.worldbank.org/icsid>.

On 1993 Convention for the Conservation of Anadromous Stocks in the North Pacific Ocean, see 1952 International Convention for the High Seas Fisheries of the North Pacific Ocean *supra*.

On Convention for the Conservation of Southern Bluefin Tuna, Canberra, 10 May 1993 [in force: 20 May 1994, 1819 UNTS 360; *UN LOS Bull.* 57 (1994

No.26); *Southern Bluefin Tuna* Award, para.23] and Australia/CSBT Commission Headquarters Agreement, 20 January 1998 [in force: 10 March 1999, 2076 UNTS 528], see *Southern Bluefin Tuna (Provisional Measures)* Order, President T.A. Mensah, ITLOS Cases Nos 3 and 4, 38 ILM 1624 (1999) <www.itlos.org>; 2000 *Southern Bluefin Tuna (Jurisdiction)* Pleadings and Award, President S.M. Schwebel, 39 ILM 1359 (2000) <www.worldbank.org/icsid>; 2001 *Ireland v. UK Mox Plant (Provisional Measures)* Separate O. Vice-President Nelson, para.5; Oral Hearings, ITLOS/PV.01/07, 11-12 [Counsel Lowe, 19 Nov 2001] <www.itlos.org>.

On FAO Agreement to Promote Compliance with International Conservation and Management Measures by Fishing Vessels on the High Seas, Rome, 24 Nov 1993 [in force: 24 April 2003, 2221 UNTS 91; 33 ILM 968 (1994); 90 AJIL 267 (1996)], see *Gabcikovo* Hearings, CR 97/2 [trans.], 12 n.11 [Agent Szenasi, 3 March 1997]; *Spain v. Canada (Jurisdiction)* Judgment, ICJ Rep. 1998, 461, para.70, Dissents Bedjaoui, 544, paras 75-77, Ranjeva, 562-565, paras 23-25, 30, Vereshchetin, 577, para.15, Torres Bernardez, 705, para.339, at 716-717, paras 375, 377, at 721, para.386; Pleadings, 295 n.301 [Canada's Counter-Memorial], 511 [Co-Agent Hankey, 11 June 1998] <www.icj-cij.org>; *M/V Saiga* Judgment, 38 ILM 1323 (1999), para.85; *Southern Bluefin Tuna (Jurisdiction)* Japan's Memorial, para.141, Hearings, Vol.I [Counsel Lauterpacht, 7 May 2000] <www.worldbank.org/icsid>.

On Convention on the Conservation and Management of Pollock Resources in the Central Bering Sea of 16 June 1994 [in force: 8 Dec 1995, 34 ILM 67 (1995)], see *Southern Bluefin Tuna (Jurisdiction)* Japan's Memorial, para.37 <www.worldbank.org/icsid>.

On Eritrea/Yemen Memorandum of Understanding on Cooperation in the Areas of Maritime Fishing, Trade and Transportation of 1994, see 1999 *Eritrea/Yemen Maritime Delimitation (Phase II)* Award, paras 29, 90, 107, 111, and Annexes II & III [40 ILM 983 (2001) <www.pca-cpa.org>].

On 1994 UK/France Agreement on Fishing Rights in Waters Between Guernsey and French Coasts, see *Minquiers and Ecrehos* Judgment *supra*.

On 1995 EC/Canada Fisheries Agreement, see Participation by International Organizations *infra*.

On UN Agreement for the Implementation of the Provisions of the United Nations Convention on the Law of the Sea of 10 Dec 1982 Relating to the Conservation and Management of Straddling Fish Stocks and Highly Migratory Fish Stocks (UN 1995 Fish Stocks Agreement), New York, 4 Dec 1995 [in force: 11 Dec 2001, 2167 UNTS 3; 34 ILM 1542 (1995); 90 AJIL 270 (1996)], see *Spain v. Canada (Jurisdiction)* Judgment, ICJ Rep. 1998, 432, paras 20, 64-65, 70, 81, Separate O. Oda, paras 14-15, Dissents Vice-President Weeramantry, para.39, Bedjaoui, para.89, Ranjeva, paras 23-30, Vereshchetin, paras 14-16, Torres Bernardez, paras

180, 339, 363, 376-378, 386, 396, 408-409; Pleadings, 44-45, 100-104, 123-126, 137 [Spain's Memorial], 249-250, 265, 294 n.301 [Canada's Counter-Memorial], Hearings, CR 98/9 [trans.], 31-32 [Counsel Rodriguez, 9 June 1998], CR 98/10, 16 [Counsel Highet, 10 June], CR 98/11 [trans.], 5, 16 [Agent Kirsch, 11 June], 35 [Co-Agent Hankey], 59-60 [Counsel Willis], CR 98/12, 11 [12 June], CR 98/14 [Hankey, Willis, 17 June 1998]; *M/V Saiga* Judgment, 38 ILM 1323 (1999), paras 85, 156, Separate O. Nelson, n.4; *Southern Bluefin Tuna (Provisional Measures)* Separate Os Laing, para.19, Treves, paras 10-11 [38 ILM 1624 (1999)]; *Southern Bluefin Tuna (Jurisdiction)* Award, paras 38(i) and 71, 39 ILM 1359 (2000); Japan's Memorial, paras 143, 172, A/NZ Reply, para.70, 178, Hearings, Vol.I [Counsel Lauterpacht, Lowe, 7 May 2000], Vol.II [Counsel Burmester, Irwin, Jennings, 8 May], Vol.IV [Agent Caughley, 11 May 2000] <www.worldbank.org/icsid>; 2002 *Belize /Guatemala* OAS Proposals, B-para.8 <www.belize-guatemala.gov .bz>; 2002 *Russia v. Australia Volga* Dissent Shearer, para.11, 42 ILM 159 (2003); Annex VII *Mox Plant* UK Counter-Memorial, 141, 153 <www.pca-cpa.org>. See also FAO Agreement on Port State Measures to Prevent, Deter and Eliminate Illegal, Unreported and Unregulated Fishing of 25 Nov 2009 <www.un.org/apps/ news/story.asp?NewsID=33064&Cr=fishing&Cr1 & www.fao.org/news/story/en/ item/37627/icode/>; UNGA Adopts Two Oceans Resolutions, UN Doc.GA/10899 of 4 Dec 2009 <www.un.org/News/Press/docs//2009/ga10899.doc.htm>.

On Inter-American Convention for the Protection and Conservation of Sea Turtles, Bahia, 5 Sep 1996 [in force: 2 May 2001, 2164 UNTS 29; 12 IJMCL 554 (1997)], see *US – Import Prohibition of Certain Shrimp and Shrimp Products* Report AB-1998-4, WTO Appellate Body, WT/DS58/AB/R, 12 October 1998, paras 167-171, 38 ILM 100 (1999); 94 AJIL 361 (2000); Report AB-2001-4, WT/ DS58/AB/RW, 22 October 2001, paras 111-134, 41 ILM 149 (2001); 96 AJIL 685 (2002).

On Agreement on the Conservation of Cetaceans of Black Sea, Mediterranean Sea and Contiguous Atlantic Ocean, Monaco, 24 Nov 1996 [in force: 1 June 2001, 2183 UNTS 304; 36 ILM 777 (1997)], see *Southern Bluefin Tuna (Jurisdiction)* Japan's Memorial, paras 37, 140, Hearings, Vol.III [Question 9 of Arbitrators, 10 May 2000], Written Answers of the Parties to Question 9 [26 May 2000] <www .worldbank.org/icsid>.

On Eritrea/Yemen Treaty on the Joint Committee for Bilateral Cooperation of 16 October 1998, see 1999 *Eritrea/Yemen Maritime Delimitation (Phase II)* Award, paras 29, 90, 107, 111, and Annexes II & III [40 ILM 983 (2001) <www .pca-cpa.org>].

On Iceland/Norway/Russia Fisheries (Barents Sea Loophole) Agreement and Protocol, Saint Petersburg, 15 May 1999 [in force: 15 July 1999, 2070 UNTS 204; 2073 UNTS 253; 14 IJMCL 484 (1999)], see *Southern Bluefin Tuna (Jurisdiction)*

Hearings, Vol.I [Counsel Lauterpacht, 7 May 2000] <www.worldbank.org/icsid>.

On 2000 UK/France Fisheries in the Bay of Granville and Delimitation (France/Jersey) Agreements (superseding 1839 and 1951 UK/France Agreements *supra*), see *Minquiers and Ecrehos* Judgment *supra.*

On Memorandum of Understanding on the Conservation of Marine Sea Turtles and Their Habitats of the Indian Ocean and Southeast Asia, 14 July 2000 [in force: 1 September 2001 <www.wcmc.org.uk/cms/TurtlesSEA_MOU_intro.htm>], see *US – Import Prohibition of Certain Shrimp and Shrimp Products* Report AB-2001-4, WT/DS58/AB/RW, 22 Oct 2001, paras 131-134, 41 ILM 149 (2001); 96 AJIL 685 (2002).

On Framework Agreement for the Conservation of Living Marine Resources of the High Seas of the South-East Pacific, Galapagos, 14 August 2000 [*UN LOS Bull.* 70 (2001 No.45)] and Modification Protocol of Agreement's Article 19(1) of 27 Nov 2003, see suspended *EC/Chile Swordfish*, ITLOS Case No.7, 40 ILM 475 (2001), WTO Panel, WT/DS193/3 and Add.1, 6 and 9 April 2001 <www.europa.eu.int/comm/trade/miti /dispute/swordfish.htm>; Annex VII *Mox Plant* UK Counter-Memorial, 153; Hearings, 9 [Counsel Plender, 12 June 2003] <www.pca-cpa.org>; ITLOS Orders of 16 Dec 2003, 29 Dec 2005, 11 Dec 2008 and 15 Dec 2009 <www.itlos.org>.

On 1853 *UK/USA The Washington* Award, see Internal Waters, Territorial Sea and Baselines, Bays, and Regime of Islands *supra.*

On 1877 *UK/USA Fishery Rights (Halifax Commission)* [No.96/Stuyt], see *Gulf of Maine* Pleadings, Vol.I, 190-192 [Canada's Memorial], Vol.II, 27 [US Memorial].

On 1888 *The Araunah* [82 BFSP 1058], see *SS Lotus* PCIJ Series A, No.10 (1927) – Dissent Moore, 80-81, 83; *Gulf of Maine* Pleadings, Vol.V, 648, 651, 652 [US Reply].

On 1893 *UK/USA Behring Sea Fur Seal* Award [*supra*], see *SS Lotus* PCIJ Series A, No.10 (1927) – Dissent Moore, 89; *Eastern Greenland* Pleadings, 491 [Norway's Counter-Memorial]; *Anglo/Norwegian Fisheries* Pleadings, Vol.I, 270, 352 [Norway's Counter-Memorial], Vol.II, 79-80, 465, 602 [UK Reply], Vol.III, 479, 485-486 [Norway's Rejoinder]; *Nuclear Tests* Pleadings (Australia), 339-340 [Memorial]; *Gulf of Maine* Pleadings, Vol.V, 510 [US Reply]; *Denmark v. Norway* Oral Hearings, CR 93/5, 29 [Agent Tresselt, 15 Jan 1993]; *Gabcikovo* Hearings, CR 97/4, 18 [Counsel Crawford, 5 March 1997], CR 97/9, 65-66 [Counsel McCaffrey, 25 March], CR 97/10, 10-12, 15 [26 March 1997]; Annex VII *Mox Plant* UK Rejoinder, 135 <www.pca-cpa.org>; 2006 *Barbados/Trinidad & Tobago*

(Jurisdiction and Merits) Award, para.134; Barbados' Memorial, para.120 <www.pca-cpa.org>; 2009 *Abyei Boundary* Award, para.759 <www.pca-cpa.org>.

On 1902 *USA v. Russia Cape Horn Pigeon, James Hamilton Lewis, C.H. White & Kate and Anna* Award [RIAA IX, 59; No.236/Stuyt; 22 AJIL 509 (1928); Appendix/Simmonds], see 2006 *Barbados/Trinidad & Tobago* Award, para.291 n.27 <www.pca-cpa.org>.

On 1906 *Mortensen v. Peters (The Niobe*; Moray Firth) Judgment [14 S.L.T. 227; (1906) 8 F. (Ct. of Sess.) 93; 43 S.L.R. 872; 1 AJIL 526 (1907); No.68/Simmonds], see *Anglo/Norwegian Fisheries* Dissent Read, ICJ Rep. 1951, 192; Pleadings, Vol.I, 64, 92 [UK Memorial], Vol.III, 252, 328-330 [Norway's Rejoinder], Vol.IV, 87-88 [Agent Sir Eric Beckett, 27 Sep 1951]; *Tunisia/Libya* Pleadings, Vol.IV, 338 [Libya's Reply].

On 1909 *Norway v. Sweden Grisbadarna* Award, see Equitable Maritime Boundary Delimitation *supra.*

On 1909 and 1910 Judgments on fishing rights (the Hawar Islands) of Bahraini courts, see *Qatar v. Bahrain (Merits)* Oral Hearings, CR 2000/8, 26 [Counsel Shankardass, 5 June 2000], 32 [Counsel Sinclair], CR 2000/13, 16, 46 [Counsel Volterra, 13 June 2000].

On 1910 *UK/USA North Atlantic Coast Fisheries* Award [*supra*], see *Corfu Channel* Dissent Krylov, ICJ Rep. 1949, 74, Dissent Azevedo 101; *Corfu* Pleadings, Vol.II, 137 [Counter-Memorial of Albania], 293 [UK Reply], Vol.III, 274-275, 276 [Agent Sir Eric Beckett, 11 Nov 1948], 377, 382, 386 [Counsel Cot, 18 Nov 1948], Vol.IV, 543, 553 [Beckett, 18 Jan 1949], 673 [Cot, 22 Jan 1949]; *Anglo/Norwegian Fisheries* Dissent Read, ICJ Rep. 1951, 188; *Anglo/Norwegian* Pleadings, Vol.I, 63-64, 69 [UK Memorial], 423-424, 427-437, 443, 444, 450, 477-478, 504-506, 554-555, 569, 573 [Norway's Counter-Memorial], Vol.II, 451, 468, 471-473, 475-477, 479-488, 527-528, 562-564, 576, 602-603, 617-619, 622, 629, 638 [UK Reply], Vol.III, 318, 322-328, 341, 356, 486 [Norway's Rejoinder], Vol.IV, 72, 82-85, 87 [Agent Sir Eric Beckett, 27 Sep 1951], 268, 272-275, 507 [Counsel Bourquin, 11 and 26 Oct 1951]; *US Nationals in Morocco* Pleadings, Vol.I, 65-67 [France's Memorial], Vol.II, 172-173 [Agent Gros]; *Minquiers and Ecrehos* Pleadings, Vol.II, 88 [Counsel Fitzmaurice, 21 Sep 1953]; *North Sea* Separate O. Ammoun, ICJ Rep. 1969, 113 n.4; *Fisheries Jurisdiction* Pleadings (UK), 489 [Counsel Slynn, 29 March 1974]; *Tunisia/Libya* Pleadings, Vol.IV, 117 n.2, 322-324, 327, 337-338 [Libya's Reply]; *Gulf of Maine* Pleadings, Vol.I, 195-197 [Canada's Memorial], Vol.II, 25 [US Memorial], Vol.V, 99 n.79 [Canada's Reply], 509, 517 [US Reply]; 1986 *Canada/France* Award [*supra*]; *Gulf of Fonseca* Judgment, ICJ Rep. 1992, 591-592, Dissent Oda, 736, 747, 750-751; *Libya/Chad Territorial Dispute* Separate O. Ajibola, ICJ Rep. 1994, 72; *M/V Saiga* Counter-Memorial (M) Guinea, para.116, Reply (M) Saint Vincent and the Grenadines, para.63 n.1; *Cameroon v. Nigeria (Preliminary Objections)* Judgment, ICJ Rep. 1998, 296; *Spain v. Canada (Jurisdiction)* Dissent Torres Bernardez, ICJ Rep. 1998, 682-683, para.270; *Panama v. France Camuco* Separate O. Nelson, n.5 [39 ILM 666 (2000) <www.itlos.org>]; *Qatar v. Bahrain (Merits)* Joint Dissent Bedjaoui, Ranjeva, Koroma, para.94 n.27, ICJ Rep. 2001, 175; *Cameroon v. Nigeria; Equatorial Guinea Intervening (Merits)* Dissent Ajibola, para.9, ICJ Rep.2002, 541 <www.icj-cij.org>; 2002 *Russia v. Australia Volga* Separate O. Cot, para.20 <www.itlos.org>; *Costa Rica v. Nicaragua San Juan River* Hearings, CR 2009/4, 33-34, para.63 [Counsel Brownlie, 5 March 2009] <www.icj-cij.org>.

On 1927 *The Deutschland* and 1934 *The St. Just* Judgments, see Internal Waters, Territorial Sea and Baselines – Straight Baselines, *supra*.

On 1954 *In Re Sauger et al.* Judgment, see Exclusive Economic (/Fishery) Zone – Evolution *supra*.

On 1962 *Denmark/UK The Red Crusader (The Niels Ebbesen)* Report of the Commission of Inquiry, see Use of Force in Enforcement at Sea *infra*.

On 1986 *Canada/France Filleting in the Gulf of St. Lawrence* Award [*supra*], see *Gulf of Fonseca* Oral Hearings, C 4/CR 91/4 [trans.], 33 [Counsel Weil, 18 April 1991]; *Canada/France* Award, para.86 [31 ILM 1173-1174 (1992)]; *M/V Saiga* Dissent Ndiaye, [38 ILM 1323 (1999)], para.36; Memorial (M) Saint Vincents, para.133, Counter-Memorial (M) Guinea, paras 107, 116 n.45; *Southern Bluefin Tuna (Jurisdiction)* A/NZ Reply, para.148 n.164 <www.worldbank.org /icsid>; 2002 *Russia v. Australia Volga* Separate O. Cot, paras 19-20 <www.itlos.org>; Annex VII *Mox Plant* UK Counter-Memorial, 145 <www.pca-cpa.org>; *Congo v. France (Provisional Measures)* Dissent de Cara, ICJ Rep. 2003, 140 n.68 <www .icj-cij.org>; 2006 *Barbados/Trinidad & Tobago* Award, para.291 n.26 <www .pca-cpa.org>; *Costa Rica v. Nicaragua San Juan River* Hearings, CR 2009/4, 52, para.6 n.70 [Counsel Pellet, 5 March 2009] <www.icj-cij.org>.

On 2000 *Southern Bluefin Tuna* Award [*supra*], see 2001 *Mox Plant (Provisional Measures)* Separate O. Vice-President Nelson, paras 5-7 [41 ILM 405 (2002)]; Annex VII *Mox Plant (Jurisdiction)* Hearings, 28, 32 [Counsel Plender, 12 June 2003], 40-42, 43, 47 [Counsel Bethlehem], 78 [Counsel Sands], 5 [Arbitrator Crawford, 13 June 2003] <www.pca-cpa.org>; 2003 UNCITRAL *CME Czech Republic B.V. (The Netherlands) v. The Czech Republic* Award, paras 201-202 [<http://ita.law.uvic .ca/documents/CME-2003-Final_000.pdf & www.asil.org/ilib0607.htm> Dispute Settlement – Choice of Procedure *infra*]; *Malaysia v. Singapore (Provisional Measures)* Hearings, ITLOS/PV.03/05, 21 [Counsel Lauterpacht, 27 Sep 2003] <www.itlos.org>; 2006 *Barbados/Trinidad & Tobago (Jurisdiction and Merits)* Award, President S.M. Schwebel, para.200 [RIAA XXVII, 147 <www.un.org/law/ riaa & http://untreaty.un.org/cod/riaa/cases/vol_XXVII/147-251.pdf>; 45 ILM

800 (2006); <www.pca-cpa.org>]; Barbados' Reply, para.91 n.184, para.101 n.198; *Guyana/Suriname* Suriname's Rejoinder, paras 2.74, 4.9; Hearings, 45 [Counsel Rosenne, 8 July 2005], Day 5, 770-771 [Counsel Greenwood, 13 Dec 2006], Day 7, 1134-1135 [Counsel Murphy, 15 Dec 2006] <www.pca-cpa.org>.

See also Exclusive Economic (/Fishery) Zone; Continental Shelf - Sedentary Species; Equitable Maritime Boundary Delimitation - Fishery Resource Factors; and Regime of Islands - Sovereignty Over Island Territory and Joint Fishery Rights, *supra*; Dispute Settlement - Automatic Exemption of Fishery Disputes *infra*.

SUBMARINE CABLES AND PIPELINES

1958 HSC, Articles 2(3) and 26-29; 1958 CSC, Article 4
1982 UNCLOS, Part IV, Article 51, Part V, Article 56(3), Part VI, Article 79, Part VII, Articles 87(1)(c) and 112-115, Part X, Article 124(2):

Corfu Channel Pleadings, Vol.I, 22 [UK Memorial], Vol.III, 279 [Agent Sir Eric Beckett, 11 Nov 1948]; *Antarctica* Pleadings, 25-26 [UK Application]; *North Sea* Judgment, ICJ Rep. 1969, 39, para.65, Separate O. Jessup, 68; Pleadings, Vol.II, 66 [Agent Jaenicke, 25 Oct 1968], 129-130 [Agent Riphagen, 30 Oct], 243 [Reply by Counsel Waldock to Questions Fitzmaurice, 8 Nov 1968]; *Aegean Sea* Pleadings, 438 [Counsel Economides, 16 Oct 1978]; *Gulf of Maine* Pleadings, Vol.III, 58 [Canada's Counter-Memorial]; *Gabcikovo* Oral Pleadings, CR 97/5, 66 [Counsel Sands, 6 March 1997]; *Spain v. Canada (Jurisdiction)* Dissents Weeramantry, ICJ Rep. 1998, 506, para.40, Torres Bernardez, 715, para.371; *Oil Platforms (Merits)* Judgment, ICJ Rep. 2003, 192, 203, paras 65, 88; Hearings, CR 2003/7, 12-13, 18 [Counsel Bundy, 19 Feb 2003], CR 2003/9, 12 [Agent Taft, 21 Feb], CR 2003/11, 38 [Counsel Murphy, 25 Feb], CR 2003/17, 34 [5 March 2003]; *Romania v. Ukraine* Hearings, CR 2008/19, 51, para.114 [Counsel Crawford, 3 Sep 2008] <www.icj-cij.org>.

See also High Seas - Freedom of the High Seas (*Iran v. USA Oil Platforms*) *supra*.

1985 *Guinea/Guinea-Bissau* Award, paras 25, 105 [25 ILM 266, 295 (1986)]; *M/V Saiga* Separate O. Laing [38 ILM 1323 (1999)], para.32; 2005 *Belgium/Netherlands Iron Rhine* Award, para.80 <www.pca-cpa.org>, relying on the 1977 *Netherlands (PTT) and the Post Office (London) v. Ned Lloyd* [74 ILR 212].

On UK/France Sumbarine Telegraph Convention of 2 January 1859 [*Minquiers and Ecrehos* Pleadings, Vol.I, 209-212], see *Minquiers and Ecrehos* Judgment, ICJ Rep. 1953, 60; Pleadings, Vol.I, 55-56, 118-119 [UK Memorial].

On Convention for the Protection of Submarine Cables, Paris, 14 March 1884 [in force: 1 March 1888, 163 CTS 391], see *SS Lotus* Pleadings, PCIJ Series C, No.13-II, 79 [Agent Basdevant, 3 August], 133 [Agent Bey, 8 August 1927], 162 [Basdevant, 9 Aug 1927], 206, 208 [France's Memorial], 237 [Observations Fedozzi]; 2005 *Belgium/Netherlands* Award, para.80 <www.pca-cpa.org>.

On the first Monterey Accelerated Research System's (MARS) 32 miles long cable, see 13 March 2007 <http://news.bbc.co.uk/2/hi/science/nature/6445611.stm>. On the Mediterranean Undersea Cables, see 20/22 Dec 2008 <www.voanews.com/english/2008-12-20-voa11.cfm & http://news.bbc.co.uk/2/hi/technology/7794868.stm>; 23 Dec 2008 <http://news.bbc.co.uk/2/hi/technology/7797162.stm>.

See also Access to, Jurisdiction and Treatment in Ports – Ports/Oil and Gas Development *supra*.

ENCLOSED OR SEMI-ENCLOSED SEAS

1982 UNCLOS, Part IX, Articles 122-123
1995 SSA, Article 15

North Sea Continental Shelf ICJ Rep. 1969, 3 – Judgment, 13, Separate O. President Bustamante y Rivero, 58, 61, Separate O. Padilla Nervo, 89-90, Dissent Morelli, 199-200; Pleadings, Vol.I, 17, 39, 71-74, 76-80 [FRG Memorial], 205-209 [Denmark's Counter-Memorial], 353, 358-362 [NL Counter-Memorial], 417-432 [FRG Reply], Vol.II, 37-40, 66-67 [Agent Jaenicke, 24 and 25 Oct 1968], 129-131 [Agent Riphagen, 30 Oct], 186, 188 [Jaenicke, 4 Nov 1968]; *Aegean Sea* case – see Equitable Maritime Boundary Delimitation *supra*; *Tunisia/Libya (Merits)* Judgment, ICJ Rep. 1982, 34-35, 41-42; Pleadings, Vol.I, 482-485 [Libya's Memorial], Vol.II, 48 [Tunisia's Counter-Memorial], Vol.V, 362 [Counsel Vallat, 19 Oct 1981]; *Gulf of Maine* Judgment, ICJ Rep. 1984, 343-344; *Libya/Malta (Intervention)* Judgment, ICJ Rep. 1984, 11, Dissents Sette-Camara, 78, 81-83, Schwebel, 133, Sir Robert Jennings, 151, *(Merits)* Judgment, ICJ Rep. 1985, 20-22, 40, 42, 50, 52, Joint Separate O., 78-81, Separate O. Valticos, 113, Dissents Mosler, 115-116, 121, Oda, 155, Schwebel, 182; Pleadings, Vol.I, 28-36, 127, 130, 153-157 [Libya's Memorial], Vol.II, 68, 143 [Libya's Counter-Memorial], Vol.III, 183, 206, 211-213, 218 [Malta's Reply], 444, 473 [Counsel Brownlie, 3 Dec 1984]; *Great Belt* case – see Straits Used for International Navigation *supra*; *Gulf of Fonseca* Dissent Oda, ICJ Rep. 1992, 760; Hearings, C 4/CR 91/40, 28-29 [Counsel Lauterpacht, 5 June 1991], CR 91/43, 80 [Counsel Brownlie, 7 June 1991]; *Denmark v. Norway* Separate O. Oda, ICJ Rep. 1993, 103-105; Hearings, CR 93/5, 39 [Agent Tresselt, 15 Jan 1993], CR 93/6, 45 [Agent Haug, 18 Jan], CR 93/7, 27-34 [Counsel Brownlie, 19 Jan], CR 93/10, 50 [Counsel Bowett, 25 Jan 1993]; *Botswana/Namibia* Dissent Vice-President Weeramantry, ICJ Rep.

1999, 1190-1191, para.109; *Qatar v. Bahrain (Merits)* Judgment, ICJ Rep. 2001, 52, para.35 – see Equitable Maritime Boundary Delimitation *supra*; *Cameroon v. Nigeria (Preliminary Objections)* Judgment, ICJ Rep. 1998, 322-325, *(Merits)* Judgment, ICJ Rep. 2002, 303, paras 30, 272, 280, 296-297; Hearings, CR 98/2, 39-44 [Counsel Crawford, 3 March 1998] <www.icj-cij.org>; 2009 *Romania v. Ukraine* Judgment – see Equitable Maritime Boundary Delimitation *supra*.

2001 *Ireland v. UK Mox Plant (Provisional Measures)* Order and Pleadings, ITLOS Case No.10 <www.itlos.org>; 2003 OSPAR *Mox Plant* Award and Annex VII *Mox Plant* <www.pca-cpa.org>; 2002 *Newfoundland/Nova Scotia (Phase II)* Award, paras 4.1/2, 5.3 <www.gov.ns.ca>; 2003 *Malaysia v. Singapore (Provisional Measures)* Order (No.12), ITLOS Rep.2003, 9 <www.itlos.org> and 2005 Annex VII *Malaysia v. Singapore* Award and Settlement Agreement of 26 April 2005, 2324 UNTS 23; <http://internet-stg1.mfa.gov.sg/internet/press/land/frm_main_land.htm> & <www.pca-cpa.org>; 2006 *Barbados/Trinidad & Tobago (Jurisdiction and Merits)* Award and Pleadings <www.pca-cpa.org>; 2006 ECJ *EC v. Ireland Mox Plant* Judgment <http://curia.eu.int/jrisp/cgi-bin/form.pl?lang=EN&Submit=rechercher&numaff=C-459/03>.

See also Equitable Maritime Boundary Delimitation – *Denmark v. Norway* case, 1965 Denmark/Norway Agreement *supra*.

On the Caspian Sea, see *Great Belt* Hearings, CR 91/10, 15 [Co-Agent Koskenniemi, 1 July 1991], CR 91/14, 27 [Agent Magid, 5 July 1991]; Caspian Oil Maps <www.rigzone.com/news/image_results.asp?ctry_id=173>.

RIGHT OF ACCESS OF LAND-LOCKED STATES TO AND FROM THE SEA AND FREEDOM OF TRANSIT

1958 HSC, Article 3
1982 UNCLOS, Part X, Articles 124-132

Jurisdiction of the European Commission of the Danube Between Galatz and Braila PCIJ Series B, No.14 (1927) – Advisory Opinion, 6, President M. Huber concurring; *UK, Czechoslovak Republic, Denmark, France, Germany, Sweden/Poland Territorial Jurisdiction of the International Commission of the River Oder* PCIJ Series A, No.23 (1929) – Judgment, 5, President D. Anzilotti; *Railway Traffic Between Lithuania and Poland (Railway Sector Landwarów-Kaisiadorys* PCIJ Series A/B, No.42 (1931) – Advisory Opinion, 108; *Access To, Or Anchorage In, The Port of Danzig, of Polish War Vessels* PCIJ Series A/B, No.43 (1931) – Advisory Opinion, 142-144; *Polish War Vessels* Pleadings, PCIJ Series C, No.55, 70, 75-76 [Statement Free City of Danzig], 113-115 [Report Permanent Commission], 120-121 [Report Ishii], 164-165 [Poland's Memorial], 235-236, 267 [Agent Williams, 9 and 10 Nov 1931], 332-333, 342 [Williams, 12 Nov], 367,

368 [Counsel de Visscher, 14 Nov 1931], 377 [Question of Judge van Eysinga]; *Legal Status of Eastern Greenland* PCIJ Series A/B, No.53 (1933) – Judgment, 52; *Eastern Greenland* Pleadings, PCIJ Series C, No.63, 1107-1108 [Norway's Rejoinder]; PCIJ Series C, No.67, 3337 [Agent Steglich-Petersen, 17 Jan 1933]; *Oscar Chinn* PCIJ Series A/B, No.63 (1934) – Judgment, 65; *Portugal v. India Right of Passage over Indian Territory (Preliminary Objections)* and *(Merits)* Judgments, ICJ Rep. 1957, 125 and 1960, 6 [cf. 2006 *Barbados/Trinidad & Tobago* Award, para.281 <www.pca-cpa.org>]; *IMCO* Pleadings, 216-218 [Switzerland]; *North Sea* Judgment, ICJ Rep. 1969, 42, Dissent Tanaka, 176, Dissent Lachs, 227; Pleadings, Vol.I, 408 [FRG Reply], Vol.II, 118 [Counsel Sir Humphrey Waldock, 30 Oct 1968], 122 [Agent Riphagen], 137-138 [Riphagen, 31 Oct], 160 [Agent Jacobsen, 1 Nov 1968]; *Aegean Sea (Jurisdiction)* Judgment, ICJ Rep. 1978, 25-27, Dissent Stassinopoulos, 78; Pleadings, 140 [Counsel O'Connell, 27 Aug 1976]; Pleadings, 268 [Greece's Memorial (Jurisd.)], 343 [Counsel O'Connell, 10 Oct 1978], 429 [Counsel Economides, 13 Oct 1978]; *Libya/Malta* Pleadings, Vol.I, 480-482, 554-569 [Malta's Memorial], Vol.II, 68-71 [Libya's Counter-Memorial], Vol.III, 147-148, 166 [Malta's Reply]; *Great Belt* Hearings, CR 91/13, 21 [Agent Gronberg, 4 July 1991]; *Gabcikovo* Judgment, ICJ Rep. 1997, 18; *Oil Platforms (Preliminary Objection)* Judgment, ICJ Rep. 1996, 819, Separate O. Higgins, 859-860, Dissent Vice-President Schwebel, 887-888, *(Counter-Claim)* Order, ICJ Rep. 1998, 204; *Benin/Niger* Hearings, C5/CR 2005/1, 15, para.1.4 [Agent Biaou, 7 March 2005]; eight *Legality of Use of Force (Preliminary Objections)* Separate Os Kreca, para.45 [quoting *Territorial Jurisdiction of the International Commission of the River Oder* Judgment, PCIJ Series A, No.23, p.19 (1929)], ICJ Rep. 2004, Belgium, 402, Canada, 548, France, 693, Germany, 838, Italy, 984, NL, 1133, Portugal, 1280, UK, 1425 and *Bosnia & Herzegovina v. Serbia & Montenegro (Jurisdiction and Merits)* Separate O. Kreca, para.43, ICJ Rep. 2007; *Costa Rica v. Nicaragua San Juan River* Judgment, ICJ Rep. 2009, para.19 <www.icj-cij.org>.

1925 *Chile/Peru Tacna-Arica* Award – see Equitable Maritime Boundary Delimitation *supra*; *M/V Saiga* Separate O. Laing [38 ILM 1323 (1999)], paras 24, 30; *Southern Bluefin Tuna (Jurisdiction)*, President S.M. Schwebel, Japan's Memorial, para.119, Hearings, Vol.II [Counsel Irwin, 8 May 2000] <www.worldbank/icsid>; Sir Elihu Lauterpacht, Judge Stephen M. Schwebel, Shabtai Rosenne and Francisco Orrego, *Joint Legal Opinion on Guatemala's Territorial Claim to Belize*, Summary, paras 4, 7(vii), 13, 27, 124-125, 139 (Jan 2002) <www.belize-guatemala.gov.bz/> and <www.bwp-bookcenter.com>; 2005 *Belgium/Netherlands* Award, President Rosalyn Higgins <www.pca-cpa.org> & <www.asil.org/ilib050614.htm>.

2002 *Eritrea/Ethiopia Delimitation of the Border (Merits)* Decision, paras 2.7, 6.30/6.31, 41 ILM 1057 (2002); <www.pca-cpa.org>, <www.un.org/NewLinks/eebcarbitration/> and Equitable Maritime Delimitation *supra.*

For Eritrea/Ethiopia Transit & Port Agreement of 27 September 1993 and 1994 Djibouti/Ethiopia Port Agreement, see *UN LOS Bull.* 56, 58 (1998 No.38).

On previous demands of the Ethiopian Democratic Party (EDP, in opposition to the ruling Tigray People's Liberation Front – TPLF) to assure access to the sea through the port of Assab as part of the UN Commission's Decision, see Africa News of 11 Feb 2002 <http://library.northernlight.com/FC20020211860000132.html?cb=0&dx=1006&sc=0>, Ethiopians in USA Lobby of 15 Feb <http://globalarchive.ft.com/globalarchive/article. html?id=020215002553> and Ethiopia Will Abide by Border Ruling of 2 April 2002 <http://globalarchive.ft.com/globalarchive/article.html?id=020402004215&query= eritrea>. On confirmation after the *Eritrea/Ethiopia* Decision's delivery that the port of Assab remains part of Eritrea's territory, see BBC News of 16 April 2002 <http://news.bbc.co.uk/hi/english/world/africa/newsid_1933000/1933451.stm> and 22 April 2003 <www.meskerem.net/bm4-22.htm>. See also Ethio/Djibouti Corridor of 29 August 2003 <http://allafrica.com/stories/200308290339.html>; Ethiopia/India Trade of 19 March 2004 <http://eri24.com/news4702.htm>; Ethiopia's Access to the Sea of 9 July 2004 <www.ethiomedia.com/release/access_to_sea_070904.html> and 14 Jan 2006 <http://allafrica.com/stories/200601160531.html>.

UN *Ethiopia/Eritrea Ports (Claim 6)* Final Award of the Eritrea/Ethiopia Claims Commission of 19 Dec 2005, 111 RGDIP 198-202 (2007); <www.pca-cpa.org/ & www.asil.org/ilib060127.htm>; 101 AJIL 622 (2007).

On FCN Treaties, see Internal Waters, Territorial Sea and Baselines *supra.*

On Convention and Statute on Freedom of Transit, Barcelona, 20 April 1921 [in force: 31 Oct 1922, 7 LNTS 13], see *SS Wimbledon* Pleadings, PCIJ Series C, No.3 – Additional Volume, 47 [Germany's Counter-Memorial], 83 [Reply of Four Powers]; *Corfu Channel (Merits)* ICJ Rep. 1949, 4 – Dissent Azevedo, 98, 102, 105; *Great Belt* Pleadings, 249 [Finland's Memorial].

On Declaration Recognizing the Right to a Flag of States Having no Sea Coast, Barcelona, 20 April 1921 [in force: 20 April 1921, 7 LNTS 73], see *IMCO* Pleadings, 88 [Liberia].

On Convention and Statute on the Regime of Navigable Waterways of International Concern, Barcelona, 20 April 1921 [in force: 31 Oct 1922, 7 LNTS 36], see *SS Wimbledon* Pleadings, 83 [Reply of Four Powers], 143, 145, 155 [Germany's Rejoinder]; *Anglo/Norwegian Fisheries* Individual O. Alvarez, ICJ Rep. 1951, 151; *M/V Saiga* Separate O. Laing [38 ILM 1323 (1999)], para.24.

On Convention on the Regime of Navigation on the Danube, Belgrade, 18 August 1948 [in force: 11 May 1949, 33 UNTS 181], see *Gabcikovo-Nagymaros Project* Judgment, ICJ Rep. 1997, 72; Hearings, CR 97/2 [trans.], 37-38 [Counsel Kiss, 3 March 1997], CR 97/5 [trans.], 7-8 [6 March], CR 97/6, 46 [Counsel Sands, 7 March], CR 97/11, 20-21 [Counsel Watts, 27 March 1997]; *Legality of Use of Force (Provisional Measures)* Orders (in all 10 cases), para.3, ICJ Rep. 1999, 126, 261, 365, 424, 483, 544, 658, 763, 828, 918 <www.icj-cij.org>.

On 1994 Danube Convention, see Protection and Preservation of the Marine Environment *infra*.

On Croatia/Bosnia-Herzegovina Agreement on Free Transit Through the Territory of Republic of Croatia to and from the Port of Ploce and Through the Territory of Bosnia and Herzegovina at Neum, Zagreb, 22 Nov 1998, see UN Doc.A/53/762-S/1998/1118 (1998); *ITLOS Yearbook 1998*, at 41.

On UN Office of the High Representative for the Least Developed Countries and Landlocked Developing States (OHRLLS <www.unohrlls.org>) and 2003 Almaty High-Level Programme of Action, see UN Seeks to Help Landlocked States of 1 Oct 2008 <www.un.org/apps/news/story.asp?NewsID=28391&Cr=landlocked&Cr1> and 3 Oct 2008 <www.un.org/apps/news/story.asp?NewsID=28427&Cr=landlocked&Cr1 & www.un.org/News/Press/docs/2008/ga10762.doc.htm>; UN Doc .GA/EF/3271 of 25 Nov 2009 <www.un.org/News/Press/docs//2009/gaef3271.doc.htm>.

See also Equity – Equitable Sharing of International Watercourses *infra*.

OVERFLIGHT

1958 TSC, Article 2; HSC, Article 2(4); 1982 UNCLOS, Part II, Article 2, Part III, Articles 36, 38(2), 39(1) and (3), Part IV, Article 53(1)-(3), Part V, Article 58, Part VII, Article 87(1)(b), Part XII, Articles 212 and 222:

Corfu Channel (Merits) Dissent Azevedo, ICJ Rep. 1949, 101; *Nuclear Tests (Interim Measures)* Orders, ICJ Rep. 1973, 103-104, 139-140, Dissents Ignacio-Pinto, 129, 163; *Nuclear Tests* Judgments, ICJ Rep. 1974, 258, 462, Dissent Gros, 281, Joint Dissents, 361, 370, 513, 522, Dissent Barwick, 425-426, 434, 438; Pleadings (Australia), 13-14 [Application], 43-44, 56 [Request], 330, 331 [Memorial], 514-522 [Counsel Byers, 9 July 1974], (New Zealand), 6-7 [Application], 49, 53, 58 [Request], 204, 209 [Memorial], 267 [Counsel Finlay, 10 July 1974]; *Aegean Sea* Pleadings, 90 [Counsel O'Connell, 26 Aug 1976], 421 [Counsel Weil, 13 Oct], 433-434, 437 [Counsel Economides, 13 and 16 Oct 1978]; *Tunisia/Libya (Merits)* Dissent Oda, ICJ Rep. 1982, 223-224; Pleadings, Vol.II, 464; *Nicaragua v. USA (Merits)* Judgment, ICJ Rep. 1986, 111, para.212; *Great Belt* Pleadings, 576-577

[Denmark's Counter-Memorial]; *New Zealand v. France* Dissent Weeramantry, ICJ Rep. 1995, 326-327; *Indonesia/Malaysia (Merits)* Judgment, ICJ Rep. 2002, 679-680, 683, paras 130, 138-139, Dissent Franck, 696, para.17; Hearings, CR 2002/28, 36-39 [Counsel Soons, 3 June 2002]; *Nicaragua v. Honduras (Merits)* Judgment, ICJ Rep. 2007, paras 95, 185, 220-221; Hearings, CR 2007/7, 40, para.47 [Counsel Brotons, 8 March 2007], CR 2007/11, 63, para.32 [Counsel Oude Elferink, 19 March], CR 2007/13, 50, para.34 [Counsel Sands, 22 March 2007]; *Malaysia/Singapore (Merits)* Judgment, ICJ Rep. 2008, paras 247-248; *Romania v. Ukraine* Hearings, CR 2008/30, 41, para.31 [Co-Agent Dinescu, 15 Sep 2008]; *Ecuador v. Colombia Alleged Aerial Spraying by Colombia of Toxic Herbicides over Ecuadorian Territory*, ICJ Rep. 2008 <www.icj-cij.org>.

1977 *Anglo/French* Decision [18 ILM 397 (1979)], paras 163, 175; 1998 *Eritrea/Yemen (Phase I)* Award, paras 358-359, 507 <www.pca-cpa.org>; *M/V Saiga* Separate O. Laing [38 ILM 1323 (1999)], para.32; 2001 *Ireland v. UK Mox Plant (Provisional Measures)* Ireland's Request & Statement, paras 40, 42, UK Response, paras 67-68, 208; Hearings, ITLOS/PV.01/08, 9-10 [Counsel Goldsmith, 20 Nov 2001], 29 [Counsel Plender] <www.itlos.org>; 2002 *Belize/Guatemala* OAS Proposals, D-para.2 <www.belize-guatemala.gov.bz>; *Guyana/Suriname* Guyana's Memorial, para.5.8 <www.pca-cpa.org>.

On US Air Defense Identification Zones [ADIZs – since 1940, which – like CADIZ – are loosely based on the 1944 ICAO Convention, as Amended (Article 11), *infra* and are acquiesced in by other states], see *Gulf of Maine* Pleadings, Vol.II, 47 [US Memorial], Vol.III, 19, 168-169, 374, 374-380 [Canada's Counter-Memorial], Vol.V, 78 [Canada's Reply], Vol.VIII, 106 [Fig.18]; *Libya/Malta* Pleadings, Vol.IV, 36 [Counsel Briggs, 7 Dec 1984].

On Convention on International Civil Aviation, Chicago, 7 Dec 1944 [in force: 4 April 1947, 15 UNTS 295] and Protocols of 30 Sep 1977 [in force: 17 August 1999, 2133 UNTS 44] and 26 Oct 1990 [in force: 28 Nov 2002, 2216 UNTS 483], see *Nicaragua v. USA (Merits)* Judgment, ICJ Rep. 1986, 111, para.212; *Iran v. USA Aerial Incident of 3 July 1988* – Settlement of Disputes, Preventive Diplomacy C) *infra*; *Spain v. Canada* Pleadings, 450 [Counsel Rodriguez, 9 June 1998]; *M/V Saiga* Separate O. Laing [38 ILM 1323 (1999)], para.28 n.21; *DR Congo v. Uganda (Provisional Measures)* Order, para.7, ICJ Rep. 2000, 113; *DR Congo v. Rwanda New Application (Provisional Measures)* Order, para.6(c), ICJ Rep. 2002, 222 and *(Jurisdiction)* Judgment, ICJ Rep. 2006, para.11(c) <www.icj-cij.org>.

On International Air Services Transit Agreement, Chicago, 7 Dec 1944 [in force: 30 Jan 1945, 84 UNTS 389], see *IMCO* Pleadings, 61 [Liberia], 402 [L, 3 May 1960].

On International Air Transport Agreement, Chicago, 7 Dec 1944 [in force: 8 Feb 1945, 171 UNTS 387], see *IMCO* Pleadings, 61 [Liberia].

On 1971 Montreal Convention and 1988 Protocol, see Peaceful Uses of the Sea, Maritime Terrorism *infra.*

See also Continental Shelf – Superjacent Waters and Air Space *supra*; Protection and Preservation of the Marine Environment – Pollution From or Through the Atmosphere; and Peaceful Uses of the Sea – Nuclear Weapon Tests *infra.*

PROTECTION AND PRESERVATION OF THE MARINE ENVIRONMENT

1958 CSC, Article 5(7); 1958 HSC, Articles 24-25
1972 UN Stockholm Declaration and Action Plan
1982 UNCLOS, Preamble, Part I, Article 1(1), Parts II-IX, Part V, Article 56(1)(b)(iii), Part XII, Articles 192-237
1992 UNCED Rio Declaration and Agenda 21, Chapter 17
1994 Agreement
2002 WSSD Johannesburg Declaration and Plan of Implementation, paras 29-34

Concept of the Protection of the Environment for Present and Future Generations
1972 Stockholm Principles 1-2; 1982 UNCLOS, Preamble; 1992 Rio Principle 3; 2002 Johannesburg Declaration:

Nuclear Tests Pleadings (Australia), 377 [Memorial], (New Zealand), 210 [Memorial]; *Denmark v. Norway* Separate O. Weeramantry, ICJ Rep. 1993, 276-277; *New Zealand v. France* Dissent Weeramantry, ICJ Rep. 1995, 341-342, Dissent Sir Geoffrey Palmer, 406, 419-420; *Nuclear Weapons (WHO)* Dissent Weeramantry, ICJ Rep. 1996, 141, *(UNGA)* Advisory Opinion, 241-242, para.29, *as reaffirmed* by *Gabcikovo-Nagymaros Project* Judgment, President S.M. Schwebel, ICJ Rep. 1997, 41, para.53, at 68, para.112, and at 78, para.140, Separate O. Vice-President Weeramantry, 102, 108, Dissent Herczegh, 176, 179; *Botswana/Namibia* Dissent Vice-President Weeramantry, para.82, ICJ Rep. 1999, 1180; *Argentina v. Uruguay Pulp Mills on the River Uruguay (Provisional Measures)* Order, ICJ Rep. 2006, 132, para.72, Dissent Vanuesa, 148 <www.icj-cij.org>.

Minors Oposa v. Secretary of the Department of Environment and Natural Resources Decision of the Supreme Court of the Philippines, 33 ILM 173 (1994); *Ireland v. UK Mox Plant (Provisional Measures)* Ireland's Request & Statement, para.92; Hearings, ITLOS/PV.01/06, 36 [Counsel Sands, 19 Nov 2001] (relying on the *Gabcikovo-Nagymaros Project* Judgment *supra*); 2002 *Russia v. Australia Volga* Declaration Marsit, para.3 <www.itlos.org>; Annex VII *Mox Plant* UK Counter-Memorial, 114-115 <www.pca-cpa.org>; 2005 *Belgium/Netherlands Iron Rhine* Award, para.58; *Barbados/Trinidad & Tobago* Hearings, President S.M. Schwebel, Day-6, 73 [Agent Mottley, 25 Oct 2005] <www.pca-cpa.org>.

See also UNGA Resolution 55/2 on United Nations Millenium Declaration of 8 Sep 2000, reaffirming commitment for the principles of sustainable development, including those set out in the UNCED Agenda 21 (para.22); UNGA Adopts Two Oceans Resolutions, UN Doc.GA/10899 of 4 Dec 2009 <www.un.org/News/Press/docs//2009/ga10899.doc.htm>.

Obligation to Protect and Preserve the Marine Environment
1958 HSC, Articles 24-25; 1972 Stockholm Principle 7; 1982 UNCLOS, Articles 192-193; 1992 Rio Principle 2; 1994 Agreement:

Nuclear Tests (Interim Measures) Orders, ICJ Rep. 1973, 104-105, 140-141, Declarations Jiménez de Aréchaga, 108, 144, Declarations Sir Garfield Barwick, 110, 147, Dissents Gros, 122, 156-157, Dissents Ignacio-Pinto, 130-131, 163; *Nuclear Tests* Judgments, ICJ Rep. 1974, 258-260, 461-464, Separate Os Petren, 303-306, 488-490, Joint Dissents, 360-363, 512-514, Dissents Barwick, 389, 425, 431-439, 525; *Nuclear Tests* Pleadings (Australia), 8-14 [Application], 43-57 [Request], 149-152 [Fiji's Application], 337 [Memorial], 514-522 [Counsel Byers, 9 July 1974], (New Zealand), 5-9 [Application], 49-59 [Request], 89-92 [Fiji's Application]; *Gulf of Maine* Judgement, ICJ Rep. 1984, 344; Pleadings, Vol. III, 83, 197-198, 352 [Canada's Counter-Memorial], Vol.IV, 152-153, 166 [US Counter-Memorial]; *Denmark v. Norway* Separate O. Weeramantry, ICJ Rep. 1993, 277-278; *New Zealand v. France Nuclear Tests (Request for an Examination of the Situation)* ICJ Rep. 1995, 288 – Order, 290-291, 294, 298-299, 306, paras 63-64 (referring to the 1986 UNEP SPREP Convention, *infra*), *as reaffirmed* by *Nuclear Weapons (UNGA)* Advisory Opinion, ICJ Rep. 1996, 242, para.30, and 243, para.32; *New Zealand v. France* Declaration Oda, ICJ Rep. 1995, 310, Separate O. Shahabuddeen, 312-313, Dissents Weeramantry, 319, 326-330, 339-358, Koroma, 369-379, Palmer, 384-392, 400-413; NZ Request (Examination of the Situation); Hearings, CR 95/19, 51-53, 59-60 [Co-Agent McGrath, 11 Sep 1995], CR 95/20, 46 [Questions Weeramantry, 12 Sep], NZ and France's Written Replies of 15 Sep 1995; *Nuclear Weapons (WHO)* Advisory Opinion, ICJ Rep. 1996, 76-77, Dissents Weeramantry, 104, 139-143, Koroma, 175-187, *(UNGA)* Dissent Weeramantry, 452-471; Hearings, CR 95/28, 57 [Attorney-General East/NZ, 9 Nov 1995], CR 95/31, 29 [Ambassador Slade/Samoa, also on behalf of the Marshalls and Solomons, 13 Nov], CR 95/32, 65 [Sands/Solomons, 14 Nov 1995]; *Oil Platforms* Hearings, CR 96/12, 55 [Counsel Lowenfeld, 16 Sep 1996]; *Gabcikovo* Judgment, ICJ Rep. 1997, 18, 31-37, 64-68, 73-74, 77-80, Separate O. Weeramantry, 88-119, Dissents Oda, 159-161, 168, Herczegh, 176-189; *Botswana/Namibia* Dissent Vice-President Weeramantry, ICJ Rep. 1999, 1179-1183, paras 80-90 <www.icj-cij.org>.

See also *Nauru v. Australia Certain Phosphate Lands in Nauru* case [Settlement of Disputes – Preventive Diplomacy B) *infra*], which dealt with the issue of environmental degradation, as referred to in the *Nuclear Tests* Dissent Weeramantry, ICJ Rep. 1995, 362 n.1, Dissent Palmer, 408; *East Timor* Judgment, ICJ Rep. 1995, 104, para.33, Dissent Weeramantry, 197-204; Hearings, CR 95/3 [trans.], 17-19 [Counsel Dupuy, 31 Jan 1995], 73-74 [Co-Agent Teles], CR 95/4 [trans.], 69-71 [1 Feb], CR 95/6, 53 [Dupuy, 3 Feb], CR 95/14, 70 [Counsel Crawford, 16 Feb 1995].

The environmental (in general) claims of Yugoslavia in this respect were referred to in paras 1-7 of each of the ten *Legality of Use of Force (Provisional Measures)* Orders, as well as in Orders in the cases with Belgium, paras 34-35, Canada, paras 33-34, the Netherlands, paras 34-35, Portugal, paras 34-35, and the United Kingdom, paras 29-30; in Orders in the cases with France, Germany and Italy, paras 21-22; and in *Yugoslavia v. Belgium* Dissent of Vice-President Weeramantry, applicable *mutatis mutandis* to his Dissents from Orders in the cases with Canada, the Netherlands and Portugal, ICJ Rep. 1999, 124, 259, 363, 422, 481, 542, 656, 761, 826, 916; *(Preliminary Objections)* Judgments, ICJ Rep. 2004, in cases with Belgium, paras 22-23, 128, Canada, Italy and France, paras 21-22, 115, UK and Germany, paras 20-21, 114, the Netherlands, paras 21-22, 127 and Portugal, paras 21-22, 118 <www.icj-cij.org>.

1977 *Anglo/French* Decision [18 ILM 397 (1979)], paras 163, 175; *United States – Import Prohibition of Certain Shrimp and Shrimp Products* Report AB-1998-4, WTO Appellate Body, President F. Feliciano, WT/DS58/AB/R, 12 October 1998, paras 67-68 [EC], paras 127-134, 168-171 [AB], 38 ILM 100 (1999); 94 AJIL 361 (2000); and Report AB-2001-4, President J. Bacchus, WT/DS58/AB/RW, 22 October 2001, paras 111-134, 41 ILM 149 (2001); 96 AJIL 685 (2001); *Southern Bluefin Tuna (Jurisdiction)*, President S.M. Schwebel, Japan's Memorial, paras 119, 139 <ww.worldbank/icsid>; 2001 *Ireland v. UK Mox Plant (Provisional Measures)* Order and Pleadings, President P.Ch. Rao, Case No.10, ITLOS Rep. 2001, 89; 41 ILM 405 (2002) <www.itlos.org>; 2003 OSPAR *Mox Plant* Award, paras 101-103, Dissent Griffith, para.30; Ireland's Reply, para.42, UK Rejoinder, para.21, Hearings, Vol.I, 57 [Counsel Sands, 21 Oct 2002]; 2002 *Russia v. Australia (Prompt Release)* Judgment, President L.D.M. Nelson, Case No.11, para.67, Declarations Vice-President Vukas, para.7, Marsit; 2003 *Malaysia v. Singapore (Provisional Measures)* Order, President L.D.M. Nelson, Case No.12, ITLOS Rep. 2003, 9; Hearings, ITLOS/PV.03/05, 21 [Counsel Lauterpacht, 27 Sep 2003] <www.itlos.org>; 2006 ECJ *EC v. Ireland Mox Plant* Judgment, paras 89, 114 <http://curia.eu.int/jrisp/cgi-bin/form.pl?lang=EN&Submit=rechercher&numaff=C-459/03> 2005 *Belgium/Netherlands Iron Rhine* Award, paras 23, 58-59 (citing 1997 *Gabcikovo* Judgment, para.140), 70-71, 79-80, 87-96, 106, 114, 116, 118, 121-141, 144, 151, 159, 168-176, 189-192, 215, 220-229, 234-235, 243 <www.pca-cpa.org>

& <www.asil.org/ilib050614.htm> and *Costa Rica v. Nicaragua San Juan River* Declaration Guillaume, ICJ Rep. 2009, para.12 n.31 <www.icj-cij.org>.

Permanent Sovereignty over Natural Resources

[UNGA Res.1803(XVII) of 14 Dec 1962 and Res.3281(XXIX) on the Charter of Economic Rights and Duties of States of 12 Dec 1974] 1977 *Texaco v. Libya* Award, 53 ILR 389; Stuyt/No. A 1.77; 1982 *Kuwait v. American Independent Oil Company (Aminoil)* Award, 21 ILM 976 (1982); Stuyt/No.A 1.83; *DR Congo v. Uganda Armed Activities on the Territory of the Congo (Merits)* Judgment, ICJ Rep. 2005, 168, paras 28, 166, 222-250, 259, Declaration Koroma, para.11, Dissent Kateka, paras 50-56 <www.icj-cij.org>.

See also UNSC Presidential Statement S/PRST/2007/22 on Maintenance of International Peace and Security: Natural Resources and Conflict of 25 June 2007 <www.un.org/ga/president/61/statements/statement20070625.shtml & www .un.org/apps/news/story.asp?NewsID=23027&Cr=conflict&Cr1>.

Sic utere tuo ut alienum non laedas
1972 Stockholm Principles 21-22; 1982 UNCLOS, Article 194(2); 1992 Rio Principles 2 and 13:

SS Lotus Dissent Moore, PCIJ Series A, No.10 (1927), 88, invoking 1887 *US v. Arjona* Judgment [120 US 479]; *Corfu Channel (Merits)* ICJ Rep. 1949, 4 – Judgment, 18, 22-23, Individual O. Alvarez, 44-46, Dissent Winiarski, 52-54 [invoking the *Lotus* Dissent Moore], Dissent Azevedo, 90; *Anglo/Norwegian Fisheries* Pleadings, Vol.II, 427, 430 [UK Reply]; *North Sea* Pleadings, Vol.II, 200 [Counsel Shigeru Oda, 5 Nov 1968]; *Nuclear Tests (Interim Measures)* Dissents Ignacio-Pinto, ICJ Rep. 1973, 130-131, 163; *Nuclear Tests* Judgments, ICJ Rep. 1974, 270, 475, Separate Os Gros, 276-277, 279, 288, 480, Separate Os Petren, 303-304, 488, Joint Dissents, 318-320, 361-363, 368-371, 500-502, 512-514, 520-523, Dissents de Castro, 388-389, 524, Dissent Barwick, 431-434; *Nuclear Tests* Pleadings (Australia), 49 [Request], 524 [Questions Sir Humphrey Waldock], 525-527 [Replies Byers, 11 July 1974], (New Zealand), 56 [Request], 291 [Questions Waldock, 11 July 1974], 429-431 [Replies Agent, 15 July 1974]; *Aegean Sea* Pleadings, 107 [Counsel O'Connell, 26 Aug 1976]; *Nicaragua v. USA (Merits)* Dissents Schwebel, ICJ Rep. 1986, 380-381, paras 239-241 and Jennings, 536; *Great Belt (Provisional Measures)* Separate O. Shahabuddeen, ICJ Rep. 1991, 32-33; *New Zealand v. France Nuclear Tests* Order, ICJ Rep. 1995, 290-291, 294, 298-299, Dissents Weeramantry, 327, 346-358, 362 n.1, Koroma, 370-371, 378-379, Palmer, 400-412; Hearings, CR 95/20, 11-12 [Counsel Keith, 11 Sep 1995], CR 95/20 [transl.], 67-68, 73-74 [De Brichambaut], CR 95/21, 50 [Sir Arthur Watts]; *Nuclear Weapons (UNGA)* Advisory Opinion, ICJ Rep. 1996, 241, para.27, and

242, para.29, *as reaffirmed* by *Gabcikovo-Nagymaros Project* Judgment, ICJ Rep. 1997, 41, para.53; *Nuclear Weapons (WHO)* Dissents Weeramantry, ICJ Rep. 1996, 141-142, Koroma, 208, *(UNGA)* Dissents Vice-President Schwebel, 320-321, Shahabuddeen, 381-383, Weeramantry, 496, 502-506, 517, Koroma, 566-570; Hearings, CR 95/34, 55 [15 Nov 1995, UK]; *Gabcikovo-Nagymaros Project* Judgment, ICJ Rep. 1997, 39-46 [incl. 41, para.53 *supra*], 59, para.94, at 62, para.97, at 73-75, paras 125-129, Separate O. Weeramantry, 102, Dissents Oda, 160, Herczegh, 176, 193; *Legality of Use of Force (Provisional Measures)* Orders – see Obligation to Protect and Preserve the Marine Environment *supra*; *DR Congo v. Uganda (Merits)* Judgment, ICJ Rep. 2005, 262, para.277, Declaration Tomka, 351-352, para.2, Dissent Kateka, 372, para.36; *Argentina v. Uruguay Pulp Mills on the River Uruguay (Provisional Measures)* Orders, ICJ Rep. 2006, 132, para.72, Dissent Vanuesa, 148, and ICJ Rep. 2007, 35, Dissent Torres Bernardez, para.28; *Ecuador v. Colombia Alleged Aerial Spraying by Colombia of Toxic Herbicides over Ecuadorian Territory*, ICJ Rep. 2008 <www.icj-cij.org>.

2001 *Ireland v. UK Mox Plant (Provisional Measures)* Order and Pleadings, ITLOS Case No.10 <www.itlos.org>; 2003 OSPAR *Mox Plant* Award; Annex VII *Mox Plant* UK Counter-Memorial, 207-208 <www.pca-cpa.org>; *Malaysia v. Singapore (Provisional Measures)* Hearings, ITLOS/PV.03/02/Corr.1, 17, 19 [Counsel Schrijver, 25 Sep 2003] <www.itlos.org>; 2005 *Belgium/Netherlands Iron Rhine* Award, paras 222-223, 243 <www.pca-cpa.org>.

On 1941 *Trail Smelter* and 1956 *Lake Lanoux* Awards, see *infra.*

Environmental Impact Assessment/Notification/Consultation

1972 Stockholm Principle 18 and UNGA Resolutions 2995(XXVII)1972 and 3129(XXVIII)1973; 1982 UNCLOS, Part XII, Articles 198, 204-206, 210(5) and 211(7), Part XVI, Article 302; 1992 Rio Principles 17-19:

Gulf of Maine Judgment, ICJ Rep. 1984, 282; Pleadings, Vol.II, 36-37 [US Memorial], Vol.III, 355-359 [Canada's Counter-Memorial], Vol.IV, 260, 265 [US Counter-Memorial], Vol.V, 65, 71-72, 114-115 [Canada's Reply], Vol.VI, 95 [Counsel Binnie, 4 April 1984], Vol.VII, 101 [Counsel Bowett, 5 May], 117 [Counsel Fortier, 5 May 1984]; *Great Belt* Hearings, CR 91/14, 32 [Agent Magid, 5 July 1991]; *Nuclear Tests* Order, ICJ Rep. 1995, 290-291, 298-299, Dissents Weeramantry, 339, 344-358, Koroma, 368-370, Palmer, 401-407, 411-412; NZ Request and Further Request and France's Aide Mémoire (Examination of the Situation); *Nuclear Tests* Hearings, CR 95/19, 27-28, 37-38 [Agent East, 11 Sep 1995], 60 [Counsel McGrath], 88 [Counsel Lauterpacht], CR 95/20, 10 [Counsel Keith, 12 Sep 1995], 23-43 [Co-Agent MacKay], 40-41 [Agent East], CR 95/20 [transl.], 67-68 [De Brichambaut]; *Gabcikovo* Judgment, ICJ Rep. 1997, 32-35, 44, 66-68, 73, 77-79, Separate O. Weeramantry, 111-115, Dissents Oda, 168,

Skubiszewski, 233; Hearings, CR 97/9, 37-42 [Counsel McCaffrey, 25 March 1997]; *Argentina v. Uruguay (Provisional Measures)* Orders, ICJ Rep. 2006, 113 and 2007, 3; *Nicaragua v. Honduras* Hearings, CR 2007/13, 50, para.32 [Counsel Sands, 22 March 2007]; *Ecuador v. Colombia Toxic Herbicides* case <www.icj-cij.org>.

Cf. Sir Elihu Lauterpacht CBE QC, The 1972-1974 and 1995 *Nuclear Tests* Cases, in *Nuclear Weapons in International Law and Politics*, BIICL London, 16 March 2007 <www.biicl.org/files/2593_16th_march_programme.pdf & www.biicl.org/events/view/-/id/137/>.

EC Measures Concerning Meat and Meat Products (Hormones) Report AB-1997-4, WTO Appellate Body, President F. Feliciano, WT/DS26/AB/R-WT/DS48/AB/R, 16 Jan 1998, paras 26-31 [EC], 48-51 [USA], 65-67 [Canada], 89-91 [Australia], 178-209 and 253(j) [AB], defining the concept of risk assessment.

2001 *Ireland v. UK Mox Plant (Provisional Measures)* Order and Pleadings, President P.Ch. Rao, Case No.10, ITLOS Rep. 2001, 89; 2003 OSPAR *Mox Plant* Award <www.pca-cpa.org>; 2005 *Belgium/Netherlands Iron Rhine* Award, paras 21-22, 118, 121-137, 154-159, 173, 179 <www.pca-cpa.org>. 2003 *Malaysia v. Singapore (Provisional Measures)* Order, ITLOS Case No.12 <www.itlos.org>; 2005 Annex VII *Malaysia v. Singapore* Award and Settlement Agreement <http://internet-stg1.mfa.gov.sg/internet/press/land/frm_main_land.htm> & <www.pca-cpa.org>; *European Commission v. Ireland Mox Plant* Case C-459/03, OJEC C/24 (2004) <http://europa.eu.int/eur-lex/pri/en/oj/dat/2004/c_007/c_00720040110en00240024.pdf> and Opinion of Advocate General Poiares Maduro of 12 Jan 2006 [*UNSG Oceans Report*, UN Doc. A/61/63, para.275 (2006)] and the ECJ *EC v. Ireland Mox Plant* Judgment of 30 May 2006 [<http://curia.eu.int/jrisp/cgi-bin/form.pl?lang=EN&Submit=rechercher&numaff=C-459/03> & Cases since 1989 at <http://curia.eu.int/en/content/juris/index.htm> and PR No.45/06 <http://curia.eu.nt/en/actu/communiques/cp060045en.pdf>]; Annex VII *Ireland v. UK Mox Plant (Suspension of Periodic Reports by the Parties)* Order No.5 of 22 Jan 2007 and PR of 21 Feb 2007 and *Mox Plant (Termination of Proceedings)* Order No.6 of 6 June 2008 <www.pca-cpa.org>; Dismantling and Clean-Up of Sellafield by US-France-UK Nuclear Management Partners (NMP) Until 2030 of 24 Nov 2008 <http://news.bbc.co.uk/2/hi/business/7733487.stm & www.kentucky.com/473/story/603962.html>.

UN ECE *Romania/Ukraine Danube-Black Sea (Bystroe) Canal* Opinion of Commission of Inquiry under the 1991 Espoo EIA Convention (Art.3 & Appendix IV) [1989 UNTS 310; 30 ILM 802 (1991)] of 11 July 2006 <www.unece.org/env/eia/inquiry.htm> and press comments <www.mosnews.com/news/2006/07/11/canaldisp.shtml & www.cceg.ro/2006stiri/UN.htm>.

On Article 34 of the 1957 EURATOM Treaty, see Peaceful Uses of the Sea – Nuclear Weapon Tests *infra*.

On Article 6 of Directive 80/836/EURATOM [OJEC L 246/1 (1980)], as amended by Directive 84/467/EURATOM [OJEC L 265/4 (1984) and C 267/211 (1991)], as replaced by Directive 96/29 *infra*, see *Nuclear Tests* Dissent Koroma, ICJ Rep. 1995, 370; NZ Request (Examination of the Situation), para.87; Hearings, CR 95/18, 84-85 [Counsel Lauterpacht, 11 Sep 1995]; 2001 *Ireland v. UK Mox Plant (Provisional Measures)* Ireland's Request & Statement, para.24, UK Response, paras 37, 55(2), 174, 189 <www.itlos.org>; 2003 OSPAR *Mox Plant* Award, paras 19, 30, Dissent Griffith, paras 99, 104; Ireland's Memorial, paras 38, 44, UK Counter-Memorial, para.1.11/13, Ireland's Reply, para.34; Hearings, Vol.I, 6 [Agent O'Hagan, 21 Oct 2002]; Annex VII *Mox Plant* UK Counter-Memorial, 6, 20, 24, 140 <www.pca-cpa.org>; 2006 ECJ *EC v. Ireland Mox Plant* Judgment, paras 26-27 [*supra*].

On Directive 96/29/EURATOM [OJEC L 159/114 (1996)], see 2001 *Ireland v. UK Mox Plant (Provisional Measures)* Ireland's Request & Statement, para.24, UK Response, paras 30, 55(2), 167-168, 174, 189; Hearings, ITLOS/PV.01/07, 31, 37 [Counsel Goldsmith, 19 Nov 2001] <www.itlos.org>; 2003 OSPAR *Mox Plant* Award, paras 18, 33, 41; Dissent Griffith, paras 99, 104-106; UK Counter-Memorial, paras 1.15, 1.24, Ireland's Reply, para.34; Hearings, Vol.I, 6 [Agent O'Hagan, 21 Oct], Vol.II, 53 [Counsel Plender, 22 Oct], Vol.IV, 8, 17 [Counsel Brady, 24 Oct 2002]; Annex VII *Mox Plant (Provisional Measures)* Hearings, 24 [Lord Goldsmith, 20 June 2003], 33-34 [Counsel Wordsworth], 31 [Counsel Plender, 21 June 2003]; UK Counter-Memorial, 6, 9, 33, 73, 101, 125, 163, 203; UK Rejoinder, 33, 38, 55, 63, 79; Hearings, 20 [Counsel Plender, 12 June 2003] <www.pca-cpa.org>; 2006 ECJ *EC v. Ireland Mox Plant* Judgment, paras 27, 37, 147, 150 [*supra*].

On EC Council Directive 85/337/EEC on the Assessment of the Effects of Certain Public and Private Projects on the Environment of 27 June 1985 [OJEC L 175 (1985)], as amended by Directive 97/11/EEC, see 1995 NZ Request (Examination of the Situation), paras 88, 92; *Nuclear Tests* Oral Hearings, CR 95/20, 26 [Co-Agent MacKay, 12 Sep 1995]; *Gabcikovo* Separate O. Weearamntry, ICJ Rep. 1997, 111 n.78; Oral Hearings, CR 97/9, 39 n.54 [Counsel McCaffrey, 25 March 1997]; 2001 *Ireland v. UK Mox Plant (Provisional Measures)* Ireland's Request & Statement, paras 70, 85, 87, 89, UK Response, paras 13(2), 172, 220; Hearings, ITLOS/PV.01/07, 26-27 [Counsel Lord Goldsmith, 19 Nov 2001], ITLOS/PV.01/08, 23-24 [Counsel Plender, 20 Nov 2001] <www.itlos. org>; Annex VII *Mox Plant (Provisional Measures)* Hearings, 24 [Lord Goldsmith, 20 June 2003], 33-35 [Counsel Wordsworth]; Ireland's Memorial, I, 117, 120, 122, 127, 129; UK Counter-Memorial, 3, 6, 20, 22, 33, 71, 101, 110, 112-113, 118, 120, 122-124, 129-130, 133, 140; UK Rejoinder, 35, 50, 62, 63, 77-78, 80-81, 85-86;

Hearings, 19 [Counsel Plender, 12 June 2003] <www.pca-cpa.org>; 2005 *Belgium/Netherlands* Award, para.118 <www.pca-cpa.org> & <www.asil.org/ilib/2005/06/ilib050614.htm>; 2006 ECJ *EC v. Ireland Mox Plant* Judgment, paras 37, 111-115, 119, 142, 147, 150 [*supra*].

Cf. 1994 *R. v. Secretary of State* Judgment *infra*.

On EC Council Directive 90/313/EEC on Access to Environmental Information of 7 June 1990 [OJEC L 158/56 (1990)], including its exceptions with respect to commercially confidential information, as being amended [COM(2000)402 Final, OJEC L 337E/156 (2000) <http://europa.eu.int/eur-lex/en/com/pdf/2000/en 500PC0402.pdf>] as repealed by Directive 2003/4/EC of 28 January 2003 [OJEC L 41/26 (2003) <http://europa.eu.int/eur-lex/pri/en/oj/dat/2003/l-041/l_04120030214en00260032.pdf>], see 2003 OSPAR *Mox Plant* Award, paras 30, 95-96, 104, 109-126, 133, 140-143, 151-156, 172, 177, Declaration Chairman Reisman, paras 10-11, 20, Dissent Griffith, paras 23, 26, 49, 51, 117-118, 121; Ireland's Memorial, paras 57, 64, 102, 124, 127, UK Counter-Memorial, paras 3.9/12, 4.10/12, 5.20/24, 5.34, Ireland's Reply, paras 8/9, 20, 42, UK Rejoinder, para.13; Hearings, Vol.I, 28-30, 32, 43, 47-52, 58-60, 64-65, 69, 71 [Counsel Sands, 21 Oct], 80, 82 [Counsel Fitzsimons], Vol.II, 53 [Counsel Plender, 22 Oct], 80-81, 83-84, 86, 89, 91-92, 95-97 [Counsel Wordsworth], Vol.III, 5, 29 [Counsel Bethlehem, 23 Oct], Vol.IV, 8, 21-22, 24 [Counsel Brady, 24 Oct], 62 [Sands], Vol.V, 4-6 [Sands, 25 Oct 2002], 11-14, 20 [Plender]; Annex VII *Mox Plant* UK Rejoinder, 55, 63; Hearings, 19, 23 [Counsel Plender, 12 June 2003] <www.pca-cpa.org>; 2006 ECJ *EC v. Ireland Mox Plant* Judgment, paras 117-119, 142, 147 [*supra*].

On EC Council Directive 92/43/EEC on the Conservation of Natural Habitats and of Wild Fauna and Flora of 21 May 1992 [OJEC L 206/7 (1992)], see *Ireland v. UK Mox Plant (Provisional Measures)* Oral Hearings, ITLOS/PV.01/06, 23 [Counsel Fitzsimons, 19 Nov 2001] <www.itlos.org>; 2005 *Belgium/Netherlands Iron Rhine* Award, paras 118, 121-137, 151-152, 159, 189 <www.pca-cpa.org>.

On EC Council Directive 2003/4/EC [*supra*], see 2003 OSPAR *Mox Plant* Declaration Chairman Reisman, para.11, Dissent Griffith, paras 26-29, 31, 120-123 <www.pca-cpa.org>.

On EIA Mox Plant Opinion of the EC Commission of 25 February 1997 [OJEC C 86/03, C 291/9 (1997)], see 2001 *Ireland v. UK Mox Plant (Provisional Measures)* Separate O. Anderson, para.3; UK Response, paras 11, 36, 57, 183, 200, 220, 226(2) and Annex 3; Oral Hearings, ITLOS/PV.01/06, 22 [Counsel Fitzsimons, 19 Nov 2001], 30 [Counsel Sands], ITLOS/PV.01/07, 23, 32-33, 35-37 [Counsel Lord Goldsmith], ITLOS/PV.01/08, 7, 11, 34-35 [Goldsmith, 20 Nov 2001], ITLOS/PV.01/09, 19 [Counsel Wordsworth] <www.itlos.org>; 2003 OSPAR *Mox Plant*

Award, paras 17-19; UK Counter-Memorial, para.2.6; Annex VII *Mox Plant (Provisional Measures)* Hearings, 24 [Lord Goldsmith, 20 June 2003], 33-34 [Counsel Wordsworth]; Ireland's Memorial, I, 122, 128; UK Counter-Memorial, 19, 23-24, 57, 61, 122, 125, 130-133, 137, 163; UK Rejoinder, 46-47, 87, 113-114 <www.pca-cpa.org>; 2006 ECJ *EC v. Ireland Mox Plant* Judgment, para.25 [*supra*].

On 1974 *National Parks & Conservation Association v. Morton* Judgment, 498 F.2d 765 (D.C. Cir. 1974), see 2002 OSPAR *Mox Plant* UK Counter-Memorial, Appendix B-25/27 and Annex 25 <www.pca-cpa.org>.

On 1976 *National Parks II v. Kleppe* Judgment, 547 F.2d 673 (1976), see 2002 OSPAR *Mox Plant* Ireland's Reply, Appendix A.23/24.

On 1976 *Department of the Air Force v. Rose* Judgment of US Supreme Court, 425 U.S. 352 (1976) and *Gulf and Western Industries Inc v. US* Judgment, 1999 US App. D.C. 1, 615 F.2d 527 (D.C. Cir. 1976), see 2002 OSPAR *Mox Plant* Ireland's Reply, Appendix A.18, A.21, A.23.

On 1983 *Public Citizen Health Research Group v. Food and Drug Administration* Judgment, 704 F. 2d 1280 (1983), see 2002 OSPAR *Mox Plant* Ireland's Reply, Appendix A.24; Hearings, Vol.II, 105 [Counsel Bethlehem, 22 Oct], Vol.III, 4 [23 Oct 2002].

On 1984 *Fletcher Timber v. Attorney-General* [1984] 1 NZLR 290, and 1985 *Brightwell v. ACC* [1985] 1 NZLR 132, Judgments of New Zealand Court of Appeal, see 2002 OSPAR *Mox Plant* Ireland's Reply, Appendix A.8.

On 1988 *Saarl and Others v. Minister for Industry, Post and Telecommunications and Trade and Others* Judgment of the European Court of Justice, Case 187/87: [1988] ECR 5013, see 2003 OSPAR *Mox Plant* Award, para.16; Annex VII *Mox Plant (Provisional Measures)* Hearings, 33 [Lord Goldsmith, 20 June 2003] <www.pca-cpa.org>.

On 1989 *Rubin v. Canada (Minister of Transport)* [1989] 1 F.C. 265, and *Canada Packers Inc. v. Canada (Minister of Agriculture)* [1989] 1 F.C. 47, Judgments, see 2002 OSPAR *Mox Plant* Ireland's Reply, Appendix A.11/13; Oral Hearings, Vol.I, 84-85 [Counsel Fitzsimons, 21 Oct 2002].

On 1992 *Critical Mass Energy Project v. NRC* Judgment, 975 F.2d 871 (D.C. Cir. 1992), see 2002 OSPAR *Mox Plant* UK Counter-Memorial, Appendix B-25/27 and Annex 26, Ireland's Reply, Appendix A.19.

On 1994 *R. v. Secretary and Others, ex Parte Greenpeace* Judgment, see *infra*.

On 1995 *R. v. British Coal Corporation, ex Parte Ibstock Building Products Ltd.*, [1995] JPL 836; Env. LR 227, see 2002 OSPAR *Mox Plant* Ireland's Memorial, para.130, Annex 15, UK Counter-Memorial, para.5.8; Oral Hearings, Vol.I, 30 [Counsel Sands, 21 Oct 2002].

On 1997 *Dagg v. Canada (Minister of Finance)* Judgment of Canada's Supreme Court, [1997] 2 S.C.R. 403, see 2002 OSPAR *Mox Plant* Ireland's Reply, Appendix A.10.

On 1998 *Occam Marine Technologies v. The National Research Council of Canada* [1998] FC T-146-98, see 2002 OSPAR *Mox Plant* Ireland's Reply, Appendix A.13.

On 1998 *Secretary of State for the Environment, Transport and the Regions and Another, ex Parte Alliance Against the Birmingham Northern Relief Road and Others* Judgment of Justice Sullivan, [1998] All ER (D) 386, see 2002 OSPAR *Mox Plant* Ireland's Memorial, paras 131-138, 142-143 Annex 15; Hearings, Vol.I, 39-40, 50-51, 68 [Counsel Sands, 21 Oct], Vol.IV, 52, 56, 63-64 [24 Oct 2002].

On 1999 *R. v. Secretary of State for the Environment, Transport and Regions, ex Parte Alliance Against the Birmingham Northern Relief Road* Judgment of Justice Sullivan, [1999] JPL 231; ELR 447, see 2003 OSPAR *Mox Plant* Dissent Griffith, paras 49-50; UK Counter-Memorial, paras 5.8/11, 5.26, Annex 14, UK Rejoinder, para.19; Hearings, Vol.II, 98 [Counsel Wordsworth, 22 Oct], Vol.III, 23-24 [Bethlehem, 23 Oct], Vol.V, 21-22 [Counsel Plender, 25 Oct 2002].

On 1999 *Public Citizen Health Research Group v. Food and Drug Administration* Judgment, 185 F.3d 898 (D.C. Cir. 1999), see 2002 OSPAR *Mox Plant* UK Counter-Memorial, Appendix B-27 and Annex 27.

On 1999 *Mecklenburg v. Kreis Pinneberg der Landrat* Judgment of the European Court of Justice, Case C-321/96: [1999] 2 CMLR 418, see 2003 OSPAR *Mox Plant* Award, paras 150, 156, 172, 177, Dissent Griffith, paras 47, 77, 113, 130; Ireland's Memorial, para.102, Annex 15, UK Counter-Memorial, paras 4.10/11; Hearings, Vol.I, 40, 58, 64 [Counsel Sands, 21 Oct], 96 [Counsel Wordsworth, 22 Oct], Vol.III, 14 [Counsel Bethlehem, 23 Oct], Vol.IV, 53, 56, 63 [Sands, 24 Oct], Vol.V, 20 [Conusel Plender, 25 Oct 2002].

On 2001 *London Regional Transport and London Underground Limited v. The Mayor of London and Transport for London* Judgment of the Court of Appeal, [2001] EWCA Civ.1491, see 2002 OSPAR *Mox Plant* Ireland's Memorial, paras 141-143, 155, 158, Annex 15, UK Counter-Memorial, paras 5.14/18, 5.26, UK Rejoinder, para.20; Hearings, Vol.I, 70 [Counsel Sands, 21 Oct], Vol.III, 24-25 [Counsel Bethlehem, 23 Oct], Vol.V, 22 [Counsel Plender, 25 Oct 2002].

On the *R. (Friends of the Earth Ltd. and Greenpeace Ltd.) v. Secretary of State for the Environment, Food and Rural Affairs and Secretary of State for Health* Judgment of Justice Collins, High Court of Justice Administrative Court of 15 November 2001, [2001] EWHC Admin 914; <www.foe.co.uk/pubsinfo/infoteam/pressrel/2001/20011115111838. html>, see 2001 *Ireland v. UK Mox Plant (Provisional Measures)* UK Response, paras 47-49, 168 and Annex 9; Hearings,

ITLOS/PV.01/06, 26 [Counsel Fitzsimons, 19 Nov 2001], ITLOS/PV.01/07, 30, 33 [Counsel Goldsmith], ITLOS/PV.01/08, 28-29 [Counsel Plender, 20 Nov 2001] <www.itlos.org>; 2003 OSPAR *Mox Plant* Award, para.19; UK Counter-Memorial, para.1.24 and Annex 7; Hearings, Vol.II, 68 [Counsel Plender, 22 Oct], Vol.III, 25 [Counsel Bethlehem, 23 Oct 2002]; Annex VII *Mox Plant* UK Counter-Memorial, 26 <www.pca-cpa.org>.

On the Court of Appeal's Judgment of 7 Dec 2001, [2001] EWCA Civ. 1847; <www.rte.ie/news/2001/1207/sellafield.html>, see 2003 OSPAR *Mox Plant* Award, para.37; UK Counter-Memorial, para.1.24 and Annex 8; Hearings, Vol.II, 68 [Counsel Plender, 22 Oct], Vol.III, 25 [Counsel Bethlehem, 283 Oct 2002]; Annex VII *Mox Plant* UK Counter-Memorial, 26 <www.pca-cpa.org>.

Pollution from Land-Based Sources

1982 UNCLOS, Part XII, Articles 207, 212 and 213, 222; 2002 Johannesburg Plan of Implementation, paras 23-28 (Freshwater), paras 29, 32 (Oceans):

Nuclear Tests Pleadings (Australia), 520 [Counsel Byers, 9 July 1974]; *Gabcikovo* Judgment, ICJ Rep. 1997, 18; *Spain v. Canada* Pleadings, 251 [Canada's Counter-Memorial]; 2001 *Ireland v. UK Mox Plant (Provisional Measures)* Order and Pleadings, ITLOS Case No.10 <www.itlos.org>; 2003 OSPAR *Mox Plant* Award <www.pca-cpa.org> and 2006 *EC v. Ireland Mox Plant* Judgment, para.14 [*supra*].

Environmental Protection of Lakes and Rivers

Gulf of Maine Pleadings, Vol.III, 360-361 [Canada's Counter-Memorial]; *Gabcikovo* Judgment, ICJ Rep. 1997, 18, 31-46, 59, 62, 64-68, 73-74, 77-80, Separate O. Weeramantry, 88-119, Dissents Oda, 159-161, 168, Herczegh, 176-189; *Legality of Use of Force (Provisional Measures)* Orders – see Obligation to Protect and Preserve the Marine Environment *supra*; *Kasikili/Sedudu Botswana/Namibia* Judgment, ICJ Rep. 1999, 1054, 1095, 1106, 1108, paras 12, 76, 102-103, Dissent Vice-President Weeramantry, 1155, 1169, 1177-1195, paras 4-5, 47, 76-119; 2004 *France/Netherlands* Award [1976 Rhine Convention, 16 ILM 265 (1977)], awarding Euro 19mln to the NL, President K. Skubiszewski (Poland), Judges G. Guillaume, Declaration (France/ICJ) and P.H. Kooymans (NL/ICJ) <www.pca-cpa.org> & <www.asil.org/ilib0718.htm>; RIAA XXV, 267 <http://untreaty.un.org/cod/riaa/vol_XXV.htm> and Award's text in English and French with Introduction by L. Boisson de Chazournes, in *PCA Awards Series*, Vol.IV (2007) <www.asserpress .nl & www.pca-cpa.org/showpage.asp?pag_id=1056>; *Benin/Niger* Judgment, ICJ Rep. 2005, 147, para.137; Hearings, C5/CR 2005/1, 23, para.2.5 [Counsel Pellet,

7 March], C5/CR 2005/3, 14, para.9 [Agent Mindaoudou, 8 March], C5/CR 2005/6, 48-49, paras 10, 13 [Counsel Klein, 11 March] <www.icj-cij.org>, including Niger's "W" Park under the 1971 Ramsar Wetlands Convention <www.ramsar.org/profiles_niger.htm> and <http://whc.unesco.org/sites/749.htm>; UN ECE *Romania/Ukraine Danube-Black Sea (Bystroe) Canal* Opinion of Commission of Inquiry under the 1991 Espoo EIA Convention (Art.3 & Appendix IV) [1989 UNTS 310; 30 ILM 802 (1991)] of 11 July 2006 <www.unece.org/env/eia/inquiry.htm> and press comments <www.mosnews.com/news/2006/07/11/canaldisp.shtml & www.cceg.ro/2006stiri/UN.htm>; *Argentina v. Uruguay (Provisional Measures)* Orders, ICJ Rep. 2006, 113 and 2007, 3; *Costa Rica v. Nicaragua San Juan River* Order, ICJ Rep. 2005, 165 and Judgment, ICJ Rep. 2009, paras 86-90, 104, 109, 118, 127, 141, Declaration Guillaume, paras 3, 15; Hearings, CR 2009/2, 13, para.4 [Agent Ugalde-Alvarez, 2 March 2009], CR 2009/5, 16-27, paras 25-49 [Counsel Reichler, 6 March], CR 2009/7, 54, para.42 [Reichler, 12 March 2009]; *Ecuador v. Colombia Toxic Herbicides*, ICJ Rep. 2008 <www.icj-cij.org>; 2009 *Abyei Boundary* Award, paras 357-371, referring to environmental considerations in land boundary delimitation <www.pca-cpa.org>.

Pollution from Sea-Bed Activities
1958 CSC, Article 5(7); 1982 UNCLOS, Part V, Article 56(1)(b)(iii), Part XII, Articles 208 and 214:

Gulf of Maine Judgment, ICJ Rep. 1984, 279, 344; Pleadings, Vol.I, 106-107, 162 [Canada's Memorial], Vol.II, 34-38 [US Memorial], Vol.III, 58, 137, 170, 352-361 [Canada's Counter-Memorial], Vol.IV, 152-153, 166, 259-271 [US Counter-Memorial], Vol.V, 64-65, 342-343 [Canada's Reply], 440 [US Reply], Vol.VI, 450-455 [Counsel Colson, 19 April 1984], Vol.VII, 117, 123-124 [Counsel Fortier, 5 May], 154, 269 [Agent Robinson, 9 and 11 May], 192 [Counsel Stevenson, 9 May 1984]; *Great Belt* Pleadings, 511, 522 [Denmark's Counter-Memorial]; *Oil Platforms* Hearings, CR 96/14, 17 [Counsel Zeinoddin, 19 Sep 1996]; *Spain v. Canada* Pleadings, 251 [Canada's Counter-Memorial] <www.icj-cij.org>; *Barbados/Trinidad & Tobago* Barbados' Reply, para.157 <www.pca-cpa.org>.

Pollution from Activities in the Area
1982 UNCLOS, Part XII, Articles 209 and 215; 1994 Agreement:

New Zealand v. France Nuclear Tests (Interim Measures) Order, ICJ Rep. 1973, 139-140; Pleadings (Australia), 519 [Counsel Byers, 9 July 1974], (NZ), 7, 8 [Application], 49, 55, 77 [Request], 204 [Memorial]; *New Zealand v. France* Dissent Weeramantry, ICJ Rep. 1995, 326.

Pollution by Dumping
1982 UNCLOS, Part I, Article 1(1)5, Part XII, Articles 210 and 216:

Nuclear Tests Pleadings (Australia), 519 [Counsel Byers, 9 July 1974]; *Gulf of Maine* Pleadings, Vol.I, 35 n.7 [Canada's Memorial], Vol.III, 355 [Canada's Counter-Memorial], Vol.VII, 192 [Counsel Stevenson, 9 May 1984]; *Great Belt* Pleadings, 156 [Agent Fergo, 2 July 1991]; *New Zealand v. France* Dissents Weeramantry, ICJ Rep. 1995, 343, 345, Koroma, 370-371; NZ Request (Examination of the Situation), paras 101-102; Oral Hearings, CR 95/20, 16-21 [Counsel Keith, 12 Sep 1995].

Nuclear-Powered Ships and Ships Carrying Dangerous Substances
1982 UNCLOS, Part II, Articles 22(2) and 23, Part XII, Articles 194(3)(b), 211 and 217; 2002 Johannesburg Plan of Implementation, paras 29, 33.bis:

IMCO Pleadings, 208-209 [Panama, *The Savannah*]; *Great Belt* Pleadings, 150 [Counsel de Arechaga, 2 July 1991], 247, 356 [Finland's Memorial], 529, 599, 616 [Denmark's Counter-Memorial]; *Nuclear Tests* Dissent Palmer, ICJ Rep. 1995, 388; *Nuclear Weapons (UNGA)* Dissent Vice-President Schwebel, ICJ Rep. 1996, 320; 2001 *Ireland v. UK Mox Plant (Provisional Measures)* Order and Pleadings, ITLOS Case No.10, President P. Ch. Rao, 41 ILM 405 (2002) <www.itlos.org>; 2003 OSPAR *Mox Plant* Award, President W.M. Reisman <www.pca-cpa.org>; 2006 *EC v. Ireland Mox Plant* Judgment, para.114-117 [*supra*]. Cf. 22 July 2002 <www.nuclearfreeflotilla.org/late_news.htm>.

Pollution from Vessels
1958 HSC, Articles 24-25; 1982 UNCLOS, Article 94(4)(c) and (5)-(7), Article 194(3)(b), Articles 211 and 217-233; 2002 Johannesburg Plan of Implementation, paras 29, 33:

IMCO Advisory Opinion, ICJ Rep. 1960, 170; *IMCO* Pleadings, 48-49, 52, 93 [Liberia], 257 [India] (See also High Seas, Nationality of Ships – Genuine Link *supra*); *Gulf of Maine* Pleadings, Vol.I, 35 n.7 [Canada's Memorial], Vol.III, 137 n.26, 359-360 [Canada's Counter-Memorial], Vol.V, 65, 342-343 [Canada's Reply], 381, 532 [US Reply]; *Great Belt* Pleadings, 149-150 [Counsel de Arechaga, 2 July 1991]; *Gabcikovo* Hearings, CR 97/10, 10-11 [Counsel McCaffrey, 26 March 1997]; 1998 *Eritrea/Yemen (Phase I)* Award, President R.Y. Jennings, para.312 <http://www.pca-cpa.org>; *M/V Saiga* Judgment, President T.A. Mensah [38 ILM 1323 (1999)], para.105, Separate O. Laing, paras 38, 45, 47, 49; *Southern Bluefin Tuna (Jurisdiction)*, President S.M. Schwebel, Japan's Memorial, para.119 <www.worldbank.org/icsid>; *Oil Platforms (Merits)* Hearings, CR 2003/9, 28,

36 [Counsel Mathias, 21 Feb 2003], 38 [Counsel Neubauer], CR 2003/13, 20-21 [Counsel Matter, 26 Feb 2003] <www.icj-cij.org>; 2006 *EC v. Ireland Mox Plant* Judgment, para.114-117 [*supra*]; 2007 *Guyana/Suriname* Award, para.316 <www.pca-cpa.org>; ECJ Grand Chamber *International Association of Independent Tank Owners (Intertanko) v. Secretary of State for Transport*, Case C-308/06 of 3 June 2008 <http://eur-lex.europa.eu>; 103 AJIL 555 (2009).

On IMO's role, see *Finland v. Denmark (Provisional Measures)* Declaration Tarassov, ICJ Rep. 1991, 24; Pleadings, 5, 24 [Finland's Application, para.15 and Annex 10], 115 [Co-Agent Koskenniemi, 1 July 1991], 145 [Counsel Gimsing, 2 July], 183 [Agent Gronberg, 4 July], 211-212, 218 [Agent Magid, 5 July 1991].

See also Settlement of Disputes – 1982 LOSC, Article 287(1)(d) *infra*.

Port State Jurisdiction

SS Lotus Judgment, PCIJ Series A, No.10 (1927) was unprecedented in involving a prosecution by a port state of a foreign-flagged vessel in respect of a collision on the high seas; 2007 *Guyana/Suriname* Award, para.316 <www.pca-cpa.org>.

See also Access to and Jurisdiction and Treatment in Ports; High Seas – Status of Ships/Criminal Jurisdiction *supra*; Settlement of Disputes – Prompt Release of Vessels and Crews *infra*; FAO Agreement on Port State Measures to Prevent, Deter and Eliminate Illegal, Unreported and Unregulated Fishing of 25 Nov 2009 <www.un.org/apps/news/story.asp?NewsID=33064&Cr=fishing&Cr1 & www.fao.org/news/story/en/item/37627/icode/>.

Pollution from or through the Atmosphere
1982 UNCLOS, Article 194(3)(a) and Articles 212, 222:

Ecuador v. Colombia Alleged Aerial Spraying by Colombia of Toxic Herbicides over Ecuadorian Territory, ICJ Rep. 2008 <www.icj-cij.org>.

On 1963 Moscow Treaty, see Peaceful Uses of the Sea *infra*.

On on 1979 UN ECE Air Pollution Convention, 1985 UNEP Ozone Convention and 1992 UN Climate Convention, see *infra*.

See also Pollution From Land-Based Sources *supra*; Peaceful Uses of the Sea – Nuclear Weapon Tests *infra*.

Ice-Covered Areas
1982 UNCLOS, Article 234:

North Atlantic Ice Patrol (IMO SOLAS Convention, Chapter V) *IMCO* Pleadings, 113 [Liberia], 125 [USA], 191 [Panama], 271 [L, 26 April 1960], 325 [USA, 28 April 1960]. See also High Seas – 1912 *Titanic* disaster *supra*.

Gulf of Maine Pleadings, Vol.III, 358 [Canada's Counter-Memorial], Vol.IV, 153 n.3 [US Counter-Memorial]; *Denmark v. Norway* Judgment, ICJ Rep. 1993, 44, 72-73, 76, Separate Os Schwebel, 120, Weeramantry, 271; Hearings, CR 93/2, 32-33 [Counsel Lynge, 12 Jan 1993], CR 93/7, 20-21 [Counsel Brownlie, 19 Jan 1993]; 2005 US Supreme Court's *Alaska v. US* Opinion <www.supremecourtus.gov/opinions/opinions.html>.

On 1998 *Sellers v. Maritime Safety Inspector*, see *infra*.

See also Exclusive Economic (/Fishery) Zone – Protection and Preservation of the Marine Environment, 1970 Canada's Arctic Waters Act and Optional Clause Declaration *supra*; Environmental Factors in Disputes Over Territorial Sovereignty in this section *infra*.

Precautionary Approach

1982 UNCLOS, Part II, Article 23; 1992 Rio Principle 15, and Agenda 21, Chapter 17, paras 17.1 and 17.22; 1995 SSA, Articles 5(c) and 6, and Annex II; 2002 Johannesburg Plan of Implementation, paras 22, 64(e), 103(f):

New Zealand v. France Nuclear Tests Order, ICJ Rep. 1995, 290, 298-299, Dissents Weeramantry, 342-344, Palmer, 407, 410-412; NZ Request and France's Aide-Mémoire (Examination of the Situation); *Nuclear Tests* Hearings, CR 95/19, 37-38 [Agent East, 11 Sep 1995], CR 95/20 [transl.], 67-68, 71-73 [De Brichambaut, 12 Sep 1995], CR 95/20, 10, 15, 20-21 [Counsel Keith], 36-38 [Co-Agent MacKay], 40-41 [Agent East], 47 [Question 2 Shahabuddeen], NZ and France's Written Replies of 15 Sep 1995; *Nuclear Weapons (WHO)* Dissent Weeramantry, ICJ Rep. 1996, 138.

Gabcikovo-Nagymaros Project Judgment, ICJ Rep. 1997, 62, para.97, at 68, para.113, at 78, para.141; Hearings, CR 97/9, 33-37 [Counsel McCaffrey, 25 March 1997]. The required precautionary measures should be construed as included into the Court's guidance concerning the future arrangements of the Parties. See ICJ Rep. 1997, 75-81 (Settlement of Disputes – Preventive Diplomacy A) *infra*) and ILC Report, UN Doc. A/55/10, para.716 (2000) <www.un.org/law>.

EC Measures Concerning Meat and Meat Products (Hormones) Report AB-1997-4, WTO Appellate Body, President F. Feliciano, WT/DS26/AB/R-WT/DS48/AB/R, 16 January 1998, paras 16 [EC], 43 [USA], 60 [Canada], 120-125 and 253(c) [AB]; *US – Import Prohibition of Certain Shrimp and Shrimp Products* Report AB-1998-4, para.67 [Obligation to Protect and Preserve Marine Environment *supra*].

Southern Bluefin Tuna (Provisional Measures) Order, President T.A. Mensah, ITLOS Cases Nos 3/4, 38 ILM 1624 (1999), paras 67, 70-71, 74, 77, 79-80, Joint

Declaration, Separate Os Laing, paras 11-18, Shearer <www.itlos.org>; *Australia and New Zealand v. Japan Southern Bluefin Tuna (Jurisdiction)* Award, President S.M. Schwebel, paras 31, 33-34, 41(f) and 50; A/NZ Reply, paras 37, 68-70; Hearings, Vol.III [Question 1 of Arbitrators, 10 May], Written Answers of the Parties to Question 1 [26 May 2000] <www.worldbank.org/icsid>.

2001 *Ireland v. UK Mox Plant (Provisional Measures)* Order, President P.Ch. Rao, ITLOS Case No.10, paras 71-76, 84, Joint Declaration Caminos, Yamamoto, Park, Akl, Marsit, Eiriksson and Jesus, Separate Os Treves, paras 8-9, Szekely; Ireland's Request & Statement, paras 48, 88, 96-105, 112, UK Response, paras 150, 183-184, 207-208; Hearings, ITLOS/PV.01/06, 10, 13 [Agent O'Hagan, 19 Nov 2001], 30, 32-33, 40 [Counsel Sands], ITLOS/PV.01/08, 18 [Counsel Bethlehem, 20 Nov 2001], 25 [Counsel Plender] <www.itlos.org>; 2003 OSPAR *Mox Plant* Dissent Griffith, paras 73-78; Ireland's Memorial, paras 82, 98; Hearings, Vol. IV, 24 [Counsel Brady, 24 Oct 2002]; Annex VII *Mox Plant* Ireland's Memorial, I, 105-107, UK Counter-Memorial, 183, 198-203; UK Rejoinder, 125-132 <www.pca-cpa.org>; 2003 *Malaysia v. Singapore (Provisional Measures)* Order, President L.D.M. Nelson, ITLOS Case No.12, paras 22(2), 74/75, 99, Separate O. Rao, paras 5, 25 <www.itlos.org>; and 2005 Annex VII *Malaysia v. Singapore* Award <www.pca-cpa.org>.

Argentina v. Uruguay (Provisional Measures) Dissent Vinuesa, ICJ Rep. 2006, 152 <www.icj-cij.org>.

On a risk assessment, see EIA/Notification/Consultation *supra*.

Marine Biodiversity

1982 UNCLOS, Preamble, Part XII, Articles 192-196 and 237; 1992 Rio Agenda 21, Chapter 15, and Chapter 17, para.17.86; 1995 SSA, Article 5(g); 2002 Johannesburg Plan of Implementation, paras 29(d), 31, 39(c), 42:

2002 *Belize/Guatemala* OAS Proposals, B-paras 1, 12, C and Annex A <www.belize-guatemala.gov.bz>; 2005 *Belgium/Netherlands* Award, para.126 <www.pca-cpa.org>; *Argentina v. Uruguay (Provisional Measures)* Order, para.11(1)(d-e), ICJ Rep. 2006, 116 and Order, para.3(1)(d-e), ICJ Rep. 2007, 4; *Ecuador v. Colombia Toxic Herbicides* case, ICJ Rep. 2008 <www.icj-cij.org>.

On EC Council Habitats Directive 92/43/EEC, see Environmental Impact Assessment/Notification/Consultation *supra*

On 1992 UNEP Convention on Biodiversity, see *infra*; UNGA Adopts Two Oceans Resolutions, UN Doc.GA/10899 of 4 Dec 2009 <www.un.org/News/Press/docs//2009/ga10899.doc.htm>.

Erga Omnes *Rights and Obligations*

Reparation for Injuries Suffered in the Service of the United Nations Advisory Opinion, ICJ Rep. 1949, 183; *North Sea* Judgment, ICJ Rep. 1969, 20, para.14, and 28, para.35, Separate O. Ammoun, 102, Dissents Tanaka, 190, Morelli, 205; *North Sea* Pleadings, Vol.I, 507 [Common Rejoinder of Denmark/NL], Vol.II, 80, 99, 104-105, 109 [Counsel Sir Humphrey Waldock, 28 and 29 Oct 1968], 246 [Reply by Waldock to Questions Fitzmaurice, 8 Nov], 281 [Waldock, 11 Nov 1968]; *Fisheries Jurisdiction (Merits)* Declarations Nagendra Singh, ICJ Rep. 1974, 39, 212, Joint Separate Os, 45, 47, 217, 219, Separate O. Dillard, 55-56, 60, 61, Separate Os de Castro, 96, 225, Separate Os Waldock, 119-120, 227, Dissent Gros, 137; *Tunisia/Libya (Intervention)* Separate O. Oda, ICJ Rep. 1981, 32; *Libya/ Malta (Intervention)* Separate O. de Arechaga, ICJ Rep. 1984, 70, Dissent Oda, 108-109.

Ethiopia v. South Africa; Liberia v. South Africa South West Africa (Preliminary Objections) and *(Second Phase)* Separate O. Jessup, ICJ Rep. 1962, 425-426, and 1966, 387-388, and *Belgium v. Spain Barcelona Traction, Light and Power Company, Limited (Second Phase)* Judgment, ICJ Rep. 1970, 32, paras 33-34, as relied upon by *Nuclear Tests* Judgments, ICJ Rep. 1974, 269, 474, Separate O. Gros, 288, 290, Dissents Petren, 303, 487-488, Dissents Petren, 310, 493, Joint Dissents Onyeama, Dillard, Jiménez de Aréchaga, and Sir Humphrey Waldock, 362, 370, 513-514, 521, Dissents de Castro, 386-387, 524, Dissent Barwick, 436-438; *Nuclear Tests* Pleadings (Australia), 326-330, 334-335, 343 [Memorial], (New Zealand), 205-208, 210, 211 [Memorial], 262-266 [Counsel Finlay, 10 July 1974]; *Nicaragua v. USA (Provisional Measures)* Dissent Schwebel, ICJ Rep. 1984, 197-198 and *(Jurisdiction and Admissibility)* Dissent Schwebel, 627-628, para.116; *Portugal v. Australia East Timor* Judgment, ICJ Rep. 1995, 102, para.29, Dissents Weeramantry, 172, 202, 213-216, Skubiszewski, 244; Hearings, CR 95/3 [trans.], 27 [Counsel Dupuy, 31 Jan 1995], CR 95/5, 25-26 [Counsel Higgins, 2 Feb], 46-48 [Co-Agent Teles], CR 95/8 [trans.], 26-33 [Counsel Pellet, 7 Feb 1995]; *New Zealand v. France Nuclear Tests* Order, ICJ Rep. 1995, 305, para.61, Dissent Palmer, 414-415; Oral Hearings, CR 95/21 [trans.], 17-18 [Dupuy, 12 Sep 1995]; *Nuclear Weapons (WHO)* Dissent Weeramantry, ICJ Rep. 1996, 140-143, *Nuclear Weapons (UNGA)* Dissent Koroma, 573; Hearings, CR 95/22, 68 [Australian Foreign Minister Evans, 30 Oct 1995], CR 95/25, 60 [Mexico, 3 Nov], CR 95/32, 64-65 [Solomon I., 14 Nov 1995].

Gulf of Fonseca (Intervention) Judgment, ICJ Rep. 1990, 120; *Great Belt* Pleadings, 225 [Agent Lehmann, 5 July 1991]; *Denmark v. Norway* Separate O. Oda, ICJ Rep. 1993, 100, 110; *Application of the Convention on the Prevention and Punishment of the Crime of Genocide (Preliminary Objections)* Judgment,

ICJ Rep. 1996, 616, para.31; *Gabcikovo* Judgment, ICJ Rep. 1997, 62, Separate O. Weeramantry, 117-118; *Spain v. Canada (Jurisdiction)* Dissent Vereshchetin, ICJ Rep. 1998, 575, para.11; *Yugoslavia v. USA Legality of Use of Force (Provisional Measures)* Separate Os Oda, ICJ Rep. 1999, para.22 at 154, 288, 387, 452, 513, 566, 686, 792, 859, 943 Dissent Kreca, para.9 at 144, 346, 415, 474, 535, 630, 744, 824, 905, 963, (in all 10 Orders); *Pakistan v. India (Jurisdiction)* Dissent Pirzada, para.89, ICJ Rep, 2000, 102; *Qatar v. Bahrain (Merits)* Dissent Torres Bernardez, paras 363 [de Visscher], 555, ICJ Rep. 2001, 387, 447; *Indonesia/Malaysia (Intervention)* Separate O. Franck, para.9, ICJ Rep. 2001, 655; Hearings, CR 2001/1, 10 [Counsel Reisman, 25 June 2001]; *Oil Platforms (Merits)* Hearings, CR 2003/8, 42 [Counsel Crawford, 19 Feb 2003], CR 2003/14, 27-28, 31 [Counsel Pellet, 28 Feb], CR 2003/19, 27 [7 March 2003]; *Israel Wall* Advisory Opinion, ICJ Rep. 2004, 199, para.155, Separate Os Higgins, 216, para.37, Kooymans, 229, 231, paras 33, 40; *DR Congo v. Uganda (Merits)* Separate O. Simma, ICJ Rep. 2005, 349-350, paras 39-41; *DR Congo v. Rwanda New Application (Provisional Measures)* Order, ICJ Rep. 2002, 219, paras 22, 31, 36, 40, 71, Separate O. Mavungu, 289, para.66 and *(Jurisdiction)* Judgment, ICJ Rep. 2006, paras 56-70, 121-124, Separate O. Dugard <www.icj-cij.org>.

1998 *Eritrea/Yemen (Phase I)* Award, para.153 <www.pca-cpa.org>; *Southern Bluefin Tuna (Jurisdiction)*, President S.M. Schwebel, A/NZ Reply, para.26, Hearings, Vol.I [Counsel Rosenne, 7 May 2000] <www.worldbank.org/icsid>.

On EURATOM Treaty of 25 March 1957 [in force: 1 Jan 1958, 298 UNTS 167; 51 AJIL 955 (1957)], see 2001 *Ireland v. UK Mox Plant (Provisional Measures)* Order, ITLOS Case No.10, paras 40-50, Separate O. Anderson, paras 1-3; UK Response, paras 3, 11, 36, 57, 166-167, 218; Oral Hearings, ITLOS/PV.01/07, 9 [Counsel Lowe, 19 Nov 2001], 31, 35 [Counsel Lord Goldsmith], ITLOS/PV.01/08, 24 [Counsel Plender, 20 Nov 2001], ITLOS/PV.01/09, 20-21 [Plender] <www.itlos .org>; 2003 OSPAR *Mox Plant* Award, paras 16-19, 141; UK Counter-Memorial, para.2.6; Hearings, Vol.II, 62-63 [Counsel Plender, 22 Oct 2002], 98 [Counsel Wordsworth]; 2003 Annex VII *Mox Plant (Suspension of Proceedings)* Orders Nos 3 & 4; 2008 Annex VII *Mox Plant* (Termination of Proceedings) Order; Ireland's Memorial, I, 97-98, 122, 128; UK Counter-Memorial, 23-24, 32-33, 97-98, 100-102, 130-133; UK Rejoinder, 33, 53, 58-62 <www.pca-cpa.org>; *European Commission v. Ireland Mox Plant* Case C-459/03, OJEC C/24 (2004) <http:// europa.eu.int/eur-lex/pri/en/oj/dat/2004/c_007/c_00720040110en00240024.pdf> and Opinion of Advocate General Poiares Maduro of 12 Jan 2006 [*UNSG Oceans Report*, UN Doc. A/61/63, para.275 (2006)] and the ECJ *EC v. Ireland Mox Plant* Judgment of 30 May 2006 [<http://curia.eu.int/jrisp/cgi-bin/form.pl?lang=EN &Submit=rechercher&numaff=C-459/03> & Cases since 1989 at <http://curia.

eu.int/en/content/juris/index.htm> and PR No.45/06 <http://curia.eu.nt/en/actu/communiques/cp060045en.pdf>].

See also Peaceful Uses of the Sea – Nuclear Weapon Tests *infra*.

On African Convention on the Conservation of Nature and Natural Resources, Algiers, 15 Sep 1968 [in force: 16 June 1969, 1001 UNTS 3], as Amended on 11 July 2003 <www.fao.org/docrep/007/y5636e/y563e04.htm> & <www.iucn.org/themes/law>, see *Botswana/Namibia* Dissent Vice-President Weeramantry, ICJ Rep. 1999, 1194, para.113 <www.icj-cij.org>.

On Agreement for Cooperation in Dealing with Pollution of the North Sea by Oil, Bonn, 9 June 1969 [in force: 9 August 1969, 704 UNTS 3; as superseded by Agreement for Cooperation in Dealing with Pollution of the North Sea by Oil and Other Harmful Substances, Bonn, 13 Sep 1983, in force: 1 Sep 1989, 1605 UNTS No.28022; Cmnd.9104, as Amended by Denmark/Norway/Sweden Agreement, Stockholm, 25 Jan 1994, in force: 9 April 1995, 2090 UNTS 229], see *Gulf of Maine* Pleadings, Vol.III, 170 [Canada's Counter-Memorial].

On Convention on Wetlands of International Importance Especially as Waterfowl Habitat, Ramsar, 2 Feb 1971 [in force: 21 Dec 1975, 11 ILM 963 (1972)] and Protocol, Paris, 3 Dec 1982 [in force: 1 Oct 1986, 22 ILM 698 (1983) <www.ramsar.org/>], see *Botswana/Namibia* Dissent Vice-President Weeramantry, paras 81 and 112, ICJ Rep. 1999, 1179, 1193; Hearings, CR 99/6, 22 [Counsel Selepeng, 22 Feb 1999]; *Benin/Niger Frontier Dispute* [see Regime of Islands – Environmental Factors in Disputes over Territorial Sovereignty *supra*]; *Costa Rica v. Nicaragua San Juan River* Judgment, ICJ Rep. 2009, para.88 <www.icj-cij.org>.

On Convention for the Prevention of Marine Pollution by Dumping From Ships and Aircraft, Oslo, 15 Feb 1972 [in force: 7 April 1974, 932 UNTS 3] and Protocol of 2 March 1983 [in force: 1 Sep 1989, Cmnd 8942], as superseded by the 1992 Paris Convention [*infra*], see *Great Belt* Pleadings, 156 [Agent Fergo, 2 July 1991], 348, 349 n.1 [Finland's Memorial], 594 [Denmark's Counter-Memorial]; 2003 OSPAR *Mox Plant* Award, para.10, Declaration President Reisman, para.9; Annex VII *Mox Plant* Ireland's Memorial, I, 103, 140, 193 n.35; UK Counter-Memorial, 103 <www.pca-cpa.org>.

On IMO Convention on the Prevention of Marine Pollution by Dumping of Wastes and Other Matter, London, 29 Dec 1972 [in force: 30 August 1975, 1046 UNTS 120; 11 ILM 1291 (1972), as Amended] and Protocol of 8 Nov 1996 [36 ILM 1 (1997); 97 AJIL 979 (2003)], see *Great Belt* Pleadings, 156 [Agent Fergo, 2 July 1991], 347 n.4, 349 n.1 [Finland's Memorial]; *Nuclear Tests* Dissent Palmer, ICJ Rep. 1995, 411; NZ Request (Examination of the Situation), para.102; Hearings, CR 95/20, 16, 18 [Counsel Keith, 12 Sep 1995]; *Nuclear Weapons (UNGA)* Dissent Weeramantry, ICJ Rep. 1996, 455; *Spain v. Canada* Pleadings,

253 n.156 [Canada's Counter-Memorial]; Annex VII *Mox Plant* UK Counter-Memorial, 103, 140, 193 n.35 <www.pca-cpa.org>.

On Convention on International Trade in Endangered Species of Wild Fauna and Flora (CITES), Washington, 3 March 1973 [in force: 1 July 1975, 27 UST 1087], as Amended on 22 June 1979 and 30 April 1983 [in force: 13 April 1987, TIAS 11079], see *Nuclear Weapons (UNGA)* Dissent Weeramantry, ICJ Rep. 1996, 455; *Botswana/Namibia* Dissent Vice-President Weeramantry, para.81, ICJ Rep. 1999, 1179; Oral Hearings, CR 99/6, 22 [Counsel Selepeng, 22 Feb 1999], CR 99/10, 15-16 [Agent Kawana, 1 March 2000]; *Costa Rica v. Nicaragua San Juan River* Judgment, ICJ Rep. 2009, para.88 <www.icj-cij.org>.

On IMO International Convention for the Prevention of Pollution from Ships (MARPOL), London, 2 Nov 1973, and Protocol of 1 June 1978 [Convention and Protocol in force: 2 Oct 1983, 1340 UNTS 61, 2041 UNTS 448], see *Great Belt* Pleadings, 348-349, 352 [Finland's Memorial], 594 [Denmark's Counter-Memorial]; *M/V Saiga* Judgment [38 ILM 1323 (1999)], para.78, Separate O. President Mensah, para.22; 2002 *Volga* Dissent Anderson, para.17 <www.itlos.org>; Annex VII *Mox Plant* Ireland's Memorial, I, 102-103; UK Counter-Memorial, 103, 152 <www.pca-cpa.org>; ECJ Grand Chamber *International Association of Independent Tank Owners (Intertanko) v. Secretary of State for Transport*, Case C-308/06 of 3 June 2008 <http://eur-lex.europa.eu>; 103 AJIL 555 (2009).

On Convention on the Protection of the Environment, Stockholm, 19 Feb 1974 [in force: 5 Oct 1976, 13 ILM 591 (1974)], see *Gabcikovo* Separate O. Weeramantry, ICJ Rep. 1997, 111 n.78.

On USA/Canada Agreement on the Establishment of Joint Pollution Contingency Plans for Spills of Oil and Other Noxious Substances of 19 June 1974 [in force: 10 June 1974, *Gulf of Maine* Pleadings, Vol.V, 342-343], see *Gulf of Maine* Pleadings, Vol.III, 359 [Canada's Counter-Memorial], Vol.V, 65 [Canada's Reply].

On Convention on the Regulation of Water Management Issues, Budapest, 31 May 1976, see *Gabcikovo* Judgment, ICJ Rep. 1997, 52, 61, 73, Dissent Herczegh, 193, 202; Hearings, CR 97/2 [trans.], 36 [Counsel Kiss, 3 March 1997], CR 97/5 [trans.], 6-7, 17 [6 March], CR 97/6, 23, 27, 31-34 [Counsel Sands, 7 March], CR 97/7, 53-55 [Counsel McCaffrey, 24 March], CR 97/9, 28 [25 March], CR 97/11, 19-20 [Counsel Watts, 27 March 1997].

On Convention on the Protection of the Rhine Against Pollution by Chlorides, Bonn, 3 December 1976 [in force: 5 July 1985, 16 ILM 265 (1977)] and Protocol, Brussels, 25 Sep 1991 [in force: 1 Nov 1994], see Pollution From Land-Based Sources – 2004 *France/Netherlands* Award *supra*.

On 1976 Environmental Modification Techniques Convention, see Peaceful Uses of the Sea *infra*.

On UNEP Convention for the Protection of the Mediterranean Sea Against Pollution and two Protocols on Pollution Emergencies and Ocean Dumping, Barcelona, 16 Feb 1976 [in force: 12 Feb 1978, 1102 UNTS 27; 15 ILM 290 (1976)], Land-Based Pollution Protocol, Athens, 17 May 1980 [in force: 17 June 1983, 19 ILM 869 (1980)], Protected Areas Protocol, Geneva, 3 April 1982 [in force: 23 March 1986], and Continental Shelf Protocol, Madrid, 14 Oct 1994, see *Libya/Malta* Pleadings, Vol.I, 30-31 [Libya's Memorial]; *Great Belt* Pleadings, 349 n.1 [Finland's Memorial].

On 10 June 1995, the 1976 Barcelona Convention – retitled into: for the Protection of the Marine Environment and the Coastal Region of the Mediterranean – and its Dumping Protocol were amended, and the new Specially Protected Areas and Biological Diversity Protocol was adopted [in force: 12 Dec 1999, 11 IJMCL 101 (1996); superseded the 1982 Geneva Protocol]. On 1 Oct 1996, Protocol on Transboundary Movements of Hazardous Wastes, Izmir, was adopted. See *Spain v. Canada (Jurisdiction)* Dissent Bedjaoui, ICJ Rep. 1998, 548, para.87; *Botswana/Namibia* Dissent Vice-President Weeramantry, ICJ Rep. 1999, 1191, para.109 <www.icj-cij.org>; 2002 OSPAR *Mox Plant* UK Counter-Memorial, para.5.32, Appendix A-11 <www.pca-cpa.org>.

On UN ECE Convention on Lange-Range Transboundary Air Pollution, Geneva, 13 Nov 1979 [in force: 16 March 1983, 18 ILM 1442 (1979)] and Protocols, Geneva, 18 Nov 1991, Oslo, 14 June 1994 [in force: 5 Aug 1998, 33 ILM 1273 (1994)], Arhaus, 24 June 1998 [37 ILM 505 (1998); Review of all Protocols, UN Doc.EB.AIR/WG.5/2001/1, 18 May 2000], see *Gabcikovo* Separate O. Weeramantry, ICJ Rep. 1997, 112; Oral Hearings, CR 97/2 [trans.], 12 n.11 [Agent Szenasi, 3 March 1997]; *Southern Bluefin Tuna (Jurisdiction)* Hearings, Vol.III [Question 9 of Arbitrators, 10 May 2000], Written Answers of the Parties to Question 9 [26 May 2000] <www.worldbank.icsid>.

On UNEP Convention for the Conservation of the Marine Environment of the Red Sea and Gulf of Aden and Protocol on Pollution Emergencies, Jeddah, 14 Feb 1982 [in force: 20 August 1985, 9 EPL 56 (1982) and 10 EPL 28 (1983)], see *Great Belt* Pleadings, 349 n.1 [Finland's Memorial]; 1999 *Eritrea/Yemen (Phase II)* Award, para.108 <www.pca-cpa.org>.

On UNEP Convention for the Protection and Development of the Marine Environment of the Wider Caribbean Region and Protocol on Pollution Emergencies, Cartagena de Indias, 24 March 1983 [in force: 11 Oct 1986, 22 ILM 221 (1983)] and Protocols on Specially Protected Areas, Kingston, 18 Jan 1990 [in force: 18 June 2000, 5 IJMCL 370 (1990)] and Land-Based Pollution, Aruba, 6 Oct 1999 [<www.cep.unep.org/law/sub_law.htm>, see *Southern Bluefin Tuna (Jurisdiction)* Hearings, Vol.I [Counsel Lauterpacht, 7 May 2000], Vol.II [Counsel Irwin, 8 May], Vol.III [Question 9 of Arbitrators, 10 May], Written Answers of the Parties to Question 9 [26 May 2000] <www.worldbank.icsid>.

On Canada/USA Treaty on the Skagit River and Ross Lake, and the Seven Mile Reservoir on the Pend d'Oreille River of 2 April 1984 [TIAS 11088], see *Gabcikovo* Oral Hearings, CR 97/10, 11-12 [Counsel McCaffrey, 26 March 1997].

On UNEP Convention for the Protection of the Ozone Layer, Vienna, 22 March 1985 [in force: 22 Sep 1988, 26 ILM 1516 (1987)] and its Montreal Protocol of 16 September 1987 [in force: 1 January 1989, 1522 UNTS 3; 26 ILM 1541 (1987)], as Amended [32 ILM 874, 880-881 (1993); 2020 UNTS 111], see *Nuclear Weapons* Oral Hearings, CR 95/29, 37-38 [Qatar, 10 Nov 1995], CR 95/34, 81 [USA, 15 Nov 1995]; *Gabcikovo* Separate O. Weeramantry, ICJ Rep. 1997, 112; Hearings, CR 97/2 [trans.], 12 n.11 [Agent Szenasi, 3 March 1997], CR 97/9, 34 n.42 [Counsel McCaffrey, 25 March 1997].

On UNEP Convention for the Protection of the Natural Resources and Environment of the South Pacific Region (SPREP) and two Protocols on Pollution Emergencies and Ocean Dumping, Noumea, 25 Nov 1986 [in force: 22 August 1990, 26 ILM 38 (1987); 1982 UNTS 4], see *New Zealand v. France* Order, ICJ Rep. 1995, 290, para.5, 298-299, paras 34-35, 306, para.63, Dissents Weeramantry, 347, Koroma, 368, 369-371, Palmer, 388, 410-411; NZ Request (Examination of the Situation); *Nuclear Tests* Hearings, CR 95/19, 26-28, 37 [Agent East, 11 Sep 1995], CR 95/20, 12-14, 17 [Counsel Keith, 12 Sep 1995], 30-35, 37 [Co-Agent MacKay], 41 [Agent East], [transl], 67-68 [De Brichambaut]; *Nuclear Weapons (UNGA)* Advisory Opinion, ICJ Rep. 1996, 243, para.32; Hearings, CR 95/28, 56-57 [NZ, 9 Nov 1995], CR 95/31, 26 [Samoa, 13 Nov], CR 95/32, 33 [Solomons, 14 Nov 1995]; *Southern Bluefin Tuna (Jurisdiction)* Hearings, Vol.I [Counsel Lauterpacht, 7 May 2000], Vol.III [Question 9 of Arbitrators, 10 May], Written Answers of the Parties to Question 9 [26 May 2000] <www.worldbank.org/icsid>.

On France's reservation upon signing the SPREP Convention, see *Nuclear Tests* Hearings, CR 95/19, 26 [Agent East, 11 Sep], CR 95/20, 34 [MacKay, 12 Sep 1995].

On UNEP Convention on the Control of Transboundary Movements of Hazardous Wastes and Their Disposal, Basel, 22 March 1989 [in force: 5 May 1992, 28 ILM 649 (1989); 1673 UNTS 126; 85 AJIL 674 (1991)], as amended (Annex I) and supplemented (Annexes VIII/IX), 6 November 1998 [2046 UNTS 123], and Liability and Compensation Protocol of 10 December 1999 <www.basel.int/> [30 EPL 43 (2000)], see *Gabcikovo* Hearings, CR 97/2 [trans.], 12 n.11 [Agent Szenasi, 3 March 1997]; *Spain v. Canada* Pleadings, 252-253 n.156 [Canada's Counter-Memorial]; *Southern Bluefin Tuna (Jurisdiction)* Hearings, Vol.I [Counsel Lauterpacht, 7 May 2000] <www.worldbank. org/icsid>; Annex VII *Mox Plant* UK Counter-Memorial, 152 <www.pca-cpa.org>.

On UN ECE Convention on Environmental Impact Assessment (EIA) in a Transboundary Context, Espoo, 25 Feb 1991 and Kiev Protocol on Strategic

Environmental Assessment (SEA) of 21 May 2003 [in force: 10 Sep 1997 <www.unece.org/env/eia/welcome.html>; 1989 UNTS 310; 30 ILM 802 (1991); SEA Protocl <www.unece.org/env/eia/sea_protocol.htm], see *Nuclear Tests* Dissent Koroma, ICJ Rep. 1995, 370; NZ Request (Examination of the Situation), para.92; CR 95/20, 29 [Co-Agent Mackay, 12 Sep 1995], [transl.], 67 [De Brichambaut]; *Gabcikovo* Separate O. Weeramantry, ICJ Rep. 1997, 111 n.78; Hearings, CR 97/2 [trans.], 12 n.11 [Agent Szenasi, 3 March 1997], CR 97/5 [trans.], 15 [Counsel Kiss, 6 March], CR 97/9, 39 n.54, 41 n.59 [Counsel McCaffrey, 25 March 1997]; *Southern Bluefin Tuna (Jurisdiction)* Hearings, Vol.III [Question 9 of Arbitrators, 10 May 2000], Written Answers of the Parties to Question 9 [26 May 2000] <www.worldbank.org/icsid>. 2001 *Ireland v. UK Mox Plant (Provisional Measures)* Ireland's Request & Statement, paras 70, 89; Hearings, ITLOS/PV.01/07, 26 [Counsel Goldsmith, 19 Nov 2001] <www.itlos.org>; 2002 OSPAR *Mox Plant* UK Counter-Memorial, para.5.32, Appendix A-11; Annex VII *Mox Plant (Provisional Measures)* Hearings, 63 [Counsel Sands, 17 June 2003]; Ireland's Memorial, 104, 117-118; UK Counter-Memorial, 103, 112, 118, 150-151; UK Rejoinder, 83, 85 <www.pca-cpa.org>; UN ECE *Romania/Ukraine Danube-Black Sea (Bystroe) Canal* Opinion of Commission of Inquiry under the 1991 Espoo EIA Convention (Art.3 & Appendix IV) of 11 July 2006 <www.unece.org/env/eia/inquiry.htm> and press comments <www.mosnews.com/news/2006/07/11/canaldisp.shtml & www.cceg.ro/2006stiri/UN.htm>.

On Protocol on Environmental Protection to the 1959 Antarctic Treaty, Madrid, 4 Oct 1991 [in force: 14 Jan 1998, 402 UNTS 71; 30 ILM 1455 (1991)] and Liability Annex, 17 June 2005 [45 ILM 1 (2006)], see *Nuclear Tests* Dissent Koroma, ICJ Rep. 1995, 370; NZ Request (Examination of the Situation), para.92; Hearings, CR 95/20, 29 [Co-Agent Mackay, 12 Sep 1995]; *Gabcikovo-Nagymaros Project* Hearings, CR 97/2 [trans.], 12 n.11 [Agent Szenasi, 3 March 1997] <www.icj-cij.org>. See also Signature, Ratification and Accession – Provisional Application *supra.*

On Treaty on European Union, Maastricht, 7 Feb 1992 [in force: 1 Nov 1993, OJEC C 224/1 (1992); 31 ILM 247 (1992)], as amended by Treaty of Amsterdam of 2 Oct 1997 [in force: 1 May 1999, 37 ILM 56 (1998); OJEC C 340/1 (1997); OJEC C 325/33 (2002)], as amended by Treaty of Lisbon of 17 Dec 2007 [in force: 1 Dec 2009, <http://news.bbc.co.uk/1/hi/world/europe/6901353.stm & www.consilium.europa.eu/showPage.aspx?id=1296&lang=en>], see *Nuclear Tests* Dissent Weeramantry, ICJ Rep. 1995, 343-344; 1995 NZ Request (Examination of the Situation), para.107 n.98; *Gabcikovo* Separate O. Weeramantry, ICJ Rep. 1997, 93 n.11, 94; *Oil Platforms (Preliminary Objection)* Separate O. Rigaux, ICJ Rep. 1996, 871-872; *Spain v. Canada* Pleadings, 60 [Spain's Memorial], 215, 266 [Canada's Counter-Memorial]; 2001 *Ireland v. UK Mox Plant (Provisional*

Measures) Order, ITLOS Case No.10, paras 40-50, Separate O. Anderson, paras 1, 3; UK Response, paras 3, 166-167, 218; Hearings, ITLOS/PV.01/07, 9 [Counsel Lowe, 19 Nov 2001], 21 [Counsel Lord Goldsmith], ITLOS/PV.01/08, 21-28 [Counsel Plender, 20 Nov 2001], ITLOS/PV.01/09, 14-15 [Lowe], 20-21, 26-27 [Plender] <www.itlos.org>; 2003 OSPAR *Mox Plant* Award, paras 109-110, 140-141; UK Counter-Memorial, paras 3.11, 3.13/15, Ireland's Reply, para.8, UK Rejoinder, para.2; Hearings, Vol.I, 47-49 [Counsel Sands, 21 Oct], Vol.II, 84, 86-87 [Counsel Wordsworth, 22 Oct], Vol.V, 12-13 [Counsel Plender, 25 Oct 2002]; 2003 Annex VII *Mox Plant (Suspension of Proceedings)* Orders Nos 3 & 4; Ireland's Memorial, I, 97-98; UK Counter-Memorial, 97-98, 100-102; UK Rejoinder, 49-62 <www.pca-cpa.org>; 2005 *Belgium/Netherlands Iron Rhine* Award, President R. Higgins, paras 4, 13-15, 28, 97-159, 189 <www.pca-cpa.org>; *European Commission v. Ireland Mox Plant* Case C-459/03, OJEC C/24 (2004) <http://europa.eu.int/eur-lex/en/index.html> & <http://europa.eu.int/eur-lex/pri/en/oj/dat/2004/c_007/c_00720040110en00240024.pdf> and Opinion of Advocate General Poiares Maduro of 12 Jan 2006 [*UNSG Oceans Report*, UN Doc. A/61/63, para.275 (2006)] and the ECJ *EC v. Ireland Mox Plant* Judgment of 30 May 2006 [<http://curia.eu.int/jrisp/cgi-bin/form.pl?lang=EN&Submit=rechercher&numaff=C-459/03> and PR No.45/06 <http://curia.eu.nt/en/actu/communiques/cp060045en.pdf>]; Annex VII *Ireland v. UK Mox Plant (Suspension of Periodic Reports by the Parties)* Order No.5 of 22 Jan 2007 and PR of 21 Feb 2007 and *Mox Plant (Termination of Proceedings)* Order No.6 of 6 June 2008 <www.pca-cpa.org>; ECJ Grand Chamber *International Association of Independent Tank Owners (Intertanko) v. Secretary of State for Transport*, Case C-308/06 of 3 June 2008 <http://eur-lex.europa.eu>; 103 AJIL 555 (2009).

On UN ECE Convention on the Protection and Use of Transboundary Watercourses and International Lakes, Helsinki, 17 March 1992 [in force: 6 Oct 1996, 1936 UNTS 270, 31 ILM 1312 (1992)], see *Gabcikovo* Hearings, CR 97/2 [trans.], 12 n.11 [Agent Szenasi, 3 March 1997], CR 97/5 [trans.], 15 [Counsel Kiss, 6 March 1997] <www.icj-cij.org>; 2002 OSPAR *Mox Plant* UK Counter-Memorial, para.5.32, Appendix A-11 <www.pca-cpa.org>

On UN ECE Convention on the Transboundary Effects of Industrial Accidents, Helsinki, 17 March 1992 [in force: 19 April 2000, 31 ILM 1330 (1992); 2105 UNTS 457], *Gabcikovo* Hearings, CR 97/2 [trans.], 12 n.11 [Agent Szenasi, 3 March 1997] <www.icj-cij.org>; 2002 OSPAR *Mox Plant* UK Counter-Memorial, para.5.32, Appendix A-11 <www.pca-cpa.org>.

On Convention on the Protection of the Marine Environment of the Baltic Sea Area, Helsinki, 9 April 1992, as Amended [in force: 17 Jan 2000, 1507 UNTS 167; 1887 UNTS 248, 2055 UNTS 255; 2099 UNTS 163, 196; 2117 UNTS 479; 2213 UNTS 277], see *Nuclear Tests* Dissent Weeramantry, ICJ Rep. 1995, 343; 1995 NZ

Request (Examination of the Situation); *Southern Bluefin Tuna* Hearings, Vol.II [Counsel Irwin, 8 May 2000] <www.worldbank.org/icsid>; 2002 OSPAR *Mox Plant* UK Counter-Memorial, para.5.32 <www.pca-cpa.org>.

On UNEP Convention on Biological Diversity, Rio de Janeiro, 5 June 1992 [in force: 29 Dec 1993, 1760 UNTS 143; 31 ILM 818 (1992)] and Cartagena Biosafety Protocol of 29 Jan 2000 [in force: 11 Sep 2003, 39 ILM 1027 (2000)], see *Nuclear Tests* Dissents Koroma, ICJ Rep. 1995, 370, Palmer, 410; NZ Request (Examination of the Situation), paras 92, 101; Hearings, CR 95/20, 29 [Co-Agent Mackay, 12 Sep 1995]; *Nuclear Weapons* Hearings, CR 95/29, 37-38 [Qatar, 10 Nov 1995], CR 95/32, 74 [Solomon I., 14 Nov], CR 95/34, 82 [USA, 15 Nov 1995]; *Gabcikovo* Judgment, ICJ Rep. 1997, 73, para.125, Separate O. Weeramantry, ICJ Rep. 1997, 93 n.9; Hearings, CR 97/2 [trans.], 12 n.11 [Agent Szenasi, 3 March 1997], CR 97/5 [trans.], 13 [Counsel Kiss, 6 March], CR 97/5, 71 [Counsel Sands], CR 97/6 [trans.], 70-71 [Counsel Dupuy, 7 March 1997]; *United States – Import Prohibition of Certain Shrimp and Shrimp Products* Report AB-1998-4, WTO Appellate Body, President F. Feliciano, WT/DS58/AB/R, 12 October 1998, paras 130, 168; *Botswana/Namibia* Dissent Vice-President Weeramantry, paras 81, 84, 87-88 and 116, ICJ Rep. 1999, 1096 <www.icj-cij.org>; 2003 OSPAR *Mox Plant* Dissent Griffith, para.73 <www.pca-cpa.org>; *Costa Rica v. Nicaragua San Juan River* Judgment, ICJ Rep. 2009, para.88 <www.icj-cij.org>; UNGA Adopts Two Oceans Resolutions, UN Doc.GA/10899 of 4 Dec 2009 <www.un.org/News/Press/docs//2009/ga10899.doc.htm>.

On UN Framework Convention on Climate Change, Rio de Janeiro, 5 June 1992 [in force: 21 March 1994, 31 ILM 849 (1992); 1771 UNTS 108] and Kyoto Protocol of 11 Dec 1997 [in force: 16 Feb 2005 <www.un.org/News/Press/docs/2005/sgsm9721.doc.htm>, 37 ILM 22 (1998); 95 AJIL 648 (2001); 96 AJIL 487 (2002); <http://unfccc.int/2860.php>], see *Nuclear Weapons* Hearings, CR 95/32, 74 [Solomon I., 14 Nov 1995], CR 95/34, 81-82 [USA, 15 Nov 1995]; *Gabcikovo* Separate O. Weeramantry, ICJ Rep. 1997, 93 n.9; Hearings, CR 97/2 [trans.], 12 n.11 [Agent Szenasi, 3 March 1997]; 2003 OSPAR *Mox Plant* Dissent Griffith, para.73 <www.pca-cpa.org>; UNGA Adopts Two Oceans Resolutions, UN Doc. GA/10899 of 4 Dec 2009 <www.un.org/News/Press/docs//2009/ga10899.doc .htm>; UNGA Resolution on UN Framework Convention on Climate Change, UN Doc.GA 10900 of 7 Dec 2009 <www.un.org/News/Press/docs//2009/ga10900 .doc.htm & http://www1.voanews.com/english/news/environment/UN-chief-climate-Copenhagen-08DEC09--78785532.html>.

On Convention on the Protection of the Marine Environment of the North-East Atlantic (OSPAR Convention), Paris, 22 Sep 1992 [in force: 25 March 1998, 32 ILM 1069 (1993) <www.ospar.org>], see *Nuclear Tests* Dissent Weeramantry, ICJ Rep. 1995, 343, 345, Dissent Palmer, 410; 1995 NZ Request (Examination of the Situation), para.101; *Southern Bluefin Tuna (Jurisdiction)* Japan's Memorial, paras 139, 151 <www.worldbank.org/icsid>; 2001 *Ireland v. UK Mox Plant (Provisional Measures)* Order, ITLOS Case No.10, paras 40-50, Separate Os Anderson, paras 1, 3, Jesus; Ireland's Request & Statement, paras 25, 54, 70-75, 87-90, 102-105, 136-138, UK Response, paras 3, 13, 38, 106-107, 123-124, 163-165, 176-182, 188, 190, 218; Hearings, ITLOS/PV.01/06, 10 [Agent O'Hagan, 19 Nov 2001], 24 [Counsel Fitzsimons], 38 [Counsel Sands], ITLOS/PV.01/07, 8-13 [Counsel Lowe], 21, 25-27, 30, 32-33 [Counsel Goldsmith], ITLOS/PV.01/08, 21-28 [Counsel Plender, 20 Nov 2001], 34 [Goldsmith], ITLOS/PV.01/09, 14 [Lowe], 25-27 [Plender] <www.itlos.org>; 2003 OSPAR *Mox Plant* and Annex VII *Mox Plant (Provisional Measures)* Hearings, 34, 38-39 [Counsel Wodsworth, 20 June 2003]; Ireland's Memorial, I, 97-98, 102-104-106; UK Counter-Memorial, 33-34, 97-98, 103, 194-203; UK Rejoinder, 39-42, 55, 60 <www.pca-cpa.org>; *European Commission v. Ireland Mox Plant* Case C-459/03, OJEC C/24 (2004) <http://europa.eu.int/eur-lex/en/index.html> and Opinion of Advocate General Poiares Maduro of 12 Jan 2006 [*UNSG Oceans Report*, UN Doc. A/61/63, para.275 (2006)] and the ECJ *EC v. Ireland Mox Plant* Judgment of 30 May 2006 [<http://curia.eu.int/jrisp/cgi-bin/form.pl?lang=EN&Submit=rechercher&numaff=C-459/03> and PR No.45/06 <http://curia.eu.nt/en/actu/communiques/cp060045en.pdf>].

On Convention on Civil Liability for Damage Resulting from Activities Dangerous to the Environment, Lugano, 21 June 1993 [32 ILM 1228 (1993)], see 2003 OSPAR *Mox Plant* Award, para.66; UK Counter-Memorial, para.5.32, Appendix A-11 <www.pca-cpa.org>.

On Convention on Cooperation for the Protection and Sustainable Use of the Danube River, Sofia, 29 June 1994 [in force: 22 Oct 1998], see *Gabcikovo* Oral Hearings, CR 97/2 [trans.], 42 [Counsel Kiss, 2 March 1997].

On IAEA Convention on Nuclear Safety, Vienna, 20 Sep 1994 [in force: 24 Oct 1996, 33 ILM 1518 (1994); 1963 UNTS 293], see 2002 OSPAR *Mox Plant* UK Counter-Memorial, para.5.32, Appendix A-11; Annex VII *Mox Plant (Provisional Measures)* Hearings, 63 [Counsel Sands, 17 June 2003]; Ireland's Memorial, I, 102, 104; UK Counter Memorial, 28-29 <www.pca-cpa.org>.

On European Energy Charter Treaty (ECT) and Protocol on Energy Efficiency and Related Environmental Aspects of 17 Dec 1994 [in force: 16 April 1998, in 34 ILM 360 (1995); Charter, in 2080 UNTS 95; Protocol, in 2081 UNTS 3; <www.encharter.org/index.jsp>], see Signature, Ratification and Accession – Provisional Application, UNCITRAL *Yukos and GML (previously Menatep) et al. v. Russian Federation* and ICSID *Ioannis Kardassopoulos v. Georgia* Arbitrations *infra.*

On UN Convention on the Law of the Non-Navigation Uses of International Watercourses, 21 May 1997 [36 ILM 700 (1997); <www.un.org/law/cod/watere.htm>], see *Nuclear Tests* Hearings, CR 95/20, 29 [Co-Agent MacKay, 12 Sep

1995]; *Gabcikovo* Judgment, ICJ Rep. 1997, 56, para.85, at 80, para.147, Dissents Herczegh, 189-191, 202, Skubiszewski, 235; Hearings, CR 97/5 [trans.], 15 [Counsel Kiss, 6 March 1997]; *Botswana/Namibia* Separate O. Kooymans, paras 25-38, ICJ Rep. 1999, 1148-1152; Hearings, CR 99/5 [trans.], 33-35 [Counsel Cot, 18 Feb 1999] <www.icj-cij.org>; *Malaysia v. Singapore (Provisional Measures)* Hearings, ITLOS/PV.03/03, 29-30 [Counsel Reisman, 26 Sep 2003] <www.itlos.org>.

On UN ECE Convention on Access to Information, Public Participation in Decision-Making and Access to Justice in Environmental Matters, Aarhus, 25 June 1998 [in force: 30 Oct 2001, 2161 UNTS 447; 38 ILM 517 (1999)], see 2003 OSPAR *Mox Plant* Award, paras 97, 104, 150, 155, Dissent Griffith, paras 7-19, 25, 29, 31, 113-122; Ireland's Memorial, paras 100, 118, 122, 127, UK Counter-Memorial, paras 4.10, 4.13, 5.22, 5.30, 5.32, Appendix A-11, Ireland's Reply, para.42, UK Rejoinder, para.21; Hearings, Vol.I, 28, 58, 60-61, 65 [Counsel Sands, 21 Oct], Vol.II, 53 [Counsel Plender, 22 Oct], 89-93 [Counsel Wordsworth], Vol.III, 26 [Counsel Bethlehem, 23 Oct], Vol.V, 20 [Plender, 25 Oct 2002] <www.pca-cpa.org>.

On Eritrea/Yemen Treaty on the Joint Committee for Bilateral Cooperation of 16 October 1998, see Protection and Preservation of the Marine Environment *supra*.

On the IAEA/IMO International Code for the Safe Carriage of Packaged Irradiated Nuclear Fuel, Plutonium and High-Level Radioactive Wastes on Board Ships (INF Code) of 28 May 1999 [in force: 1 Jan 2001, Resolution MSC.88(71), UN Doc. IMO MSC 71/23, Annex 4, 2 June 1999], as Amended [in force: 1 Jan 2003, Resolution MSC.118(74), MSC 74/24, at 24, 27 and Annex 3, 13 June 2001] see 2001 *Ireland v. UK Mox Plant (Provisional Measures)* Separate O. Anderson, para.4 n.13; UK Response, paras 33-34, 65; Oral Hearings, ITLOS/PV.01/07, 32 [Counsel Goldsmith, 19 Nov 2001], ITLOS/PV.01/08, 7-8 [Goldsmith, 20 Nov 2001] <www.itlos.org>; Annex VII *Mox Plant* Ireland's Memorial, 109; UK Counter-Memorial, 31, 47, 50-52, 95-96, 173 <www.pca-cpa.org>.

On UNEP Convention for Cooperation in the Protection and Sustainable Development of the Marine and Coastal Environment of the Northeast Pacific, Antigua, 19 February 2002 [*UN LOS Bull.* 46 (2002 No.48); reservation of El Salvador as protested by Honduras, UN Doc. S/2002/251], see Equitable Maritime Boundary Delimitation – 1992 *Gulf of Fonseca* Judgment (Honduras Request of 20 Jan 2002) *supra*.

On 1856 *Blyth v. Birmingham Water Works* [11 Exchequer 781, 156 ER 1047 (1856)], see *Nuclear Tests* Dissent Palmer, ICJ Rep. 1995, 405.

On 1938 and 1941 *USA v. Canada Trail Smelter* Awards [RIAA III, 1905, 1965; 32 AJIL 785 (1938); 33 AJIL 182 (1939); 35 AJIL 684 (1941); Nos 290 and 403/Stuyt], see *Nuclear Tests* Dissent de Castro, ICJ Rep. 1974, 388-389; 1994

Laguna del Desierto Award, para.68 [113 ILR 43]; *New Zealand v. France* Dissent Weeramantry, ICJ Rep. 1995, 346, 362 n.1, Dissent Palmer, 408; *Gabcikovo* Separate O. Vice-President Weeramantry, ICJ Rep. 1997, 111-112; Hearings, CR 97/2 [trans.], 40-42 [Counsel Kiss, 2 March 1997]; *M/V Saiga* Memorial of Saint Vincents, para.168; Annex VII *Mox Plant* UK Rejoinder, 135 <www.pca-cpa.org>; *El Salvador v. Honduras (Revision)* Hearings, C6/CR 2003/3, 19 n.10 [Counsel Dupuy, 9 Sep 2003] <www.icj-cij.org>; *Malaysia v. Singapore (Provisional Measures)* Hearings, ITLOS/PV.03/02/Corr.1, 19 [Counsel Schrijver, 25 Sep 2003] <www.itlos.org>; 2009 *Abyei Boundary* Award, para.512 <www.pca-cpa.org>. On 2004 *Trail Smelter* II, see *Colville Confederated Tribes v. Teck Cominco Metals Ltd.* of 21 July 2004 <www.newsday.com/news/nationworld/wire/sns-ap-columbia-pollution,0,2311579.story?coll=sns-ap-nationworld-headlines> and <www.teckcominco.com/news/04-archive/04-21-tc.htm>; Teck Cominco Files Motion to Dismiss Colville Tribes' Lawsuit of 26 August at: www.teckcominco.com/news/04-archive/04-24-tc.htm; and News at <www.teckcominco.com/ & www.topix.net/us/epa>.

On 1947 *US v. Carroll Towing Co.* [159 Fed. Rep. 2d 169], see *Nuclear Tests* Dissent Palmer, ICJ Rep. 1995, 405.

On 1954 *The Diago Fukurya Maru*, see Peaceful Uses of the Sea – Nuclear Weapon Tests *infra*.

On 1956 *Spain/France Lake Lanoux* Award, President Petren [RIAA XII, 285; 24 ILR 101; 53 AJIL 156 (1959); No.425/Stuyt], see *Nuclear Tests* Joint Dissent, ICJ Rep. 1974, 330, 334; *Aegean Sea* Pleadings, 123 [Counsel Pinto, 26 Aug 1976], 203-204 n.1 [Greece's Memorial (Jurisd.)], 271 [Greece's Memorial (Merits)]; *Tunisia/Libya (Merits)* Dissent Gros, ICJ Rep. 1982, 145; *Denmark v. Norway* Separate O. Weeramantry, ICJ Rep. 1993, 247; *Nuclear Tests* Dissent Palmer, ICJ Rep. 1995, 408; *Gabcikovo* Dissent Skubiszewski, ICJ Rep. 1997, 235-238; Hearings, CR 97/2 [trans.], 40 [Counsel Kiss, 2 March 1997]; 2001 *Ireland v. UK Mox Plant (Provisional Measures)* Ireland's Request & Statement, para.61; Hearings, ITLOS/PV.01/06,38 [Counsel Sands, 19 Nov 2001], ITLOS/PV.01/07, 18 [Counsel Lowe], 29 [Counsel Goldsmith] <www.itlos.org>; Annex VII *Mox Plant* Ireland's Memorial, I, 252 <www.pca-cpa.org>; 2003 *Malaysia v. Singapore (Provisional Measures)* Declaration President L.D.M. Nelson, para.5; Hearings, ITLOS/PV.03/01, 22 [Counsel Sir Elihu Lauterpacht, 25 Sep 2003], PV.03/02/Corr.1, 19 [Counsel Schrijver] <www.itlos.org>; 2005 *Belgium/Netherlands* Award, para.54 <www.pca-cpa.org>; 2006 *Barbados/Trinidad & Tobago (Jurisdiction and Merits)* Award, President S.M. Schwebel, para.292 <www.pca-cpa.org>.

On 1958 Judgment of District Court of Columbia [164 F. Supp. 390; Court of Appeals, 1960, 278 F. Rep. 2nd Ser. 252], see *Nuclear Tests* Separate O. Gros, ICJ Rep. 1974, 289.

On 1974 *National Parks* as well as 1976 *National Parks II, Department of the Air Force* and *Gulf and Western Industries Inc* Judgments, see EIA/Notification/Consultation *supra*.

On 1983 *Public Citizen*, 1984 *Fletcher Timber* and 1985 *Brightwell* Judgments, see EIA/Notification /Consultation *supra*.

On 1986 *Chernobyl* disaster, see *Nuclear Tests* Dissent Weeramantry, ICJ Rep. 1995, 340, 356; Hearings, CR 95/20 [transl.], 53 [De Brichambaut, 12 Sep 1995]; *Nuclear Weapons (WHO)* Dissents Weeramantry, ICJ Rep. 1996, 116, Koroma, 177, 199, *(UNGA)* Dissent Weeramantry, 459, 464, 544; Hearings, CR 95/22, 9 [WHO, 30 Oct], CR 95/35, 27 [Zimbabwe, 15 Nov 1995]; *Ireland v. UK Mox Plant (Provisional Measures)* Ireland's Request & Statement, para.11 <www.itlos.org>. Cf. UNGA Resolution 55/171 on Closure of the Chernobyl Nuclear Power Plant of 14 Dec 2000 and Resolutions 56/109 and 58/119 on Chernobyl Consequences of 14 Dec 2001 and 17 Dec 2003; IAEA/Chernobyl Facts of 6 April 2004 <www.unwire.org/UNWire/20040406/449_22545.asp>; Chernobyl/Belarus of 31 July <http://news.bbc.co.uk/2/hi/europe/3943013.stm>; Chernobyl Caused Sweden Cancers of 20 Nov 2004 <http://news.bbc.co.uk/1/hi/world/europe/4028729.stm>; UNSG Kofi Annan's Statement of 26 April 2005 <www.un.org/apps/sg/sgstats.asp?nid=1419> and Chernobyl 20 Years On of 25 April 2006 <www.voanews.com/english/Chernobyl-2006.cfm>, <http://news.bbc.co.uk/1/hi/world/europe/4942828.stm> & <www.un.org/apps/news/story.asp?NewsID=18188&Cr=nuclear&Cr1>.

On 1986/90 *The Rainbow Warrior* Mediation and Arbitration, see Access to and Jurisdiction and Treatment in Ports *supra*.

On 1988 *Saarl and Others v. Minister for Industry*, see EIA/Notification / Consultation *supra*.

On 1989 *Rubin v. Canada* and *Canada Packers Inc.* Judgments, see EIA/Notification /Consultation *supra*.

On 1991 *Alabama et al. v. US Environmental Protection Agency* [925 F.2d 385 (11th Cir.], see *Great Belt* Pleadings, 173 [Agent Magid, 2 July 1991].

On 1992 *Critical Mass Energy* Judgment, see EIA/Notification/Consultation *supra*.

On 1994 *R. v. Secretary and Others, ex parte Greenpeace and Lancashire County Council* Judgment [(1994) 4 All ER 352; *Journal Env'l L.* 312 (1994)], see *Nuclear Tests* Dissent Palmer, ICJ Rep. 1995, 405; 1995 NZ Request (Examination of the Situation), paras 87, 94-95; 2003 OSPAR *Mox Plant* Award, para.19; Ireland's Memorial, para.40; Annex VII *Mox Plant* UK Counter-Memorial, 20, 71 n.46; UK Rejoinder, 35, 78-79, 89 n.53 <www.pca-cpa.org>.

On 1995 *R. v. British Coal Corporation*, 1998 *Secretary of State for the Environment* and 1999 *Mecklenburg* Judgments, see EIA/Notification/Consultation *supra*.

On 1997 *Dagg v. Canada (Minister of Finance)* and 1998 *Occam Marine Technologies* Judgments, see EIA/Notification /Consultation *supra*.

On 1998 *Sellers v. Maritime Safety Inspector* Judgment of the New Zealand Court of Appeal [120 ILR 585], see *Southern Bluefin Tuna (Jurisdiction)* Hearings, Vol.III [Lauterpacht, 10 May 2000] <www.worldbank.org/icsid/bluefintuna/main .htm>.

On 1999 *R. v. Secretary of State* and *Public Citizen*, as well as 2001 *London Regional Transport* Judgments, see EIA/Notification/Consultation *supra*.

On 2001 *R. (Friends of the Earth Ltd. and Greenpeace Ltd.) v. Secretary of State for the Environment* Judgment and the Court of Appeal's Judgment, see EIA/Notification /Consultation *supra*.

On 2004 *France/Netherlands* Award, see Pollution From Land-Based Sources *supra*.

On 2005 Annex VII *Malaysia v. Singapore Land Reclamation In and Around the Straits of Johor* Award, including Settlement Agreement, Arbitrators: President Christopher Pinto (Sri Lanka), Sir Arthur Watts KCMG QC (UK), Kamal Hossain (Malaysia), Bernard H. Oxman (USA), Ivan Shearer (Australia) <www.pca-cpa.org>; 2324 UNTS 23, see 2003 *Malaysia v. Singapore (Provisional Measures)* Order, President L.D.M. Nelson, ITLOS Case No.12; Malaysia's Request for Provisional Measures, paras 2, 9, 20; Singapore's Response, paras 4, 11, 66, 82, 178/181; Hearings, ITLOS/PV.03/01, 18, 24 [Counsel Sir Elihu Lauterpacht, 25 Sep 2003], PV.03/02/Corr.1, 21-23 [Counsel Crawford, 25 Sep], PV.03/03, 11 [Counsel Chan, 26 Sep], 33 [Counsel Reisman], PV.03/04, 9 [Reisman], 12, 16 [Counsel Lowe], PV.03/05, 21 [Lauterpacht, 27 Sep 2003], 30 [Reisman], 37 [Agent Koh] <www.itlos.org>; 9 Jan 2005 <http://news.bbc.co.uk/1/hi/world/ asia-pacific/4173405.stm> & *Malaysia v. Singapore* Settlement Agreement of 26 April 2005 <http://internet-stg1.mfa.gov.sg/internet/press/land/frm_main_land. htm>; *UN LOS Bull.* 30 (2006 No.59) & <www.pca-cpa.org>; *Guyana/Suriname* Suriname's Rejoinder, para.2.74; Hearings, 45 [Counsel Rosenne, 8 July 2005] <www.pca-cpa.org>; *Malaysia/Singapore* Hearings, CR 2007/24, 17, para.36 [Agent Kadir, 13 Nov 2007] <www.icj-cij.org>.

On 2003 OSPAR *Ireland v. UK Mox Plant* Award (1992 OSPAR Convention *supra*), Arbitrators: Chairman W. Michael Reisman (USA), Gavan Griffith QC (Australia) and Lord Mustill PC (UK) [<www.pca-cpa.org>; 42 ILM 1118 (2003)], see 2001 *Ireland v. UK Mox Plant (Provisional Measures)* Order, para.40, Case No.10, Separate O. Jesus, para.6 [ITLOS Rep. 2001, 89; 41 ILM 405 (2002)]; Ireland's Request & Statement, paras 25, 54, 74-75, 136-137, UK Response, paras 3, 38, 106-107, 123-124, 163-165, 176-182, 188, 190; Hearings, ITLOS/PV.01/06, 10 [Agent O'Hagan, 19 Nov 2001], 24 [Counsel Fitzsimons], ITLOS/PV.01/07, 8-14 [Counsel Lowe], 21, 25-27 [Counsel Lord Goldsmith], ITLOS/PV.01/08, 21-23 [Counsel Plender, 20 Nov

2001], 34 [Goldsmith], ITLOS/PV.01/09, 27 [Plender] <www.itlos.org>; 2006 ECJ *EC v. Ireland Mox Plant* Judgment, paras 30, 32, 49, 118, 178 <http://curia.europa.eu/jurisp/cgi-bin/form.pl?lang=EN&Submit=rechercher&numaff=C-459/03>; 2007 *Channel Tunnel Group Ltd & France-Manche S.A./United Kingdom/France Eurotunnel* Partial Award, para.152 <www.pca-cpa.org>; *Guyana/Suriname* Hearings, 31 [Co-Agent Reichler, 6 July 2005] <www.pca-cpa.org>; Dismantling and Clean-Up of Sellafield by US-France-UK Nuclear Management Partners (NMP) Until 2030 of 24 Nov 2008 <http://news.bbc.co.uk/2/hi/business/7733487.stm & www.kentucky.com/473/story/603962.html>.

On Annex VII *Ireland v. UK Mox Plant (Suspension of Proceedings and Provisional Measures)* Order No.3 of 24 June and Order No.4 of 14 Nov 2003, *Mox Plant (Suspension of Periodic Reports by the Parties)* Order No.5 of 22 Jan 2007 and PR of 21 Feb 2007 <www.pca-cpa.org/PDF/MOX%20Order%20No.5.pdf> and *Mox Plant (Termination of Proceedings)* Order No.6 of 6 June 2008, Arbitrators: President Thomas A. Mensah (Ghana), James Crawford SC (Australia), Sir Arthur Watts KCMG, QC (UK), L. Yves Fortier CC QC, (Canada) Gerhard Hafner (Austria) <www.asil.org/ilib060706.cfm & www.pca-cpa.org/>, see 2001 *Mox Plant (Provisional Measures)* Order, ITLOS Case No.10, paras 31-32, 58, 77 [41 ILM 405 (2002)]; Ireland's Request & Statement, paras 1, 52, 129-131; UK Response, paras 8, 152; Hearings, ITLOS/PV.01/06, 15 [Agent O'Hagan, 19 Nov 2001] <www.itlos.org>; 2003 OSPAR *Mox Plant* Dissent Griffith, para.85 <www.pca-cpa.org>; 2005 *Belgium/Netherlands Iron Rhine* Award, paras 14, 101 and Award's text in English and French with Introduction by Colin Warbrick, in *PCA Awards Series*, Vol.III (2007) <www.asserpress.nl & www.pca-cpa.org/showpage.asp?pag_id=1056>; *European Commission v. Ireland Mox Plant* Case C-459/03, OJEC C 7/24 (2004) and 2006 ECJ *EC v. Ireland Mox Plant* Judgment, paras 34-48 *infra*; 2007 *Channel Tunnel Group Ltd & France-Manche S.A./United Kingdom/France Eurotunnel* Partial Award, para.152 <www.pca-cpa.org>; *Guyana/Suriname* Suriname's Rejoinder, para.2.74; Hearings, 7, 31, 45 [Counsel Rosenne, 8 July 2005] <www.pca-cpa.org>; Dismantling and Clean-Up of Sellafield by US-France-UK Nuclear Management Partners (NMP) Until 2030 of 24 Nov 2008 <http://news.bbc.co.uk/2/hi/business/7733487.stm & www.kentucky.com/473/story/603962.html>.

On Answer by the European Commission to Parliamentary Question H-0256/03 by Proinsias de Rossa of 15 May 2003 on Sellafield Nuclear Plant <http://www3.europarl.eu. int/omk/omnsapir.so/searchdeb?LANGUE=EN&ARG=questnum&QUEST=yes&YEAR =03&RECHERCHE=h0256%2F03&LEG=L5>, see Annex VII *Mox Plant (Suspension of Proceedings and Provisional Measures)* Order of 24 June 2003, paras 14-28, esp. para.21; Hearings, 4 [Counsel Plender, 12 June], 13 [President Mensah's Statement, para.7, 13 June 2003]; and *Mox Plant (Termination of Proceedings)* Order No.6 of 6 June 2008 <www.pca-cpa.org>.

On plutonium shipment by the *Pacific Pintail* and *Pacific Teal* throughout 26 April-17 September 2002, see BNFL Nuclear Transport, 26 April <http://pub112.ezboard.com/fpuntersloungegeneral.showMessage?topicID=658.topic>, 22 July <www.nuclearfree flotilla.org/late_news.htm>, 17 Sep 2002 <www.radicus.net/news/wed/ar/Qbritain-japan-nuclear.RRTw_CSH.asp>.

On *European Commission v. Ireland Mox Plant* Case C-459/03, OJEC C/24 (2004) <http://europa.eu.int/eur-lex/pri/en/oj/dat/2004/c_007/c_00720040110en00240024.pdf> and Opinion of Advocate General Poiares Maduro of 12 Jan 2006 [*UNSG Oceans Report*, UN Doc. A/61/63, para.275 (2006)] and the ECJ *EC v. Ireland Mox Plant* Judgment of 30 May 2006 [<http://curia.europa.eu/jurisp/cgi-bin/form.pl?lang=EN&Submit=rechercher&numaff=C-459/03> & Cases since 1989 at <http://curia.eu.int/en/content/juris/index.htm> and PR No.45/06 <http://curia.eu.nt/en/actu/communiques/cp060045en.pdf> & www.asil.org/ilib060706.cfm], see 2005 *Belgium/Netherlands Iron Rhine* Award, paras 14,101 <www.pca-cpa.org; RIAA XXVII, 35>; Annex VII *Ireland v. UK Mox Plant (Suspension of Periodic Reports by the Parties)* Order No.5 of 22 Jan 2007 and PR of 21 Feb 2007 and *Mox Plant (Termination of Proceedings)* Order No.6 of 6 June 2008 <www.pca-cpa.org>; Dismantling and Clean-Up of Sellafield by US-France-UK Nuclear Management Partners (NMP) Until 2030 of 24 Nov 2008 <http://news.bbc.co.uk/2/hi/business/7733487.stm & www.kentucky.com/473/story/603962.html>; Sellafield Returns Nuclear Waste to Japan of 20 Jan 2010 <http://news.bbc.co.uk/2/hi/business/8469249.stm>. See also ECJ Grand Chamber *International Association of Independent Tank Owners (Intertanko) v. Secretary of State for Transport*, Case C-308/06 of 3 June 2008 <http://eur-lex.europa.eu>; 103 AJIL 555 (2009).

On UN ECE *Romania/Ukraine Danube-Black Sea (Bystroe) Canal* Opinion of Commission of Inquiry under the 1991 Espoo EIA Convention (Art.3 & Appendix IV) [1989 UNTS 310; 30 ILM 802 (1991)], see 11 July 2006 <www.unece.org/env/eia/inquiry.htm> and press comments <www.mosnews.com/news/2006/07/11/canaldisp.shtml & www.cceg.ro/2006stiri/UN.htm>.

For emphasis on importance of international environmental (including oceans) law in Statements of the ICJ Presidents, see: Judge Sir Robert Jennings' Statement to the UN Conference on Environment and Development (UNCED), Rio de Janeiro, 3-14 June 1992, *ICJ Yearbook 1991-1992* 212-218 (No.46); ICJ President Stephen M. Schwebel's Statement to the 52nd UNGA, UN Doc. A/52/PV.36, at 1-5, 27 October 1997, *reprinted in* 92 AJIL 612-615 (1998), *ICJ Yearbook 1997-1998* 288-295 (No.52); ICJ President Gilbert Guillaume's Statement to the UN 6th Legal Committee, 30 Oct 2002, <www.un.org/News/Press/docs/2002/gal3221.doc.htm>, *reprinted in ICJ Yearbook 2002-2003* 335-343 (No.57); ICJ President Rosalyn Higgins' Statement to the 61st UNGA, 26 Oct 2006 quoted under Chamber for Environmental Matters *infra*; ICJ President Hisashi Owada's

Statement to the 6th Legal Committee, 30 Oct 2009, p. 4 <www.un.org/News/Press/docs//3009/gal3377.doc.htm>; ICJ <www.icj-cij.org/court/index.php?p1=1&p2=3>.

On the ICJ Chamber for Environmental Matters established, under Article 26(1) of the ICJ Statute, in a follow-up to the Rio Agenda 21, Chapter 39.10 [*ICJ Press Releases* Nos 93/20, 94/10, 95/13, 2000/3, 2002/8, 2003/11, 2005/10, 22 April 2005], see *Nuclear Tests* Dissent Palmer, ICJ Rep. 1995, 408-409; *Nuclear Weapons* Hearings, CR 95/22, 55 [Foreign Minister Evans, 30 Oct 1995], CR 95/32, 65 [Solomon Islands, 14 Nov 1995]; *Gabcikovo* Hearings, CR 97/2 [trans.], 12-13 [Agent Szenasi, 3 March 1997]. As in its 13 years of existence, no state had asked for a case to be heard by this Chamber, the ICJ decided not to reconstitute it in 2006, but to establish it under Article 26(2) of the Court's Statute if the parties so request in the future. See Statement of ICJ President Rosalyn Higgins the 61st UNGA, *ICJ Press Release* No.2006/34 of 26 Oct 2006 <www.icj-cij.org>, *summarized in* <www.un.org/apps/news/story.asp?NewsID=20391&Cr=international&Cr1=court> and UN Doc.GA/10523 of 26 Oct 2006 <www.un.org/News/Press/docs/2006/ga10523.doc.htm>.

See also Exclusive Economic (/Fishery) Zone – Protection and Preservation of the Marine Environment, and Rational Conservation and Optimum Utilization of Fisheries; Equitable Maritime Boundary Delimitation – Economic Factors, Environmental Factors; Regime of Islands – Environmental Factors in Disputes over Territorial Sovereignty: and Fisheries *supra*; Use of Force in Enforcement at Sea; Settlement of Disputes – Standard of Preventing Serious Harm to the Marine Environment; Peaceful Uses of the Sea – Prohibition of Threat or Use of Force (Necessity and Countermeasures) and Nuclear Weapon Tests; Equity; and Relation to Other Conventions *infra.*

USE OF FORCE IN ENFORCEMENT AT SEA

1982 UNCLOS, Part V, Article 73, Part XII, Article 225, Part XV, Article 298(1)(b)
1995 SSA, Article 22(1)(f):

Legal Status of Eastern Greenland PCIJ Series A/B, No.53 (1933) – Dissent Vogt, 103; *Eastern Greenland* Pleadings, PCIJ Series C, No.63, 686-690 [Reply of Denmark]; *Fisheries Jurisdiction (Interim Measures)* Orders, ICJ Rep. 1972, 13, 31, Dissents Padilla Nervo, 20-21, 37-38, *(Jurisdiction)* Dissents Padilla Nervo, ICJ Rep. 1973, 37, 46-47, 82, 91, *(Continuance of Interim Protection)* Declarations Ignacio-Pinto, 305, 316, Dissents Gros, 307, 317, Dissents Petren, 310, 318, *(Merits)*

Judgments, ICJ Rep. 1974, 7, 179, 203-205, 206 (para.77(5)), Declaration Dillard, 207-208, Separate O. de Castro, 225-226, Separate O. Waldock, 229-233, Dissent Gros, 236-237, Dissent Petren, 242-243, Dissent Onyeama, 250-251; *Fisheries Jurisdiction* Pleadings (UK), 155 [Iceland's Note], 273, 286, 375-378, 421-432 [Memorial (Merits)], 447 [Counsel Silkin, 25 March 1974], (FRG), 29-31 [Request], 260-265, 277-284 [Memorial (Merits)]; *Aegean Sea (Intermin Measures)* Order, ICJ Rep. 1976, 5, 7-8, 11-13, Separate Os Mosler, 26, Elias, 29; Pleadings, 7-9 [Greece's Application], 63-66 [Request], 92 [Counsel O'Connell, 25 Aug 1976]; *Libya/Malta* Pleadings, Vol.I, 373-374 [Libya's Memorial]; *Spain v. Canada Fisheries (Jurisdiction)* Judgment, ICJ Rep. 1998, 432, paras 15-22, 24, 35, 53, 61-63, 78-84, Separate O. President Schwebel, 470, Dissent Vice-President Weeramantry, 496; Pleadings, 49 [Spain's Memorial], Hearings, CR 98/9 [trans.], 6-9, 11, 13 [Agent Pastor Ridruejo, 9 June 1998], 17-23, 27-32, 46-48 [Counsel Rodriguez], CR 98/10, 17-20, 35 [Counsel Highet, 10 June], CR 98/11 [trans.], 12-15 [Agent Kirsch, 11 June], 40 [Co-Agent Hankey], 60-62 [Senior Counsel Willis], CR 98/12, 9-10, 16-17 [12 June], CR 98/12 [trans.], 29-44 [Counsel Weil], CR 98/13, 10-11 [Pastor Ridruejo, 15 June], CR 98/13, 61-63 [Counsel Dupuy, 15 June], CR 98/14 [Willis, Hankey, 17 June 1998]; *Oil Platforms (Merits)* Judgment, ICJ Rep. 2003, 161; Hearings, CR 2003/14, 53-54 [Counsel Crawford, 28 Feb 2003], CR 2003/17, 39 [Counsel Murphy, 5 March 2003], both quoting ICJ Rep. 1974, 204, para.76 [*supra*]; *Nicaragua v. Colombia* Nicaragua's Written POs Statement, para.12 <www.icj-cij.org>.

M/V Saiga Judgment, ITLOS Case No.2, President T.A. Mensah [38 ILM 1323 (1999)], paras 26, 28-29, 33, 91, 153-159, 176, Separate O. Anderson; 2004 *Juno Trader* Judgment, Case No.13, President L.D.M. Nelson, paras 36-40, 95, Separate O. Treves <www.itlos.org>; 2006 *Barbados/Trinidad & Tobago (Jurisdiction and Merits)* Award, paras 89-91, 98, 263, 270; Day-4, 24-25 [Counsel Wordsworth, 21 Oct 2005], Day-5, 53-54 [Counsel Fietta, 24 Oct], Day-8, 86, 89 [Wordsworth, 28 Oct 2005] <www.pca-cpa.org>; *Guyana/Suriname* Award – see Peaceful Uses of the Sea – Prohibition of Threat or Use of Force *infra*.

On 1935 *Canada/USA I'm Alone (The Wolcott, The Dexter)* Award [RIAA III, 1609; 29 AJIL 296, 326 (1935); 54 AJIL 89 (1960); No.357/Stuyt], see *South West Africa (Preliminary Objections)* Separate O. Jessup, ICJ Rep. 1962, 425; *Barcelona Traction (Second Phase)* Separate O. Fitzmaurice, ICJ Rep. 1970, 79 n.24; *Nuclear Tests* Pleadings (Australia), 328 [Memorial]; *Spain v. Canada* Pleadings, 622 [Counsel Willis, 17 June 1998] <www.icj-cij.org>; *M/V Saiga* Judgment [38 ILM 1323 (1999)], para.156; Memorial of Saint Vincent and the Grenadines, paras 97, 170, 174, 197, Counter-Memorial of Guinea, paras 75-76, 151, 192, Reply of Saint Vincents, para.198, Rejoinder of Guinea, para.153 n.198, paras 163-164; Hearings

ITLOS PV.99/1, 12 [Agent Joseph, 8 March 1999], 99/17, 19 [Counsel Plender, 19 March 1999] <www.itlos.org>; *Oil Platforms (Merits)* Hearings, CR 2003/14, 33-34, 35 [Counsel Pellet, 28 Feb 2003] <www.icj-cij.org>; 2007 *Guyana/Suriname* Award, para.445 n.518; Suriname's Rejoinder, para.4.61 <www.pca-cpa.org>; 2009 *Abyei Boundary* Award, para.476 <www.pca-cpa.org>.

On 1962 *Denmark/UK The Red Crusader (The Niels Ebbesen)* Report of the Commission of Inquiry [35 ILR 485; No.C 5/Stuyt], see *Spain v. Canada Fisheries Jurisdiction* Pleadings, 622 [Senior Counsel Willis, 17 June 1998] [http://www.icj-cij.org]; *M/V Saiga* Judgment [38 ILM 1323 (1999)], para.156; Memorial of Saint Vincent and the Grenadines, paras 97, Counter-Memorial of Guinea, paras 148, 151-152 <www.itlos.org>; *Guyana/Suriname* Award, para.445 n.518; Suriname's Rejoinder, para.4.61 <www.pca-cpa.org>.

See also Settlement of Disputes – Disputes Concerning Military Activities and Law Enforcement, and Involvement of the UN Security Council; Peaceful Uses of the Sea – Prohibition of Threat or Use of Force (2007 *Guyana/Suriname* Award, Necessity, Countermeasures and Clean Hands) *infra*.

MARINE SCIENTIFIC RESEARCH AND TECHNOLOGY TRANSFER

1958 CSC, Article 5(1)
1982 UNCLOS, Part XIII, Articles 238-265, Part XIV, Articles 266-278; Final Act Annex VI
1994 Agreement
1995 SSA, Article 14, and Annex I
2002 WSSD Johannesburg Declaration and Plan of Implementation, paras 34, 52-55, 99-125

Development of Marine Scientific Research

Legal Status of Eastern Greenland PCIJ Series A/B, No.53 (1933) – Judgment, 40-41, 62-63; *Eastern Greenland* Pleadings, PCIJ Series C, No.62, 16, 38-39, 58-59, 61 [Memorial of Denmark], 226-229, 261-262, 269-278, 283-284 [Norway's Counter-Memorial], No.63, 1073-1077 [Norway's Rejoinder], No.66, 2768 [Agent Steglich-Petersen, 24 Nov 1932], 2960-2966 [Counsel Rygh, 5 Dec 1932]; *Minquiers and Ecrehos* ICJ Rep. 1953, 47 – Judgment, 70; Pleadings, Vol.I, 401 [France's Counter-Memorial], 557 [UK Reply], Vol.II, 184 [Counsel Harrison, 24 Sep 1953]; *Antarctica* Pleadings, 13-14, 18, 20-21, 22-23, 27-31, 53-60, 62-63, 66-67 [UK Applications]; *North Sea* Pleadings, Vol.I, 311 [NL Counter-Memorial]; *Gulf of Fonseca* Judgment, ICJ Rep. 1992, 549, 589, Separate O. Bernardez, 669; *Indonesia/Malaysia (Merits)* Judgment, ICJ Rep. 2002, 625, paras 26, 102, 104, 117, 130;

Hearings, CR 2002/28, 34 [Counsel Soons, 3 June], CR 2002/31, 57-58 [Counsel Schrijver, 7 June], CR 2002/32, 13 [Counsel Sir Elihu Lauterpacht], CR 2002/33, 35-37 [Soons, 10 June 2002]; *Nicaragua v. Honduras (Merits)* Judgment, ICJ Rep. 2007, para.80; Hearings, CR 2007/1, 53-54, paras 18-20 [Counsel Oude Elferink, 5 March 2007], CR 2007/3, 48-49, para.32 [7 March 2007] <www.icj-cij.org>.

Other Relevant Jurisprudence

Fisheries Jurisdiction (Interim Measures) Orders, ICJ Rep. 1972, 17, 34, *(Merits)* Judgments, ICJ Rep. 1974, 7, 14, 26, 31, 34 (para.79(4)(e)), 194, 200, 206 (para.77(4)(e)), Declarations Nagendra Singh, 40, 213 [see also ICES *infra*]; Pleadings (UK), 463 [Counsel Silkin, 25 March 1974]; *Nuclear Tests (Interim Measures)* Orders, ICJ Rep. 1973, 105, 141, Declarations Sir Garfield Barwick, 110, 146, Dissent Ignacio-Pinto, 164; *Nuclear Tests* Judgments, ICJ Rep. 1974, 258, 462, Dissent Gros, 285-286, Joint Dissents, 368, 520; Pleadings (Australia), 12 [Application], 45-49 [Request], (NZ), 51 [Request]; *Gulf of Maine* Judgment, ICJ Rep. 1984, 278-281, 305-307, 340-341; Pleadings, Vol.I, 56-57, 89-90 [Canada's Memorial], Vol.II, 43-46 [US Memorial], Vol.III, 156-159, 162-165, 225, 343-345, 372-363 [Canada's Counter-Memorial], Vol.IV, 137, 301-303 [US Counter-Memorial], Vol.V, 78, 104 [Canada's Reply], 464-470 [US Reply], Vol.VI, 140 [Counsel Bowett, 5 April 1984], 278-279 [Counsel Stevenson, 12 April], 351-353 [Counsel Rashkow, 16 April 1984]; *New Zealand v. France* Order, ICJ Rep. 1995, 290, 298, Dissents Weeramantry, 328-330, 339-340, 348-358, Koroma, 366-367, Palmer, 401-405; 1995 NZ Request (Examination of the Situation) <www.icj-cij.org>; 1998 *Eritrea/Yemen Territorial Sovereignty and Scope of the Dispute (Phase I)* Award, paras 44, 52-53, 69, 256, 278-279, 334, 407-408 [40 ILM 900 (2001) <www.pca-cpa.org>]; *El Salvador v. Honduras Gulf of Fonseca (Revision)* Hearings, C6/CR 2003/4, 23 [Counsel Mendelson, 10 Sep 2003]; *Nicaragua v. Honduras (Merits)* Hearings, CR 2007/7, 40, para.48 [Counsel Sands, 13 March 2007] <www.icj-cij.org>; *Malaysia/Singapore (Merits)* Judgment, ICJ Rep. 2008, paras 167, 235, 260, 265, Dissent Dugard, para.21; Hearings, CR 2007/22, 21-23, paras 41-47 [Counsel Bundy, 8 Nov 2007], CR 2007/22 [transl.], 46, para.10 [Counsel Pellet], CR 2007/23, 19, paras 41-42 [Bundy, 9 Nov], CR 2007/26, 60-65, paras 20-21 & 26-33 [Counsel Crawford, 15 Nov], CR 2007/27, 28, para.58 [Counsel Schrijver, 16 Nov 2007] <www.icj-cij.org>. See also UNGA Adopts Two Oceans Resolutions, UN Doc.GA/10899 of 4 Dec 2009, Statements of Canada and Russia at 15-17 <www.un.org/News/Press/docs//2009/ga10899 .doc.htm>.

High Seas Freedom of Scientific Research
1958 HSC, Article 2; 1982 UNCLOS, Part VII, Article 87(1)(f), Part XIII, Articles 238-244, 246(3):

Nuclear Tests Pleadings (Australia), 341 [Memorial]; *Aegean Sea* Pleadings, 89 [Counsel O'Connell, 25 Aug 1976]; *M/V Saiga* Separate O. Laing [38 ILM 1323 (1999)], para.32; 2000 *Australia and New Zealand v. Japan Southern Bluefin Tuna (Jurisdiction and Admissibility)* Award [Fisheries *supra*] – experimental fishing programme (EFP), 39 ILM 1359 (2000) <www.worldbank.org/icsid>.

Scientific Research within the EEZ/CS
1958 CSC, Article 5(8); 1982 UNCLOS, Part V, Article 56(1)(b)(ii), Part XIII, Articles 246-255:

Aegean Sea (Interim Measures) Order, ICJ Rep. 1976, 4, 6-11, Separate O. Mosler, 25-26, Dissent Stassinopoulos, 35-40, *(Jurisdiction)* Judgment, ICJ Rep. 1978, 6-8; Pleadings, 3-11 [Greece's Application], 63-66 [Request], 89-91, 107-110 [Counsel O'Connell, 25 Aug 1976], 128-131 [Counsel Pinto, 26 Aug], 141-142 [O'Connell, 27 Aug 1976]; *Tunisia/Libya (Merits)* Dissent Oda, ICJ Rep. 1982, 228; Pleadings, Vol.I, 39-45 [Tunisia's Memorial]; *Gulf of Maine* Pleadings, Vol.III, 343-345 [Canada's Counter-Memorial]; *Libya/Malta* Pleadings, Vol.I, 80-84 [Libya's Memorial], Vol.II, 19-20 [Libya's Counter-Memorial]; 1998 *Eritrea/Yemen (Phase I)* Award, para.407-408 [40 ILM 900 (2001)]; *M/V Saiga* Separate O. Laing [38 ILM 1323 (1999)], para.49; *Cameroon v. Nigeria (Merits)* Hearings, CR 2002/20, 56 [Counsel Crawford, 15 March 2002] <www.icj-cij.org>; 2006 *Barbados/Trinidad & Tobago (Jurisdiction and Merits)* Award, paras 182, 362-364; Barbados' Reply, paras 157-158; Trinidad's Rejoinder, paras 175-176; Hearings Day-4, 60-61 [Counsel Crawford, 21 Oct 2005], Day-5, 25-26 [Counsel Volterra, 24 Oct 2005] <www.pca-cpa.org>; 2007 *Guyana/Suriname (Jurisdiction and Merits)* Award, paras 467-470, 479-484.

Fundamental Scientific Research
1958 CSC, Article 5(8); 1982 UNCLOS, Part VII, Article 87(1)(f), Part XIII, Article 246(3):

Aegean Sea Pleadings, 108-110 [Counsel O'Connell, 26 Aug 1976].

Transfer of Marine Technology
1982 UNCLOS, Part XIV, Articles 266-278:

Libya/Malta Pleadings, Vol.I, 480-482, 554-569 [Malta's Memorial], Vol.II, 68-71 [Libya's Counter-Memorial], Vol.III, 147-148 [Malta's Reply]; *Denmark v. Norway* Separate O. Weeramantry, ICJ Rep. 1993, 259.

On International Council for the Exploration of the Sea (ICES), see *Fisheries Jurisdiction (Interim Measures)* Orders, ICJ Rep. 1972, 13, 17, 31, 35, *(Merits)* Separate O. Dillard, ICJ Rep. 1974, 53; Pleadings (UK), 73 [Request], 413 [map], 455-456 [Counsel Silkin, 25 March 1974], (FRG), 27 [Request], 244, 252 [Memorial (Merits)]; *Gulf of Maine* Pleadings, Vol.III, 154 [Canada's Counter-Memorial], Vol.V [Annex 89], Vol.VI, 97 [Counsel Binnie, 4 April 1984]; *Denmark v. Norway* Oral Hearings, CR 93/2, 50-52 [Counsel Trolle, 12 Jan 1993], CR 93/5, 53, 62 [Agent Tresselt, 15 Jan 1993]; *Ireland v. UK Mox Plant (Provisional Measures)* Separate O. Anderson, para.3 <www.itlos.org>.

On El Nino, see *Gulf of Maine* Pleadings, Vol.IV, 80 [US Counter-Memorial]. Cf. UN Docs A/55/99-E/2000/86 (2000), A/57/189 (2002) and UNGA Resolutions 55/197 and 57/255 on International Cooperation to Reduce the Impact of the El Nino Phenomenon of 20 Dec 2000 & 20 Dec 2002 and 59/232 of 22 Dec 2004.

On Jan Mayen's LORAN-C meteorological station, see Equitable Maritime Boundary Delimitation – *Denmark v. Norway* case *supra.*

On Scientific Research Installations or Equipment, see Exclusive Economic (/Fishery) Zone – Artificial Islands, Installations and Structures; on Precautionary Approach, see Protection and Preservation of the Marine Environment *supra.*

See also Equitable Maritime Boundary Delimitation – Economic Factors; Protection and Preservation of the Marine Environment – Precautionary Approach and EIA/Notification/Consultation *supra.*

INTERNATIONAL SEABED AREA

1982 UNCLOS, Part I, Article 1(1), Part XI, Articles 133-191, Part XVII, Articles 311(6) and 314, Annexes III and IV; Final Act Annex I
1994 Agreement

Speech of Ambassador Arvid Pardo (Malta) to the UNGA

[UN Doc. A/6695 (1967) & UN GAOR, 22nd Sess., Annex 3, 1st Comm., 1515th mtg at 1, UN Doc. A/C.1/PV.1515 (1 Nov 1967)] *North Sea* Pleadings, Vol.I, 353 [NL Counter-Memorial]; *Tunisia/Libya (Merits)* Dissent Oda, ICJ Rep. 1982, 212; *Denmark v. Norway* Separate O. Vice-President Oda, ICJ Rep. 1993, 98; *Guyana/Suriname* Hearings Day 1, 14-15 [Agent Insanally, 7 Dec 2006] <www.pca-cpa.org>.

A Map of the US Congress Foreign Affairs Committee

[9th US Congress' First Session, House Report 999, at 88-89] *North Sea* Pleadings, Vol.II, 33-35 [Agent Jaenicke, 24 Oct], 127 [Agent Riphagen, 30 Oct 1968].

UN Sea-Bed Committee

North Sea Separate O. Ammoun, ICJ Rep. 1969, 100, 109 n.3, 111 n.4, 142, Dissent Sorensen, 249; Pleadings, 35 [Agent Jaenicke, 24 Oct 1968], 79 [Counsel Sir Humphrey Waldock, 28 Oct 1968], 126-128 [Agent Riphagen, 30 Oct], 172, 178 [Jaenicke, 4 Nov], 197-198 [Counsel Shigeru Oda, 5 Nov], 244 [Reply by Waldock to Questions Fitzmaurice, 8 Nov 1968]; *Fisheries Jurisdiction (Jurisdiction)* Dissents Padilla Nervo, ICJ Rep. 1973, 45, 90, *(Merits)* Separate Os de Castro, 97 n.3, 225; Pleadings (FRG), 306 [Agent Jaenicke, 28 March 1974]; *Aegean Sea* Pleadings, 455 [Counsel O'Connell, 16 Oct 1978]; *Tunisia/Libya (Merits)* Dissent Oda, ICJ Rep. 1982, 161-162, 164, 171, 213-216; *Gulf of Maine* Pleadings, Vol.VII, 154 [Agent Robinson, 9 May 1984]; *Libya/Malta (Merits)* Dissent Oda, ICJ Rep. 1985, 140; 2002 *Russia v. Australia Volga* Declaration Vice-President Vukas, para.10 <www.itlos.org>.

Gulf of Maine Pleadings, Vol.VII, 148 [Agent Robinson, 9 May 1984]; *Libya/Malta* Pleadings, Vol.I, 480-482 [Malta's Memorial], Vol.II, 69 [Libya's Counter-Memorial]; *Denmark v. Norway* Separate O. Weeramantry, ICJ Rep. 1993, 259; Oral Hearings, CR 93/1Corr., 16 [Agent Lehmann, 11 Jan 1993] <www.icj-cij.org>; *Canada/France (St. Pierre & Miquelon)* Award, para.78 [31 ILM 1160, 1172 (1992)] and 2002 *Newfoundland and Labrador/Nova Scotia (Phase II)* Award, paras 2.29-2.34 <www.gov.ns.ca/>, as both relied upon in 2006 *Barbados/Trinidad & Tobago (Jurisdiction and Merits)* Award, President S.M. Schwebel, para.82; Trinidad's Counter-Memorial, paras 265-269, 287-288; Barbados' Reply, paras 132-145; Day-1, 85-87 [Counsel Reisman, 17 Oct 2005], 94-95, 105 [Counsel Volterra], Day-4, 94, 97-100, 107-108 [Counsel Crawford, 21 Oct], Day-6, 45 [Reisman, 25 Oct], Day-8, 39-40, 58 [Crawford, 28 Oct 2005] <www.pca-cpa.org>.

On 1994 Agreement on Part XI, see *Southern Bluefin Tuna (Jurisdiction)*, President S.M. Schwebel, Hearings, Vol.I [Counsel Lauterpacht, 7 May 2000] <www.worldbank.org/icsid>.

See also Protection and Preservation of the Marine Environment – Pollution From Activities in the Area *supra*; Archaeological and Historical Objects; Privileges and Immunities of the UNCLOS Institutions *infra*.

SETTLEMENT OF DISPUTES

1958 HSFC, Articles 9-12; 1958 DSP

1982 UNCLOS, Part XV, Articles 279-299, Part XVI, Article 302, and Annexes V-VIII and Annex IX, Article 7; 1994 Agreement, Annex (Secs 3, 6)

1992 UNCED Rio Declaration and Agenda 21

1995 SSA, Part VIII, Articles 27-32

Obligation to Settle Disputes by Peaceful Means

1945 United Nations Charter, Articles 2(3) and 33; 1982 UNCLOS, Article 279; 1992 Rio Principle 26, Agenda 21, Chapter 39, para.39.10; 1995 SSA, Article 27:

Interpretation of Judgments Nos 7 and 8 (Factory at Chorzow) Judgment, PCIJ Series A, No.13, 10-11 (1927); *Corfu Channel (Merits)* Dissent Krylov, ICJ Rep. 1949, 75; *Anglo/Norwegian Fisheries* Individual O. Alvarez, ICJ Rep. 1951, 151; *North Sea* Judgment, ICJ Rep. 1969, 34, para.50, 36, para.55, 47, para.86, Separate O. Padilla Nervo, 88, 92, 98, 99, Separate O. Ammoun, 146, Dissent Morelli, 216; *North Sea* Pleadings, Vol.I, 181 [Denmark's Counter-Memorial], Vol.II, 70 [Agent Riphagen, 28 Oct 1968]; *Fisheries Jurisdiction (Jurisdiction)* Judgments, ICJ Rep. 1973, 10-16, 21, 56-60, *(Merits)* Judgments, ICJ Rep. 1974, 25, 26, 194, Declarations Nagendra Singh, 40, 213, Separate O. Dillard, 67, Separate Os de Castro, 95, 102, 225, Separate Os Waldock, 125, 227, Dissent Gros, 143, 148-149; *Nuclear Tests* Judgments, ICJ Rep. 1974, 270-272, 476-477, *as reaffirmed* by *New Zealand v. France* Order, ICJ Rep. 1995, 304, para.56, Declaration Vice-President Schwebel, 309, Separate O. Shahabuddeen, 312-316, Dissent Palmer, 416-420; *Aegean Sea (Interim Measures)* Order, ICJ Rep. 1976, 6, 11-13, Dissent Stassinopoulos, 35-36, *(Jurisdiction)* Judgment, ICJ Rep. 1978, 38; Pleadings, 107, 115, 117 [Counsel O'Connell, 25 and 26 Aug 1976], 322-323 [9 Oct 1978]; *Tunisia v. Libya (Revision)* Judgment, ICJ Rep. 1985, 217-218; *Gulf of Maine* Judgment, ICJ Rep. 1984, 266; Pleadings, Vol.IV, 99-100 [US Counter-Memorial]; *Libya/Malta (Intervention)* Judgment, ICJ Rep. 1984, 20, Separate O. de Arechaga, 63; *Guinea-Bissau v. Senegal Arbitral Award* Separate O. Lachs, ICJ Rep. 1991, 95, Dissent Aguilar and Ranjeva, 120-121; *Gulf of Fonseca* Judgment, ICJ Rep. 1992, 555, Separate O. Bernardez, 658-659; *Denmark v. Norway* Separate O. Shahabuddeen, ICJ Rep. 1993, 204-210; *Qatar v. Bahrain (Jurisdiction and Admissibility)* Dissent Shahabuddeen, ICJ Rep. 1995, 51-52; *East Timor* Judgment, ICJ Rep. 1995, 99-100; *Nuclear Weapons (UNGA)* Advisory Opinion, ICJ Rep. 1996, 233-236; *Bosnia and Herzegovina v. Yugoslavia (Preliminary Objections)* Judgment, ICJ Rep. 1996, 614-615; *Lockerbie (Preliminary Objections)* Judgments, ICJ Rep. 1998, 17 [*Libya v. UK*], 122-123 [*Libya v. USA*], Dissents President Schwebel, 65-66, 156-157; *Spain v. Canada (Jurisdiction)* Judgment, ICJ Rep. 1998, 456, para.56, Separate O. Kooymans, 492, para.10; *Yugoslavia v. Belgium* (para.48), *Yugoslavia v. Canada* (para.44), *Yugoslavia v. France* (para.36), *Yugoslavia v. Germany* (para.35), *Yugoslavia v. Italy* (para.36), *Yugoslavia v. Netherlands* (para.48), *Yugoslavia v. Portugal* (para.47), *Yugoslavia v. Spain* (para.37), *Yugoslavia v. UK* (para.40), and *Yugoslavia v. USA* (para.31) *Legality of Use of Force (Provisional Measures)* Orders, and Declarations Koroma (all ten Orders), ICJ Rep. 1999 124, 259, 363, 422, 481, 542, 656, 761, 826, 916; *Cameroon v. Nigeria (Preliminary Objections)* Judgment, ICJ Rep. 1998, 314-315, Separate O. Kooymans, 356-357, *Cameroon v. Nigeria; Equatorial Guinea Intervening* Dissent Ajibola, paras 1-10, 175, ICJ Rep. 2002, 538-541, 594; *LaGrand* Separate O. Parra-Aranguren, ICJ Rep. 2001, 545-546, para.8, quotig the 1998 Judgment *supra*; *DR Congo v. Belgium Arrest Warrant of 11 April 2000* Judgment, ICJ Rep. 2002, 12-15; *Oil Platforms (Merits)* Hearings, CR 2003/9, 10 [Agent Taft IV, 21 Feb 2003]; *Liechtenstein v. Germany (Preliminary Objections)* Judgment, ICJ Rep. 2005, 6-19, 27, paras 1-27 and operative para.54(1)(a), Dissents Kooymans, 29-31, paras 1-6, Owada, 47-62, paras 1-44, Berman, 70-72, paras 1-5, Declaration Fleischhauer, 69; *DR Congo v. Rwanda (Jurisdiction)* Judgment, ICJ Rep. 2006, para.90; *Nicaragua v. Colombia (Preliminary Objections)* Judgment, ICJ Rep. 2007, paras 33-59; *Mexico v. USA Interpretation of 2004 Avena Judgment (Provisional Measures)* Order, paras 53-54, ICJ Rep. 2008, Joint Dissent Owada, Tomka and Sir Kenneth Keith, paras 19-20; *Belgium v. Senegal Obligation to Prosecute or Extradite (Provisional Measures)* Order, ICJ Rep. 2009, paras 42-55, Joint Separate O. Al-Khasawneh and Skotnikov, paras 7-16, Separate O. Sur, paras 13-15 <www.icj-cij.org>.

2000 *Southern Bluefin Tuna (Jurisdiction and Admissibility)* Award, President S.M. Schwebel, 39 ILM 1359 (2000), paras 48, 53, 67-71, Separate O. Keith; Japan's Memorial, paras 110-115, A/NZ Reply, paras 42-53, 96, Hearings, Vol.I [Counsel Rosenne, Lowe, 7 May 2000], Vol.II [Counsel Burmester, Mansfield, Agent Caughley, 8 May], Vol.IV [Counsel Crawford, 11 May 2000] <www.worldbank.org/icsid>; 2001 *Ireland v. UK Mox Plant (Provisional Measures)* Separate O. Vice-President Nelson <www.itlos.org>; 2006 *Barbados/Trinidad & Tobago (Jurisdiction and Merits)* Award, President S.M. Schwebel, paras 67-68, 75, 80, 191, 196-198, 200, 204-209, 213-215, 275, 291-293 <www.pca-cpa.org>; 2007 *Guyana/Suriname (Jurisdiction and Merits)* Award, President L.D.M. Nelson, paras 164-165, 168, 263, 267, 408, 428, 449; 2009 *Abyei Boundary* Award, President P.M. Dupuy, paras 407, 453-466, 767 <www.pca-cpa.org>.

On Optional Protocol of Signature Concerning the Compulsory Settlement of Disputes, Geneva, 29 April 1958 [in force: 30 September 1962, 450 UNTS 169], see *North Sea* Dissent Sorensen, ICJ Rep. 1969, 256; 1977 *Anglo/French Continental*

Shelf Decision [18 ILM 397 (1979)], paras 34, 42-44; *Tunisia/Libya (Merits)* Dissent Oda, ICJ Rep. 1982, 189; *Passage Through the Great Belt (Provisional Measures)* Order, ICJ Rep. 1991, 13; Finland's Application, para.9; *Denmark v. Norway* Separate O. Vice-President Oda, ICJ Rep. 1993, 97; *East Timor* Application of Portugal, para.17; *Qatar v. Bahrain (Jurisdiction and Admissibility)* Koroma, ICJ Rep. 1995, 70; *Oil Platforms (Preliminary Objection)* Dissent Oda, ICJ Rep. 1996, 895.

On 1982 UNCLOS, Part XV, see *Cameroon v. Nigeria (Preliminary Objections)* Judgment, ICJ Rep. 1998, 321-322, *as reaffirmed* by *Cameroon v. Nigeria; Equatorial Guinea Intervening (Merits)* Judgment, ICJ Rep. 2002, 422-424, paras 239, 241-244, Declaration Oda, paras 28-29, Separate O. Mbaye, paras 102-105 <www.icj-cij.org>. See also Articles 281-283, Choice of Procedure and Montreaux Clause *infra*.

On dispute settlement procedures under the 1957 EURATOM Treaty and the 1992 EU Treaty as Amended, see references to these treaties in Protection and Preservation of the Marine Environment *supra*.

On dispute settlement procedure under the 1995 UN Fish Stocks Agreement [Fisheries *supra*], see *Spain v. Canada* Pleadings, 528 [Senior Counsel Willis, 12 June 1998]; 2000 *Southern Bluefin Tuna (Jurisdiction)* Award, paras 38(i) and 71, 39 ILM 1359 (2000); Japan's Memorial, paras 143, 172, A/NZ Reply, para.178, Hearings, Vol.I [Counsel Lauterpacht, Lowe, 7 May 2000], Vol.II [Counsel Burmester, Irwin, Jennings, 8 May 2000] <www.worldbank.org/icsid>; *UNSG Fish Stocks Agreement Reports* A/62/260 (2007) & A/63/128 (2008) & A/64/305 (2009) <www.un.org/Depts/los>.

See also UNGA Resolution 55/2 on United Nations Millennium Declaration of 8 Sep 2000, reaffirming commitment to the purposes and principles of the Charter of the United Nations and to resolution of disputes by peaceful means and in conformity with the principles of justice and international law (paras 1-4 and 30), and resolving "to strengthen the International Court of Justice, in order to ensure justice and the rule of law in international affairs" (para.30); WWSD Johannesburg Declaration and Plan of Implementation of 4 Sep 2002 <www.iisd.ca/wssd/portal.html> and UN Doc. A/CONF.199/20 (2002); General Assembly Resolution 57/26 on Prevention and Peaceful Settlement of Disputes of 19 Nov 2002 and UN Security Council Statement on The Role of the Security Council in the Pacific Settlement of Disputes, UN Doc. S/PRST/2003/5 of 13 May 2003; 2005 *UN World Summit Outcome*, reaffirming [para.3] dedication to the UN Millennium Declaration and [paras 5, 73, 134(f)] "the important role of the ICJ, the principal judicial organ of the United Nations" in pacific settlement of disputes <http://www.un.org/summit2005/>; UN Security Council High-Level Meeting on Mediation and Settlement of Disputes – Presidential Statement, UN Doc. S/PRST/2008/36 of 23 Sep 2008 <www.un.org/News/Press/docs//2008/sc9452.doc.htm> and UN Secretary-General's Statement <www.un.org/News/Press/docs//2008/sgsm11807.doc.htm, www.un.org/apps/news/story.asp?NewsID=28189&Cr=ki-moon&Cr1 & www.un.org/apps/sg/sgstats.asp?nid=3416>.

Definition of Obligation to Negotiate

Railway Traffic Between Lithuania and Poland Advisory Opinion, PCIJ Series A/B, No.42, 116 (1931), *as reaffirmed* by the *North Sea* Judgment, ICJ Rep. 1969, 47-48, paras 85-87, Separate O. President Bustamante y Rivero, 58, 65, Separate Os Padilla Nervo, 88, 92, 98, Ammoun, 146-147, Dissents Tanaka, 184-185, 195-196, Morelli, 216-217, Lachs, 219, Sorensen, 253-254; *North Sea* Pleadings, Vol.I, 393-394 [FRG Reply]; *Fisheries Jurisdiction (Merits)* Judgments, ICJ Rep. 1974, 31-33, 34 (para.79(2)-(3)) [*UK v. Iceland*], 201-202, 205-206 (para.77(2)-(3)) [*FRG v. Iceland*], Declarations Nagendra Singh, 41, 214, Separate O. Dillard, 67, 71, Separate Os de Castro, 104, 225, Dissent Gros, 143-146; *Fisheries Jurisdiction* Pleadings (UK), 373-374 [Memorial (Merits)]; *Aegean Sea (Interim Measures)* Order, ICJ Rep. 1976, 12-13, *(Jurisdiction)* Separate O. Nagendra Singh, ICJ Rep. 1978, 47-48; Pleadings, 70 [Turkey's Response], 116-117 [Counsel O'Connell, 26 Aug 1976], 167 [Turkey's Statement], 324-326 [O'Connell, 9 Oct 1978]; *Tunisia/Libya (Merits)* Dissent Gros, ICJ Rep. 1982, 144-147, also invoking [145] the 1957 *Lake Lanoux* Award [24 ILR 101, esp.133-138], *Tunisia v. Libya (Revision)* Judgment, ICJ Rep. 1985, 229; *Gulf of Maine* Judgment, ICJ Rep. 1984, 291-293; Pleadings, Vol.IV, 99-100 [US Counter-Memorial], Vol.V, 402-403 [US Reply]; *UN Headquarters Agreement* Advisory Opinion, ICJ Rep. 1988, 33-34, invoking *Mavrommatis Palestine Concessions* Judgment, PCIJ Series A, No.2, 13 (1924); *Gulf of Fonseca* Judgment, ICJ Rep. 1992, 406; Hearings, C 4/CR 91/46, 14 [Counsel Lauterpacht, 11 June 1991]; *Nuclear Weapons (UNGA)* Advisory Opinion, ICJ Rep. 1996, 263-264; *Gabcikovo-Nagymaros Project* Judgment, ICJ Rep. 1997, 66, paras 107-108, at 78, para.141, Separate O. Bedjaoui, 140-141, Dissent Herczegh, 190-191; *Cameroon v. Nigeria (Preliminary Objections)* Dissent Ajibola, ICJ Rep. 1998, 414; *Qatar v. Bahrain (Jurisdiction and Admissibility)* Judgment, ICJ Rep. 1994, 126; Hearings, CR 2000/16, 39 [Counsel Weil, 15 June 2000] <www.icj-cij.org>; 2000 *Southern Bluefin Tuna (Jurisdiction)* Award, President S.M. Schwebel, paras 53-55 and 67-71 [39 ILM 1359 (2000) <www.worldbank.org/icsid>]; *Malaysia v. Singapore (Provisional Measures)* Hearings, ITLOS/PV.03/03, 34 [Counsel Reisman, 26 Sep 2003], PV.03/05, 30 [Agent Koh, 27 Sep 2003] <www.itlos.org>; *DR Congo v. Rwanda (Jurisdiction)* Judgment, ICJ Rep. 2006, paras 80-93 <www.icj-cij.org>; 2006 *Barbados/Trinidad & Tobago (Jurisdiction and Merits)* Award, President S.M. Schwebel, paras 69-85, 100-101, 112, 188-217,

291-293; Barbados' Reply, paras 66-106; Hearings Day-1, 66-79 [Counsel Reisman, 17 Oct 2005], Day-7, 17-18, 50 [Questions Sir Arthur Watts, 27 Oct 2005], 45-64 [Counsel Wordsworth] <www.pca-cpa.org>.

See also Equitable Maritime Boundary Delimitation – 1982 UNCLOS, Articles 74(1)-(2)/83(1)-(2) *supra*.

Preventive Diplomacy – Parallel Pursuance of Negotiations and Judicial Settlement

A) Generally:

Free Zones of Upper Savoy and the District of Gex (First Phase) Order, PCIJ Series A, No.22, 13 (1929), *as reaffirmed* by *North Sea* Judgment, ICJ Rep. 1969, 47, para.87, *Burkina Faso/Mali Frontier Dispute* Judgment, ICJ Rep. 1986, 577, para.46, and *Finland v. Denmark Passage Through the Great Belt (Provisional Measures)* Order, ICJ Rep. 1991, 20, paras 35-36, Declaration Tarassov, 23-24, Separate Os Vice-President Oda, 27, Broms, 38-39, *(Discontinuance)* Order, ICJ Rep. 1992, 348; *Nottebohm (Second Phase)* Judgment, ICJ Rep. 1955, 19-20; *North Sea* Separate O. Ammoun, ICJ Rep. 1969, 146-147; Pleadings, Vol.II, 9-10 [Agent Jaenicke, 23 Oct 1968], 78-79 [Counsel Sir Humphrey Waldock, 28 Oct], 167 [Jaenicke, 4 Nov 1968]; *Trial of Pakistani Prisoners of War (Interim Protection)* Order, ICJ Rep. 1973, 347; *Fisheries Jurisdiction (Jurisdiction)* Dissents Padilla Nervo, ICJ Rep. 1973, 45, 90, *(Continuance Interim Measures)* Orders, 303, 314, Dissents Gros, 308-309, 317, *(Merits)* Judgment, ICJ Rep. 1974, 17-20, Declarations Nagendra Singh, 41-42, 214-215, Separate O. de Castro, 77, 104, Dissents Gros, 143-149, 238-239, Dissents Petren, 154-160, 241, Dissents Onyeama, 173, 249; *Western Sahara* Declaration Gros, ICJ Rep. 1975, 75-77; *Tunisia/Libya (Merits)* Dissent Gros, ICJ Rep. 1982, 153, *(Revision and Interpretation)* Judgment, ICJ Rep. 1985, 218; *Gulf of Maine* Dissent Gros, ICJ Rep. 1984, 385, 389; *Aegean Sea (Interim Measures)* Order, ICJ Rep. 1976, 11-13, Separate Os President de Aréchaga, 16, Lachs, 19-20, Elias, 30, Dissent Stassinopoulos, 38-40, and *(Jurisdiction)* Judgment, ICJ Rep. 1978, 10-13, 12, para.12, *as reaffirmed* by *Nicaragua v. USA Military and Paramilitary Activities (Jurisdiction and Admissibility)* Judgment, ICJ Rep. 1984, 440, para.106, and *Cameroon v. Nigeria (Preliminary Objections)* Judgment, ICJ Rep. 1998, 302-303, para.56; *Aegean Sea (Jurisdiction)* Separate Os Vice-President Nagendra Singh, ICJ Rep. 1978, 47-48, Lachs, 52-53; Pleadings, 116 [Counsel O'Connell, 26 Aug 1976]; *Lockerbie (Provisional Measures)* Dissents Bedjaoui, ICJ Rep. 1992, 49, 159, Dissents Ranjeva, 75, 182; *Gabcikovo-Nagymaros Project* Judgment, ICJ Rep. 1997, 75-81; *Yugoslavia v. Belgium Legality of Use of Force (Provisional Measures)* Dissent Vice-President Weeramantry, ICJ Rep. 1999,

195-199, applicable *mutatis mutandis* to his Dissents from Orders in the cases with Canada, the Netherlands and Portugal; *Pakistan v. India Aerial Incident of 10 August 1999 (Jurisdiction)* Judgment, para.52, ICJ Rep. 2000, 33; *Congo v. Belgium (Provisional Measures*, paras 74-76, ICJ Rep. 2000, 201-202; *Qatar v. Bahrain (Merits)* Joint Dissent Bedjaoui, Ranjeva, Koroma, ICJ Rep. 2001, 200-201, paras 178-179; *Indonesia/Malaysia (Application of the Philippines for Permission to Intervene)* Separate O. Weeramantry, para.22, ICJ Rep. 2001, 642-643 <www.icj-cij.org>; 2003 *Malaysia v. Singapore (Provisional Measures)* Order, ITLOS Case No.12, para.52, *reaffirming Cameroon v. Nigeria (Preliminary Objections)* Judgment, ICJ Rep. 1998, 303 [*supra*], Separate Os Ndiaye, Jesus <www.itlos.org>; eight *Legality of Use of Force (Preliminary Objections)* Separate Os Higgins, paras 4-12, ICJ Rep. 2004 – Belgium, 336-339, Canada, 482-485, France, 627-630, Germany, 772-775, Italy, 918-921, Netherlands, 1067-1070, Portugal, 1214-1217, UK, 1359-1362 <www.icj-cij.org>.

Statements of President Sir Robert Jennings to the 46th and 48th UNGA – UN Doc. A/46/PV.44, 1-5 (8 November 1991), *reprinted in ICJ Yearbook 1991-1992* 205-212 (No.46); and UN Doc.A/48/PV.31, 1-5 (15 October 1993), *reprinted in ICJ Yearbook 1993-1994* 219-223 (No.48); Statements of President Stephen M. Schwebel to the 52nd, 53rd and 54th UNGA – UN Doc. A/52/PV.36, 1-5 (27 October 1997), *reprinted in* 92 AJIL 612-615 (1998), *ICJ Yearbook 1997-1998* 288-295 (No.52); UN Doc. A/53/PV.44, 1-5 (27 October 1998), *ICJ Press Release* No.98/33, *reprinted in ICJ Yearbook 1998-1999* 316-323 (No.53); and UN Doc. A/54/PV.39, 1-5 (26 October 1999), *ICJ Press Release* No.99/46, *reprinted in ICJ Yearbook 1999-2000* 282-288 (No.54) <www.icj-cij.org>.

2000 *Southern Bluefin Tuna (Jurisdiction)* Award, President S.M. Schwebel, paras 67-71 [RIAA XXIII, 1; 39 ILM 1359 (2000); 119 ILR 508 <www.worldbank.org/icsid>]; *Oceans and the Law of the Sea – Report of the Secretary-General*, UN Doc. A/56/58, 80-81 (2001).

For Statement of Australia's Minister of Foreign Affairs and Trade of 29 May 2001, announcing resolution of the dispute, see <www.dfat.gov.au/media/releases/foreign/2001/fa065_01.html>. Note ratification of the 1995 UN Fish Stocks Agreement by Australia on 23 December 1999 and NZ on 18 April 2001 <www.un.org/Depts/los>. For the 57th UNGA Statement of Ambassador Shabtai Rosenne of 9 December 2002 on the Occassion of the UNCLOS's 20th Anniversary [referring to the Award at 5-7], see <*id.*>; Statement of NZ Foreign Affairs Consultant and other MFA items <www.mft.govt.nz/support/legal/disputes/seapol.html>.

2001 *Newfoundland and Labrador/Nova Scotia (Phase I)* Award, para.3.16 <www.gov.ns.ca/petro/documents/TribunalAwardPhaseI.pdf>; *Panama v. Yemen Chaisiri Reefer 2 (Discontinuance)* Order, ITLOS Case No.9 <www.itlos.org>.

B) Cases which were withdrawn after the Court rendered its first decision(s):

Passage Through the Great Belt (Provisional Measures) Order, ICJ Rep. 1991, 20, paras 35-36, and *(Discontinuance)* Order of President Sir Robert Jennings, ICJ Rep. 1992, 348 – see Straits Used for International Navigation *supra*.

See also *Nauru v. Australia Certain Phosphate Lands in Nauru (Preliminary Objections)* Judgment, ICJ Rep. 1992, 240, Separate O. Shahabuddeen, 270, Dissent President Sir Robert Jennings, 301, Dissent Vice-President Oda, 303, Dissent Schwebel, 329, and *(Discontinuance)* Order, ICJ Rep. 1993, 322; Orders, ICJ Reports 1991, 3, 1992, 345, 1993, 316; *Oil Platforms (Merits)* Hearings, CR 2003/13, 14 [Counsel Murphy, 26 Feb 2003] <www.icj-cij.org>.

For Australia/Nauru Agreement of 10 August 1993, see 1770 UNTS 380; 32 ILM 1471 (1993). For UK/Australia Agreement of 24 March 1994, see 1820 UNTS 6. For Australia/New Zealand Agreement of 23 May 1994, see 1820 UNTS 14. See also 65 *British YIL* 625 (1994); 15 *Australian YIL* 652 (1994), and 16 *Australian YIL* 544, 577, 580 (1995). Cf. *East Timor* Hearings, CR 95/7, 72-73 [Counsel Crawford, 6 Feb 1995]; Australia Takes Control in Nauru of 26 July 2004 <http://news.bbc.co.uk/2/hi/business/3926497.stm & 24 July <www.abc.net.au/news/newsitems/200407/s1160902.htm>.

Nicaragua v. Honduras Border and Transborder Armed Actions (Provisional Measures) Order, ICJ Rep. 1988, 9, *(Jurisdiction and Admissibility)* Judgment, 69, and *(Discontinuance)* Order, ICJ Rep. 1992, 222; *Paraguay v. USA Vienna Convention on Consular Relations (Provisional Measures)* Order, ICJ Rep. 1998, 248, Declaration President Schwebel, 259, Declarations Oda, 260, Koroma, 263, and *(Discontinuance)* Order, 426; pair of the *Libya v. UK; Libya v. USA Lockerbie* cases [see Peaceful Uses of the Sea – Maritime Terrorism *infra*]; *Congo v. Burundi (Discontinuance)* and *Congo v. Rwanda (Discontinuance)* Orders, ICJ Rep. 2001, 3, 6 <ww.icj-cij.org>.

2001 *EC/Chile Swordfish* case – suspended after establishment of ITLOS Chamber, Case No.7, ITLOS Rep. 2001, 4; 40 ILM 475 (2001) and WTO Panel, WT/DS193/3 and Add.1, 6 and 9 April 2001 <www.europa.eu.int/comm/trade/miti/dispute/swordfish.htm>; Orders of 16 Dec 2003 and 29 Dec 2005 further suspending proceedings until 1 Jan 2008 and *Swordfish (Discontinuance)* Order of 17 Dec 2009 <www.itlos.org>.

C) Cases in which the normal course of the proceedings was suspended to allow for negotiations between the parties which finally led to the removal of these cases from the Court's General List:

Arbitral Award of 31 July 1989 (Provisional Measures) Order, ICJ Rep. 1990, 64, Judgment, ICJ Rep. 1991, 53; *Maritime Delimitation Between Guinea-Bissau and Senegal (Discontinuance)* Order, ICJ Rep. 1995, 423 – see Equitable Maritime Boundary Delimitation *supra.*

See also *Iran v. USA Aerial Incident of 3 July 1988* Orders, ICJ Rep. 1989, 132, 1990, 86, 1991, 6, 1992, 225, and *(Discontinuance)* Order, ICJ Rep. 1996, 9.

For the Partial Award of the Iran-US Claims Tribunal of 22 February 1996, see 35 ILM 553 (1996). Cf. 83 AJIL 912-913 (1989).

Oil Platforms (Preliminary Objection) Hearings, CR 96/12, 37 [Cdr Neubauer, 16 Sep 1996]; *Oil Platforms (Merits)* Hearings, CR 2003/5, 55 [Counsel Bundy, 17 Feb 2003], CR 2003/7, 18 [19 Feb], CR 2003/14, 40 [Counsel Pellet, 28 Feb], CR 2003/16, 35 [Agent Zahedin-Labbaf, 3 March], CR 2003/17, 12-13 [Agent Taft, 5 March], CR 2003/19, 17 [Counsel Sellers, 7 March 2003] <www.icj-cij.org>.

Annex VII *Ireland v. UK Mox Plant (Suspension of Proceedings)* Orders of 24 June & 14 Nov 2003 <www.pca-cpa.org>; ECJ *EC v. Ireland Mox Plant* Judgment of 30 May 2006 <http://curia.eu.int/>; Annex VII *Mox Plant (Suspension of Periodic Reports by the Parties)* Order No.5 of 22 Jan 2007 and Press Release of 21 Feb 2007 and *Mox Plant (Termination of Proceedings)* Order No.6 of 6 June 2008 <www.pca-cpa.org>; Dismantling and Clean-Up of Sellafield by U.S.-France-UK Nuclear Management Partners (NMP) Until 2030 of 24 Nov 2008 <http://news.bbc.co.uk/2/hi/business/7733487.stm & www.kentucky.com/473/story/603962.html>.

Cf. 2005 *Eureko BV v. Poland (PZU)* Partial Award <www.investmentclaims.com/decisions/Eureko-Poland-LiabilityAward.pdf>; <www.asil.org/ilib050913.cfm>; Eureko/Poland Agreement Concerning PZU SA of 2 Oct 2009 <www.msp.gov.pl/portal/en/16/695/State_Treasury_and_Eureko_BV_reach_theagreement_on_PZU_SA_Poland_to_regain_cont.html> & Treasury's News in English <www.msp.gov.pl/portal/em/16>; Poland Settles Dispute with Netherlands' Eureko of 2 Oct 2009 <www.cnbc.com/id/33135699/site/14081545/for/cnbc/>; *Eureko BV v. Poland (Discontinuance)* Order of Tribunal's President L. Yves Fortier of 4 Dec 2009 <www.msp.gov.pl/portal.php?serwis=pl&dzial=298id=8255&poz=drukuj=1>; Eureko <www.eureko.net/polish/index.asp>.

D) Cases in which the Court defined the fundamental legal parameters within which the parties pursued their further negotiations:

Fisheries Jurisdiction (Merits) Judgments, ICJ Rep. 1974, 33-35, paras 78-79 [*UK v. Iceland*], 202, 205-206, paras 69 and 77 [*FRG v. Iceland*];

Gabcikovo-Nagymaros Project Judgment, ICJ Rep. 1997, 78, para. 141, and 83, para.155(2)(B), and Slovakia's Request, *ICJ Communiques* Nos 98/28 and 98/31 of 3 Sep and 7 Oct 1998; Statement of President Stephen M. Schwebel to the 52nd UNGA [UN Doc. A/52/PV.36, 2-3 (27 Oct 1997), *reprinted in* 92 AJIL 613-614 (1998); *ICJ Yearbook 1997-1998* 288-295 (No.52)]; *ICJ Report 1 August 2001-31 July 2002*, UN Doc.A/57/4, at 47-52 (2002); *ICJ Report 1 August 2007-31 July 2008*, UN Doc.A/63/4, at 19 (2008); *ICJ Report 1 August 2008-31 July 2009*, UN Doc.A/64/4, at 25 (2009) <www.icj-cij.org>;

Yugoslavia v. Belgium Legality of Use of Force (Provisional Measures) Dissent Vice-President Weeramantry, ICJ Rep. 1999, 195-199, applicable *mutatis mutandis* to his Dissents from Orders in the cases with Canada, the NL and Portugal; 2000 *Southern Bluefin Tuna (Jurisdiction)* Award – see A) *supra*; 2005 Annex VII *Malaysia v. Singapore* Award and Settlement Agreement <www.pca-cpa.org> & <http://internet-stg1.mfa.gov.sg/internet/press/land/frm_main_land.htm>; *DR Congo v. Uganda (Merits)* Judgment, paras 260, 261 and 344, operative para.345(6) & (14), ICJ Rep.2005, 168 and *ICJ Report 1 August 2008-31 July 2009*, UN Doc.A/64/4, at 26 (2009) <www.icj-cij.org>; 2006 *Barbados/Trinidad and Tobago (Jurisdiction and Merits)* Award, paras 285-293 & *dispositif* para.385(3) <www.pca-cpa.org>; *Nicaragua v. Honduras (Merits)* Judgment, ICJ Rep. 2007, *dispositif* para.321(4) <www.icj-cij.org>.

1982 UNCLOS, Articles 281 and 283 (No Settlement Reached):

1999 *Southern Bluefin Tuna (Provisional Measures)* Order, ITLOS Cases Nos 3/4, President T.A. Mensah, para.60, ITLOS Rep. 1999, 280; 38 ILM 1624 (1999).

2000 *Southern Bluefin Tuna (Jurisdiction)* Award, President S.M. Schwebel, paras 26-28, 34, 38-39, 41-43, 49, 53-55 [RIAA XXIII, 1; 39 ILM 1359 (2000); 119 ILR 508]; Japan's Memorial, paras 155-156, A/NZ Reply, paras 10, 18-19, 88, 92, Hearings, Vol.I [Counsel Rosenne, 7 May 2000], Vol.II [Agent Campbell, Counsels Burmester, Mansfield, 8 May], Vol.IV [Burmester, 11 May 2000] <www.worldbank.org/icsid>.

2001 *Ireland v. UK Mox Plant (Provisional Measures)* Order, President P.Ch. Rao, ITLOS Case No.10, paras 54-60, Separate Os Anderson, para.1, Treves, para.4 [41 ILM 405 (2002); Ireland's Request & Statement, paras 49, 134, UK Response, paras 5-7, 120-125, 136, 160-161, 186-196; Hearings, ITLOS/PV.01/07, 7-8, 13-15 [Counsel Lowe, 19 Nov 2001], 23, 27-29 [Counsel Goldsmith], ITLOS/PV.01/08, 11, 15 [Counsel Bethlehem, 20 Nov 2001], 25-26 [Counsel Plender], ITLOS/PV.01/09, 15-17 [Lowe] <www.itlos.org>; 2003 OSPAR *Mox Plant* Award and Annex VII *Mox Plant* Ireland's Memorial, I, 95-96 <www.pca-cpa.org>; 2003 *Malaysia v. Singapore (Provisional Measures)* Order, Case No.12 <www.itlos.org>.

2006 *Barbados/Trinidad & Tobago (Jurisdiction and Merits)* Award, President S.M. Schwebel, paras 69-85, 100-101, 112, 188-217, 291-293; Barbados' Reply, paras 66-106; Hearings Day-1, 66-79 [Counsel Reisman, 17 Oct 2005], Day-7, 17-18, 50 [Questions Sir Arthur Watts, 27 Oct 2005], 45-64 [Counsel Wordsworth] <www.pca-cpa.org>; 45 ILM 800 (2006); RIAA XXVII, 147; 2007 *Guyana/Suriname* Award, President L.D.M. Nelson, paras 165, 269, 408-410, 457; Suriname's Rejoinder, para.4.9; Hearings, 45 [Counsel Rosenne, 8 July 2005], Day 5, 770-771 [Counsel Greenwood, 13 Dec 2006] Day 7, 1134-1135 [Counsel Murphy, 15 Dec 2006] <www.pca-cpa.org>.

See also Equitable Maritime Boundary Delimitation – 1982 UNCLOS, Articles 74(2)/83(2) *supra*; Relation to Other Conventions *infra*.

1982 UNCLOS, Article 281 (Self-Contained Settlement Clauses):

2000 *Southern Bluefin Tuna (Jurisdiction)* Award, President S.M. Schwebel, 39 ILM 1359 (2000), paras 23, 26-28, 38-39, 41, 53, 56-65 and 70-71, Separate O. Sir Kenneth Keith; Japan's Memorial, paras 137-145 and Annex 47, Hearings, Vol.I [Counsel Sir Elihu Lauterpacht, 7 May 2000], Vol.II [Counsels Crawford, Irwin, 8 May], Vol.III [Questions 6-9 of Arbitrators, Lauterpacht, 10 May], Vol.IV [Question 10 of Sir Kenneth Keith, Counsel Mansfield, 11 May], Written Answers of the Parties to Questions 6-10 [26 May 2000] <www.worldbank.org/icsid>; 2001 *Ireland v. UK Mox Plant (Provisional Measures)* Separate Os Vice-President Nelson, paras 5-7, Treves, para.4; Ireland's Request & Statement, para.138, UK Response, para.136; Hearings, ITLOS/PV.01/07, 10-12 [Counsel Lowe, 19 Nov 2001], ITLOS/PV.01/08, 21-22 [Counsel Plender, 20 Nov 2001] <www.itlos.org>; Annex VII *Mox Plant* UK Counter-Memorial, 99-100; UK Rejoinder, 61 <www.pca-cpa.org>; 2006 *Barbados/Trinidad & Tobago (Jurisdiction and Merits)* Award, President S.M. Schwebel, para.200 [RIAA XXVII, 147; 45 ILM 800 (2006); <www.pca-cpa.org>]; *Guyana/Suriname* Suriname's Rejoinder, para.2.74 <www.pca-cpa.org>.

1982 UNCLOS, Article 281 (De Facto Agreements):

2003 *Malaysia v. Singapore (Provisional Measures)* Order, President L.D.M. Nelson, paras 54-57, Separate O. Jesus, ITLOS Rep. 2003, 9 <www.itlos.org>; 2006 *Barbados/Trinidad & Tobago (Jurisdiction and Merits)* Award, President S.M. Schwebel, para.200 <www.pca-cpa.org>. See also 1982 UNCLOS, Articles 281 and 283 (No Settlement Reached) *supra*.

1982 UNCLOS, Article 282 (Optional Clause):

2000 *Southern Bluefin Tuna (Jurisdiction)* Award, President S.M. Schwebel, para.39(c) [39 ILM 1359 (2000)]; Hearings, Vol.I [Counsel Rosenne, 7 May

2000], Vol.II [Counsel Burmester, 8 May], Vol.III [Question 2 of Arbitrators, Counsel Lowe, 10 May], Vol.IV [Burmester, 11 May], Written Answer of Japan to Question 2 [26 May 2000] <www.worldbank.org/icsid>; *Ireland v. UK Mox Plant (Provisional Measures)* Separate O. Treves, paras 3-4; UK Response, para.136 <www.itlos.org>; Annex VII *Mox Plant (Jurisdiction)* Hearings, 29 [Counsel Plender, 12 June 2003 <www.pca-cpa.org>.

2006 *Barbados/Trinidad & Tobago (Jurisdiction and Merits)* Award, President S.M. Schwebel, paras 204, 208; Hearings Day-3, 22-23 [Counsel Crawford, 20 Oct 2005] <www.pca-cpa.org>.

1982 UNCLOS, Article 282 (General, Regional or Bilateral Agreements)

Southern Bluefin Tuna (Provisional Measures) Order, President T.A. Mensah, ITLOS Cases Nos 3/4, para.54 [38 ILM 1624 (1999)]; *Southern Bluefin Tuna (Jurisdiction)* Award, President S.M. Schwebel, para.36 [RIAA XXIII, 1; 39 ILM 1359 (2000); 119 ILR 508], Hearings, Vol.III [Question 6 of Arbitrators, 10 May], Written Answer of Japan to Question 6 [26 May 2000] <www.worldbank. icsid>; 2001 *Ireland v. UK Mox Plant (Provisional Measures)* Order, President P.Ch. Rao, Case No.10, paras 38-53, 61, Separate Os Vice-President Nelson, Anderson, para.1, Treves, paras 1-6, Jesus [ITLOS Rep. 2001, 89; 41 ILM 405 (2002)]; Ireland's Request & Statement, paras 135-139, UK Response, paras 1-4, 136, 160-185; Hearings, ITLOS/PV.01/07, 8-13 [Counsel Lowe, 19 Nov 2001], ITLOS/PV.01/08, 15 [Counsel Bethlehem, 20 Nov 2001], 20-28 [Counsel Plender], ITLOS/PV.01/09, 14-15 [Lowe] <www.itlos.org>.

Annex VII *Mox Plant* Ireland's Memorial,I, 97-98; UK Counter-Memorial, 100-103; UK Rejoinder, 49-62; Annex VII *Mox Plant (Jurisdiction)* Hearings [10-13 June 2003] <www.pca-cpa.org>. On 2003 OSPAR *Ireland v. UK Mox Plant* Award (PCA), 2003 EC Answer on Sellafield, 2006 ECJ *European Commission v. Ireland Mox Plant* Judgment and 2007 Annex VII *Ireland v. UK Mox Plant* Orders Nos 5 & 6 (PCA) – see Protection and Preservation of the Marine Environment *supra*.

2006 *Barbados/Trinidad & Tobago (Jurisdiction and Merits)* Award, President S.M. Schwebel, para.200 [RIAA XXVII, 147; 45 ILM 800 (2006); *Guyana/Suriname* Suriname's Rejoinder, para.2.74 <www.pca-cpa.org>.

See also Relation to Other Conventions *infra*.

Choice of Procedure
1982 UNCLOS, Article 287(1) and Annexes VI-VIII:

Aegean Sea Pleadings, 323, 345-346 [Counsel O'Connell, 9 and 10 Oct 1978]; *Cameroon v. Nigeria (Preliminary Objections)* Judgment, ICJ Rep. 1998, 321-322.

Saint Vincent and the Grenadines v. Guinea M/V Saiga (Provisional Measures) Order, unanimous [37 ILM 1202 (1998)], and *M/V Saiga* Judgment, ITLOS Case No.2, President T.A. Mensah [38 ILM 1323 (1999) <www.itlos.org>].

2000 *Southern Bluefin Tuna (Jurisdiction)* Pleadings and Award, President S.M. Schwebel [39 ILM 1359 (2000) <www.worldbank.org/icsid>]; 2005 Annex VII *Malaysia v. Singapore* Award, President M.C.W. Pinto; 2006 *Barbados/Trinidad & Tobago (Jurisdiction and Merits)* Award, President S.M. Schwebel <www.pca-cpa.org>; 2007 *Guyana/Suriname* Award, President L.D.M. Nelson.

2001 *EC/Chile Swordfish*, suspended Case No.7, President P. Ch. Rao [ITLOS Rep. 2001, 4; 40 ILM 475 (2001)] and WTO Panel, WT/DS193/3 and Add.1, 6 and 9 April 2001 <www.europa.eu.int/comm/trade/miti/dispute/swordfish.htm>; Orders of 16 Dec 2003 and 29 Dec 2005 further suspending proceedings until 1 Jan 2008, ITLOS Rep. 2003, 69 and Orders of 30 Nov 2007, 11 Dec 2008 and 17 Dec 2009 <www.itlos.org>.

Montreux (Riphagen) Clause/Arbitral Tribunal
1982 UNCLOS, Article 287(1)(c) and (5) and Annex VII:

M/V Saiga (Provisional Measures) Order, ITLOS Case No.2 [37 ILM 1202 (1998)] – before the parties agreed to transfer their dispute to the ITLOS, they contemplated bringing it to the arbitral tribunal under Annex VII in pursuance of that provision, and requested provisional measures under Article 290(5) changed subsequently into request under 290(1).

Southern Bluefin Tuna (Provisional Measures) Order, ITLOS Cases Nos 3 and 4 [38 ILM 1624 (1999) <www.itlos.org>]; *Southern Bluefin Tuna (Jurisdiction)* Award [39 ILM 1359 (2000) <www.worldbank.org/icsid>].

2001 *Ireland v. UK Mox Plant (Provisional Measures)* Order, Case No.10 [ITLOS Rep. 2001, 89; 41 ILM 405 (2002); 2003 EC Answer on Sellafield Nuclear Plant – see Participation by International Organizations *infra*; 2003 OSPAR *Mox Plant* Award <www.pca-cpa.org>; 2003 *Malaysia v. Singapore (Provisional Measures)* Order (No.12), ITLOS Rep. 2003, 9 <www.itlos.org> and 2005 Annex VII *Malaysia v. Singapore* Award <www.pca-cpa.org>.

2003 Annex VII *Mox Plant (Suspension of Proceedings and Provisional Measures)* Orders Nos 3 & 4; Ireland's Memorial, 96-97; *Mox Plant (Suspension of Periodic Reports by the Parties)* Order No.5 of 22 Jan 2007 and PR of 21 Feb 2007 and *(Termination of the Proceedings)* Order No.6 of 6 June 2008 <www .pca-cpa.org>.

2006 *Barbados/Trinidad & Tobago (Jurisdiction and Merits)* Award [RIAA XXVII, 147; 45 ILM 800 (2006); <www.pca-cpa.org>]; 2007 *Guyana/Suriname (Jurisdiction and Merits)* Award, para.168 <www.pca-cpa.org>.

Cf. *Certain German Interests in Polish Upper Silesia (Jurisdiction)* Judgment, PCIJ Series A, No.6, 20 (1925); 1929 *USA v. Mexico American Bottle Company* Award, RIAA IV, 437; No.354/Stuyt; 1985 ICSID *SSP (ME) Ltd. v. Egypt (Jurisdiction)* Decision, 106 ILR 529; which were all quoted in [para.435] 2003 UNCITRAL *CME Czech Republic B.V. (The Netherlands) v. The Czech Republic* Award, Tribunal's Members: Chairman Wolfgang Kuhn (Germany), Stephen M. Schwebel (USA) and Sir Ian Brownlie (UK), paras 201-202, 433-437, also quoting [paras 201-202] 2000 *Southern Bluefin Tuna (Jurisdiction)* Award and [para.433] 2001 *Mox Plant (Provisional Measures)* Order [*supra*] <http://ita.law.uvic.ca/documents/CME-2003-Final_000.pdf>, as upheld by 2003 UNCITRAL *The Czech Republic v. CME Czech Republic B.V. (The Netherlands)* Judgment of the Svea Court of Appeals (Sweden), at 95-98, 42 ILM 919 (2003) <www.chamber.se/arbitration/english/current/Svea_Court_8735-01.pdf>; <www.asil.org/ilib0607.htm & www.asil.org/ilib0612.htm>, as analyzed by 2004 ILA Committee on International Commercial Arbitration, Rapporteur Audley Sheppard <www.ila-hq.org>; Final Report on International Commercial Arbitration, in *Report of the 73rd ILA Conference, Rio de Janeiro*, 17-21 August 2008, 850 (2008).

First Woman Judge and President Rosalyn Higgins in the PCIJ-ICJ History:

H.E. President Rosalyn Higgins (2006-2009) <www.icj-cij.org/court/index.php?p1=1&p2=2&p3=1&judge=6>, <www.asil.org/awardarchives.cfm#HudsonAwards>, <http://wikipedia.org/wiki/Rosalyn_Higgins>; *ICJ Press Release* No.2006/5, 6 Feb 2006 <www.un.org/News/Press/docs/2006/icj620.doc.htm> & UK Foreign Secretary Welcomes Dame Rosalyn Higgins as the ICJ President <www.gnn.gov.uk/Content/Detail.asp?ReleaseID=186724&NewsAreaID=2>; UN Secretary-General Ban Ki-Moon's Visit to the Court, *ICJ Press Release* No.2007/3 of 1 Feb 2007 <www.un.org/av/photo/detail/0138476.asp?sid=&browse=/av/photo/cats/secretary-general_official_travel.asp> and H.M. Queen Elizabeth's II Visit to the ICJ, No.2007/4 of 5 Feb 2007 <www.icj-cij.org>; *Romania v. Ukraine Maritime Delimitation in the Black Sea* Judgment, President Rosalyn Higgins, ICJ Rep. 2009, rendered unanimously in the very end (almost the last day) of her triennium in appreciation of Judge Higgins' outstanding Presidency and her being the first woman in the World Court's history; *Selected Writings of H.E. President Rosalyn Higgins* (2009) <www.oup.com/>.

For visits to the Court of previous UN Secretary-General Kofi A. Annan, see President Stephen M. Schwebel: 2-3 March 1997 and 17 May 1999 – *ICJ Press Releases* No.97/5 of 24 Feb 1997 and No.99/21 of 17 May 1999; President Gilbert Guillaume – No.2002/35 of 22 Nov 2002; President Rosalyn Higgins – 12 April 2006 <www.icj-cij.org/presscom/index.php?p1=6&p2=1>.

See also Former ICJ President Higgins Appointed as Adviser to the UK Iraq Inquiry Committee of 14 Oct 2009 <www.iraqinquiry.org.uk/news/091013advisers_appointed.aspx, www.guardian.co.uk/politics/blog/2009/oct/14/iraq-inquiry-adviser-opposed-war & www.ejiltalk.org/uk-inquiry-to-consider-legality-of-iraq-war-and-appoints-former-icj-president-dame-rosalyn-higgins-as-international-law-adviser/>.

Judges Ad Hoc
1982 UNCLOS, Annex VI, Article 17 (ITLOS Statute); Article 31 ICJ Statute:

Application of the Convention on the Prevention and Punishment of the Crime of Genocide (Provisional Measures) and *(Counter-Claims)* Separate Os Sir Elihu Lauterpacht, ICJ Rep. 1993, 408-409 and 1997, 278, as *reaffirmed* by *New Zealand v. France* Dissent Sir Geoffrey Palmer, ICJ Rep. 1995, 420-421; *Congo v. Belgium Arrest Warrant of 11 April 2000* Separate O. Bula-Bula, ICJ Rep. 2002, 101, paras 3-4; *Indonesia/Malaysia (Merits)* Dissent Franck, *id.*, 693-695, paras 9-12; *Yugoslavia v. Bosnia & Herzegovina (Revision of 1996 Judgment)* Separate O. Mahiou, ICJ Rep.2003, 75, para.14; *Liechtenstein v. Germany (Preliminary Objections)* Dissent Sir Franklin Berman, ICJ Rep. 2005, 71, para.1; *Benin/Niger (Merits)* Dissent Bennouna, ICJ Rep. 2005, 153, para.3; *DR Congo v. Uganda Armed Activities on the Territory of the Congo (Merits)* Dissent Kateka, ICJ Rep. 2005, 361, para.2; *Belgium v. Senegal Obligation to Prosecute or Extradite (Provisional Measures)* Separate O. Sur, para.2, ICJ Rep. 2009 <www.icj-cij.org>.

Botswana/Namibia Judgment's, ICJ Rep.1999, 1045, model of neither of the parties appointing a Judge *Ad Hoc*; Statement of ICJ President Rosalyn Higgins to the 63rd UNGA of 30 Oct 2008, at 5-6 <www.icj-cij.org>; 103 AJIL 540 (2009).

Provisional Measures
1982 UNCLOS, Article 290, and Annex VI (ITLOS Statute), Article 25; Article 41 ICJ Statute:

Denmark/Norway Legal Status of the Southeastern Territory of Greenland (Interim Measures) Order, PCIJ Series A/B, No.48, 284 (1932) [It was one of six cases in total where the Permanent Court considered the requests for interim measures and one of four cases where such requests were dismissed]; *United Kingdom v. Anglo-Iranian Oil Co. (Interim Protection)* Order, ICJ Rep. 1951, 89; *Switzerland v. USA Interhandel (Interim Protection)* Order, ICJ Rep. 1957, 105; *Fisheries Jurisdiction (Interim Protection)* Orders, ICJ Rep. 1972, 12 [*UK v. Iceland*], 30 [*FRG v. Iceland*], and (*Continuance of Interim Measures of Protection*) Orders, ICJ Rep. 1973, 302, 313; *Nuclear Tests (Interim Protection)* Orders, ICJ Rep. 1973, 99 [*Australia v. France*], 135 [*New Zealand v. France*]; *Pakistan v. India Trial of*

Pakistani Prisoners of War (Interim Protection) Order, ICJ Rep. 1973, 328; *Greece v. Turkey Aegean Sea Continental Shelf (Interim Protection)* Order, ICJ Rep. 1976, 3; *USA v. Iran United States Diplomatic and Consular Staff in Tehran (Provisional Measures)* Order, ICJ Rep. 1979, 7; *Libya/Malta (Intervention)* Dissent Schwebel, ICJ Rep. 1984, 143; *USA v. Nicaragua Military and Paramilitary Activities (Provisional Measures)* Order, ICJ Rep. 1984, 169; *Burkina Faso/Mali Frontier Dispute (Provisional Measures)* Order, ICJ Rep. 1986, 3; *Nicaragua v. Honduras Border and Transborder Armed Actions (Provisional Measures)* Order, ICJ Rep. 1988, 9 [in this case the request was withdrawn]; *Guinea-Bissau v. Senegal Arbitral Award of 31 July 1989 (Provisional Measures)* Order, ICJ Rep. 1990, 64; *Finland v. Denmark Passage Through the Great Belt (Provisional Measures)* Order, ICJ Rep. 1991, 12; *Questions of Interpretation and Application of the 1971 Montreal Convention Arising From the Aerial Incident at Lockerbie (Provisional Measures)* Orders, ICJ Rep. 1992, 3 [*Libya v. UK*], 114 [*Libya v. USA*]; *Bosnia and Herzegovina v. Yugoslavia Application of the Convention on the Prevention and Punishment of the Crime of Genocide (Provisional Measures)* Orders, ICJ Rep. 1993, 3, 325; *New Zealand v. France Nuclear Tests (Request for an Examination of the Situation)* Order, ICJ Rep. 1995, 291-292, paras 8-9, 301, para.41, 306-307, para.67 and para.68(2), Declaration Vice-President Schwebel, 309, Dissent Weeramantry, 321-322, 330, 332-333, 339, 356, 358, Dissent Koroma, 373-374, 379-380, Dissent Palmer, 388-389, 394, 408; *Cameroon v. Nigeria Land and Maritime Boundary (Provisional Measures)* Order, ICJ Rep. 1996, 13; *Paraguay v. USA Vienna Convention on Consular Relations (Provisional Measures)* Order, ICJ Rep. 1998, 248; *Germany v. USA LaGrand (Provisional Measures)* Order, ICJ Rep. 1999, 9 <www.icj-cij.org>.

The ten *Legality of Use of Force (Provisional Measures)* Orders, ICJ Rep. 1999, 124 [*Yugoslavia v. Belgium*], 259 [*Yugoslavia v. Canada*], 363 [*Yugoslavia v. France*], 422 [*Yugoslavia v. Germany*], 481 [*Yugoslavia v. Italy*], 542 [*Yugoslavia v. Netherlands*], 656 [*Yugoslavia v. Portugal*], 761 [*Yugoslavia v. Spain*], 826 [*Yugoslavia v. United Kingdom*], and 917 [*Yugoslavia v. USA*], provided the first instance of the Court's dismissal of the requests due to the lack of *prima facie* jurisdiction, which has previously always been recognized even when the Court ultimately dismissed the requests concerned. The cases with the United States and Spain were ordered to be removed from the General List, as the Court manifestly lacked jurisdiction to entertain those cases <www.icj-cij.org>.

DR Congo v. Belgium Arrest Warrant of 11 April 2000 (Provisional Measures) Order, ICJ Rep. 2000, 182; *Germany v. USA LaGrand* Judgment, President Gilbert Guillaume, ICJ Rep. 2001, 483-484, para.45, 487, para.57, 501-506, paras 98-109 and operative para.128(2)(c) and (5); *Indonesia/Malaysia (Intervention)* Judgment, para.21, ICJ Rep. 2001, 575; *Cameroon v. Nigeria; Equatorial Guinea Intervening*

(Merits) Judgment, ICJ Rep. 2002, 453, para.321; 2002 *Eritrea/Ethiopia (Interim Measures)* Order <www.pca-cpa.org>; *Mexico v. USA Avena and Other Mexican Nationals (Provisional Measures)* Order, Declaration Oda, ICJ Rep. 2003, 77, 93, 96; *Congo v. France (Provisional Measures)* Order, ICJ Rep. 2003, 10, Joint Separate O. Koroma and Vereshchetin, 113, Dissent de Cara, 116, 143; *DR Congo v. Uganda Armed Activities on the Territory of the Congo (Provisional Measures)* Order, ICJ Rep. 2000, 111; and *(Merits)* Judgment, ICJ Rep. 2005, 258-259, paras 262-265, at 281, *dispositif* para.345(7), Dissent Kateka, 379, paras 59-61; *DR Congo v. Rwanda New Application (Provisional Measures)* Order, ICJ Rep. 2002, 219, 299 and *(Jurisdiction)* Judgment, para.25, ICJ Rep. 2006; *Argentina v. Uruguay (Provisional Measures)* Orders, ICJ Rep. 2006, 113 and 2007, 3, of which the 2007 Order involved the first Request for Provisional Measures by a Respondent in the Court's history; *Bosnia & Herzegovina v. Serbia & Montenegro (Jurisdiction and Merits)* Judgment, President Higgins concurring, ICJ Rep. 2007, paras 451-458, 471(7); *Mexico v. USA Interpretation of 2004 Avena Judgment (Provisional Measures)* Order, President Higgins concurring, ICJ Rep. 2008 and Judgment, President Higgins concurring, ICJ Rep. 2009; *Georgia v. Russian Federation Ethnic Cleansing (Provisional Measures)* Order, President Higgins concurring, ICJ Rep. 2008; *Belgium v. Senegal President Habre (Provisional Measures)* Order, President Hisashi Owada, ICJ Rep. 2009 <www.icj-cij.org>.

Emilio Agustin Maffezini v. Kingdom of Spain (Provisional Measures) Order of 28 October 1999, para.9, President F. Orrego Vicuna, Arbitrators: Thomas Buergenthal and Sir Maurice Wolf [Germany's *LaGrand* Application was of 2 March 1999 <www.icj-cij.org>] <www.investmentclaims.com/decisions/Maffezini-Spain-ProvisionalMeasures-28Oct1999-Eng.pdf>.

Saint Vincent and the Grenadines v. Guinea M/V Saiga (Provisional Measures) Order, ITLOS Case No.2, unanimous, President T.A. Mensah, Declaration Vukas, Declaration Warioba, Separate O. Laing [ITLOS Rep. 1998, 24; 37 ILM 1202 (1998)]; *Southern Bluefin Tuna (Provisional Measures)* Order, President T.A. Mensah, ITLOS Cases Nos 3/4, Joint Declaration Vice-President Wolfrum and Judges Caminos, Marrotta Rangel, Yankov, Anderson and Eiriksson, Declaration Warioba, Separate O. Laing, Separate O. Treves, Joint Separate O. Yamamoto and Park, Separate O. Shearer, Dissents Vukas, Eiriksson [ITLOS Rep. 1999, 280; 38 ILM 1624 (1999)]; as revoked by 2000 *Southern Bluefin Tuna (Jurisdiction)* Award, President S.M. Schwebel, paras 28, 30, 35, 66, 72(2), which recommended, para.70 *in fine*, that the parties abstain "from any unilateral act that may aggravate the dispute while its solution has not been achieved" [39 ILM 1359 (2000) <www.worldbank.org/icsid>]; 1999 *Nicaragua v. Honduras (Provisional Measures)* Order of CACJ – see Equitable Maritime Boundary Delimitation – *Nicaragua v.*

Honduras case *supra*; 2003 *Malaysia v. Singapore (Provisional Measures)* Order, Case No.12, Declarations President Nelson, Anderson, Joint Declaration Hossain and Oxman, Separate Os Rao, Ndiaye, Jesus, Cot, Lucky <www.itlos.org>.

2001 *Ireland v. UK Mox Plant (Provisional Measures)* Order, President Ch. Rao, Case No.10, Joint Declaration Caminos, Yamamoto, Park, Akl, Marsit, Eiriksson and Jesus, Separate Os Vice-President Nelson, Judges Mensah, Anderson, Wolfrum, Treves, Jesus and Szekely, ITLOS Rep. 2001, 89; 41 ILM 405 (2002) <www.itlos.org>; 2003 Annex VII *Mox Plant (Suspension of Proceedings and Provisional Measures)* Orders Nos 3 & 4 <www.pca-cpa.org>; 2006 ECJ *EC v. Ireland Mox Plant* Judgment, paras 16, 38-40, 138 <http://curia.eu.int/jrisp/cgi-bin/form.pl?lang=EN&Submit=rechercher&numaff=C-459/03>; Annex VII *Ireland v. UK Mox Plant (Suspension of Periodic Reports by the Parties)* Order No.5 of 22 Jan 2007 and PR of 21 Feb 2007 and *Mox Plant (Termination of Proceedings)* Order No.6 of 6 June 2008 <www.pca-cpa.org>; EC *Croatia/Slovenia Land and Maritime Boundary Delimitation* Arbitration Agreement of 4 Nov 2009, Art.10(2) *supra.*

Standard of Preventing Serious Harm to the Marine Environment 1982 UNCLOS, Article 290(1):

Nuclear Tests (Interim Protection) Orders, Vice-President F. Ammoun Acting President concurring, ICJ Rep. 1973, 99 [*Australia v. France*], 135 [*New Zealand v. France*], as referred to in the *New Zealand v. France* Order and its Opinions, ICJ Rep. 1995, *supra*, set up the basis for that standard; *Argentina v. Uruguay Pulp Mills on the River Uruguay (Provisional Measures)* Orders, ICJ Rep. 2006, 155 and 2007, 3 <www.icj-cij.org>.

On the ICJ Chamber for Environmental Matters, see Protection and Preservation of the Marine Environment *supra.*

M/V Saiga (Provisional Measures) Separate O. Laing, paras 21, 25 n.42, para.36 [37 ILM 1218 (1998)]; 1999 *Eritrea/Yemen (Phase II)* Award, Annex I: Arbitration Agreement of 3 Oct 1996, Article 11(1) <www.pca-cpa.org>; *Southern Bluefin Tuna (Provisional Measures)* Order, President T.A. Mensah, ITLOS Cases Nos 3/4, [38 ILM 1624 (1999)]; as revoked by 2000 *Southern Bluefin Tuna (Jurisdiction)* Award, President S.M. Schwebel, paras 28, 30, 35, 66, 72(2) [RIAA XXIII, 1; 39 ILM 1359 (2000) <www.worldbank.org/icsid>]; 2003 *Malaysia v. Singapore (Provisional Measures)* Order, President L.D.M. Nelson, Case No.12, ITLOS Rep. 2003, 9 <www.itlos.org>.

2001 *Ireland v. UK Mox Plant (Provisional Measures)* Order, President Ch. Rao, ITLOS Case No.10; 2003 Annex VII *Mox Plant (Suspension of Proceedings and Provisional Measures)* Order, President T.A. Mensah <www.pca-cpa.org>;

Mox Plant (Suspension of Periodic Reports by the Parties) Order No.5 of 22 Jan 2007 and PR of 21 Feb 2007 and *Mox Plant (Termination of Proceedings)* Order No.6 of 6 June 2008 <www.pca-cpa.org>.

Provisional Measures Pending the Establishment of an Arbitral Tribunal 1982 UNCLOS, Article 290(5):

M/V Saiga (Provisional Measures) Order, ITLOS Case No.2 [37 ILM 1202 (1998)], were originally requested under Article 290(5), but after the parties agreed to transfer their dispute to the ITLOS, the provisional measures became an incidental phase thereof in pursuance of Article 290(1); *Southern Bluefin Tuna (Provisional Measures)* Order, ITLOS Cases Nos 3 and 4 [38 ILM 1624 (1999) <www.itlos.org>].

Cf. 2000 *Southern Bluefin Tuna (Jurisdiction)* Pleadings and Award [39 ILM 1359 (2000) <www.worldbank.org/icsid>].

2003 *Malaysia v. Singapore (Provisional Measures)* Order <www.itlos.org>; 2001 *Ireland v. UK Mox Plant (Provisional Measures)* Order, ITLOS Case No.10; 2003 Annex VII *Mox Plant (Suspension of Proceedings and Provisional Measures)* Order and 200- Award <www.pca-cpa.org>; 2006 ECJ *EC v. Ireland Mox Plant* Judgment, paras 16, 38-40, 138 [*supra*]; Annex VII *Ireland v. UK Mox Plant (Suspension of Periodic Reports by the Parties)* Order No.5 of 22 Jan 2007 and PR of 21 Feb 2007 and *Mox Plant (Termination of Proceedings)* Order No.6 of 6 June 2008 <www.pca-cpa.org>.

Site Visit (Descente sur les lieux)
1982 UNCLOS, Annex VI (ITLOS Statute), Article 27; Article 48 ICJ Statute; Article 81 ITLOS Rules; Article 44 ICJ Statute and Article 66 ICJ Rules:

Diversion of Water from the Meuse (Site Visit) Order, President J.G. Guerrero, PCIJ Series C, No.81, 553 (1937) and minutes of this unprecedented site visit (*descente sur les lieux*) effected by the Court on 13-15 May 1937, *id.*, at 222, Judgment, PCIJ Series A/B, No.70, 9 (1937) and 31 AJIL 696 (1937), 32 AJIL 1-2 (1938); *Corfu Channel (An Expert Opinion)* Order, President Guerrero, ICJ Rep. 1948, 124, *(Merits)* Judgment, Acting President Guerrero, ICJ Rep. 1949, 9, 151; *South West Africa (Site Visit)* Order, President Sir Percy Spender, ICJ Rep. 1965, 9-10, *(Second Phase)* Judgment, ICJ Rep. 1966, 9; *Gulf of Maine* Pleadings, Vol.VII, 328-332, 334-335, 341-342, 353-356, 372 [Correspondence] and 79 AJIL 578, 596-597 (1985); *El Salvador/Honduras; Nicaragua Intervening Gulf of Fonseca (Merits)* Judgment, President J. Sette-Camara, ICJ Rep. 1992, 361-362, para.22; Hearings, C 4/CR 91/50, 22-23 [President Sette-Camara, 14 June 1991]; *Gabcikovo-Nagymaros Project (Site Visit)* Order, President M. Bedjaoui, ICJ

Rep. 1997, 3, Judgment, President S.M. Schwebel, ICJ Rep. 1997, 13-14, para.10, referring to *descente sur les lieux* effected by the Court on 1-4 April 1997, for the first time since such visit held 60 years earlier in the *Diversion from the Meuse* case [*supra*]; Hearings, CR 97/2, 14 [President Schwebel, 3 March 1997], CR 97/11, 57 [27 March], CR 97/12, 10 [President Schwebel, 10 April 1997] <www.icj-cij.org> and 92 AJIL 133-140 (1998).

Statement of President Stephen M. Schwebel to the 52nd UN General Assembly, UN Doc. A/52/PV.36, 1-5, at 2 (27 Oct 1997), *reprinted in* 92 AJIL 612-617 (1998), *ICJ Yearbook 1997-1998* 288-300 (No.52); Statement of President Rosalyn Higgins to the UN 6th Legal Committee of the 62nd UN General Assembly (2 Nov 2007), at 4 <www.un.org/News/Press/docs/2007/gal3333.doc.htm> & <www.icj-cij.org>.

1909 *Grisbadarna* Award, President J.A. Loeff, RIAA XI, 147; 4 AJIL 229 (1910) – the very first site visit (*descente sur les lieux*) effected on 14-20 July 1909; 1966 *Rio Palena* Award, President Lord McNair, RIAA XVI, 109, 149; 1977 *Beagle Channel* Award, President Sir Gerald Fitzmaurice, 52 ILR 116; 17 ILM 641 – a site visit effected in March 1976; 1988 *Taba* Award, President G. Lagergren, 80 ILR 226, para.7 – a site visit effected on 17 February 1988; 1994 *Laguna del Desierto* Award, President R. Nieto Navia, 113 ILR 17, paras 10-11 – a site visit effected on 3-4 February 1994; UN *Eritrea/Ethiopia Boundary* Commission, President Sir Elihu Lauterpacht, UN Doc. S/2001/1194, Annex I: Third Report on the Work of the Commission, para.4 (13 December 2001) – a site visit contemplated in October 2001, but not effected <www.pca-cpa.org>; UN Mixed *Cameroon/Nigeria* Commission [see Equitable Maritime Boundary Delimitation – *Cameroon v. Nigeria; Equatorial Guinea Intervening* Judgment *supra*]; 2007 *Guyana/Suriname* Award, paras 120-126, 309 – Hydrographer's Site Visit on 31 May-1 June 2007 <www.pca-cpa.org & http://cgxenergy.ca/Stabroek-May26-07.html>.

Intervention

1982 UNCLOS, Annex VI (ITLOS Statute), Article 31; Articles 62 and 63 ICJ Statute:

France, Britain, Italy, Japan v. Germany SS Wimbledon (Question of Intervention by Poland) Judgment [unanimous], PCIJ Series A, No.1, 11 (1923), President B.C.J. Loder, Article 63; *Denmark v. Norway Legal Status of Eastern Greenland* case – since Iceland contemplated but abandoned intervention under Article 62 of the ICJ Statute, *Eastern Greenland* Pleadings, PCIJ Series C, No.67, 4081-4082, 4118-4119, *Eastern Greenland* Judgment referred to the factor of "the extent to which the sovereignty is also claimed by some other power", PCIJ Series A/B, No.53, 46 (1933); *Corfu Channel (Merits)* Judgment, ICJ Rep. 1949, 15-17, Individual O. Alvarez, 49-51, Dissents Badawi Pacha, 58-60, Krylov, 68, Ecer, 116-117 – the alleged involvement of Yugoslavia did not form part of submissions of the parties and was not proved; *Anglo/Norwegian Fisheries* case – Iceland might have been contemplating intervention, but no measures to this effect were initiated; *Colombia/Peru Haya de la Torre* Judgment, ICJ Rep. 1951, 71, President J. Basdevant, Article 63; *North Sea* Judgment, ICJ Rep. 1969, 54, para.101(D)(3); Pleadings, Vol.II, 270 [Counsel Sir Humphrey Waldock, 11 Nov 1968]; *Monetary Gold Removed From Rome in 1943 (Preliminary Question)* Judgment, ICJ Rep. 1954, 32, Article 62; *Nuclear Tests (Application of Fiji for Permission to Intervene)* Orders, ICJ Rep. 1973, 320 [*Australia v. France*], 324 [*New Zealand v. France*], and ICJ Rep. 1974, 530 [*Australia v. France*], 535 [*New Zealand v. France*], President M. Lachs, Article 62; *Nicaragua v. USA Military and Paramilitary Activities (Declaration of Intervention of El Salvador)* Order, ICJ Rep. 1984, 215, President T.O. Elias, Article 63, *(Jurisdiction and Admissibility)* Judgment, 431, Dissent Schwebel, 604 and *(Merits)* Dissent Schwebel, ICJ Rep. 1986, 273-283, paras 17-41, at 312-314, paras 107-114, at 320-394, paras 128-272, Factual Appendix at 432-527 [see also Peaceful Uses of the Sea – "Clean Hands" Doctrine *infra*];

Tunisia/Libya Continental Shelf (Application of Malta for Permission to Intervene) Judgment [unanimous], ICJ Rep. 1981, 3, President Sir Humphrey Waldock, Article 62, Separate Os Morozov, 22, Oda, 23, Schwebel, 35, *(Merits)* Judgment, ICJ Rep. 1982, 42, 62, 91, 93-94, para.133 B(1) and C(3), Dissent Oda, 249-251; *Canada/USA Gulf of Maine* Judgment, ICJ Rep. 1984, 246 – whereas no attempt at intervention appeared in the record of the case, possible interests of France might have been affected [cf. Equitable Maritime Boundary Delimitation – 1992 *Canada/France (St. Pierre & Miquelon)* Award *supra*]; *Libya/Malta Continental Shelf (Application of Italy for Permission to Intervene)* Judgment, ICJ Rep. 1984, 3, President T.O. Elias, Article 62, Separate Os Morozov, 30, Nagendra Singh, 31, Mbaye, 35, Jiménez de Aréchaga, 55, Dissent Vice-President Sette-Camara, 71, Dissents Oda, 90, Ago, 115, Schwebel, 131, Sir Robert Jennings, 148, *(Merits)* Judgment, ICJ Rep. 1985, 22, 24-28, 53, 55, Separate O. Valticos, 104, 113, Dissents Mosler, 116-117, Oda, 129-131, 135, 137, Schwebel, 172-178, 179, 184;

On differences between the ICJ and ITLOS Statutes, see *Libya/Malta (Intervention)* Separate O. de Arechaga, ICJ Rep. 1984, 64, Dissent Vice-President Sette-Camara, 88-89;

Burkina Faso/Mali Frontier Dispute Judgment, ICJ Rep. 1986, 578-580; *El Salvador/Honduras Land, Island and Maritime Frontier Dispute (Application by Nicaragua for Permission to Intervene)* Order, President M. Ruda, ICJ Rep. 1990, 3, and Judgment [unanimous], ICJ Rep. 1990, 92, Chamber's President J. Sette-Camara, Separate O. Oda, 138, *(Merits)* Judgment, ICJ Rep. 1992, 359-360, 580-610, Separate O. Bernardez, 712-731 – the first instance of granting a state (Nicaragua) permission to intervene as a non-party under Article 62 of the ICJ Statute; *Nauru v. Australia Certain Phosphate Lands in Nauru (Preliminary Objections)* Judgment, ICJ Rep. 1992, 259-262, Separate O. Shahabuddeen, 292-300, Dissent President Sir Robert Jennings, 301-302, Dissent Schwebel, 329-343; *Denmark v. Norway* Separate O. Schwebel, ICJ Rep. 1993, 125; *Australia v. Portugal East Timor* Judgment, President M. Bedjaoui concurring, ICJ Rep. 1995, 100-105, Separate Os Oda, 113, Shahabuddeen, 119-127, Dissents Weeramantry, 156-170, Skubiszewski, 242-245; *New Zealand v. France Nuclear Tests (Request for an Examination of the Situation)* Order, President M. Bedjaoui, Articles 62 and 63 of the ICJ Statute, ICJ Rep. 1995, 292, para.11, 301, para.41, 306-307, para.67 and para.68(3), Dissents Weeramantry, 323, 356, 358-359, Koroma, 379-380, Palmer, 388-389; *Nuclear Weapons* Hearings, CR 95/22, 68 [Foreign Minister Evans, 30 Oct 1995], CR 95/28, 55 [NZ Attorney-General East, 9 Nov 1995]; *Qatar v. Bahrain (Merits)* Judgment, ICJ Rep. 2001 (in press), paras 221-222, 249-251; *Cameroon v. Nigeria (Preliminary Objections)* Judgment, President S.M. Schwebel, ICJ Rep. 1998, 286, 310-311, 322-325, Separate Os Higgins, 346-347, Kooymans, 360-361, Dissent Ajibola, 400-401, 415, *(Application of Equatorial Guinea for Permission to Intervene)* Order [unanimous], President S.M. Schwebel, ICJ Rep. 1999, 1029; Hearings, CR 98/2, 40-44, 48-61 [Counsel Crawford, 3 March 1998], CR 98/4 [trans.], 8-9 [Counsel Cot, 6 March 1998], CR 98/4, 56-59 [Counsel Highet], *Cameroon v. Nigeria; Equatorial Guinea Intervening (Merits)* Judgment, President G. Guillaume, ICJ Rep. 2002, 303, paras 15, 18, 28-30, 226-238, 241, 243-245, 269, 277-278, 284, 291-292, 307, Declaration Herczegh, Separate O. Mbaye, paras 132-136, Dissent Ajibola, para.172; *Indonesia/Malaysia (Application of the Philippines for Permission to Intervene)* Judgment, President G. Guillaume, ICJ Rep. 2001, 575, Article 62; Hearings, CR 2001/1-4 [25-29 June 2001], *(Merits)* Judgment, ICJ Rep. 2002, 625; *Liechtenstein v. Germany (Preliminary Objections)* Judgment, ICJ Rep. 2005, 12, para.11, Dissents Kooymans, 37-38, paras 32-35, Owada, 65-66, paras 52-56, Berman, 80-81, paras 25-27; *DR Congo v. Uganda (Merits)* Judgment, ICJ Rep. 2005, 236-238, paras 197-204;

Copies of the *Nicaragua v. Honduras* pleadings were – upon the parties' agreement – furnished to Colombia and Jamaica but refused to El Salvador, as referred to, in *Nicaragua v. Honduras (Merits)* Judgment, ICJ Rep. 2007, paras 9-11, 21-23, 222-225, 246, 249-251, 255-258, 312-319, *dispositif* para.321(3) *in fine*, Dissent Torres Bernardez, paras 63, 154-157; Hearings CR 2007/1, 13 [President Rosalyn Higgins, 5 March 2007], 49, para.6 [Counsel Oude Elderink], CR 2007/3,

47-49, paras 28-30, 33 [Oude Elferink, 7 March], CR 2007/5, 24-25, paras 72-74 [Counsel Pellet, 9 March], CR 2007/11, 37, para.19 [Pellet, 19 March 2007], 61, para.28, at 63, para.33 [Oude Elferink]; Application of Costa Rica to Intervene in *Nicaragua v. Colombia (Merits)* of 25 Feb 2010 <www.icj-cij.org>.

1917 *El Salvador v. Nicaragua Gulf of Fonseca* Judgment – see Equitable Maritime Boundary Delimitation *supra*; 1977 *Anglo/French Continental Shelf* Decision [18 ILM 397 (1979)], paras 23-29; 1985 *Guinea/Guinea-Bissau* Award, paras 93-94, 100-104, 108 [25 ILM 291, 294-295, 297 (1986)]; *M/V Saiga (Provisional Measures)* Separate O. Laing [37 ILM 1218 (1998)], para.24; 1999 *Eritrea/Yemen Maritime Delimitation (Phase II)* Award, President R.Y. Jennings, paras 39, 44-46, 136, 149, 164, 167 [40 ILM 983 (2001) <www.pca-cpa.org>]; *Southern Bluefin Tuna (Provisional Measures)* Order, President T.A. Mensah, ITLOS Cases Nos 3/4, para.76 [38 ILM 1624 (1999)]; 2000 *Southern Bluefin Tuna (Jurisdiction)* Award, President S.M. Schwebel, paras 22 and 69 [39 ILM 1359 (2000)]; Japan's Memorial, paras 17, 97, 163, 178-180, A/NZ Reply, paras 134, 173-176, Hearings, Vol.I [Counsel Lauterpacht, 7 May 2000], Vol.II [Counsel Serdy, 8 May 2000] <www.worldbank.org/icsid>; 2001 *Lance Paul Larsen v. The Hawaiian Kingdom* [119 ILR 566; 95 AJIL 927 (2001)] <www.pca-cpa.org>.

2006 *Barbados/Trinidad & Tobago (Jurisdiction and Merits)* Award, President S.M. Schwebel, para.10 & Map I: Guyana's request for Application/Statement of Claim by Barbados rejected; otherwise interests of third states, in paras 40, 42-45, 51, 63, Map II, 85-86, 117, 154, 157, 163-165, 168, Map III, 218, 324, 339-349, 358, 374, 381-383 and Maps V-VII, *dispositif* para.385, Technical Report; Hearings Day-8, 25-31 [Counsel Crawford, 28 Oct 2005], replying at 29-31 to President Schwebel's Question, Day-7, 32 [27 Oct 2005] <www.pca-cpa.org>.

Interpretation or Application
1982 UNCLOS, Annex VI (ITLOS Statute), Article 32; Article 60 (Interpretation) and Article 61 (Revision) ICJ Statute:

Interpretation of Judgments Nos 7 and 8 (Factory at Chorzów) Judgment, Article 60, PCIJ Series A, No.13 (1927), *as reaffirmed by Mexico v. USA Interpretation of 2004 Judgment (Provisional Measures)* Order, para.54, ICJ Rep. 2008, Joint Dissent Owada, Tomka and Keith, paras 19-20; *Interpretation of Article 179, Annex, Paragraph 4 of the Peace Treaty of Neuilly* Judgments, Article 60, PCIJ Series A, No. 3 (1924) and No.4 (1925); *Colombia/Peru Asylum (Request for Interpretation of the 1950 Judgment)* Judgment, President J. Basdevant, Article 60, ICJ Rep. 1950, 395, Dissent Caicedo Castilla, 404; *North Sea* Separate O. Jessup, ICJ Rep. 1969, 84; *Tunisia/Libya Continental Shelf (Merits)* Dissent Gros, ICJ Rep. 1982, 146-147, *(Application for Revision and Interpretation)* Judgment [unanimous], ICJ Rep. 1985, 192, President Nagendra Singh, Separate Os Ruda,

232, Oda, 236, Schwebel, 246, de Bastid, 247 – the first instance of finding the (Tunisian) request for interpretation under Article 60 of the ICJ Statute partly admissible, and the only instance in the Court's jurisprudence of the request for revision under Article 61, which request was found inadmissible; *Qatar v. Bahrain (Jurisdiction and Admissibility)* Dissent Shahabuddeen, ICJ Rep. 1995, 61; *New Zealand v. France Nuclear Tests (Request for an Examination of the Situation)* Order, President M. Bedjaoui, Articles 60 and 61, ICJ Rep. 1995, 295, para.23, 299, para.36, 300, para.40, 301, para.43, 303, paras 50-52, Declaration of Vice-President Schwebel, 309, Separate O. Shahabuddeen, 312, Dissents Weeramantry, 320-321, Koroma, 369, 372, 375-376, Palmer, 393, 399; *Nigeria v. Cameroon Land and Maritime Boundary (Request for Interpretation of the Cameroon v. Nigeria Judgment of 11 June 1988)* Judgment, President S.M. Schwebel, ICJ Rep. 1999, 31 – the first instance of a request for the interpretation of a judgment on preliminary objections which the Court found as falling under Article 60 which makes no distinction as to the type of judgment that can be the object of a request for interpretation; *El Salvador/Honduras; Nicaragua Intervening (Revision of the 1992 Judgment)*, ICJ Rep. 1992, 351, *(Formation of Chamber)* Order, ICJ Rep. 2002, 618, Judgment, 2003, 392, President Guillaume, Dissent Paolillo, 413 – revision under Article 61 was found inadmissible; *Yugoslavia v. Bosnia and Herzegovina (Revision of the 1996 Preliminary Objections Judgment)* Judgment, ICJ Rep. 1996, 595, ICJ Rep. 2003, 7, President G. Guillaume, Declaration Rezek, 51, Separate Os Koroma, 34, Mahiou, 70, Dissents Vereshchetin, 39, Dimitrijevic, 53 – revision under Article 61 was found inadmissible; as relied upon by eight *Legality of Use of Force (Preliminary Objections)* Judgments, ICJ Rep. 2004, 279, 429, 575, 720, 865, 1011, 1160, 1307, in cases with Belgium, paras 39, 80-91, Britain and Germany, paras 37, 76-89, Canada, Italy, France, Netherlands and Portugal, paras 38, 79-90, and eight 7-Power Joint Declaration, para.10, Separate Os Kooymans, paras 8-11, Elaraby, paras 9-13, Kreca, paras 9, 17-19; *Bosnia & Herzegovina v. Serbia & Montenegro (Jurisdiction and Merits)* Judgment, President Rosalyn Higgins concurring, ICJ Rep. 2007, paras 114-141, Dissent Vice-President Al-Khasawneh, paras 22-29; *Mexico v. USA Interpretation of 2004 Avena Judgment (Provisional Measures)* Order, ICJ Rep. 2008 and *(Interpretation of 2004 Avena Judgment)* Judgment, President Rosalyn Higgins concurring, ICJ Rep. 2009 <www.icj-cij.org>.

1978 *Anglo/French Continental Shelf* Decision [54 ILR 213], 1995 *Argentina/Chile Laguna del Desierto* Award [113 ILR 194] and 2002 *Eritrea/Ethiopia Boundary (Interpretation)* Decision – see Equitable Maritime Boundary Delimitation *supra.*

2002 *Compania de Aguas del Aconquija S.A. and Vivendi Universal v. Argentine Republic (Annulment of 2000 Award)* Decision, President L. Yves Fortier CC QC, ICSID Case No.ARB/97/3, [41 ILM 1135 (2002); <www.worldbank.org/

icsid/cases/vivendi_annul.pdf>, partly annulling the 2000 *Vivendi v. Argentina (Jurisdiction & Merits)* Award <www.worldbank.org/icsid/cases/ada_Awardofthe Tribunal.pdf>] and 2003 *Vivendi v. Argentina (Supplementation and Rectification of 2002 Decision)* Decision, President Fortier, rejecting Argentina's Requests [<www.worldbank.org/icsid/cases/vivendi-supp.pdf>]; *as reaffirmed* by 2009 *Abyei Boundary* Award, President P.M. Dupuy, para.405 n.812, paras 418, 526-528 <www.pca-cpa.org>.

I-ACHR Judgment of 8 February 2006 dismissing Suriname's Request for Interpretation of *Moiwana Village v. Suriname* Judgment of 15 June 2005 <www .corteidh.or.cr/seriecpdf/seriec_124_esp.pdf> & <www.asil.org/ilib060321.htm>.

Holdings on the *Abyei* ABC Experts' interpretation and implementation of their mandate in partial excess thereof, in 2009 *Abyei Boundary* Award <www .pca-cpa.org>.

On 1875 *Mexico/USA Schreck* Award [Stuyt/No.82], see *Yugoslavia v. Bosnia and Herzegovina (Revision)* Dissent Vereshchetin, ICJ Rep. 2003, 44, para.12, Separate O. Mahiou, 73-74, para.9 <www.icj-cij.org>.

On 1910 *USA/Venezuela Orinoco Steamship Company* Award [PCA 1999, 69; PCA Awards <www.haguejusticeportal.net>; Stuyt/No.292; 3 AJIL 436, 985 and Supp. 224 (1909); 4 AJIL 676 (1910); 5 AJIL 32, 35, 230 (1911); 18 RGDIP, 166 (1911); 24 AJIL 74 (1930)], see *Tunisia v. Libya* Pleadings, 173 [Counsel Dupuy, 14 June 1985], 226 [Counsel Queneudec, 18 June 1985]; *Guinea-Bissau v. Senegal Arbitral Award* Separate O. Shahabuddeen, ICJ Rep. 1991, 110-111, Dissent Weeramantry, 160, 163, 168; Hearings, CR 91/3, 68-69 [Counsel Highet, 4 April 1991]; *Denmark v. Norway* Separate O. Weeramantry, ICJ Rep. 1993, 231; *El Salvador v. Honduras (Revision)* Hearings, C6/CR 2003/3, 19, para.12 [Counsel Dupuy, 9 Sep 2003] <www.icj-cij.org>; 2009 *Abyei Boundary* Award, President P.M. Dupuy, paras 416, 487 <www.pca-cpa.org>. See also 2008-200- ICSID *ConocoPhillips v. Venezuela Orinoco Oil Nationalization* Arbitration, President Sir Kenneth Keith, Arbitrators L. Yves Fortier and Ian Brownlie <http://icsid .worldbank.org/ICSID/Ondex.jsp & www.globalarbitrationreview.com/news/ article/4692/conocophillips-tribunal-constituted/>.

On 1914 *Costa Rica/Panama Boundary* Award, see Equitable Maritime Boundary Delimitation *infra*.

On 1927 *France/Germany Baron de Neuflize* Award, see *Tunisia v. Libya (Revision)* Pleadings, 226-227 [Counsel Queneudec, 18 June 1985]; *Yugoslavia v. Bosnia and Herzegovina (Revision)* Separate O. Mahiou, para.5, ICJ Rep. 2003, 71-72; *El Salvador v. Honduras (Revision)* Hearings, C6/CR 2003/2, 33, para.27 [Counsel Mendelson, 8 Sep 2003] <www.icj-cij.org>.

On *Medellin v. Texas* Judgment of U.S. Supreme Court, Overruling President Bush of 25 March 2008 [<http://travel.state.gov/law/consular_4199.html>; 47 ILM 281 (2008); <www.asil.org/ilib080331.htm, www.iht.com/articles/2008/03/25/america/scotus.php & http://news.bbc.co.uk/2/hi/americas/7313228.stm>; 102 AJIL 551-562 (2008)], see *Mexico v. USA Interpretation of 2004 Avena Judgment (Provisional Measures)* Order, paras 3-5, 34-36, 49, ICJ Rep. 2008, Dissent Buergenthal, paras 14-16, Joint Dissent Owada, Tomka and Sir Kenneth Keith, paras 5-7, 14 and *(Interpretation of 2004 Avena Judgment)* Judgment, ICJ Rep. 2009, paras 31-35, Dissent Sepulveda-Amor, paras 7, 24-27, 40 <www.icj-cij.org>.

Examination of the Situation
1982 UNCLOS, Annex VI (ITLOS Statute), Article 27; Article 48 ICJ Statute:

Nuclear Tests Judgments, ICJ Rep. 1974, 272, para.60 [*Aus v. France*], 477, para.63 [*NZ v. France*]; *New Zealand v. France Request for an Examination of the Situation in Accordance with Paragraph 63 of the Court's Judgment of 20 December 1974 in the Nuclear Tests Case* Order, ICJ Rep. 1995, 288, reciting in the initial phrase Article 48 of the Statute, and relying, 302-304, paras 44-54, and 306, para.66, on a "special procedure", Declaration Vice-President Schwebel, 309, Dissents Koroma, 376, Palmer, 383, 399; Oral Hearings, CR 95/20, 45 [Questions Vice-President Schwebel, 12 Sep], 46-47 [Questions Koroma], NZ and France's Written Replies of 15 Sep 1995; Sir Elihu Lauterpacht CBE QC, The 1972-1974 and 1995 *Nuclear Tests* Cases, in *Nuclear Weapons in International Law and Politics*, BIICL London, 16 March 2007 <www.biicl.org/files/2593_16th_march_programme.pdf & www.biicl.org/events/view/-/id/137/>.

Prompt Release of Vessels and Crews
1982 UNCLOS, Part XV, Article 292, and Part V, Article 73(2), Part XII, Articles 220(6)-(8), 226(1):

Tunisia/Libya (Merits) Dissent Oda, ICJ Rep. 1982, 230.

Saint Vincent and the Grenadines v. Guinea M/V Saiga Judgment, relying in para.51 on *Greece v. United Kingdom Ambatielos (Merits: Obligation to Arbitrate)* Judgment, ICJ Rep. 1953, 18, Case No.1, Dissent President Mensah, Joint Dissent Vice-President Wolfrum and Yamamoto, Dissent Anderson, Joint Dissent Park, Nelson, Rao, Vukas and Ndiaye [ITLOS Rep. 1997, 16: 37 ILM 360 (1998)]; *M/V Saiga* Judgment, Case No.2, President T.A. Mensah, paras 163-166, Separate O. Laing, paras 57-58 [ITLOS Rep. 1999, 10; 38 ILM 1323 (1999)]; *Panama v. France Camouco* Judgment, Case No.5, President Rao concurring, Declarations Mensah, Laing, Ndiaye, Separate O. Vice-President Nelson, Dissents Anderson,

Vukas, Wolfrum, Treves [ITLOS Rep. 2000, 10; 39 ILM 666 (2000)]; *Seychelles v. France M/V Monte Confurco* Judgment, Case No.6, President Rao concurring, Declarations Mensah, Vukas, Ndiaye, Separate Os Vice-President Nelson, Dissents Anderson, Laing, Jesus [ITLOS Rep. 2000, 86]; 2001 *Belize v. France Grand Prince* Judgment, Case No.8, President Rao concurring, Declarations Vice-President Nelson, Wolfrum, Cot, Separate Os Anderson, Laing, Treves, Joint Dissent Caminos, Marotta Rangel, Yankov, Yamamoto, Akl, Vukas, Marsit, Eiriksson and Jesus [ITLOS Rep. 2001, 11]; *Panama v. Yemen Chaisiri Reefer 2 (Discontinuance)* Order, Case No.9, President Rao [ITLOS Rep. 2001, 76]; 2002 *Russia v. Australia Volga* Judgment, Case No.11, President L.D.M. Nelson concurring, Declarations of Vice-President Vukas, Marsit, Separate O. Cot, Dissents Anderson, Shearer [ITLOS Rep. 2002, 4; 42 ILM 159 (2003)]; 2004 *Saint Vincent & the Grenadines v. Guinea-Bissau Juno Trader* Judgment, ITLOS Case No.13, President L.D.M. Nelson, Declaration Kolodkin, Joint D. Kolodkin, Anderson, Cot, Separate Os Park, Rao, Treves, Lucky, Joint Separate O. Mensah and Wolfum [ITLOS Rep. 2004, 17; 44 ILM 498 (2005)]; 2007 *Japan v. Russia Hoshinmaru* Judgments, ITLOS Case No.14, President R. Wolfrum, Declarations Kolodkin, Treves, Lucky, Turk, Separate O. Yanai [ITLOS Rep. 2005-2007, 18]; 2007 *Japan v. Russia Tomimaru* Judgment, ITLOS Case No.15, President R. Wolfrum, Declarations Nelson, Yanai, Separate Os Jesus, Lucky [ITLOS Rep. 2005-2007, 74; <www.itlos.org>].

2004 *Saint Vincent v. Guinea-Bissau (Prompt Release)* Judgment, para.77 (ITLOS Case No.13), relies upon "elementary considerations of humanity", without invoking their original exposition by the *Corfu Channel (Merits)* Judgment, ICJ Rep. 1949, 22; as *reaffirmed* by *Nicaragua v. USA (Merits)* Judgment, ICJ Rep. 1986, 112 and *Nuclear Weapons (UNGA Request)* Advisory Opinion, ICJ Rep. 1996, 257, para.79; as *reaffirmed* by *Israel Wall* Advisory Opinion, ICJ Rep. 2004, 199, para.157 <www.icj-cij.org>.

Exhaustion of Local Remedies
1982 UNCLOS, Article 295:

Mavrommatis Palestine Concessions Judgment, PCIJ Series A, No.2 (1924); *Panevezys-Saldutiskis Railway* Judgment, PCIJ Series A/B, No.76, 4 (1939); *Greece v. United Kingdom Ambatielos (Preliminary Objection)* Judgment, Vice-President J.G. Guerrero, Acting President concurring, ICJ Rep. 1952, 28, Dissent President Sir Arnold McNair, 58, *Greece v. UK (Merits: Obligation to Arbitrate)* Judgment, ICJ Rep. 1953, 10, Dissent President McNair and Judges Basdevant, Klaestad and Read, 25; 1956 *Greece v. UK Ambatielos Claim* Award, Separate O. President R.J. Alfaro, Dissent Spiropoulos [RIAA XII, 83; 23 ILR 306 and 24 ILR 291; No.422/Stuyt]; *France v. Norway Certain Norwegian Loans (Preliminary*

Objections) Judgment, President G.H. Hackworth concurring, ICJ Rep. 1957, 9, 15, 17, 20, 27, Separate O. Sir Hersch Lauterpacht, 34-35, 38-41, Dissent Read, 79, 97-99; *Switzerland v. USA Interhandel (Interim Protection)* Order [unanimous], President A. Badawi, ICJ Rep. 1957, 105, and *Interhandel (Preliminary Objections)* Judgment, President H. Klaestad, ICJ Rep. 1959, 6, 26-27, Dissents Armand-Ugon, 85, Sir Hersch Lauterpacht, 95 [*as reaffirmed* by 2007 *Guinea v. DR Congo (Preliminary Objections)* Judgment, *infra*, para.42]; *USA v. Italy Eletronica Sicula S.p.A. (ELSI)* Judgment, Chamber's President M. Ruda, ICJ Rep. 1989, 15, 42-44, Separate O. Oda, 83, Dissent Schwebel, 94 [*as reaffirmed* by 2007 *Guinea v. DR Congo (Preliminary Objections)* Judgment, *infra*, para.44]; *Oil Platforms (Counter-Claim)* Dissent Rigaux, ICJ Rep. 1998, 228; *Spain v. Canada* Pleadings, 296 [Canada's Counter-Memorial]; *Congo v. Belgium Arrest Warrant of 11 April 2000* Judgment, ICJ Rep. 2002, 16-18, paras 37-40; *Mexico v. USA (Jurisdiction and Merits)* Judgment, ICJ Rep. 2004, 12, President Shi Jiuyong concurring, paras 38-40, 111, Separate Os Vereshchetin, 79, Parra-Aranguren, 84, paras 16-28, Tomka, 94-97, paras 4-13, Sepulveda, 99, paras 17, 25-31; *Liechtenstein v. Germany (Preliminary Objections)* Judgment, ICJ Rep. 2005, 12, para.11, Dissents Kooymans, 38-39, paras 37-42, Owada, 66-68, paras 57-62; *DR Congo v. Uganda (Merits)* Judgment, ICJ Rep. 2005, 276, para.330, Separate O. Simma, 348, para.36; *Guinea v. DR Congo (Preliminary Objections)* Judgment, ICJ Rep. 2007, paras 11-12, 32-48, 68-75, 81, 85, 95, Declaration Mahiou, Separate O. Mampuya <www.icj-cij.org>. Cf. *Report of the 54th ILC*, UN Doc.A/57/10, 131-166 (2002); 101 AJIL 418-420 (2007).

M/V Saiga (Provisional Measures) Separate O. Laing, paras 9, 42 [37 ILM 1218 (1998)]; *Saint Vincent and the Grenadines v. Guinea M/V Saiga* Judgment, ITLOS Case No.2, paras 89-102, Separate Os Wolfrum, paras 46-55, Rao, paras 13-16 [38 ILM 1323 (1999)]; *Panama v. France Camouco* Judgment, ITLOS Case No.5, paras 55-58, Dissent Anderson [39 ILM 666 (2000) <www.itlos.org>]; 2002 *Compania de Aguas del Aconquija S.A. and Vivendi Universal v. Argentine Republic* Decision on Annulment, paras 51-55, ICSID Case No.ARB/97/3 [41 ILM 1135 (2002)] and 2003 *Mondev International Ltd. v. United States*, ICSID Case No.ARB(AF)/99/2 [42 ILM 85 (2003); 98 AJIL 155-163 (2004); www.state.gov/documents/organization/14442.pdf & www.law.cam.ac.uk/rcil/mondev_award.pdf] <www.worldbank.org/icsid>.

On 1934 *Finland v. UK Finnish Ships* Award of Judge Bagge (Sweden) [RIAA III, 1479; No.397/Stuyt], see *Ambatielos* Pleadings, 16 [Greece's Memorial], 266 [UK Rejoinder], 443-444 [Counsel Sir Frank Soskice, 28 March 1953], 492-493 [Counsel Fawcett, 30 March 1953]; 1956 *Greece v. UK Ambatielos Claim* Award; *France v. Norway Certain Norwegian Loans* Pleadings, Vol.II, 161-165 [Counsel Bourquin, 22 May 1957]; *Switzerland v. USA Interhandel (Preliminary Objections)*

Dissent Armand Ugon, ICJ Rep. 1959, 87; *USA v. Italy ELSI* Pleadings, Vol.II, 27-28, 265 [Counter-Memorial of Italy], 374 n.1 [US Reply].

On 1956 *Greece v. UK Ambatielos Claim* Award [RIAA XII, 83; 23 ILR 306 and 24 ILR 291; No.422/Stuyt], see *France v. Norway Certain Norwegian Loans* Pleadings, Vol.II, 74 [Agent Gros, 14 May 1957], 161-165 [Counsel Bourquin, 22 May 1957]; *USA v. Italy ELSI* Pleadings, Vol.II, 27-28 [Italy's Counter-Memorial], 374 n.2 [US Reply]; *Oil Platforms* Hearings, CR 96/15, 54 [Counsel Crawford, 20 Sep 1996].

Automatic Exemption of Fishery Disputes
1982 UNCLOS, Article 297(3):

On Australia's reservation of 6 February 1954 to its Optional Clause Declaration, excluding from the ICJ jurisdiction its dispute with Japan over pearl fisheries, see *Nicaragua v. USA (Jurisdiction and Admissibility)* Separate Os Oda, ICJ Rep. 1984, 493, Sir Robert Jennings, 551; *Spain v. Canada (Jurisdiction)* Separate O. Kooymans, ICJ Rep. 1998, 491, para.8.

On Canada's reservation of 7 April 1970 to its Optional Clause Declaration, see Exclusive Economic (/Fishery) Zone – Evolution *supra*.

On New Zealand's reservation of 22 September 1977 to its Optional Clause Declaration, excluding from the ICJ jurisdiction "disputes arising out of, or concerning, the jurisdiction or rights claimed or exercised by New Zealand in respect of the exploration, exploitation, conservation or management of the living resources in marine areas beyond and adjacent to the territorial sea of New Zealand but within 200 nautical miles from the baselines", see *Spain v. Canada* Pleadings, 118, 120-121 [Spain's Memorial]; *Southern Bluefin Tuna (Jurisdiction)* Award, President S.M. Schwebel, para.39(c) [39 ILM 1359 (2000)], Hearings, Vol. I [Counsel Rosenne, 7 May 2000], Vol.II [Counsel Burmester, 8 May], Vol.III [Counsel Lowe, 10 May], Vol.IV [Burmester, 11 May 2000] <www.worldbank.org/icsid>.

On Canada's reservation of 10 May 1994 to its Optional Clause Declaration, excluding from the ICJ jurisdiction "disputes arising out of or concerning conservation and management measures taken by Canada with respect to vessels fishing in the NAFO Regulatory Area…and the enforcement of such measures", see *Spain v. Canada (Jurisdiction)* Judgment, ICJ Rep. 1998, 432, Separate O. President Schwebel, 470; *Southern Bluefin Tuna (Jurisdiction)* Japan's Memorial, paras 4-7, 99, A/NZ Reply, paras 49-51, Hearings, Vol.II [Counsel Burmester, 8 May 2000] <www.worldbank.org/icsid>.

M/V Saiga (Provisional Measures) Separate O. Laing, 37 ILM 1218 (1998), paras 22, 42; *M/V Saiga* Judgment, ITLOS Case No.2, President T.A. Mensah, 38 ILM 1323 (1999), para.44; *Southern Bluefin Tuna (Provisional Measures)* Order,

President T.A. Mensah, ITLOS Cases Nos 3/4 [38 ILM 1624 (1999)] and ITLOS/PV.99/20, 10-11 [Counsel Williams, 18 Aug 1999] – applicability of exemption under Article 297(3) LOSC was denied by the applicants claiming that the disputes concerned only the high seas part of the stock, and this issue was not addressed by ITLOS; 2000 *Southern Bluefin Tuna (Jurisdiction)* Award, President S.M. Schwebel, paras 41(b)(c) and 60-62 [39 ILM 1359 (2000)]; A/NZ Reply, paras 28-30, 35, 59, 116, Hearings, Vol.I [Counsel Rosenne, 7 May 2000], Vol.II [Counsels Burmester, Crawford, 8 May], Vol.III [Counsel Lowe, 10 May], Vol.IV [Counsel Crawford, 11 May 2000] <www.worldbank.org/icsid>; 2001 *EC/Chile Swordfish*, discontinued ITLOS Case No.7 [40 ILM 475 (2001)] and WTO Panel, WT/DS193/3 and Add.1 (2001) <www.europa.eu.int/comm/trade/miti/dispute/swordfish. htm>; Orders of 16 Dec 2003 and 29 Dec 2005 (until 1 Jan 2008), ITLOS Rep. 2003, 69; ITLOS Order of 17 Dec 2009 <www.itlos.org>.

2006 *Barbados/Trinidad & Tobago (Jurisdiction and Merits)* Award, President S.M. Schwebel, paras 79, 215-217, 258, 272-283, *dispositif* paras 384(iii) & 385(3); Hearings Day-5, 72 [Lowe's Question, 24 Oct 2005], Day-8, 15 [Counsel Greenwood, 28 Oct], 69-70 [Counsel Wordsworth], 119-121, 125 [Greenwood], 129 [Agent Jeremie] <www.pca-cpa.org>; 2007 *Guyana/Suriname* Award, President L.D.M. Nelson, para.414.

Maritime Boundary Delimitation Disputes
1982 UNCLOS, Article 298(1)(a):

Denmark v. Norway Separate O. Vice-President Oda, ICJ Rep. 1993, 113; 2000 *Southern Bluefin Tuna (Jurisdiction)* Award, para.61 [39 ILM 1359 (2000) <www.worldbank.org/icsid>]; 2003 *Malaysia v. Singapore (Provisional Measures)* Order, Case No.12, para.28; Hearings, ITLOS/PV.03/02/Corr.1, 7 [Counsel Crawford, 25 Sep 2003] <www.itlos.org>; 2006 *Barbados/Trinidad & Tobago (Jurisdiction and Merits)* Award, President S.M. Schwebel, paras 2, 67-68, 73, 78, 192, 204 <www.pca-cpa.org>; 2007 *Guyana/Suriname* Award, President L.D.M. Nelson, paras 2, 167, 330, 413-414.

See also Continental Shelf – 1982 UNCLOS, Article 76(10); and Equitable Maritime Boundary Delimitation – 1982 UNCLOS, Articles 15 and 74/83 *supra*.

On Malta's reservation of 23 January 1981 to its Optional Clause Declaration, accepting the ICJ jurisdiction with respect to the continental shelf delimitation disputes, and on Malta's reservation of 2 September 1983, excluding from the ICJ jurisdiction disputes concerning: its territory, including the territorial sea and the status thereof; the continental shelf or any other zone of maritime jurisdiction and the resources thereof; the determination or delimitation of any of the above; and the prevention or control of pollution or contamination of the marine environment, see *Nicaragua v. USA (Jurisdiction and Admissibility)* Separate Os

Oda, ICJ Rep. 1984, 494, Sir Robert Jennings, 551-552; *Libya/Malta* Pleadings, Vol.II, 621 [Counsel Lauterpacht, 30 Jan 1984]; *Spain v. Canada* Pleadings, 118 [Spain's Memorial].

For Australia's reservation to its Optional Clause excluding from the ICJ jurisdiction disputes over maritime boundary delimitation or the exploitation of an area in dispute or adjacent to that area, as well as its Declaration under Article 298(1)(a), both of 25 March 2002, see <www.foreignminister.gov.au/releases/2002/fa039j_02.html>; *UN LOS Bull.* 16 (2002 No.48). Cf. Equitable Maritime Boundary Delimitation – Mineral Resources Factors, 2002-2003 Australia/East Timor Dili and 2006 Treaties *supra*.

Military Activities and Law Enforcement Disputes **1982 UNCLOS, Articles 298(1)(b) and 302:**

Military Activities Disputes

On France's reservation of 20 May 1966 to its Optional Clause Declaration, excluding from the ICJ jurisdiction "disputes concerning activities connected with national defence", see the 1973/74 *Nuclear Tests* and 1995 *France v. New Zealand* cases [Peaceful Uses of the Sea, Nuclear Weapon Tests *infra*].

2000 *Southern Bluefin Tuna (Jurisdiction)* Hearings, Vol.III [Question 9 of Arbitrators, 10 May 2000], Vol.IV [Question 10 of Sir Kenneth Keith, 11 May], Written Answers of Australia and New Zealand to Question 9, paras.9.4/5, and Question 10 of Arbitrators [26 May 2000] <www.worldbank/icsid.org>; 2001 *Ireland v. UK Mox Plant (Provisional Measures)* Hearings, ITLOS/PV.01/06, 14 [Agent O'Hagan, 19 Nov 2001] <www.itlos.org>; *Israeli Wall* Advisory Opinion, ICJ Rep. 2004, 136 <www.icj-cij.org>; ASIL ILIB of 9 July 2004 <www.asil.org/ilib0712.htm>; U.S. Legal Adviser John B. Bellinger, The United States and the UNCLOS, 3 Nov 2008 <www.state.gov/s/l/rls/111587.htm>.

Cf. Protection and Preservation of the Marine Environment – EIA/Notification /Consultation *supra*.

Law Enforcement Disputes

Tunisia/Libya (Merits) Dissent Oda, ICJ Rep. 1982, 230.

2000 *Southern Bluefin Tuna (Jurisdiction)* Award, para.61 [39 ILM 1359 (2000) <www.worldbank.org/icsid>].

Involvement of the UN Security Council
1982 UNCLOS, Article 298(1)(c):

SC Resolution 19 of 27 February 1947 and Resolution 22 of 9 April 1947: *Corfu Channel (Preliminary Objection)* Judgment, ICJ Rep. 1947-1948, Separate Opinion Basdevant, Alvarez, Winiarski, Zoricic, de Visscher, Badawi Pascha and Krylov, 31, Dissent Daxner, 33; *Corfu Channel (Merits)* ICJ Rep. 1949, 4 – Judgment, 24, Individual O. Alvarez, 41, Dissents Winiarski, 55, Badawi Pascha, 61-62, 66, Azevedo, 87-88, 90, 92, 94, 96-98, 111-112; *Corfu* Pleadings, Vol.I, 30-37, 41-42 [UK Memorial], Vol.III, 296 [Agent Sir Eric Beckett, 12 Nov 1948]; *North Sea* Separate O. Ammoun, ICJ Rep. 1969, 146-147.

During the pair of the 1972/1974 *Fisheries Jurisdiction* cases (see Fisheries *supra*) and thereafter the British/Icelandic incidents of the Second and Third Cod Wars were brought in May 1973 and Dec 1975 to the attention of the Security Council which, however, took no decision on either occasion. See *Fisheries Jurisdiction (Continuance of Interim Protection)* Dissents Gros, ICJ Rep.1973, 307, 317; Pleadings (UK), 286, 375-378, 421-432 [Memorial (Merits)], (FRG), 260-263, 277-284 [Memorial (Merits)]; UN Doc. S/1975/11907; British/Icelandic Cod Wars Remembered of 10 Oct 2008 <http://news.bbc.co.uk/2/hi/uk_news/politics/7662827.stm>.

Western Sahara – see Equitable Maritime Boundary Delimitation *supra*.

SC Resolution 395 of 25 August 1976: *Aegean Sea (Interim Measures)* Order, ICJ Rep. 1976, 12-13, Separate Os President de Aréchaga, 16, Lachs, 19-20, Elias, 27, 29-30, Tarazi, 33-34, Dissent Stassinopoulos, 38-39 *(Jurisdiction)* Judgment, ICJ Rep. 1978, 10-11; Pleadings, 131-133 [Counsel Pinto, 26 Aug 1976], 135 [Question President de Aréchaga], 137 [Reply of Agent Karandreas, 27 Aug 1976], 138 [Question Lachs], 194-197 [Greece's Memorial (Jurisd.)], 320-326 [Counsel O'Connell, 9 Oct 1978], 503-510 [texts], 578 [Written Reply to Lachs, 28 August 1976].

Basic elements of SC 395 were incorporated in the Berne Agreement of 11 November 1976 [*Aegean Sea* Pleadings, 280, *reprinted in* UN Doc. S/1987/18766, Annex II]. Cf. Doc. S/1987/18759.

The oil rig *Saipem II* incident in August 1980 was brought to the attention of the Security Council and good offices of UN Secretary-General Kurt Waldheim [UN Docs S/1980/14228, 14229 and 14256; 26 AFDI 422 (1980); and S/1981/14786] were instrumental in persuading Libya and Malta to bring their dispute to the Court. See *Libya/Malta* Pleadings, Vol.I, 90-92 [Libya's Memorial], 375 [S/1980/14140], 377 [S/1980/14145], 378 [S/1980/14256], 381-382 [S/PV.2294th Meeting, 30 July 1981], 383-386 [S/1981/14786], 428 [Malta's

Memorial], Vol.II, 21-23, 143, 169 [Libya's Counter-Memorial]; *Annual Review of United Nations Affairs 1980* 90 (1981) and *1981* 113 (1983).

Armed incidents in the Bakassi Peninsula were brought to the attention of the Security Council in 1994 and 1996 [S/1994/228, 258, 351 and 519; S/1996/125, 140, 150] and good offices of UN Secretary-General Boutros Boutros-Ghali [S/1996/390, 391, 891 and 892], which paralleled the *Cameroon v. Nigeria (Provisional Measures)* proceedings, resulted in a peaceful settlement of the conflict. See *Cameroon v. Nigeria (Provisional Measures)* Order, ICJ Rep. 1996, 23-24, Separate O. Ajibola, 42-43; *1996 SC Resolutions and Decisions* 91-92 (S/INF/52, UN 1998); *Cameroon v. Nigeria (Preliminary Objections)* Judgment, ICJ Rep. 1998, 297-298, 306-307, *Cameroon v. Nigeria; Equatorial Guinea Intervening (Merits)* Judgment, ICJ Rep. 2002, 448-453, paras 308-324, Dissent Ajibola, paras 4, 53 <www.icj-cij.org>.

In his Statement to the 53rd UNGA, President Schwebel exemplified the possibility of political and judicial resolution of disputes working in parallel by the fact that both the Security Council and the Court called on the parties to respect a ceasefire and to take the necessary steps to return their forces to the position that they had occupied before the outbreak of the fighting. See UN Doc. A/53/PV.44, 2-3 (27 Oct 1998), *reprinted in ICJ Yearbook 1998-1999* 316, 319 (No.53) <www.icj-cij.org>; Equitable Maritime Boundary Delimitation – *Cameroon v. Nigeria; Equatorial Guinea Intervening* case *supra.*

On Request of the Ministry of Foreign Affairs of Honduras to the President of the United Nations Security Council of 20 Jan 2002, see Equitable Maritime Boundary Delimitation – 1992 *Gulf of Fonseca* Judgment *supra.*

See also *United Kingdom v. Anglo-Iranian Oil Co. (Interim Protection)* Order, ICJ Rep. 1951, 89; *Legal Consequences for States of the Continued Presence of South Africa in Nambia (South West Africa) Notwithstanding Security Council Resolution 276 (1970)* Advisory Opinion, ICJ Rep. 1971, 16; *USA v. Iran United States Diplomatic and Consular Staff in Tehran (Provisional Measures)* Order, ICJ Rep. 1979, 7; *Nicaragua v. USA Military and Paramilitary Activities (Provisional Measures)* Order, ICJ Rep. 1984, 169, *(Jurisdiction and Admissibility)* Judgment, 431-436, paras 89-98, *(Merits)* Judgment, ICJ Rep. 1986, 26-28, paras 32-35, Dissent Schwebel, 284-293, paras 43-68, at 309-311, paras 103-106, at 374-377, paras 225-230, UN Docs S/18230, S/18250, S/18415, S/18428 and USA/Nicaragua Agreement of Friendship & Cooperation, 6 January 1992 [in force: by signature, 2211 UNTS 441]; *Guinea-Bissau v. Senegal (Provisional Measures)* Dissent Thierry, ICJ Rep. 1990, 81; *Libya/Chad Territorial Dispute* Judgment, ICJ Rep. 1994, 36-37, Separate O. Ajibola, 57, 82; *Nuclear Weapons (WHO)* Dissent Weeramantry, ICJ Rep. 1996, 150.

Questions of Interpretation and Application of the 1971 Montreal Convention Arising From the Aerial Incident at Lockerbie (Provisional Measures) ICJ Rep. 1992, [*Libya v. UK*] Order, 3, Joint D. Evensen, Tarassov, Guillaume and Aguilar Mawdsley, 24, Separate Os Lachs, 26, Shahabuddeen, 28, Dissent Bedjaoui, 33, Dissents Weeramantry, 50, Ranjeva, 72, Ajibola, 78, El-Kosheri, 94, [*Libya v. USA*] Order, 114, [Opinions, as above]; and *(Preliminary Objections)* ICJ Rep. 1998, [*Libya v. UK*] Judgment, 9, Joint D. Bedjaoui, Guillaume and Ranjeva, 32, Joint D. Bedjaoui, Ranjeva and Koroma, 46, Joint D. Guillaume and Fleischhauer, 47, Declaration Herczegh, 51, Separate Os Kooymans, 54, Rezek, 61, Dissent President Schwebel, 64, Dissents Oda, 82, Sir Robert Jennings, 99; [*Libya v. USA*] Judgment, 115, Joint D. Bedjaoui, Ranjeva and Koroma, 138, Joint D. Guillaume and Fleischhauer, 139, Declaration Herczegh, 143, Separate Os Kooymans, 144, Rezek, 152, Dissent President Schwebel, 155, Dissent Oda, 173, *(Discontinuance)* Orders, Preident Shi, ICJ Rep. 2003, 150, 152. Cf. *Spain v. Canada Fisheries (Jurisdiction)* Pleadings, 606-607 [Co-Agent Hankey, 17 June 1998].

With respect to reaffirmation in each of the ten *Legality of Use of Force (Provisional Measures)* Orders of 2 June 1999 that "when such a dispute gives rise to a threat to the peace, breach of the peace or act of aggression, the Security Council has special responsibilities under Chapter VII of the Charter" (last paragraph before the *dispositif*), Judge *ad hoc* Kreca remarked in each of his nine Dissents and in his one Separate Opinion that this formulation "leaves the impression that the Court is elegantly attempting to drop the ball in the Security Council's court", ICJ Rep. 1999, 256, 360, 418, 477, 538, 652, 758, 823, 913, 971. The Security Council adopted its Resolutions S/RES/1244 and 1247 on 10 and 18 June 1999. See also eight *(Preliminary Objections)* Judgments, ICJ Rep. 2004, Belgium, 279, Canada, 429, France, 575, Germany, 720, Italy, 865, Netherlands, 1011, Portugal, 1160, UK, 1307.

Pakistan v. India Aerial Incident of 10 August 1999 (Jurisdiction) Judgment, ICJ Rep. 2000, 12; *DR Congo v. Belgium (Provisional Measures)* Order, ICJ Rep. 2000, 182; *Oil Platforms (Merits)* Judgment, ICJ Rep. 2003, 161, paras 23, 37; Hearings, CR 2003/5, 61-62 [Counsel Bundy, 17 Feb 2003], CR 2003/9, 13, 16 [Agent Taft IV, 21 Feb], CR 2003/10, 13-14 [Counsel Mattler, 24 Feb], CR 2003/12, 36, 49, 52 [Counsel Matheson, 26 Feb], CR 2003/14, 21 [Counsel Sellers, 28 Feb], CR 2003/15, 19-23 [Counsel Momtaz, 3 March], 41-42 [Bundy], CR 2003/16, 23, 27-29 [Counsel Pellet], CR 2003/17, 21-22 [Co-Agent Bettauer, 5 March], 43 [Counsel Murphy], CR 2003/18, 16 [Counsel Mathias], 27, 28-29 [Matheson], 33 [Taft], CR 2003/19, 17 [Sellers, 7 March 2003]; *Israeli Wall* Advisory Opinion, ICJ Rep. 2004, 136 <www.icj-cij.org>; ASIL/ILIB of 9 July 2004 <www.asil.org/ilib/ilib0712.htm>; *DR Congo v. Uganda (Provisional Measures)* Order, ICJ Rep. 2000, 111, Declaration Koroma, 134 and *(Merits)* Judgment, ICJ Rep. 2005, 168, paras

60, 70, 100, 142-154, 208, Declaration Koroma, paras 9-12; *DR Congo v. Rwanda (Provisional Measures)* Order, ICJ Rep. 2002, 219 and *(Jurisdiction)* Judgment, ICJ Rep. 2006, paras 1, 63, 86.

Application of the Convention on the Prevention and Punishment of the Crime of Genocide [Bosnia & Herzegovina v. Yugoslavia (Serbia & Montenegro)] (Provisional Measures) Orders, ICJ Rep. 1993, 3, 325, Declaration Oda, Separate Os Shahabuddeen, Weeramantry, Ajibola, Lauterpacht, Dissents Tarassov, Kreca, *Bosnia & Herzegovina v. Yugoslavia (Preliminary Objections)* Judgment, ICJ Rep. 1996, 595, Declaration Oda, 625, Joint D. Shi and Vereshchetin, 631, Declaration Lauterpacht, 633, Separate Os Shahabuddeen, 634, Weeramantry, 640, Parra-Aranguren, 656, Dissent Kreca, 658, *(Counter-Claims)* Order, President S.M. Schwebel, ICJ Rep. 1997, 243, *Bosnia & Herzegovina v. Yugoslavia (Revision of the 1996 Judgment)* Judgment, President G. Guillaume, ICJ Rep. 2003, 7, *Bosnia & Herzegovina v. Serbia & Montenegro (Jurisdiction and Merits)* Judgment, President R. Higgins, ICJ Rep. 2007 <www.icj-cij.org>.

1998 *Eritrea/Yemen Territorial Sovereignty (Phase I)* Award, paras 270, 306, 505 [40 ILM 900 (2001)]; 2002 *Eritrea/Ethiopia Boundary* Decision, paras 3.7, 3.33 <www.un.org/NewLinks/eebcarbitration/>, <www.pca-cpa.org> and Equitable Maritime Boundary Delimitation *supra*.

See also U.S. Legal Adviser John B. Bellinger, The United States and the UNCLOS, 3 Nov 2008 <www.state.gov/s/l/rls/111587.htm>; Peaceful Uses of the Sea *infra*.

1982 UNCLOS, Article 287(1)(d) and Annex VIII

The *IMCO* Advisory Opinion, ICJ Rep. 1960, 150 [High Seas, Nationality of Ships – Genuine Link *supra*] underlined prominence of the IMCO which, under Assembly Resolution 450(11) of 1979, was renamed into the International Maritime Organization (IMO) and has evolved to the principal international organization responsible for the issues pertaining to navigation and marine-based sources of pollution. Cf. *Great Belt* Pleadings, 347 [Finland's Memorial]; Annex VII *Mox Plant* UK Counter-Memorial, 30-31 <www.pca-cpa.org>. All references throughout the 1982 LOSC to "international organization" in singular form in the context of those matters apply to the IMO. Other three principal international organizations listed in Annex VIII include the UNEP, FAO and IOC/UNESCO, responsible for environment, fisheries and marine scientific research respectively.

On the IMO's role, see also Straits Used for International Navigation – *Great Belt* case; Protection and Preservation of the Marine Environment – Pollution From Vessels *supra*; and Relation to Other Conventions *infra*.

Southern Bluefin Tuna (Jurisdiction) Hearings, Vol.II [Counsel Jennings, 8 May 2000] <www.worldbank.org/icsid>.

Cf. UN ECE *Romania/Ukraine Danube-Black Sea (Bystroe) Canal* Opinion of Commission of Inquiry under the 1991 Espoo EIA Convention (Art.3 & Appendix IV) [1989 UNTS 310; 30 ILM 802 (1991)] of 11 July 2006 <www.unece.org/env/eia/inquiry.htm> and press comments <www.mosnews.com/news/2006/07/11/canaldisp.shtml & www.cceg.ro/2006stiri/UN.htm>.

Annual Statements of the ICJ Presidents to the United Nations General Assembly are published in the *ICJ Yearbooks* and are also available at the Court's Internet address <www.icj-cij.org>. For Message of President Gilbert Guillaume on the Occasion of the 20th Anniversary of the UN Convention on the Law of the Sea, see *ICJ Press Release* No.2002/38, 10 Dec 2002 <*id.*>; and for Statement of President L. Dolliver M. Nelson of 9 Dec 2002, see <www.itlos.org>.

See also Privileges and Immunities of the UNCLOS Institutions *infra.*

GOOD FAITH AND ABUSE OF RIGHTS

1945 United Nations Charter, Article 2(2)
1982 UNCLOS, Part XVI, Article 300
1992 UNCED Rio Declaration, Principle 27
1995 SSA, Article 34

Corfu Channel (Merits) Dissent Azevedo, ICJ Rep. 1949, 103, Dissent Ecer, 119; *Anglo/Norwegian Fisheries* Individual O. Alvarez, ICJ Rep. 1951, 150, 152, 153; *Rights of Nationals of the USA in Morocco* Judgment, ICJ Rep. 1952, 212; *North Sea* Judgment, ICJ Rep. 1969, 46, para.85, Separate O. President Bustamante y Rivero, 58, Separate O. Ammoun, 102; Pleadings, Vol.I, 455, 516 [Common Rejoinder of Denmark/NL]; *Fisheries Jurisdiction (Merits)* Judgments, ICJ Rep. 1974, 33, 34 (para.79(2)), 202, 205 (para.77(2)), Separate O. Dillard, 71; *Nuclear Tests* Joint Dissent, 362; *Tunisia/Libya (Merits)* Dissent Gros, ICJ Rep. 1982, 145; *Gulf of Maine* Judgment, ICJ Rep. 1984, 305; *Great Belt* Pleadings, 629-639 [Denmark's Counter-Memorial]; *Libya/Chad Territorial Dispute* Separate O. Ajibola, ICJ Rep. 1994, 71-74; *France v. New Zealand* Oral Hearings, CR 95/21 [transl.], 18 [Dupuy, 12 Sep 1995]; *Nuclear Weapons (UNGA)* Advisory Opinion, ICJ Rep. 1996, 264-265; *Gabcikovo* Judgment, ICJ Rep. 1997, 66, 78-79, Dissent Fleischhauer, 205-206, 210; *Cameroon v. Nigeria (Preliminary Objections)* Dissent Ajibola, ICJ Rep. 1998, 398; *Spain v. Canada* Pleadings, 240-241 [Canada's Counter-Memorial], 479-480, 487 [Counsel Dupuy, 10 June 1998].

Cameroon v. Nigeria Land and Maritime Boundary (Preliminary Objections) Judgment, ICJ Rep. 1998, 296-297, paras 38-39, *reaffirming* 1910 *UK/USA North*

Atlantic Coast Fisheries Award [RIAA XI, 167, 188; No.291/Stuyt]; *Factory of Chorzów (Merits)* Judgment No.13, PCIJ Series A, No.17, 30 (1928); *Free Zones of Upper Savoy and the District of Gex (Second Phase)* Order, PCIJ Series A, No.24, 12 (1930), and *(Final Phase)* Judgment, PCIJ Series A/B, No.46, 167 (1932); *Rights of Nationals of the USA in Morocco* Judgment, ICJ Rep. 1952, 212; *FRG v. Iceland Fisheries Jurisdiction (Jurisdiction)* Judgment, ICJ Rep. 1973, 18; *Nuclear Tests* Judgments, ICJ Rep. 1974, [*Australia v. France*] 268, [*New Zealand v. France*] 473; *Nicaragua v. Honduras Transborder Armed Actions (Jurisdiction and Admissibility)* Judgment, ICJ Rep. 1988, 105.

For reaffirmation of the 1910 *North Atlantic Coast Fisheries* holding, see also 1986 *Canada/France* Award [Fisheries *supra*].

United States – Import Prohibition of Certain Shrimp and Shrimp Products Report AB-1998-4, WTO Appellate Body, President F. Feliciano, WT/DS58/AB/R, 12 October 1998, para.158; *Southern Bluefin Tuna (Provisional Measures)* Order, ITLOS Cases Nos 3/4, President Mensah [38 ILM 1624 (1999)]; 2000 *Southern Bluefin Tuna (Jurisdiction)* Award, President Schwebel paras 34, 41(c), 64 [39 ILM 1359 (2000)]; Japan's Memorial, paras 115, 168, A/NZ Reply, paras 38, 181-184, Hearings, Vol.I [Counsel Lowe, 7 May 2000], Vol.II [Counsel Geddis, 8 May 2000] <www.worldbank.org/icsid>; 2001 *EC/Chile Swordfish*, ITLOS Case No.7, President Rao [40 ILM 475 (2001)] <www.itlos.org>.

Sir Elihu Lauterpacht, Judge Stephen M. Schwebel, Shabtai Rosenne and Francisco Orrego, *Joint Legal Opinion on Guatemala's Territorial Claim to Belize*, paras 17, 88, Annex II, para.28 (Jan 2002) <www.belize-guatemala.gov.bz/> and <http://vandeplaspublishing.com>; *Cameroon v. Nigeria; Equatorial Guinea Intervening (Merits)* Hearings, CR 2002/7, 44-46 [Counsel Corten, 26 Feb 2002]; *Oil Platforms (Merits)* Judgment, President Shi concurring, ICJ Rep. 2003, 196, para.73, Dissent Elaraby, 302; Hearings, CR 2003/8, 25 [Counsel Pellet, 19 Feb 2003] <www.icj-cij.org>; Annex VII *Mox Plant* UK Counter-Memorial, 143-146 <www.pca-cpa.org>; 2003 *Malaysia v. Singapore (Provisional Measures)* Order, paras 31, 74, Declarations of President Nelson, Anderson, Separate Os Rao, para.5, Cot, para.7; Hearings, ITLOS/PV.03/03, 31 [Counsel Reisman, 26 Sep 2003], PV.03/05, 23 [Counsel Sir Eli Lauterpacht, 27 Sep 2003] <www.itlos.org>; 2004 *France/Netherlands* Award, President K. Skubiszewski <www.pca-cpa.org> & <www.asil.org/ilib0718.htm>; 2004 *Juno Trader (Prompt Release)* Separate O. Treves, para.5, Case No.13 <www.itlos.org>; 2005 *Belgium/Netherlands Iron Rhine* Award, President Rosalyn Higgins, paras 23, 48, 85-86, 157,162, 202-203 <www.pca-cpa.org>; *Benin/Niger Territorial Dispute* Judgment, ICJ Rep. 2005, 124, para.60; Hearings, C5/CR 2005/2, 18, para.9.11 [Counsel Pellet, 7 March 2005] <www.icj-cij.org>; 2006 *Barbados/Trinidad & Tobago (Jurisdiction and*

Merits) Award, President S.M. Schwebel, paras 88-102, 105, 208, 292-293, *dispositif* para.385(3); Barbados' Reply, paras 107-117; Hearings Day-7, 64-68 [Counsel Wordsworth, 27 Oct 2005] <www.pca-cpa.org>; *Argentina v. Uruguay Pulp Mills on the River Uruguay (Provisional Measures)* Order, ICJ Rep. 2006, 122, 124, paras 39, 46, and Order, ICJ Rep. 2007, 16, para.53 <www.icj-cij.org>; *Djibouti v. France Certain Questions of Mutual Assistance in Criminal Matters (Jurisdiction and Merits)* Declaration of Judge Keith, para.6, ICJ Rep. 2008; *Costa Rica v. Nicaragua San Juan River* Judgment, ICJ Rep. 2009, para.150 <www.icj-cij.org>.

PEACEFUL USES OF THE SEA

Prohibition of Threat or Use of Force

1945 United Nations Charter, Articles 2(4) and 51; 1982 UNCLOS, Preamble, Part II, Article 19(2)(a), Part III, Article 39(1)(b), Part VII, Article 88, Part XVI, Article 301:

Corfu Channel (Merits) ICJ Rep. 1949, 4 – Judgment, 30-31, 34-35, Individual O. Alvarez, 42, 47, Dissent Krylov, 76-77, Dissents Azevedo, 108-109, 112, Ecer, 115-116, 129-131; *Corfu Channel* Pleadings, Vol.I, 44-45 [UK Memorial], Vol.II, 115-116 [Albania's Counter-Memorial], 281-284 [UK Reply], 367-375 [Albania's Rejoinder], Vol.III, 265, 290-296 [Agent Sir Eric Beckett, 11 and 12 Nov 1948], 404-422 [Counsel Cot, 18 and 19 Nov 1948], Vol.IV, 580-584 [Agent Beckett, 19 Jan 1949], 675-679 [Counsel Cot, 22 Jan 1949]; *North Sea* Separate O. Ammoun, ICJ Rep. 1969, 118, Dissent Tanaka, 172; *Nuclear Tests (Interim Measures)* Dissents Ignacio-Pinto, ICJ Rep. 1973, 132, 163; *Aegean Sea (Interim Measures)* Order, ICJ Rep. 1976, 6-8, 11-13, Separate Os President de Aréchaga, 16, Mosler, 26, Elias, 27-30, Dissent Stassinopoulos, 35-40, *(Jurisdiction)* Dissent Stassinopoulos, ICJ Rep. 1978, 79; *Libya/Malta (Merits)* Judgment, ICJ Rep. 1985, 42; *Nicaragua v. USA (Provisional Measures)* Order, ICJ Rep. 1984, 170, para.1(b) and (e), 181, para.28, 187, para.41(B)(1), Dissent Schwebel, 190, 199, *(Jurisdiction and Admissibility)* Judgment, ICJ Rep. 1984, 424, para.73, *as reaffirmed* by *Nicaragua v. USA (Merits)* Judgment, ICJ Rep. 1986, 93, para.174, also *id.* 46-53, paras 76-92, and 111-112, para.213, Dissent Schwebel, 259, and *Nuclear Weapons (UNGA)* Advisory Opinion, ICJ Rep. 1996, 244-247, Dissents Vice-President Schwebel, 322-329, Koroma, 557.

Legality of the Use by a State of Nuclear Weapons In Armed Conflict ICJ Rep. 1996 – Advisory Opinion, 66, Declaration Ranjeva, 86, Declaration Ferrari Bravo, 87, Separate O. Oda, 88, Dissents Shahabuddeen, 97, Weeramantry, 101, Koroma, 172; *Legality of the Threat or Use of Nuclear Weapons* ICJ Rep. 1996 – Advisory

Opinion, 226, Declaration President Bedjaoui, 268, Declarations Herczegh, 275, Shi, 277, Vereshchetin, 279, Ferrari Bravo, 282, Separate Os Guillaume, 287, Ranjeva, 294, Fleischhauer, 305, Dissent Vice-President Schwebel, 311, Dissents Oda, 330, Shahabuddeen, 375, Weeramantry, 429, Koroma, 556, Higgins, 583.

See also 2001 *Greenock* Judgment of the Scottish Court of Appeal, 51 ICLQ 171-176 (2002); UNGA Resolutions 54/54-Q of 1 Dec 1999, 56/24-S of 29 Nov 2001, 57/85 of 22 Nov 2002, 58/46 of 8 Dec 2003 and 59/83 of 3 Dec 2004 on Follow-Up to the ICJ *Legality of the Threat or Use of Nuclear Weapons* Advisory Opinion, UN Docs A/53/208 & Add.1 (1998), A/54/161 & Add.1 (1999), A/55/131 & Add.1(2000), A/56/130 & Add.1(2001), A/57/95 & Add.1-2 (2002); Statement of President Gilbert Guillaume to the Sixth Committee, 30 Oct 2002 <www.un.org/News/Press/docs/2002/gal3221.doc.htm>; UN Doc. A/58/162 & Add.1-2 (2003), A/59/136 & Add.1-2 (2004); UNGA Resolution 62/39 of 5 Dec 2007 on Follow-Up to the ICJ *Legality of the Threat or Use of Nuclear Weapons* Advisory Opinion <www.un.org/law>.

Spain v. Canada Fisheries (Jurisdiction) Judgment, ICJ Rep. 1998, 432, paras 24, 35, 53, 78-84, Separate O. President Schwebel, 470; Pleadings, 538-557 [Counsel Weil, 12 June 1998], 559-560 [Agent Pastor Ridruejo [15 June], 599-600, 604 [Co-Agent Hankey, 17 June 1998] <www.icj-cij.org>.

In each of the ten 1999 *Legality of Use of Force (Provisional Measures)* Orders, the Court expressed its profound concern with the use of force in Yugoslavia which "raises very serious issues of international law", and deemed it necessary to emphasize that "all parties appearing before it must act in conformity with their obligations under the United Nations Charter and other rules of international law, including humanitarian law", ICJ Rep. 1999, 140, 273, 374, 433, 492, 557, 671, 773 [Spain – No.112 removed from the General List], 839, 925 [USA – No.114 removed from the General List]; and in each of the eight *Kosovo (Preliminary Objections)* Judgments – including in the cases with Belgium paras 22-23, 128, Canada, Italy and France, paras 21-22, 115, UK and Germany, paras 20-21, 114, the Netherlands, paras 21-22, 127 and Portugal, paras 21-22, 118, ICJ Reports 2004, Belgium, 279, Canada, 429, France, 575, Germany, 720, Italy, 865, Netherlands, 1011, Portugal, 1160, UK, 1307 – the Court reaffirmed the *Spain v. Canada* holdings, ICJ Rep. 1998, 456, paras 55-56, Separate O. President Schwebel, 470-473 and *Pakistan v. India (Jurisdiction)* holdings, ICJ Rep.2000, 33, para.33, that "Whether or not the Court finds that it has jurisdiction over a dispute, the parties "remain in all cases responsible for acts attributable to them that violate the rights of other States" <www.icj-cij.org>.

Qatar v. Bahrain (Merits) Judgment, President G. Guillaume, ICJ Rep. 2001, 40, paras 48, 55, 76, 84, 96, Joint Dissent Bedjaoui, Ranjeva, Koroma, paras

134-135, Dissent Torres Bernardez, paras 92-94, 104, 114, 118-130, 193, 200, Separate O. Fortier, paras 35-41; *Congo v. Rwanda New Application (Provisional Measures)* Order, ICJ Rep. 2002, 219, 299.

Cameroon v. Nigeria (Provisional Measures) Order, ICJ Rep. 1996, 13, *(Preliminary Objections)* Judgment, ICJ Rep. 1998, 275, *Nigeria v. Cameroon (Interpretation)* Judgment, ICJ Rep. 1999, 31, *Cameroon v. Nigeria; Equatorial Guinea Intervening (Merits)* Judgment, ICJ Rep. 2002, 450-452, 457, paras 310-316, 325.V, Separate O. Mbaye, 534-537, paras 138-150, Dissent Ajibola, 539, 593-601, paras 4, 173-202.

Iran v. USA Oil Platforms (Preliminary Objection) Judgment, ICJ Rep, 1996, 803, *(Counter-Claim)* Order, ICJ Rep. 1998, 190, *Oil Platforms (Merits)* Judgment, ICJ Rep. 2003, 161, Declarations Vice-President Ranjeva, 220, Koroma, 223, Separate Os Higgins, 225, Parra-Aranguren, 241, Kooijmans, 246, Buergenthal, 270, Owada, 306, Simma, 324, Rigaux, 362 Dissents Al-Khasawneh, 266, Elaraby, 290; Hearings, CR 2003/5-19, 17 February-7 March 2003; *El Salvador v. Honduras (Revision)* Hearings, C6/CR 2003/3, 16 [Counsel Dupuy, 9 Sep], 52-53 [Counsel Sanchez Rodriguez], C6/CR 2003/4, 21 [Counsel Mendelson, 10 Sep 2003] <www.icj-cij.org>; 2003 *Malaysia v. Singapore (Provisional Measures)* Separate O. Jesus <www.itlos.org>.

Legal Consequences of the Construction of a Wall in the Occupied Palestinian Territory (Composition of the Court) Order, ICJ Rep. 2004, 3, Dissent Buergenthal, 7 and Judge Elaraby's Interview <http://weekly.ahram.org.eg/2001/547/profile.htm>, *Israel Wall* Advisory Opinion, President Shi concurring, ICJ Rep. 2004, 136, 171, 182, 194-195, paras 86-87, 117, 138-142, Dissent Buergenthal, 240, Separate Os Koroma, 204, Higgins, 207, Kooymans, 219, Al-Khasawneh, 235, Elaraby, 246, Owada, 260 <www.icj-cij.org>; ASIL ILIB of 9 July 2004 <www.asil.org/ilib040712.cfm>; UN SC Res.1566 of 8 Oct 2004 <www.un.org/News/Press/docs/2004/sc8214.doc.htm & www.un.int/usa/04_186.htm>; 2004 *Beit Sourik Village Council v. Israel* Judgment, 42 ILM 1099 (2004); 99 AJIL 6, 19 (2005); <www.asil.org/insights/insigh140.htm> & 2005 *Mara'Abe v. Prime Minister of Israel* Judgment, 45 ILM 202 (2006); 100 AJIL 895-901 (2006) & <www.asil.org/ilib050929.cfm>; 2006 *Public Committee Against Torture in Israel v. Israel* Judgment of Israel Supreme Court, 46 ILM 373 (2007) & <www.asil.org/ilib070119.cfm>; UN Register of Israeli War Damage of 10 May 2007 <www.un.org/apps/news/story.asp?NewsID=22518&Cr=Palestin&Cr1 & www.un.org/News/Press/docs/2007/sga1064.doc.htm> and 27 June 2008 <www.un.org/apps/news/story.asp?NewsID=27193&Cr=palestin&Cr1 & www.un.org/News/Press/docs/2008/sga1141.doc.htm>; Israel Agrees to Barrier Reroute of 29 July 2008 <http://news.bbc.co.uk/2/hi/middle_east/7530336.stm> and 22 August 2008 <http://news.bbc.co.uk/2/hi/middle_east/7575782.stm>; Five Years After *Israel Wall* Advisory

Opinion of 8 July 2009 <www.un.org/apps/news/story.asp?NewsID=31410&Cr =palestin&Cr1>; Israel Security Fence <http://securityfence.mfa.gov.il/mfm/web/ main/missionhome.asp?MissionID=45187>.

DR Congo v. Uganda (Provisional Measures) Order, ICJ Rep. 2000, 111, Declarations Oda, 131, Koroma, 134, *(Counter-Claims)* Order, ICJ Rep.2001, 660 and *(Merits)* Judgment, ICJ Rep. 2005, 168, Declarations Koroma, 284, Tomka, 351, Verhoeven, 355, Separate Os Parra-Aranguren, 292, Kooymans, 306, Elaraby, 327, Simma, 334, Dissent Kateka, 361.

Bosnia & Herzegovina v. Yugoslavia (Provisional Measures) Orders, ICJ Rep. 1993, 3, 325, *(Preliminary Objections)* Judgment, ICJ Rep. 1996, 595, *(Counter-Claims)* Order, ICJ Rep. 1997, 243, *Yugoslavia v. Bosnia & Herzegovina (Revision of 1996 Judgment)* Judgment, ICJ Rep. 2003, 7, *Bosnia & Herzegovina v. Serbia & Montenegro (Jurisdiction and Merits)* Judgment, President Rosalyn Higgins concurring, ICJ Rep. 2007; *Georgia v. Russia (Provisional Measures)* Order, President Rosalyn Higgins concurring, ICJ Rep. 2008; *Croatia v. Serbia (Jurisdiction)* Judgment, President Rosalyn Higgins concurring, ICJ Rep. 2008 <www.icj-cij.org>.

2007 *Guyana/Suriname Maritime Delimitation (Jurisdiction and Merits)* Award, President L.D.M. Nelson – incident with CGX's oil rig and drill ship *C.E. Thornton*, 2-3 June 2000, Award, paras 150-151, 183, 201-202, 263-278, 401-452, 474-477, 484, *dispositif* paras 487(ii), 488(2); Guyana's Memorial, paras 1.10, 5.8/5.12, 7.1/7.9, 10.1/10.33, Suriname's Counter-Memorial, paras 7.1/7.45, Guyana's Reply, paras 2.47/2.48, 8.10/8.19, Suriname's Rejoinder, paras 2.81/2.120, 4.1/4.79; *Guyana/Suriname* Hearings Day 1, 43-44 [Co-Agent Ramphal, 7 Dec 2006], Day 4, 546-589 [Co-Agent Akhavan, 11 Dec], Day 7, 1074-1150 [Counsel Murphy, 15 Dec], Day 9, 1440-1468 [Akhavan, 18 Dec 2006] <www.pca-cpa .org>. See also Equitable Maritime Boundary Delimitation – 1982 LOSC, Articles 74(3)/83(3) *supra.*

On 1797 *UK/USA The Betsey* Award [1 C.Rob.93; No.3/Stuyt], see eight *Legality of Use of Force (Preliminary Objections)* Separate Os Kreca, para.45, ICJ Rep. 2004, Belgium, 402, Canada, 548, France, 693, Germany, 838, Italy, 984, NL, 1133, Portugal, 1280, UK, 1425; *Bosnia & Herzegovina v. Serbia & Montenegro (Jurisdiction and Merits)* Separate O. Kreca, para.23, ICJ Rep. 2007 <www.icj-cij.org>.

On 1837 *USA/Canada The Caroline* incident [J.B. Moore, 2 *Digest of Int. Law* 409-414 (1906)], see *Oil Platforms (Merits)* Iran's Reply, paras 7.51/56; US Rejoinder, paras 5.35/38; Hearings, CR 2003/12, 50 [Counsel Matheson, 26 Feb 2003] <www.icj-cij.org>

For 1904 *UK/Russia Dogger Bank* Report of International Commission of Inquiry, see 2 AJIL 929 (1908); PCA 1999, 297; No.C 1/Stuyt.

On 1915 *The Kim and Other Vessels (The Alfred Nobel, The Bjornstjerne Bjornson, The Fridland)* Judgment of the British Prize Court [P.215; 3 Lloyd's Prize Cases 167; 9 AJIL 913, 979 (1915); 11 AJIL 251-269 (1917); 24 AJIL 86 (1930)], see *Oil Platforms (Merits)* Hearings, CR 2003/5, 49 [Counsel Momtaz, 17 Feb 2003] <www.icj-cij.org>.

On 1935 *Canada/USA I'm Alone* Award, see Use of Force in Enforcement at Sea *supra*.

On 1962 *Denmark/UK The Red Crusader*, see Use of Force in Enforcement at Sea *supra*.

For codification of the principle of *Neutrality*, see *Nuclear Weapons (UNGA)* Advisory Opinion, ICJ Rep. 1996, 260-261, paras 88-89, Dissent Shahabuddeen, 387-389; *Oil Platforms (Merits)* Hearings, CR 2003/13, 35-46 [Counsel Murphy, 26 Feb 2003], 51 [Agent Taft], CR 2003/17, 11 [Taft, 5 March 2003] <www.icj-cij.org>. See also High Seas – 1872 *UK/USA The Alabama (The Kaersage)* Award *supra*.

For codification of the rules on *State of Necessity*, see *Gabcikovo-Nagymaros Project* Judgment, President S.M. Schwebel, ICJ Rep. 1997, 35-42, paras 40-54, and at 45-46, para.57, relying on Draft Articles on the International Responsibility of States, Article 33, *ILC Yearbook* 1980-II, 32. See also 1797 *UK/USA The Betsey* Award and 1837 *Caroline* incident *supra*; *New Zealand v. France Rainbow Warrior* Award, 82 ILR 554-555; RIAA XX, 217, at 253 [Access to and Jurisdiction and Treatment in Ports *supra*]; *M/V Saiga (Merits)* Judgment, ITLOS Case No.2, President T.A. Mensah, paras 129 and 132-136, 38 ILM 1323 (1999); *Oil Platforms (Merits)* Judgment, ICJ Rep. 2003, 196-199, paras 73-78; *Israel Wall* Advisory Opinion, ICJ Rep. 2004, 194-195, paras 140-142, reaffirming the 1997 *Gabcikovo* holdings *supra* <www.icj-cij.org>; 2005 ICSID *CMS Gas Transmission Company v. Argentine Republic* Award, President F. Orrego Vicuna, paras 304-394, reaffirming the 1997 *Gabcikovo* holdings, *supra*, 44 ILM 1205 (2005); 2006 ICSID *LG&E Energy Corp., G&E Capital Corp., LG&E International Inc. v. Argentine Republic* Award, paras 245-265, reversing the 2005 *CMS* Award's necessity holdings [*supra*], 46 ILM 36 (2007); and 2007 ICSID *CMS Gas v. Argentina (Annulment)* Decision, President Gilbert Guillaume, who did not invalidate but strongly criticized the 2005 *CMS Gas* Award [*supra*] on the ground of "manifest error of law" <http://icsid.worldbank/ICSID/index.jsp/ & www.asil.org/insights/2007/12/insights071220.html>.

Cf. Sir Arthur Watts, *The International Law Commission 1994-1998*, Vol.I, 13 (Oxford 1999); Second Report on State Responsibility, J. Crawford Special Rapporteur, UN Doc. A/CN.4/498/Add.2, 28-30 and 31 (1999); *Report of the 53rd ILC*, UN Doc. A/56/10, 169-170 (paras 2-3), 199-203 (paras 11, 15-16), 210-211 (paras

3, 5) (2001) and UNGA Resolution 56/83 (2001); *UNSG Report on Responsibility of States for Internationally Wrongful Acts: Decisions of International Courts, Tribunals and Other Bodies*, UN Doc. A/62/62, at 55-66 (2007) and UK Comments-Table, in UN Doc. A/62/63, at 18-23 (2007) <www.un.org/law>.

For codification of the rules on *Countermeasures*, see *Gabcikovo-Nagymaros Project* Judgment, ICJ Rep. 1997, 55-57, paras 82-88, relying on ILC Draft Articles on State Responsibility, Articles 47-50, UN Doc. A/51/10, 144-145 (1996), as well as on: 1978 *USA/France Interpretation of Air Transport Services Agreement of 27 March 1946* Award, 54 ILR 311; RIAA XVIII, 421, at 443 et seq.; No.439/Stuyt; and on *Nicaragua v. USA (Merits)* Judgment, ICJ Rep. 1986, 127, para.249. See also *Gabcikovo* Dissent Vereshchetin, ICJ Rep. 1997, 219-226; Sir Elihu Lauterpacht, Judge Stephen M. Schwebel, Shabtai Rosenne and Francisco Orrego, *Joint Legal Opinion on Guatemala's Territorial Claim to Belize*, para.214 (January 2002) <www.belize-guatemala.gov.bz/>; *Guyana/Suriname* Award, para.446; Hearings Day 4, 582-583 [Co-Agent Akhavan, 11 Dec], Day 7, 1126-1130 [Counsel Murphy, 15 Dec 2006] <www.pca-cpa.org>.

Cf. Second Report on State Responsibility, J. Crawford Special Rapporteur, UN Doc. A/CN.4/498/Add.4, 10-13 (1999); Third Report on State Responsibility, J. Crawford, UN Doc. A/CN.4/507/Add.4, 19 n.792 (2000); *Report of the 53rd ILC*, UN Doc. A/56/10, 35-36 (paras 51, 55), 180-182 (paras 2, 5), 325 (para.3), 329-330 (paras 2, 4), 343 (para.4), 346 (para.3) (2001) and UNGA Resolution 56/83 (2001); Judge S.M. Schwebel, in 101 AJIL 237, 238 (2007); *UNSG Report on Responsibility of States for Internationally Wrongful Acts: Decisions of International Courts, Tribunals and Other Bodies*, UN Doc. A/62/62, at 80-85 (2007) and UK Comments-Table, in UN Doc. A/62/63, at 18-23 (2007) <www.un.org/law>.

On the *"Clean Hands" Doctrine*, see *Diversion of Water from the Meuse* Judgment, PCIJ Series A/B, No.70, 25 (1937) – Dissents Anzilotti, 50 and Manley O. Hudson, 76-77, as relied upon, in *Nicaragua v. USA Military and Paramilitary Activities In and Against Nicaragua (Merits)* Dissenting Opinion of Judge Stephen M. Schwebel, ICJ Reports 1986, 266, para.1, at 272, para.14, at 313, para.111, at 380-381, paras 239-240, at 392-394, paras 268-272 [also: *Iran v. USA Oil Platforms (Preliminary Objection)* Dissent of Vice-President Schwebel, ICJ Rep. 1996, 878, 888-889 and Schwebel, in 95 AJIL 465-466 (2001)], as relied upon, in *Yugoslavia v. Belgium (Provisional Measures)* Order, ICJ Rep. 1999, 124, Dissent of Vice-President Weeramantry, 184 and President S.M. Schwebel, Clean Hands Doctrine, in *The World Bank, International Financial Institutions, and the Development of International Law* 74-78 (ASIL 1999); as further relied upon, in *Congo v. Belgium Arrest Warrant of 11 April 2000* Dissent Van den Wyngaert, ICJ Rep. 2002, 160, para.35; *Oil Platforms (Merits)* Judgment, ICJ Rep. 2003,

176-177, paras 27-29, at 208, para.100; US Rejoinder, para.2.13 and n.169; Hearings, CR 2003/8, 26, para.4, at 29, para.13, at 30-31, paras 19-21, at 35, para.31, at 38-39 [Counsel Pellet, 19 Feb 2003], CR 2003/11, 32, paras 14.24/27 [Counsel Mathias, 25 Feb], CR 2003/16, 24-26 [Pellet, 3 March], CR 2003/18, 14 [Mathias, 5 March 2003]; *Israeli Wall* Advisory Opinion, ICJ Rep. 2004, 163-164, paras 63-64 <www.icj-cij.org> & <www.asil.org/ilib040712.cfm>; 2007 *Guyana/Suriname Maritime Delimitation (Jurisdiction and Merits)* Award, paras 173, 182-184, 268, 417-422, 457; Suriname's Preliminary Objections, paras 1.10, 7.1/7.9, Guyana's Reply, paras 2.47/2.48, Suriname's Rejoinder, paras 2.81/2.120; Hearings Day 1, 44 [Co-Agent Ramphal, 7 Dec 2006], Day 4, 551, 582 [Co-Agent Akhavan, 11 Dec], Day 7, 1100-1101 [Counsel Murphy, 15 Dec 2006] <www .pca-cpa.org> – see also Prohibition of Threat or Use of Force (2007 *Guyana/ Suriname* Award) *supra.*

See also the "Clean Hands" Doctrine in BIT State-Investor Arbitrations of 30 October 2009 <www.globalarbitrationreview.com/news/article/19249/ should-clean-hands-factor-investment-arbitration-/>.

Nuclear (Atmospheric and Underground) Weapon Tests

Nuclear Tests (Interim Protection) Orders, ICJ Rep. 1973, 99 [*Australia v. France*], 135 [*New Zealand v. France*], Vice-President F. Ammoun Acting President concurring, Declarations Sir Garfield Barwick, 110, 146, Dissents Forster, 111, 148, Dissents Gros, 115, 149, Dissents Petren, 124, 159, Dissents Ignacio-Pinto, 128, 163, *(Application of Fiji for Permission to Intervene)* Orders, ICJ Rep. 1973, 320 [*Aus v. France*], 324 [*NZ v. France*], and ICJ Rep. 1974, 530 [*Aus v. France*], 535 [*NZ v. France*], President M. Lachs concurring, Declarations (dissenting) Gros, Petren, Onyeama, Ignacio-Pinto, 322, 326, Declarations (concurring) Gros, Onyeama, 531, 536, Dillard and Sir Humphrey Waldock, Jiménez de Aréchaga, 532, 537, Barwick, 533, 538, and *Nuclear Tests* Judgments, ICJ Rep. 1974, 253 [*Aus v. France*], 457 [*NZ v. France*], Declaration President Lachs, 273, Separate Os Forster, 275, 479, Separate Os Gros, 276, 480, Separate Os Petren, 298, 483, Separate Os Ignacio-Pinto, 308, 493, Joint Declaration and Joint Dissents Bengzon, Onyeama, Dillard, de Aréchaga and Sir Humphrey Waldock, 273, 311, 494, Dissents de Castro, 372, 524, Dissents Barwick, 391, 525; Orders, ICJ Rep. 1973, 338, 341; *Nuclear Tests* Pleadings (Australia), 333 [Memorial], 524 [Question Waldock, 9 July 1974], 525-527 [Reply Counsel Byers, 11 July], (New Zealand), 291 [Question Waldock, 11 July], 429-431 [Reply Agent, 15 July 1974].

Fisheries Jurisdiction (Continuance of Interim Measures) Dissents Petren, ICJ Rep. 1973, 310-311, 318; *Aegean Sea (Jurisdiction)* Separate O. Lachs, ICJ Rep. 1978, 50-51, Dissent Stassinopoulos, 79; Pleadings, 102-103, 111-112 [Counsel O'Connell, 25 Aug 1976], 125 [Counsel Pinto, 26 Aug 1976], 266, 276 [Memorial of Greece], 438 [Counsel Economides, 16 Oct 1978], 455-456 [O'Connell]; *Tunisia/Libya (Intervention)* Judgment, ICJ Rep. 1981, 16, Separate O. Oda, 32-33; *Gulf of Maine* Pleadings, Vol.V, 531, 536 [US Reply]; *Nicaragua v. USA (Jurisdiction and Admissibility)* Judgment, ICJ Rep. 1984, 418; *Libya/Malta (Intervention)* Dissent Oda, ICJ Rep. 1984, 111; *Burkina Faso/Mali Frontier Dispute* Judgment, ICJ Rep. 1986, ICJ Rep. 1986, 573-574; *Nicaragua v. Honduras (Jurisdiction and Admissibility)* Judgment, ICJ Rep. 1988, 105-106; *Great Belt (Provisional Measures)* Separate O. Shahabuddeen, ICJ Rep. 1991, 32-33; Hearings, CR 91/9, 31-32, 37-39, 47 [Counsel Sinclair, 1 July 1991], Pleadings, 249, 328 [Finland's Memorial]; *New Zealand v. France Request for an Examination of the Situation in Accordance with Paragraph 63 of the Court's Judgment of 20 December 1974 in the Nuclear Tests Case* Order, ICJ Rep. 1995, 288, President M. Bedjaoui concurring, Declaration Vice-President Schwebel, 309, Declarations Oda, Ranjeva, 310, 311, Separate O. Shahabuddeen, 312, Dissents Weeramantry, 317, Koroma, 363, Sir Geoffrey Palmer, 381 [Pleadings (written/oral) and the Order reprinted, in *New Zealand at the International Court of Justice: French Nuclear Testing in the Pacific* (NZ Ministry of Foreign Affairs 1996); *Legality of the Threat or Use of Nuclear Weapons (WHO)* Dissent Koroma, ICJ Rep. 1996, 179-180, 217, *(UNGA)* Advisory Opinion, 226, 243, 265, Declaration President Bedjaoui, 268, Dissent Vice-President Schwebel, 311; Hearings, CR 95/22, 67-68 [Foreign Minister Evans, 30 Oct 1995], CR 95/27, 55, 61, 65 [Malaysia, 7 Nov], CR 95/28, 20, 39-41, 50, 53-59 [NZ Attorney-General East, 9 Nov], CR 95/31, 26-29 [Samoa, 13 Nov], CR 95/32, 32-33 [Solomon Islands, 14 Nov 1995]; 2001 *Ireland v. UK Mox Plant (Provisional Measures)* UK Response, paras 133, 227-228; Hearings, ITLOS/PV.01/06, 32-33 [Counsel Sands, 19 Nov 2001], ITLOS/PV.01/08, 14, 17 [Counsel Bethlehem, 20 Nov 2001] <www.itlos.org>; *Mexico v. USA (Provisional Measures)* Hearings, CR 2003/2, 36-37 [Counsel Sir Elihu Lauterpacht, 21 Jan 2003] <www.icj-cij.org>.

See also *ILC Yearbook* 1956-II, 278 [Article 27: Freedom of the High Seas], 286 [Article 48: Pollution of the High Seas], 295 [Article 66: Contiguous Zone]; and 1960-II, 65; Sir Arthur Watts, *The International Law Commission 1949-1998*, Vol.I, 58-59, 75-76 (Oxford 1999); Sir Elihu Lauterpacht CBE QC, The 1972-1974 and 1995 *Nuclear Tests* Cases, in *Nuclear Weapons in International Law and Politics*, BIICL London, 16 March 2007 <www.biicl.org/files/2593_16th_march_programme.pdf & www.biicl.org/events/view/-/id/137/>.

On compensation paid (without admitting any liability) by the USA to Japan in 1955 and to inhabitants of Rongelap Atoll (Pacific Islands Trust Territory) in 1964 for injuries caused by the US nuclear tests conducted in 1954 on Enewetak and Bikini Atolls respectively, see *Nuclear Tests* Dissent Gros, ICJ Rep. 1974, 281-282; Pleadings (Australia), 332 [Memorial], 520 [Counsel Byers, 9 July 1974];

Nuclear Weapons (UNGA) Dissent Weeramantry, ICJ Rep. 1996, 462-463, 469, Dissent Koroma, 569; Oral Hearings, CR 95/32, 19-31 [Marshall Islands, 14 Nov 1995].

On 1954 *The Diago Fukurya Maru* (Japanese fishing boat affected by US nuclear tests in Bikini Atoll; US paid *ex gratia* compensation), see *Nuclear Tests* Pleadings (Australia) 332 [Memorial], 521 [Counsel Byers, 9 July 1974]; *Nuclear Weapons (WHO)* Dissent Weeramantry, ICJ Rep. 1996, 120.

See also *ILC Report 47th Session* 231-232 (A/50/10, 1995); *Danielsson, Largenteau and Haoa v. Commission*, EC Court of Justice, Case T 219/95; *In the Matter of the People of Enewetak, et al., Claimants for Compensation* Award of Marshall Islands' Nuclear Claims Tribunal, 39 ILM 1214 (2000).

On French nuclear tests carried in Algeria in 1960/63 in compliance with Article 34 of the EURATOM Treaty of 25 March 1957 [in force: 1 Jan 1958, 51 AJIL 955 (1957)], see *Nuclear Tests* Pleadings (Australia), 3 [Application], 315, 333 [Memorial], (New Zealand), 288-289 [Counsel Quentin-Baxter, 10 July 1974]; *New Zealand v. France* Dissent Palmer, ICJ Rep. 1995, 386; NZ Request (Examination of the Situation), paras 94-95 n.88; Hearings, CR 95/19, 64 [Counsel Lauterpacht], 11 Sep 1995]. Cf. *Nicaragua v. USA (Merits)* Dissent Schwebel, ICJ Rep. 1986, 371, para.218.

On *AALCC Report on the Legality of Nuclear Tests* (New Delhi 1964), see *Nuclear Tests* Joint Dissent, ICJ Rep. 1974, 362; Pleadings (Australia), 334 n.1, 377 [Memorial].

For a map showing the French Pacific Tests Centre (Centre d'expérimentations du Pacifique), opened in 1963 in Mururoa and Fangataufa Atolls (Tuamotu Archipelago, French Polynesia), including prohibited and dangerous zones for aircraft and shipping, see *Nuclear Tests* Pleadings (Australia), 3 [Application], Annex 1, 16, (NZ), 3 [Application], Annex 1, 10. Cf. *Nuclear Tests* Judgments, ICJ Rep. 1974, 258, 461.

For the Lists of French Atmospheric Nuclear Tests in 1966/74 and Underground Nuclear Tests in 1975/91, see *Nuclear Tests* Pleadings (Australia), 4 [Application]; 1995 NZ Request (Examination of the Situation), Annex 4.

On Statement of President Jacques Chirac of 13 June 1995 that France would conduct a final series (18th since 1975) of eight underground nuclear weapon tests in the South Pacific starting in September, see *Nuclear Tests* Order, ICJ Rep. 1995, 289, Dissent Palmer, 390; 1995 NZ Request (Examination of the Situation), para.57, Annex I; Hearings, CR 95/19, 20-21 [Agent East, 11 Sep 1995], 65 [Counsel Lautrepacht]. *Nuclear Weapons* Hearings, CR 95/22, 67-68 [Foreign Minister Evans, 30 Oct 1995].

After the Court rendered its 1995 *New Zealand v. France Nuclear Tests* Order, ICJ Rep. 1995, 288, President Chirac announced on 29 Jan 1996 that with its 6th explosion on 27 Jan, France concluded its current series of the South Pacific tests. On results of the Study of the Radiological Situation at the Atolls of Mururoa and Fangataufa, see IAEA Resolution GC(42)/RES/14 of 25 Sep 1998.

On France's withdrawal from Optional Clause on 2 Jan 1974 [83 RGDIP 822 (1974)], see *Nuclear Tests* Pleadings (Australia), 441 [Counsel Lauterpacht]; 1995 NZ *Aide-Mémoire*, para.55; *New Zealand v. France* Dissent Palmer, ICJ Rep. 1995, 420; Oral Hearings, CR 95/19, 49 [Counsel McGrath, 11 Sep 1995], CR 95/21, 53 [Watts, 12 Sep 1995]; *Legality of Use of Force* Separate Os Oda, para.11 (all 10 Orders), ICJ Rep. 1999, 149, 283, 388, 447, 508, 567, 681, 854, 938 <www .icj-cij.org>.

On France's denunciation on 2 Jan 1974 of the 1928 General Act for the Pacific Settlement of International Disputes [93 LNTS 344], see *Nuclear Tests* Judgments, ICJ Rep. 1974, 272, para.60, 477, para.63; *Aegean Sea (Jurisdiction)* Judgment, ICJ Rep. 1978, 16, Dissent Stassinopoulos, 72-73; Pleadings, 209 [Greece's Memorial (Jurisd.)]; *New Zealand v. France* Order, ICJ Rep. 1995, 289, para.3, 293, para.18, 302, para.45, Dissents Weeramantry, 337-338, Koroma, 368, 374-375, Palmer, 394-395; Hearings, CR 95/19, 46-49 [Counsel McGrath, 11 Sep 1995].

See also Statements of France, in *UNCLOS III Off. Rec.*, Vol.I: Jeannel, 37th Meeting-11 July 1974, 155 (1975); Vol.V, de Lacharriere, 59th Meeting-5 April 1976, 13-14 (1976).

On France's Declaration upon signing the 1982 UNCLOS and ensuing 1983 Statement [*UNCLOS III Off. Rec.*, Vol.XVII, 86-87, 241 (1984)], see *New Zealand v. France* Oral Hearings, CR 95/20, 28 [Co-Agent MacKay, 12 Sep 1995].

On France's reservation upon signing the 1986 SPREP Convention, see Protection and Preservation of the Marine Environment *supra*.

See also *Nuclear Weapons (UNGA)* Dissent Oda, ICJ Rep. 1996, 338-339 (France), 340 (Australia), 341; Hearings, CR 95/24, 33 [Vice-President Schwebel's Question to France, 2 Nov 1995], 71 [to Mexico]; UK/France Nuclear Cooperation Treaty of 9 February 2001 [in force: *id.*, 2186 UNTS 21].

On Resolution I on Nuclear Tests on the High Seas [*UNCLOS I Off. Rec.* 1958-II, 143], see *Nuclear Tests* Dissent de Castro, ICJ Rep. 1974, 390; Pleadings (Australia), 378-380.

On Resolution 3(I) of the 1972 UN Stockholm Conference on the Human Environment and Principle 26 of the Stockholm Declaration, see *Nuclear Tests* Joint Dissents, ICJ Rep. 1974, 361, 514, 520; Pleadings (Australia), 48-49 [Request], 334, 370, 372 [Memorial], (NZ), 8 [Application], 55 [Request], 203 [Memorial]; *New Zealand v. France* Dissent Palmer, ICJ Rep. 1995, 407.

On Principle 24 of the 1992 UNCED Rio Declaration, see *Nuclear Weapons (WHO)* Dissents Weeramantry, ICJ Rep. 1996, 141, Koroma, 187, 216, *(UNGA)* Advisory Opinion, 242.

On 1986/90 *The Rainbow Warrior* Mediation and Arbitration, see Access to and Jurisdiction and Treatment in Ports *supra*.

Maritime Terrorism

Corfu Channel (Merits) Dissent Ecer, 115.

The seizure of the Italian cruise ship *Achille Lauro* by Palestinian guerrillas in Egyptian territorial waters on 7 Oct 1985 and the brutal murder of the US national Leon Klinghoffer on 8 Oct 1985 [24 ILM 1509-1565 (1985); http//news.bbc.co.uk/onthisday/hi/dates/stories/october/7/newsid_2518000/2518697.stm] led to the adoption of the 1987 US Anti-Terrorism Act [Pub.L. No.100-204, paras 1001-1005, 101 Stat. 1406 (codified at 22 USCA paras 5201-5203 (West Supp. 1988)] targeted at the PLO Permanent Observer Mission in New York. Intended closure of this Mission by the United States became the subject of the *Applicability of the Obligation to Arbitrate Under Section 21 of the United Nations Headquarters Agreement of 26 June 1947* Advisory Opinion, ICJ Rep. 1988, 12, Separate O. Schwebel, 42. See also *Achille Lauro* Hijacker Abu Abbas Dies in Iraq of 10 March 2004 <http://news.bbc.co.uk/2/hi/middle_east/3502416.stm & *id.* /2952879.stm>; The Youngest and Stateless *Achillo Lauro* Hijacker Released of 7 July 2008 <http://news.bbc.co.uk/2/hi/europe/7494586.stm>.

The *Achille Lauro* affair led to the adoption of the IMO Convention for the Suppression of Unlawful Acts Against the Safety of Maritime Navigation (SUA Convention) and Protocol for the Suppression of Unlawful Acts Against the Safety of Fixed Platforms Located on the Continental Shelf, Rome, 10 March 1988 [in force: 1 March 1992, 27 ILM 668, 685 (1988); 1678 UNTS 202, 304]; the IMO Code of Practice for the Investigation of the Crimes of Piracy and Armed Robbery Against Ships, Assembly Resolution 922(22) of 29 Nov 2001 [UN Doc. A/57/72 (2002)]; and IMO SUA Convention and Protocol of 14 Oct 2005 <www.imo.org/conventions/mainframe.asp?topic_id=259&doc_id=686>, signed by the USA on 17 Feb 2006, 100 AJIL 225 (2006); <www.state.gov/r/pa/prs/ps/2006/61506.htm>. On the Rome Convention, see *Great Belt* Pleadings, 349, 353 [Finland's Memorial]; *Congo v. Belgium Arrest Warrant of 11 April 2000* Separate O. President Guillaume, ICJ Rep. 2002, 39, para.8. The 1988 IMO Convention and Protocol are modelled on the Convention for the Suppression of Unlawful Acts Against the Safety of Civil Aviation, Montreal, 23 Sep 1971 [in force: 26 January 1973, 974 UNTS 177; 10 ILM 1151 (1971)] and Protocol for the Suppression of Unlawful Acts of Violence at Airports Serving

International Civil Aviation, Montreal, 24 Feb 1988 [in force: 6 August 1989, 27 ILM 627 (1988)].

Cf. *Nuclear Weapons (UNGA)* Dissent of Vice-President Schwebel, ICJ Rep. 1996, 323-329; *Questions of Interpretation and Application of the 1971 Montreal Convention Arising From the Aerial Incident at Lockerbie (Provisional Measures)* Orders, ICJ Rep. 1992, 3 [*Libya v. UK*], 114 [*Libya v. USA*], *(Preliminary Objections)* Judgments, ICJ Rep. 1998, 9 [*Libya v. UK*], 115 [*Libya v. USA*], Orders, ICJ Rep. 2000, 140, 143 and *(Discontinuance)* Orders, ICJ Rep. 2003, 150, 152 <www.icj-cij.org>, and UN SC Resolution S/RES/1506 of 12 Sep 2003 <www.un.org/Docs/sc>; 1998 UK/Netherlands Agreement, 2062 UNTS 82; 38 ILM 926 (1999); Opinion of the High Court of Justiciary at Camp Zeist, *id.*, 942; 40 ILM 582 [Opinion] (2001). See also UN SC Resolutions S/RES/1373 of 28 Sep 2001 and S/RES/1456 of 20 Jan 2003 [42 ILM 510 (2003)]; 46 AFDI 643 (2000); 95 AJIL 405, 839-843 (2001); 96 AJIL 237, 899, 964, 981 (2002); 97 AJIL 315-341, 987-991 (2003); <www.ltb.org.uk/>; *Oil Platforms (Merits)* Hearings, CR 2003/5, 58-59 [Counsel Bundy, 17 Feb 2003], CR 2003/12, 49 [Counsel Matheson, 26 Feb], CR 2003/15, 12, 16 [Bundy, 3 March] 59 [Bothe], CR 2003/18, 27 [Matheson, 5 March], CR 2003/19, 34 [Agent Zahedin-Labbaf, 7 March 2003]; 98 AJIL 195-197 (2004); Libya to Resolve Claims with United States of 31 May 2008 <http://news.bbc.co.uk/2/hi/africa/7428901.stm>; 17 June 2008 <http://news.bbc.co.uk/2/hi/uk_news/scotland/south_of_scotland/7459727.stm>; U.S. President Bush Signs Libya Claims Resolution Act of 4 August 2008 <www.asil.org/pdfs/ilib080814_2.pdf & www.asil.org/ilib080814.cfm>, <www.state.gov/secretary/rm/2008/08/107623.htm & http://news.bbc.co.uk/2/hi/americas/7542568.stm>; USA/Libya Comprehensive Claims Settlement Agreement of 14 August 2008 <www.state.gov/r/pa/prs/ps/2008/aug/108251.htm>, <www.iht.com/articles/2008/08/14/africa/libya.php, http://news.bbc.co.uk/2/hi/americas/7561271.stm & http://edition.cnn.com/2008/WORLD/africa/08/14/lockerbie/index.html>; Lockerbie Marks 20th Anniversary of 21/22 Dec 2008 <http://news.bbc.co.uk/2/hi/uk_news/scotland/south_of_scotland/7794771.stm & www.cnn.com/2008/WORLD/europe/12/21/scotland.lockerbie.anniversary/indexz.html>.

Israel Wall (Composition of the Court) Order, ICJ Rep. 2004, 3 and Judge Elaraby's Interview <http://weekly.ahram.org.eg/2001/547/profile.htm>; *Israel Wall* Advisory Opinion, President Shi concurring, ICJ Rep. 2004, 136, paras 46, 54-55, 63, 116, 127, 138-142, 162, Separate Os Higgins, 211-212, paras 15-20, Kooymans, 219, paras 13, 35-36, Dissent Buergenthal, 240-245 <www.icj-cij.org>; <www.asil.org/ilib040712.cfm>; 2004 *Beit Sourik Village Council v. Israel* Judgment, 42 ILM 1099 (2004); 99 AJIL 6, 19 (2005); <www.asil.org/insights/insigh140.htm> & 2005 *Mara'Abe v. Prime Minister of Israel* Judgment, 45 ILM 202 (2006); 100 AJIL 895-901 (2006) & <www.asil.org/ilib050929.cfm>; UN SC Res.1566 of 8 Oct 2004 <www.un.org/News/Press/docs/2004/sc8214.doc.htm>

& <www.un.int/usa/04_186.htm>; 2006 *Public Committee Against Torture in Israel v. Israel* Judgment of Israel Supreme Court, 46 ILM 373 (2007) & <www.asil.org/ilib070119.htm>; UN Register of Israeli War Damage of 10 May 2007 <www.un.org/apps/news/story.asp?NewsID=22518&Cr=Palestin&Cr1 & www.un.org/News/Press/docs/2007/sga1064.doc.htm> and 27 June 2008 <www.un.org/apps/news/story.asp?NewsID=27193&Cr=palestin&Cr1 & www.un.org/News/Press/docs/2008/sga1141.doc.htm>; Israel Agrees to Barrier Reroute of 29 July 2008 <http://news.bbc.co.uk/2/hi/middle_east/7530336.stm> and 22 August 2008 <http://news.bbc.co.uk/2/hi/middle_east/7575782.stm>; Five Years After *Israel Wall* Advisory Opinion of 8 July 2009 <www.un.org/apps/news/story.asp?NewsID=31410&Cr=palestin&Cr1>; Israel Security Fence <http://securityfence.mfa.gov.il/mfm/web/main/missionhome.asp?MissionID=45187>.

DR Congo v. Uganda (Merits) Judgment, ICJ Rep. 2005, 168, paras 162-164, 277, 300-304, Declaration Koroma, para.10, Separate Os Kooymans, paras 16-35, Simma, paras 4-15, 27 <www.icj-cij.org> & 100 AJIL 525-550 (2006); 2007 *Guyana/Suriname* Award, para.316 <www.pca-cpa.org>; U.S. Mission to the UN – International Law <www.un.int/usa/> and <http://usinfo.state.gov/is/international_security/terrorism.html>; PSI, 98 AJIL 355-357, 526-545, 588-590 (2004); <http://usinfo.state.gov/products/pubs/proliferation/, www.proliferationsecurity.info & http://en.wikipedia.org/wiki/Proliferation_Security_Initiative>.

On the 1971 Montreal Convention, see also *Iran v. USA Aerial Incident of 3 July 1988* – Settlement of Disputes, Preventive Diplomacy C) *supra*; *Congo v. Uganda (Provisional Measures)* Order, paras 5 and 7, ICJ Rep. 2000, 112-113; *DR Congo v. Belgium Arrest Warrant of 11 April 2000* Separate O. President Guillaume, ICJ Rep. 2002, 39, para.8, Dissent van den Wyngaert, 174, para.59; *DR Congo v. Rwanda New Application (Provisional Measures)* Order, President Guillaume concurring, ICJ Rep. 2002, 219, paras 2, 6(c), 28, 48, 63, 86-88, Declaration Elaraby, 260, paras 7, 11-14, Separate Os Dugard, 268-269, para 9-10, Mavungu, 272, paras 21, 33-38 and *DR Congo v. Rwanda (Jurisdiction)* Judgment, President Shi concurring, ICJ Rep. 2006, 6, paras 1, 7, 11, 15, 110-119.

On UN International Convention for the Suppression of Terrorist Bombings, New York, 15 Dec 1997 [in force: 23 May 2001, 2149 UNTS 257; <www.un.org/law/cod/terroris.htm>] and UN InternationalConvention for the Suppression of the Financing of Terrorism, New York, 9 Dec 1999 [in force: 10 April 2002, 2178 UNTS 198; <www.un.org/law/cod/finterr.htm>], see *DR Congo v. Belgium Arrest Warrant of 11 April 2000* Separate O. President Guillaume, ICJ Rep. 2002, 39, para.8; *Bosnia & Herzegovina v. Serbia & Montenegro (Jurisdiction & Merits)* Judgment, ICJ Rep. 2007, para.429, Declaration Skotnikov, n.1 <www.icj-cij.org>.

Nuclear Terrorism

2001 *Ireland v. UK Mox Plant (Provisional Measures)* Order, President P.Ch. Rao, ITLOS Case No.10, paras 26, 69 [41 ILM 405 (2002)]; Ireland's Request and Statement, paras 28, 35, 39-43, 50, 66, 83, 101, 106-107, 118-121, UK Response, paras 6, 15, 17, 41(7), 67-71, 94(2), 116-119, 124-125, 180, 216, 220(6); Hearings, ITLOS/PV.01/06, 9-10 [Agent O'Hagan, 19 Nov 2001], 22 [Counsel Fitzsimons], 29, 34 [Counsel Sands], ITLOS/PV.01/08, 9-10 [Counsel Goldsmith, 20 Nov 2001], 27-28 [Counsel Plender] <www.itlos.org>; Annex VII *Mox Plant*; UK Counter-Memorial, 174-178, 233-234; UK Rejoinder, 106-111 <www.pca-cpa.org>; 2006 ECJ *EC v. Ireland Mox Plant* Judgment, paras 35(5), 134 <http://curia.eu.int/jrisp/cgi-bin/form.pl?lang=EN&Submit=rechercher&numaff=C-459/03>. Cf. *IMO News* 18-23 (2001 No.4) <www.imo.org>; *IAEA Press Releases* No.26 of 30 Nov 2001, 2002/4 <www.iaea.org>; IAEA Measures, 41 ILM 737 (2002) and 3 June 2004 <www.unwire.org/UNWire/20040603/449_24500.asp>.

On UN International Convention for the Suppression of Acts of Nuclear Terrorism, New York, 4 April 2005 [44 ILM 815 (2005); 99 AJIL 712 (2005); <www.un.org/law/lindex.htm>], see *Bosnia & Herzegovina v. Serbia & Montenegro (Jurisdiction & Merits)* Declaration Skotnikov, n.1, ICJ Rep.2007 <www.icj-cij.org>.

On 1986/90 *The Rainbow Warrior*, see Access to, Jurisdiction and Treatment in Ports *supra*.

See also High Seas, Piracy *supra*.

On 1921 Convention on the Non-Ratification and Neutralization of the Aaland Islands, see Straits Used for International Navigation – Longstanding International Conventions in Force *supra*.

On Treaty Banning Nuclear Weapon Tests in the Atmosphere, in Outer Space and Under Water (Partial Nuclear Test Ban Treaty), Moscow, 5 August 1963 [in force: 10 Oct 1963, 480 UNTS 43; 2 ILM 883 (1963); 57 AJIL 1026 (1963); a substantive session of the Amendment Conference of States Parties was held at UN/New York on 7-18 Jan 1991], see *Nuclear Tests (Interim Measures)* Dissents Ignacio-Pinto, ICJ Rep. 1973, 132, 163; *Nuclear Tests* Dissent Gros, ICJ Rep. 1974, 282, 286-288, Dissents Petren, 305, 490, Joint Dissents, 361, 368, 519, Dissent de Castro, 388 n.1, 427, Dissent Barwick, 449; *Nuclear Tests* Pleadings (Australia), 12 [Application], 47, 49 [Request], 333-334, 370, 372 [Memorial], 520 [Counsel Byers, 9 July 1974], (New Zealand), 8 [Application], 51, 52, 55 [Request], 203 [Memorial], 264 [Counsel Finlay, 10 July 1974]; *New Zealand v. France* Dissents Weeramantry, ICJ Rep. 1995, 328, Koroma, 371, 378, Palmer, 415; 1995 NZ Request (Examination of the Situation), paras 60, 109-110; *Nuclear Weapons*

(UNGA) Advisory Opinion, ICJ Rep. 1996, 249, 252, Dissents Oda, 356-357, 360-361, Weeramantry, 534; Annex VII *Mox Plant* UK Counter-Memorial, 103, 196 n.34 <www.pca-cpa.org>.

On *Communiqué* of the ANZUS Council [1951 ANZUS Treaty, in force: 29 April 1952, 131 UNTS 85] of 5 April 1968, see *Nuclear Tests* Dissent Gros, ICJ Rep. 1974, 282.

On Treaty on the Non-Proliferation of Nuclear Weapons (NPT), 1 July 1968 [in force: 5 March 1970, 729 UNTS 161; 7 ILM 809 (1968); 62 AJIL 954 (1968); as extended indefinitely by the NPT Review and Extension Conference of the Parties on 11 May 1995, 34 ILM 959-74 (1995); 2005 NPT Review Conference <www.un.org/events/npt2005/>, <www.iaea.org/NewsCenter/News/2005/npt_2005.html> & <www.state.gov/t/np/wmd/nnp/c10602.htm>; 2010 NPT Review Conference <www.un.org/News/Press/docs/2007/note6075.doc.htm>], see *Nuclear Tests* Pleadings (New Zealand), 8 [Application], 51 [Request], 203 [Memorial]; 1995 NZ Request (Examination of the Situation), para.57 n.63, para.59; *New Zealand v. France* Oral Hearings, CR 95/20, 22 [Counsel Keith, 12 Sep 1995]; *Nuclear Weapons (WHO)* Dissent Weeramantry, ICJ Rep. 1996, 160, *(UNGA)* Advisory Opinion, 245-246, 249, 251-253, 263-265, Declaration Ferrari Bravo, 284-285, Separate O. Guillaume, 292-293, Dissents Vice-President Schwebel, 312-317, 329, Oda, 358-359, 360-369, Shahabuddeen, 378-379, 381-382, 384, 400, 411, 414-420, Weeramantry, 441, 448, 488, 530-531, 534, 536-542, Koroma, 581, Higgins, 593; *Yugoslavia v. Bosnia and Herzegovina (Revision)* Dissent Dimitrijevic, para.33, ICJ Rep. 2003, 61 <www.icj-cij.org>.

On Treaty for the Prohibition of Nuclear Weapons in Latin America and the Caribbean, Tlatelolco, 14 Feb 1967 [in force: 22 April 1968, 634 UNTS 281; 6 ILM 521 (1967); Status of Treaty and its Additional Protocols I and II – 28 ILM 1400 (1989); Amendments of 3 July 1990, 10 May 1991 and 26 August 1992 – UN Docs A/47/467, Annex (1992) and NPT/Conf.1995/10, Annex C], see *Nuclear Tests* Joint Dissents, ICJ Rep. 1974, 368, 520; Pleadings (Australia), 12 [Application], (New Zealand), 8 [Application], 51 [Request], 203 [Memorial]; *Nuclear Weapons (WHO)* Dissents Weeramantry, ICJ Rep. 1996, 140, Koroma, 209-210, *(UNGA)* Advisory Opinion, 249, 252-253, 263, Separate Os Guillaume, 291-292, Fleischhauer, 308, Dissents Vice-President Schwebel, 318, Oda, 359-360, 363, Shahabuddeen, 384, 415-416, Weeramantry, 534, 536, Koroma, 566; Hearings, CR 95/33, 28-29 [Costa Rica, 14 Nov 1995].

See also IAEA/USA Agreement for the Application of Safeguards in Connection with the Tlatelolco Treaty of 17 February 1989 [in force: 6 April 1989, 28 ILM 1345 (1989)].

On Treaty on the Prohibition of the Emplacement of Nuclear Weapons and Other Weapons of Mass Destruction on the Sea-Bed and Ocean Floor and in the

Subsoil Thereof, London, Moscow and Washington, 11 Feb 1971 [in force: 18 May 1972, 955 UNTS 115; 10 ILM 146 (1971)], see *Aegean Sea* Pleadings, 439 [Counsel Economides, 16 Oct 1978], 455-456 [Counsel O'Connell]; *Gulf of Maine* Pleadings, Vol.V, 520 [US Reply]; *Nuclear Tests* Dissent Koroma, ICJ Rep. 1995, 379; *Nuclear Weapons (UNGA)* Advisory Opinion, ICJ Rep. 1996, 249, Dissent Weeramantry, 534.

On UK/Malta Defence Agreement of 26 March 1972 [for 7 years, until withdrawal of British forces in 1979, 76 RGDIP 1196 (1972); 80 RGDIP 1261 (1976)], see *Libya/Malta* Pleadings, Vol.I, 27 [Libya's Memorial]. On Declaration on Malta's Neutrality of 15 May 1981 [Pleadings, Vol.I, 514], see *id.* 420, 483, 498-499 [Malta's Memorial], Vol.II, 74-75 [Libya's Counter-Memorial].

On USA/USSR Treaty on the Limitation of Underground Nuclear Weapon Tests of 3 July 1974 [in force: 11 Dec 1990, UN Doc. A/9698, Annex I (1974)], Protocol of 1 June 1990 as Amended on 31 Dec 1992/2 Feb 1993 [1714 UNTS 124], see *Nuclear Tests* Dissent Gros, ICJ Rep. 1974, 287-288.

On USA/USSR Treaty on Underground Nuclear Explosions for Peaceful Purposes of 28 May 1976, Protocol of 1 June 1990 [in force: 11 Dec 1990, 1714 UNTS 388], see *New Zealand v. France* Dissent Weeramantry, ICJ Rep. 1995, 328.

On Convention on the Prohibition of Military or Any Other Hostile Use of Environmental Modification Techniques of 10 Dec 1976 [in force: 5 Oct 1978, 1108 UNTS 151], see *Nuclear Weapons (WHO)* Dissent Koroma, ICJ Rep. 1996, 216, *(UNGA)* Advisory Opinion, 241, Dissent Weeramantry, 503.

On South Pacific Nuclear Free Zone Treaty, Rarotonga, 6 August 1985 [in force: 11 Dec 1985, Protocols 1-3, 24 ILM 1440 (1985); status, 28 ILM 1599 (1989); Joint Declaration of 20 Oct 1995, UN Docs NPT/Conf.1995/11 and A/50/665-S/1995/877; Protocols 1-3 signed by France, UK and USA on 25 March 1996], see *Great Belt* Pleadings, 328 [Finland's Memorial]; *Nuclear Tests* Dissent Palmer, ICJ Rep. 1995, 389; the 1995 NZ Request (Examination of the Situation), para.60; *Nuclear Tests* Oral Hearings, CR 95/19, 23-24 [NZ, 11 Sep 1995], CR 95/23 [transl.], 35 [France, 1 Nov], CR 95/28, 42 [NZ, 9 Nov], CR 95/31, 28 [Samoa, 13 Nov], CR 95/34, 60 [UK, 15 Nov 1995]; *Nuclear Weapons (UNGA)* Advisory Opinion, ICJ Rep. 1996, 249-251, 253, 263, Separate Os Guillaume, 291, Fleischhauer, 308, Dissents Vice-President Schwebel, 318, Oda, 360, 363, Shahabuddeen, 385, Weeramantry, 534.

On Convention on the Prohibition of the Development, Production, Stockpiling and Use of Chemical Weapons and on Their Destruction, Paris, 13 Jan 1993 [in force: 29 April 1997, 1974 UNTS 46; 32 ILM 800 (1993)], Agreement on the Relationship Between the UN and the OPCW, New York, 17 Oct 2000 [in force: 26 Sep 2001, 2160 UNTS 207], UK/OPCW Agreement on Privileges and Immunities of the OPCW, The Hague, 26 Oct 2000 [in force: 28 Feb 2002, 2207 UNTS 15] and Austria/OPCW Agreement on Privileges and Immunities of the OPCW, Vienna, 10 July 2001 [in force: 1 Sep 2002, 2197 UNTS 3], see *Nuclear Weapons (WHO)* Dissents Weeramantry, ICJ Rep. 1996, 134-135, 152-153, Koroma, 183, *(UNGA)* Advisory Opinion, 248, para.57, Separate O. Guillaume, 292, Dissent Vice-President Schwebel, 323-329 [328: 1993 Convention]; *Gabcikovo* Oral Hearings, CR 97/2 [trans.], 12 n.11 [Agent Szenasi, 3 March 1997]; *Oil Platforms (Merits)* Hearings, CR 2003/5, 20 [Agent Zahedin-Labbaf, 17 Feb], 61-62 [Counsel Bundy], CR 2003/16, 28 [Counsel Pellet, 3 March 2003], 35 [Zahedin-Labbaf] <www.icj-cij.org>.

On Southeast Asia Nuclear Weapon Free Zone Treaty, Bangkok, 15 Dec 1995 [35 ILM 635 (1996)], see *Nuclear Weapons (UNGA)* Advisory Opinion, ICJ Rep. 1996, 253, Dissents Vice-President Schwebel, 318, Oda, 363, Shahabuddeen, 385.

On African Nuclear Weapon Free Zone Treaty, Cairo, 11 April 1996 [35 ILM 698 (1996)], see *Nuclear Weapons (UNGA)* Advisory Opinion, ICJ Rep. 1996, 253, Dissents Vice-President Schwebel, 318, Oda, 363-364, Shahabuddeen, 385, Weeramantry, 534.

On UN Comprehensive Nuclear Test Ban Treaty, New York, 24 Sep 1996 [35 ILM 1439 (1996); <www.fas.org/nuke/control/ctbt/>], Austria/PrepCom CNTBTO Agreement, Vienna, 18 March 1997 [in force: 1 Nov 1997, 1998 UNTS 4] and UN/PrepCom CNTBTO Agreement, New York, 26 May 2000 [in force: 15 June 2000, 2110 UNTS 217] see *Nuclear Weapons (UNGA)* Dissents Oda, ICJ Reports 1996, 339, 357, 361-362, Weeramantry, 534. See also Changes Anticipated at CNTBTO of 22 July 2004 <www.unwire.org/UNWire/20040722/449_26084 .asp>; UN Ministerial Meeting on CNTBTO's Entry Into Force of 24 Sep 2008 <www.un.org/News/Press/docs//2008/sgsm11809.doc.htm & www.un.org/News/briefings/docs//2008/080924_CTBT.doc.htm>.

On 1997 UN International Convention for the Suppression of Terrorist Bombings, see Maritime Terrorism *supra*.

On 1999 UN International Convention for the Suppression of the Financing of Terrorism, see Maritime Terrorism *supra*.

On 2005 UN International Convention for the Suppression of Acts of Nuclear Terrorism, see Nuclear Terrorism *supra*.

On 1939 Declaration of Panama, see Exclusive Economic (/Fishery) Zone, Evolution *supra*.

On NATO shipping and treaties, see *IMCO* Pleadings, 428 [USA, 4 May 1960]; *Fisheries Jurisdiction (Merits)* Dissent Gros, ICJ Rep. 1974, 142; *Nuclear Tests* Pleadings (New Zealand), 286-288 [Counsel Quentin-Baxter, 10 July 1974]; *Gulf of Maine* Pleadings, Vol.III, 169, 374, 381 [Canada's Counter-Memorial]; *Nicaragua v. USA (Merits)* Dissent Schwebel, ICJ Rep. 1986, 309-310, para.104; *Nuclear Weapons (UNGA)* Dissents Shahabuddeen, ICJ Rep. 1996, 384, Weeramantry, 510; *Legality of Use of Force (Provisional Measures)* Orders, ICJ Rep. 1999, 124, 259, 363, 422, 481, 542, 656, 761, 826, 916; *Georgia v. Russia (Provisional Measures)* Order, ICJ Rep. 2008; *Macedonia v. Greece* <www.icj-cij.org>; NATO <www.nato.int/> & <www.asil.org/insights081229.cfm>.

See also Inter-Oceanic Canals; Exclusive Economic Zone – Military Installations; Equitable Maritime Boundary Delimitation – Security Factors; Use of Force in Enforcement; Settlement of Disputes – Military Activities and Law Enforcement Disputes as well as Involvement of the UN Security Council *supra*.

ARCHAEOLOGICAL AND HISTORICAL OBJECTS

1982 UNCLOS, Part XI, Article 149, Part XVI, Article 303

SS Lotus PCIJ Series A, No.10 (1927) – Dissent Moore, 85; *Tunisia/Libya* Pleadings, Vol.I, 112-116 [Tunisia's Memorial], Vol.II, 153-155 [Libya's Counter-Memorial]; *Botswana/Namibia* Dissent Vice-President Weeramantry, paras 86, 91, ICJ Rep. 1999, 1181, 1184; *Romania v. Ukraine* Hearings, CR 2008/29, 51 [Judge Oxman's Question 2, 12 Sep 2008], CR 2008/31, 42-43, paras 2-7 [Counsel Lowe's Reply to Question 2], 55, para.2(g) [Agent Aurescu's Corrig. to Lowe's Reply, 16 Sep], CR 2008/32, 18, para.14 [Counsel Sir Michael Wood, 18 Sep 2008] <www.icj-cij.org>; *Nicaragua v. Colombia* Nicaragua's Memorial, 201 <www.icj-cij.org>.

M/V Saiga Separate O. Laing [38 ILM 1323 (1999)], paras 11, 45 <www.itlos.org>.

2007 ICSID *Malaysian Historical Salvors (MHS), SDN, BHD v. Malaysia Sunken Treasure (Jurisdiction)* Award of Sole Arbitrator Michael Hwang (Singapore), as annulled by the 2009 *MHS v. Malaysia (Annulment)* Decision, President Stephen M. Schwebel (USA), Arbitrators Mohamed Shahabuddeen (Guyana) and Peter Tomka (Slovakia) <www.globalarbitrationreview.com/news/article/15229/icsid-award-annulled/ & www.investmenttreatynews.org/cms/news/archive/2009/04/23/malaysian-historical-salvors-jurisdictional-award-annulled-committee-split-on-question-of-economic-development-as criteria-of-icsid-investments.aspx>; 48 ILM 1081 (2009); and 20-- *MHS v. Malaysia Sunken Trea-sure (Merits)* Award <http://icsid.worldbank.org/ICSID/FrontServlet & www.arbitration.fr/5.html>.

On Convention on the Protection of the World Cultural and Natural Heritage, Paris, 23 November 1972 [in force: 17 Dec 1975, 1037 UNTS No.15511; 27 UST 37], see *Nuclear Weapons (UNGA)* Dissent Weeramantry, ICJ Rep. 1996, 455.

On UNESCO Convention on the Protection of the Underwater Cultural Heritage, Paris, 6 Nov 2001, in force: 2 Jan 2009, amplifying UNCLOS Article 303

[41 ILM 40 (2002); U.S. position, shared by EU, Japan, Australia and other States, 96 AJIL 419, 468 (2002); 100 AJIL 649 (2006); <www.unesco.org>; <http://en.wikipedia.org/wiki/UNESCO_Convention_on_the_Protection_of_the_Underwater_Cultural_Heritage>; Shipwrecks <http://en.wikipedia.org/wiki/List_of_shipwrecks & http://en.wikipedia.org/wiki/Shipwreck>], see Replies to Judge Oxman's Question 2, in *Romania v. Ukraine* Hearings in this section *supra*; 2001 UNESCO Convention Will Enter Into Force on 2 Jan 2009 of 14 Oct 2008 <www.un.org/apps/news/story.asp?NewsID=28566&Cr=unesco&cr1>.

EQUITY

1982 UNCLOS, Preamble 4 and 5, Part V, Articles 59, 69(1), 69(3), 70(1), 70(4) and 74(1), Part VI, Articles 82(4) and 83(1), Part XI, Article 140(2), Part XIV, Articles 266(3) and 269(b):

Relevant Jurisprudence

Diversion of Water from the Meuse Judgment, PCIJ Series A/B, No.70, 25 (1937) – Dissents Anzilotti, 50 and Manley O. Hudson, 76-77, as relied upon by *North Sea* Separate O. Jessup, ICJ Rep. 1969, 84, Separate O. Ammoun, 138, 142, 145; Pleadings, Vol.II, 200 [Counsel Shigeru Oda, 5 Nov 1968]; *Fisheries Jurisdiction (Merits)* Separate O. Dillard, ICJ Rep. 1974, 63 n.1; Pleadings (UK), 473 [Counsel Silkin, 25 March 1974]; *Tunisia/Libya (Merits)* Dissent Evensen, ICJ Rep. 1982, 290-291; Pleadings, Vol.I, 166-167 [Tunisia's Memorial], Vol.IV, 417 [Counsel Sir Robert Jennings, 16 Sep 1981]; *Nicaragua v. USA (Provisional Measures)* Dissent Schwebel, ICJ Rep. 1984, 198-199, and (*Merits*) Dissent Schwebel, ICJ Rep. 1986, 259, 380-381, paras 239-240, at 392-393, paras 268-272; *Denmark v. Norway* Separate O. Weeramantry, ICJ Rep. 1993, 234-236, 255 n.1; *Gabcikovo* Separate O. Koroma, ICJ Rep. 1997, 149-152, Dissent Skubiszewski, 238-239; *Oil Platforms (Merits)* Hearings, CR 2003/11, 27-28, 34-35 [Counsel Mathias, 25 Feb 2003], CR 2003/16, 25 [Counsel Pellet, 3 March], CR 2003/18, 11, 16 [Mathias, 5 March 2003] <www.icj-cij.org>.

Corfu Channel (Compensation) ICJ Rep. 1949, 244 [the first instance of applying by the Court of equity in the field of quantification of monetary sums due in reparation claims and related types of cases] – Judgment, 249, Dissent Ecer, 253-256, *as reaffirmed* by *Judgments of the Administrative Tribunal of the I.L.O. Upon Complaints Made Against UNESCO* Advisory Opinion, ICJ Rep. 1956, 100; and *North Sea Continental Shelf* Judgment, ICJ Rep. 1969, 48-49, para.88; as relied upon by *Gulf of Maine* Dissent Gros, ICJ Rep. 1984, 383; *Denmark v. Norway* Separate O. Shahabuddeen, ICJ Rep. 1993, 192, 194.

Belgium v. Spain Barcelona Traction, Light and Power Company, Limited (Second Phase) Judgment, ICJ Rep. 1970, 48-50, Separate O. Sir Gerald Fitzmaurice, 85-86, Separate O. Ammoun, 332-333; as relied upon by *Gulf of Maine* Dissent Gros, ICJ Rep. 1984, 384; Pleadings, Vol.VII, 30-31 [Counsel Weil, 3 May 1984]; *Libya/Malta* Pleadings, Vol.II, 316 n.3 [Malta's Counter-Memorial]; *Denmark v. Norway* Separate O. Weeramantry, ICJ Rep. 1993, 232 n.1, 233, 238 n.3, 240; Hearings, CR 93/8 [trans.], 64 [Counsel Weil, 20 Jan 1993]; *Guinea v. DR Congo (Preliminary Objections)* Judgment, ICJ Rep. 2007, paras 82-87.

Fisheries Jurisdiction (Jurisdiction) Separate Os Fitzmaurice, ICJ Rep. 1973, 33 n.16, 77 n.16, *(Merits)* Judgments, ICJ Rep. 1974, 33-35, paras 78-79(3) [*UK v. Iceland*], 202, 205-206, paras 69 and 77(3) [*FRG v. Iceland*], Declarations Ignacio-Pinto, 36, 209, Separate O. Dillard, 63-66, 70-71, Separate Os de Castro, 99, 103-104, 225, Dissent Gros, 136, 138-139, 146-147; *Fisheries Jurisdiction* Pleadings (UK), 372-374 [Memorial (Merits)], 473 [Counsel Silkin, 25 March 1974], (FRG), 257-259 [Memorial (Merits)]. Cf. *Gulf of Maine* Dissent Gros, ICJ Rep. 1984, 384-385; Pleadings, Vol.I, 119 [Canada's Memorial], Vol.III, 196-197, 206, 218 [Canada's Counter-Memorial], Vol.V, 15, 30-31 [Canada's Reply], Vol.VI, 90-91 [Counsel Binnie, 4 April 1984], 171 [Counsel Weil, 6 April], Vol.VII, 28 [Weil, 3 May], 88-91 [Binnie, 4 May 1984]; *Libya/Malta* Pleadings, Vol.III, 375 [Counsel Weil, 29 Nov 1984], Vol.IV, 97-98 [Counsel Colliard, 11 Dec 1984]; *Denmark v. Norway* Separate O. Weeramantry, ICJ Rep. 1993, 236, 238-239; *Gabcikovo* Dissent Skubiszewski, ICJ Rep. 1997, 239; *Botswana/Namibia* Separate O. Kooymans, para.24, ICJ Rep. 1999, 1148; Hearings, CR 99/5 [trans], 30 [Counsel Cot, 18 Feb 1999] <www.icj-cij.org>; *Southern Bluefin Tuna (Jurisdiction)* Hearings, Vol. I [Counsel Lowe, 7 May 2000] <www.worldbank.org/icsid>; 2006 *Barbados/ Trinidad & Tobago (Jurisdiction and Merits)* Award, President S.M. Schwebel, para.280 <www.pca-cpa.org>.

Interpretation of the Agreement of 25 March 1951 Between the WHO and Egypt Advisory Opinion, ICJ Rep. 1980, 96, para.49, as relied upon by *Great Belt* Pleadings, 642-643 [Denmark's Counter-Memorial]; *Panama v. France Camouco* Separate O. Vice-President Nelson, n.6, ITLOS Case No.5, 39 ILM 666 (2000) <www.itlos.org>.

Burkina Faso/Mali Frontier Dispute Judgment, ICJ Rep. 1986, 567-568, 631-633, Separate O. Abi-Saab, 662, as relied upon by the *Gulf of Fonseca* Judgment, ICJ Rep. 1992, 396, 514; *Denmark v. Norway* Separate Os Shahabuddeen, ICJ Rep. 1993, 188, Ajibola, 296-297; *Botswana/Namibia* Hearings, CR 99/5 [trans], 30 [Counsel Cot, 18 Feb 1999]; *Guinea v. DR Congo (Preliminary Objections)* Judgment, ICJ Rep. 2007, para.79.

Libya/Chad Separate O. Ajibola, ICJ Rep. 1994, 59; *East Timor* Dissent Weeramantry, ICJ Rep. 1995, 203; *Nuclear Weapons* Hearings, CR 95/20, 65-66 n.53 [Australia, 30 Oct 1995]; *Cameroon v. Nigeria; Equatorial Guinea Intervening (Merits)* Dissent Ajibola, paras 3-9, ICJ Rep. 2002, 538-541; *Oil Platforms (Merits)* Hearings, CR 2003/12, 32 [Counsel Weil, 26 Feb 2003]; *Guinea v. DR Congo (Preliminary Objections)* Judgment, ICJ Rep. 2007, paras 79-94 <www.icj-cij.org>.

1997 *Inter-Entity Boundary in Brcko Area* Award, paras 87-94, President Roberts B. Owen, 36 ILM 369 (1997) [1999 Final Award, 38 ILM 534 (1999) and 39 ILM 879 (2000); <www.state.gov/www/regions/eur/bosnia/brcko_arb.html>; 100 AJIL 825-826 (2006)];

1998 *Eritrea/Yemen Territorial Sovereignty (Phase I)* Award, President Sir Robert Jennings, paras 108-113 [40 ILM 900 (2001) <www.pca-cpa.org>; 2000 *Australia and New Zealand v. Japan Southern Bluefin Tuna (Jurisdiction)* Award, President Stephen M. Schwebel, Award, paras 41(c) and 64, 39 ILM 1359 (2000); A/NZ Reply, paras 38, 68 and 180-184 <www.worldbank.org/icsid>; Sir Elihu Lauterpacht, Judge Stephen M. Schwebel, Shabtai Rosenne and Francisco Orrego, *Joint Legal Opinion on Guatemala's Territorial Claim to Belize*, paras 164-165, 222, Annex II, paras 28, 30 (January 2002) <www.belize-guatemala.gov.bz/>;

2001 *Mox Plant (Provisional Measures)* Separate O. Vice-President Nelson, para.8 <www.itlos.org>;

2002 *Eritrea/Ethiopia Boundary* Decision, paras 3.14-3.15, President Sir Elihu Lauterpacht, 41 ILM 1057 (2002); <www.un.org/NewLinks/eebcarbitration/>; 2002 *Compania de Aguas del Aconquija S.A. and Vivendi Universal v. Argentine Republic (Annulment of 2000 Award)* Decision, paras 51-55, President L. Yves Fortier CC QC, ICSID Case No.ARB/97/3, [41 ILM 1135 (2002); <www.worldbank.org/icsid/cases/vivendi_annul.pdf> and 2000 *Vivendi v. Argentina (Jurisdiction & Merits)* Award <www.worldbank.org/icsid/cases/ada_AwardoftheTribunal.pdf>] and 2003 *Vivendi v. Argentina (Supplementation and Rectification of 2002 Decision)* Decision, President Fortier <www.worldbank.org/icsid/cases/vivendi-supp.pdf>;

2004 *Juno Trader (Prompt Release)* Separate O. Lucky, para.30, Case No.13 <www.itlos.org>;

2005 *Belgium/Netherlands Iron Rhine* Award, paras 23, 157, 162, 202-205, 208, 220, 226 <www.pca-cpa.org>.

"Clean Hands" Doctrine – see Peaceful Uses of the Sea *supra*.

Equitable Sharing of International Waterways

Territorial Jurisdiction of the International Commission of the River Oder Judgment, PCIJ Series A, No.23, 27 (1929), *as reaffirmed* by *Gabcikovo* Judgment, ICJ Rep. 1997, 56, para.85; *Botswana/Namibia* Separate O. Kooymans, para. 30, ICJ Rep.

1999, 1150; eight *Legality of Use of Force (Preliminary Objections)* Separate Os Kreca, para.42, ICJ Rep. 2004, 400, 546, 691, 836, 982, 1131, 1278, 1423 <www.icj-cij.org>.

Oscar Chinn Judgment, PCIJ Series A/B, No.63 (1934), 65; 1937 *Diversion of Water from the Meuse* Judgment and Dissent Hudson [see *supra*]; *North Sea* Separate O. Jessup, ICJ Rep. 1969, 82; Pleadings, Vol.I, 464-465 [Common Rejoinder of Denmark/NL], Vol.II, 128 [Agent Riphagen, 30 Oct 1968], 178-179 [Agent Jaenicke, 4 Nov], 215-216 [Riphagen, 7 Nov 1968]; *Gulf of Maine* Pleadings, Vol.III, 189, 198, 201 [Canada's Counter-Memorial]; *Libya/Malta* Pleadings, Vol.I, 124 [Libya's Memorial]; *Great Belt* Pleadings, 316 [Finland's Memorial], 556-557 [Denmark's Counter-Memorial]; *Gulf of Fonseca* Judgment, ICJ Rep. 1992, 602; *Denmark v. Norway* Separate O. Weeramantry, ICJ Rep. 1993, 247, 248-249, 262, 277; *Oil Platforms (Preliminary Objection)* Judgment, ICJ Rep. 1996, 819, Separate O. Higgins, 859-860, Dissent Vice-President Schwebel, 887-888; *Oil Platforms (Merits)* Hearings, CR 2003/6, 22, 23-25 [Counsel Pellet, 18 Feb], CR 2003/16, 32 [3 March 2003] <www.icj-cij.org>.

Hungary/Slovakia Gabcikovo-Nagymaros Project Judgment, ICJ Rep. 1997, 8, Declaration President S.M. Schwebel, 85, Declaration Rezek, 86, Separate Os Vice-President Weeramantry, 88, Bedjaoui, 120, Koroma, 142, Dissents Oda, 153, Ranjeva, 170, Herczegh, 176, Fleischhauer, 204, Vereshchetin, 219, Parra-Aranguren, 227, Skubiszewski, 232; Orders, ICJ Rep. 1994, 151, 1997, 3 (*Site Visit*).

For Czechoslovakia/Hungary Agreement on Mutual Assistance in the Construction of the Gabcikovo-Nagymaros System of Locks of 16 Sep 1977 [in force: 30 June 1978], as Amended by Protocol of 10 Oct 1983 [in force: 7 Feb 1984] and Protocol of 6 Feb 1989 [terminating 1983 Protocol], see 1724 UNTS 120; 32 ILM 1247 (1993). For Czech and Slovak Federation/EC/Hungary Agreement on the Gabcikovo-Nagymaros Project of 28 Oct 1992, see 32 ILM 1291 (1993). For Hungary/Slovakia Special Agreement of 7 April 1993 [in force: 26 June 1993], see 1725 UNTS 226; 32 ILM 1293 (1993).

Slovakia's Request for an additional Judgment, *ICJ Communiques* Nos 98/28 and 98/31 of 3 Sep and 7 Oct 1998; *ICJ Report 1 August 2001-31 July 2002*, UN Doc.A/57/4 (2002), at 47-52, paras 178-196; *ICJ Report 1 August 2007-31 July 2008*, UN Doc.A/63/4 (2008), at 19, paras 93-95; *ICJ Report 1 August 2008-31 July 2009*, UN Doc.A/64/4 (2009), at 25, paras 104-106 <www.icj-cij.org>.

Cf. *Oil Platforms (Merits)* Hearings, CR 2003/8, 36-37 [Counsel Pellet, 19 Feb 2003], CR 2003/11, 30-31, 33 [Counsel Mathias, 25 Feb], CR 2003/12, 28 [Counsel Weil, 26 Feb], CR 2003/16, 21 (n.39), 22-24 [Pellet, 3 March], CR 2003/18, 15 [Mathias, 5 March 2003] <www.icj-cij.org>; Annex VII *Mox Plant (Provisional Measures)* Hearings, 14 [Counsel Crawford and Sands, 18 June 2003] <www

.pca-cpa.org>; *Malaysia v. Singapore (Provisional Measures)* Hearings, ITLOS/PV.03/02/Corr.1, 24 [Counsel Crawford, 25 Sep 2003] <www.itlos.org>; *Israel Wall* Advisory Opinion, ICJ Rep. 2004, 195, para.140 <www.icj-cij.org>; *Croatia v. Serbia (Preliminary Objections)* Separate O. Tomka, para.14, Dissent Owada, para.21, ICJ Rep. 2008.

1999 *Botswana/Namibia Kasikili Sedudu* Judgment, 2002 *Cameroon v. Nigeria; Equatorial Guinea Intervening (Merits)* Judgment, 2002 UN *Eritrea/Ethiopia Boundary* Decision (para.7.3), 2002 *Belize/Guatemala* OAS Facilitators' Proposals (D-para.2) and *Benin/Niger Frontier Dispute* – see Equitable Maritime Boundary Delimitation, Thalweg Principle/Lakes and Rivers *supra*; *Qatar v. Bahrain (Merits)* Joint Disent Bedjaoui, Ranjeva, Koroma, ICJ Rep. 2001, 200-201, paras 177-180.

The violation of "obligation to respect freedom of navigation on international rivers" was alleged in Applications of Yugoslavia of 29 April 1999 to form part of each of its disputes with 10 NATO Member States, of which disputes with Spain and the USA were removed from the General List, ICJ Rep. 1999, 761, 916, while the eight *Legality of Use of Force (Preliminary Objections)* Judgments, ICJ Rep. 2004, found that the Court had no jurisdiction over the merits of these disputes. See Peaceful Uses of the Sea – Prohibition of Threat or Use of Force *supra*.

Argentina v. Uruguay Pulp Mills on the River Uruguay (Provisional Measures) Orders, ICJ Rep. 2006, 113 and 2007, 3 <www.icj-cij.org>; 46 ILM 311 (2007).

Costa Rica v. Nicaragua San Juan River Order, ICJ Rep. 2005, 165 and Judgment, ICJ Rep. 2009. Cf. *Nicaragua v. Colombia (Preliminary Objections)* Hearings, CR 2007/16, 50-52, paras 16-23 [Counsel Stephen M. Schwebel, 4 June 2007], CR 2007/18, 15, paras 13-14 [Counsel Schwebel, 6 June], CR 2007/19, 16, paras 30-31 [Agent Arguello, 8 June 2007] and *Costa Rica v. Nicaragua San Juan* Judgment, ICJ Rep. 2009, paras 1, 27-28 <www.icj-cij.org>.

M/V Saiga Separate O. Laing [38 ILM 1323 (1999)], paras 24-26; 2000 *Southern Bluefin Tuna (Jurisdiction)*, President S.M. Schwebel, Japan's Memorial, para.122 n.91 <www.worldbank.org/icsid>; 2001 *Ireland v. UK Mox Plant (Provisional Measures)* Ireland's Request & Statement, paras 92-93 <www.itlos.org>; *Indonesia/Malaysia (Merits)* Judgment, ICJ Rep. 2002, 652, para.50 <www.icj-cij.org>; 2003 *Kaiser Aluminium & Chemical Corporation (Kaiser) and the Volta Aluminium Company (Valco) v. Government of Ghana and the Volta River Authority (VRA)* Mediation by Judge Stephen M. Schwebel <www.mclglobal.com/History/May2003/09e2003/09e3r.html>, at 2-6 and <http://allafrica.com/stories/200305070811.html> and 20 Nov 2008 <www.ghanaweb.com/GhanaHomePage/NewsArchive/artikel.php?ID=153342.

UN ECE *Romania/Ukraine Danube-Black Sea (Bystroe) Canal* Opinion of Commission of Inquiry under the 1991 Espoo EIA Convention (Art.3 & Appendix IV) [1989 UNTS 310; 30 ILM 802 (1991); <www.unece.org/env/eia/welcome.html>] of 11 July 2006 <www.unece.org/env/eia/inquiry.htm> and press comments <www.mosnews.com/news/2006/07/11/canaldisp.shtml & www.cceg.ro/2006stiri/UN.htm>; *Guyana/Suriname* Suriname's Counter-Memorial, para.3.33, Suriname's Rejoinder, para.2.54 <www.pca-cpa.org>.

On Costa Rica/Nicaragua (Canas Jerez) Treaty of 15 April 1858 [UN Docs A/53/882 and 905 (1999); A/56/770 (2002)], see *Nicaragua v. Colombia* Nicaragua's Memorial, 75; *Costa Rica v. Nicaragua San Juan River* Judgment, ICJ Rep. 2009, paras 19-21 <www.icj-cij.org>. See also Inter-Oceanic Canals – 1888 *Costa Rica/Nicaragua* Award of U.S. President Cleveland *supra*.

On 1921 Barcelona and 1948 Danube Conventions, see Rights of Access of Land-Locked States to and from the Sea and Freedom of Transit *supra*.

On 1954 USA/Canada Great Lake Fisheries Convention, see Fisheries *supra*.

On 1958 Danube Fishing Convention, see Fisheries *supra*.

On Fort Lamy (N'Djamena) Convention and Statute on the Development of the Lake Chad Basin, Yaounde, 22 May 1964, as Amended on 22 Oct 1972, see *Cameroon v. Nigeria (Preliminary Objections)* Judgment, ICJ Rep. 1998, 285, 288, 304-313, Dissent Ajibola, 404-407, 417; Hearings, CR 98/1, 63-75 [Counsel Brownlie, 2 March 1998]; *Cameroon v. Nigeria; Equatorial Guinea Intervening (Merits)* Judgment, ICJ Rep. 2002, 303, paras 36, 40-47, 53-57, 63-64, Separate O. Mbaye, paras 40-43, 51, 63, Dissent Ajibola, paras 11-18, 32-47 and UN *Cameroon/Nigeria* Mixed Commission [Equitable Maritime Boundary Delimitation *supra*]; *Benin/Niger* Hearings, C5/CR 2005/5, 22, para.3.14 [Counsel Forteau, 10 March 2005] <www.icj-cij.org>.

On Argentina/Uruguay River Uruguay Boundary Treaty of 7 April 1961 [in force: 19 Feb 1966] and Argentina/Uruguay Statute of the River Uruguay of 26 Feb 1975 [in force: 18 Sep 1976], see *Argentina v. Uruguay Pulp Mills on the River Uruguay (Provisional Measures)* Orders, ICJ Rep. 2006, 113 and 2007, 3 <www.icj-cij.org>.

On 1976 Budapest Convention and 1984 Canada/USA Treaty, see Protection and Preservation of the Marine Environment *supra*.

On 1992 UN ECE Watercourses Convention, 1994 Danube Convention, 1976 Pollution of the Rhine by Chlorides Convention and 1997 UN International Watercourses Convention, see Protection and Preservation of the Marine Environment *supra*.

On the River Niger Basin Authority [NBA <www.diplomatie.gouv.fr/actu/article. gb.asp?ART=41711; Paris NBA Conference, 26-27 April 2004 <www.un.org/News /Press/docs/2004/sgsm9277.doc.htm>, <www.unwire.org/UNWire/

20040427/449_23216. asp>], see *Benin/Niger Frontier Dispute* – Equitable Maritime Boundary Delimitation, Thalweg Principle/Lakes and Rivers *supra*.

See also Internal Waters, Territorial Sea and Baselines – Mouth of Rivers; Equitable Maritime Boundary Delimitation – Thalweg Principle/Lakes and Rivers; Regime of Islands – Islands in Lakes and Rivers; Protection and Preservation of the Marine Environment – Environmental Protection of Lakes and Rivers *supra*.

On 1888 *Costa Rica/Nicaragua* Award of U.S. President Grover Cleveland, see Inter-Oceanic Canals *supra*.

On 1892 Judgment of the French Cour de Cassation, see *North Sea* Separate O. Ammoun, ICJ Rep. 1969, 126 n.1.

On 1902 *France/Venezuela Frederick & Co.* Award [No.260/Stuyt], see *North Sea* Separate O. Ammoun, ICJ Rep. 1969, 142 n.4.

On 1910 *USA/Venezuela Orinoco Steamship Company* Award, see Settlement of Disputes – Interpretation or Application *supra*.

On 1913 *UK/USA The Yukon Lumber* Award [7 AJIL 687, 885 (1913); No.303/Stuyt], see *Eastern Greenland* Pleadings, PCIJ Series C, No.62, 493, 520 [Norway's Counter-Memorial], No.63, 841 [Denmark's Reply]; *Ambatielos* Pleadings, 101 [Greece's Memorial]; *Gulf of Maine* Pleadings, Vol.IV, 105-106 [US Counter-Memorial], Vol.V, 86 n.27 [Canada's Reply], Vol.VI, 374 [Counsel Rashkov, 16 April 1984].

On 1914 *Netherlands/Portugal Island of Timor* Award, see Regime of Islands, Sovereignty Over Island Territory *supra*.

On 1916 CAC *Costa Rica v. Nicaragua* Judgment, see Inter-Oceanic Canals *supra*.

On 1922 *Norway/USA Norwegian Shipowners' Claim* Award, see High Seas *supra*.

On 1926 *UK v. USA Cayuga Indians* Award [RIAA VI, 173, 179-184; 20 AJIL 574 (1926); No.303/Stuyt], see *Barcelona Traction (Second Phase)* Separate O. Sir Gerald Fitzmaurice, ICJ Rep. 1970, 84; *Aegean Sea (Jurisdiction)* Separate O. Lachs, ICJ Rep. 1978, 50; 1997 *Brcko* Award [*supra*], para.88; *Cameroon v. Nigeria* Hearings, CR 98/1, 35 [Counsel Sir Arthur Watts, 2 March 1998]; *Oil Platforms (Merits)* Hearings, CR 2003/11, 40 [Counsel Murphy, 25 Feb 2003] <www.icj-cij.org>.

On 1928 *UK/Turkey W.J. Armstrong & Co. Ltd. v. Vickers Ltd.* Award, see *North Sea* Separate O. Ammoun, ICJ Rep. 1969, 142 n.4.

On 1928 *France v. Mexico Georges Pinson* Award [RIAA V, 327; No.363/Stuyt], see *Denmark v. Norway* Separate O. Weeramantry, ICJ Rep. 1993, 247 n.3; 2006 *Barbados/Trinidad & Tobago* Award, para.291 n.27 <www.pca-cpa.org>.

On 1928 *Portugal v. Germany Naulilaa* Award, see High Seas *supra.*

On 1929 *USA McMahan v. Mexico Rio Grande* Award, see Equitable Maritime Boundary Delimitation *supra.*

On 1934 *New Jersey v. Delaware* Judgment, see Equitable Maritime Boundary Delimitation *supra.*

On 1968 *India/Pakistan Rann of Kutch* Award, see Regime of Islands, Sovereignty Over Island Territory *supra.*

See also Equitable Maritime Boundary Delimitation *supra.*

PRIVILEGES AND IMMUNITIES OF THE UNCLOS INSTITUTIONS AND THEIR RELATIONSHIP WITH THE UNITED NATIONS

CLCS

– 1982 UNCLOS, Part VI, Article 76(8), and Annex II; Legal Opinion of the United Nations Legal Counsel Hans Corell on the Applicability of the Convention on the Privileges and Immunities of the United Nations of 13 Feb 1946 [1 UNTS 15 and 90 UNTS 327] to the Members of the Commission, UN Docs CLCS/5 (1998) and SPLOS/28 (1998); Opinion of UN Legal Counsel Nicolas Michel <http://untreaty.un.org/ola-internet/olahome.html>, Doc. CLCS/46 (2005); UNCLCS Rules of Procedure, UN Docs CLCS/40 (2004) and CLCS/40/Rev.1 (2008); Submissions and Preliminary Information (and related Comments by other states) pursuant to UNCLOS Article 76 <www.un.org/Depts/los/clcs_new/clcs_home.htm>.

See also Continental Shelf – 1982 UNCLOS, Article 76(8) *supra.*

ISBA

– 1982 UNCLOS, Part XI, Articles 176-183, and Annex IV, Article 13; Agreement on Relationship Between the United Nations and the International Seabed Authority, New York, 14 March 1997 [in force: 26 Nov 1997, UNGA Resolution 52/27, 1967 UNTS 256; 36 ILM 1492 (1997)] and Protocol on the Privileges and Immunities of the International Seabed Authority, Kingston, 26 March 1998 [in force: 31 May 2003, 2214 UNTS 133]; Headquarters Agreement Between the International Seabed Authority and the Government of Jamaica, Kingston, 26 August 1999 and Supplementary Agreement, 17 Dec 2003 <www.isa.org.jm/en/documents/basic>.

UN Joint Staff Pension (JSP) Board/ISBA Agreement as to the Conditions Governing the Admission of the ISBA to Membership in the United Nations JSP Fund, New York, 27 May and 17 June 1998 [in force (retroactively): 1 Jan 1998, 2019 UNTS 564]; Special Agreement Extending the Jurisdiction of the Administrative Tribunal of the United Nations to the International Seabed Authority with Respect to Applications by Staff Members of the ISBA Alleging

Non-Observance of the Regulations of the United Nations Joint Staff Pension Fund, New York, 24 June 1998 [in force (retroactively): 1 Jan 1998, 2019 UNTS 572] & New York, 13 March 2003 [2209 UNTS 455]; ISA <www.isa.org.jm/en/documents/basic>.

ITLOS

– 1982 UNCLOS, Annex VI, Article 10; Agreement on the Privileges and Immunities of the International Tribunal for the Law of the Sea, New York, 23 May 1997 [in force: 30 December 2001, 2167 UNTS 294]; pending adoption of Headquarters Agreement Between the International Tribunal for the Law of the Sea and the Federal Republic of Germany on 14 Dec 2004 [in force: 1 May 2007], German Ordinance on the Privileges and Immunities of the ITLOS of 10 Oct 1996 applied, *mutatis mutandis*, the relevant provisions of the UN Convention on the Privileges and Immunities of the Specialized Agencies, New York, 21 Nov 1947 [in force: 16 August 1949, 33 UNTS 261].

Agreement on Cooperation and Relationship Between the United Nations and the International Tribunal for the Law of the Sea, New York, 18 December 1997 [in force: 8 September 1998, UNGA Resolution 52/251]. See *Saint Vincent and the Grenadines v. Guinea Saiga (Merits)* Judgment, para.3, Case No.2, ITLOS Rep. 1999, 10; 38 ILM 1323 (1999); *Panama v. France Camouco (Prompt Release)* Judgment, para.7, Case No.5, ITLOS Rep. 2000, 10; 39 ILM 666 (2000); *Seychelles v. France Monte Confurco (Prompt Release)* Judgment, para.7, Case No.6, ITLOS Rep. 2000, 86; *Belize v. France Grand Prince (Prompt Release)* Judgment, para.5, Case No.8, ITLOS Rep. 2001, 11; *Ireland v. UK Mox Plant (Provisional Measures)* Order, para.10, Case No.10, ITLOS Rep. 2001, 89; 41 ILM 405 (2002); 2002 *Russia v. Australia Volga (Prompt Release)* Judgment, para.5, Case No.11, ITLOS Rep. 2002, 4; 42 ILM 159 (2003); 2003 *Malaysia v. Singapore (Provisional Measures)* Order, para.9, Case No.12, ITLOS Rep. 2003, 9; 2004 *Saint Vincent v. Guinea-Bissau Juno Trader (Prompt Release)* Judgment, para.6, Case No.13; 2007 *Japan v. Russia Hoshinmaru (Prompt Release)* Judgment, Case No.14, para.8 and *Tomimaru (Prompt Release)* Judgment, Case No.15, para.8 <www.itlos.org>.

Special Agreement Extending the Jurisdiction of the Administrative Tribunal of the United Nations to the International Tribunal for the Law of the Sea with Respect to Applications by Staff Members of the ITLOS Alleging Non-Observance of the Regulations of the United Nations Joint Staff Pension Fund, Hamburg, 25 Feb 1998 [in force (retroactively): 1 Jan 1997, 2006 UNTS 494]; ITLOS <www.itlos.org>.

Cf. *Applicability of Article VI, Section 22, of the Convention on the Privileges and Immunities of the United Nations ('Mazilu')* Advisory Opinion, ICJ Rep. 1989, 177; *Legality of the Use by a State of Nuclear Weapons in Armed Conflict* Advisory

Opinion, President M. Bedjaoui concurring, ICJ Rep. 1996, 78-79, para.25; *Difference Relating to Immunity From Legal Process of a Special Rapporteur of the Commission on Human Rights* Advisory Opinion, ICJ Rep. 1999, 62, President S.M. Schwebel concurring, Separate Os Vice-President Weeramantry, 92, Oda, 99, Rezek, 109, Dissent Koroma, 111; UN Docs ECOSOC Resolutions 1999/64 and 2000/208, Letters of the UN Secretary-General to the ECOSOC President, UN Docs E/1999/121 and 1999/124 of 21 Oct and 15 Dec 1999, E/2000/105, 24 July 2000.

SIGNATURE, RATIFICATION AND ACCESSION

1958 TSC, Articles 26-28, 31; 1958 HSC, Articles 31-33, 36; 1958 HSFC, Articles 15-17, 21; 1958 CSC, Articles 8-10, 14; 1958 DSP, Articles V-VI
1982 UNCLOS, Part I, Article 1(2), Part XVII, Articles 305-307, 319, and Annex IX
1994 Agreement, Articles 2-8
1995 SSA, Articles 1(2), 37-39 and 47

Relevant Jurisprudence

UK, Czechoslovak Republic, Denmark, France, Germany, Sweden/Poland Territorial Jurisdiction of the International Commission of the River Oder PCIJ Series A, No.23 (1929) – Judgment, President D. Anzilotti, 5, at 19 *as reaffirmed* by *Croatia v. Serbia (Preliminary Objections)* Dissent Kreca, para.51, ICJ Rep. 2008; *Corfu Channel* Pleadings, Vol.III, 269-271 [Agent Sir Eric Beckett, 11 November 1948]; *Reservations to the Convention on the Prevention and Punishment of the Crime of Genocide* Advisory Opinion, ICJ Rep. 1951, 28-29; *Anglo/Norwegian Fisheries* Pleadings, Vol.I, 395-396 [Norway's Counter-Memorial], Vol.II, 432-439 [UK Reply], Vol.III, 301-302 [Norway's Rejoinder]; *North Sea* ICJ Rep. 1969, 3 – Judgment, 42-43, paras 73-74, 43, para.76, Separate O. Padilla Nervo, 89, 94-95, 99, Separate O. Ammoun, 102-103, 128, 129-130, Dissents Tanaka, 173, 175-176, Morelli, 197, Lachs, 226-229, 232-233, 238, Sorensen, 241, 246; *North Sea* Pleadings, Vol.I, 192 [Denmark's Counter-Memorial], 343 [NL Counter-Memorial], 399-401, 407-410 [FRG Reply], 490-491, 507-508 [Common Rejoinder of Denmark/NL], Vol.II, 100-101, 102, 105 [Counsel Sir Humphrey Waldock, 29 Oct 1968]; *Fisheries Jurisdiction* Pleadings (UK), 468-469 [Counsel Silkin, 25 March 1974], (FRG), 295-296 [Agent Jaenicke, 28 March 1974]; *Tunisia/Libya (Merits)* Dissent Oda, ICJ Rep. 1982, 162, 170-171; *Libya/Malta (Merits)* Judgment, ICJ Rep. 1985, 29-30, Separate O. Vice-President Sette-Camara, 68, Dissent Oda, 140; *Guinea-Bissau v. Senegal (Provisional Measures)* Separate O. Evensen, ICJ Rep. 1990, 72; *Denmark v. Norway* Judgment, ICJ Rep. 1993, 59, Declaration Evensen, 84,

Separate Os Shahabuddeen, 131-132, Ajibola, 288-289; Hearings, CR 93/6, 39-40 [Agent Haug, 18 Jan 1993]; *Qatar v. Bahrain (Merits)* Judgment, President G. Guillaume, ICJ Rep. 2001, 91, para.167, Dissent Torres Bernardez, 266, para.10; *Cameroon v. Nigeria; Equatorial Guinea Intervening (Merits)* Judgment, ICJ Rep. 2002, 423-430, 440, paras 253, 258-264, 285, Separate O. Mbaye, 526-532, paras 110-126, Dissent Ajibola, 590-593, paras 160-168; Hearings, CR 2002/6, 25 [Counsel Tomuschat, 25 Feb 2002]; *Nicaragua v. Honduras (Merits)* Judgment, ICJ Rep. 2007, paras 4, 261; *Romania v. Ukraine* Judgment, ICJ Rep. 2009, paras 3, 31; Hearings, CR 2008/18, 28-29, paras 39-45 [Agent Aurescu, 2 Sep 2008], CR 2008/20, 53-54, paras 73-79 [Counsel Lowe, 4 Sep], CR 2008/29, 19-21, paras 61-69 [Counsel Malintoppi, 12 Sep], CR 2008/30, 16-17, para.19 [Agent Aurescu, 15 Sep], CR 2008/31, 17-18, paras 31-33 [Counsel Lowe, 16 Sep], CR 2008/32, 55-56, paras 33-38 [Malintoppi, 18 Sep 2008]; *Croatia v. Serbia (Preliminary Objections)* Judgment, President Rosalyn Higgins concurring, paras 96-119 and *dispositif* para.146(2), Dissent Kreca, ICJ Rep. 2008 <www.icj-cij.org>.

1977/1978 *Anglo/French Continental Shelf* Decisions and 1985 *Guinea/Guinea-Bissau* Award – see Equitable Maritime Boundary Delimitation *supra*; 1999 *Eritrea/Yemen (Phase II)* Award, President Sir Robert Jennings, para.130 [40 ILM 983 (2001) <www.pca-cpa.org>]; 2000 *Southern Bluefin Tuna (Jurisdiction)* Pleadings and Award, President S.M. Schwebel [39 ILM 1359 (2000) <www.worldbank.org/icsid>]; 2006 *Barbados/Trinidad & Tobago (Jurisdiction and Merits)* Award, President S.M. Schwebel, para.191; Barbados Reply, paras 3, 31 <www.pca-cpa.org>.

For the lists of signatures, ratifications and accessions to the four 1958 Geneva Conventions as at 31 December 2001, see UN Doc. ST/LEG/SER.E/20 (2002).

For the lists of signatures, ratifications and accessions to the 1982 LOSC, the 1994 Agreement and the 1995 SSA, see *id*; and <www.un.org/Depts/los/>.

Unratified Treaties

Corfu Channel Pleadings, Vol.III, 269-271 [Agent Sir Eric Beckett, 11 Nov 1948]; *Reservations to the Convention on the Prevention and Punishment of the Crime of Genocide* Advisory Opinion, ICJ Rep. 1951, 28; *Anglo/Norwegian Fisheries* Pleadings, Vol.I, 395-396 [Norway's Counter-Memorial]; *Ambatielos (Preliminary Objection)* Judgment, ICJ Rep. 1952, 43-44; *Belgium/Netherlands Sovereignty over Certain Frontier Land* Judgment, ICJ Rep. 1959, 229-230; *Gulf of Maine* Judgment, ICJ Rep. 1984, 286-287; Pleadings, Vol.IV, 97-100, 137-140 [US Counter-Memorial], Vol.V, 33, 98-99 [Canada's Reply]; *El Salvador/Honduras; Nicaragua Intervening Gulf of Fonseca (Merits)* Judgment, ICJ Rep. 1992, 514-515, paras 262-263; *Libya/Chad Territorial Dispute* Judgment, President Sir Robert Jennings, ICJ Rep. 1994, 28, para.57; *Qatar v. Bahrain (Merits)* Judgment,

President G. Guillaume, ICJ Rep. 2001, 57, 68, paras 45-47, 88-89, Dissent Torres Bernardez, 348-349, paras 255-257; Hearings, CR 2000/17, 52 [Counsel Bundy, 20 June 2000], quoting 1998 *Eritrea/Yemen (Phase I)* Award, paras 172 and 183; Sir Elihu Lauterpacht, Judge Stephen M. Schwebel, Shabtai Rosenne and Francisco Orrego, *Joint Legal Opinion on Guatemala's Territorial Claim to Belize*, paras 201-207 (January 2002) <www.belize-guatemala.gov.bz/>; eight *Legality of Use of Force (Preliminary Objections)* Separate Os Kreca, para.45 [quoting *Territorial Jurisdiction of the International Commission of the River Oder* Judgment, PCIJ Series A, No.23, p.19 (1929)], ICJ Rep. 2004, Belgium, 402, Canada, 548, France, 693, Germany, 838, Italy, 984, NL, 1133, Portugal, 1280, UK, 1425 and *Bosnia & Herzegovina v. Serbia & Montenegro (Jurisdiction and Merits)* Separate O. Kreca, para.43, ICJ Rep. 2007 <www.icj-cij.org>.

Nicaragua v. Honduras and *Nicaragua v. Colombia* cases, involving until 2001 unratified Colombia/Costa Rica Delimitation and Cooperation Treaty of 17 March 1977 [*The Law of the Sea – Maritime Boundary Agreements 1970-1984* 154 (UN 1987); Charney/ASIL Report No.2-1 (Nweihed)] and Protocol on the Pacific Ocean of 6 April 1984 adopted by an Exchange of Notes of 29 May 2000 [both in force: 20 Feb 2001, *UN LOS Bull.* 81 (2001 No.46)] and Colombia/Honduras Maritime Delimitation (Lopez-Ramirez) Treaty of 2 August 1986, ratified by Colombia and Honduras on 30 Nov and 2 Dec 1999, but claimed by Nicaragua to be invalid [*UN LOS Bull.* 103 (1987 No.10); Charney/ASIL Report No.2-4 (Nweihed)]; *Nicaragua v. Honduras (Merits)* Judgment, ICJ Rep. 2007, paras 18, 59-71, 222-225, 246, 251, 255, 313-317, Dissent Torres Bernardez, paras 63, 154-157, 162; Hearings, CR 2007/1, 29, para.47 [Agent Arguello, 5 March 2007], CR 2007/8, 23, para.26 [Counsel Queneudec, 14 March], CR 2007/10, 32, para.153 [Counsel Colson, 16 March], CR 2007/11, 13, para.9, at 21, para.45 [Arguello, 19 March], 37, para.19 [Counsel Pellet]; *Nicaragua v. Colombia* Colombia's Preliminary Objections, paras 1.5/1.6, 2.61 and Costa Rica's Application to Intervene under Art. 62 of the ICJ Statute of 25 Feb 2010 <www.icj-cij.org> [Equitable Maritime Boundary Delimitation *supra*].

Costa Rica v. Nicaragua San Juan River Hearings, CR 2009/3, 14, para.25 [Counsel Crawford, 3 March 2009]; Costa Rica's Memorial, Annex 15 [Soto-Carazo Treaty of 26 July 1887, ratified by Costa Rica but not by Nicaragua] <www.icj-cij.org>.

1998 *Eritrea/Yemen (Phase I)* Award, President Sir Robert Jennings QC, para.172, 183 [40 ILM 900 (2001]; 2001 *Newfoundland and Labrador/Nova Scotia (Phase I)* Award, paras 3.13/15 and 6.3 <www.gov.ns.ca/petro/documents/TribunalAwardPhaseI.pdf> and 2002 *(Phase II)* Award, para.3.3 <www.gov.ns.ca/>; 2003 OSPAR *Mox Plant* Dissent Griffith, paras 15-16 <www.pca-cpa.org>; 2007 *Guyana/Suriname* Award, para.312 <www.pca-cpa.org>.

Cf. unsigned Slovenia/Croatia Maritime Delimitation (Bay of Piran) Treaty of 25 June 2001, as referred to in, e.g., Slovenia's Note Verbale of 30 August 2004 with Map, *UN LOS Bull.* 139 (2005 No.56); 2005 Croatia's Note Verbale, *id.* 125 (2005 No.57); Slovenia's White Paper on Border with Croatia of 19 June 2006 <www.csees.net/?page=news&news_id=53452&country_id=7 & www.mzz.gov.si/fileadmin/pageuploads/Novinarsko_sredisce/Sporocila_za_javnost/AIDE_MEMOIRE-ang.pdf>; Equitable Maritime Boundary Delimitation – *Croatia/Slovenia Land and Maritime Boundary Delimitation*, Arbitration Agreement of 4 Nov 2009 *supra.*

Provisional Application

2005 *Belgium/Netherlands Iron Rhine* Award, President R. Higgins, paras 1 and 12, noting the Award's delivery (on 24 May 2005) during provisional application of the Arbitration Agreement (until its entry into force on 1 July 2005), even though by the time of the Award's delivery, the necessary ratification procedures in each country and the mutual notification thereof had already been completed <www.pca-cpa.org>.

2007 ICSID *Ioannis Kardassopoulos v. Georgia (Jurisdiction)* Award, President L. Yves Fortier CC QC, Arbitrators Sir Arthur Watts KCMG QC and Francisco Orrego Vicuna, upholding unanimously Jurisdiction *Ratione Temporis* under the ECT Article 45 <www.investmentclaims.com/decisions/Kardassopoulos-Georgia-Jurisdiction.pdf> and ITN of 10 August 2007, pp.3-7 at <www.iisd.org/pdf/2007/itn_aug10_2007.pdf>; and other websites listed under *Yukos and GML et al. v. Russia* Arbitration *supra.*

UNCITRAL *Yukos and GML (previously Menatep) et al. v. Russian Federation* Arbitration, President L. Yves Fortier QC, Arbitrators Stephen M. Schwebel and Francois Poncet (replacing as of 1 July 2007 Daniel M. Price), instituted under the European Energy Charter Treaty (ECT), Article 45 and Protocol on Energy Efficiency and Related Environmental Aspects of 17 Dec 1994 [in force: 16 April 1998, in 34 ILM 360 (1995); Charter, in 2080 UNTS 95; Protocol, in 2081 UNTS 3; <www.encharter.org/index.jsp>], which Russia did not ratify; 26 July 2005 <www.akm.ru/eng/news/2005/july/26/ns1510838.htm & www.supportmbk.com/update/7_28_2005_briefing.cfm>; 5 Sep 2006 <www.timesonline.co.uk/article/0,,29390-2342684,00.html>; 8 Nov 2006 <www.timesonline.co.uk/article/0,,5-2442854,00.html>; BIICL Investment Treaty Forum's Seminar on Russia and the Energy Charter, London, 24 Jan 2007 <www.biicl.org/events/view/-id/126 & www.biicl.org/itf> & p.9 at <www.iisd.org/pdf/2006/itn_nov2_2006.pdf>; ICSID/SCC Conference on the Energy Charter Treaty, Washington D.C., 18 May 2007 <www.worldbank.org/icsid/highlights/conf-flyer.pdf & www.encharter.org/index.php?id=221>; 4 Jan 2008 <www.telegraph.co.uk/news/main.jhtml?xml=news/2008/01/03/nlaw103.xml>; UNCITRAL *Yukos and GML et al. v.*

Russian Federation Hearings, PCA, The Hague, 17-30 Nov 2008 <www.pca-cpa.org & www.globalarbitrationreview.com/news/article/14948/>; ECT Dispute Resolution Conference in Brussels, 22-23 Oct 2009 <www.biicl.org/events/view/-id/403>; *Yukos and GML et al. v. Russian Federation (Jurisdiction)* Awards of 30 Nov 2009 <www.globalarbitrationreview.com/news/article/19521/tribunal-says-yukos-case-proceed-/ & www.globalarbitrationreview.com/news/article/19544/yukos-result-positive-energy-investors-/>, <www.kyivpost.com/news/business/bus_general/detail/54071 & www.nytimes.com/2009/12/02/business/global/02yukos.html> and <http://en.rian.ru/business/20091201/157051114.html, www.ft.com/cms/s/0/256d0276-de0e-11de-b8e2-00144feabdc0.html & www.guardian.co.uk/business/2009/nov/30/yukos-shareholders-russian-government-oil>; updated list of 3 Yukos cases <www.encharter.org/index.php?id=213>; ICSID <http://icsid.worldbank/ICSID/index.jsp & www.investmentclaims.com>; LCIA <www.lcia-arbitration.com>; World's Top 10 Arbitrators <www.americanlawyer.com/focuseurope/scorecard0605.html>; TDM <www.transnational-dispute-management.com/>; Investment Treaty Forum (ITF) <www.biicl.org/itf>; ECT Disputes <www.encharter.org/index.php?id=213>; Top 50 Treaty Disputes of 13 June 2007 <www.law.com/jsp/article.jsp?id=1181639136817> and Top 50 Treaty Disputes of 15 July 2009 <www.law.com/jsp/tal/PubArticleTAL.jsp?id=1202431684674&slreturn=1&hbxlogin=1; ITN <www.iisd.org/investment/itn>; Arbitration Data Base <www.arbitration.fr/5.html>.

On provisional application of the Russia/USA Bering Sea and Arctic Maritime Boundary Agreement of 1 June 1990 [29 ILM 941 (1990); 2009 U.S. Presidential Arctic Directive, See III D <www.whitehouse.gov/>], see each of the three *Yukos and GML et al. v. Russian Federation (Jurisdiction)* Awards of 30 Nov 2009, para. 184 [Respondent's Witness M. Nordquist] and para. 202 [Claimant's Witness v. Gladyshev] <www.encharter.org/index.php?id=213> *supra.*

See also 1994 UN Part XI Agreement, Article 7 [in force: 28 July 1996, 1936 UNTS 3; 33 ILM 1309 (1994); <www.un.org/Depts/los>]; Final Act of 1991 Protocol on Environmental Protection to the 1959 Antarctic Treaty [in force: 14 Jan 1998, 402 UNTS 71; 30 ILM 1455 (1991)] listed in Protection and Preservation of the Marine Environment *supra.*

RESERVATIONS AND DECLARATIONS

1958 HSFC, Article 19; 1958 CSC, Article 12
1982 UNCLOS, Part XVII, Articles 309-310, and Annex IX
1994 Agreement, Article 2(2)
1995 SSA, Articles 42-43 and 47

Reservations to the Convention on the Prevention and Punishment of the Crime of Genocide Advisory Opinion, ICJ Rep. 1951, 15; *Anglo/Norwegian Fisheries*

Judgment, ICJ Reports 1951, 139; *Ambatielos (Preliminary Objection)* Judgment, ICJ Rep. 1952, 43-44; *North Sea* Judgment, ICJ Reports 1969, 26-27, paras 29-33, and 38-40, paras 63-66, 41, para.67, 42, para.72, as relied upon by *Yugoslavia v. USA Legality of Use of Force (Provisional Measures)* Dissent Kreca, ICJ Rep. 1999, 965, para.10; *North Sea* Separate O. President Bustamante y Rivero, ICJ Rep. 1969, 57, Separate Os Padilla Nervo, 87, 88-89, 92, 94, 95, 97-98, Ammoun, 114, 130, Dissent Vice-President Koretsky, 163, Dissents Tanaka, 182, Morelli, 198, Lachs, 223-225, Sorensen, 248, 252-253; *North Sea* Pleadings, Vol.I, 56-58 [FRG Memorial], 187, 190-191 [Denmark's Counter-Memorial], 312-313, 339-340, 343-345 [NL Counter-Memorial], 401, 409-413 [FRG Reply], 513-517 [Common Rejoinder of Denmark/NL], Vol.II, 17-20, 25 [Agent Jaenicke, 23 Oct 1968], 87-88, 106-109 [Sir Humphrey Waldock, 28 and 29 Oct], 175, 206 [Jaenicke, 4 and 5 Nov], 243 [Reply by Waldock to Questions Fitzmaurice, 8 Nov 1968]; *Aegean Sea (Jurisdiction)* Judgment, ICJ Rep. 1978, 23, para.55, 33, para.80, Dissents de Castro, 68-71, Stassinopoulos, 74-81; Pleadings, 238-259 [Greece's Memorial (Jurisd.)], 341-346 [Counsel O'Connell, 10 Oct 1978], 381-425 [Counsel Weil, 12 and 13 Oct 1978], 426-439 [Counsel Economides]; *Gulf of Maine* Judgment, ICJ Rep. 1984, 279-281, 301, Dissent Gros, 375; Pleadings, Vol.V, 398 [US Reply]; *Libya/Malta* Pleadings, Vol.I, 450-451 [Malta's Memorial]; *Nicaragua v. USA (Jurisdiction and Admissibility)* Dissent Schwebel, ICJ Rep. 1984, 603-616 and *(Merits)* Dissent Schwebel, ICJ Rep. 1986, 296-306, paras 78-99; *Nicaragua v. Honduras (Jurisdiction)* Judgment, ICJ Rep. 1988, 69, para.39; *Yugoslavia v. USA* (paras 21-25) and *Yugoslavia v. Spain* (paras 29-33) *Legality of Use of Force (Provisional Measures)* Orders, ICJ Rep. 1999, 772, 923-924; *Cameroon v. Nigeria; Equatorial Guinea Intervening* Judgment, ICJ Rep. 2002, 426, para.253; *Yugoslavia v. Bosnia and Herzegovina (Revision)* Judgment, ICJ Rep. 2003, 7, paras 52-53, 57, 62; *DR Congo v. Rwanda New Application (Provisional Measures)* Order, ICJ Rep. 2002, 219, paras 22, 39-41, 69-72 and *(Jurisdiction)* Judgment, ICJ Rep. 2006, paras 45-79, Joint Separate O. Higgins, Kooymans, Elaraby, Owada and Simma; *Nicaragua v. Colombia* Nicaragua's Memorial, 151-153, 175-178, concerning Protocol (Esguerra-Irias) of Exchange of Ratifications of 5 May 1930 to Colombia/ Nicaragua Territorial Questions (Barcenas-Esguerra) Treaty of 24 May 1928 [16 LNTS 340] and *Nicaragua v. Colombia (Preliminary Objections)* Judgment, ICJ Rep. 2007, paras 18-20, 28, 63-64, 69-72, 75-81, 117 and Declaration Tomka, paras 6-13; *Romania v. Ukraine* Judgment, ICJ Rep. 2009, paras 35, 39, 42; Hearings, CR 2008/18, 28-29, paras 39-45 [Agent Aurescu, 2 Sep 2008], CR 2008/20, 53-54, paras 73-79 [Counsel Lowe, 4 Sep], CR 2008/29, 19-21, paras 61-69 [Counsel Malintoppi, 12 Sep], CR 2008/30, 16-17, para.19 [Agent Aurescu, 15 Sep], CR 2008/31, 17-18, paras 31-33 [Counsel Lowe, 16 Sep], CR 2008/32, 55-56, paras 33-38 [Malintoppi, 18 Sep 2008] <www.icj-cij.org>.

1977/1978 Anglo/French Continental Shelf Decisions – see Equitable Maritime Boundary Delimitation *supra*; *M/V Saiga* Separate O. Vukas [38 ILM 1323 (1999)], para.18; 2000 *Southern Bluefin Tuna (Jurisdiction)*, President S.M. Schwebel, A/NZ Reply, para.144 <www.worldbank.org/icsid>; *Malaysia v. Singapore (Provisional Measures)* Hearings, ITLOS/PV.03/05, 24 [Counsel Sir Elihu Lauterpacht, 27 Sep 2003] <www.itlos.org>.

For reservations and declarations concerning the four 1958 Geneva Conventions as at 31 December 2001, see UN Doc. ST/LEG/SER.E/20 (2002).

For declarations and statements concerning the 1982 UNCLOS, the 1994 Agreement and the 1995 SSA, see *id*; and <www.un.org/Depts/los/>.

On declarations made under the 1982 UNCLOS, see *Oceans and the Law of the Sea – Reports of the United Nations Secretary-General*, UN Docs A/54/429, para.16 (1999), A/56/58, para.23 (2001), A/57/57, para.22 (2002), A/59/62 (2004), para.12, A/60/63 (2005), paras 3-4, A/61/63 (2006), para.3 and A/61/63/Add.1 (2006), paras 3-5, A/62/66 (2007), paras 4-7, A/62/66 (2007), paras 7-9 and A/62/66/Add.1 (2007), paras 5-8, A/64/66, paras 6-9 (2009) <www.un.org/Depts/los>.

AMENDMENT AND REVISION

1958 TSC, Articles 30 and 31(c); 1958 HSC, Articles 35 and 36(c); 1958 HSFC, Articles 20 and 21(c); 1958 HSC, Articles 13 and 14(c)
1982 UNCLOS, Part XVII, Articles 312-316 and 319; 1994 Agreement, S 4
1995 SSA, Article 45

North Sea Judgment, ICJ Rep. 1969, 42, para.72, Separate O. Padilla Nervo, 87; Pleadings, Vol.II, 198 [Counsel Shigeru Oda, 5 Nov 1968].

2000 *Southern Bluefin Tuna (Jurisdiction)*, President S.M. Schwebel, A/NZ Reply, para.144 <www.worldbank.org/icsid>.

PARTICIPATION BY INTERNATIONAL ORGANIZATIONS

1982 UNCLOS, Part I, Article 1(2), Part XVII, Articles 305(1)(f), 306-307 and Annex IX
1994 Agreement, Articles 3-5, 7 and 8(2)
1995 SSA, Article 47

North Sea Pleadings, Vol.II, 269 [Sir Humphrey Waldock, 11 Nov 1968]; *Nuclear Tests* Dissent Gros, ICJ Rep. 1974, 284; *Spain v Canada Fisheries (Jurisdiction)* Judgment, ICJ Rep. 1998, 447, paras 25, 27, Dissent Vereshchetin, 573, para.7; Oral Hearings, CR 98/9 [transl.], 8, 13 [Agent Pastor Ridruejo, 9 June 1998], 24 [Counsel Rodriguez], 35-43 [Counsel Brotons], CR 98/12 [trans.], 44-53 [Counsel Weil, 12 June], CR 98/13, 11-12 [Pastor Ridruejo, 15 June 1998], 25-28 [Brotons] <www.icj-cij.org>.

The Queen v. The Secretary of State for Trade and Industry, Ex Parte Greenpeace Ltd. Judgment, Justice Maurice Kay, Case No. CO/1336/1999 [120 ILR 617]; 2000

Southern Bluefin Tuna (Jurisdiction) Japan's Memorial, para.90 <www.worldbank.org/icsid>; Annex VII *Mox Plant (Jurisdiction)* Oral Hearings, 3-32 [Counsel Plender, 12 June 2003], 32-61 [Counsel Bethlehem], 9-10 [Bethlehem, 13 June 2003], 10-11 [Agent Wood], 11-14 [President Mensah's Statement] <www.pca-cpa.org>.

On French nuclear tests carried in Algeria in 1960/63 in compliance with the 1957 EURATOM Treaty, see Peaceful Uses of the Sea – Nuclear Weapon Tests *supra*. On the EURATOM Treaty, see also Protection and Preservation of the Marine Environment *supra*.

On Directive 80/836/EURATOM, as amended by Directive 84/467/EURATOM, on Directive 96/29/EURATOM, on Council Directive 85/337/EEC as amended by Directive 97/11/EEC, on the 1997 EIA Mox Plant Opinion of the EC Commission, and on Council Directive 90/313/EEC as amended by Directive 2003/4/EC and on the related case law, see Protection and Preservation of the Marine Environment – EIA/Notification/Consultation *supra*.

See also *Nuclear Weapons (UNGA)* Dissent Oda, ICJ Rep. 1996, 338, 339.

On Protocol 6 (Article 2) to EC/Iceland Free Trade Agreement of 22 July 1972 [in force: 1 April 1973], see *Fisheries Jurisdiction (Merits)* Dissents Gros, ICJ Rep. 1974, 139-140, 141, 142, 235-236; Pleadings (FRG), 474 [Question Judge Gros, 25 March 1974], (UK), 505-506 [Reply Counsel Slynn, 29 March 1974]; (FRG), 350, 352-353 [Question Gros, 28 March, and Reply Agent Jaenicke, 2 April 1974].

After previous repeated suspension of the application of Protocol 6 to Icelandic fish products, the Community ultimately allowed, under the EC Council Regulation No.76 of June 1976 amending Protocol 6, customs duties on imports of fish from Iceland to be reduced [OJEC L 217/1 (1976)], as followed by the EC Council's Hague Resolution on 200-mile EFZs [15 ILM 1425 (1976); OJEC C 105/1 (1981)].

On EC/Norway Agreement of 14 May 1973 [in force: 1 July], see *Fisheries Jurisdiction (Merits)* Dissent Gros, 140, 141-142.

On the EC Common Fisheries Policy in 1977/1983, see *Aegean Sea* Pleadings, 338 [Counsel O'Connell, 10 Oct 1978]; *Tunisia/Libya* Pleadings, Vol.II, 203 [Libya's Counter-Memorial]; *Gulf of Maine* Pleadings, Vol.VII, 260-262 [Counsel Colson, 11 May 1984]; *Denmark v. Norway* Hearings, CR 93/2, 45-51 [Counsel Trolle, 12 Jan 1993]; *Spain v. Canada* Pleadings, 60-63 [Spain's Memorial].

On EC/Denmark(Greenland) Fisheries Agreement of 29 Jan 1985 [signed on 13 March 1984, OJEC L 29/8 (1985); Council Regulation No.3926, OJEC L 397/65 (1992), No.3363, OJEC L 363 (1994)] and Protocol of 30 June 1989 [1 January 1990/31 December 1994, OJEC L 389/80 (1989) and L 252/2 (1990)], see *Denmark v. Norway* Judgment, ICJ Rep. 1993, 71, Dissent Fischer, 311;

Denmark's Memorial, paras 139-145, 176-177, 308, Denmark's Reply, paras 118-130, 305-306; Hearings, CR 93/2, 29-31 [Counsel Lynge, 12 Jan 1993], 46-49, 54-55 [Counsel Trolle], CR 93/5, 65 [Agent Tresselt, 15 Jan 1993].

On EC/Morocco Fisheries Agreements of 25 February 1988 [OJEC L 72/50 99/45, 181/1, 301/67 (1988); L 208/39, 333/66 (1990)] and 30 March 1992 [OJEC L 21, 91, 218, 407/1 (1992)], see *East Timor* Oral Hearings, CR 95/4 [trans.], 64-65 [Co-Agent Teles, 1 Feb 1995], CR 95/9, 82-87 [Co-Agent Burmester, 8 Feb], CR 95/10, 8-11 [9 Feb], CR 95/12, 77-82 [Co-Agent Correia, 13 Feb], CR 95/14, 63-67, 69 [Counsel Crawford, 16 Feb 1995]; 24 June 2004 <www .arabicnews.com/ansub/Daily/Day/040624/2004062419.htm>.

Cf. Morocco, Spain and Fishing <www.american.edu/TED/ice/morspain.htm>; Equitable Maritime Boundary Delimitation – 1975 *Western Sahara* Advisory Opinion *supra*; Morocco/EU-France, Spain, Portugal Fisheries Agreement of 18 Dec 2004 <www.arabicnews.com/ansub/Daily/Day/041218/2004121826.html>; 15 Jan 2005 <www.arabicnews.com/ansub/Daily/Day/050115/2005011522.html>; EC/Morocco Fisheries Partnership Agreement of 9 May 2006 and Protocol of 29 May 2006, OJEC L 141/4 & 9 (2006); 16 May 2006 <www.arso.org/ UEpescero160506.htm & www.fishelsewhere.org/home_e.html>.

On EC/USA Fisheries Agreements of 1977, 1984, 1989 and 1991 [1087 UNTS No.16649, 2021 UNTS No.34822, 2024 UNTS No.16649, 2194 UNTS 475; OJEC L 141/2 (1977), L 272/1 (1984) and L 63/22 (1989); 2232 UNTS 378], see *Southern Bluefin Tuna (Jurisdiction)* Hearings, Vol.I [Counsel Sir Elihu Lauterpacht, 7 May 2000], Vol.III [Question 9 of Arbitrators, 10 May], Vol.IV [Question 10 of Sir Kenneth Keith, 11 May], Written Replies of the Parties to Questions 9-10 of Arbitrators [26 May 2000] <www.worldbank.org/icsid>.

On EC/Canada Fisheries Agreement of 20 April 1995 [OJEC L 327/20 (1995)], see *Spain v. Canada (Jurisdiction)* Judgment, ICJ Rep. 1998, 437, para.12, at 444-447, paras 21-22, 25-27, at 468, para.88, Separate O. Oda, 484, para.18, Dissent Torres Bernardez, 589, 594, paras 19, 35; Pleadings, 63-67, 130-136 [Spain's Memorial], 215 n.10, 222 n.34, 266, 291-296 [Canada's Counter-Memorial], Hearings, CR 98/9 [trans.], 13 [Agent Pastor Ridruejo, 9 June 1998], 35-41, 47-48 [Counsel Brotons], CR 98/12 [trans.], 46-47, 50-53 [Counsel Weil, 12 June], CR 98/13, 11-12 [Pastor Ridruejo, 15 June 1998].

On EC protest against the *Estai*'s arrest, see Judgment, ICJ Rep. 1998, 444, para.20, Dissents Weeramantry, para.40, Torres Bernardez, paras 33-35, 42; Pleadings, 32-40 [Spain's Memorial], Hearings, CR 98/9 [trans.], 23 [Counsel Rodriguez, 9 June 1998], CR 98/12 [trans.], 48-49 [Counsel Weil, 12 June 1998] <www.icj-cij.org>.

On EC Council Regulation No.3760 on a Community System for Fisheries and Aquaculture of 20 Dec 1992 [OJEC L 389/1 (1992); as Amended by No.1181, in OJEC L 164/1 (1998)] and Regulation No.894 Laying Down Certain Technical Measures for the Conservation of Fisheries Resources of 29 April 1997 [OJEC

L 132/1 (1997); as superseded by EC Council Regulations Nos 2341 and 2371 of 20 Dec 2002 [OJEC L 356/12 and L 358/59 (2002)], see *Spain v. Canada (Jurisdiction)* Judgment, ICJ Rep. 1998, 461, para.70; Pleadings, 60 n.58 [Spain's Memorial], 295 n.302; 2001 *Ireland v. UK Mox Plant (Provisional Measures)* Separate O. Anderson, para.3; Ireland's Request & Statement, para.5 <www.itlos. org>; 2005 EU Fishing Quotas of 22 Dec 2004 <http://news.bbc.co.uk/1/hi/world/ europe/4116887.stm>; 2006 ECJ *EC v. Ireland Mox Plant* Judgment, paras 8, 122-125, 154-155, 177 <http://curia.europa.eu/jurisp/cgi-bin/form.pl?lang=EN& Submit=rechercher&numaff=C-459/03>; 2009 EU Fishing Quotas of 19 Dec 2008 <http://news.bbc.co.uk/2/hi/europe/7792088.stm>; Common Fisheries Policy <http://europa.eu.int/comm/fisheries/policy_en.htm & http://europa.eu/pol/fish/ index_en.htm>.

On EC position on armed incidents in the Bakassi Peninsula, see *Cameroon v. Nigeria (Provisional Measures)* Separate O. Ajibola, ICJ Rep. 1996, 39, 43; Oral Hearings, CR 96/2, 54 [Counsel Pellet, 5 March 1996].

On the 1992 Maastricht Treaty, as amended by the 1997 Amsterdam Treaty, as amended by 2007 Treaty of Lisbon, see Protection and Preservation of the Marine Environment *supra*.

On Article 177 (preliminary ruling), presently Article 234, of the EC Treaty, see *Oil Platforms (Preliminary Objection)* Separate O. Rigaux, ICJ Rep. 1996, 871-872. On the practice on "the margin of appreciation" of the Court of Justice of the European Communities, see *Oil Platforms (Merits)* Hearings, CR 2003/12, 31 [Counsel Weil, 26 Feb 2003], CR 2003/16, 16 [Counsel Crawford, 3 March 2003] <www.icj-cij.org>; 2005 *Belgium/Netherlands Iron Rhine* Award, President R. Higgins, paras 101-105, 119-120, 137, 206 <www.pca-cpa.org> & <www.asil .org/ilib050614.htm>. See also preliminary ruling rendered by means of ECJ Grand Chamber *International Association of Independent Tank Owners (Intertanko) v. Secretary of State for Transport*, Case C-308/06 of 3 June 2008 <http://eur-lex .europa.eu>; 103 AJIL 555 (2009).

On EC mediation with respect to the Gabcikovo-Nagymaros Project, see *Gabcikovo* Judgment, ICJ Rep. 1997, 27, 48-50, 73, 79, Dissents Herczegh, 184, Vereshchetin, 222; Hearings, CR 97/2, 38-39 [Agent Szenasi, 3 March 1997], CR 97/5 [trans.], 9-10 [Counsel Kiss, 6 March], CR 97/6, 27 [Counsel Sands, 7 March], CR 97/6, 62 [Counsel Dupuy], CR 97/7 [trans.], 33 [Co-Agent Mikulka, 24 March], CR 97/7, 55 [Counsel McCaffrey], CR 97/10, 41-51 [Counsel Refsgaard, 26 March], 51-56 [Counsel Watts], CR 97/11, 10, 21-22 [27 March 1997], 25-26 [Mikulka] <www.icj-cij.org>. For London Agreement of 28 October 1992, see 32 ILM 1291 (1993).

On EC Council Habitats Directive 92/43/EEC, see Protection and Preservation of the Marine Environment – Environmental Impact Assessment/Notification/ Consultation *supra*.

On 1994 European Energy Charter Treaty (ECT), see Signature, Ratification and Accession – Provisional Application, UNCITRAL *Yukos, GML (previously Menatep) et al. v. Russian Federation* and ICSID *Ioannis Kardassopoulos v. Georgia* Arbitrations *supra.*

On 1999 *Macklenburg v. Kreis Pinneberg der Landrat* Judgment (ECJ), see Protection and Preservation of the Marine Environment – EIA/Notification/ Consultation *supra.*

On EU 1999 International Pollution Prevention and Control (IPPC), see *Argentina v. Uruguay Pulp Mills on the River Uruguay (Provisional Measures)* Order, paras 45, 56, ICJ Rep. 2006 <www.icj-cij.org>.

On *EC/Chile Swordfish,* suspended ITLOS Case No.7, President Rao, 40 ILM 475 (2001); ITLOS Rep. 2003, 69; WTO Panel, WT/DS193/3 and Add.1 (2001) <www.europa.eu.int/comm/trade/miti/dispute/swordfish.htm> and 2008 ITLOS Order (further suspending proceedings until 1 Jan 2010); *EC/Chine (Discontinuance)* Order of 17 Dec 2009 <www.itlos.org> – see Fisheries *supra.*

On EU policy on arrest warrants, see *Congo v. Belgium Arrest Warrant of 11 April 2000* Joint Separate O. Higgins, Kooymans, Buergenthal, ICJ Rep. 2002, 76-77, para.47, Dissent van den Wyngaert, 150-151, 180-181, paras 22, 78 <www .icj-cij.org>.

On EU policy on Eritrea/Ethiopia Peace Process, see Equitable Maritime Boundary Delimitation – 2002 *Eritrea/Ethiopia Delimitation of the Border* Decision *supra.*

On EU policy on the former Yugoslavia (SFRY and FRY), see *Yugoslavia v. Bosnia and Herzegovina (Revision)* Dissent Dimitrijevic, paras 25-32, ICJ Rep. 2003, 59-61. On EU policy on legality of Kosovo's Declaration of Independence of 17 Feb 2008, 47 ILM 461 (2008), see *Kosovo* Advisory Opinion, ICJ Rep. 2010; Hearings, CR 2009/32, 37-46 [UK Agent Bethlehem, 10 Dec 2009], 46-55 [UK Counsel Crawford] <www.icj-cij.org>.

On EU policy on international trade in crude oil and refined oil products, see *Oil Platforms (Merits)* Judgment, ICJ Rep. 2003, 205-207, 215-217, paras 93-97, 120, Separate O. Simma, 339-342, paras 29-34; Hearings, CR 2003/11, 47, 52 [Counsel Murphy, 25 Feb 2003], CR 2003/13, 49 [Agent Taft, 26 Feb], CR 2003/17, 37-38 [Murphy, 5 March 2003] <www.icj-cij.org>.

On EU transport policy, see *Great Belt* Pleadings, 446-449, 578-579 [Denmark's Counter-Memorial]. On EU Trans-European Networks (TEN), see 2005 *Belgium/Netherlands Iron Rhine* Award, paras 106-120, 137 <www.pca-cpa.org/. On *Channel Tunnel Group Ltd & France-Manche S.A./United Kingdom/France Eurotunnel* Partial Award <www.pca-cpa.org>, see Straits Used for International Navigation – Relevant Jurisprudence *supra.*

On EU-ACP (African, Caribbean and Pacific) States Partnership Agreement, Cotonou, 23 June 2000 [*ACP-EU Courier, Special Issue,* Sep 2000 <www.acpsec

.org/en/treaties.htm>; the Cotonou Agreement superseded the Fourth EC-ACP States Convention, Lomé, 15 Dec 1989, 29 ILM 783 1990), as amended by Mauritius Agreement of 4 Nov 1995, *ACP-EU Courier* No.155, Jan 1996], see *Congo v. France Certain Criminal Proceedings in France (Provisional Measures)* Hearings, CR 2003/20, 11 [Agent Obia, 28 April], CR 2003/22, 21-22 [29 April 2003] <www.icj-cij.org>.

On EC *Croatia/Slovenia Land and Maritime Boundary Delimitation*, see Equitable Maritime Boundary Delimitation *supra*

See also Communication from the Commission on an Integrated Framework for Fisheries Partnership Agreements with Third Countries, Brussels, 23 Dec 2002, COM (2002)637 Final; Equitable Maritime Boundary Delimitation – 2002 UN *Eritrea/Ethiopia Delimitation of the Border* Decision [2003 ACP-EU Joint Parliamentary Assembly Resolution and EU CFSP Declarations on Ethiopia and Eritrea] *supra*; Financing of the ACP-EU Cotonou Partnership Agreement in 2008/2013 of 7 June 2006 <www.consilium.europa.eu/ueDocs/cms_Data/docs/pressData/en/er/89928.pdf>.

For Declaration made by the European Community upon its signature of the 1982 UNCLOS on 7 Dec 1984, see *UN LOS Bull.* 16 (1985 No.4), and for Declaration made upon its formal confirmation of the 1982 UNCLOS and the 1994 Agreement on 1 April 1998, see *id.* 7 (1998 No.37) <www.un.org/Depts/los/> and Council Decision 98/392/EC of 23 March 1998, OJEC L 179/1 (1998). For Declaration made by the European Community upon its signature of the 1995 SSA on 27 June 1996, see *id.* 26 (1996 No.32).

Cf. *Spain v. Canada (Jurisdiction)* Dissent Bernardez, ICJ Rep. 1998, 728, para.409; 2001 *Ireland v. UK Mox Plant (Provisional Measures)* UK Response, paras 168-170 and Annex 18; Hearings, ITLOS/PV.01/08, 23-24 [Counsel Plender, 20 Nov 2001], ITLOS/PV.01/09, 15 [Counsel Lowe] <www.itlos.org>; Annex VII *Mox Plant* UK Counter-Memorial, 101-102, UK Rejoinder, 49-62; Hearings, 3-32 [Counsel Plender, 12 June 2003], 11-14 [President Mensah's Statement, 13 June]; and on EC Commission's Parliamentary Answer to Question H-0256/03 of 15 May 2003, see *id.*, 4 [Plender, 12 June 2003] <www.pca-cpa.org>; *Nicaragua v. Honduras (Merits)* Judgment, ICJ Rep. 2007, para.4 <www.icj-cij.org>; *Romania v. Ukraine* Judgment, ICJ Rep. 2009, para.3 <www.icj-cij.org>; ECJ Grand Chamber *International Association of Independent Tank Owners (Intertanko) v. Secretary of State for Transport*, Case C-308/06 of 3 June 2008 <http://eur-lex.europa.eu>; 103 AJIL 555 (2009).

On Parliamentary Answer on Sellafield Nuclear Plant of the European Commission of 15 May 2003 and *European Commission v. Ireland Mox Plant* Case C-459/03, OJEC C 7/24 (2004) and ECJ Judgment of 30 May 2006 – see Protection and Preservation of the Marine Environment – Annex VII *Ireland v. UK Mox Plant* Arbitration *supra*.

EC Commission Green Paper: Towards a Future EU Maritime Policy, COM (2006)275Final, Vol.II – Annex <http://ec.europa.eu/maritimeaffairs/policy_en.html & http://eur-lex.europa.eu/LexUriServ/site/en/com/2006/com2006_0275Ben01.pdf>; The EU Integrated Maritime Policy – Priorities for the Next Commission of 15 Oct 2009 <http://ec.europa.eu/maritimeaffairs/press/press_rel151009_en.html & http://ec.europa.eu/maritimeaffairs/whatsnew_en.html>.

RELATION TO OTHER CONVENTIONS

1958 TSC, Article 25; 1958 HSC, Article 30
1982 UNCLOS, Part XII, Article 237, Part XV, Article 293, Part XVII, Articles 311 and 319(2)(c)
1995 SSA, Article 44

Gulf of Maine Pleadings, Vol.VII, 189 [Counsel Stevenson, 9 May 1984]; *Great Belt* Pleadings, 152 [Counsel de Arechaga, 2 July 1991], 324 [Finland's Memorial], 624 [Denmark's Counter-Memorial]; *Denmark v. Norway* Separate O. Shahabuddeen, ICJ Rep. 1993, 132; Norway's Counter-Memorial, para.314; Hearings, CR 93/6, 48-49 [Agent Haug, 18 Jan 1993]; *Romania v. Ukraine* Judgment, ICJ Rep. 2009, para.71; Hearings, CR 2008/28, 11, para.7 [Counsel Sir Michael Wood, 11 Sep 2008] <www.icj-cij.org>.

1986 *Canada/France* Award, para.51 [see Fisheries *supra*]; 2000 *Australia and New Zealand v. Japan Southern Bluefin Tuna (Jurisdiction)* Arbitral Tribunal: President Stephen M. Schwebel (USA/ICJ), Chusei Yamada (Japan), Sir Kenneth Keith (New Zealand), Florentino P. Feliciano (Philippines), Per Tresselt (Norway) – Award, 39 ILM 1359 (2000), paras 27-34, 38, 41, 47-52, 54; Japan's Memorial, paras 116-131, A/NZ Reply, paras 39-53, 106, 143-148, 152-163, Hearings, Vol.I [Sir Elihu Lauterpacht, 7 May 2000], Vol.II [Counsels Crawford, Irwin, 8 May], Vol.III [Questions of Arbitrators, Lauterpacht, 10 May], Vol.IV [Counsel Mansfield, 11 May]; Written Answers of the Parties to Questions of Arbitrators [26 May 2000] <www.worldbank.org/icsid>; 2001 *Ireland v. UK Mox Plant (Provisional Measures)* Separate Os Vice-President Nelson, paras 5-7, Treves, para.4; Ireland's Request & Statement, para.138, UK Response, para.136; Hearings, ITLOS/PV.01/07, 10-14 [Counsel Lowe, 19 Nov 2001], ITLOS/PV.01/08, 21-22 [Counsel Plender, 20 Nov 2001]; 2002 *Russia v. Australia Volga (Prompt Release)* Declaration Vice-President Vukas, para.9 <www.itlos.org>; *Guyana/Suriname* Suriname's Counter-Memorial, para.2.17, Guyana's Reply, para.7.9 <www.pca-cpa.org>.

Cf. Settlement of Disputes – 1982 UNCLOS, Article 281 and Article 282 *supra*.

See also T. Scovazzi *et al.* eds, *Index of Multilateral Treaties on the Law of the Sea* (Milano 1985); Summary Information on the Role of International Fishery and Other Bodies with Regard to the Conservation and Management of Living Resources of the High Seas, UN Doc. FAO Fisheries Circular No.908 (1996); *The Law of the Sea – Multilateral Treaties: A Reference Guide to Multilateral Treaties and Other International Instruments Related to the United Nations Convention on the Law of the Sea (Revised and Updated as of 31 December 1996)* (United Nations: New York 1997); *Register of International Treaties and Other Agreements in the Field of the Environment 1996* (UNEP 1997); Status of Multilateral Conventions and Instruments in Respect of Which the IMO or Its Secretary-General Performs Depositary Functions as at 31 Dec 2000, UN Doc. IMO J/7772; *Millennium Summit Multilateral Treaty Framework: An Invitation to Universal Participation* (United Nations: New York 2000); *International Instruments Related to the Prevention and Suppression of International Terrorism* (United Nations: New York 2001) <www.untreaty.un.org/English/terrorism.asp>; *Compendium of International Arrangements on Transfer of Technology: Selected Instruments* (United Nations: New York and Geneva 2001); *Implications of the UN Convention on the Law of the Sea for the IMO*, UN Doc. IMO LEG/MISC/3/Rev.1 (6 Jan 2003); *Multilateral Treaty Framework: An Invitation to Universal Participation – Focus 2005: Responding to Global Challenges* (United Nations: New York 2005); 60 Years of UN's Role in World Maritime Shipping of 24 Sep 2008 <www.un.org/apps/news/story.asp?NewsID=28232&Cr=maritime&Cr1>.

For recent developments, see *UN LOS Bull.* and *UN LOSIC*; *The Law of the Sea – A Bibliography 2005* (United Nations: New York 2006), issued annually; and the annual *Oceans and the Law of the Sea – Reports of the United Nations Secretary-General*, of which the latest are UN Docs A/56/58 & Add.1 (2001), A/57/57 & Add.1 (2002), A/58/65 & Add.1 (2003), A/59/62 & Add.1 (2004), 60/63 & Add.1 (2005), 61/63 & Add.1 (2006), 62/66 & Add.1/2 (2007), A/63/63 & Add.1 (2008) and A/64/66 & Add.1/2 (2009) at UNDOALOS <www.un.org/Depts/los/>; UN Treaties <http://treaties.un.org>; UN Law <www.un.org/law/lindex.htm>.